OVERSIZE

W9-CGX-677

1997 v.4

AMERICAN ERAS

DEVELOPMENT OF A NATION

1 7 8 3 - 1 8 1 5

AMERICAN ERAS

DEVELOPMENT OF A NATION

1 7 8 3 - 1 8 1 5

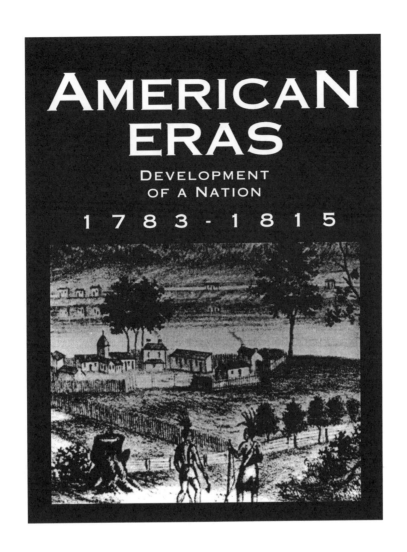

EDITED BY

ROBERT J. ALLISON

A MANLY, INC. BOOK

GALE

DETROIT   NEW YORK   TORONTO   LONDON

AMERICAN ERAS

1783-1815

Matthew J. Bruccoli and Richard Layman, Editorial Directors
Karen L. Rood, Senior Editor

CONTENTS

OVERVIEW

Best of Times, Worst of Times. "It was the best of times, it was the worst of times," Charles Dickens described these years; "it was the age of wisdom, it was the age of foolishness, it was the epoch of belief, it was the epoch of incredulity, . . . it was the spring of hope, it was the winter of despair, we had everything before us, we had nothing before us, we were all going direct to Heaven, we were all going direct the other way." It is hard to imagine a period of greater contrasts, unless we think of our own time. In Europe Wolfgang Amadeus Mozart, Ludwig van Beethoven, and Franz Joseph Haydn were creating the most enduring music in human history; Johann Wolfgang von Goethe, Friedrich Schiller, Robert Burns, and William Wordsworth were writing the world's greatest literature. Scientists were finding ways to prevent smallpox and other devastating diseases and were unlocking the secrets of electricity, steam power, and the elements. Much of the world as we know it today was being created in these tumultuous years.

Age of Inventions. In 1800 the everyday life of people around the world had changed little since the year 1000. By 1900 the Industrial Revolution had transformed the world's economy, bringing all the world into close contact. Prototypes of the inventions that shape our lives today were first created in these years by men and women who could not have foreseen all their consequences. Benjamin Franklin, American minister to France, was awed by the first balloon flight in 1784. Another spectator, who did not see the significance of this first controlled flight, dismissed it by asking, "What good is it?" Franklin replied, "What good is a new born baby?"

Progress. The balloon would help speed communications, and the steam engine would drive power looms and ultimately ships and wagons. Robert Koch and Edward Jenner developed a vaccine to prevent smallpox, a deadly disease that could wipe out an entire population. Allessandro Volta developed a cell for storing electricity, which ultimately became the battery. Gian Domenico Romagnosi made an electric current move through a wire. Richard Trevethick used a steam engine to power a carriage. In France, Franklin was hailed as the genius who had "wrested lightening from the sky, and the sceptre from the hand of the tyrant." These inventions and discoveries, made by men in different countries, seemed to usher in a new world, where people would not be divided by national lines, but be united in a common quest to better the human race.

Politics. But science and progress could not be divorced from politics and in fact could be used for political ends. The British navy sought ways to prevent scurvy, a disease we now know to be caused by a vitamin deficiency. At sea for months, the sailors lost teeth to the painful disease. The discovery that scurvy could be prevented by adding citrus juice to the daily ration of rum meant that British warships would carry limes and lemons, and that the British navy could spend longer periods at sea, controlling the trade routes. Without a large fleet, France hired American mechanic Robert Fulton to develop submarines and torpedoes, weapons to use against the British ships. The French also experimented with vacuum-packing food to preserve it indefinitely. This would ultimately change the diets of people all over the world, but the immediate purpose was to allow France's armies to carry their food with them as they conquered Europe. In America, Eli Whitney invented a gun that could be mass-produced, a development with profound effects on both manufacturing and on warfare. Whitney's cotton gin made it easier to clean cotton, but also made the institution of slavery more profitable. Inventors and scientists could not always control the uses of their inventions, nor could they escape politics. In 1794 Joseph Priestley, the discoverer of oxygen, was forced to leave England for America, and the French executed the great chemist Antoine Lavoisier, accusing him of being an aristocrat. Mathematician Joseph-Louis Lagrange commented after Lavoisier's death, "It required but a moment to sever that head, and perhaps a century will not be sufficient to produce another like it."

American Genius. The great achievement of Americans in this era was to create a government that would not destroy genius, but would allow it to flourish. While the Americans could boast of scientists such as Franklin and David Rittenhouse, the most creative Americans of the era were political thinkers. John Adams wrote the Constitution of Massachusetts in 1780 and wrote prolifically on the problems of establishing stable governments. Thomas Jefferson of Virginia drafted model constitutions for Virginia and Kentucky and never stopped reminding his countrymen that the basic purpose of any government was to protect human rights. James Madison combined the profound and subtle mind of a scholar with the shrewd insight of a master politician. George Washington, soldier and planter, prevented the other officers in the Continental Army from staging a coup d'état in 1783; he used his considerable influence and prestige to keep the United States together during the 1780s, and as the first president Washington helped establish the dignity of republican government. Franklin embodied the best parts of the era's spirit: curious, optimistic, rational, he was an active player in the life of the country up to the day of his death, and afterward, with the publication of his *Autobiography* (1793), he continued to influence the lives of Americans.

Creating the Government. Following the Revolution the thirteen independent states argued over their respective shares of the war debt (estimated at $42 million). Each state also created a new system of government, relying heavily on representative legislatures, with relatively weak governors. In 1787 delegates from twelve states met to plan a nation. They designed the Constitution of the United States, which created a unique system of government, with responsibilities divided between state and federal authorities, and the federal powers distributed among the legislative, executive, and judicial branches. In 1791 they added the Bill of Rights, guaranteeing the American people religious freedom, trial by jury, free speech, and protection against unreasonable government interference in their lives.

Problems of Independence. As long as they had been subjects of the British king, Americans enjoyed protection by the British navy and free trade in all British ports, including the West Indies. Most American trade was with the British West Indian colonies, bringing supplies and food to the sugar plantations of Barbados and Jamaica, carrying away molasses that they could process into sugar or rum. After the Revolution, the British forbade Americans to trade in her other colonies and also prevented Americans from trading in the Mediterranean. Some Americans sought other trading opportunities, sailing to China, to Java, and to Arabia. In 1802 Nathaniel Bowditch of Salem, Massachusetts, published a new atlas of navigation, correcting thousands of errors in the standard British works. Apprentice navigators in Salem learned to find their bearings by studying Bowditch's manual and writing out voyage logs for imaginary journeys along the coast of East Africa to the port of Aden. Independence had created a problem, but Americans were able to find a solution.

Neutrality. In creating their government, the Americans had taken into account the experience of Europe, rejecting the prevailing political wisdom about how to construct a government and to contain its power. In setting the government in motion, the Americans also tried to steer clear of European politics, not wanting to come under the influence of England or France. France had lost the Seven Years' War to England in 1763; French military assistance had helped the American colonies become independent. In 1789 the French people, burdened by the debts of these two wars, rose up to throw off their government, abolishing the aristocracy, executing the king, and declaring themselves free to create a new system of government, just as the Americans had done. Many Americans applauded this revolution, but others feared the turmoil and anarchy brought on by the end of the old order. When the French leaders began executing their opponents, killing thousands, American leaders feared the consequences of such brutal equality. In 1793 France and England went to war; and ultimately revolutionary France went to war with every nation in Europe. Which side the United States would take was not certain. France was on the side of liberty and against the old monarchies. On the other hand, many Americans feared the disorder and anarchy of France and still retained strong feelings for England. President Washington and Secretary of State Thomas Jefferson proposed a policy of neutrality. The United States would, according to Jefferson, cultivate "peace, commerce, and honest friendship with all nations—entangling alliances with none." This was a wise policy, as the nations of Europe engaged in a long series of wars brought about by their confusing relationships of mutual support and defense. The Americans were able to trade with all the powers engaged in the European conflict, as well as to find markets with European merchants distracted or destroyed by war.

France and England Respond. France and England did not welcome American neutrality. When the United States entered into a trade agreement with England in 1795, France retaliated by attacking American ships. Neither side declared war, but between 1797 and 1799 American and French ships fought one another at sea. This "Quasi-War" marked the birth of the U.S. Navy and ended with an agreement in 1800. France could benefit from American trade, particularly after the British had begun blockading European ports. Napoleon Bonaparte, who took power in France in 1799, controlled most of continental Europe by 1806. He forbade merchants trading with Britain to trade with continental ports. England, for her part, reciprocated. In order to maintain her fleet, the British needed a constant supply of sailors. The Royal Navy was notorious for its tough discipline and strenuous labor; sailors often jumped ship to serve in the less demanding, and better-paying, American merchant fleet or even the U.S. Navy. England insisted on her right to detain American ships to find any deserters who might be serving on board. The United States did not like this policy, but could not challenge the British navy. In 1807 the British ship *Leopard* ordered the American frigate *Chesapeake* to stop and be searched. The American captain did not answer quickly enough, and the British opened fire, killing three Americans, wounding eighteen, and forcing the American captain to allow his ship to be searched. One British deserter and three Americans who had been impressed into British service were found, and the British took them off the *Chesapeake*.

The Embargo. The Jefferson administration knew the United States did not have the resources to fight the British. Instead, Jefferson decided to use the greatest weapon available to the Americans, their agricultural supplies. Without American rice, corn, and wheat, the British could not feed their people or their army and navy; without American cotton the British textile industry would collapse. By withholding American goods from Europe, the Americans could convince both the English and the French, who had embarked on a devastating war in Europe and in the rest of the world, that there were other ways to resolve disputes. Jefferson called for an embargo on all American trade on 22 December 1807. Nothing would enter or leave American ports for one year. The embargo did not work as Jefferson had hoped. It did not bring France or England to their senses; instead, it simply created an economic depression in the United States, even though it forced Americans to begin manufacturing the kinds of goods they otherwise would have bought from England or France. Jefferson left office in 1809, and the embargo expired. Three years later the United States declared war on England.

The War of 1812. When the United States went to war against England, the British were preoccupied fighting against Napoleon. The British were most heavily involved in Spain, but were also involved in a war between India, most of which was now under the control of the East India Company, and Nepal. Napoleon had invaded Russia and was in Moscow waiting for the czar to surrender. The Americans hoped to invade Canada but were turned back by a force of British and Native Americans. In the Ohio River valley the Shawnee leader Tecumseh and his brother Tenskwatawa led a massive Indian alliance against the Americans, supported by the British. The Shawnee and their allies fought in the North, the Creek in the South. At sea the Americans were more successful: American seamanship, learned both in trading around the world and in fighting against France (1798–1799) and Tripoli (1801–1805) helped the Americans win some crucial naval battles. The U.S.S. *Constitution* defeated the larger and more heavily armed

British frigate *Guerrière* in August 1812. Naval victories boosted American spirits, but not enough to offset the devastating losses: Detroit was seized; Maine was declared part of Canada; and in August 1814 a British force captured Washington, D.C., burning the capitol and the executive mansion, forcing President James Madison to flee. Another British army, fifteen thousand veterans of the Duke of Wellington's army that had defeated the French in Spain, with fifty British battleships and frigates, was on its way to the Mississippi River valley, where it was likely to seize the port of New Orleans and support the Creek and Shawnee in their war against the Americans. That fall a convention of the New England states discussed seceding from the Union and forming their own confederation, which would be allied with the British.

Triumph of 1815. The New Englanders arrived at the burned capital city to present their demands to President Madison. They arrived on the same day as two other pieces of news. First, in Ghent, Holland, American and British negotiators had agreed to peace terms: Britain once again recognized American independence, and the United States would keep all of the territory it had held before the war began. This was a tremendous diplomatic victory for the American negotiators, led by a new generation of leaders, John Quincy Adams, Albert Gallatin, and Henry Clay. The Americans might have lost the war on the battlefield, but they won it at the negotiating table. On the same day, though, even more exciting news arrived in Washington: at New Orleans, Andrew Jackson and a force of Kentucky and Tennessee volunteers, pirates, Choctaw, free blacks, and French-speaking Creoles had destroyed the well-trained, seasoned British army. This final military victory, which came after the peace treaty had been signed, turned the War of 1812 from an American defeat into a resounding victory. For the victorious Americans, the war concluded a period of international tension and internal doubt of whether the new republic could survive in the tempestuous world of power and violence. Jackson and other generals, the negotiators at Ghent, the small but vital navy, the political leaders who resisted the temptation to enlarge their own powers, and citizens who remained committed to the ideals of republican government provided a decisive answer.

ACKNOWLEDGMENTS

This book was produced by Manly, Inc. Anthony J. Scotti and Karen L. Rood were the in-house editors.

Production manager is Samuel W. Bruce.

Office manager is Kathy Lawler Merlette.

Administrative support was provided by Ann M. Cheschi and Brenda A. Gillie. Bookkeeper is Joyce Fowler.

Copyediting supervisor is Jeff Miller. The copyediting staff includes Phyllis A. Avant, Patricia Coate, Christine Copeland, Thom Harman, and William L. Thomas Jr.

Editorial associates are L. Kay Webster and Mark McEwan.

Layout and graphics staff includes Marie L. Parker and Janet E. Hill.

Photography editor is Margaret Meriwether. Photographic copy work was performed by Joseph M. Bruccoli.

Software specialist is Marie L. Parker. Systems manager is Chris Elmore.

Typesetting supervisor is Kathleen M. Flanagan. The typesetting staff includes Pamela D. Norton and Patricia Flanagan Salisbury.

Walter W. Ross, Steven Gross, and Mark McEwan did library research. They were assisted by the following librarians at the Thomas Cooper Library of the University of South Carolina: Linda Holderfield and the interlibrary-loan staff; reference-department head Virginia Weathers; reference librarians Marilee Birchfield, Stefanie Buck, Stefanie DuBose, Rebecca Feind, Karen Joseph, Donna Lehman, Charlene Loope, Anthony McKissick, Jean Rhyne, Kwamine Simpson, and Virginia Weathers; circulation-department head Caroline Taylor; and acquisitions-searching supervisor David Haggard.

AMERICAN ERAS

DEVELOPMENT OF A NATION

1783 - 1815

WORLD EVENTS:

SELECTED OCCURRENCES OUTSIDE THE UNITED STATES

MAJOR POWERS AND LEADERS

Austria-Hungary (Holy Roman Empire)—Joseph II (1780–1790); Leopold II (1790–1792); Francis II (1792–1835)

China—Emperors Qian-lung (1735–1796) and Jia-qing (1796–1820)

France—King Louis XVI (1774–1792; beheaded 1793); National Convention (1792–1795); Committee of Public Safety (1793–1795), Maximilien Robespierre, president (1793–1794); Directorate, five members (1795–1799); Napoleon Bonaparte, first consul (1799–1804), emperor (1804–1814; 1815); King Louis XVII (1814–1815; 1815–1824)

Great Britain—King George III (1760–1820); George, Prince of Wales (later George IV) regent, (1811–1820); Prime Ministers William Petty, second Earl of Shelburne (1782–1783), William Henry Cavendish Bentinck, third Duke of Portland (1783; 1807–1809), William Pitt the Younger (1783–1801; 1804–1806), Henry Addington (1801–1804), William Wyndham Grenville, first Baron Grenville (1806–1807), Spencer Perceval (1809–1812), and Robert Banks Jenkinson, second Earl of Liverpool (1812–1827)

Japan—Emperor Kokaku (1779–1816); Shoguns Ieharu (1760–1786) and Ienari (1786–1837)

Ottoman Empire (Turkey)—Abdulhamid I (1774–1789); Selim III (1789–1807); Mustafa IV (1807–1808); Mahmud II (1808–1839)

Prussia—Frederick II, the Great (1740–1786); Frederick William II (1786–1797); Frederick William III (1797–1840)

Russia—Czarina Catherine II, the Great (1762–1796); Paul I (1796–1801); Alexander I (1801–1825)

Spain—Charles III (1759–1788); Charles IV (1788–1808); Ferdinand VII (1808; 1813–1833); Joseph Bonaparte (brother Napoleon I of France, 1808–1813)

MAJOR CONFLICTS

1767–1799—Mysore Wars: Britain and Mughals versus Mysore, a southern Indian state

1775–1782; 1803–1805; 1817–1818—Mahratta Wars: Britain and allied Indian states versus Maharashtra

1788–1791—Russian-Turkish War

1791–1802—Wars of the French Revolution: Britain and Austria versus France

1792–1804—War for Haitian independence

1797–1799—Quasi-War: United States versus France

1801–1805—Tripolitan War: United States versus Tripoli

1803–1815—Napoleonic Wars: Britain, Austria, and Russia versus France

1804–1810—West African Jihad

1809–1826—Wars for Latin American Independence: Spain versus Mexico, Paraguay, Ecuador, Bolivia, Venezuela, and Guatemala

1812–1815—War of 1812: United States versus Britain

1813–1814—Creek War: United States versus the Creek

1783

- The Kingdoms of Kartli and Kakheti in Georgia ask Russia to protect them against the Ottomans.

- The army of Oyo, a powerful state in West Africa, is defeated by an army from neighboring Borgu; this event will lead to the weakening of the Oyo state.

- Russia annexes Crimea and expels the Turks.

- A famine begins in Japan which will kill nearly one million people in ten years.

4 Feb.   An earthquake in Calabria, Italy, kills thirty thousand people.

6 Feb.   Spain ends its siege of Gibraltar, allowing the British to maintain a fortress there.

1 Mar.   Olaudah Equiano, a former slave living in London, informs British philanthropist Granville Sharp of an incident on the slave ship *Zong.* Sharp unsuccessfully tries to prevent the ship's owners from collecting insurance for drowned slaves, and public outcry leads to a campaign against the slave trade.

9 Apr.   Tipu Sultan of India captures Bedmore from the East India Company.

1 June   The Order of Saint Patrick is founded in Ireland.

3 Sept.   The United States and Great Britain sign a peace treaty, ending the Revolutionary War and establishing American independence. British and French land claims in Africa are also recognized.

1784

- The University of Lemberg in Austria-Hungary is founded.

- Immanuel Kant publishes *Notion of Universal History in a Cosmopolitan Sense* and "What is Enlightenment?"

- Bodawpaya, the king of Burma, conquers Arakan and begins a war with Thailand, envisioning the conquest of Southeast Asia.

- Serfdom is abolished in Denmark.

- The first school for the blind opens in Paris.

- Antoine Lavoisier and Pierre Simon measure the oxygen consumed and the carbon dioxide produced by breathing and burning.

6 Jan.   In the Treaty of Constantinople, Turkey accepts the Russian annexation of Crimea.

28 Feb.   John Wesley, the father of Methodism, organizes chapels and preachers.

11 May   The British East India Company makes peace with Tipu Sultan.

4 July   Joseph II abrogates Hungary's constitution, suppressing the courts and taking the crown jewels to Vienna.

13 Aug.   Parliament passes the India Act, making the directors of the East India Company answerable to a board appointed by the king.

Oct.   Mughal emperor Shāh 'Alam II appoints Sindhia, leader of Marāthās, to be regent, helping to secure Delhi against revolt.

1785

- Sweden declares war on Russia; Denmark attacks Sweden.

- The Emerald Buddha chapel is completed in Bangkok.

- John Molson of Montreal opens a beer brewery, which his family will run for the next six generations.

- The Boulton and Watt rotating steam engine is installed for the first time in an English textile mill.

7 Jan. John Jeffries and François Blanchard make the first aerial crossing of the English Channel in a hot-air balloon.

1 May Wolfgang Amadeus Mozart's opera, *The Marriage of Figaro*, premieres in Vienna.

23 May Benjamin Franklin publishes a description of bifocal glasses, which he invented.

July Swedish and Russian naval fleets battle off Hogland.

23 July Frederick II of Prussia forms the Fürstenbund, a league of German princes, against Joseph II of Austria-Hungary; England joins the alliance.

1786

- Thomas Clarkson publishes *On the Slavery and Commerce of the Human Species*, an attack on the slave trade.

- Russian navigator Gavril Pribylov discovers and names Pribilof Islands (Fur Seal Islands) in the Bering Sea.

- The English Committee for the Relief of the Black Poor is formed to organize the settlement of free blacks in Sierra Leone.

- Scottish millwright Andrew Meikle develops a threshing machine to harvest grain.

- The Ottoman Turks send a fleet to restore authority in Egypt.

11 May Starving Japanese peasants break into rice warehouses in Osaka, and within a week they will raid warehouses in thirty other cities.

25 May Pedro III of Portugal dies and is succeeded by Maria I.

14 July British subjects start evacuating the Mosquito Coast of Nicaragua.

11 Aug. The British establish a trading post at Penang, Malaya Peninsula.

17 Aug. Frederick the Great of Prussia dies and is succeeded by his nephew, Frederick William II.

1787

- The Central University of Ecuador is founded in Quito.

- A plague in Algiers kills seventeen thousand people.

- The Society for the Abolition of the Slave Trade is formed in England.

- The first balloon ascension using hydrogen occurs in France.

Jan.	Joseph II of Austria-Hungary, Holy Roman Emperor, provokes rebellions by clergy in the Netherlands by abolishing feudal and clerical courts.
13 Feb.	The French foreign minister Charles Gravier de Vergennes dies.
22 Feb.– 12 May	France's Assembly of Notables convenes and rejects reform proposals.
4 Apr.	Robert Burns publishes *Poems, Chiefly in the Scottish Dialect.*
May	Catherine the Great inspects the Russian fleet being built in the Crimea and meets with Joseph II of Austria-Hungary.
13 May	The British government sends 756 convicts to New South Wales, Australia, to establish a colony.
15 May	Four hundred former slaves from British colonies establish the "Province of Freedom" at Saint George's Bay, West Africa; disease and hostility of natives lead to the colony's abandonment three years later.
June	Dutch republicans arrest Princess Wilhelmina, wife of Dutch Stadtholder William V, and niece of Frederick the Great.
8 Aug.	Austria and Russia declare war on Turkey.
17 Aug.	Riots occur in Paris.
5 Sept.	The Mughal emperor Shāh 'Alam II appoints Ghulam Qadir regent after Ghulam drives Sindhia's forces from Delhi, India.
13 Sept.	The Prussians invade the Netherlands, and the British prepare a fleet to support them.
10 Oct.	A Dutch rebellion ends with William V returning to power.
29 Oct.	The premiere in Prague of Wolfgang Amadeus Mozart's *Don Giovanni.*
15 Nov.	Christoph Willibald Gluck, imperial composer to the Holy Roman Emperor, dies at age seventy-three; Joseph II appoints Mozart to succeed him.

1788

•	The Marylebone Cricket Club is founded in England and codifies the rules of the game.
•	Great Britain, Holland, and Prussia form the Triple Alliance.
•	University of King's College, now Windsor University, Canada, is founded.
•	British abolitionists mount a petition drive to end the slave trade; by May tens of thousands of signatures are collected. Olaudah Equiano presents the petition to Queen Charlotte, and he writes his autobiography, *Interesting Narrative of Olaudah Equiano.*
•	In France the antislavery *Société des Amis des Noirs* is formed.
1 Jan.	The first issue of *The Times* of London appears.
18 Jan.	The British convict fleet reaches Botany Bay, Australia; after finding it unsuitable for colonization, it moves to Port Jackson and renames the settlement Sydney.
Feb.	Austria declares war against Turkey.

June	The African Association is formed in London to promote exploration of central Africa.
July	Gustavus III of Sweden invades Finland.
30 July	In Delhi, Ghulam Qadir deposes Shāh ʿAlam II.
22 Aug.	King Naimbanna of Sierra Leone confirms a grant of land from Frenchman's Bay to white settlers.
6 Oct.	The Polish Diet meets to revise the national constitution.
Dec.	The Nguyen Family usurps power and seizes Hanoi, Vietnam, but a Chinese army quickly recaptures the city.
14 Dec.	Carlos III of Spain dies after ruling twenty-nine years and is succeeded by Carlos IV.

1789

Jan.	While Chinese troops celebrate the new year, Nguyen forces attack and drive them from Hanoi; Hung-li recognizes Nguyen Quang Trong as the legitimate king of Annam.
29 Jan.	The Duc de Lauzan of France captures Saint Louis, Senegal.
7 Apr.	Selim III becomes the Ottoman sultan.
28 Apr.	Sailors on H.M.S. *Bounty,* in the South Pacific gathering breadfruit trees, mutiny and cast Capt. William Bligh and eighteen others adrift in a lifeboat. The mutineers marry Tahitian women and land on Pitcairn Island. Bligh and eleven men survive forty-five days in the open boat, crossing thirty-six hundred miles of ocean; they reach Timor and ultimately return to England. The mutineers are not discovered until 1808.
11 July	Louis XVI dismisses finance minister Jacques Necker, leading to popular demonstrations against the king.
14 July	A Parisian mob storms the Bastille, seizing weapons and releasing prisoners.
4 Aug.	The French Assembly abolishes feudal privileges, declaring legal and fiscal equality.
4 Aug.	The English Privy Council issues a report on the slave trade recommending strict regulation of the traffic.
26 Aug.	The French Assembly adopts the Declaration of the Rights of Man.
10 Sept.	The French Assembly decides to create a unicameral legislature and to give the king veto power.
1 Oct.	An uprising occurs in the Austrian Netherlands, which proclaims its independence as the Belgian Republic.
9 Oct.	Ottoman forces in Belgrade surrender to the Russians and Austrians.
2 Nov.	The French Assembly nationalizes church property.
14 Dec.	The French Assembly allows communes to elect municipal officials and replaces the former provinces with eighty-three departments which are divided into districts.

1790

- Jacob Schweppe in Geneva manufactures the first carbonated beverages.
- Planters suppress a mulatto uprising in Santo Domingo.
- Gurkhas from Nepal attack Tibet.

30 Jan.   Prussia and the Ottoman Empire form an alliance.

13 Feb.   Monastic institutions in France are dissolved.

20 Feb.   Joseph II of Austria-Hungary dies and is succeeded by Leopold III.

29 Mar.   Prussia and Poland form a defensive alliance.

July   England and Spain resolve their dispute over Nootka Sound.

12 July   The French Assembly passes the Civil Constitution of Clergy, making religious dioceses subordinate to civil government.

15 Aug.   Russia and Sweden make peace.

Nov.   Edmund Burke writes *Reflections on the Revolution in France.*

27 Nov.   The French Assembly requires all clergymen to take oaths to support the Civil Constitution of the Clergy; half of the clergy, and all but seven bishops, refuse to do so.

Dec.   The Belgian Republic is suppressed.

1791

- An Oyo army is defeated by Nupe.
- The University of Stuttgart is founded.
- The Society of United Irishmen forms to push for Irish independence.
- Berlin's Brandenburg Gate is completed and is copied from the Propylea at Athens.
- Parliament rejects the abolition of the slave trade.
- Thomas Paine writes *Vindication of the Rights of Man* in response to Edmund Burke's *Reflections on the Revolution in France.*

Mar.   Robert Burns publishes his poem "Tam O'Shanter" in *Edinburgh Magazine.*

21 Mar.   Lord Charles Cornwallis captures Bangalore, India.

13 Apr.   Pope Pius VI condemns the Civil Constitution of Clergy.

3 May   A new Polish constitution is proclaimed, converting the elected monarchy into a hereditary monarchy. Russia opposes the constitution, and Frederick Augustus III of Saxony declines an offer to the Polish throne.

15 May   The French Assembly grants the right to vote to free mulattoes in the French West Indies.

15 May   Lord Charles Cornwallis defeats Tipu Sultan at Arikera.

24 May   The papal nuncio leaves France.

6 July   Leopold II of Austria-Hungary calls on all monarchs to resist revolution.

22 Aug.   A slave revolt breaks out in Santo Domingo.

30 Aug.	Austria-Hungary and Turkey sign the Treaty of Sistova.
14 Sept.	Louis XVI accepts a new French constitution.
30 Sept.	The premiere of Wolfgang Amadeus Mozart's opera *The Magic Flute* in Vienna.
	The French National Assembly is dissolved.
5 Dec.	Wolfgang Amadeus Mozart dies at age thirty-five.
15 Dec.	The U.S. Bill of Rights is ratified.
21 Dec.	The British take the Indian fortress of Savandroog.
26 Dec.	The Canada Act takes effect, dividing the country at the Ottawa River into primarily English Upper Canada and primarily French Lower Canada.

1792

- French revolutionaries open Louvre Palace as an art museum.
- Cao Xueqin's novel *Dream of the Red Chamber* is published.
- Mary Wollstonecraft publishes *Vindication of the Rights of Woman.*
- The Russian ship *Ekaterina* sails to the Kurile Islands from Okhotsk, unsuccessfully seeking trade with Japan.
- Over ten thousand Japanese die as Mount Unzen-Dake erupts.
- The New York Stock Exchange is formed.
- The Chinese army drives the Nepalese Gurkhas out of Tibet.
- Nepal and India sign a commercial treaty; a British Resident is sent to reside at Katmandu but is recalled two years later.

9 Jan.	In the Treaty of Jassy, Turkey cedes to Russia all land east of the Dniester River and recognizes Russian suzerainty over Georgia.
Feb.–Mar.	Approximately eleven hundred former British slaves arrive in Sierra Leone.
7 Feb.	Leopold II of Austria and Frederick William II of Prussia form an alliance.
24 Feb.	Tipu Sultan, after a defeat at Seringapatam, makes peace with the British. He cedes half of his territories and pays an indemnity of £ 3.3 million.
Mar.	Freetown, Sierra Leone, is founded by freed American slaves who had been in Nova Scotia since the American Revolution.
1 Mar.	Leopold II dies; his son, Francis II, succeeds as king of Austria-Hungary and Holy Roman Emperor.
Apr.	Parliament votes to end the slave trade by 1796.
29 Mar.	Gustavus III of Sweden dies two weeks after being shot in the back at the Stockholm Opera House; his son Gustavus, age thirteen, becomes king.
4 Apr.	The French Assembly extends the right to vote to free blacks in the West Indies.
20 Apr.	France declares war on Austria.

24 Apr.	French army officer Rouget de Lisle writes "La Marseillaise," a patriotic song celebrating France's war against Prussia and Austria.
19 May	Russia invades Poland.
20 June	Angered by Louis XVI's dismissal of Minister of the Interior Jean-Marie Roland, a Paris crowd invades the Tuileries palace.
11 July	Francis II of Austria-Hungary leads an invasion of France.
27 July	The Duke of Brunswick threatens to destroy Paris if King Louis XVI is harmed.
9 Aug.	A Paris mob overthrows the municipal government and establishes a commune.
10 Aug.	A French crowd storms the Tuileries and kills the Swiss Guard. The Assembly suspends the king and calls for a national convention to be elected by all adult men.
19 Aug.	The Marquis de Lafayette defects from France to the Austrians.
Sept.	France sends a six-thousand-man army to the West Indies.
2 Sept.	Verdun falls to the Austrians. A Paris crowd slaughters twelve hundred prisoners.
20 Sept.	A French army turns back the Austrians at Valmy.
21 Sept.	The French Convention abolishes the monarchy.
22 Sept.	The Convention declares France a republic. It abolishes the old calendar and installs a new calendar with twelve months of thirty days each, beginning 22 September, Year One; every tenth day is a holiday.
10 Nov.	The French government prohibits the worship of God and creates a cult of Reason.
14 Nov.	French troops occupy Brussels.
19 Nov.	The French decree support to all people struggling for freedom.
11 Dec.	The trial of Louis XVI starts.

1793

Jan.	The Catholic Relief Act removes restrictions from Irish Catholics, though they still cannot hold public office.
14 Jan.	The French Convention unanimously finds Louis XVI guilty of treason and by a vote of 361–321 sentences him to death.
21 Jan.	King Louis XVI is executed on the guillotine.
1 Feb.	The Convention declares war on England and Holland.
Mar.	France annexes Belgium, the Rhineland, and Basel.
23 Apr.	President George Washington declares American neutrality.
1 Aug.	France adopts the decimal system.
5 Sept.	The beginning of the Reign of Terror in France, in which forty thousand will be executed by July 1794.

7 Oct.	The emperor orders Earl George Macartney to leave China and decides neither to establish diplomatic relations with England nor allow British merchants to trade anywhere but Canton.
16 Oct.	Marie-Antoinette is guillotined.

1794

•	On a twenty-three-week voyage from London to Madras, a British naval squadron successfully tests the theory of James Lind that citrus fruits will prevent scurvy. The Royal Navy thereafter will carry limes to prevent the vitamin deficiency linked to the disease as well as mix lime juice with rum rations.
10 Feb.	In London the first performance of Joseph Haydn's Symphonies 99 and 100 occurs.
Mar.	Thaddeus Kosciusko leads a Polish uprising.
May	France outlaws slavery in its colonies and extends citizenship to all adult males. Toussaint L'Ouverture, a former slave fighting for the Spanish, joins French forces on Santo Domingo to oppose a British invasion and a possible re-establishment of slavery.
8 May	French chemist Antoine-Laurent Lavoisier is guillotined.
19 July	A revolt occurs in Geneva in support of the French Revolution.
28 Sept.–13 Oct.	The French Navy attacks the British colony at Freetown.
7 Nov.	The Russians capture Warsaw.

1795

•	After a mob attacks King George III's carriage, Parliament passes the Treason and Sedition Bills, punishing by deportation anyone whose writing or speaking excites hatred of the king or constitution and forbidding meetings of more than fifty people without a magistrate's permission.
•	Āghā Mohammad Khān, founder of the Persian Qajar dynasty, occupies Tbilisi, Kakheti, and Kartli; Catherine II of Russia sends troops to retake the area.
•	A second maroon war breaks out in Jamaica.
22 May	British explorer Mungo Park sails for West Africa to map the Niger River; he returns to London two years later.
22 July	France and Spain make peace.
16 Sept.	The British take Cape Colony, South Africa, from the Dutch.
21 Sept.	A riot between Catholics and Protestants occurs in Armagh, Ireland.
1 Oct.	Belgium is incorporated into France.
5 Oct.	Napoleon crushes an uprising in Paris.
15 Oct.	Hung-li, the longest-reigning monarch in China's history (since 1736), abdicates in favor of his son Yung-yen, but continues to hold power.
25 Nov.	King Stanislaw II Augustus Poniatowski of Poland abdicates. Poland is partitioned among Russia, Prussia, and Austria.

1796

- Edward Jenner uses a cowpox vaccination against smallpox.

- The House of Commons defeats a bill abolishing the slave trade.

- Tehran becomes the capital of Persia.

12 Feb. A British treaty with the king of Kandy establishes a British protectorate over Ceylon.

16 Feb. British authorities expel Dutch colonists from Ceylon and make it part of Madras, but a rebellion occurs and Ceylon becomes a royal colony instead.

31 Mar. Johann Wolfgang von Goethe's *Egmont* premieres in Weimar.

19 Aug. France and Spain make an alliance.

5 Oct. Spain declares war on England.

Nov. With Spain and France allied, England withdraws its fleet from the Mediterranean.

16 Nov. Catherine II of Russia dies and is succeeded by her son, Paul I.

15 Dec. Forty-three French ships embark fifteen thousand men for an invasion of Ireland.

1797

- The Persian ruler Āghā Mohammad Khān is assassinated and is succeeded by his nephew, Fath 'Ali Shāh.

- Toussaint-Louverture, leading Haiti's blacks, drives the British from the island.

26 Jan. Another partition of Poland occurs.

4 Feb. An earthquake in the Andes kills forty-one thousand in Peru and Ecuador.

Mar. The British begin suppressing the United Irish revolt.

9 Mar. The doge of Venice, Luigi Manin, is deposed, and Venice is annexed by Austria.

Aug. Toussaint-Louverture expels French representatives from Santo Domingo.

16 Apr. British sailors mutiny at Spithead.

2 May British sailors at The Nore in the Thames estuary mutiny.

Oct. France prepares for an invasion of England.

31 Oct. The Directory bans British goods from countries France controls.

Nov. Frederick William II of Prussia dies and is succeeded by his grandson, Frederick William III.

1798

- London hatter John Hetherington makes a top hat of silk, thus contributing to the reduced demand for beaver pelts.

- The Persian emperor leases the islands of Hormuz and Qeshm to Muscat.

- Thomas Robert Malthus publishes *Essay on Principles of Population,* arguing that the world's population increases faster than the capacity to feed it. Accordingly, the world will ultimately face starvation.

- A typhoid epidemic in England kills thousands. In addition, poor harvests and rising food prices lead to mass starvation.

- Samuel Taylor Coleridge publishes "'Rime of the Ancient Mariner" and "Kubla Khan."

9 Jan.	The last meeting of the Irish Parliament occurs.
15 Feb.	With a French army outside Rome, Italian revolutionaries proclaim the Roman Republic. Pope Pius VI is driven into exile, and French officers loot the Vatican treasury.
19 Feb.	The premiere in Paris of the opera *Leonore,* with an overture by Ludwig van Beethoven.
30 Mar.	Martial law is proclaimed in Ireland.
20 Apr.	A British fleet is sent to the Mediterranean to protect Naples.
24 May	Rebellion breaks out in Ireland.
June	British sailors riot in the Mediterranean.
21 June	British forces suppress the Irish rebellion.
2 July	Napoleon and forty thousand French troops occupy Alexandria, Egypt.
3 July	Dr. Francisco de Lacerda of Portugal begins exploring the Zambezi River in southern Africa. He journeys as far inland as Cazembe, where he dies in October.
1–2 Aug.	A British fleet under Horatio Nelson defeats the French at the Battle of the Nile.
Sept.	The Russian czar sends a fleet to the Mediterranean to cooperate with Turkey.
21 Oct:	The British East India Company enters an agreement with the imam of Muscat to exclude French traders.
Oct.	Frederick North arrives in Ceylon as the first British governor.
21–24 Oct.	Two thousand die in an uprising in Cairo as sheiks and the elite resist the re-forming efforts of the French.
4 Dec.	France declares war against Naples.
29 Dec.	Russia and England form an alliance.

1799

- Scottish explorer Mungo Park publishes *Travels in the Interior of Africa.*
- The Second Coalition of Britain, Austria, Russia, Naples, and Ottoman Porte is formed.

9 Jan.	The first British income tax is enacted.
Feb.	Napoleon invades Syria, but a plague forces the French army back to Egypt.
7 Feb.	The Emperor Qian-lung, China's longest ruling monarch, dies.

12 Mar.	France declares war on Austria.
19 Mar.	The first performances of Franz Joseph Haydn's *Die Schöpfung (The Creation)* and Ludwig van Beethoven's *Sonata Pathetique.*
6 May	Tipu Sultan is killed storming Seringapatam, and the Hindu royal family resumes power in Mysore.
5 July	Sierra Leone becomes an independent British colony.
12 July	The British Parliament suppresses corresponding and debating societies and reading rooms, requires printing presses and type foundries to register with the government, and forbids meetings of workers.
25 July	At Abukir Napoleon defeats a Turkish army supported by England.
24 Aug.	Napoleon leaves Egypt for France.
29 Aug.	Pope Pius VI, pope since 1775 and exiled by Napoleon since 1798, dies.
26 Sept.	A French victory at Zurich forces the Russians to sue for peace.
Nov.	Naples recaptures Rome from the French.
9–10 Nov.	Napoleon dissolves legislative councils and becomes First Consul of the French Republic.
25 Dec.	A new constitution for France provides a ten-year term for the First Consul.

1800

•	Colonists in Freetown rebel against the Sierra Leone Company.
•	Toussaint-Louverture defeats a mulatto army, gains control of the French half of Hispaniola, and invades the Spanish area of the island.
•	Italian physicist Allessandro Volta invents the "voltaic cell," the prototype of the electric battery.
Feb.	France ratifies the new constitution.
13 Feb.	The Banque de France is founded.
13 Mar.	Gregorio Barnabo Chiaramonte becomes Pope Pius VII.
20 Mar.	The French defeat the Turks at Heliopolis.
20 Mar.–21 Apr.	Pashas in Egypt lead a revolt against the French.
5 Apr.	The British capture the island of Gorée off Senegal from France.
14 June	Napoleon defeats the Austrians at Marengo.
5 Sept.	The French garrison on Malta surrenders to the English.
1 Oct.	In the secret Treaty of San Ildefonso, Spain cedes the Louisiana Territory to France.
3 Dec.	French forces defeat the Austrians at Hohenlinden.

1801

Jan.	The Act of Union creates the United Kingdom of Great Britain. England and Ireland are to be governed by one parliament.
26 Jan.	Toussaint-Louverture captures the Spanish capital of Santo Domingo. France sends an army to recapture the colony.
9 Feb.	Austria and France sign the Treaty of Lunéville in which France is to control Italy west of Venice.
11 Mar.	Russia's insane Czar Paul I is murdered and replaced by his son, Alexander I; the new czar withdraws from the war against France.
21 Mar.	At the Battle of Alexandria a British and Turkish army defeat a French force.
2 Apr.	A British fleet defeats the Danes at the Battle of Copenhagen.
10 June	Tripoli declares war on the United States.
July	Toussaint-Louverture sends a constitution to France for Napoleon's approval.
15 July	Napoleon and Pius VII reach an agreement by which the French government will nominate bishops to be consecrated by the pope. Meanwhile, the pope is restored to Rome.
Aug.	French forces in Egypt capitulate.
18 Nov.	Ten Freetown settlers are killed and forty-two, including the governor, wounded when Temnes warriors attack the settlement.
24 Dec.	Richard Trevithick in England uses a steam engine to power a carriage.

1802

- Portuguese traders begin the first successful crossing of the African continent from Angola to the Zambezi River, reaching Tete in 1811.

- Italian inventor Gian Domenico Romagnosi observes an electric current moving through a wire.

- Marie Grosholtz Tussaud, a Swiss wax modeler who had been commissioned in 1793 to make death masks of guillotine victims, opens a wax museum in London.

- The British Parliament passes the Factory Act to protect apprentices in textile mills.

- Nathaniel Bowditch of Salem, Massachusetts, publishes *New American Practical Navigator,* correcting eight thousand errors in an earlier English text on navigation.

- Thomas Wedgwood, son of British potter Josiah Wedgwood, produces the first photographic image on paper coated with silver nitrate; however, the image fades quickly.

27 Mar.	England and France sign the Treaty of Amiens. England accepts France's conquests in Europe and gives up Malta, Elba, Minorca, and Cape Colony, but keeps Ceylon and Trinidad.
11 Apr.	Freetown settlers repulse Temnes warriors.
1 June	Nguyen Phuc Anh proclaims himself Emperor Gia Long, changes the name of his country from Annam to Vietnam, and establishes the capital at Hue.
10 June	Toussaint-Louverture is arrested and taken to France.

14 June	Napoleon orders slavery to be reestablished in Santo Domingo and other French colonies.
2 Aug.	A French plebiscite elects Napoleon Consul for life.
1 Nov.	Gen. Victor-Emmanuel Leclerc, sent to Santo Domingo to restore slavery and French power, dies of yellow fever.

1803

•	King Kamehameha I unites the eight islands of Hawaii.
•	Wahhabi fundamentalists capture Mecca.
•	Maryland farmer Thomas Moore patents the icebox.
•	English chemist John Dalton arranges a table of atomic weights.
•	Cotton becomes the leading export of the United States.
20 Feb.	The British seize Kandy, Ceylon, and leave a small force to protect their puppet king.
7 Apr.	Toussaint-Louverture dies in a French prison.
16 May	After Britain refuses to surrender Malta, France and England resume war.
23–24 June	British troops are massacred after an uprising in Kandy, Ceylon.
23 July	An uprising in Ireland fails.
23 Sept.	At the Battle of Assaye, British forces defeat the Mahrathas.
Dec.	British capture Pondicherry from the Mahrathas.

1804

•	The Universities of Kazan and Kharkov in Russia are founded.
•	The first vacuum-bottling factory, or cannery, is opened near Paris.
Feb.	French authorities discover a plot by royalists to depose Napoleon.
21 Feb.	In West Africa Uthman dan Fodio accuses Hausa kings of laxity in Islamic observance and declares a jihad, or holy war. By 1810 he will control all of the Hausa territory and form the Sokoto Empire.
17 Mar.	Johann Schiller's play *Wilhelm Tell* premieres.
21 Mar.	The Code Napoleon, civil laws based on Roman statutes and egalitarian concepts of the French Revolution, is promulgated.
Oct.	The Russian warship *Nadezhda* enters the harbor at Nagasaki, Japan, but is told to leave.
Oct.	British seize the Spanish treasure fleet carrying gold valued at $3 million.
8 Oct.	Jean-Jacques Dessalines proclaims himself Emperor Jacques I of Santo Domingo.
2 Dec.	The Pope crowns Napoleon emperor of France.

1805

•	Kebbi and Zaria fall to Uthman's forces.
•	The British House of Lords defeats a bill to abolish the slave trade.
•	In Arabia, Wahhabi capture Medina.
7 Apr.	The premiere of Ludwig van Beethoven's Third Symphony in Vienna. Beethoven had dedicated this "heroic" symphony to then-consul and antimonarchist Napoleon, but tore up the dedication when Napoleon was crowned emperor of France.
11 Apr.	Russia allies itself with England.
26 May	Napoleon is crowned king of Italy.
4 June	The United States and Tripoli sign a peace treaty.
26 July	An earthquake kills thousands in Naples.
9 Aug.	Austria and England become allies.
9 Oct.	France and Naples agree to neutrality.
15–20 Oct.	A French army captures an Austrian force at New Ulm.
21 Oct.	At Trafalgar the Royal Navy under Horatio, Lord Nelson destroys two-thirds of the French and Spanish fleets.
13 Nov.	Napoleon occupies Vienna.
19 Nov.	Natives kill Mungo Park while he is on a second exploration of the Niger River.
20 Nov.	Premier of the opera *Fidelio,* music by Ludwig van Beethoven, in Vienna.
2 Dec.	Napoleon defeats Russians and Austrians at Austerlitz.
26 Dec.	Francis II of Austria cedes Venetia, Istria, and Dalmatia to France.

1806

12 Jan.	French forces leave Vienna.
19 Jan.	British forces arrive in South Africa to take Cape Colony.
23 Jan.	A French army forces King Ferdinand of Naples to flee; Joseph Bonaparte becomes king of Naples the next month.
16 May	British foreign minister Charles James Fox orders a naval blockade of the European continent.
27 June	A British force from the Cape of Good Hope captures Buenos Aires.
July	A Sepoy mutiny occurs at Velore, India, and one thousand are killed or wounded.
10 July	A peace treaty between settlers at Sierra Leone and Temnes King Tom and King Firama, who cede lands to the colony.
13 Sept.	The Prussian army moves into Thuringia.
Aug.	A Spanish force from Montevideo recaptures Buenos Aires.

6 Aug.	Napoleon has German states withdraw from the Holy Roman Empire and form the Confederation of the Rhine. In addition, he forces Francis II of Austria to abdicate the title of Roman Emperor.
17 Oct.	Jacques I of Santo Domingo is assassinated; Henri Christophe takes control of the northern part of the island; and Alexandre Pétion captures the southern part.
19 Oct.	The French win a stunning victory over the Prussians at Jena and Auerstadt.
27 Oct.	Napoleon occupies Berlin.
21 Nov.	Napoleon's Berlin Decree closes the European continent to British trade and bars British subjects from Europe. The Prussian army and Frederick William III flee to East Prussia.
Dec.	Russia and Turkey go to war.
27 Dec.	The Russians capture Bucharest.

1807

- Katsina falls to Uthman's forces.
- Russians attack Japanese settlements on Sakhalin Island and Hokkaidō.
- William Wordsworth publishes *Poems in Two Volumes*.

7 Jan.	England joins the war against Turkey.
7–8 Feb.	Russian and Prussian forces halt Napoleon's advance at Eylau.
19 Feb.	A British fleet breaks through Turkish defenses at the Dardanelles.
25 Mar.	Parliament bars British subjects from participating in the slave trade.
31 Mar.	The British attempt to invade Egypt but are defeated at Rosetta.
29 May	Janissaries in Turkey depose and kill Sultan Selim III, installing Mustapha IV as sultan.
14 June	Napoleon's troops defeat the Russians at Friedland.
7–9 July	Prussia cedes west Elbean possessions to France's German satellites and yields Polish territories to Grande Duchy of Warsaw; Frederick August of Saxony becomes Grand Duke of Warsaw; Prussia joins the Continental System and remains garrisoned by Napoleon; and Czar Alexander recognizes French conquests.
Aug.	A truce occurs between Russia and Turkey.
16 Aug.	Gaslights are used on London streets for the first time.
7 Sept.	A Danish fleet surrenders to the British after a bombardment of Copenhagen.
17 Dec.	Napoleon issues the Milan Decree on seizing ships.

1808

- The Imperial University, or University of France, and the Universities of Lyon and Rennes are founded.

1 Jan.	Sierra Leone becomes a royal British colony.
19 Mar.	Carlos IV of Spain abdicates in favor of Ferdinand, who relinquishes the crown to Napoleon in May.
17 Apr.	In the Bayonne Decree, Napoleon orders the seizure of American ships entering French, Italian, or Hanseatic ports; French will eventually seize $10 million of American ships and cargo.
2 May	A Spanish uprising starts against the French.
June	Muhammad Ali begins the conquest of upper Egypt.
15 July	Joachim Murat becomes king of Naples after Joseph Bonaparte abdicates to become king of Spain.
20 July	French troops occupy Madrid but are driven out by the Spanish.
28 July	Mahmud II becomes Sultan of Turkey.
Sept.–Oct.	The Franco-Russian alliance is reaffirmed at Erfurt.
Nov.	Napoleon leads two hundred thousand men into Spain.
2 Dec.	Napoleon occupies Madrid, and the royal family is imprisoned three days later.
22 Dec.	The first performance of Ludwig van Beethoven's Symphonies 5 and 6 occur in Vienna.

1809

•	Uthman dan Fodio takes Kano in northern Nigeria. He founds the city of Sokoto and establishes control of the Islamic movement over the entire Hausa region.
•	Finland becomes an autonomous grand duchy of the Russian empire.
•	Economist David Ricardo publishes *High Price of Bullion a Proof of the Depreciation of Bank Notes.*
•	Samuel Somering invents the electric telegraph.
Jan.	Parliament learns that the mistress of the Duke of York is selling army commissions.
12 Mar.	England and Persia form an alliance.
13 Mar.	A coup d'état in Sweden deposes King Gustavus IV.
5 June	The duke of Sudermania becomes King Charles XIII of Sweden.
Apr.	Austrians invade Bavaria and are defeated by Napoleon.
25 Apr.	The East India Company signs a treaty with Ranjit Singh, ruler of Lahore.
1 May	Napoleon annexes the Papal States to France.
3 May	Russia declares war on Austria.
12 May	Napoleon captures Vienna.
21–22 May	Napoleon is defeated at Aspern.

12 June	Napoleon is excommunicated by the Catholic Church.
5–6 July	At Wagram the French army defeats the Austrians, with high casualties on both sides: 23,000 French dead or wounded, 7,000 missing; 19,110 Austrians dead or wounded, 6,740 missing.
5 July	Napoleon imprisons Pope Pius VII.
14 July	The British seize Saint-Louis, Senegal, from France.
27–28 July	A British army under Sir Arthur Wellesley defeats Joseph Bonaparte's Spanish army at Talevera de Reina, and as a result Wellesley becomes Viscount Wellington of Talavera.
26 Sept.	The Turks defeat the Russians at Silisteria.
14 Oct.	Austria and France make peace.
16 Dec.	Napoleon divorces Josephine.

1810

	The University of Berlin is founded.
	Portugal agrees to gradual abolition of the slave trade.
	The German Rudolph Ackermann invents the differential gear, a steering mechanism to allow carriages to turn sharp corners.
	French chemist Louis-Nicolas Vauquelin identifies nicotine as the active chemical in tobacco.
6 Jan.	Peace between France and Sweden is declared.
17 Feb.	Rome is declared the second city of the French Empire.
11 Mar.	Napoleon marries Maria Luisa, an eighteen-year-old Austrian archduchess.
6 Apr.	Rioting in England occurs after the reformer Sir Francis Burdett is committed to the Tower of London for criticizing the government.
15 June	The first performance of Johann Wolfgang von Goethe's play *Egmont*, with music by Ludwig von Beethoven.
9 July	Napoleon annexes Holland.
25 Aug.	Muhammad 'Alī Pasha asks the Ottoman Empire to grant Egypt autonomy.
16 Sept.	Don Miguel Hidalgo y Costilla, a priest in Dolores, Mexico, begins a rebellion against the Spanish government.
16 Dec.	Representatives of New Spain present grievances to the Spanish Cortes.
31 Dec.	Czar Alexander withdraws from the Continental System.

1811

	The University of Christiania, Norway, is founded.
	Spain debates abolishing the slave trade; Cuban planters object and defeat the move.
	English engineer John Blenkinsop invents a two-cylinder steam locomotive.

•	Jane Austen publishes *Sense and Sensibility*.
5 Feb.	The Prince of Wales is appointed regent for King George III, who has gone completely mad.
Mar.	"Luddite" riots occur in Nottingham, England, as unemployed workers destroy textile machinery which has put them out of work.
1 Mar.	Muhammad 'Alī Pasha, Ottoman viceroy in Egypt, massacres rebellious Mamluks.
21 Mar.	Father Miguel Hidalgo is captured in Mexico.
7 Jul	A general congress in Venezuela declares independence.
31 July	Father Miguel Hidalgo y Costilla is executed at Chihuahua.
14 Aug.	Paraguay declares independence.
18 Sept.	The Dutch surrender Java to the British.

1812

•	Russia and Sweden sign a secret alliance.
•	The University of Genoa is founded.
•	Swiss Orientalist J. L. Burckhardt begins an ascent of the Nile to Korosko, then travels through the desert to the Red Sea and eventually Mecca.
•	Dingiswayo, Zulu chief, begins consolidating military forces in southern Africa.
8 Jan.	Nicaraguan rebels capture Fort San Carlos.
Mar.	A devastating earthquake strikes Venezuela.
8 May	The Spanish Cortes produces a democratic constitution.
11 May	British Prime Minister Spencer Perceval is assassinated in the House of Commons lobby.
28 May	In the Treaty of Bucharest, Turkey cedes Moldavian lands to Russia, grants amnesty to Serbian rebels, but maintains a garrison in Serbia.
18 June	The United States declares war on Great Britain.
24 June	Napoleon invades Russia.
12 July	After Napoleon seizes Swedish Pomerania, Sweden allies itself with England.
9 Aug.	Two thousand Muslim pilgrims returning from Mecca die in a windstorm in Arabia.
17 Aug.	The French defeat the Russians at Smolensk Oblast.
7 Sept.	A Russian army is defeated at Borodino, seventy-five miles west of Moscow.
14 Sept.	Napoleon enters Moscow and waits for the czar to sue for peace.
15 Oct.	The Russians burn Moscow.
19 Oct.	Napoleon withdraws from Moscow.

1813

•	Muhammad Ali sends an army to Arabia to retake holy cities from Muslim fundamentalists.
17 Mar.	Calling on all German people to rise up against Napoleon, Frederick William of Prussia allies with Russia and declares war against France.
Apr.	Napoleon invades Germany.
4 June	Napoleon agrees to an armistice that lasts until 10 August.
21 June	Wellington occupies Madrid and begins fighting in northern Spain, preparing for an invasion of France.
27 June	Austria agrees to support the allies if Napoleon does not accept conditions for peace.
14 Sept.	The first Congress of Mexican rebels meets, elects José Maria Morelos y Pavón, priest from Caracuaro, general in chief.
8 Oct.	Wellington's army enters France through the Pyrenees.
14–19 Oct.	The allies defeat Napoleon at Leipzig.
6 Nov.	The Mexican Congress declares independence and emancipates slaves.
21 Dec.	Leaders of the Guatemalan independence movement are arrested.

1814

•	The Mazrui dynasty in Mombasa, East Africa, appeals to the British in India for support against the sultan of Oman.
•	War begins between the British in India and Nepal.
Jan.	Naples allies itself with Austria against Napoleon.
14 Mar.	Ferdinand VII is restored to the Spanish throne.
31 Mar.	The allies occupy Paris.
2 Apr.	The Imperial Senate deposes Napoleon.
6 Apr.	Napoleon abdicates, and the Imperial Senate calls on the younger brother of King Louis XVI to be king.
24 Apr.	Louis XVIII arrives in Paris.
17 May	Norway declares independence from Sweden.
30 May	The First Treaty of Paris restores France to its 1792 borders and imposes mild indemnities. The English receive the Cape Colony.
4 June	Louis XVIII grants a charter retaining legal equality, religious freedom, and revolutionary land settlements; it also makes parliament subordinate to the monarch.
16 July	Swedish troops enter Norway.
7 Aug.	Pope Pius VII returns to Rome and restores the Order of Jesus, dissolved by Clement XIV in 1773.
Sept.	At the Congress of Vienna foreign ministers of allied powers meet to restore international order.

10 Oct.	The Norwegian Diet elects Charles Frederick, Duke of Holstein, to be king, but he abdicates.
22 Oct.	The Mexican Congress drafts a Constitution, creating a republic.
4 Nov.	King Charles XIII of Sweden accepts the Norwegian constitution, guaranteeing Norway its independence as a free state united to Sweden; he is proclaimed king of Norway.

1815

•	The University of Groningen, Netherlands is founded.
•	An estimated twelve thousand people in Java die as volcano Mount Tamboro erupts.
Feb.	Vikrama, king of Kandy, Ceylon, attacks British merchants.
14 Feb.	The British take control of Kandy.
27 Feb.	Napoleon escapes from exile on Elba.
1 Mar.	Napoleon enters France and quickly advances north.
2 Mar.	All chiefs on Ceylon submit to British rule.
15 Mar.	Joachim Murat of Naples declares war on Austria.
20 Mar.	Louis XVIII flees Paris, and Napoleon issues a new constitution for France before invading Belgium.
30 Apr.	The central provinces of Poland are made into the Kingdom of Poland under the protection of the Russian czar.
22 May	Joachim Murat of Naples flees to France; he attempts to return to Naples in October but is captured and shot.
18 June	The allies defeat Napoleon at Waterloo, Belgium.
22 June	Napoleon abdicates.
8 July	Louis XVIII returns to Paris and begins the second restoration of monarchy.
20 Nov.	The second Treaty of Paris imposes a 700-million-franc indemnity on France, removes border territories from French control, and initiates a military occupation of the country.
5 Nov.	Royalist troops capture Mexican rebel José Maria Morelos y Pavan.
27 Nov.	Cracow, Poland is declared a free republic.
Dec.	The British and Nepalese sign the Treaty of Saguali, alowing the British envoy to live in Katmandu if he does not interfere with Nepalese affairs.
22 Dec.	Morelos is executed by firing squad.

Letter from "JL" to George Washington informing him of his election as president of the United States (National Archives)

CHAPTER TWO

THE ARTS

by EILEEN KA-MAY CHENG

CONTENTS

Sidebars and tables are listed in italics.

1783

Literature	Jupiter Hammon, *An Evening's Improvement;* David Humphreys, *The Glory of America.*
Music	Oliver Brownson, *Select Harmony;* Andrew Law, *A Collection of Hymns for Social Worship* and *The Rudiments of Music;* John Friedrich Peter, *A Psalm of Joy.*
3 Apr.	Fiction writer Washington Irving is born in New York City.

1784

Literature	Jeremy Belknap, *The History of New-Hampshire. Volume I;* Hugh Henry Brackenridge, *Narratives of a Late Expedition Against the Indians;* Samuel Low, *Winter Display'd, A Poem;* Peter Markoe, *The Patriotic Chief. A Tragedy;* Phillis Wheatley, *Liberty and Peace, A Poem.*
Music	Andrew Law, *Select Harmony,* second edition; Joshua Smith, *Divine Hymns or Spiritual Songs;* Abraham Wood, *An Anthem on Peace.*
24 June	The Virginia legislature votes to commission a marble statue of George Washington and appoints Benjamin Franklin and Thomas Jefferson to choose a sculptor. They recommend Frenchman Jean-Antoine Pélissier.
23 Dec.	New York is designated the temporary capital of the United States.

1785

Literature	Timothy Dwight, *The Conquest of Canäan: A Poem;* David Ramsay, *The History of the Revolution of South-Carolina.*
Music	Silas Ballou, *New Hymns on Various Subjects;* Daniel Read, *The American Singing-Book;* Timothy Swan, *The Federal Harmony.*
•	German organist-composer John Christopher Mollar immigrates to the United States, where he becomes organist at the Zion German Lutheran Church of Philadelphia in 1786.
20 May	Charles Willson Peale opens an exhibition of his moving pictures at his Philadelphia gallery, using special machinery and lighting with transparent pictures to create the illusion of movement. The exhibition closes in 1787.

1786

Literature	Mathew Carey, *The Plagi-Scurriliad: A Hudibrastic Poem;* Thomas Coombe, *The Peasant of Auburn;* Philip Freneau, *The Poems of Philip Freneau. Written Chiefly during the late War;* David Humphreys, *A Poem on the Happiness of America;* St. George Tucker, *The Knight and Friars: An Historical Tale;* Phillis Wheatley, *Poems on Various Subjects, Religious and Moral. First American Edition.*
Music	William Billings, *The Suffolk Harmony;* John F. Peter, *The Lord Is in His Holy Temple;* Isaiah Thomas, ed., *The Worcester Collection of Sacred Harmony.*
•	John Jacob Astor opens the first music store in New York City.
•	British-born composer Alexander Reinagle immigrates to the United States and settles in Philadelphia.

• John Trumbull completes his paintings *The Death of General Warren at the Battle of Bunker's Hill* and *The Death of General Montgomery at the Battle of Quebec*. He also begins work on *The Declaration of Independence*.

25 Sept. Theater performances in Philadelphia are banned.

26 Oct. The *New Haven Gazette* publishes first installment of the mock epic *The Anarchiad,* by Joel Barlow, David Humphreys, John Trumbull, Lemuel Hopkins, and other members of a group of poets known as the Connecticut Wits.

1787

Literature Joel Barlow, *The Vision of Columbus: A Poem in Nine Books;* Philip Freneau, *A Journey from Philadelphia to New-York;* David Humphreys, *Select Poems by Col. Humphreys, Aid-de-Camp to Gen. Washington.*

Music Andrew Adgate, *Select Psalms and Hymns for the Use of Mr. Adgate's Pupils and Proper for All Singing Schools;* John Aitken, *A Compilation of the Litanies and Vespers, Hymns and Anthems, As They Are Sung in the Catholic Church;* William Brown,*Three Rondos for the Piano Forte or Harpsichord;* Daniel Read, *A Supplement to the American Singing-Book;* William Tuckey, *Anthem from the 97th Psalm.*

• William Dunlap writes his first play, *The Modest Soldier.*

Jan. Mathew Carey of Philadelphia publishes the first issue of the *American Museum.*

16 Apr. Royall Tyler's comedy *The Contrast* opens in New York City.

1788

Literature Timothy Dwight, *The Triumph of Infidelity: A Poem;* Philip Freneau, *The Miscellaneous Works;* David Humphreys, *An Essay on the Life of the Honorable Major-General Israel Putnam;* St. George Tucker, *Liberty, A Poem.*

Music Andrew Adgate, *Rudiments of Music;* Daniel Bayley, *The New Harmony of Zion;* Oliver Holden, *The Federal Harmony»* Francis Hopkinson, *Seven Songs for the Harpsichord or Forte Piano;* Simeon Jocelin, *The Chorister's Companion;* Alexander Reinagle, *Federal March* and *A Collection of Federal Songs;* Timothy Swan, *The Federal Harmony.*

• A group of musician founds the New York Musical Society.

1789

Literature William Hill Brown, *The Power of Sympathy;* David Ramsay, *The History of the American Revolution;* George Richards, *The Political Passing Bell: An Elegy.*

Music Andrew Adgate, *The Philadelphia Songster* and *Philadelphia Harmony;* Jacob French, *The New American Melody;* John Hubbard, *Harmonia Selecta;* Johann Friedrich Peter, *Six String Quartets;* Abraham Wood, *Divine Songs* and *Ode to Spring.*

• Harvard graduate Samuel Holyoke begins teaching music.

• Piano maker Charles Albrecht begins work in Philadelphia, and the Bacon Piano Company is established in New York City.

2 Mar. The Philadelphia antitheater law is repealed.

7 Sept.	William Dunlap's play *The Father, or American Shandy-ism* has its premiere in New York City.
15 Sept.	Novelist James Fenimore Cooper is born in Burlington, New Jersey.
24 Nov.	Dunlap's *Darby's Return* opens in New York City.
28 Dec.	Novelist Catherine Maria Sedgwick is born in Stockbridge, Massachusetts.

1790

Literature	Sarah Wentworth Morton, *Ouâbi, or The Virtues of Nature. An Indian Tale in Four Cantos;* Jedidiah Morse, *The History of America;* Mercy Otis Warren, *Poems, Dramatic and Miscellaneous.*
Music	John Antes, *String Trios, Opus 3;* Samuel Holyoke, *Washington;* Daniel Read, *An Introduction to Psalmody.*
•	Peter Markoe publishes his comic opera *The Reconciliation.*
31 May	President George Washington signs the first U.S. copyright law.
10 July	The House of Representatives votes to locate the nation's capital on the Potomac River.
6 Dec.	The nation's capital moves temporarily to Philadelphia.

1791

Literature	Jeremy Belknap, *The History of New-Hampshire. Volume II;* Mathew Carey, ed., *The Beauties of Poetry, British and American;* Benjamin Young Prime, *Columbia's Glory, or British Pride Humbled: A Poem on the American Revolution;* Susanna Rowson, *Charlotte, A Tale of Truth.*
Music	Hans Gram, *America* (march) and *The Death Song of an Indian Chief;* Samuel Holyoke, *Harmonia Americana.*
•	Musicians in Boston found the Philo-Harmonic Society.
•	Jeremy Belknap founds the Massachusetts Historical Society, the first group of this sort in the United States.
9 May	Author-composer Francis Hopkinson dies in Philadelphia.
1 Sept.	Poet Lydia Howard Sigourney is born in Norwich, Connecticut.

1792

Literature	Jeremy Belknap, *The Foresters, An American Tale* and *The History of New-Hampshire. Volume III;* Hugh Henry Brackenridge *Modern Chivalry,* Part I, volumes 1 and 2; Francis Hopkinson, *The Miscellaneous Essays and Occasional Writings.*
Music	Anna Beeman, *Hymns on Various Subjects;* James Hewitt, *Overture in 9 Movements Expressive of a Battle;* Oliver Holden, *American Harmony* and *Coronation* ("All Hail the Power of Jesus' Name"); G. Richards and O. W. Lane, *Psalms, Hymns and Spiritual Songs: Selected and Original.*
•	British conductor-composer James Hewitt immigrates to the United States and becomes conductor at the Park Street Theater in New York City.

•	British organist-composer Raynor Taylor immigrates to the United States.
•	French composer and horn player Victor Pélissier arrives in Philadelphia.
13 Oct.	The cornerstone is laid for the building later known as the White House, the first public building to be constructed in Washington, D.C.
22 Dec.	Massachusetts repeals its antitheater law.

1793

Literature	Hugh Henry Brackenridge, *Modern Chivalry*, Part I, volume 3; Michel Guillaume Jean de Crèvecoeur (J. Hector St. John), *Letters From an American Farmer*, first American edition; George Richards, *The Declaration of Independence: A Poem*; Elihu Hubbard Smith, ed., *American Poems, Select and Original*; Royall Tyler, *The Origin of Evil. An Elegy*.
Music	Benjamin Cook, *Three Songs from Shakespeare*; Jacob French, *The Psalmodist's Companion*; James Hewitt and Mary Ann Pownall, *A Book of Songs*; Oliver Holden, *The Union Harmony*; Jacob Kimball, *The Rural Harmony*; Andrew Law, *The Musical Primer*, revised edition; John Christopher Moller, *Sinfonia*; Daniel Read, *The Columbian Harmonist*, no. 1; Nehemiah Shumway, *The Amercan Harmony*; Stephen Storace and James Cobb, *The Favorite Songs from the Last New Comic Opera, Called The Pirates*; A. Wood and J. Stone, *The Columbian Harmony*.

•	Susanna Rowson returns to America as an actress for a Philadelphia theater company and writes her play *Slaves in Algiers; or, A Struggle for Freedom*, which becomes an immediate hit when it is staged on 30 June 1794 with music by popular composer Alexander Reinagle.
•	The New Theatre Opera House opens in Philadelphia.
•	British singer-pianist-composer Benjamin Carr immigrates to the United States, where he settles in Philadelphia and stages his light opera *The Caledonia Frolic*.
•	Alexander Reinagle helps to form a comic-opera company in New York City.
•	American artist Gilbert Stuart returns to the United States from England, where he has made a name for himself as a portrait painter.
18 Sept.	The cornerstone is laid for the U.S. Capitol.

1794

Literature	Joel Barlow, *The Conspiracy of Kings: A Poem*; Jeremy Belknap, *American Biography*; Timothy Dwight, *Greenfield Hill: A Poem in Seven Parts*; Philip Freneau, *The Village Merchant: A Poem*; David Humphreys, *A Poem on Industry*; Susanna Rowson, *Charlotte, A Tale of Truth*, first American edition, and *The Fille de Chambre*.
Music	Supply Belcher, *The Harmony of Maine*; William Billings, *The Continental Harmony*; Benjamin Carr, *Four Ballads* and *Federal Overture*; James Hewitt, *Overture, Storm at Sea*; Andrew Law, *The Art of Singing*; John Christopher Moller, *Dank und Gebet*; Alexander Reinagle, music for *Slaves in Algiers* and *Overture, St. Patrick's Day*; Reinagle and Susanna Rowson, "America, Commerce and Freedom"; Raynor Taylor, *An Ode to the New Year*, *An Anthem for Public or Private Worship*, and *The Wounded Sailor*.

• James Hewitt stages his ballad operas *Tammany, or the Indian Chief* and *The Patriots.*

• Alexander Reinagle stages his operas *Robin Hood* and *The Spanish Barber.*

3 Nov. Poet William Cullen Bryant is born in Cummington, Massachusetts.

29 Dec. Under the leadership of Charles Willson Peale, the Columbianum in Philadelphia, one of the earliest art academies in the United States, is formed.

1795

Literature Jeremy Belknap, ed., *Sacred Poetry;* Philip Freneau, *Poems Written between the Years 1768 & 1794;* Lemuel Hopkins, *The Democratiad. A Poem;* John Blair Linn, *Miscellaneous Works, Prose and Poetical;* Susanna Rowson, *Trials of the Human Heart.*

Music Amos Bull, *The Responsary;* Benjamin Carr, *Macbeth* (incidental music); Oliver Holden, Hans Gram, and Samuel Holyoke, *The Massachusetts Compiler of Theoretical Principles;* John Christopher Moller, *Overture to Auld Robin Gray, Overture to Harlequin's Invasion,* and *Quartet for Glass Harmonica, Two Violas and Cello;* Daniel Read, *The Columbian Harmonist,* no. 2–3; Raynor Taylor, *La Petite Piedmontese* (ballet).

• Raynor Taylor becomes organist at St. Peter's Church in Philadelphia.

• Alexander Reinagle produces a melodrama, *The Purse,* and an opera, *The Volunteers.*

• Gilbert Stuart paints his first portrait of George Washington.

2 Mar. Judith Sargent Murray's play *The Medium* is performed in Boston.

22 May The first exhibition of the Columbianum opens in Philadelphia.

4 July Construction begins on the Massachusetts State House, designed by Charles Bulfinch.

22 Sept. Humor writer Augustus Baldwin Longstreet is born in Augusta, Georgia.

1796

Literature Joel Barlow, *The Hasty-Pudding: A Poem, in Three Cantos;* Lemuel Hopkins, *The Guillotina, or a Democratic Dirge: A Poem;* John Blair Linn, *The Poetical Wanderer;* St. George Tucker, *The Probationary Odes of Jonathan Pindar.*

Music Benjamin Carr, *Six Piano Sonatas;* Carr and Susanna Rowson, "In Vain the Verdure of Spring"; James Hewitt, *Three Sonatas for the Piano Forte, Opus 5;* Victor Pélissier, *The Mysterious Monk* (incidental music); Alexander Reinagle, *Overture to the Lucky Escape* and *Pierre de Provence and La belle Magulone* (ballet); Raynor Taylor, *New Overture* and *Violin Concerto.*

• John Christopher Moller becomes conductor of the New York City Concerts.

• Gilbert Stuart paints two more portraits of George Washington.

• William Dunlap invests in the Old American Company, a theater company in New York City, where he and Benjamin Carr produce their new opera, *The Archers.*

•	Jean-Antoine Houdon's sculpture of George Washington is installed in the Virginia State House.
Mar.	The English-born architect Benjamin Latrobe arrives in the United States.
9 Mar.	Judith Sargent Murray's play *The Traveller Returned* is performed in Boston.
4 May	Historian William Hickling Prescott is born in Salem, Massachusetts.
19 Dec.	Victor Pélissier and Elihu Hubbard Smith's comic opera, *Edwin and Angelina*, has its premiere in New York City.

1797

Literature	Hugh Henry Brackenridge, *Modern Chivalry*, Part I, volume 4; Hannah Foster, *The Coquette*; Sarah Wentworth Morton, *Beacon Hill: A Local Poem*; Robert Treat Paine Jr., *The Ruling Passion: An Occasional Poem*; Royall Tyler, *The Algerine Captive*.
Music	John Aitken, ed., *Scot's Musical Museum*; Daniel Belknap, *Harmonist's Companion*, "A View of the Temple," "A Masonic Ode," "Spring," and "Summer"; Oliver Brownson, *A Collection of Sacred Harmony*; James Hewitt, *The Battle of Trenton*; Oliver Holden, *The Worcester Collection*; Richard Merrill, *The Musical Practitioner*; Raynor Taylor, *Sonata for Piano with Violin* and *Symphony*; Peter Van Hagen, *Federal Overture*.
•	Victor Pélissier stages a melodrama, *Ariadne Abandoned by Theseus in the Isle of Naxos*.
•	Alexander Reinagle produces a melodrama, *Columbus*, and a musical farce, *The Savoyard*.
•	Raynor Taylor composes two operas, *The Iron Chest* and *The Shipwreck'd*.
17 Feb.	John Daly Burk's play *Bunker-Hill, or the Death of General Warren* has its premiere in Boston.

1798

Literature	Charles Brockden Brown, *Alcuin* and *Wieland*; Hannah Foster, *The Boarding School*; Judith Sargent Murray, *The Gleaner*; Susanna Rowson, *Reuben and Rachel*.
Music	Joseph Hopkinson and Philip Phile, "Hail Columbia"; Jacob Kimball, *The Village Harmony*; Robert Treat Paine Jr., "Adams & Liberty"; Alexander Reinagle, *The Itallian Monk* and *The Gentle Shepherd* (incidental music); Susanna Rowson and Benjamin Carr, "The Little Sailor Boy."
30 Mar.	William Dunlap's play *André* opens in New York City.

1799

Literature	Richard Alsop, Theodore Dwight, and Lemuel Hopkins, *The Political Greenhouse for the Year 1798*; Charles Brockden Brown, *Ormond, Arthur Mervyn*, Part I, and *Edgar Huntly*; Mathew Carey, *A Plumb Pudding* and *The Porcupiniad*; Sarah Wentworth Morton, *The Virtues of Society*.

Music   Jonathan Benjamin, *Harmonia coelestis;* Benjamin Carr, *Three Ballads, Opus 2;* Stephen Jenks, *The New England Harmonist;* David Merrill, *Psalmodist's Best Companion;* Robert Treat Paine Jr. and Peter Van Hagen Jr., "To Arms Columbia"; Alexander Reinagle, "I Have a Silent Sorrow Here"; Raynor Taylor, *Monody on the Death of George Washington.*

• James Hewitt creates two ballad operas, *Columbus* and *The Mysterious Marriage.*

• Musician Filippo Traetta, a political prisoner in Italy, escapes to the United States, settling first in Boston.

Apr.   Charles Brockden Brown founds the *Monthly Magazine and American Review.*

1800

Literature   Richard Alsop, *A Poem Sacred to the Memory of George Washington;* John Blair Linn, *The Death of Washington. A Poem;* Robert Treat Paine Jr., *An Eulogy on the Life of General George Washington;* George Richards, ed., *Hymns and Odes, Composed on the Death of Gen. George Washington;* Mason Locke Weems, *A History of the Life and Death, Virtues, and Exploits of General George Washington;* Sarah Wood, *Julia and the Illuminated Baron.*

Music   Daniel Belknap, *The Evangelical Harmony, Funeral Ode, Autumn,* and *Winter;* Benjamin Carr, *Dead March and Monody for General Washington;* John Cole, *Episcopalian Harmony;* James Hewitt, *The Musical Repository* and "The Wounded Hussar"; Oliver Holden, *From Vernon's Mount Behold the Hero Rise* and *Plain Psalmody;* Samuel Holyoke, *The Instrumental Assistant I;* John Hodgkinson, *Let Washington Be Our Boast;* Jonathan Huntington, *The Albany Collection;* Jacob Kimball, *The Essex Harmony;* Alexander Reinagle, *Masonic Overture, Pizarro* (incidental music) and *Rosa;* Timothy Swan, *Songster's Assistant;* Abraham Wood, *Funeral Elegy on the Death of General George Washington.*

• Designed by Benjamin Latrobe, the Bank of Pennsylvania building, the first U.S. public edifice in the Greek Revival style, is completed in Philadelphia.

• James Hewitt stages his operas *Robin Hood* and *The Wild Goose Chase.*

• Alexander Reinagle produces a dramatic sketch, *A Wreath for American Tars,* and a musical farce, *The Double Disguise.*

• Peter Van Hagen writes the musical drama *Columbus.*

• The Library of Congress is founded in Washington, D.C., the new, permanent capital of the United States.

3 Oct.   Historian George Bancroft is born in Worcester, Massachusetts.

1801

Literature   Charles Brockden Brown, *Clara Howard* and *Jane Talbot;* John Blair Linn, *The Powers of Genius: A Poem;* Tabitha Gilman Tenney, *Female Quixotism: Exhibited in the Romantic Opinions and Extravagant Adventures of Dorsina Sheldon;* Sarah Wood, *Dorval.*

Music   Richard Allen, *A Collection of Spiritual Songs and Hymns;* Uri K. Hill, *The Vermont Harmony;* James Hewitt, *The Fourth of July (A Grand Military Sonata);* George Jackson, *Freedom and Our President (Jefferson's March);* Alexander Reinagle, *Edwy and Elgiva* (incidental music); Nehemiah Shumway, *American Harmony;* Timothy Swan, *New England Harmony.*

•	Benjamin Carr becomes organist at St. Augustine's Catholic Church in Washington, D.C.
3 Jan.	Joseph Dennie of Philadelphia publishes the first issue of the periodical *Port Folio*.

1802

Literature	Sarah Wood, *Amelia*.
Music	Henry Alline, *Hymns and Spiritual Songs;* Daniel Belknap, *The Middlesex Collection;* Jacob French, *The Harmony of Harmonies;* James Hewitt, *Collection of Most Favorite Country Dances* and *Grand Sinfonie Characteristic of the Peace of the French Republic;* Samuel Holyoke, *Columbian Repository of Sacred Harmony;* Abraham Maxim, *Oriental Harmony;* Victor Pélissier, *Gil Blas;* Peter Van Hagen Jr., "Anna" and "Gentle Zephyr"; Peter Weldon, *The New York Serenading Waltz*.
•	The American Academy of the Fine Arts (originally known as the Society of Fine Arts) is founded in New York City.
11 Feb.	Novelist Lydia Maria Child is born in Medford, Massachusetts.

1803

Literature	Thomas Green Fessenden, *Terrible Tractoration;* William Wirt, *The Letters of the British Spy*.
Music	Anonymous, "Jefferson and Liberty"; John Cole, *Cole's Collection of Psalm Tunes and Anthems;* Uri K. Hill, *A Number of Original Airs, Duetto's and Trio's;* Oliver Holden, *Charlestown Collection of Sacred Songs;* George K. Jackson, *President Jefferson's New March and Quick Step;* Victor Pélissier, *La fille hussar;* Timothy Swan, *The Singer's Museum;* Filippo Traetta, *Sinfonia Concertata;* David Zeisberger, *A Collection of Hymns for the Use of the Christian Indians of the Mission of the United Brethren of North America*.
•	Victor Pélissier stages his melodrama *A Tale of Mystery*.
25 May	Poet and essayist Ralph Waldo Emerson is born in Boston.
Oct.	Charles Brockden Brown begins publishing the *Literary Magazine and American Register*.
Nov.	*The Monthly Anthology and Boston Review* is founded by David Phineas Adams in Boston.

1804

Literature	Hugh Henry Brackenridge, *Modern Chivalry,* Part II, volume 1; Thomas Green Fessenden, *Original Poems;* Susanna Rowson, *Miscellaneous Poems;* Sarah Wood, *Ferdinand and Elmira*.
Music	Benjamin Carr, *The Siege of Tripoli;* Ebenezer Child, *The Sacred Musician;* Samuel Holyoke, *The Christian Harmonist;* George K. Jackson, *Ode for General Hamilton's Funeral* and *David's Psalms*.
•	Alexander Reinagle produces *The Sailor's Daughter,* a musical comedy.
•	Charles S. Ashworth becomes conductor of the U.S. Marine Band.

| 4 July | Novelist Nathaniel Hawthorne is born in Salem, Massachusetts. |
| 29 Nov. | The New York Historical Society is founded by John Pintard, DeWitt Clinton, Egbert Benson, and David Hosack. |

1805

Literature	Hugh Henry Brackenridge, *Modern Chivalry*, Part II, volume 2; John Davis, *The First Settlers of Virginia: An Historical Novel;* John Blair Linn, *Valerian: A Narrative Poem;* Thomas Green Fessenden, *Democracy Unveiled;* Mercy Otis Warren, *History of the Rise, Progress, and Termination of the American Revolution.*
Music	Jeremiah Ingalls, *The Christian Harmony;* George K. Jackson, *Ode to Harmony* and *Ode to Peace;* Stephen Jenks, *The Delights of Harmony;* Stith Mead, *Hymns and Spiritual Songs;* David S. Mintz, *Spiritual Song Book;* Timothy Olmstead, *The Musical Olio;* Alexander Reinagle, *Overture to The Wife of Two Husbands* and *The Voice of Nature* (incidental music).
•	Victor Pélissier stages *Valentine and Orson,* a melodrama.
Feb.	William Dunlap's New York theater company goes bankrupt.
June	The Pennsylvania Academy of Fine Arts is founded in Philadelphia.
6 Sept.	Sculptor Horatio Greenough is born in Boston.
28 Dec.	Fourteen-year-old John Howard Payne founds the *Thespian Mirror,* one of the first magazines covering New York theater. He continues to publish it until 31 May 1806.

1806

Literature	Susanna Rowson, *A Present for Young Ladies; Containing Poems, Dialogues, Addresses . . . ;* Noah Webster, *A Compendious Dictionary of the English Language.*
Music	Daniel Belknap, *The Village Compilation;* Abijah Forbush, *Psalmist's Assistant;* Gottlieb Graupner, *Rudiments of the Art of Playing the Piano Forte;* James Hewitt, *Theme with Thirty Variations in D Major;* Uri K. Hill, *The Sacred Minstrel;* Jonathan Huntington, *The Apollo Harmony;* Stephen Jenks, *Laus Deo;* Timothy Olmstead, *Martial Music;* Daniel Read, *Litchfield Collection;* Oliver Shaw, *A Favorite Selection of Music.*
•	Alexander Reinagle stages his opera *Mary, Queen of Scots.*
7 Feb.	John Howard Payne's first play, *Julia, or The Wanderer,* is produced in New York City.
17 Apr.	Novelist William Gilmore Simms is born in Charleston, South Carolina.

1807

| Literature | Richard Alsop, Mason F. Cogswell, Theodore Dwight, Lemuel Hopkins, and Elihu Hubbard Smith, *The Echo, with Other Poems;* Joel Barlow, *The Columbiad;* William Hill Brown, *Ira and Isabella; or, The Natural Children;* David Ramsay, *The Life of George Washington.* |

Music	Joseph Herrick, *The Instrumental Preceptor;* Oliver Holden, *Vocal Companion;* Samuel Holyoke, *Instrumental Assistant II;* John Hubbard, *Essay on Music;* George K. Jackson, *Thirteen Easy Canons;* Stephen Jenks, *The Hartford Collection of Sacred Harmony;* Elias Mann, *Massachusetts Collection of Sacred Harmony;* Timothy Olmstead, *Martial Music;* Oliver Shaw, *For the Gentlemen: A Favorite Selection of Instrumental Music.*
•	James Nelson Barker and John Bray's musical *Tears and Smiles,* a play notable for its use of American character types, is produced in Philadelphia.
•	James Hewitt stages a ballad opera, *The Tars from Tripoli.*
•	Alexander Reinagle produces his opera *The Travellers.*
24 Jan.	Washington Irving, William Irving, and James Kirke Paulding begin publishing *Salmagundi,* a series of satirical essays; the last number appears on 25 January 1808.
27 Feb.	Poet Henry Wadsworth Longfellow is born in Portland, Maine.
17 Dec.	Poet John Greenleaf Whittier is born on a farm near Haverhill, Massachusetts.

1808

Literature	William Cullen Bryant, *The Embargo;* Mason Locke Weems, *The Life of George Washington,* enlarged edition.
Music	Anonymous, *The Missouri Songster;* William Emerson, *A Collection of Psalms and Hymns;* Charles Hupfield, *Musical Preceptor;* George K. Jackson, *Ode for the Fourth of July;* David Moritz Michael, *Psalm 103;* Oliver Shaw, *The Columbian Sacred Harmonist.*
•	James Nelson Barker and John Bray's musical *The Indian Princess,* the first dramatization of the story of John Smith and Pocahontas, is performed in Philadelphia.

1809

Literature	Washington Irving, *A History of New York;* David Ramsay, *History of South Carolina;* Royall Tyler, *The Yankey in London;* Mason Locke Weems, *The Life of Gen. Francis Marion in the Revolutionary War.*
Music	Daniel Belknap, *Belknap's March;* Benjamin Carr, *Applicazione adolcita, Opus 6;* Joel Harmon Jr., *The Columbian Sacred Minstrel;* Andrew Law, *The Art of Playing the Organ and Pianoforte;* Hezekiah Moors, *The Province Harmony;* Oliver Shaw, *Thanksgiving Anthem;* William Smith, *The Churchman's Choral Companion;* Solomon Watt, *Impartial Selection of Hymns and Spiritual Songs,* Peter Weldon, *President Madison's March.*
19 Jan.	Poet and fiction writer Edgar Allan Poe is born in Boston.
24 Feb.	John Howard Payne makes his professional acting debut, playing Young Norval in a New York production of *Douglas,* a tragedy by Scotsman John Home.
29 Aug.	Poet, novelist, and essayist Oliver Wendell Holmes is born in Cambridge, Massachusetts.

1810

Literature Charles Jared Ingersoll, *Inchiquin, The Jesuit's Letters;* Isaiah Thomas, *History of Printing in America.*

Music Benjamin Carr, *Six Ballads from "The Lady of the Lake";* Elkanah K. Dare, *The Periodical Harmony;* James Hewitt, *Yankee Doodle with Variations;* Thomas S. Hinde, *The Pilgrim Songster;* Jesse Mercer, *The Cluster;* Nahum Mitchell, *Brattle Street Collection;* Peter K. Moran, *Variations on a Swiss Waltz;* John Wyeth, *Repository of Sacred Music.*

• Benjamin Carr, Raynor Taylor, and George Schetky give a concert in Philadelphia that the local press calls "the greatest musical event" that has ever occurred in that city.

22 Feb. Novelist Charles Brockden Brown dies.

May A group of artists in Philadelphia form the Society of Artists.

28 May Author and editor Margaret Fuller is born in Cambridgeport, Massachusetts.

1811

Literature Isaac Mitchell, *The Asylum;* Robert Treat Paine Jr., *A Monody on the Death of Lieut. General Sir John Moore.*

Music Benjamin Carr, *Lessons and Exercises in Vocal Music, Opus 8;* Starke Dupuy, *Hymns and Spiritual Songs;* Victor Pélissier, *Columbian Melodies;* Edward Riley, *Riley's New Instructions for the German Flute;* Oliver Shaw, *A Plain Introduction to the Art of Playing the Pianoforte.*

• James Hewitt leaves New York for Boston, where he becomes music director at the Federal Street Theater.

Jun. The last issue of the *Monthly Anthology* appears.

14 June Novelist Harriet Beecher Stowe is born in Litchfield, Connecticut.

1812

Literature Robert Treat Paine Jr., *The Works in Verse and Prose;* James Kirke Paulding, *The Diverting History of John Bull and Brother Jonathan.*

Music Benjamin Carr, *Six Progressive Sonatas;* Eliakim Doolittle, "The Hornet Stinging the Peacock"; Jonathan Huntington, *Classical Church Musick;* Nahum Mitchell, *Templi Carmina;* H. W. Pilkington, *A Musical Dictionary;* James Sanderson, "Hail to the Chief."

• James Hewitt becomes organist at Trinity Church in Boston.

• Jonathan Huntington becomes a singing instructor in Boston.

1813

Literature James Kirke Paulding, *The Lay of the Scottish Fiddle;* Susanna Rowson, *Sarah, or The Exemplary Wife.*

Music Jacob Eckhard Jr., "Naval Song (The Pillar of Glory)"; Solomon Warriner, *Springfield Collection of Sacred Music;* John Wyeth, *Repository of Sacred Music II.*

• Novelist and abolitionist William Wells Brown is born into slavery on a plantation near Lexington, Kentucky.

30 Mar.	Novelist Ann Sophia Stephens is born in Humphreysville, Connecticut.
28 Aug.	Poet Jones Very is born in Salem, Massachusetts.

1814

Literature	William Dunlap, *A Narrative of the Events Which Followed Bonaparte's Campaign in Russia;* William Wirt and others, *The Old Bachelor.*
Music	Benjamin Carr, *The History of England, Opus 11;* John Cole, *The Devotional Harmony;* Joel Harmon Jr., *A Musical Primer;* Uri K. Hill, *The Handelian Repository;* Andrew Law, *Essays on Music;* Francis Scott Key, "The Star-Spangled Banner" (set to John Stafford Smith's "To Anacreon in Heaven"); Raynor Taylor, *The Aethiop* (occasional music).
20 Mar.	Humor writer George Washington Harris is born in Allegheny City, Pennsylvania.
19 Oct.	Historian and dramatist Mercy Otis Warren dies in Plymouth, Massachusetts.

1815

Literature	Hugh Henry Brackenridge, *Modern Chivalry,* complete and revised edition; Philip Freneau, *A Collection of Poems, on American Affairs, and a Variety of Other Subjects;* William Dunlap, *The Life of Charles Brockden Brown;* James Kirke Paulding, *The United States and England;* John Howard Payne, *Juvenile Poems;* Lydia Howard Sigourney, *Moral Pieces in Prose and Verse.*
Music	Micah Hawkins, "Backside of Albany, or, The Siege of Plattsburg"; Oliver Shaw, *Christian Psalmody;* Filippo Traetta, *Peace.*
26 Apr.	The new Handel and Haydn Society in Boston adopts a constitution.
May	Richard Henry Dana founds *The North American Review* in Boston.
1 Aug.	Richard Henry Dana Jr., future author of *Two Years Before the Mast,* is born in Boston.
25 Dec.	The Handel and Haydn Society of Boston performs its first concert.

OVERVIEW

National Identity. As inhabitants of a new nation, Americans faced a particularly daunting task. Devoting much of their energy and most of their resources to survival, they had little time or money for cultural pursuits. As John Adams put it in 1780, "It is not indeed the fine Arts, which our Country requires. The Usefull, the mechanic Arts, are those which We have occasion for in a young Country." He added that "the Art of Legislation and Administration and Negotiation, ought to take Place, indeed to exclude in a manner all other Arts.—I must study Politicks and War that my sons may have liberty to study Mathematicks and Philosophy. My sons ought to study Mathematicks and Philosophy . . . in order to give their children a right to study Painting, Poetry, Musick, Architecture, Statuary, Tapestry and Porcelaine." While Adams and many other Americans believed that the nation had to establish itself as a political entity before turning its attention to art and literature, others considered culture an integral part of any nation's identity. These Americans hoped the establishment of a vital national culture would contribute to a stronger sense of American nationality that would counteract the forces threatening to drive Americans apart. For them the achievement of true political independence required America to free itself from the models of British art and literature. As Noah Webster put it in 1783, "America must be as independent in *literature* as she is in *politics*."

Cultural Independence. Before the American Revolution, colonists had viewed themselves as Englishmen, looking to England for cultural standards. As a result, citizens of the new United States lacked a strong indigenous cultural tradition that could provide a starting point for a national culture. Indeed, a sense of cultural inferiority persisted throughout the postrevolutionary period, and Americans continued to defer to the cultural achievements of the Old World. Although Americans still depended on European models, however, they also sought cultural independence from Europe. A powerful sense of nationalism, which began to materialize in the early years of the new republic, was expressed Americans' artistic and literary endeavors.

Translatio Studii. Americans had long believed in the potential of the New World for cultural greatness. They based their belief on the idea of the *translatio studii*, or *translatio imperii*—the idea that civilization inevitably moves from east to west. This theory had a long lineage, and Enlightenment thinkers had given it renewed vigor in the eighteenth century. The most eloquent exponent of this theory was Anglican bishop George Berkeley, who summed it up in "Verses by the Author on the Prospect of Planting Arts and Learning in America" (1752):

> Westward the course of empire takes its way;
>   The first four acts already past,
> A fifth shall close the drama with the day;
>   Time's noblest offspring is the last.

Americans took this doctrine to mean that the New World would eventually be a center of cultural greatness.

Republican Ideology. Further complicating American cultural development was the complex relationship between the arts and Americans' republican ideals. Rooted in classical political theory and the ideas of eighteenth-century British opposition thinkers, republicanism was a central ingredient in the ideology of the American Revolution and continued to exert a powerful influence on citizens of the new nation. According to this ideology the ultimate goal of government was to preserve liberty, which was most threatened by luxury and corruption. Believing that the fine arts were a form of luxury that could thrive only in a wealthy society, republican thinkers considered the arts antithetical to republican virtue, the willingness to sacrifice individual interests for the public good. John Adams demanded of Thomas Jefferson, "Will you tell me how to prevent luxury from producing effeminacy, intoxication, extravagance and folly? It is vain to think of restraining the fine arts. Luxury will follow riches and the fine arts will come with luxury in spite of all that wisdom can do." Republican theorists warned against the development of the fine arts as both a sign and a cause of social degeneracy. They feared that the fine arts would encourage a taste for sensual pleasures and would weaken the spirit and vigilance necessary to maintain liberty. Yet, as an extension of their belief that liberty was conducive to social and political prosperity, republican thinkers also argued that liberty was favorable to artistic achievement. John Trenchard and Thomas Gordon, two of the most influential exponents of British opposition ideology, made this link when they declared, *"Polite Arts and Learning [are] naturally produced in Free States, and marred by such as are not free."*

Liberal Capitalism. Republican ideology was itself undergoing modification in this period as Americans began to turn to a liberal capitalistic ethos that stressed private profit rather than public good. According to liberal ideology, a social order arose unintentionally from the interaction of individuals who pursued their own private interests. This emerging ideology reflected and furthered the rise of a capitalist economy in the United States. Liberal capitalism coexisted uneasily with republicanism and posed its own problems for artistic development. In one sense liberal capitalism was favorable to the arts, for it viewed luxury and wealth as beneficial and natural results of the pursuit of private interest, rather than as enemies to virtue. Consequently, the liberal capitalist did not regard art and luxury as signs of degeneracy. Yet, as contemporary commentators recognized, liberal capitalism threatened the arts in another way. By placing such a premium on profit, it encouraged a sense of materialism that endangered an appreciation for aesthetic and intellectual pursuits.

Democracy. Republican and liberal ideologies both encouraged a belief in equality, which elevated the status of the people and gave primacy to popular judgment. Republicanism was based on the idea of equality, as virtue was only possible in a society of independent and equal individuals. Liberal capitalism emphasized the centrality of self-interest, which it portrayed as a universal trait, discrediting a belief in inherent differences based on birth or social status. As a result, a democratic spirit increasingly took hold in the new nation, a development that had dual implications for American arts and letters.

Democratic Art. Artists and writers of the new republic embraced and drew inspiration from these democratic currents, seeing themselves as pioneers. Just as the Revolution had established popular government, they would establish a popular foundation for art. Consistent with democratic ideals, they hoped to free the arts from their traditional reliance on aristocratic patrons. Instead of depending on wealthy individuals to sponsor them and commission their works, artists and writers would rely on public support. Yet the trend toward democracy also posed problems for cultural development. Artists who were freed from aristocratic patrons became subject to the vicissitudes of popular opinion, which could deprive them of their means of support and endanger their creative independence. Democracy therefore created a quandary for artists, who wondered how to preserve their artistic integrity while accommodating popular tastes. Furthermore, with popular preference as the ultimate standard of judgment, a democratic culture threatened the possibility of higher aesthetic standards and values. In his well-known analysis of American democracy Frenchman Alexis de Tocqueville ascribed American artistic mediocrity to democratic society. He argued that while "the productions of artists are more numerous," the "merit of each production is diminished," concluding, "No longer able to soar to what is great, they cultivate what is pretty and elegant, and appearance is more attended to than reality."

ARCHITECTURE: CLASSICAL REVIVAL

Background. Americans achieved their first artistic successes in architecture, which appears in many ways to have been the form of art best suited to a republican nation. Because architecture served a practical purpose, it was exempted from traditional republican objections to art as a decadent product of aristocratic luxury. Their ideological concerns infused even the architectural styles that Americans favored, and the classical style was compatible with republican ideals. It was only fitting for Americans to imitate the architecture of the ancient Greek and Roman republics, whose political institutions had provided the models for the system of government in the United States.

Benjamin Latrobe. One of the most influential figures in the classical revival was Benjamin Latrobe, a British architect who immigrated to the United States in 1796. He designed the building for the Bank of Pennsylvania, the first public edifice built in the Greek Revival style. Believing that the grandeur and imperial connotations of Roman architecture made it incompatible with American ideals and culture, Latrobe expressed the democratic spirit of America through the simplicity of Greek architecture, itself the product of democracy. He stated firmly, "my principles of good taste are rigid in Grecian architecture. . . . Wherever therefore the Grecian style can be copied without impropriety I love to be a *mere*, I would say a *slavish* copyist." Latrobe did not follow Greek models slavishly, however, for he recognized that "the *forms* and the *distribution* of the Roman and Greek buildings which remain, are in general inapplicable to the objects and uses of our public buildings." Latrobe's design for the Bank of Pennsylvania used Greek details, but it did not strictly conform to Greek models. By adapting their classical forms to American circumstances he created a unique American style.

Greek Revival. The completion of the Bank of Pennsylvania building in 1800 launched the Greek Revival movement that dominated American architecture from 1820 to 1860. Latrobe's students Robert Mills and William Strickland carried on and extended his affinity for Greek forms in their designs. The distinguishing feature

The Bank of Pennsylvania in Philadelphia, designed by Benjamin Latrobe and completed in 1800 (engraving after a drawing by George Strickland)

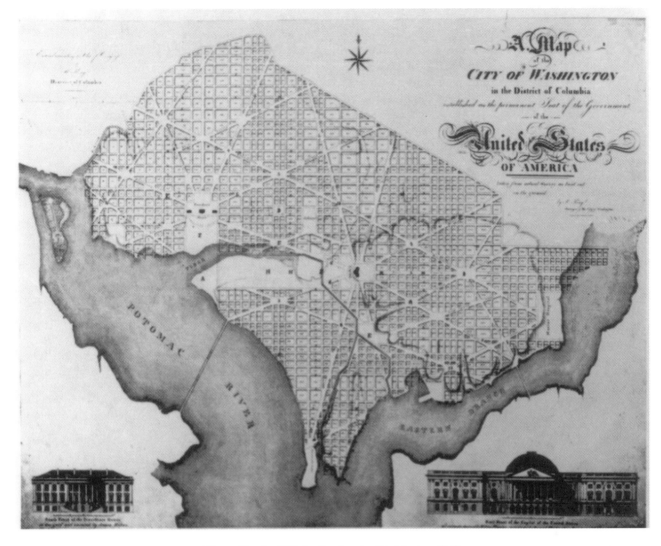

Pierre Charles L'Enfant's plan for Washington, D.C.

of Greek Revival architecture, the white classical portico of the Greek temple, became a common sight on public buildings and private residences throughout the country.

Sources:

Talbot Hamlin, *Benjamin Henry Latrobe* (New York: Oxford University Press, 1955);

Hamlin, *Greek Revival Architecture in America* (New York: Oxford University Press, 1947);

J. Meredith Neil, *Toward a National Taste: America's Quest for Aesthetic Independence* (Honolulu: University Press of Hawaii, 1975);

Russel Blaine Nye, *The Cultural Life of the New Nation, 1776–1830* (New York: Harper & Row, 1960).

ARCHITECTURE: THE NATIONAL CAPITAL

Public Architecture. American architecture did more than reflect Americans' political and cultural aspirations; it would also help the nation achieve them. Modeled on the Maison Carrée, a Roman temple in Nîmes, France, Thomas Jefferson's classical design for the new Virginia State House in Richmond would serve a dual purpose, he argued in 1785. Jefferson, whose preference for Roman classicism was influenced by the writings of the sixteenth-century Venetian architect Andrea Palladio,

called the design for the new state capitol "very simple," but added, "it is noble beyond expression, and would have done honour to our country as presenting to travellers a morsel of taste in our infancy promising much for our maturer age." Furthermore, he asked, "how is a taste in this beautiful art to be formed in our countrymen, unless we avail ourselves of every occasion when public buildings are to be erected, of presenting to them models for their study and imitation." Jefferson's vision prevailed, and the Virginia capitol was built essentially according to his design.

Washington, D.C. Similar concerns gave even greater import to the architecture and design of Washington, D.C. As secretary of state, Jefferson took an active interest in the planning and development of this city, playing a key role in the political compromise of 1790 that heavily influenced the decision to locate the federal capital on the Potomac. Jefferson involved himself in the layout and building of Washington, supervising and advising Pierre Charles L'Enfant, the French architect in charge of designing the new city. Jefferson expressed his hope that the U.S. Capitol building would be "worthy of the first temple dedicated to the sovereignty of the people, embellishing with Athenian taste the course of a nation looking far beyond the range of Athenian destinies." The orderly layout of the streets and buildings also conformed to classical ideals of rationality and uniformity. L'Enfant's plan for the city, however, closely resembles the layout of Versailles—the seat of French absolute monarchy and the antithesis of republican ideals. Indeed, in many ways L'Enfant's design betrayed the republican values it was supposed to symbolize. Everything in the city was designed to facilitate the display of authority and reinforce the majesty of government. L'Enfant planned the city around public buildings and monuments, while the "grand avenues" that extended across the city served little practical function. His plans for Washington left little room for the ordinary people to go about their everyday lives.

Problems. L'Enfant's conception of the capital ultimately contributed to its failure to become a national cultural center. Without any means to attract commerce and people to it, the capital languished. Rather than becoming an American Athens, Washington became a cultural and social backwater, whose only reason for being was the business of government. Latrobe ridiculed the capital as a "Gigantic Abortion." The implications of the design for American culture were not what its planners intended. Unlike European capitals, Washington did not become an acknowledged center for American cultural life. The result was a physical separation between American artists and politicians that contributed to a split between politics and culture in America and undermined public support for the arts. Artists remained scattered throughout different regions of the country, hindering the process of intellectual exchange within the artistic community. Thus divided, artists continued to maintain regional ties that often conflicted with and obstructed their efforts to establish a national identity and culture.

Sources:
Stanley Elkins and Eric McKitrick, *The Age of Federalism: The Early American Republic, 1788–1800* (New York: Oxford University Press, 1993);
Gordon Wood, ed., *The Rising Glory of America, 1760–1820* (New York: Braziller, 1971).

ARCHITECTURE: FEDERAL STYLE

An American Style. The classical and federal styles dominated American architecture in the early republic. Closely related to one another, they used classical elements in different ways. Classical architecture is monumental and austere in character, patterning itself after ancient temples. In contrast, federal architecture is lighter and more intricate, with delicate details and ornaments. The leading practitioner of federal style was Bostonian Charles Bulfinch (1763–1844), who developed his interest in English neoclassical architecture while in

The Massachusetts State House, Boston. The central portion of the building was designed by Charles Bulfinch and built in 1795–1797.

London. In particular he looked for models to two leading figures in the English neoclassical tradition: Robert Adam and William Chambers, modifying and adapting their style to American circumstances. On his return to Boston in 1787, Bulfinch executed his first design, the Hollis Street Church. This project was followed by designs for many other private and public buildings, including the Connecticut State House (1793–1796) and the Federal Street Theater (1793–1794) in Boston. Through such designs he helped to establish the dominance of federal-style architecture in New England.

Amateur to Professional. American architects of this period were either gentlemen amateurs, for whom architecture was a hobby, or builders, for whom design was a secondary aspect of construction. From a wealthy background, Bulfinch started out as an amateur and remained one until the failure of one of his most ambitious projects, the Tontine Crescent (1793–1794) in Boston. Inspired by English examples, the Tontine Crescent was a row of connected houses built according to a coherent design, the first such development in America. Because he began work on this project during a recession, Bulfinch had been unable to attract enough investors and ended up financing it with his own money. After going bankrupt in 1796, he turned to architecture to make a living, helping to transform architecture into a professional occupation. In his wife's words, "My husband . . . made Architecture his business, as it had been his pleasure."

The Massachusetts State House. The most important and best-known of Bulfinch's designs is the Massachusetts State House (1795–1797). Modeled on William Chambers's design for Somerset House in England, the Massachusetts State House design is notable for its central dome, a feature that was widely imitated in designs for other state capitols. Contemporary commentary on the Massachusetts State House suggests how this building adapted British styles for American nationalistic purposes. A writer for the *Columbian Centinel* declared in 1798, "Too much praise cannot be bestowed upon the Agents who have directed the construction of this superb edifice, for their economy, liberality and patriotism.—The materials are mostly of the produce of our country, and the composition ornaments were made and moulded on the spot." The intersection between public affairs and Bulfinch's architectural interests culminated with his appointment as architect of the U.S. Capitol in 1817, taking over from Benjamin Latrobe the task of rebuilding of the Capitol after it was burned by the British during the War of 1812. Work was completed in 1827.

Sources:

Fiske Kimball, *American Architecture* (Indianapolis & New York: Bobbs-Merrill, 1928);

Harold Kirker, *The Architecture of Charles Bulfinch* (Cambridge, Mass.: Harvard University Press, 1969);

Charles A. Place, *Charles Bulfinch, Architect and Citizen* (New York: Da Capo Press, 1968);

Joseph J. Thorndike Jr., ed., *Three Centuries of American Architects* (New York: American Heritage Publishing, 1981);

Marcus Whiffen, *American Architecture Since 1780: A Guide to the Styles* (Cambridge, Mass.: MIT Press, 1969);

Whiffen and Frederick Koeper, *American Architecture, 1607–1976* (Cambridge, Mass.: MIT Press, 1981).

ART: AMERICAN PORTRAITURE

Background. Without aristocratic patronage and with limited public interest in the arts, American artists faced a serious problem in finding financial support. Widespread demand for portraits made portraiture the most viable way for them to earn a living, and many artists turned to this form of art. The business and commercial aspects of artistic endeavor were especially conspicuous in portrait painting. Artists had traditionally regarded history painting as at the top of the artistic hierarchy and portraiture as at the bottom. Despite the financial opportunities it offered, artists aspired to higher forms of art, seeing portrait painting as limiting and demeaning, as the artist was often required to sacrifice art to accommodate the subject's personal vanity.

Gilbert Stuart. As one of the most successful and prolific American portraitists of the early republic, Gilbert Stuart (1755–1828), a Rhode Island native, did not share his contemporaries' qualms about portrait painting, realizing its commercial potential to its fullest. Best known for his portraits of George Washington, Stuart had established his reputation as a portrait painter in England, where he trained under Benjamin West. Despite his artistic success there, he fell into debt because of his extravagant way of life.

AN AFRICAN AMERICAN PAINTER

Joshua Johnson was the first known African American portrait painter in the United States. There is little certain information on his back—ground. He was probably born in the West Indies and seems to have come to America sometime in the 1770s as a slave or indentured servant to the family of Philadelphia artist Charles Willson Peale. Johnson eventually achieved his freedom and worked in Baltimore from about 1796 to 1825. By his own account Johnson was a "self-taught genius" in painting. Johnson painted more than eighty portraits, including *Sarah Ogden Gustin* (circa 1798–1802), his only signed work. His subjects ranged from members of the wealthiest Baltimore families to middle- and working-class individuals. Johnson's portraits combined sophistication with folk simplicity, reflecting at once the artistic influence of the Peales and his lack of formal training.

Gilbert Stuart's "Lansdowne portrait" of George Washington (1796), commissioned by William Bingham of Philadelphia as a gift for William Petty, Marquis of Lansdowne

The Washington Portraits. Forced to return to the United States in 1793 to escape his creditors, Stuart undertook the project of portraying George Washington. "I expect to make a fortune by Washington alone," he declared. "I calculate upon making a plurality of portraits, wholelengths, that will enable me to realize. And if I should be fortunate I will repay my English and Irish creditors." The results more than lived up to these expectations of profit. Stuart painted several different portraits of Washington and turned the sizable demand for repli-cas into a highly lucrative enterprise. The first version (1795)—called the "Vaughan type" after its owner, Samuel Vaughan—was followed by the most popular and influential of his Washington portraits, the "Athenaeum portrait" (1796), so called because the Boston Athenaeum bought it shortly after Stuart's death. Stuart used the head from the "Athenaeum portrait" for his best-known full-length painting of Washington, the "Lansdowne portrait" (1796)—named after its owner William Petty, Marquis of Lansdowne—and for all of his subse-

The Death of General Warren at the Battle of Bunker's Hill (1786), the first painting in John Trumbull's Revolutionary War series, which helped to shape Americans' perceptions of the war

quent replicas. While profit motivated Stuart's portraits of Washington, he produced works of lasting importance that helped to fix Washington's image in the American mind. In particular, the simplicity and austerity of the Athenaeum portrait confirmed the perception of Washington as the embodiment of republican dignity.

Sources:

James Thomas Flexner, *America's Old Masters: First Artists of the New World* (New York: Viking, 1939);

Neil Harris, *The Artist in American Society: The Formative Years, 1790–1860* (New York: Braziller, 1966);

Richard McLanathan, *Gilbert Stuart* (New York: Abrams, 1986);

Charles Merrill Mount, *Gilbert Stuart: A Biography* (New York: Norton, 1964).

ART: HOUDON'S SCULPTURE OF WASHINGTON

Background. The prominence of sculpture among the ancient Greeks and Romans made sculpture appealing as an ideal way to commemorate the achievements of American Revolutionary heroes. Yet America was slow to develop sculptors, and European artists filled the demand for sculpture well into the nineteenth century. In 1784 the Virginia legislature voted to commission a marble statue of George Washington for the state capitol and appointed Benjamin Franklin and Thomas Jefferson to choose an artist. They recommended Jean-Antoine Houdon, a leading French sculptor, whose works included portrait busts of other prominent Americans, including themselves. Houdon initially planned to execute the commission in Paris, using Charles Willson Peale's portrait of Washington as a model. Although Peale sent Houdon the portrait, Houdon ended up coming to the

United States to take the bust of Washington from life. He worked with Washington at Mount Vernon in 1785 and completed the statue in 1791. It was installed in the Virginia capitol in 1796.

Antique or Modern Dress? Houdon faced a major dilemma: whether to portray Washington in antique or modern dress. Traditionally, artists depicted their subjects in classical garb, but historical painter Benjamin West had established the precedent of using historically accurate contemporary costume instead. Houdon ultimately decided to follow West's lead. Jefferson approved this decision, finding Houdon's Washington "strongly reminiscent of West, Copley, Trumbull, and Brown. I think a modern in antique dress as just an object of ridicule as a Hercules or Marius with a periweg and chapeau-bras." Horatio Greenough's statue of Washington, completed in 1841, later became such an object of ridicule because he portrayed Washington as a classical deity, bare-chested and draped in ancient robes.

Cincinnatus. Though Houdon clothed his statue in modern costume, he modeled his Washington on a classical hero—the Roman general Cincinnatus, who was widely regarded as the ideal republican leader. After leading his army to military victory, Cincinnatus had turned down the opportunity to become a dictator and returned to his civilian life as a farmer. For many Americans Washington's greatest act was his decision to relinquish power after the American Revolution. In doing so, they believed, he had made possible the preservation of republicanism in America. Houdon's Washington is wearing military garb, but he also has a plow, representing his decision to give up military power for the life of a

Jean-Antoine Houdon's statue of George Washington, installed in the Virginia State House in Richmond in 1796

John S. Hallam, "Houdon's Richmond Statue of Washington," *American Art Journal*, 10 (November 1978): 73–80;

Garry Wills, *Cincinnatus: George Washington and the Enlightenment* (Garden City, N.Y.: Doubleday, 1984).

ART: THE PENNSYLVANIA ACADEMY OF FINE ARTS

Early Academies. Inspired by the prestigious Royal Academy in Great Britain, American artists and patrons looked to the creation of art institutions as a way to promote artistic development in the United States. The Society of Fine Arts in New York (later renamed the American Academy of the Fine Arts) was the first major American art academy, established in 1802 under the auspices of Robert and Edward Livingston. Early American academies quickly fell prey to internal divisions and factionalism, stemming largely from tensions between patrons and artists. Wealthy patrons were necessary to establish and maintain the academies, but artists resented and resisted control by laymen whom they considered insensitive to their interests. Yet artists and art academies were unable to free art from reliance on private patronage despite republican prescriptions to the contrary.

The Pennsylvania Academy. The Pennsylvania Academy of Fine Arts in Philadelphia achieved an unusual degree of success and stability. Founded in 1805, it offered instruction to artists and sought to raise public awareness and interest through public art exhibitions. As one of its founders, Charles Willson Peale, explained, its goal was "to promote the cultivation of the Fine Arts in the U.S.A. by introducing correct and elegant copies from the first masters in Sculpture and Painting . . . by occasionally conferring moderate but honorable premiums, and otherwise assisting the studies and exciting the efforts of the Artists, gradually to unfold, enlighten, and invigorate the talents of our countrymen."

The Society of Artists. With the exception of Peale, most of the founders of the Pennsylvania Academy of Fine Arts were not artists but wealthy patrons of art such as Joseph Hopkinson and Horace Binney. Though not immune to the tensions that beset other academies, the Pennsylvania Academy was more sensitive to the interests of artists than its counterparts and so avoided many of the conflicts that divided and weakened other art academies. In 1810 a group of artists, resenting patron domination of the Pennsylvania Academy of Fine Arts, formed their own organization, the Society of Artists. Yet instead of allowing this development to immobilize its operations, the Pennsylvania Academy made greater efforts to address the needs of artists. The Academy thus neutralized the Society, which had effectively dissolved by 1815.

gentleman farmer at Mount Vernon. Since republican ideology glorified farming as an occupation uniquely favorable to virtue, Houdon's plow helped to fix Washington's image as the embodiment of republican ideals.

Sources:
Wayne Craven, *Sculpture in America* (New York: Crowell, 1968);

Sources:
Neil Harris, *The Artist in American Society: The Formative Years, 1790–1860* (New York: Braziller, 1966);

Design for the Triumphal Arch that Philadelphia artist Charles Willson Peale built from wood and paper for the celebration of the signing of the Treaty of Paris, January 1784 (drawing by Lester Headley Sellers, based on descriptions in contemporary newspapers and Peale's *Autobiography*

Lillian B. Miller, *Patrons and Patriotism: The Encouragement of the Fine Arts in the United States, 1790–1860* (Chicago: University of Chicago Press, 1966);

J. Meredith Neil, *Toward a National Taste: America's Quest for Aesthetic Independence* (Honolulu: University Press of Hawaii, 1975).

DRAMA: MORALITY AND THE THEATER

Background. For Americans of the early republic, theater was the most suspect of all the fine arts. A deeply rooted belief in the immorality of theater, dating from the Puritans, led some colonies to prohibit stage productions before the Revolution. Following the war, theatrical companies that had ceased to operate because of wartime restrictions tried to revive themselves. They first had to petition state legislatures for permission to perform, often provoking sharp opposition. The debate was especially fierce in Philadelphia, and similar disputes took place in New York, Charleston, Boston, and other cities. Opponents saw the theater as conducive to dissipation and vice. Plays came under fire for their often bawdy language and for plots involving immoral topics, especially seduction. Actors were portrayed as people of loose morals, prone to debauchery.

Democratic Audiences. Critics found the composition and behavior of theater audiences equally objectionable. They condemned, in particular, the presence of prostitutes in the audience. Theaters set aside special boxes for prostitutes in order to shield respectable women from contact with them, but critics charged that by admitting prostitutes at all, theaters turned them-

selves into nothing better than "Hot Beds of Vice" and "disguised Brothels." Elite distrust of the masses (possibly fueled by their anxieties about democracy) also contributed to antitheater sentiments. The theater brought together large crowds of people from many social classes. Although hierarchical distinctions were preserved by the arrangement and division of seats into different price categories, the physical proximity of people made some wealthy patrons uneasy. The often rowdy behavior of such crowds confirmed elite prejudice against the vulgar masses and fed fears that their presence in such numbers would encourage social disorder. Audiences actively participated in theatrical performances and were uninhibited about expressing their approval or disapproval of what was happening on stage. Performances were frequently disrupted by rowdy audience members who shouted abusive obscenities or pelted actors and fellow patrons with objects such as apples and nuts.

Republican Concerns. Critics of theater feared its ability to undermine virtue and so endanger republicanism itself. A healthy republic, they said, depended on the moral character of the people. In making this argument they drew on the traditional view of drama as a cause and sign of decay and corruption in republican societies. The groundswell of hostility to theater reached a crescendo in 1786 with the passage in Pennsylvania of a bill prohibiting the building of theaters or the performance of plays in Philadelphia. This law was one in a series of statutes passed to ban or restrict theater in American cities after the Revolution.

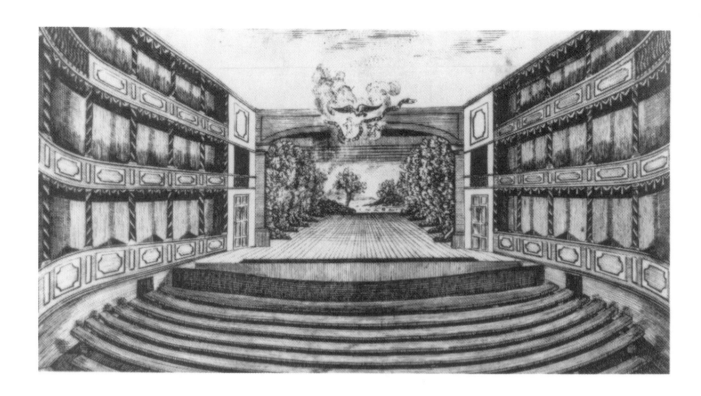

Interior and exterior of the Chestnut Street Theater, Philadelphia, designed by Benjamin Latrobe and completed in 1794

Defenders of Theater. In defiance of such strictures, defenders of theater persisted in asserting the legitimacy of this art form and gradually gained ground over their opponents. Advocates of theater shared many of the critics' objectives. Both sought to create a virtuous republican citizenry. Playwrights did not disagree with their opponents' moral concerns, arguing instead that their plays would actually foster virtue in their audiences and assure the vitality of republican ideals. They also depicted theater as a valuable expression of American genius that would disprove European indictments of the deficiency of American culture. Furthermore, they pointed out that suppressing theater violated republican principles of freedom of expression. Petitioners for the legalization of theater in Philadelphia reasoned that if theater were banned, "every freeman must incur a forfeiture of a natural right, which he ought to possess—the right of acting as he pleases, in a matter perfectly indifferent to the well-being of the community." These arguments eventually won the day, and the Pennsylvania Assembly repealed the antitheater law in 1789. In 1792 Massachusetts repealed its ban on theater, which dated back to 1750.

Sources:

Joseph J. Ellis, *After the Revolution: Profiles of Early American Culture* (New York: Norton, 1979);

David Grimsted, *Melodrama Unveiled: American Theater and Culture, 1800–1850* (Chicago: University of Chicago Press, 1968);

Kenneth Silverman, *A Cultural History of the American Revolution* (New York: Crowell, 1976);

Gordon Wood, ed., *The Rising Glory of America, 1760–1820* (New York: Braziller, 1971).

DRAMA: THE EMERGENCE OF AMERICAN THEATER

The Contrast. Playwright Royall Tyler benefited from and contributed to the growing acceptance of the theater among early national Americans, becoming the nation's first successful playwright. His play *The Contrast,* first performed in New York on 16 April 1787, was a critical and popular success, commanding many repeat performances. Reviewers saw Tyler's play as an illustration of the advantages of theater and praised his achievement as living proof of American cultural vitality. The prologue to *The Contrast* proclaimed its nationalist purposes, describing the play as a "piece, which we may fairly call our own." The play took conventional plots and characters from eighteenth-century British drama and gave them a distinctively American cast. As a realistic depiction of American social life and manners, Tyler's play contributed to the quest for a literature based on American topics and themes.

Virtue versus Luxury. In *The Contrast* Tyler expressed Americans' political and ideological concerns about their nation's republican character. The central theme is the conflict between virtue and luxury. The plot centers on the arranged engagement of the virtuous and sentimental Maria Van Rough and the dissolute Billy

---

JONATHAN VISITS THE THEATER

In *The Contrast* Royall Tyler used the character Jonathan to satirize the naive innocence of rural Americans and to offer a fresh point of view on the ways of more sophisticated city dwellers. In the following scene Jonathan describes his first visit to a theater:

Jonathan: So I went right in, and they shewed me away, clean up to the garret, just like meeting-house gallery. And so I saw a power of topping folks, all sitting round in little cabbins, "just like father's corn-cribs"; and then there was such a squeaking with the fiddles, and such a tarnal blaze with the lights, my head was near turned. At last the people that sat near me set up such a hissing—hiss—like so many mad cats; and then they went thump, thump, thump, just like our Peleg threshing wheat, and stampt away, just like the nation; and called out for one Mr. Langolee,—I suppose he helps act the tricks. . . .

Jessamy: Well, and did you see the man with his tricks?

Jonathan: Why, I vow, as I was looking out for him, they lifted up a great green cloth and let us look right into the next neighbor's house. Have you a good many houses in New-York made so in that 'ere way?

Jenny: Not many; but did you see the family?

Jonathan: Yes, swamp it; I see'd the family.

Jenny: Well, and how did you like them?

Jonathan: Why, I vow they were pretty much like other families;—there was a poor, good-natured, curse of a husband, and a sad rantipole of a wife. . . .

Jenny: Well, Mr. Jonathan, you were certainly at the play-house.

Jonathan: I at the play-house!—Why didn't I see the play then?

Jenny: Why, the people you saw were players.

Jonathan: Mercy on my soul! did I see the wicked players?—Mayhap that 'ere Darby that I liked so was the old serpent himself, and had his cloven foot in his pocket. Why, I vow, now I come to think on't, the candles seemed to burn blue, and I am sure where I sat it smelt tarnally of brimstone.

Jessamy: Well, Mr. Jonathan, from your account, which I confess is very accurate, you must have been at the play-house.

Jonathan: Why, I vow, I began to smell a rat. When I came away, I went to the man for my money again; you want your money? says he; yes, says I for what? says he; why, says I, no man shall jocky me out of my money; I paid my money to see sights, and the dogs a bit of a sight have I seen, unless you listening to people's private business a sight. Why, says he, it is the School for Scandalization—The School for Scandalization!—Oh! ho! no wonder you New-York folks are so cute at it, when you go to school to learn it; and so I jogged off.

Source: Royall Tyler, *The Contrast: A Comedy* (Philadelphia: From the Press of Pritcahrd & Hall and published by Thomas Wignell, 1790).

Dimple, who has learned his rakish ways during a trip to England. Maria's father, a merchant whose constant refrain is "mind the main chance," is preoccupied with commercial opportunity. He arranges Maria's engagement because he believes that Dimple's fortune makes him a good match. Tyler introduces Maria singing "The Death Song of Alknomook," a lament on the nobility of a dying Indian, setting up a contrast between Maria's sentimentality and her father's shrewd practicality. The situation is complicated by the arrival of the courageous and honest Col. Henry Manly, a hero of the American Revolution. Although Manly and Maria fall in love, they are bound by Maria's engagement to Dimple to deny their feelings for one another. While Manly embodies the self-sacrificing virtue considered essential to republicanism, Dimple personifies the qualities that endangered these ideals—luxury and hypocrisy. The play ends happily after it is revealed that Dimple has squandered his fortune in England and plans to jilt Maria so that he can marry an unattractive but wealthy woman while taking one of Maria's friends as his mistress. In the final scene Maria's father approves of the marriage of Maria and Manly and bestows his fortune on them. Manly's victory over Dimple represents the victory of republican virtue over European corruption. Critics commended *The Contrast* for this republican moral, which validated arguments in favor of theater as a stimulus to republican virtue. As one critic concluded, the point of *The Contrast* was "to render superlatively ridiculous the cox-comical extravagance of the age, and the subversion of *natural simplicity*, into the *imp of luxury*—and holding high to view, in letters of the purest gold, all the virtues of the human heart."

Manly and Jonathan. Tyler set up another contrast, however, that complicated the message of *The Contrast*: the opposition between Manly and his servant Jonathan. While Manly represents classical republicanism, Jonathan exemplifies the independent and democratic Yankee. Tyler furthered this characterization of Jonathan by having him sing "Yankee Doodle" in the first known stage performance of the lyrics to this song. While Jonathan's rustic, backwoods dialect is often a source of comedy in the play, Tyler also made Manly's formality and pomposity the object of mockery. Clearly Tyler did not favor either of these character types as the ideal American, suggesting that he possessed a more detached perspective on republican ideals than his contemporaries may have realized.

Sources:

Ada Lou Carson and Herbert L. Carson, *Royall Tyler* (Boston: Twayne, 1979);

Emory Elliott, ed., *American Writers of the Early Republic, Dictionary of Literary Biography*, volume 37 (Detroit: Gale Research, 1985);

Kenneth Silverman, *A Cultural History of the American Revolution* (New York: Crowell, 1976);

G. Thomas Tanselle, *Royall Tyler* (Cambridge, Mass.: Harvard University Press, 1967).

FICTION: THE FIRST AMERICAN NOVEL

Background. During the 1780s Americans developed a growing interest in the relatively new literary form of the novel, reading books by British novelists such as Daniel Defoe, Samuel Richardson, and Henry Fielding, as well as European authors. One particular favorite was German writer Johann Wolfgang von Goethe's *The Sorrows of Young Werther* (1774), the story of a sensitive, alienated young romantic who commits suicide. The novel became especially popular after an American edition was published in Philadelphia in 1784. Yet despite the rise of novel reading, Americans in general remained highly ambivalent about the novel.

The Question of Morality. Some critics called novels frivolous and immoral diversions and expressed the fear that fiction would lure popular attention away from serious and edifying works such as history or religion. They also distrusted novels because of their imaginative quality, a deeply rooted prejudice with origins in the Puritan

Frontispiece for *The Power of Sympathy* (1789), illustrating the subplot based on a scandal involving two prominent Boston families

view that works of fiction were essentially lies. A more immediate source of this distrust was Scottish common-sense philosophy, which had an immense influence in early-national American thought and culture. Common-sense philosophers such as Thomas Reid, Dugald Stewart, and Henry Home, Lord Kames, gave primacy to actual experience over the realm of the possible or the ideal as the embodiment of reality. As a result, they were skeptical about the realm of the imagination, which dealt only with possible experience. In their view, then, novels were dangerous because they lacked any grounding in reality and truth.

The Power of Sympathy. In January 1789 a twenty-four-year-old Bostonian, William Hill Brown, a younger half brother of composer Mather Brown, sought to capitalize on the popularity of the novel—in particular *The Sorrows of Young Werther*—by publishing *The Power of Sympathy,* a tale of seduction generally considered the first American novel. Written in the epistolary, or novel-in-letters, form employed by Richardson in his widely read seduction novels *Pamela* (1740–1742) and *Clarissa* (1747–1748), Brown's book received little attention. Aware of the deeply rooted social and philosophical misgivings about novels, Brown had tried to address concerns about the morality of fiction by giving his novel a didactic purpose: "to represent the specious causes, and to expose the fatal consequences, of seduction; to inspire the female mind with a principle of self complacency, and to promote the economy of human life." Brown used the main plot—the story of Harriot and Harrington—to convey this lesson. Harrington is a rake who plots to seduce the beautiful Harriot, an orphan without wealth or social connections. Although Harrington repents of this scheme and decides to marry Harriot, the news that they are half brother and half sister results in the death of both characters: Harrington commits suicide with a copy of *The Sorrows of Young Werther* by his side, and Harriot dies from shock. While Brown expressed the hope that the tragic consequences of Harrington's plans to seduce Harriot would serve as a warning against such immoral behavior, the sensationalistic appeal of his novel undermined his stated moral objectives.

Imagination and Reality. Brown also sought to legitimize his work by emphasizing its basis in fact, highlighting this quality with his subtitle, "The Triumph of Nature. Founded in Truth." One of the subplots in his novel was based on a true story—the local scandal caused by the affair between Perez Morton, husband of poet Sarah Wentworth Morton, and the poet's sister, Fanny Apthorp, who gave birth to her brother-in-law's child. Brown drew directly on this series of events, which led to Fanny Apthorp's suicide, in his story of Ophelia's seduction by her brother-in-law Mr. Martin and her eventual suicide.

The Rise of the Novel. Brown's novel went largely unnoticed—owing at least in part to attempts by the Apthorps and Mortons to suppress its publication. Yet, as Kenneth Silverman has pointed out, the publication of *The Power of Sympathy* marks the beginning of a huge upswing in Americans' novel reading. Between 1744, when Benjamin Franklin published an American edition of *Pamela,* and 1789, fifty-six foreign novels were reprinted in America. Between the appearance of *The Power of Sympathy* and 1800 there were some 350 American editions of such works.

Sources:

Alexander Cowie, *The Rise of the American Novel* (New York: American Book Company, 1948);

Cathy N. Davidson, *Revolution and the Word: The Rise of the Novel in America* (New York: Oxford University Press, 1986);

Emory Elliott, ed., *American Writers of the Early Republic, Dictionary of Literary Biography,* volume 37 (Detroit: Gale Research, 1985);

Terence Martin, *The Instructed Vision: Scottish Common Sense Philosophy and the Origins of American Fiction* (Bloomington: Indiana University Press, 1961);

Kenneth Silverman, *A Cultural History of the American Revolution* (New York: Crowell, 1976).

FICTION: WOMEN AND THE NOVEL

Women Readers. Because they possessed the ability to expand the horizons of their readers, novels achieved great popularity among women, who discovered that fiction gave them access to a sphere beyond that of their own homes and families, exposing them to new experiences and possibilities. More entertaining and easier to read than traditional forms of literature such as philosophy or history, novels served an educational purpose for their readers. The process of reading improved women's literacy and encouraged them to think for themselves, making them part of an intellectual world that had traditionally excluded them.

Criticism of Novels. Deeply rooted presumptions about female inferiority fed continuing hostility to the novel. Critics charged that novels were dangerous because they encouraged women to follow their passions and emotions, inviting women to immorality and corrupting the minds of weak women ill-equipped to resist the lures of fiction. The author of an 1802 essay, "Novel Reading, a Cause of Female Depravity," declared, "Without the poison instilled [by novels] into the blood, females in ordinary life would never have been so much the slaves of vice."

Women Authors. During the early republican period there were several popular American female novelists, most notably Hannah Webster Foster, Helena Wells, S. S. B. K. Wood, Tabitha Tenney, Judith Sargent Murray, and Susanna Rowson, whose *Charlotte. A Tale of Truth* (1791) was the first American novel to become a best-seller. The prominence and success of these women, who violated traditional prohibitions against women's participation in the public arena, is one example of how novels allowed women to depart from their prescribed roles. Yet their books often upheld conventional assumptions about gender roles.

Historians Jeremy Belknap and David Ramsay

The Coquette. One such novel was Foster's *The Coquette*, the only other American novel to become a bestseller before 1800. The daughter of a prosperous merchant and the wife of a clergyman, Foster offered a mixed message in *The Coquette*, suggesting her own ambivalence about gender roles. Based loosely on a true story, the notorious scandal surrounding Elizabeth Whitman's seduction and death, *The Coquette* is the story of Eliza Wharton, a young woman whose defiance of traditional constraints on women similarly leads to her death. Desiring to enjoy freedoms usually denied to an unmarried woman, Eliza refuses a marriage proposal from the respectable but pompous Reverend Boyer. After becoming the mistress of Major Sanford, she dies while giving birth to an illegitimate child. By depicting the disastrous consequences of Eliza's self-assertion, Foster warned women against following in her footsteps. Yet the novelist also portrayed Eliza sympathetically, implicitly criticizing the injustices of a system that could allow such a tragedy to happen. In general, female novelists of Foster's time were divided among themselves about the role and status of women. The results of their differences illustrate the ability of the novel to serve as a subversive agent for social change and a conservative support for the status quo.

Sources:

Cathy N. Davidson, *Revolution and the Word: The Rise of the Novel in America* (New York: Oxford University Press, 1986);

Emory Elliott, ed., *American Writers of the Early Republic, Dictionary of Literary Biography*, volume 37 (Detroit: Gale Research, 1985);

Hannah Webster Foster, *The Coquette*, edited by Davidson (New York: Oxford University Press, 1986).

HISTORICAL WRITING: DOCUMENTING THE NEW NATION

Background. With the close of the American Revolution came an outpouring of histories in the new American nation. The first American writer to produce such a work was Jeremy Belknap, who published the first volume of his *History of New-Hampshire* in 1784. Belknap's contemporaries followed suit with histories of their own states, including Samuel Williams's *The Natural and Civil History of Vermont* (1794) and Hugh Williamson's *The History of North Carolina* (1812). These historians wrote partly out of a natural desire to explain the origins of their new nation. For historians such as Belknap and Williamson, this enterprise was more than a matter of disinterested intellectual inquiry. Recognizing that the bonds uniting their diverse and contentious compatriots were still fragile, they also sought to instill a more secure sense of national identity. Although these historians focused on their individual states, they emphasized the qualities that all Americans shared and made their states embody national traits.

David Ramsay. One of the most prolific and highly regarded of the early national historians was David Ramsay. After training as a doctor in Philadelphia, Ramsay settled in Charleston, South Carolina, where he served the revolutionary cause as a member of the state legislature and later as a delegate to the Continental Congress. After his first historical work, *The History of the Revolution of South-Carolina* (1785), he wrote a more general history of the Revolution (1789), as well as a biography of George Washington (1807) and a history of

South Carolina (1809). For Ramsay these books were important to defining and creating a unified sense of national identity, and he hoped that other Americans would produce histories because, "Enthusiastic as I am for the Unity of our republic I wish for every thing that tends to unite us as one people who know esteem & love each other."

Republican Consensus. In his books Ramsay tried to further national unity by emphasizing the consensus that had existed among colonial and Revolution-era Americans. In particular he pointed to their shared commitment to republican principles, which dated back to the earliest settlement of the colonies. In his history of the Revolution he concluded: "The English Colonists were from their first settlement in America, devoted to English liberty, on English principles." Through such a portrayal, he used history to combat the sectional and social divisions threatening to fragment the new republic.

Sources:

David Ramsay, *The History of the American Revolution*, edited by Lester H. Cohen (Indianapolis: Liberty Fund, 1990);

Arthur H. Shaffer, *The Politics of History: Writing the History of the American Revolution, 1783–1815* (Chicago: Precedent, 1975);

Shaffer, *To Be an American: David Ramsay and the Making of the American Consciousness* (Columbia: University of South Carolina Press, 1991).

HISTORICAL WRITING: THE WASHINGTON MYTH

Background. Even during his lifetime, Americans began to mythologize George Washington. Washington himself consciously cultivated the public image of a virtuous and self-sacrificing republican citizen. This characterization gained widespread acceptance among Americans of the early republic as they projected onto Washington the traits they desired for their new nation.

Mason Locke Weems. In 1800 Mason Locke Weems took the glorification of Washington to new heights in his biography of Washington. Ordained as an Anglican minister, Weems had become an itinerant bookseller by 1792. In this occupation Weems developed a sensitivity to popular taste, which proved useful when he wrote one of the many popular biographies of the first U.S. president that followed Washington's death in December 1799. Weems revised and expanded this immensely popular work several times as it went through some forty editions in twenty-five years and decisively shaped Washington's popular image.

The Washington Myth. Employing a lively and often colloquial style, Weems enshrined the idealized view of Washington that had already begun to develop in Washington's lifetime. He often made up anecdotes to make his praise of Washington's virtues more compelling. The best-known of these stories is the legend of Washington's voluntary admission that he had chopped down his father's cherry tree, an anecdote without any basis in fact that Weems added to a later edition to demonstrate that

WASHINGTON'S CHERRY TREE

The most famous story about George Washington as a boy was invented by biographer Mason Locke Weems, who falsely attributed the anecdote to a distant relative of Washington. Weems's version of the story is as follows:

"When George," said she, "was about six years old, he was made the wealthy master of a *hatchet*! of which, like most little boys, he was immoderately fond, and was constantly going about chopping every thing that came in his way. One day, in the garden, where he often amused himself hacking his mother's pea-sticks, he unluckily tried the edge of his hatchet on the body of a beautiful young English cherry-tree, which barked so terribly, that I don't believe the tree ever got the better of it. The next morning the old gentleman finding out what had befallen his tree, which, by the by, was a great favourite, came into the house, and with much warmth asked for the mischievous author, declaring at the same time, that he would not have taken five guineas for his tree. Nobody could tell him any thing about it. Presently George and his hatchet made their appearance. *George*, said his father, *do you know who killed that beautiful little cherry-tree yonder in the garden?* This was a *tough question;* and George staggered under it for a moment; but quickly recovered himself; and looking at his father, with the sweet face of youth brightened with the inexpressible charm of all-conquering truth, he bravely cried out, *"I can't tell a lie, Pa; you know I can't tell a lie. I did cut it with my hatchet."—Run to my arms, you dearest boy,* cried his father in transports, *run to my arms; glad am I, George, that you killed my tree; for you have paid me for it a thousand fold. Such an act of heroism in my son, is more worth than a thousand trees, though blossomed with silver, and their fruits of purest gold."*

Source: Mason Locke Weems, *The Life of Washington*, edited by Peter S. Onuf (Armonk, N.Y.: M. E. Sharpe, 1996).

even as a child Washington possessed extraordinary honesty. The point was not just to glorify Washington; Weems hoped to inculcate the same virtues in his readers.

Private Virtue. In addition to making the story of Washington's life accessible, Weems tried to make Washington's virtues a model for the people. Previous writers, Weems believed, had focused too much on Washington's public acts, which had little bearing on the lives of most children. In contrast, he said Washington's private virtues were directly relevant to everyday conduct, of importance to all children "because in these every youth may become a Washington—a Washington in piety and patriotism,—in industry and honour—and consequently a Washington, in what alone deserves the name, SELF ESTEEM AND UNIVERSAL RESPECT." Weems's treatment of Washington's religious piety, benevolence, industry, and other traits worthy of emulation established goals that ordinary people could attain in their everyday lives.

Biographer Mason Locke Weems

Sources:

Mason Locke Weems, *The Life of Washington*, edited by Peter S. Onuf (Armonk, N.Y.: M. E. Sharpe, 1996);

Garry Wills, *Cincinnatus: George Washington and the Enlightenment* (Garden City, N.Y.: Doubleday, 1984).

LITERATURE AND THE MONTHLY ANTHOLOGY

Background. The periodicals that began to materialize during the early years of the republic served as important vehicles for literary criticism, publishing reviews and essays on literary topics. One of the most important such periodicals was the *Monthly Anthology*, founded in Boston in 1803. Its first editor, David Phineas Adams, was unable to make the journal a financially viable enterprise and abandoned it after publishing six issues. In 1804 William Emerson, the father of poet and essayist Ralph Waldo Emerson, took over as editor, and the following year a group of leading Boston intellectuals—including Joseph Buckminster, William Tudor, and Joseph Tuckerman—joined Emerson. To give the enterprise a firmer institutional basis they formed the Anthology Society. In that year the subscribers to the *Anthology* numbered 440, but their efforts extended the life of the *Anthology* only temporarily, and it folded in 1811.

The Impact of the *Anthology*. Although short-lived, the *Anthology* made a significant contribution to Ameri-can literary development, offering original essays and extensive literary reviews that were pieces of literature in their own right. Helping to set the standards for literary achievement in America, these writings reflected the sectional and class biases of the *Anthology* editors. The *Anthology* therefore played a role in establishing the cultural dominance of New England over the rest of the nation, a tendency that would become even more pronounced in succeeding decades.

Patrician Authors. Reflecting their own privileged backgrounds, the members of the Anthology Society articulated a literary ideal that disdained commercial motives as incompatible with good literature. They themselves did not earn a living from their writings and received no pay for their contributions to the *Anthology*. They saw literature as a patrician enterprise, written by gentlemen amateurs who sought not wealth or fame but only the public good. They blamed the widespread concern with popularity and profit for the failure of Americans to develop literature and culture. *Anthology* contributor Winthrop Sargent lamented in 1805 that the "national maxim" was " '*get money.*' " His fellow contributor, Theodore Dehon, expressed a similar concern: "the passion for wealth, and the ardour of political contention, which are, perhaps, the predominant traits in the character of our countrymen, have retarded the ascendancy of genius, and obstructed the progress of letters." For Dehon literary critics needed to combat this tendency, for "Ignorance, or corruption, in the very important tribunals of criticism, would unquestionably impede the progress and diminish the reputation of American literature." He believed that publications such as the *Anthology* could help the United States to achieve the potential to "vie with any nation upon the earth in the pursuit of literary distinction."

Washington Irving and *Salmagundi*. Periodicals were objects of ridicule in *Salmagundi*, a series of humorous essays that New York writers Washington Irving, William Irving, and James Kirke Paulding began publishing in 1807. Although *Salmagundi*, which appeared serially as twenty small pamphlets between 24 January 1807 and 25 January 1808, satirized periodicals like the *Monthly Anthology*, the New Yorkers' work also shared the patrician outlook of that magazine. Like the founders of the *Anthology*, Washington Irving disparaged the desire for profit and popularity in literature. Yet at the same time Irving was deeply ambivalent on this subject. While he disdained commercial motives in literature, he was also one of the first American writers to make a successful living from authorship, helping to inaugurate a trend he found disturbing.

Sources:

Mary Weatherspoon Bowden, *Washington Irving* (Boston: Twayne, 1981);

Frank Luther Mott, *A History of American Magazines, 1741–1850* (New York: Appleton, 1930);

Lewis P. Simpson, ed., *The Federalist Literary Mind* (Baton Rouge: Louisiana State University Press, 1962).

William Emerson, the second editor of the *Monthly Anthology*

MUSIC: THE INDIGENOUS IDIOM

The First Tune Book. In 1770 William Billings published *The New-England Psalm Singer,* a collection of more than one hundred anthems, hymns, and psalms that he had written. This volume was the first tune book compiled by a single American composer, as well as the first published collection of exclusively American music. *The New-England Psalm Singer* prefigured an outpouring of American tune books that began during the 1780s. By 1800 more than one hundred American tune books had appeared in print. Designed for singing schools, *The New-England Psalm Singer* provided tunes and instructions for training American singers.

Fuguing Tunes. *The New-England Psalm Singer* includes the first "fuguing tunes" by an American com-

poser, which exemplify how Billings drew on English church music for his tunes but still gave them a distinctive American cast. A fuguing tune is usually a song with passages that require different voices to sing different words simultaneously. According to Billings, a "fuge" consisted of "Notes flying after each other, altho' not always the same sound. . . . Music is said to be Fuging, when one part comes in after another." Although first developed by English composers, fuguing tunes became identified as a particularly American form, and they became immensely popular after the Revolution. By 1810 American tune books included approximately one thousand different fuguing tunes.

Billings's Influence. The nationalistic impulses that inspired Billings's work were even more evident in his

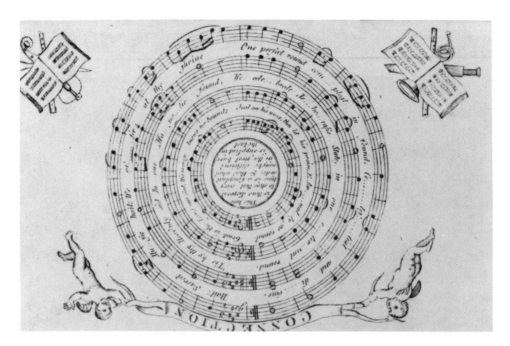

Frontispiece for William Billings's 1794 song collection *The Continental Harmony*. Billings considered tunes to be "complete circles."

next tune book, *The Singing Master's Assistant* (1778), his most popular collection, owing partly to the patriotic character of its songs. Although a composer of sacred music, Billings chose texts more for their literary quality than their spiritual message, a tendency that reflected the decline of orthodox Congregationalism in New England. The New England tune books that followed contained an increasingly secular component. Other composers included many of Billings's songs in their song collections, and his music was widely known and performed during the 1780s. He also published new tune books of his own in the 1780s and 1790s.

Democratic Music. Billings's popularity owed much to the democratic impulses at work in his music, an approach to music following naturally from his own background. A tanner who taught himself music, Billings's unpolished speech and manner reflected his humble origins. Hostile to formality and established authorities, he advised musicians, "*Nature is the best Dictator,*" and added, "For my own Part, as I don't think myself confin'd to any Rules for Composition laid down by any that went before me, neither should I think (were I to pretend to lay down Rules) that any who came after me were any ways obligated to adhere to them, any further than they should think proper: So in fact, I think it is best for every *Composer* to be his own *Carver*." The spontaneous and boisterous character of Billings's music expressed his anti-authoritarian spirit. He emphasized nature over refinement, urging singers to follow their own inclinations. Billings also drew his music from popular sources. His incorporation of folk and dance rhythms into his songs made them appealing to popular audiences and established their place in a vibrant American musical tradition.

Sources:

Gilbert Chase, *America's Music From the Pilgrims to the Present* (Urbana: University of Illinois Press, 1987);

Charles Hamm, *Music in the New World* (New York: Norton, 1983);

David McKay and Richard Crawford, *William Billings of Boston, Eighteenth-Century Composer* (Princeton: Princeton University Press, 1975);

Kenneth Silverman, *A Cultural History of the American Revolution* (New York: Crowell, 1976).

MUSIC: THE MOVEMENT FOR REFORM

Andrew Law. As the music of Billings and his followers became increasingly influential, it provoked a powerful reaction that revealed the unease with which many Americans greeted the social tendencies embodied in such music. The leader of this resistance was Andrew Law, a member of a prominent Connecticut family whose emphasis on order and gentility in music was the product of his privileged social background. Law was best known as a promoter of singing schools and a compiler of songbooks, including his own collection of psalm and hymn tunes, *Select Harmony* (1778). In contrast to Billings's emphasis on spontaneity and naturalness, Law insisted on refined singing and "good or genteel pronunciation." He sought to replace Billings's indigenous tunes with music composed in the European style. In the 1793 edition of his *Musical Primer* Law accused American composers of writing tunes that would encourage and accommodate harsh singing. Such tunes, Law declared, had proliferated "to the great prejudice of much better music, produced even in this country, and almost to the utter exclusion of genuine European compositions."

"Wild Fuges." As Law's effort to reform American music gained momentum during the early nineteenth century, its followers were especially critical of fuguing tunes, which exemplified for them all the most objectionable qualities of American music. These reformers wanted not just to refine American music, but also to restore it to an exclusively religious and spiritual purpose. In 1807 Elias Mann railed against "those wild fuges, the rapid and confused movements, which have so long been the disgrace of Congregational psalmody, and the contempt of the judicious and tasteful amateur." For such critics, fuguing tunes were primitive forms that generated a dangerous sense of excitement and enthusiasm. Warning that such feelings encouraged performers and listeners to become involved in the music for its own sake, they charged that such threatened to supplant the true function of music—to promote religious piety.

Thomas Hastings. One of the most forceful exponents of this view was Thomas Hastings. A resident of New York City for most of his life, Hastings achieved prominence as a composer, choir director, and musical compiler. His best-known compilation was *Musica Sacra* (1818), a collection of anthem, psalm, and hymn tunes. Though it was similar in format to Billings's tune books, Hastings's book excluded fuguing tunes and included many works by foreign composers such as George Frideric Handel and Joseph Haydn. In his collection Hastings warned that music used for "personal gratification, emolution, distinction, or display" is likely to awaken "some of the baser passions of the human heart." In contrast, when music "is cultivated strictly for social and beneficial purposes, and especially for the promotion of the praise and glory of God, and the edification of his people, its tendencies are necessarily and decidedly of the opposite nature."

Sources:

Gilbert Chase, *America's Music From the Pilgrims to the Present* (Urbana: University of Illinois Press, 1987);

Richard A. Crawford, *Andrew Law, American Psalmodist* (Evanston, Ill.: Northwestern University Press, 1968);

Charles Hamm, *Music in the New World* (New York: Norton, 1983).

MUSIC: MUSICAL SOCIETIES

Private Musical Societies. After a lull during the Revolution, Americans' interest in concert music continued to grow as it had before the war. Musical societies sprang up in cities throughout America and played an important role in promoting the performance of classical music. Private musical societies such as the St. Cæcilia Society in Charleston served a social and musical function. Membership was by invitation only. At society meetings members and professional musicians performed music together for invited guests, with a staged ball to end the evening. Similar organizations were formed in other cities, including the Musical Society of New York (1791) and the Philharmonic Society of Boston (1809). These private societies formed the basis for later public orchestras, but at the time their exclusiveness reflected and reinforced the elite character of patronage for instrumental concert music in early America. Only the wealthy possessed the means to develop and indulge a taste for such music, for the cost of acquiring and learning to play musical instruments was beyond the means of most ordinary individuals. In fact, most of the professional musicians who performed classical instrumental music in this period were immigrants from Europe, revealing the nation's dependence on Europe for its concert music. Likewise, virtually all the classical instrumen-

A nineteenth-century engraving of a concert conducted by William Selby at King's Chapel, Boston, on 10 January 1786. This event, which included more than seventy vocalists and musicians, is often considered the first music festival held in New England.

tal music performed in early national America was written by European composers.

The Handel and Haydn Society. Not all musical societies were so exclusive. The Handel and Haydn Society in Boston attracted large audiences to its public concerts. The society grew out of a "Peace Jubilee" organized in Boston by English-born composer and organist George K. Jackson in February 1815 to celebrate Washington's birthday and the signing of the Treaty of Ghent, which formally ended the War of 1812. This celebration brought together the greatest number of musicians ever assembled in the city to perform works by George Frideric Handel and various other composers. In the month after this triumphant concert, a group of local musicians and patrons—Gottlieb Graupner, Augustus Peabody, John Dodd, George Cushing, and Matthew Parker—decided to form a musical society to offer similar events periodically. They officially adopted a constitution for the Handel and Haydn Society on 26 April 1815.

Music and Cultural Progress. In the preamble to their constitution the founders linked the organization to the nation's political and cultural progress, arguing," While in our country almost every institution, political, civil, and moral, has advanced with rapid steps, while every other science and art is cultivated with a success flattering to its advocates, the admirers of music find their beloved science far from exciting the feelings or exercising the powers to which it is accustomed in the Old World." Seeking to advance cultural nationalism by promoting a deep admiration for European culture, the Handel and Hayden Society brought together singers from choirs throughout the area to give concerts of sacred music, particularly the music of Handel and Haydn. At its first concert, on 25 December 1815, the Handel and Haydn Society performed selections from Haydn's *Creation* and various oratorios by Handel, concluding with Handel's *Hallelujah Chorus*.

Sources:

Charles Hamm, *Music in the New World* (New York: Norton, 1983);

Charles C. Perkins, John S. Dwight, and W. F. Bradbury, *History of the Handel and Haydn Society*, 2 volumes (Boston: Mudge, 1883, 1893);

O. G. Sonneck, *Early Concert-Life in America, 1731–1800* (Leipzig: Breitkopf & Hartel, 1907).

MUSIC: PATRIOTIC SONGS

"Hail Columbia." The nationalist impulses at work in the early republican era achieved their clearest expression in patriotic songs, which in turn furthered a sense of unity among Americans. One of the best-known patriotic songs from this period was "Hail Columbia," by Philadelphian Joseph Hopkinson, the son of Francis Hopkinson, a composer and a signer of the Declaration of Independence. The younger Hopkinson wrote the words to this song at the request of singer Gilbert Fox, who performed it on 25 April 1798, to the music of the *President's March* by Philip Phile. This song was motivated by tensions between the United States and France

---

ADAMS & LIBERTY

Bostonian Robert Treat Paine Jr. wrote "Adams & Liberty" (1798) at a time when New England Federalists were campaigning for war with France and a Constitution that would establish a strong federal government. The following stanzas from Paine's song express attitudes typical of the region.

III

While FRANCE her huge limbs bathes recumbent in *blood*,

And *Society's base* threats with wide dissolution;

May PEACE, like the *Dove*, who return'd from the flood,

Find an *Ark* of abode in our mild CONSTITUTION!

But though PEACE is our aim,

Yet the boon we disclaim,

If bought by our SOV'REIGNTY, JUSTICE, or FAME.

VIII

Should the TEMPEST OF WAR overshadow our land,

Its bolts could ne'er rend FREEDOM'S *temple* asunder;

For, unmov'd, at its *portal*, would WASHINGTON stand,

And repulse, with his BREAST, *the assaults of the* THUNDER!

His *sword*, from the sleep

Of its *scabbard*, would leap,

And conduct, with its *point*, every *flash* to the deep.

IX

Let FAME to the world sound AMERICA'S voice;

No INTRIGUE *can her sons from their* GOVERNMENT *sever*;

Her PRIDE *is her* ADAMS—*her* LAWS *are his* CHOICE,

And shall flourish, till LIBERTY *slumber forever!*

Then unite, heart and hand,

Like *Leonidas'* band,

And swear to the GOD of the ocean and land,

That ne'er shall the sons of COLUMBIA *be slaves,*
While the earth bears a plant, or the sea rolls its waves.

Source: Robert Treat Paine Jr., *Adams & Liberty. The Boston Patriotic Song* (Boston: Printed by I. Thomas & E.T. Andrews, 1798).

---

that had brought the two nations to the brink of war. With France and Great Britain already at war, Americans were deeply divided, with Federalists in favor of war with France and Republicans deeply hostile to England.

ing the British bombardment of Fort McHenry on the night of 13 September 1814. The result was "The Star-Spangled Banner," which expressed Key's excitement on seeing at dawn that the Stars and Stripes was still flying as a sign that his countrymen had withstood the attack. Set, like Key's earlier lyrics, to the tune of "To Anacreon in Heaven," a popular English drinking song, "The Star-Spangled Banner" points to the complex relationship between American and England. Although inspired by nationalist pride and antagonism toward Great Britain, "The Star-Spangled Banner" at the same time reveals America's continuing cultural dependence on the mother country.

Sources:

Robert Allison, *The Crescent Obscured: The United States and the Muslim World, 1776–1815* (New York: Oxford University Press, 1995);

Gilbert Chase, *America's Music From the Pilgrims to the Present* (Urbana: University of Illinois Press, 1987);

John Tasker Howard, *Our American Music, Three Hundred Years of It* (New York: Crowell, 1930);

Burton Alva Konkle, *Joseph Hopkinson, 1770–1842* (Philadelphia: University of Pennsylvania Press, 1931);

Vera Brodsky Lawrence, *Music for Patriots, Politicians, and Presidents: Harmonies and Discords of the First Hundred Years* (New York: Macmillan, 1975);

Oscar G. Sonneck, *Report on "The Star-Spangled Banner," "Hail Columbia," "America," "Yankee Doodle"* (Washington, D.C.: U.S. Government Printing Office, 1909).

Francis Scott Key

Partisan Patriotism. As Hopkinson explained, his objective was to promote a sense of nationalism that would transcend these divisions: "to get up an American spirit which should be independent of, and above the interests, passion and policy of both belligerents, and look and feel exclusively for our honor and rights." Yet despite Hopkinson's claims to the contrary, "Hail Columbia" served a highly partisan purpose. A Federalist himself, he set the lyrics to the tune of the *President's March,* which was closely associated with George Washington and had become a rallying song for the Federalists. In giving this tune a set of patriotic lyrics Hopkinson enhanced its effectiveness and reinforced Federalist claims to patriotic nonpartisanship. One Republican paper condemned the song as a partisan tool, "which contained, amidst the most ridiculous bombast," the "vilest adulation to the anglo-monarchical party." Despite its partisan overtones, "Hail Columbia" achieved widespread popularity and was quickly established as the first American national anthem. Later the same year poet Robert Treat Paine Jr. wrote the lyrics for "Adams & Liberty," which also tapped into partisan passions against France.

"The Star-Spangled Banner." War was also the occasion for the writing of "The Star-Spangled Banner," which became the official national anthem in 1931. Francis Scott Key, a Baltimore lawyer, wrote an early version of this song in 1805 to celebrate the heroism of Stephen Decatur and the other Americans fighting in the war with Tripoli. Using the same rhyme scheme, Key rewrote the lyrics during the War of 1812, after observ-

POETRY: THE CONNECTICUT WITS

Background. At the forefront of the effort to develop a national literature was the group of poets known as the Connecticut (or Hartford) Wits, who formed the first major American literary circle. This group consisted of well-known poets such as John Trumbull, Timothy Dwight, and David Humphreys, and lesser poets, including Lemuel Hopkins, Theodore Dwight, and Richard Alsop. Almost all came from elite Connecticut families and were closely associated with Yale University. Their shared educational and social background profoundly influenced their poetry, which reveals the tensions between the Enlightenment, Protestant, and republican traditions in New England culture as a whole.

The Progress of Dulness. As products of the Enlightenment, the Wits embraced the neoclassical ideals of balance and order, repudiating religious extremism as inimical to their ideal of enlightened moderation. Yet their Calvinist origins made them equally hostile to attacks on organized religion. In his satirical poem *The Progress of Dulness* (1772, 1773) Trumbull combined Enlightenment rationalism with Protestant religiosity. While the first part of this poem satirizes ignorant ministers educated at Yale, Trumbull also affirms his respect for religion and severely mocks deism and irreligion in the second part of the poem.

Timothy Dwight. The Wits' New England origins gave their poetry a Federalist political bias in favor of a strong national government. They embraced a tradi-

Connecticut Wits John Trumbull (portrait by his second cousin John Trumbull) and David Humphreys (portrait by Julian Story)

tional notion of social order based on hierarchy and deference. Initially, they expressed optimism about the nation's republican future. In his long poem *America* (1780) Timothy Dwight, borrowing a famous phrase from Philip Freneau and Hugh Henry Brackenridge's long poem *The Rising Glory of America* (1771), confidently predicted that America's "rising glory shall expand its rays, / And lands and times unknown rehearse their endless praise." He continued to forecast a special role for the United States in his later long poem *The Conquest of Canäan* (1785).

Fear of Anarchy. Yet Dwight's fears of anarchy and infidelity ultimately prevailed over his hopes, and he became pessimistic about the nation's prospects for future improvement. In *The Triumph of Infidelity* (1788) he attacks what he perceives as forces that endanger social order, while in his pastoral poem *Greenfield Hill* (1794) he holds out the hope that his native Connecticut can show the nation "How balanc'd powers, in just gradation, prove / The means of order, freedom, peace, and love."

The Anarchiad. By the late 1780s the Connecticut Wits as a whole shared Dwight's disillusionment with the egalitarian tendencies of American society, and their writings became strident attacks on the excesses of democracy and the dangers of social unrest. The most sustained and systematic of these diatribes was *The Anarchiad.* Joel Barlow, Trumbull, Humphreys, Hopkins, and other Connecticut Wits contributed to this satirical mock-epic poem, published in twelve installments in the *New Haven Gazette* between October 1786 and September 1787. Expressing their fears about the threat of anarchy in the new nation, they were responding specifically to Shays's Rebellion of 1786, which epitomized for them the dangerous democratic forces that seemed to be employing the mob to destroy the ordered liberty of the republic. *The Anarchiad* portrays the farmers who took part in the uprising as irrational and subhuman figures, who have fallen into debt through their own laziness and taste for luxury. The Wits described their vision of the potential social disorder such a rebellion might bring in these lines: "Here shall my best and brightest empire rise, / Wild riot reign, and discord greet the skies. / Awake, my chosen sons, in folly brave, / Stab Independence! dance o'er Freedom's grave!" *The Anarchiad* was immensely popular and was republished by newspapers in Massachusetts, New York, and other states.

Later Careers. The Connecticut Wits eventually followed their interests in divergent directions. After *The Anarchiad* Trumbull turned away from poetry and increasingly devoted his attention to law and politics. Barlow ultimately repudiated the Federalist politics of the Wits altogether. Timothy Dwight became president of Yale in 1795 and used his position as a platform from

which to continue his attacks on the enemies of social order.

Sources:

Emory Elliott, ed., *American Writers of the Early Republic, Dictionary of
Literary Biography*, volume 37 (Detroit: Gale Research, 1985);

Leon Howard, *The Connecticut Wits* (Chicago: University of Chicago
Press, 1943);

Henry May, *The Enlightenment in America* (New York: Oxford University Press, 1976);

Kenneth Silverman, *A Cultural History of the American Revolution* (New
York: Crowell, 1976).

POETRY: THE QUEST FOR AN AMERICAN EPIC

Background. American poets of the early republican
era hoped to write a great American epic to consecrate
their ancestors' accomplishments and give the nation a
heroic past, just as Homer and Virgil had done for ancient Greece and Rome. Because the epic also represented the ultimate mark of cultural achievement, the
writing of a successful American epic would conclusively
put to rest doubts about the nation's cultural maturity
and contribute to the future progress of the nation.

Barlow's Epic. Joel Barlow made the most ambitious
and sustained attempt to realize these aspirations in his
epic poem *The Columbiad* (1807), a revised version of his

Joel Barlow, 1807 (portrait by Charles Willson Peale)

earlier poem *The Vision of Columbus* (1787). Barlow intended *The Vision of Columbus* to be a "philosophic"
poem about Columbus's discovery of America and its
consequences. By giving a panoramic account of American history he sought to prove that the discovery of
America had been beneficial to mankind and that
American history was a crucial stage in human progress
toward a world of peace and harmony, united in "one
great empire." Stressing God's active intervention in this
process and emphasizing the importance of religion to
social order, this version of Barlow's epic conformed to
the conservative social outlook of the Connecticut Wits.

Radical Revisions. Yet Barlow followed a different
political path from his fellow Connecticut Wits, growing
progressively more radical in his political and religious
views. This transformation coincided with Barlow's so-
journ in Europe (1788–1804). While in France and England he came under the influence of radical political
thinkers such as William Godwin and Thomas Paine
and became an ardent supporter of the French Revolution. As a result he abandoned the hierarchical social
perspective of the Connecticut Wits in favor of a democratic and egalitarian political outlook, and his revisions
to *The Vision of Columbus* reflect this transformation in
his viewpoint. For the fifth edition, published in 1793,
Barlow substantially revised the poem to reflect his
changing religious and political views, and he virtually
rewrote *The Vision of Columbus* for *The Columbiad*, in
which his efforts to make his work accessible to readers

reflect his democratic sympathies. *The Columbiad* also revealed his turn to deism, portraying humans themselves as the agents of American development and progress and reducing religion to a secondary role.

The Columbiad. The change in title signaled Barlow's epic intentions, as the word *Columbiad* evokes the ancient epics of Homer and Virgil, the *Iliad* and *Aeneid.* While Barlow sought to emulate the ancients, however, he also thought that his epic would supersede the ancient epics and remedy their moral failings. He particularly criticized Homer and Virgil for encouraging militarism and tyranny instead of sharing his desire "to encourage and strengthen, in the rising generation, a sense of the importance of republican institutions, as being the great foundation of public and private happiness, the necessary aliment of future and permanent meliorations in the condition of human nature." Believing that the safety of republican institutions depended not on military glory but on artistic achievements like his own work, Barlow urged, "This is the moment in America to give such a direction to poetry, painting and the other fine arts, that true and useful ideas of glory may be implanted in the minds of men here, to take place of the false and destructive ones that have degraded the species in other countries."

Sources:

Emory Elliott, *Revolutionary Writers: Literature and Authority in the New Republic, 1725–1810* (New York: Oxford University Press, 1982);

Elliott, ed., *American Writers of the Early Republic, Dictionary of Literary Biography,* volume 37 (Detroit: Gale Research, 1985);

Arthur L. Ford, *Joel Barlow* (New York: Twayne, 1971);

Kenneth Silverman, *A Cultural History of the American Revolution* (New York: Crowell, 1976).

HEADLINE MAKERS

HUGH HENRY BRACKENRIDGE

1748-1816
NOVELIST, LAWYER

Voice of the New Republic. Hugh Henry Brackenridge began his literary career as co-author of *The Rising Glory of America* (1772), a poem so aptly expressing the optimism of several generations of Americans that it became the prototype for dozens of other patriotic poems, including Joel Barlow's *The Prospect of Peace* (1778) and Timothy Dwight's *America* (1780). Brackenridge is best known, however, for his mock-epic novel *Modern Chivalry* (1792–1815), often called the first evenhanded satire on American democracy.

Early Life. Born in Scotland, Brackenridge and his family immigrated in 1753 to Pennsylvania, where they eked out a living on a small farm in rural York County. After five years of teaching in frontier schools he enrolled at Princeton University in 1768. At graduation ceremonies in September 1771 he and his friend Philip Freneau delivered their poem *The Rising Glory of America,* which was published in Philadelphia the following year. After graduation Brackenridge taught school while continuing his literary pursuits. He made his revolutionary sympathies clear in two anti-British plays, *The Battle of Bunkers-Hill* (1776) and *The Death of General Montgomery* (1777). After serving as a chaplain in Gen. George Washington's army (1777–1778), Brackenridge settled in Philadelphia, where he founded the *United States Magazine* as a vehicle for his patriotic fervor. The first issue appeared in January 1779. The failure of the magazine by the end of the same year helped to undermine his optimism about the nation's potential for political and cultural achievement; yet he remained a staunch patriot.

Lawyer, Politician, and Eccentric. Temporarily abandoning literature, Brackenridge studied law, and in 1781 he established a legal practice in Pittsburgh. His success as a lawyer soon brought him into political prominence. Elected to the Pennsylvania legislature in 1786, he developed a reputation as an advocate of western frontier interests. Yet he also became known for his erratic and inconsistent behavior in political and personal matters. Stories about his disheveled and skimpy dress spread throughout his life. Someone once claimed to have seen Brackenridge riding naked in the rain with his clothes tucked under saddle. Asked to explain his behavior, he said that "the storm you know, would spoil the clothes, but it couldn't spoil me." Despite such stories, Brackenridge's mercurial conduct was more than a matter of personal idiosyncrasy. His inconsistencies arose from his conscious rejection of political or ideological labels. He took this outlook into his fiction, where he analyzed and examined opposing tendencies in American culture without favoring one side over the other.

Modern Chivalry. Brackenridge's detached perspective is most evident in *Modern Chivalry*, which he began in 1788 and published in a series of volumes between 1792 and 1815. The novel is a comic account of the adventures of two fictional characters, Capt. John Farrago and his Irish servant, Teague O'Regan. As he described their travels, Brackenridge offered a vivid re-creation of life on the frontier and his own commentary on postrevolutionary American society. Farrago is a gentleman who represents the deferential social order of prerevolutionary America, while the recent immigrant Teague stands for the democratic impulses that appeared to be overtaking American society. Brackenridge's constant mocking of Teague's ignorance and foolishness reveals his reservations about these democratic trends. Yet he also recognized the power of the those forces and saw in them the wave of the future.

Incidents of the Insurrection. The Whiskey Rebellion of 1794 forced Brackenridge to grapple directly with these forces. Incensed by the federal excise tax on whiskey, passed in 1791, farmers in western Pennsylvania resorted to violent resistance. Brackenridge sympathized with their grievances, but he took a middle road and sought to moderate the conflict. Although he disavowed the rebels' violent methods, supporters of the tax charged that Brackenridge had instigated the insurrection. To defend his actions Brackenridge provided his own firsthand account of the rebellion in *Incidents of the Insurrection in Western Pennsylvania in the Year 1794* (1795).

Later Life. After successfully vindicating himself, Brackenridge continued his political and literary activities. He was appointed a judge for the Pennsylvania Supreme Court in 1799 and finished publishing *Modern Chivalry* in 1815, the year before his death.

Sources:

Hugh Henry Brackenridge, *Modern Chivalry*, edited by Lewis Leary (New Haven: College & University Press, 1965).

Emory Elliott, ed., *American Writers of the Early Republic, Dictionary of Literary Biography*, volume 37 (Detroit: Gale Research, 1985);

Joseph J. Ellis, *After the Revolution: Profiles of Early American Culture* (New York: Norton, 1979);

Daniel Marder, *Hugh Henry Brackenridge* (New York: Twayne, 1967).

CHARLES BROCKDEN BROWN

1771-1810
NOVELIST

Forging a New National Literature. Often described as the father of the American novel, Charles Brockden Brown is credited with answering the call for distinctively American fiction by transferring the horror and supernatural atmosphere of the Gothic novel from the moldering castles of Europe to New World settings. While his novels today seem derivative from his British models, in his time critics on both sides of the Atlantic praised Brown's fictional treatment of American themes and settings as the beginning of a truly American literary tradition of which his countrymen could be proud.

Background. Brown was born in 1771 to a Quaker family in Philadelphia. After a brief foray into law he turned to literature as an occupation. Brown's reputation as one of the nation's first major novelists rests on four novels: *Wieland* (1798), *Ormond* (1799), *Arthur Mervyn* (1799, 1800), and *Edgar Huntly* (1799).

Gothic Horror. Like most Gothic fiction, Brown's novels are notable for their sensationalism and violence. As Brown once wrote, "The chief point is not the virtue of a character. The prime regard is to be paid to the genius and force of mind that is displayed. Great energy employed in the promotion of vicious purposes constitutes a very useful spectacle. Give me a tale of lofty crime rather than of honest folly." Brown's fascination with the darker side of human nature reflects, in part, his own psychological makeup. Yet he was also expressing fundamental social concerns and tensions.

Wieland. Set on a pleasant country estate outside Philadelphia, Brown's first-published and best-known novel is the story of Theodore and Clara Wieland, a brother and sister orphaned from youth by the mysterious death of their father. The arrival of a stranger named Francis Carwin disrupts their peaceful existence, and the characters begin hearing mysterious voices. Theodore goes insane and kills his wife and children, believing that the voices are divine and that he is doing as they have commanded. He next attempts to murder Clara, who is saved only by Carwin's intervention. Realizing the enormity of his crime, Theodore kills himself. By emphasizing the inexplicable and the irrational, Brown reveals his belief in the limits of reason. The novel has also been interpreted as a warning not to abandon one's moral principles for the purely emotional appeal of what seems to be divine inspiration.

Yellow Fever. Both *Ormond* and *Arthur Mervyn* draw on Brown's experiences during the yellow-fever epidemics that plagued Philadelphia and New York in the

1790s. The more successful of the two books described the adventures of Arthur Mervyn, a young man left to make his own way in the world. Leaving his rural home for Philadelphia, he becomes caught up in the schemes of the unscrupulous Welbeck in the nightmarish but still alluring setting of the plague-ridden city. Arthur ultimately establishes himself financially by marrying a wealthy woman. The embodiment of the self-made individual at the heart of liberal capitalist society, Arthur is ambiguously characterized as both a virtuous innocent and an opportunistic man on the make, revealing Brown's own ambivalence about the individualistic values so cherished by his countrymen.

Later Life. Although these novels achieved critical acclaim, they enjoyed little popular success, and Brown's hopes of becoming a self-supporting author foundered. After the publication of two more novels, *Clara Howard* and *Jane Talbot,* in 1801 and the magazine serialization of "Memoirs of Carwin the Biloquist" in 1803–1805, Brown supported himself as a magazine editor, a partner in his family's mercantile business, and finally as an independent retailer before his death in 1810.

Sources:

Charles Brockden Brown, *The Novels and Related Works of Charles Brockden Brown,* Bicentennial Edition, 6 volumes, edited by Sidney J. Krause, Alexander Cowie, and S. W. Reid (Kent, Ohio: Kent State University Press, 1977–1987);

Emory Elliott, *Revolutionary Writers: Literature and Authority in the New Republic, 1725-1810* (New York: Oxford University Press, 1982);

Elliott, ed., *American Writers of the Early Republic, Dictionary of Literary Biography,* volume 37 (Detroit: Gale Research, 1985);

Donald Ringe, *Charles Brockden Brown* (New Haven: College & University Press, 1966);

Steven Watts, *The Romance of Real Life: Charles Brockden Brown and the Origins of American Culture* (Baltimore: Johns Hopkins University Press, 1994).

WILLIAM DUNLAP

1766-1839
PLAYWRIGHT, ARTIST, HISTORIAN

Pioneer Dramatist. Often considered the father of American theater, William Dunlap was a theater manager and the first American professional playwright, dominating the American stage at the end of the eighteenth century with patriotic plays on American subjects. He was also a talented painter and historian, and he dabbled in novel writing.

Early Life. Dunlap was born in Perth Amboy, New Jersey, the son of a retired British officer. His father remained loyal to Britain during the American Revolution, and in 1777, as a Loyalist refugee, he moved the family to British-occupied New York. In 1784 Dunlap traveled to England planning to study under painter Benjamin West. Once there, however, Dunlap never enrolled at West's academy and dissipated much of his time on frivolous amusements. As a result, his father demanded that his son return to the United States in 1787. When he reached home Dunlap devoted his attention to theater and wrote his first play, *The Modest Soldier,* by the end of the year. This effort did not reach the stage, but two years later two of his plays, *The Father* and *Darby's Return,* were successfully produced in New York City.

André. During the 1790s Dunlap developed a growing belief in the nation's cultural potential. Through his plays he sought to foster and contribute to America's artistic and literary advancement. Dunlap also believed that drama had an important social function: "What engine is more powerful than the theatre? No arts can be made more effectual for the promotion of good than the dramatic and the histrionic. They unite music, poetry, painting, and eloquence. The engine is powerful for good or ill—it is for society to choose." Dunlap's best-known play is *André* (1798), based on the capture and execution of Major John André as a British spy during the Revolutionary War. Rather than simplistically glorifying the Revolution, *André* depicts the moral complexities of this event. While depicting André sympathetically, however, Dunlap also justified his execution as a necessary exigency of war—deploring the tragic costs of the Revolution without questioning its overall legitimacy.

The Old American Company. Dunlap contributed to the development of American drama not only by writing plays but also by producing them. In 1796 he invested in the Old American Company, a New York theater company owned by Lewis Hallam and John Hodgkinson, and became part owner and manager. Internal conflicts and financial difficulties plagued the company from the start, and the theater failed to draw enough customers to make a profit. By 1798, as the company went further and further into debt, Dunlap had become the sole director and manager. When it went bankrupt in 1805, he was liable for all its debts and had to forfeit all of his own property to pay them. Although the failure of this enterprise tempered his optimism about American cultural development, he continued to hope that American culture would eventually live up to its promise.

Later Life. While Dunlap did not abandon theater altogether, he increasingly turned his attention to other pursuits. In 1805 he returned to painting, becoming an itinerant portrait artist and developing an interest in chronicling the development of the arts in America. After publishing a biography of novelist Charles Brockden Brown in 1815, he wrote *A History of the American Theatre* (1832) and *A History of the Rise and Progress of the Arts of Design in the United States* (1834). These works reflected his growing interest in American history in general, and his last books were *A History of New York for Schools* (1837) and *History of New Netherlands* (1839,

1840). He also wrote a temperance novel, *Thirty Years Ago; or, The Memoirs of a Water Drinker* (1836).

Sources:

Robert Canary, *William Dunlap* (New York: Twayne, 1970);

Emory Elliott, ed., *American Writers of the Early Republic, Dictionary of Literary Biography,* volume 37 (Detroit: Gale Research, 1985);

Joseph J. Ellis, *After the Revolution: Profiles of Early American Culture* (New York: Norton, 1979).

CHARLES WILLSON PEALE

1741-1827
ARTIST

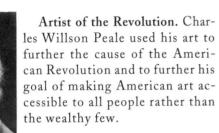

Artist of the Revolution. Charles Willson Peale used his art to further the cause of the American Revolution and to further his goal of making American art accessible to all people rather than the wealthy few.

Early Life. Born in Queen Anne's County, Maryland, Charles Willson Peale started out as a saddler before becoming an itinerant artist. Peale received formal artistic training in 1767, when he traveled to London and studied with painter Benjamin West. After returning to the colonies in 1769 he soon achieved success as a leading portrait painter. In 1772 he painted one of his best-known works, the first portrait of George Washington. With the outbreak of the Revolution, Peale eagerly took part in the revolutionary cause. He volunteered for the militia in August 1776 and participated actively in revolutionary politics, serving on various government committees in Philadelphia between 1777 and 1780. Peale also expressed his revolutionary sympathies in his art, turning his paintings into propaganda for the revolutionary cause.

Public Art. Peale's patriotic employment of his talents was consistent with his concept of "public art," which he believed should serve and be supported by the public. He advocated government subsidies for artists as an alternative to the traditional reliance on the patronage of wealthy individuals. In keeping with this ideal, Peale requested and received government support to construct a triumphal arch in Philadelphia for a celebration of the Treaty of Paris in January 1784. This structure consisted of three arches adorned with Ionic columns and transparent panels depicting a wide variety of scenes appropriate to the occasion, ranging from Washington as the American Cincinnatus to a figure representing "Confederated America." Illuminating the panels would be more than one thousand lamps. Just before the celebration, however, a rocket placed too close to the paintings set fire to them and burned them all. Although Peale was paid to re-create the arch, the fate of this project foreshadowed the later disappointment of hopes for "public art."

Moving Pictures. Peale's desire to combine patriotism and profit by creating art with both aesthetic value and popular appeal intensified in the years after the Revolution. One attempt to fulfill this goal was the exhibition of "moving pictures" he opened in Philadelphia in 1785. Using special machinery and lighting in combination with transparent pictures of scenes from history, nature, and literature, Peale was able to create the illusion of movement. He hoped that such innovations would attract a mass audience for his art not only from a desire for personal profit but also as a means to reconcile art with republican ideals. By exposing the people to the arts, Peale hoped to refute the traditional association between artistic development and social decay and establish a place for art in a republican culture. If the goal could be achieved it could free artists from their traditional dependence on wealthy patrons. Peale's "moving pictures" failed to live up to these expectations, however. After a successful start public interest in the exhibition waned, and Peale closed it in 1787.

Later Life. Peale turned his attention to the natural world and focused on a museum of natural history that he had founded the year before. Even the names of his children reflected this change of emphasis. Peale named his four oldest sons after artists—Raphaelle, Rembrandt, Titian, Rubens, and Vandyke—but the names of his next two sons—Charles Linnaeus and Benjamin Franklin—recognized men who had made achievements in the sciences. Increasingly absorbed by his work for his natural-history museum, Peale declared his retirement from painting on 24 April 1794, hoping to clear the field for his sons Raphaelle and Rembrandt, who had become artists themselves. Yet Peale did not abandon art altogether. He continued to promote American artistic development and took the lead in establishing the Columbianum, a fine-arts academy founded by and for artists. Peale hoped this academy would promote the instruction and professional advancement of artists of all sorts, but, weakened by internal divisions from the start, the Columbianum did not long survive its first exhibition in 1795. In 1804 Peale returned to painting and continued to be active until his death in 1827.

Sources:

Joseph J. Ellis, *After the Revolution: Profiles of Early American Culture* (New York: Norton, 1979);

Edgar P. Richardson, Brooke Hindle, and Lillian B. Miller, *Charles Willson Peale and His World* (New York: Abrams, 1983);

Charles Coleman Sellers, *Charles Willson Peale* (Philadelphia: American Philosophical Society, 1947).

SUSANNA HASWELL ROWSON

1762-1824
WRITER, ACTRESS, EDUCATOR

The First Best-selling American Novelist. Most often remembered as the author of *Charlotte. A Tale of Truth* (1791), a story of seduction, betrayal, and tragic death that became the first best-selling novel in the United States, Susanna Haswell Rowson was known to Americans of her time as an actress, playwright, songwriter, and educator.

Early Life. Born in Portsmouth, England, Susanna Haswell moved with her father, a lieutenant in the British navy, to Nantasket, Massachusetts, in 1767, where she spent most of her childhood. During the Revolution her family's Loyalist sympathies made their situation there difficult, and they returned to England as part of a prisoner exchange in 1778. While in England she married William Rowson, an actor, musician, and hardware merchant, in 1786, the same year in which she published her first novel, *Victoria.*

Charlotte. Rowson followed this work with several other novels, the best known of which was *Charlotte, A Tale of Truth,* published in London in 1791. An American edition was published in 1794, the year after Rowson and her husband had joined Thomas Wignell's New Theatre Company in Philadelphia. The novel had attracted few readers in England, but it was immensely popular in the United States. According to Mathew Carey, Rowson's American publisher, it sold more than fifty thousand copies by 1812, going through at least forty-five editions during Rowson's lifetime. Probably based on the then-famous scandal of Rowson's cousin John Montrésor, who eloped with a young woman named Charlotte Stanley, Rowson's novel tells the story of Charlotte Temple, a fifteen-year-old schoolgirl who is seduced by a British army officer named Montraville. He convinces her to go with him to America, where he is to fight in the Revolution, and eventually abandons her in New York City. She dies in childbirth. Rowson's emphasis on Charlotte's weakness and folly conformed to traditional assumptions about female inferiority. Yet she also implicitly criticized society's treatment of women. The novel undoubtedly appealed to Americans because it confirmed their patriotic assumptions about the morals of British soldiers, but it affected them on a basic, purely emotional level as well. The story spawned a "Charlotte cult," and for several generations faithful readers made pilgrimages to Charlotte's supposed gravestone in Trinity Churchyard, New York.

Dramatic Career. Even before Rowson's American success with *Charlotte,* she had made a name for herself in the United States. Soon after she arrived in Philadelphia in 1793, she had written a historical drama, *Slaves in Algiers,* which became a hit when it was performed in June 1794 with music by popular composer Alexander Reinagle. In this play about the topical issues of Barbary piracy and white slavery, Rowson expressed patriotic sentiments shared by many Americans, as well as her own sentiments about gender roles: "Women were born for universal sway, / Men to adore, be silent, and obey."

Patriotic Music and Poetry. Rowson again expressed her patriotism in 1794 when she wrote the words for a popular song, "America, Commerce and Freedom," with music by Reinagle, as well as a poem, "The Standard of Liberty." In both works she glorified America's republican ideals of liberty, revealing her deep sense of attachment to her adopted nation.

Educator. The proceeds from Rowson's writing provided a source of much-needed income, as the fecklessness of her husband turned her into the family's primary means of financial support. This circumstance at the same time permitted Rowson greater freedom than most women of her time and allowed her to depart from women's traditionally subordinate role. Her husband offered no opposition to his wife's varied public pursuits, nor did he take exception to the greater success and recognition she achieved. In 1797, the year after the Rowsons moved to Boston to join the Federal Street Threatre Company, Susanna Rowson gave up her stage career. Acting on her belief in the importance of women's education, she founded the Young Ladies' Academy, one of the first schools in the United States to provide post-elementary education for girls. Among her innovations were the addition of geography, math, and science to traditional feminine subjects such as music and domestic economy. Rowson wrote her own textbooks for the school, which she also published for general use. An immediate success, Rowson's academy prospered under her direction until 1822, when poor health forced her to turn the academy over to her adopted daughter and niece. She died two years later.

Sources:

Cathy N. Davidson, *Revolution and the Word: The Rise of the Novel in America* (New York: Oxford University Press, 1986);

Emory Elliott, ed., *American Writers of the Early Republic, Dictionary of Literary Biography,* volume 37 (Detroit: Gale Research, 1985);

Patricia L. Parker, *Susanna Haswell Rowson* (Boston: Twayne, 1986);

Susanna Haswell Rowson, *Charlotte Temple,* edited by Davidson (New York: Oxford University Press, 1986);

Dorothy Weil, *In Defense of Women: Susanna Rowson (1762–1824)* (University Park: Pennsylvania State University Press, 1976).

JOHN TRUMBULL

1756-1843
ARTIST

Early Life. Son of Gov. Jonathan Trumbull, John Trumbull was born in Lebanon, Connecticut. Coming from a wealthy and privileged background, Trumbull resolved to pursue his artistic aspirations from an early age. After graduating from Harvard in 1773,

Trumbull painted his first work, *The Death of Paulus Aemilius at the Battle of Cannae*. Although its subject is classical, this painting expresses his political concerns about the escalating tensions between Britain and the colonies. Soon after the outbreak of the Revolution at the Battles of Lexington and Concord in 1775, his sympathy for the cause spurred him to join the army as an adjutant to Gen. Joseph Spencer. In 1776 Gen. Horatio Gates appointed Trumbull a deputy adjutant general, giving him the rank of colonel. The following year, however, Trumbull resigned from the army, angered by a dispute over the date of his commission from the Continental Congress. Returning to artistic activities, he traveled to London in 1780 to study with the renowned painter Benjamin West.

Revolutionary War Series. In 1784 West proposed that Trumbull take over a project that West had started: a series of paintings on the American Revolution. The resulting paintings became Trumbell's best-known works. Combining his artistic interests and revolutionary loyalties, Trumbull viewed his role in this undertaking as that of a historian "commemorating the great events of our country's revolution." He shared with historians of his time the conviction that history had to teach a lesson, not just record the past. Thus, Trumbull described his primary motives as: "to preserve and diffuse the memory of the noblest series of actions which have ever presented themselves in the history of man; to give the present and the future sons of oppression and misfortune, such glorious lessons of their rights, and of the spirit with which they should assert and support them, and even to transmit to their descendants, the personal resemblance of those who have been the great actors in those illustrious scenes, were objects which gave a dignity to the profession, peculiar to my situation." Through these paintings Trumbull made an important contribution to the artistic development of the new nation, and he helped shape American images of the Revolution.

Battle Paintings. The first of these works was *The Death of General Warren at the Battle of Bunker's Hill* (1786), portraying the death of revolutionary leader Joseph Warren, whose death at Bunker Hill turned him into a martyr for the revolutionary cause. The realistic details are drawn from Trumbull's own experience as an eyewitness at the battle, but he took important liberties with the facts. For example, he portrayed a British officer, Maj. John Small, as attempting to save General Warren. As Trumbull himself acknowledged, this incident was a "pictorial liberty," which he included to "do honor to Major Small who . . . was distinguished for his humanity and kindness to American prisoners." This approach was consistent with Trumbull's aim to inculcate moral lessons in his audience. For him these higher truths took precedence over the factual accuracy of particular details. He followed this painting with other battle scenes—*The Death of General Montgomery at the Battle of Quebec* (1786), *The Capture of the Hessians at Trenton* (1786–circa 1828), and *The Death of General Mercer at the Battle of Princeton* (circa 1789–circa 1831).

The Declaration of Independence. In 1786 Trumbull turned to a civil event for the subject of his next painting—*The Declaration of Independence*. Again he conveyed a moral message in his choice of subject: by including a nonmilitary painting in a series designed to document the American war of independence, he underscored that in contrast to other nations the United States had its origins in a rational assertion of abstract principle rather than in the violence and caprice of monarchs. As usual he painstakingly sought to achieve authentic and realistic portraits of the figures in the painting, but he also departed from the historical record, taking liberties that heightened the dramatic effect of the painting and the symbolic importance of the event. *The Declaration of Independence* conflated into one day a whole series of events related to the drafting and approval of this document. The painting depicts not the signing of the Declaration but the presentation of the document to John Hancock, the president of the Continental Congress, by the drafting committee. Trumbull placed the members of this committee—Thomas Jefferson, John Adams, Benjamin Franklin, Roger Sherman, and Robert R. Livingston—at the center of the scene to highlight their role in this event. He also included signers of the Declaration who had not actually been present on the day the document was signed. In fact, the signers were never assembled as a group in the way that Trumbull depicted them. Most of the delegates signed the Declaration of Independence on 2 August 1776, and other signatures were added until some time before the publication of the signed document on 19 January 1777.

Later Life. In 1817 the House of Representatives commissioned Trumbull to paint four pictures for the Rotunda of the U.S. Capitol. He and President James Madison decided that the subjects of these works should be the Declaration of Independence, the surrender of Gen. John Burgoyne at Saratoga, Gen. Charles Cornwallis's surrender at Yorktown, and the resignation of Gen. George Washington. The installation of these paintings in the Rotunda in 1826 was the crowning achievement of Trumbull's artistic career, and they were the last major, original history paintings before his death in 1843.

Sources:

Helen A. Cooper, ed., *John Trumbull: The Hand and Spirit of a Painter* (New Haven: Yale University Art Gallery, 1982);

Irma B. Jaffe, *John Trumbull: Patriot-Artist of the American Revolution* (Boston: New York Graphic Society, 1975).

MERCY OTIS WARREN

1728-1814
HISTORIAN, DRAMATIST

Early Life. Born in West Barnstable, Massachusetts, Mercy Otis was the daughter of James Otis Sr., a merchant and lawyer who became a prominent figure in local politics. Her brother James Otis Jr. achieved even greater renown as a leader of the revolutionary resistance to Britain. James Warren, whom she married in 1754, was also a leader in that struggle. Resisting traditional limits to women's public roles, Warren carried on the family tradition of political activism and eagerly took part in the political controversies of her day. An ardent supporter of the Revolution, like her brother and husband, she used writing as a vehicle to further her political views, seeking to win adherents to the revolutionary cause through her work as a playwright and propagandist.

Dramatic Works. Warren made clear her revolutionary sympathies in her first play, *The Adulateur: A Tragedy* (1773), which satirized the Tories as corrupt defenders of tyranny in contrast to the revolutionaries, who embodied virtuous patriotism. Warren followed this work with another play in a similar vein, *The Group* (1775). After the Revolution she continued writing plays, publishing two tragedies, *The Sack of Rome* and *The Ladies of Castile,* in her *Poems, Dramatic and Miscellaneous* (1790). Like her previous plays, these two works expressed her contemporary political opinions, in this case her concerns about the role of women in politics. In both plays she placed women at the center of political upheavals. Although she did not advocate formal political rights for women, she did not believe that women should divorce themselves from politics entirely. Through the characters in *The Sack of Rome* and *The Ladies of Castile,* Warren suggested that a healthy republic required politically conscious women who were willing to make sacrifices for the public good.

Historian of the Revolution. The culmination of Warren's literary efforts was her three-volume *History of the Rise, Progress, and Termination of the American Revolution* (1805). In this history Warren sought to do more than simply recapitulate the events of the Revolution. Embracing the didactic view of history that prevailed in the eighteenth century, Warren viewed her history as a source of moral examples that would influence the conduct of present and future generations. Concerned about what she saw as the postrevolutionary lapse from revolutionary principles, Warren hoped to provide historical models that would counteract this tendency. She analyzed the Revolution as a conflict between British corruption and American virtue, setting up an implicit contrast between the virtuous self-sacrifice of the revolutionaries and the degeneracy of her postrevolutionary contemporaries. Hoping this contrast would inspire them to imitate and revive the spirit that had effected the Revolution, she declared, "It is an unpleasing part of history, when 'corruption begins to prevail, when degeneracy marks the manners of the people, and weakens the sinews of the state.'" She added, "If this should ever become the deplorable situation of the United States, let some unborn historian, in a far distant day, detail the lapse, and hold up the contrast between a simple, virtuous, and free people, and a degenerate, servile race of beings, corrupted by wealth, effeminated by luxury, impoverished by licentiousness, and become the *automatons* of intoxicated ambition."

Later Life. The contemporary response to Warren's history was mixed. Her critical portrayal of him inspired John Adams observe to Warren that "History is not the Province of Ladies." For the most part, however, Warren's contemporaries neglected her history altogether, and her work received only one lackluster review from the *Panoplist*. The *History* was Warren's last major literary production before her death in 1814.

Sources:

Lester Cohen, "Explaining the Revolution: Ideology and Ethics in Mercy Otis Warren's Historical Theory," *William and Mary Quarterly,* 37 (April 1980): 200–218;

Mercy Otis Warren, *History of the Rise, Progress and Termination of the American Revolution,* edited by Lester Cohen (Indianapolis: Liberty Classics, 1988);

Rosemarie Zagarri, *A Woman's Dilemma: Mercy Otis Warren and the American Revolution* (Wheeling, Ill.: Harlan Davidson, 1995).

PUBLICATIONS

Asher Benjamin, *The Country Builder's Assistant* (Greenfield, Mass.: Printed by Thomas Dickman, 1797)—the first American architectural pattern book, written by a prominent New England architect to provide builders in rural areas with diagrams and precise measurements for architectural details of styles used by contemporary architects in American cities; this influential book went through several editions, as did Benjamin's next book, *The American Builder's Companion* (1806);

William Dunlap, *The Life of Charles Brockden Brown,* 2 volumes (Philadelphia: Published by James P. Parke,

1815)—the first biography of the first American professional novelist, by the "Father of the American Theater";

Charles Willson Peale, *A Descriptive Catalogue of Mr. Peale's Exhibition of Perspective Views, with Changeable Effects* (Philadelphia, 1785)—catalogue of Peale's moving-picture exhibition;

Peale and others, *Constituion of the Columbianum* (Philadelphia, 1795)—constitution of the short-lived fine-arts academy founded in Philadelphia in 1795;

"Report of a committee of the assembly of Pennsylvania," *American Museum*, 5 (1789): 185–190—recommendation that Lewis Hallam and John Henry be licensed to operate a theater in Philadelphia, thus repealing the Philadelphia antitheater law of 1786, and appended petitions arguing for and against the measure;

John Trumbull, *A Catalogue of Colonel Trumbull's Paintings, New Exhibiting at the Theatre, New York* (New York: Printed by Sage & Clough, 1804)—catalogue for the first public exhibit of Old Master paintings in the United States, works from artist John Trumbull's collection, shown with a few paintings by him.

John Trumbull, *The Surrender of Lord Cornwallis at Yorktown, October 10, 1781*, begun in 1787 and completed in the late 1820s

C H A P T E R   T H R E E

BUSINESS AND THE ECONOMY

by ROBERT J. ALLISON and JOHN O'KEEFE

CONTENTS

Sidebars and tables are listed in italics.

1783

30 Apr. Gouverneur and Robert Morris prepare a proposal on American currency, basing the new monetary unit on the value of the Spanish dollar and British pound sterling.

2 July Great Britain issues the Orders in Council closing the British West Indies to American ships and ending exports of rum, molasses, sugar, coffee, and spices to the United States.

• Great Britain and the United States sign the final terms of the Treaty of Paris, ending the American Revolution, setting the nation's western boundary at the Mississippi River, and allowing American exports of manufactured goods to the British Isles.

1784

• New York City ship carpenters form a guild.

• Oliver Evans begins constructing an automated flour mill near Philadelphia.

• Simon Willard acquires the exclusive privilege of manufacturing clock-jacks in Massachusetts.

22 Feb. *Empress of China* leaves New York for China.

17 Mar. Recognizing the importance of codfish to the state's economy, the Massachusetts House of Representatives hangs a wooden cod from the ceiling of their chamber.

15 June Elias Derby's ship *Light Horse* sails from Salem to Russia, the first ship to sail under an American flag into the Baltic Sea.

July Spain closes the lower half of the Mississippi River to American traffic.

Aug. *Empress of China* is the first American vessel to arrive in Canton, China; it earns a $37,000 profit trading American ginseng root, liquor, tar, and turpentine for Chinese tea, silk, nankeens, and porcelain.

30 Aug. France opens its West Indian ports to American shipments of salted fish and meats.

Nov. Elias Derby's ship *Grand Turk* sails for the Cape of Good Hope.

Nov. Robert Morris resigns as superintendent of finance, frustrated by Congress's inability to raise money under the terms of the Articles of Confederation.

1785

20 May Congress passes the Land Ordinance of 1785, providing for the surveying of western lands into six-mile-square tracts, each with 36 sections of 640 acres.

23 June Massachusetts forbids exports in British vessels.

1786

Sept. The *Grand Turk* reaches Canton.

11–14 Sept. An interstate commercial convention is held at Annapolis, Maryland, and calls for a revised constitution.

1787

- The first coin authorized by Congress, the Fugio cent, is minted with "Mind Your Business" as the motto.

- Massachusetts grants a fifteen-year monopoly to Boston Glass House to manufacture window and plate glass.

- A British whaler with a crew from Nantucket, Massachusetts, makes the first voyage to the Pacific Ocean to hunt sperm whales.

22 May The *Grand Turk* returns to Salem.

13 July Congress passes the Northwest Ordinance of 1787, creating one large territory and providing for the development of three to five states from it; slavery is not allowed in the area.

Sept. The first American expedition to the Pacific Northwest begins when *Columbia* and *Lady Washington* sail from Boston.

1788

- A wool-manufacturing plant is established in Hartford, Connecticut, but it closes because of the high price of wool, lack of capital, and British competition.

Mar. Massachusetts bars the export of green calf-skins to keep the tanning industry in the state.

Aug. *Columbia* and *Lady Washington* reach Nootka Sound, trading an assortment of goods for otter skins.

1789

- Congress adopts a coinage system based on the Spanish dollar rather than the British pound.

8 Apr. James Madison introduces a tariff bill into Congress.

4 July Congress grants cod fishermen a bounty on exports of dried or pickled fish.

4 July President George Washington signs the first national tariff, enacted to raise money and protect American manufacturing; it imposes a 5 percent tax on all imports.

31 July Congress establishes the value of foreign coins circulating in the United States.

2 Sept. Congress creates the Treasury Department and confirms Alexander Hamilton as the first secretary.

21 Sept. Congress requests Treasury Secretary Hamilton to report on the state of public credit.

1790

- *Columbia* returns from its voyage to Canton, China, the first American ship to circle the globe.

9 Jan. Alexander Hamilton issues the Report on Public Credit, calling for federal assumption of state Revolutionary War debts.

10 Apr.	Congress passes the first patent law, and the first patent is granted to Samuel Hopkins for a process for making potash.
12 Apr.	The House of Representatives defeats Hamilton's proposal for assumption of state debts.
31 May	President George Washington signs the first copyright act to protect written materials and maps.
22 July	The first Trade and Intercourse Act provides for the regulation of Indian trade by the federal government.
24 July	Congress agrees to build a capital city on the Potomac River, part of a compromise measure to ensure Virginia's support for assumption of state debts.
4 Aug.	Congress passes the Funding Act, consolidating federal and state Revolutionary War debts and providing for the payment of interest.

1791

•	Philadelphia carpenters unsuccessfully strike for a ten-hour workday and overtime pay.
•	Treasury Secretary Alexander Hamilton issues the Report on a National Bank, supporting the formation of a large government bank to bolster economic development.
1 Feb.	Thomas Jefferson issues the Report on Fisheries.
25 Feb.	George Washington signs a bill creating the Bank of the United States.
3 Mar.	Congress approves an excise tax on whiskey.
Aug.	Alexander Hamilton and Tenche Coxe issue a prospectus for the Society for Establishing Useful Manufactures.
Oct.	Twenty-five directors are chosen for the Bank of the United States.
5 Dec.	Hamilton issues the Report on Manufactures, an assessment of the American economy.
12 Dec.	The Bank of the United States opens in Philadelphia.

1792

•	The New York Stock Exchange is founded.
Feb.	Congress grants a subsidy to whale and cod fisheries.
Mar.	A new tariff law enacts some of Alexander Hamilton's recommendations for the economy.
Mar.	Overspeculation in Bank of the United States stock causes a financial panic.
2 Apr.	Congress passes the Coinage Act, establishing a federal mint to coin gold and silver money.
8 May	Congress authorizes the minting of copper coins.
12 May	Capt. Robert Gray of the *Columbia* discovers the Columbia River.

1793

- Salem, Massachusetts, merchants open the pepper trade in Sumatra; by 1805 Americans will handle seven-eighths of Sumatra's pepper crop, 7.5 million pounds each year.

- Eli Whitney perfects the cotton gin.

- The Lehigh Coal Mine Company is founded to extract anthracite coal in Pennsylvania.

- William Foster brings three prized Merino sheep from Spain to the United States, one of many improvements in agriculture and animal breeding in this era.

1794

- The Massachusetts legislature refuses to grant a charter to Boston mechanics who want to regulate apprentices.

22 Mar. The federal government bans the slave trade to all foreign ports.

July–Aug. The Whiskey Rebellion breaks out in western Pennsylvania in opposition to the federal tax on liquor.

1795

- The Connecticut Land Company buys a large tract of land in Ohio along Lake Erie.

- North Carolina is the first state to adopt a general incorporation law, making it easier for business associations to form.

1796

- Newburyport, Massachusetts, investors open a canal connecting their town with Chelmsford and Dracut, further inland on the Merrimac River; their corporation ultimately will form the industrial city of Lowell.

- The Massachusetts Turnpike Corporation is chartered to improve roads in western Massachusetts.

Apr. Congress establishes the factory system for trading with Native Americans.

1798

- The ship *Eliza* of New York makes the first American trading voyage to Japan.

- The ship *Recovery* from Salem, Massachusetts, opens the American coffee trade in Mocha, Arabia.

1799

- The Russian American Company is chartered to gather furs in Alaska.

1800

4 Apr.   Congress passes the first federal Bankruptcy Act, applying only to merchants and traders.

10 May   Congress passes the Land Law of 1800, reforming the procedures for selling public land in the Northwest Territory.

1801

- The *Margaret* of Salem, Massachusetts, is the last American ship to visit Japan before the 1850s.

- The Boston bark *Lydia* is chartered by the Spanish government to carry the new governor of the Mariana Islands to Guam.

1802

- Eleuthère Irénée du Pont starts a powder mill on Brandywine Creek in southern Pennsylvania; within ten years it becomes the largest industrial business in the nation.

1803

- A New York sawmill is the first American business to use steam power.

1804

- The governor of Australia forbids American whalers to build and refit vessels on the Tasmanian coast.

1807

22 Dec.   The Embargo Act is in force, forbidding American vessels to sail for foreign ports.

1808

1 Jan.   End of the transatlantic slave trade.

4 Apr.   Treasury Secretary Albert Gallatin submits a report to Congress, calling for the federal government to build better roads and canals.

6 Apr.   New York State charters John Jacob Astor's American Fur Company.

1809

1 Mar.   The Non-Intercourse Act replaces the Embargo Act and opens American shipping to all nations except France and England.

1810

- Cornelius Vanderbilt begins operating a ferry service between Staten Island and Manhattan, initiating one of the largest family businesses of the nineteenth century.

Apr. Treasury Secretary Albert Gallatin presents a report on manufactures to Congress, noting that two-thirds of rural America's clothing and linen is made at home.

1 May Macon's Bill No. 2 temporarily reopens trade with Great Britain and France.

June John Jacob Astor and partners establish the Pacific Fur Company to exploit the fur trade in the Pacific Northwest.

Sept. Astor sends the *Tonquin* from New York to establish a trading post on the Columbia River.

1811

20 Feb. Congress fails to renew the charter of the Bank of the United States.

1812

- A Boston trading firm receives a monopoly on Hawaiian sandalwood from King Kamehameha I.

19 June Congress raises taxes on imported goods and issues $5 million in bonds to fund the War of 1812.

1813

Dec. To prevent trade with English territories, Congress passes a new embargo law.

1814

- Boston Associates, headed by Francis Cabot Lowell, open a mill in Waltham, Massachusetts, that produces cotton cloth, doing both spinning and weaving in one place. The mill represents a major innovation in factory production and in labor relations, as it sets a pattern by employing young women who board nearby.

14 Apr. Congress repeals the Non-Intercourse Act, replacing it with a new system of protective tariffs.

OVERVIEW

Colonies and Empire. Before the Revolution, Americans benefited from being part of the British Empire. England's command of the seas gave American merchants access to markets in Europe, the Mediterranean, and the Caribbean. Chief American exports—salted fish, rice, wheat and grain, and tobacco—were carried throughout the world by American ships. England's growing industries made manufactured goods available to American consumers. The Seven Years' War (1756–1763) gave Britain complete control of the North American continent at a tremendous cost. The British government needed to raise taxes at home to pay for this expensive war and also decided to pay closer attention to the colonies, which were sources of wealth. Most British colonial policy had focused on the sugar-producing colonies of the West Indies, which generated more wealth than the North American colonies, and on India, which the British East India Company had recently conquered. In the 1760s England decided to regulate colonial trade so that the wealth of her colonies would flow to London rather than Paris. The British government enforced its laws against smuggling and required that colonial trade pass through London. When the British government insisted that it had the power to make the colonists pay taxes on goods they imported, such as tea, and when the British granted a monopoly on the American tea trade to the British East India Company, the colonial merchants responded with boycotts, resistance, and revolution. The colonial merchants would pay taxes to support equitable laws to protect their commerce, but they would not support monopolies or what they considered unreasonable restraints on their right to trade freely.

Postwar Depression. While the American Revolution freed American merchants from British restrictions, it also denied Americans British protection and brought American traders into direct conflict with British trade policies. Before the Revolution 75 percent of American exports went to England, Ireland, and the West Indies. After the Revolution, Britain and her colonies would buy only 10 percent of America's exports. The successful Revolution brought on a depression in the United States, as England closed her markets to American trade or raised her tariffs on American goods and poured manufactured goods into American markets, selling these goods at far lower prices than American manufacturers could charge. With no central government to make trade policies, the United States could not respond to this economic warfare.

Constitution and Trade. Before the United States could respond to England's commercial warfare, the American states had to agree to cooperate. But England was not the only competitor for American merchants. Merchants in each state competed with one another and would pressure their own state legislatures to impose tariffs on merchants from other states. New York taxed New Jersey and Connecticut merchants, and Rhode Island merchants did a swift business in smuggling goods into Massachusetts. The states, meanwhile, would not support the U.S. Congress, which had no power to impose taxes. In order to pay off the U.S. debt, Congress needed to raise revenue but could only do so by asking the states for money. Not surprisingly, the states were more intent on paying their own debts and reducing their own citizens' taxes than on paying the U.S. debt. In 1785 the United States had to default on its loan from France, and only John Adams's patient and effective diplomatic skill maintained American credit with Dutch bankers. Clearly, the United States was in trouble. English policy, to shut out American trade, was calculated on the young republic failing. Business and political leaders, such as Robert Morris, Alexander Hamilton, George Washington, and James Madison, worked to give more power to Congress to raise revenue, but the states blocked their attempts. In 1785 a group of commissioners from Maryland and Virginia met at George Washington's home to discuss their trade problems in the Potomac and Chesapeake; they decided to call a meeting of delegates from other states in the region to discuss general trade problems, and in September 1786 five states were represented at Annapolis. They reasoned that solutions to the country's economic problems could be found only if the political structure was changed, giving the U.S. government more power, and they called for a general convention of all the states to meet in Philadelphia in May 1787. The Constitution which emerged from this convention gave Congress the sole power to tax imports; regulate international trade and trade between the states; and forbid the states from repudiating debts, voiding contracts, coining money, or issuing paper money. While the Constitution established a political system, it also allowed the federal government to make commercial policy for the entire country.

Mercantilism and Free Trade. It was not clear what the United States commercial policy would be. In 1776 two remarkable events occurred. One was the American Declaration of Independence; the other was the publication of Adam Smith's *Inquiry into the Nature and Causes of the Wealth of Nations.* The Americans had declared independence from the power of England's king and Parliament; Smith's influential work argued against centralized economic power. For centuries European nations had followed a policy of mercantilism, a form of economic warfare against one another. All nations sought gold, which they saw as the basis of wealth. In order to obtain gold the nations of Europe established colonies, forcing all colonial trade through the home capital—London, Paris, Lisbon, or Madrid. In addition, nations restricted trade with their rivals, imposing high tariffs and other barriers on foreign trade. In this mercantilist system the government took a leading role in promoting and protecting trade, which in turn would enrich the nation. Smith argued that this policy, though it seemed to have enriched the European countries following it, was not the best way to promote national wealth. Instead, Smith argued for a policy of free trade, with no restrictions in the form of tariffs. He saw in the American colonies examples of merchants who had sought out markets and wealth, not because government policy directed them to do so, but because they were self-interested traders. If governments would lift trade barriers, Smith predicted, merchants would seek out the best markets. In addition, Smith insisted, gold was only a measure of wealth, not the source of wealth. Real wealth came from agriculture and trade in agricultural goods. Though Spain controlled much of the world's gold resources, Spain had lost economic ground to England and Holland, which had more merchants and traders able to bring Spain goods she would exchange for gold.

Hamilton and Mercantilism. Many Americans embraced the ideas of Smith, holding that agriculture was the real producer of wealth and that commerce would enrich the nation if it were left free of government interference. Others believed the United States could best achieve economic independence by developing industries of her own. These were the two sides of a debate over what was then called political economy, with Thomas Jefferson and James Madison holding with Smith's view that agriculture was the basic producer of wealth and that the proper policy for the American government was to find or open markets for American goods. On the other hand, Hamilton saw the proper role for the U.S. government in encouraging capital accumulation and economic development. As first secretary of the treasury, Hamilton made it a priority to achieve national economic independence. The best way to do this, Hamilton believed, was by restoring public credit and by encouraging manufacturing.

Restoring Public Credit. To restore public credit, Hamilton called for the federal government to pay the states' Revolutionary War debts. These debts circulated as certificates, payable at a certain date, usually ten years after the war, issued to veterans and creditors at the close of the war. Many veterans, needing cash to pay taxes or support their families, had sold these certificates for a fraction of their face value. Investors, believing that the government ultimately would pay off these notes, had bought them up. As Congress debated assuming the state debts, speculators set out for South Carolina and Georgia to buy up the state notes, hoping they would be redeemed. Hamilton proposed that the U.S. government pay off all these certificates at face value, thus enriching these speculators. While some veterans and politicians questioned the ethical principle of rewarding speculation, Hamilton argued that the new government needed the support of these investors and that this redemption of debt certificates would align the business community with the new national government.

The Paterson Experiment. Hamilton had a bold vision for restoring public credit and establishing economic independence. To further promote economic growth, Hamilton launched the Society for Establishing Useful Manufactures, chartered by the New Jersey legislature, which proposed building a factory city at the falls of the Passaic River. Named for New Jersey governor and later Supreme Court Justice William Paterson, this planned industrial city would include, according to Hamilton's proposal, thirteen factories to produce shoes, textiles, potter, wire, thread, carpets, and blankets. Funded by private capital, and helped by loans from the Bank of New York, which was assured by Hamilton that it would continue to be a repository of federal funds if it extended credit to the Paterson venture, the society built factories at Paterson. But a financial panic in 1792 and the inability to find workers doomed the enterprise, which collapsed finally in 1795.

Jefferson and the Fisheries. Jefferson fundamentally disagreed with Hamilton's approach. Jefferson was determined to build American independence on the existing strength of the nation rather than through creating industries in imitation of Europe. Jefferson had traveled through New England in early 1784, en route for his assignment as minister to France, and learned of the plight of Nantucket's whale fishermen. British policy had closed off markets for whale oil; the Nantucketers were being pressured by economics to move to Nova Scotia. In France, Jefferson worked with the Marquis de Lafayette to open French markets for American whale oil. Similarly, he pressed France to open her markets to American tobacco. As secretary of state, Jefferson proposed a similar policy of encouraging existing American industries, fishing, and agriculture by pressing other nations to open their markets to American goods. Since France had done so, Jefferson believed the United States should reciprocate, as it would for other nations adopting favorable trade policies toward the United States. Jefferson also proposed a bounty for exports of American fish, to encourage the growth of this industry.

Madison's Policy. Madison and Jefferson believed Hamilton's debt-financing system rewarded speculators and would put an unfair burden on other Americans. Madison also saw Hamilton's system of encouraging manufactures as a violation of free-trade principles; instead, Madison believed national economic policy should take advantage of the nation's real wealth, which came from farms, not factories. Madison believed that England and other European countries would come to depend on American grain to feed their factory workers. It would be a grave mistake, he believed, to turn independent American farmers and their wives and children into factory workers, because it would both destroy their own health and welfare and destroy the real source of American wealth. To challenge England or any other country, Madison did not believe in direct competition by building manufacturing centers in America. Instead, Madison proposed a tariff policy which would set high rates on goods coming from England or any country which did not grant Americans free trading privileges. This form of commercial coercion was not designed to promote domestic manufactures; instead, it was designed to influence international affairs.

Mixed Results. Hamilton believed Madison's proposal somewhat naive; however, in 1793 when England and France went to war, demand for American grains jumped dramatically, and for the next ten years American farmers could not keep up with the demand for their crops, nor could American shipbuilders keep up with the demand for ships to carry American grain abroad. With England and France at war, American merchants came to control much of the carrying trade between Europe and the Americas and also had a significant presence in Asia. Neither Hamilton nor Jefferson and Madison would be satisfied that their policy had been completely adopted. Hamilton would succeed in establishing a bank and securing public credit, but his manufacturing city in Paterson did not emerge until much later, and in much different form. The Republicans would sweep Hamilton and his Federalists out of office, but as Jefferson remarked, they would "never get rid of his financial system."

Yazoo Land Fraud. The United States remained an agricultural nation, but agriculture was tied inextricably to international markets. Buying land, in itself, became a vital economic activity, and throughout the 1790s land speculation was a source of both wealth and corruption. To buy land in order to resell it at a higher price drove some of the most prominent men of the day, including financier Robert Morris and Supreme Court Justice James Wilson, deeply into debt, and ultimately, for Morris, to debtor's prison. In 1795 almost the entire Georgia legislature was bribed to sell its western territories, including what is today Alabama and Mississippi, to New England land speculators. The speculators were not interested in settling the land, which was still occupied by the Choctaws, Chickasaws, and Creeks. Instead, they were determined to sell it to other speculators, who in turn would sell it to others. Georgia's citizens, outraged by this corrupt land swindle, turned their legislators out of office; the new legislature rescinded the act selling the land. This satisfied Georgians who had not been part of the deal, but in New England men and women who had bought the land in good faith now owned worthless pieces of paper. Jefferson's administration tried to settle the issue, but Republicans in Congress, determined not to reward corruption, blocked the settlement; the Supreme Court ruled that Georgia could not void a contract, and in 1815 Congress voted some compensation for holders of now-worthless land in Mississippi.

Bankruptcy Law. The increased speculation in land led to increased questioning of what kind of nation the United States was becoming late in the 1790s. For the Republicans, economic development was tied to agricul-

ture. But if selling land made more profit than farming it, how to restrain citizens from increasing their wealth? In 1792 Congress began debating a national bankruptcy law to protect debtors who had overextended themselves. Republicans opposed the law because this kind of policy was for states, not the federal government, to enact, and also because it seemed to reward speculation and signaled that the United States had become a commercial rather than agricultural nation. Republicans saw that in time the United States would develop into a commercial nation, a prospect they feared less than its developing into an industrial one, as Hamilton's Paterson scheme would have it do. But Republicans did not want to speed the process, insisting that the United States first settle all its available land before it venture too far into international trade. It would be difficult, though, to restrain Americans eager to trade. Federalists favored a bankruptcy law as a protection of debtors and creditors, and because it signaled the arrival of economic maturity. Republicans, believing nations, like people, were living creatures, saw that after economic maturity would come economic decline and death. Rather than hastening the process, they hoped to slow it. The Bankruptcy Law, passed by the Federalist Congress in 1800, was repealed by the Republicans in 1803, at the same time as the purchase of Louisiana opened more territory to agricultural settlement.

Indian Trade. Before the Revolution, England had controlled migration across the Allegheny Plateau, wanting to keep the Ohio River valley in the hands of the native people who lived in it. This was not an entirely altruistic policy: merchants involved in the fur trade also needed to keep the forests, lakes, and rivers free of farms and settlers in order to allow deer and beaver to flourish and Indians to hunt them. Trading with the Indians had been a significant source of wealth for Europeans in America: France's empire in Canada was based on the fur trade, and Pennsylvania merchants had also enjoyed a lucrative trade before the Revolution. Traders would venture west with manufactured goods, guns, alcohol, and cloth to trade with Native Americans for furs. In the southeast, firms such as Panton, Leslie and Company in Pensacola, Florida, traded with the Creeks and Choctaws and did not welcome white settlement into Indian lands. Much of the Indian trade was conducted by women, who were the principal agriculturists among most Native American groups. Merchants would secure whatever links or advantages they could with Native American trading partners. One Scottish trader, Lachlan McGillivray, married a Creek woman; their son, Alexander McGillivray, became an important leader of the Creeks in the 1780s. The Indian trade was complicated and lucrative: the Constitution gave Congress the sole power to regulate the trade, and in 1796 Congress decided that it would appoint agents to trade with the Indians, forbidding states or private individuals from doing so. After 1801 the Jefferson administration began to make its goal the removal of Native Americans from their traditional lands and the settlement of those lands by white farmers. The indebtedness of Native Americans, exacerbated by trade and the fluctuations of the fur market, made it easier to force Indians to sell their land. The purchase of the Louisiana Territory, Jefferson believed, would give the United States a place to send Indians removed from east of the Mississippi.

The Pacific Northwest. While the eastern fur trade was being dismantled, a new trade opened in the Pacific Northwest. In 1792 Capt. Robert Gray, sailing on the *Columbia,* found the Columbia River and claimed this territory for the United States. The Louisiana Territory was still controlled by Spain, which claimed all the land drained by the Mississippi and Missouri Rivers. Yet an American presence began in the Pacific Northwest, where small trading settlements named Salem and Portland formed to trade with the natives for otter skins. Competing with British traders based in Vancouver and Russians based in Sitka, Alaska, these traders carried otter pelts across the Pacific to Canton either for tea or silver, which would be brought back to Salem, Massachusetts, and Boston. This was not exactly a triangular trade, as goods from Massachusetts would be brought by way of Cape Horn to the Columbia River, there traded for otter skins, which would be brought to Canton, and traded there for tea, silks, or silver. By the early nineteenth century New England traders had brought the Hawaiian Islands into this trade network, and came to know the Pacific water routes as well as they knew Massachusetts Bay. A German immigrant, John Jacob Astor, would establish a trading colony, Astoria, on the Columbia River in 1810, and though it was surrendered to a British trading firm during the War of 1812, Astor began one of the nation's greatest fortunes in the otter trade.

Slave Trade. While only 7 percent of the Africans brought to the New World came to North America, American merchants were involved in the slave trade. Olaudah Equiano was a slave who worked during the 1760s for an American merchant on the island of Montserrat, bringing enslaved Africans to South Carolina and Georgia to trade for rice and beef to feed the slaves of the Caribbean. Rhode Island merchants were also involved in the African trade, and the Narragansett Bay town of Bristol was a center for New England slave traders. While most slaves went to South America or the Caribbean, and the overwhelming majority of slaves brought to North America were taken to the plantation colonies of Georgia, South Carolina, and the Chesapeake, all colonies had slaves, and New Jersey, Connecticut, New York, and Rhode Island had significant slave populations before the Revolution. During the Revolution Virginia had ceased its slave imports, and following the war a movement against the slave trade emerged in America, led actually by Virginia planters such as George Mason.

Antislavery Movement. The 1780s were the high point for the African slave trade, with an average of eighty-five thousand slaves brought to the New World each year. Documentation of the slave trade's horrors, provided by survivors such as Equiano, who wrote an autobiography in 1789, and by British reformers such as William Wilberforce, Thomas Clarkson, and Granville Sharp, and by American Quakers like Anthony Benezet, produced moral revulsion in many Americans. George Mason proposed at the Constitutional Convention that the United States prohibit the slave trade. Delegates

from Georgia and South Carolina protested; they still needed slaves, they said, to produce their rice crops. In the end, Georgia and South Carolina struck a bargain with the delegates from New England: Georgia and South Carolina would support New England on another issue if New England would allow the slave trade to continue until 1807. Mason was outraged and said he would sooner cut off his right hand than use it to sign the Constitution. All states but Georgia and South Carolina had banned the slave trade well before 1807, when Congress, at President Jefferson's direction, banned slaves from entering the United States.

Internal Slave Trade. While the United States barred its citizens from the international slave trade, nothing would be done about the domestic slave trade. After the invention of the cotton gin in 1793 and the opening of the southwest territories (Mississippi and Alabama), Virginians, whose soil was too depleted to continue growing tobacco profitably, began selling their slaves in greater numbers to the Southwest. The Louisiana Purchase brought a rich sugar-producing region into the union, with a need for slave labor to perform the backbreaking work of harvesting cane and turning it into sugar. Slaves from Virginia and other parts of the South would be sold to Louisiana, and with no foreign sources for slaves, Virginia planters actually became breeders of slaves for sale in these domestic markets.

Embargo. Jefferson would not move against the domestic slave trade because the Constitution did not give the federal government power to do so. However, the Constitution did give the government power to regulate international trade, and when the British and French continued to threaten American commerce in 1807, Jefferson and Secretary of State Madison, who had argued that the United States should use its commercial produce to influence British policy, responded with an embargo on American trade. No American ships were permitted to leave port; American sailors were stranded at sea, and the lucrative American commerce was destroyed. Jefferson's Embargo was calculated to deprive France's armies and England's factory workers of flour and codfish; its real effect, however, was to destroy American trade. The fact that most U.S. government revenues came from tariffs, and thus would amount to almost nothing if imports stopped, greatly alarmed Secretary of the Treasury Albert Gallatin, who did not believe the Embargo would be an effective weapon against England or France. Jefferson and Madison believed it would and further believed that the Embargo would be a Republican alternative to war and would show England that American trade was more powerful than the Royal Navy and Napoleon that American grain was more potent than his army. Better to have American ships safely bottled up in port, Jefferson reasoned, than have them destroyed by British and French ships, and better to protect the tiny American navy by keeping it at home than to risk its destruction by hostile guns. The Embargo, it turned out, was a failure. It did not force the British or French to rescind their hostile policies. Instead, it created great bitterness against Jefferson in New England and severely depleted the American treasury. One inadvertent result of the Embargo was to force Americans to begin manufacturing goods they could not import from England. New England's international traders, unable to apply their capital on foreign trade, began building the kinds of factories in Rhode Island and Massachusetts that Hamilton had hoped to see rise on the banks of the Passaic. While Jefferson applauded the development of home manufactures and American self-sufficiency, he continued to worry about the long-term consequences of industrialization. Ironically, his Embargo helped spur the process. On the day before he left office, Jefferson signed a bill repealing the Embargo.

Conclusion. Americans had been pushed to rebel against England because of England's restrictive trade policies. American leaders, once independence was secured, disagreed about the best trade policies the new nation should pursue. Hamilton believed the central government should encourage industrial development and capital accumulation; Jefferson and Madison believed the best policy was to leave merchants and farmers free to find the best international markets and to protect their rights to do so. Hamilton failed to develop an industrial infrastructure, though he did establish the nation's public credit and a national bank. Jefferson and Madison failed to dismantle Hamilton's system, yet their policies of free trade and their insistence on paying the national debt inspired the kind of industrial development Hamilton had dreamed of and which the British planners of the 1760s would have found utterly astonishing. By the end of Madison's administration, with the United States successfully concluding the War of 1812, Americans turned to business enterprise with a new vigor. Fifty years earlier a British monopoly and a tax on tea had driven American merchants to revolution; by 1815 policies of their own republican government allowed American merchants to grow rich by selling tea in Europe, at a lower price than any European trader could match.

TOPICS IN THE NEWS

BANKING AND FINANCE

Debt. As the American Revolution ended, financial problems were among the most pressing issues facing the new nation. Although the war had disrupted the economy, particularly those parts of it engaged in overseas trade, people still farmed and made a living, and in many respects life for many after the Treaty of Paris simply continued as it always had. The war had cost money, however, and the financial system of the new nation needed to be completely reconstructed to pay for it and to take account of independence. The Continental Congress and the states had issued bills of credit during the war to pay for expenses. These bills were like paper money and represented the governments' obligations to redeem them at some future time, for specie (gold and silver coin). They circulated among the public as dollar bills today do, although they were often not honored. In the case of Congress, the problem was that nothing backed the value of these bills, or "continentals." During the course of the war they depreciated rapidly, making it necessary to issue more and more of them to keep the nation afloat. An inflationary spiral ensued, bringing hardship to many and undermining the economy as a whole. Congress's superintendent of finance, Robert Morris, estimated the debt of the United States in 1783 at $30 million, but this was really just a portion of the vast amounts of loans, depreciated bills of credit, and unpaid obligations the nation faced.

Taxes. The inability of the Congress to tax under the Articles of Confederation made the financial problems worse. The Articles allowed Congress to raise money only by requisitioning the states, which were not always ready or willing to impose taxes to fulfill their obligations. Some states such as Virginia did attempt to redeem their share of the national obligations, as well as their own, making themselves seem stronger than the Union. Efforts to tax imports at the federal level failed repeatedly during the 1780s to gain the unanimous consent required by the Articles. A shortage of specie also compounded the problem. The main source of gold and silver was foreign trade, which revived after the war but not quickly enough to solve the financial crisis of the 1780s. At first, imports dominated trade as Americans consumed goods denied them during the war, which meant that specie was leaving the country, not coming in. The principal wealth of the new nation was in land, something not readily converted to cash. Congress and the states, however, did try to meet some of their obligations with land. Some Continental Army veterans received western land grants for their service.

Reform. Robert Morris made the most serious efforts to reform the country's finances while he was superintendent of finance from 1781 to 1784. Morris tried to stabilize the paper currency by making it redeemable in specie and to provide for the steady payment of interest on the national debt. He hoped these measures would inspire confidence in the new government and lay the basis for

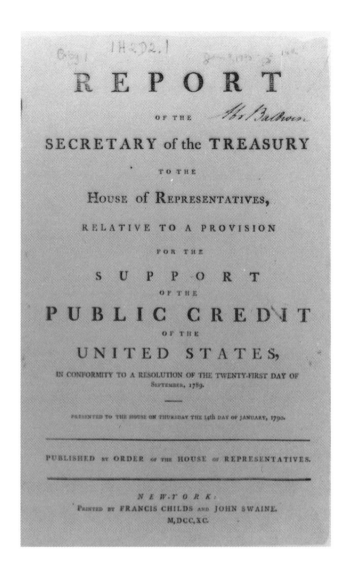

Title page for the printed version of Alexander Hamilton's
first report on the public credit

economic growth. The failure of the import duty ruined his plan, however, since it depended on the government having a steady source of income with which to redeem bills and pay interest. States instead imposed their own import taxes and rivaled each other in efforts to lure and control trade. Within the states there was unrest over economic matters as well, exhibited by Shays's Rebellion in Massachusetts in September 1786, as a group of debtor farmers, unhappy over the state's taxing policies which seemed to favor eastern merchants, attacked courthouses and the state militia. This chaotic situation and growing dissatisfaction with the weak commercial powers of Congress led to a convention of several states in Annapolis, Maryland, in 1786, which in turn called for broader constitutional reform. The Constitution that emerged in 1787 gave Congress the ability to tax and far greater direct control over the economy, powers skillfully exploited by the first secretary of the treasury, Alexander Hamilton, in the 1790s as he struggled to place the United States on firmer economic ground.

Banks. A key element in shoring up the American economy was developing a sound banking system to facilitate the circulation of money and credit. Morris took the first steps in 1781 with the chartering of the Bank of North America in Philadelphia, the first national commercial bank. The government was the principal stockholder in this enterprise, which loaned money back to the nation. It was followed by the Massachusetts Bank of Boston and the Bank of New York in 1784, all three succeeding in providing a stable currency and in making short-term loans, mainly to merchants in their respective locations. One of the centerpieces of Hamilton's economic program was a true national bank that would be sponsored by the government and could back its money with government deposits. He proposed such an institution in his January 1791 "Report on a National Bank," and Congress responded by chartering the Bank of the United States one month later.

Bank of the United States. The Bank was controversial. Jeffersonians opposed it, saying the Constitution did not grant Congress the power to charter banks, and behind this argument was a fear that the Bank would serve the interests of Federalist merchants over those of Jeffersonian farmers. The Bank was supported by many others, however, and its stock quickly sold out. It opened in Philadelphia in December 1791 with Thomas Willing as president and soon opened branches in other cities, beginning a twenty-year career supporting American business and government. It issued paper currency that held its value in specie, thus ending the inflation of the 1780s. The success of the Bank assisted Hamilton in the other major piece of his economic policy, funding the

---

PUBLIC DEBT OF THE UNITED STATES, DECEMBER 1789

Alexander Hamilton prepared this report on public credit, estimating the debts of the United States and of the states and the amount of the debt owed to Americans (domestic debt) and to foreigners (foreign debt).

Total Public Debt: $77,124,464

Foreign Debt: $11,710,307
Principal: $10,070,307
Arrears of Interest: $1,640,072

Domestic Debt: $40,414,085
Principal: $27,383,917
Arrears of Interest: $13,030,168

State Debt: $25,000,000
Ascertained: $18,201,206
Estimated Balance: $6,798,794

Source: Alexander Hamilton, *Report of the Secretary of the Treasury on the Public Credit of the United States* (New York, 1790).

public debt. The Funding Act of 4 August 1790 provided for a final settlement of debts still owed from the Revolution. The national government consolidated the remaining debts, assumed the remaining state debts, and issued new securities to replace them both. Backed by new taxes and the emerging stable banking system, the United States was able to make regular interest payments, earning the confidence of financiers and merchants for the first time. While retiring the debt was popular, the new taxes supporting it were not. In 1794 farmers in western Pennsylvania participated in an armed uprising objecting to the federal tax on liquor. This Whiskey Rebellion was quickly suppressed but indicated the depth of feeling on economic matters and the fragility of the new nation's finances.

State Banks. Events such as the Whiskey Rebellion showed that many Americans felt the merchants in the East unfairly dominated the nation's economy and used the Bank to their own advantage. One response to this feeling as well as to the success of the Bank was the formation of state-chartered banks across the country. There were twenty-nine banks in 1800 and eighty-nine by 1811. Many of these banks were located in interior regions, owned by businessmen with Jeffersonian sympathies. Many were more sensitive to the needs of farmers on the frontier hungry for long-term credit which conservative Federalist state banks in eastern cities and the Bank of the United States would not extend. Although they took greater risks, in general all these banks were secure before 1812; this was in part because of the influence of the Bank of the United States. As the only bank the federal government dealt with, it functioned informally as a central bank at the heart of a network of state banks and was able to assert some control over lending policies. Resentment of this central control over the economy grew during the Jeffersonian era, however, and state banks and their customers demanded more freedom to extend more credit. In 1811 Congress refused to recharter the Bank of the United States, despite the support of Albert Gallatin, the Jeffersonian secretary of the treasury. The Bank succumbed to its economic rivals and to the constitutional issues raised at its founding, losing by one vote in the House of Representatives and losing a tie in the Senate when Vice President George Clinton voted against it. Most of the branch offices were purchased by state banks, and shipping magnate Stephen Girard bought the Bank's main Philadelphia office and set up his own private bank. There was no longer any one bank to meet the federal government's financial needs in a unified way, however, and this combined with the disruptions of the War of 1812 to destabilize the American economy. Confusion continued until Congress chartered the Second Bank of the United States in 1816.

Sources:

Donald R. Adams Jr., *Finance and Enterprise in Early America* (Philadelphia: University of Pennsylvania Press, 1978);

Bray Hammond, *Banks and Politics in America* (Princeton, N.J.: Princeton University Press, 1957).

DOMESTIC ECONOMY

Agriculture. As important as trading was to the United States economy, the economic activity that Americans were most directly involved with was farming. Agriculture was the mainstay of this economy and the culture it supported. The early United States was overwhelmingly rural, with only 3.3 percent of the population living in cities with over eight thousand people in 1790, rising to only 4.9 percent in 1810. In the North wheat, corn, and other grains were the principal crops, and their production increased as the cities along the Atlantic coast began to grow more rapidly after 1790. Land in coastal areas was already becoming scarce by 1790, however, fueling the dispersion of the population to the west. As white Americans settled the trans-Appalachian interior, farming there began to grow as well. It was hampered at first by the difficulty of clearing land and establishing farms. The typical pioneer family would arrive at their tract with a cow, some pigs, and little else. Felling trees and building a house were the first priorities, as well as planting a first crop, usually Indian corn and pumpkins. Farming was mainly for the family's own consumption at first, although some marketing was done when possible, to provide money for tools and other manufactured necessities. Corn was the key crop, providing food and liquor for humans and fodder for animals. Meat could be hunted, but the main source was pigs, which were relatively easy to raise. As the work of clearing fields advanced, wheat could be planted once it was possible to plow the soil, and other grains such as oats and barley followed. The process was slow, however. Farmers cleared only from one to three acres a year, and it could easily take a decade of hard work before there was a well-established family farmstead to show for the effort.

Southern Farming. Staple crop production dominated southern agriculture, which participated in a much more developed agricultural market economy than the North in this era. Tobacco was historically the most important southern crop, and production peaked in 1790 when exports totaled 118,000 hogsheads. Tobacco farming quickly drains nutrients from soil, and by this period much land in tidewater Virginia and other tobacco regions was exhausted. After 1793 production declined quickly, hurt as well by the disruptions in trade caused by the Napoleonic wars. Cotton soon took its place at the center of the Southern economy. Cotton farming was limited to the coastal region of South Carolina and Georgia before 1793, when Eli Whitney per-

COTTON PRODUCTION, 1790-1815

Year	Bales of Raw Cotton
1790	3,125
1795	16,719
1800	73,145
1805	146,290
1810	177,369
1815	208,986

Source: Curtis P. Nettels, *The Emergence of a National Economy, 1775-1815* (New York: Holt, Rinehart & Winston, 1962).

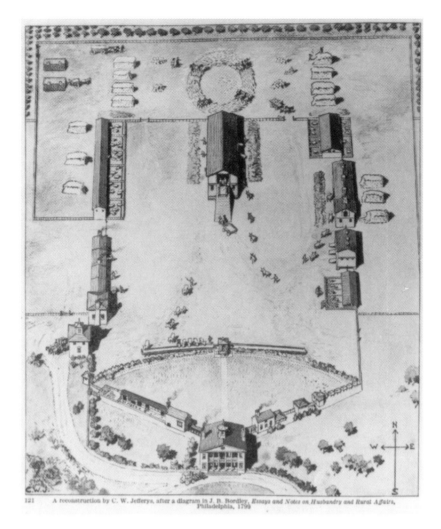

121   A reconstruction by C. W. Jefferys, after a diagram in J. B. Bordley, *Essays and Notes on Husbandry and Rural Affairs*, Philadelphia, 1799

An ideal plantation in a 1799 engraving by C. W. Jefferys

fected a cotton gin that made production of cotton easier. Production grew from three million pounds in 1793 to eighty million pounds in 1811, and it spread from the southeastern states to the Mississippi River. Cotton was a lucrative cash crop, and exports to England's textile mills boomed, growing from five hundred thousand pounds in 1793 to over forty-five million pounds in 1807. The Embargo of 1807 and the War of 1812 hurt cotton exports to Europe, but the growth of a domestic textile industry in New England began to make up the loss. Both cotton and tobacco, as well as sugar, which America began to produce after the purchase of the Louisiana Territory, were labor-intensive and relied on slavery to be profitable.

Innovations. In the early national era, the ways Americans earned their livings changed little. Almost all were engaged in farming, shipping, and fishing. Farmers used simple tools, such as the crude plow typically guided by the farmer and pulled by the team of oxen, which did no more than scrape a furrow into the topsoil. Few farmers attempted to enrich the land by rotating crops or planting clover; fertilizing was also uncommon. There was so much new land available that when the land was exhausted, many farmers simply moved and cleared new fields. At the same time, some early Americans were in-

terested in new farming techniques, and the periodical press of the era printed many articles about farming improvements. Reformers included many national leaders, such as George Washington, Thomas Jefferson, Robert Livingston, and John Taylor of Caroline. Taylor's book *Arator* (1813) publicized a system of tillage he had devised along with advice on fertilizer. George Morgan of New Jersey experimented with new varieties of corn and grains and methods to control harmful insects. Technical improvements to plows and new inventions such as the cotton gin also helped improve agriculture. Reform came slowly, however, hindered as much by its high cost as by the ready availability of new land.

Transportation. An essential part of the agricultural economy was the ability to move products to the market. Early Americans found transportation a difficult problem, given the size of the nation and its primitive road system. In upstate New York in 1804, getting wheat from the area around Rochester to the market in Albany on the Hudson River took a fourteen-day wagon trip, at a cost of more than fifty dollars a ton. Farmers in the West faced the challenge of exporting agricultural products across the mountains to the east. The Ohio and Mississippi Rivers became the principal avenues out of this area, and areas with ready access to cheap water transportation routes flourished. Major trading towns such as Cincinnati and Pittsburgh were on rivers. New Orleans became the center of trade with the Old Northwest, especially after the Louisiana Purchase in 1803 removed the threat of Spanish and French interference with river traffic. The value of goods arriving from the North in New Orleans increased from $1 million in 1799 to over $5 million in 1807. River traffic would further increase with the introduction of practical steamboats, following the experiments of John Stevens and Robert Fulton in the 1790s and early 1800s. Efforts to improve transportation also included road and canal building. In 1792 investors in Pennsylvania formed a company to build a toll road, or turnpike, between Philadelphia and Lancaster. The stone and gravel road took two years to build but was an immediate success. By 1801 there were similar companies building roads and profiting from tolls in all the states from Virginia north. Tolls also funded companies building bridges, like the fifteen-hundred-foot bridge over Boston's Charles River built in 1786. Other private companies formed to improve river navigation by building canals, like the twenty-seven-mile Middlesex Canal from Boston up the Merrimac River to New Hampshire (built between 1794 and 1803), but relatively little canal building was finished before 1815.

Indian Trade. Trading between Native Americans and European settlers had always been an important component of the economic activity of North America, and this continued to be the case during the early national period. This trade went on in the midst of the white encroachment on Indian land and the destruction of Native American cultures, making it fertile ground for conflict. On 7 August 1786 Congress passed an ordinance establishing an Indian department, mostly concerned with regulating trade with Indians. It limited trading to American citizens with licenses from the federal government. This policy proved ineffective, weakened by rivalries between the states and the central government and by individuals who pressed into western territories without regard for legal niceties, which the government had neither money nor troops to enforce. Organized trade was also often resisted by the Indians themselves, who rightly saw it as the first step in displacing them from their land. The new Constitution gave Congress clearer control over trade with Native American tribes. Under the leadership of President Washington and Secretary of War Henry Knox, the United States began forging a policy of treating with tribes for the purchase of land in an effort to avoid war. In 1790 the first of a series of trade and intercourse acts provided for trading licenses, forbade private purchases of Indian land, and set out punishments for whites committing various crimes in Indian territory. Congress strengthened these provisions in subsequent acts until the revision of March 1802 when the Intercourse Act took the form it would have for the next thirty years.

Fur and Whiskey. The main products these acts tried to regulate were fur and whiskey. After land, furs were what white Americans wanted most from Indians. Native Americans had better access to the plentiful game of the interior than any fur traders like John Jacob Astor could have, and the provision of furs was a major eco-

CONSUMER PRICE INDEX, 1783-1815

This index compares the amount it would cost to buy $100 worth of goods in 1860 with the cost in the following years. For example, these commodities would cost $28 more in 1783 than in 1860. Higher prices are not necessarily bad; since many of the commodities used to make the index were farm products and since most Americans were farmers, higher prices on this index generally meant prosperity, and lower prices meant hard times. From this index, for example, we see that prices fell in the late 1780s, a period of depression; began to rise again after the new Constitution took effect; and jumped after 1793 when American merchants capitalized on the war between France and England.

Year	C.P.I.
1783	$128
1784	123
1785	117
1786	114
1787	112
1788	107
1789	106
1790	110
1791	113
1792	115
1793	119
1794	132
1795	151
1796	159
1797	153
1798	148
1799	148
1800	151
1801	153
1802	129
1803	136
1804	142
1805	141
1806	147
1807	139
1808	151
1809	148
1810	148
1811	158
1812	160
1813	192
1814	211
1815	185

Note: One hundred dollars in 1860 would be roughly equivalent to $1,629 today.

Source: John J. McCusker, *How Much Is That in Real Money? A Historical Price Index for Use as a Deflator of Money Values in the Economy of the United States* (Worcester, Mass.: American Antiquarian Society, 1992).

nomic activity for many Indians. The extent of this trade made regulation difficult, and there was much illegal trading. Rivalries with British traders operating from Canada also made the reality of fur trading conditions far from the ideal envisioned in the intercourse acts. To further regularize the trade, Congress as early as 1796 established the factory system. The factories were government trading posts which were to deal fairly with the Indians in an effort to earn their trust and end their contacts with foreign traders. The factories were also meant to be outposts of civilization and so furthered the diplomatic goal of assimilating Indians into white culture. The factories proved unable to meet these large ambitions, in part because of the opposition of private fur traders like Astor. They also failed because of the ongoing destruction of Native American civilization, which was at least symbolized by the use of liquor. Indian traders often received whiskey for furs, and the increased availability of hard alcohol had a devastating effect on Native American societies. Efforts to control the spread of liquor to Indians began in 1803 but met with little success. However well-meant, these attempts to use trade to improve relations between whites and Indians could not prevail against the underlying political and cultural differences between the two groups.

Business. Change came as slowly to early American business as it did to agriculture. Throughout the period, most businesses were small sole proprietorships. Owners were also workers and took the risks on themselves. Some businessmen did form joint ventures to pursue larger projects. Most of these were privately formed partnerships, where all the partners shared the risk of failure. Few ventures took the form of corporations, the most common business organization today. The corporation had the advantage of limited liability for investors; if they lost money, they were liable only for their initial investment. At this time, however, corporations had to pursue some public benefit beyond the investors' profits and be chartered by special legislative acts. Most early corporations formed to build roads or canals or perform essential banking functions. Few were devoted to manufacturing goods. The numbers of corporations rose steadily over the period, especially in the North. By 1801 the states had chartered 326 corporations, and between 1800 and 1817 there were another 1,800 corporations. The passage of general incorporation laws, allowing investors to incorporate routinely rather than wait for the legislature to act, spurred the process. North Carolina passed the first of these statutes in 1795, followed by New York in 1811. The rise of corporations was also due to the general economic success of the United States before 1807. Profits from trade needed to be invested again, and the corporate venture soon became the investment of choice.

Industry. Profits came from foreign trade but also from the increasing domestic market, dominated by agricultural produce. Many early Americans made their living in retail trades as peddlers, supplying small manufactured articles to farmers too far from settled areas to have ready access to centralized markets or to the country stores springing up in the new towns on the frontier. More and more of the goods in these stores were made in America, as manufacturing slowly took a place at the center of the economy. In the cities, people worked in printing, meatpacking, sugar refining, and rum distilling. The most important industries were associated with iron, mining, smelting, and forging tools. The iron industry ran on charcoal, the first experiments using anthracite coal as a more efficient fuel not taking place until 1808. The biggest change in American industry came in association with cotton as textile milling became an important business. This industry began to mechanize with the introduction of the spinning jenny during the Revolution. Mills sprang up across New England, spurred by the Embargo of 1807. The Embargo limited exports of southern cotton to England and imports of cloth from England, and the domestic textile industry grew. A significant advance came in 1814 when Francis Cabot Lowell and his associates opened a mill in Waltham, Massachusetts, which was the first to combine spinning and weaving in one factory. The Waltham mill was just the first step toward the industrialization which would sweep the North after 1820.

Labor. As business grew and the economy expanded after 1790, labor diversified and conditions for working men and women changed accordingly. Some laborers worked in farming, helping at times when more hands were needed than the typical farm family could provide for itself. Industrial laborers usually worked in small groups; in 1815 a very large manufacturing enterprise would have at most 150 employees. Most early American wage earners were artisans or skilled workers, and they included blacksmiths, shoemakers, hatters, tailors, carpenters, and chandlers, among others. They usually worked in shops under the supervision of a master craftsman, performing specialized or routine tasks under his direction. In most main towns the master craftsmen in various trades formed craft societies, something like medieval guilds, to support each other and protect their trade. In New York in 1786, these groups associated together in a "General Society of Mechanics and Tradesmen." The journeymen and apprentices who worked for the master craftsmen also associated together, although usually to secure a wage increase, after which they would disband. In 1792 Philadelphia shoemakers banded together in support of higher wages, an association that was more permanent and more like today's labor unions. There were at least twelve strikes in the United States between 1786 and 1816, although they were hampered by the prevailing idea that organized strikes were illegal. With the rise of textile milling, women and girls became wage earners in significant numbers. The earliest mills used neighborhood women who would commute daily to the mill from home. Later mills, like Lowell's Waltham mill, sponsored closely regulated boarding homes to house young women who would move to the area while they worked in the mill for several years before returning home.

Sources:

Reginald Horsman, *Expansion and American Indian Policy, 1783–1812* (Lansing: Michigan State University Press, 1967);

Stephen Innes, ed., *Work and Labor in Early America* (Chapel Hill: University of North Carolina Press, 1988);

Drew McCoy, *The Elusive Republic* (New York: Norton, 1980);

Curtis P. Nettels, *The Emergence of a National Economy, 1775–1815* (New York: Holt, Rinehart & Winston, 1962);

Francis Paul Prucha, *American Indian Policy in the Formative Years* (Cambridge, Mass.: Harvard University Press, 1962).

EMBARGO OF 1807

Tensions. The political and military events of the early national period often had significant economic aspects, as exhibited by the Embargo of 1807. In the aftermath of the French Revolution, Britain, France, and many other European nations were at war almost constantly from 1793 to 1815. As part of this conflict, each side attempted to maintain a naval blockade of the ports of the other side, limiting their opponent's ability to send out warships and merchant vessels. The United States remained neutral in this conflict for most of this period. Because of this neutrality, American ships were permitted to trade with parties on all sides of the conflict. This was a significant advantage to American trade, still recovering from the disruption of the American Revolution, and it profited substantially from the charges for carrying goods to and from European ports. All this changed after 1805. In that year, in an admiralty case involving the American trader *Essex,* a British court held that American shipping between the West Indies and France violated a British law and left American ships open to British attacks. France's Berlin Decree (21 November 1806) and Milan Decree (17 December 1807) and Britain's Orders in Council (7 January and 11 November 1807) further threatened neutral shipping attempting to enter their enemy's ports. The British bore the brunt of Americans' anger over these trade restrictions. President Thomas Jefferson's first response was the 1806 Nonimportation Act, which barred certain imports but was largely ineffective.

The *Chesapeake*. Matters came to a head after the humiliation Americans felt in an incident involving the American warship *Chesapeake* on 22 June 1807. The *Leopard,* a man-of-war of the Royal Navy, forcibly stopped the *Chesapeake* off the Virginia coast and boarded it to search for deserters. The British took four sailors from the *Chesapeake* and impressed them, or drafted them into the navy, on the grounds that they were British citizens. This was just one of many instances of Britain impressing sailors who claimed American citizenship, as Britain refused to recognize the right of extirpation, or changing citizenship. The anger at this action was intense and widespread, but the country was not prepared for a war, and Jefferson had to seek another solution. On 22 December 1807 Congress passed the Embargo Act, banning all American trade with foreign nations.

Economic Consequences. The Embargo had an immediate effect on American trade; exports declined 75 percent and imports fell by 50 percent. New England merchants suffered the most since they were most directly involved in foreign trade. Southern farmers also suffered since they depended on exports of their staple crops, tobacco and cotton. The middle and western states were relatively unaffected since farming linked to the domestic market was the primary economic activity there. Prices and earnings fell and unemployment rose, bringing on a serious depression lasting until the end of the War of 1812. Over time Americans began to recover

THOMAS JEFFERSON ON MALTHUS

Thomas Malthus, a British political economist, had a gloomy revelation after a visit to India. The world's population, Malthus predicted, would soon face a crisis of survival. People were being born faster than new land could be cultivated to feed them all. While the world's food supply increased steadily, its population had been increasing geometrically since the 1600s and would soon exhaust the food supply. In 1804 President Thomas Jefferson was reading a new edition of Malthus's "Essay on Population" when French writer Jean-Baptiste Say sent him a copy of his own essay, *Traité d'Economie Politique* (1803). Jefferson's response reveals his own more optimistic prediction for the world's future.

The differences of circumstances between this and the old countries of Europe, furnish differences of fact whereon to reason, in questions of political economy, and will consequently produce sometimes a difference of result. There, for instance, the quantity of food is fixed, or increasing in a slow and only arithmetical ratio, and the proportion is limited by the same ratio. Supernumerary births consequently add only to your mortality. Here the immense extent of uncultivated and fertile lands enables every one who will labor, to marry young, and to raise a family of any size. Our food, then, may increase geometrically with our laborers, and our births, however multiplied, become effective. Again, there the best distribution of labor is supposed to be that which places the manufacturing hands alongside the agricultural; so that the one part shall feed both, and the other part furnish both with clothes and other comforts. Would that be the best here? Egoism and first appearances say yes. Or would it better that all our laborers should be employed in agriculture? In this case a double or a treble portion of fertile lands would be brought into culture; a double or treble creation of food be produced, and its surplus go to nourish the now perishing births of Europe, who in return would manufacture and send us in exchange our clothes and other comforts. Morality listens to this, and so invariably do the laws of nature create our duties and interests, that when they seem to be at variance, we ought to suspect some fallacy in our reasonings. In solving this question, too, we should allow its just weight to the moral and physical preference of the agricultural, over the manufacturing, man. My occupations permit me only to ask questions. They deny me the time, if I had the information, to answer them. Perhaps, as worthy the attention of the author of the *Traité d'Economie Politique,* I shall find them answered in that work. If they are not, the reason will have been that you wrote for Europe; while I shall have asked them because I think for America.

Source: Thomas Jefferson to J. B. Say, Washington, D.C., 1 February 1804, in *The Portable Thomas Jefferson,* edited by Merrill Peterson (New York: Penguin, 1975).

Federalist broadside publicizing French attacks on American merchant ships

some of their losses as southerners began to sell their cotton to northern textile mills. The mills themselves started to grow to meet the domestic demand for cloth, which previously had been supplied by British imports. Some traders found loopholes in the law or even illegal ways around the Embargo, and violations of its terms were especially common in Maine and Florida.

Political Consequences. Many Americans linked the Embargo with the policies of the Jeffersonian party. Both Jeffersonians and Federalists disliked involvement in European affairs, but Federalists had advocated that military strength was the way to deal with threats from abroad. The Jeffersonians drew on the tradition of non-importation from the American Revolution to argue that commercial policy was itself a way of affecting other countries. Thus, the Embargo was an assertion of America's importance to Britain and France, and Jefferson meant to make them reopen their trade by denying them the benefits of it. Jefferson called the Embargo a "candid and liberal experiment" in "peaceful coercion." However worthy these pacifist ideals, Europe felt the Embargo less than the United States. The act was deeply opposed by a revived Federalist Party, centered at that time in the New England cities which were most affected by the boycott. After 1808 "Mr. Jefferson's Embargo" became increasingly unpopular, as Josiah Quincy and Thomas Pickering of Massachusetts led a fight against it in Congress. They were aided from within Jefferson's party by John Randolph of Virginia. Tempers ran so high on the issue that two congressmen, George Campbell of Tennessee and Barent Gardenier of New York, even fought a duel. Most seriously, some New England Federalists threatened to have their states nullify the federal act and withdraw from the Union, making the end of the Embargo inevitable, if the nation was to survive.

Non-Intercourse Act. Congress repealed the Embargo in March 1809, three days before the end of Jefferson's term, substituting the much less stringent Non-Intercourse Act. The Non-Intercourse Act barred trade only with France and Britain, and it would resume with either or both countries once they stopped violating American neutrality. This policy left no one happy—merchants still disliked any restrictions, and President James Madison felt increasingly pressured by the loss of import duties, a main source of government money in the period. Several adjustments failed to solve the problems, and in March 1811 Madison reimposed non-intercourse, this time against Britain only. This was a tacit acknowledgment that the commercial conflict was so severe that war was unavoidable and a choice that it was better to fight Britain. The result was the War of 1812, declared the following June. The war continued to disrupt trade and put a serious strain on the nation's finances. The depression that began in 1807 did not fully ease until 1816, although the need to rely on domestic manufactured goods was a spur to American industry that would later display its true significance in the industrialization of the Jacksonian period.

Sources:

J. Van Fenstermaker and John E. Filer, "The U.S. Embargo Act of 1807: Its Impact on New England Money, Banking, and Economic Activity," *Economic Inquiry*, 28 (1990): 163–185;

Louis M. Sears, *Jefferson and the Embargo* (New York: Octagon Books, 1966).

FOREIGN TRADE

British Imports. The American Revolution ended the political connection between Great Britain and the United States, but few Americans wanted the economic ties that reached across the Atlantic to break. Britain was by far the most important trading partner of the United States both before and after the Revolution, although restoring trade relations was a difficult and lengthy process. The British were eager to resume trading with America after 1783 because that was their main market

EXPORTS OF AGRICULTURAL PRODUCTS, 1791-1815

Year	Wheat (bushels)	Corn (bushels)	Tobacco (manufactured pounds)	Rice (pounds)
1791	3,807,000	1,713,241	96,811	85,057,000
1792	4,564,000	1,964,973	127,916	80,767,000
1793	6,286,000	1,233,768	173,343	69,892,000
1794	4,504,000	1,505,977	56,785	83,116,000
1795	3,234,000	1,935,345	149,699	78,623,000
1796	3,295,000	1,173,552	296,227	36,067,000
1797	2,336,000	804,922	78,508	75,146,000
1798	2,569,000	1,218,231	256,420	66,359,000
1799	2,347,000	1,200,492	525,758	67,234,000
1800	2,966,000	1,694,327	499,166	56,920,000
1801	5,201,000	1,768,162	524,579	47,893,000
1802	5,483,000	1,633,283	276,752	49,103,000
1803	6,590,000	2,079,608	169,949	47,031,000
1804	3,722,000	1,944,873	298,139	34,098,000
1805	3,517,000	861,501	428,460	61,576,000
1806	3,609,000	1,064,263	381,733	56,815,000
1807	6,797,000	1,018,721	274,952	5,537,000
1808	1,274,000	249,533	36,332	70,144,000
1809	4,202,000	522,047	350,835	78,805,000
1810	3,919,000	1,054,252	529,285	71,614,000
1811	6,719,000	2,790,850	752,533	46,314,000
1812	6,550,000	2,039,999	586,618	72,506,000
1813	5,963,000	1,486,970	283,512	6,886,000
1814	870,000	61,284	79,377	77,549,000
1815	3,900,000	830,516	1,034,045	82,706,000

Source: Curtis P. Nettels, *The Emergence of a National Economy, 1775–1815* (New York: Holt, Rinehart & Winston, 1962).

Certificate of the "New York Mechanick Society," 1791, one of the industrial groups to protest the influx of imported goods into America

for manufactured goods. Consumer demand for those goods had built up over the revolutionary period. As fighting ended, imports resumed, and merchants rushed to provide clothing and fabrics, tableware, books, cookware, tools, and other manufactured goods, as well as some raw materials such as copper and lead. British merchants readily extended credit to their American correspondents, further helping sales. British imports quickly approached the prewar level.

Exports. Relying on Britain for consumer products was in the interest of individual Americans wanting cheaper and better products, but not for the development of the American economy. The Treaty of Paris allowed Americans to export manufactured goods to Britain, but there was a limited market for the few goods produced in the United States. Most American exports were agricultural products, and tobacco was the most important of these. Thomas Jefferson estimated in 1787 that tobacco accounted for one-third of America's exports. Tobacco production declined in the 1780s, hurt by low prices in Britain. A shortage of slave labor after 1783 also lowered the production of tobacco, as well as rice and indigo, two other major exports. Sales of naval stores plummeted as well, in the short peace before the wars of the French Revolution began. Other exports also declined: fish, furs, and whale products. American manufacturing grew slowly at first, hampered by the ready availability of British goods on both sides of the Atlantic and the high costs of starting new enterprises in America. What material was produced, such as pig iron, tended to be consumed in

the United States, and so sales did not help the American balance of trade. In 1784 British exports to the United States totaled £3.6 million sterling, five times the value of American exports to Britain.

Restricted Trade. The British made the Americans' trade imbalance even more pronounced by actions that directly struck at American economic growth. On 2 July 1783 the British government issued Orders in Council that banned American ships from the British West Indies, a major market for American fish, timber, and agricultural products. A significant portion of the pre-1775 American economy was based on the "carrying trade," as American ships carried goods to or from Britain and its other colonies, and closing the West Indies hurt that portion of the shipping industry. The British also continued to occupy military posts in the area of the Great Lakes, although by treaty they had given up that area, insisting that the United States repay prewar debts to British creditors and compensate Loyalists whose property had been confiscated. The British presence in the West was a constant irritant to the United States. It interfered with American fur trading, farming, and other economic activities west of the Appalachian Mountains and contributed to the bad feelings leading to the War of 1812.

New Markets. The Revolution and its aftermath also gave Americans the chance to develop new trading partners besides Britain. France, Spain, and the Netherlands all supported the American Revolution, in part with commercial treaties. After the war, trade with the French West Indies in the 1780s helped offset some of the loss of trade in the British West Indies. France had its own restrictive trade laws, however, banning most sales of American flour in the French Caribbean colonies in 1784. Spain was a less helpful trading partner and allowed Americans to trade with its colonies only by going through Spain itself. To further this mercantilist program, Spain closed the lower Mississippi River to American traffic in 1784, effectively blocking trade from the interior of the United States. American trade in the Mediterranean was also hampered, in this case by corsairs operating from the north coast of Africa. In 1787 Congress paid $30,000 for a treaty with the sultan of Morocco to halt pirate raids, but this was only partly successful. In 1803 Congress appropriated money for warships, and two years later Americans made peace with Tripoli. This event helped secure the area for American trade, and the Mediterranean became an important market for American fish.

Orient. In addition to European markets, Americans began developing contacts in the Far East during the 1780s. The China trade gradually became an important part of the United States trading efforts and the basis for several family fortunes. Robert Morris, at the time the United States superintendent of finance, organized the first American trading expedition to China in 1783. The *Empress of China* left New York in February 1784, carrying forty tons of ginseng, a plant valued in China for its medicinal properties. It spent four months trading at Canton and returned in May 1785 with teas, silks, nankeens, china, and other desirable luxury goods formerly available only through Britain. The trip netted a profit of $37,000, and other ships soon followed. Furs were highly valued by the Chinese, and beginning in 1787 a group of Boston traders formed a venture to send a ship westward to China, around Cape Horn, stopping in the Pacific Northwest for furs along the way. The *Columbia* was the first of these ventures, reaching Nootka Sound in what is today British Columbia in August 1788 and picking up otter pelts, and then going on to Canton and exchanging them for tea. This trade grew steadily, and in 1801 fifteen American ships brought $500,000 worth of skins to China. Americans brought other goods to the Far East as well: in 1807 Boston merchant Thomas Handasyd Perkins began shipping opium from the Middle East to China. Even before the China trade began, Americans were already trading in the Indian Ocean in 1786. Fifty American ships visited Java in 1805, and twenty went to Sumatra. Dutch traders conducted the first American ship to visit Japan in 1797, although Americans failed to establish an independent trade with that country during this period.

Recovery. After the ratification of the Constitution, the American economy entered a period of growth and development, helped in part by the economic policies of the federal government. Some state governments had already taken action, as when New York, Massachusetts, Pennsylvania, Rhode Island, and New Hampshire enacted tariffs to raise the prices of imported goods and protect local industries in the 1780s. Secretary of the Treasury Alexander Hamilton proposed similar national measures in 1791, in his Report on Manufactures, which outlined a system of federal tariffs to protect young American industries. While the value of American manufactured goods rose during this period, they never rivaled the importance of agricultural exports. American foreign trade grew steadily after 1790, reflecting the industriousness of early Americans, although various international events were even more important in determining its growth. Before 1807 the war between England and France helped the American economy. The United States was neutral and was able to sell goods to parties on both sides of the conflict. American exports rose in value from $24 million in 1793 to $49 million in 1807. American shippers benefited as well since they were able to reexport goods first imported into the United States; this kind of trade rose in value from $2 million in 1793 to $60 million in 1807. After 1807 the war hurt the American economy, as attacks on American ships led to an embargo on shipping, which produced a serious depression lasting essentially to the end of the War of 1812. Although foreign trade grew steadily during the early national period, the United States never registered a trade surplus during these years. From 1790 to 1815 America exported goods worth $847 million and imported goods worth $1.2 billion, leaving a deficit of some $380 million. These figures do not take into account the value of American shipping, however, which likely more than made up for the shortfall.

Merchants. As had been true during America's colonial period, foreign trade lay behind the growth of many large personal fortunes and sustained a class of wealthy merchants and their families, the elites of the early national era. Trade profits could be astounding. E. H. Derby Jr. made $100,000 on the 1799–1800 voyage of his *Mount Vernon* to the Mediterranean. A typical venture to the East Indies earned a return of 20 percent. Traders reaped these returns by their willingness to take risks, and in this period the "Yankee trader" became well known for his shrewd assessment of business opportunities lost to more conservative investors. The need to make each opportunity pay was partly the result of circumstances. New England especially had few natural resources to export, and merchants quickly turned to trade, banking, insurance, and manufacturing. One example was the Boston Associates, led by Francis Cabot Lowell (who had already made a fortune from foreign trade). In 1814 Lowell and his partners built a textile mill in Waltham, Massachusetts, which was the first to combine spinning and weaving under one roof, a major advance in factory production. People such as the Lowells turned their own enterprise into their capital. They set the tone for the future economic development of the nation, and their desire to accumulate wealth made that development occur more quickly than in any other Western nation. Their success is marked in the corporations, banks, and charitable institutions they funded which still survive. We can even see their success in the homes they built along America's seaboard in Salem, Boston, Philadelphia, Baltimore, and in New York City, where the mayor's official residence is a mansion built in 1799 by shipper Archibald Gracie.

Sources:
Thomas M. Doerflinger, *A Vigorous Spirit of Enterprise* (Chapel Hill: University of North Carolina Press, 1986);

Curtis P. Nettels, *The Emergence of a National Economy, 1775–1815* (New York: Holt, Rinehart & Winston, 1962);

Douglass C. North, *Economic Growth of the United States, 1790–1860* (Englewood Cliffs, N.J.: Prentice-Hall, 1961).

LAND DEVELOPMENT AND SPECULATION

Western Promises. As Americans turned their thoughts toward restoring a peacetime order after the end of the Revolution, many expressed optimism about their economic future. The most significant resource backing their hopes was land, which Americans had in abundance. Thomas Jefferson captured this feeling when he wrote in *Notes on the State of Virginia* (1787) that the "immensity of land" in the West would enrich those who farmed it as well as "preserve a republic in vigour." Some of the most significant political and military events of the era were directed toward securing control over land, and they left the United States in 1815 as one of the largest countries in the world. In 1783 the Treaty of Paris ended the Revolution and gave the United States control over all the land north of Florida, south of the Great Lakes, and east of the Mississippi River. This huge area was almost doubled in 1803 with the purchase of the Louisiana Territory from France for $15 million. This moved the western boundary to the Rockies and assured control over the Mississippi River valley, the main transportation artery for the continental interior. Land was a crucial factor for the people interested in securing a stable government in the United States. Many saw it as the best way to finance the new government, which could sell the land it controlled. It was thus a resource for paying off the new country's war debts, although it was necessary first for the federal government to assert its control over this area. There were competing claims. Although Britain had ceded its claims, the trans-Appalachian Indian tribes occupying the West had not, and the American government fought almost constantly to remove them from the course of white western settlement. Some of the government land was claimed by Revolutionary War veterans, who had been paid for their service with claims on land rather than cash. The rapid growth of emigration to the West after the end of the war threatened to undermine the government's efforts to profit from the orderly development of the area. George Washington recognized this, writing in 1784 to Richard Henry Lee, the president of the Congress, that "the spirit for emigration is great, people have got impatient, and tho' you cannot stop the road, it is yet in your power to mark the way; a little while and you will not be able to do either."

State Rivalries. Among the most complicated problems for land development were conflicting claims by many of the original states to western territory. Land claims were only one way the states competed with each other, especially before the Constitution gave the central government more authority over interstate matters. Before that time, the states not only taxed foreign trade but put up trade barriers against each other. They also refused to honor currencies issued in other states. Rival territorial claims were so important, however, that they threatened to destroy the union even before it started. Massachusetts, Connecticut, New York, Virginia, North Carolina, South Carolina, and Georgia all claimed land

WESTERN TRADE

The American author Washington Irving, best known for the story of Rip Van Winkle, wrote in 1836 an account of life in the Pacific Northwest before the War of 1812 at the request of John Jacob Astor, who controlled the fur trade there. It included this description of the fur trade to China:

The last voyage of that renowned but unfortunate discoverer, Captain Cook, had made known the vast quantities of the sea otter to be found along [the Pacific] coast, and the immense prices to be paid for its fur in China. It was as if a new gold coast had been discovered. Individuals from various countries dashed into this lucrative traffic, so that in the year 1792, there were twenty-one vessels under different flags, plying along the coast and trading with the natives. The greater part of them were American, and owned by Boston merchants. They generally remained on the coast, and about the adjacent seas for two years, carrying on as wandering and adventurous a commerce on the water as did the traders and trappers on land. Their trade extended along the whole coast from California to the high northern latitudes. They would run in near shore, anchor, and wait for the natives to come off in their canoes with peltries. The trade exhausted at one place, they would up anchor and off to another. In this way they would consume the summer, and when autumn came on, would run down to the Sandwich Islands and winter in some friendly and plentiful harbor. In the following year they would resume their summer trade, commencing at California and proceeding north; and, having in the course of the two seasons collected a sufficient cargo of peltries, would make the best of their way to China. Here they would sell their furs, take in teas, nankeens, and other merchandise, and return to Boston, after an absence of two or three years.

Source: Washington Irving, *Astoria*, volume 1 (Philadelphia: Carey, Lea, & Blanchard, 1836), pp. 32–33.

as far west as the Mississippi, based on the original royal charters establishing the colonies. States without such claims, particularly Maryland, refused to ratify the Articles of Confederation until the larger states gave up their claims. Virginia's claims were the largest, and it was their cession to the United States in 1781 that allowed the Articles to be ratified. Congress only accepted the cession in 1784, however, as competing claims from various land companies that had invested in western property were settled. It was only then that a national domain was formed. The disposition of that land would be a problem for years to come.

Western Growth. Once they were secured as part of the United States, the western territories began to grow rapidly. The first national census in 1790 revealed that 120,000 people already lived beyond the Appalachians. By this time Congress had provided for this growth with two ordinances that represent the most significant

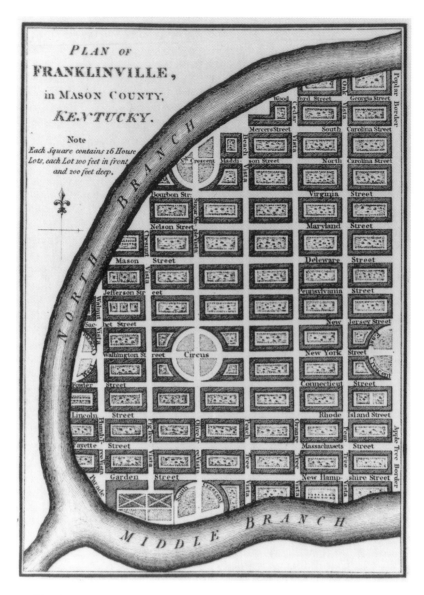

Plan for a proposed town on the North Fork of the Kentucky River, 1795

achievements of the United States government under the Articles of Confederation. The first was the Land Ordinance of 1785, which set up a system for surveying and selling the public land of the Old Northwest. The area north of the Ohio River was to be systematically surveyed and divided into townships of six miles square, each with thirty-six sections of 640 acres, which were to be auctioned off at a minimum of one dollar per acre. Some land would be reserved for public benefit, including mineral deposits, and one section in each township was reserved for maintaining a public school. The Northwest Ordinance of 1787 provided for a government for the territory north of the Ohio River, allowing for subdivision of the entire area into from three to five smaller territories each of which would eventually become a state. Territories were to be under congressional government until the population reached sixty thousand, when they could apply for statehood. Finally, slavery was banned in this area. Ohio was the first state admitted under this process, on 1 March 1803.

Speculation. Although the Northwest Ordinance was designed for selling farms to individual settlers, these accounted for a small proportion of early western land sales. Surveying was expensive and went slowly at first, and the first sale of land, in the fall of 1787, brought in less money than Congress had hoped. In an effort to realize quicker and larger profits, Congress began to sell large tracts to speculative land companies, who would also take over the cost of surveying and selling the land to individuals. This continued the practice of colonial times, when Britain had often made large land grants to individuals or companies who would turn around and sell the land in smaller plots for a profit. Selling and reselling land was a principal economic activity in early America, so much that in many areas the government post of surveyor was widely sought after for the profits a man could make. The speculators of the 1780s received very favorable deals from the government with the help of Congressmen and other government insiders who were investors in the land companies. The Ohio Company of Associates bought one million acres for less than ten cents an acre, as did the Scioto Company and others. The government continued to try to get land into the hands of individuals, but the influence of the speculating companies increased with time. For example, Washington appointed Rufus Putnam, the chief representative of the Ohio Company, as the Northwest Territory's surveyor-general in 1796, and the secretary of the territory, Winthrop Sargent, was one of the company's original organizers.

Reform. The Land Law of 1800 brought some reform. Congress established four land districts, each with its own land office, so sales of land could be conducted on the spot, instead of in Washington. Credit arrangement could also be made under the new law, passed partly at the prompting of the Northwest Territory's congressional delegate, future president William Henry Harrison. It was also supported by Albert Gallatin, soon to become secretary of the treasury and responsible for overseeing land sales. Gallatin's twelve-year tenure saw the rapid settlement of the entire Northwest Territory and the extension of the principles of land development into the area of the Louisiana Purchase. Despite reforms, the surveying and sale of land was marked by delay and fraud. There were frequent turnovers of surveyors, and most land office administrators were themselves speculating in land. The calculation and collection of sale prices were complicated by the many different currencies circulating at the time, and there were constant conflicts over prior land claims and the purchase and theft of lands from Native Americans. There was also intense pressure to sell land as quickly as possible in order to raise money for the government, especially after the beginning of the Embargo of 1807, which drastically reduced receipts from import taxes. Even with these difficulties, by the time the War of 1812 began, the government had sold more than four million acres for over $8,500,000. Sales remained strong even during the war, despite frontier conflicts with Indians and British troops.

Yazoo Land Claims. Western land speculation gave rise to one of the most important judicial decisions in the early national era, one with far-reaching effects on America's commercial development. In 1795 the Georgia legislature sold large areas of land along the Yazoo River in what is today Alabama and Mississippi to several land companies. The companies got thirty-five million acres for less than two cents per acre. Bribes and other frauds were at the heart of these sales, and they were rescinded by a new legislature in 1796. There were several legal challenges before the case reached the Supreme Court in 1810. The court upheld the original sales, despite all the accusations of fraud, and maintained that a later legislature could not undo the work of the earlier one. This was an important statement of the sanctity of contract rights and did much to stabilize commercial transactions in early America. The land business, even when fraudulent, was a symbol of the economic growth facing the new nation.

Source:
Malcolm J. Rohrbough, *The Land Office Business* (New York: Oxford University Press, 1968).

MONEY AND CURRENCY

Colonial Exchange. During the Revolutionary War the United States had experienced high inflation and economic insecurity. These problems are natural in wartime; in the new republic they were made worse by the absence of any single standard of currency. Merchants engaged in foreign trade dealt in British pounds, Spanish dollars, Portuguese Johannes, or French guineas, while colonies also issued paper money, either dollars or pounds. In addition, private banks or other businesses issued notes, which circulated as currency. With over 70 percent of the people making their living as farmers, most of the American economy was conducted in barter. Farmers traded part of their crop for necessary goods and services, and women weaved or spun to pro-

DAILY WAGE RATES IN MASSACHUSETTS, 1803-1815

	Carpenters	Masons	Painters	Laborers	Farm Laborers
1803	$1.08	$1.66	$1.33	$0.42	$0.52
1804	1.16	.89	.80		
1805	1.46	.84	.96		
1806	1.46	1.84	.93		
1807	1.50	1.50	.69		
1808	1.00	.85	.87		
1809	1.25	1.50	1.23	.54	
1810	1.08	1.20	.84	.94	
1811	1.00	1.50	1.00	.60	
1812	1.40	3.25	1.50	1.07	.85
1813	1.26	1.60	1.00	.96	
1814	1.04	1.00	.70		
1815	1.00	1.13	.99	.87	

Note: Farm wage does not include board, usually provided by the farmer.

Source: Curtis P. Nettels, *The Emergence of a National Economy, 1775–1815* (New York: Holt, Rinehart & Winston, 1962).

Rhode Island paper money, 1786

duce clothing for their families and additional trade items. Thus, the new republic had a bewildering variety of coins, paper currency, barter items, and redeemable certificates in circulation. The value of these various currencies fluctuated wildly; by April 1780 the Continental dollar was worth four hundred times less than it had been three years earlier. Gold and silver fluctuated less in value, but merchants and others would cut gold and silver pieces into smaller parts (the Spanish dollar, for example, could be cut into eight pieces, hence the expression "pieces of eight.") As George Washington said, "Without a Coinage . . . our Dollars, pistareens, &c. will be converted . . . into five quarters, and a man must travel with a pair of money scales in his pocket, or run the risk of receiving Gold at one fourth less by weight than it counts."

Gold and Silver. To finance the war Congress borrowed money from France and Holland as well as from private citizens. These debts had to be repaid in gold or silver; states also had debts which needed to be paid in hard currency. Some states required taxes to be paid in gold or silver, which placed a burden on farmers, who rarely had specie. Other states, such as Rhode Island, wanted to encourage the local economy and did not want to punish debtors and so allowed them to repay loans in vastly depreciated paper or with produce. Either way, with debts repaid in gold or silver, or repaid with corn or wheat, someone would suffer. With no single medium

of exchange and no central government able to repay international loans, the United States would not enjoy prosperity. In 1785 Congress could not make its payment on the loans from France and defaulted, which would make it impossible to borrow more. In 1786, when Massachusetts tried to raise taxes to pay its own war debts, farmers in the state revolted. In Maryland the state was torn apart by a debate over paper money, which was inflationary and beneficial to borrowers, versus hard currency, which fluctuated less in value and so helped lenders.

The Morris Plan. In April 1783 Robert Morris, the minister of finance under the Articles of Confederation, proposed an elaborate system to make sense of the U.S. currency. Morris and his assistant, cousin Gouverneur Morris, prepared a table comparing the values of all state currencies and proposed a standard monetary unit based on the pound and dollar, regulating it according to the constant value of Spanish dollars and British pounds received in the United States. The common unit would have a value of 1/1600 of a British pound, or 1/1440 of a Spanish dollar. Morris's system was tied in with his plans for a national mint, and he hired a workman, Benjamin Dudley, to begin making coins.

Complexity. The very complexity of Morris's system made it unworkable. A pound of butter, worth one-fifth of a dollar, under Morris's system would be valued at 288 units, and a horse, worth eighty Spanish dollars, would cost 115,200 units. Thomas Jefferson, a member of Congress from Virginia, proposed an alternative plan. Instead of basing the currency on a common denominator, Jefferson proposed basing an American dollar on a standard weight of gold or silver and minting coins of gold (a ten-dollar "Eagle" and a five-dollar "Half-Eagle") and of silver (dollar, half-dollar, and dime) and of copper (the cent). Jefferson based the American currency on the decimal system (dime comes from *dixième*, for a tenth, and cent from *centum*, or hundredth) rather than on the British pound, shilling, and pence. Congress approved Jefferson's plan in 1786 but was unable to take any action.

Constitution. The Constitution allowed the new government to make some sense of the complicated financial picture. Under the new Constitution only the U.S. Congress and not the states could coin money and regulate its value, emit bills of credit, or make anything but gold or silver legal tender for paying debts. This policy required a new national currency, and Secretary of the Treasury Alexander Hamilton revived the proposal for a national mint and currency.

Proposal. In 1791 Hamilton reintroduced the subject of currency, basing his proposal on Jefferson's and Congress's 1785–1786 system. Hamilton modified slightly the proposed value of the dollar, averaging the weights of various Spanish dollars then in circulation to determine the value of their gold against silver. The Coinage Act of 1792 set the silver content of the dollar at 371.25 grains and made fifteen pounds of silver equal in value to one pound of pure gold. The act also allowed private citizens to bring gold or silver to the mint to be turned into coins, free of charge.

Counterproposal. Jefferson at this time proposed a different standard for American currency. As secretary of state, Jefferson was working on a uniform system of weights and measures; he wanted to base American currency and weights on the same standard, an ounce of pure rainwater, and to regulate the dollar's value to an ounce of silver. Hamilton did not adopt this idea, but the new mint, established in 1792, created an American system of coinage which is still in operation. Instead of basing American currency on the British model, Americans adopted a system based on the decimal system, though the cent coin is still called the penny, like its British cousin.

Results. The American system of currency adopted in 1792, developed by Jefferson and Hamilton working separately, is a model of organization and rational simplicity. However, the American economy continued to be based on other currencies: bartered products, foreign currencies, banknotes, and bills of exchange. The United States would not issue its own paper currency for nearly a century, until the Civil War. The system of coinage was a step toward a national economy, though not all proponents of the measure regarded it as such.

Sources:

Julian Boyd and others, eds., *The Papers of Thomas Jefferson*, volumes 7 and 18 (Princeton, N.J.: Princeton University Press, 1953);

Herman E. Krooss, ed., *Documentary History of Banking and Currency in the U.S.*, volume 1 (New York: Chelsea House, 1969);

Arthur Nussbaum, *A History of the Dollar* (New York: Columbia University Press, 1957).

SHIPBUILDING

The Industry. While the steamboat was the most dramatic maritime innovation of the period, most commerce continued to be carried by sailing ships. Americans had become the world's best builders of boats and ships, and the rise of British maritime power was made possible by American shipwrights, who had delivered to England an average of fifty ships each year before the Revolution. In 1769 shipyards in the American colonies, mainly in New England, but also in New York and the Chesapeake, produced 389 vessels. After the war, with British markets for American ships shut off and merchants excluded from English ports, the industry declined. In 1789 the new U.S. government put a higher tariff on ships built or owned by foreigners which entered American ports, hoping to stimulate the shipbuilding industry. It succeeded, with the total tonnage of American-built ships owned by Americans more than doubling by 1790, from 123,000 tons to 364,000 tons. Because laws also forbade foreigners to buy American-built ships, more of these ships were owned by Americans, greatly increasing the United States' share of the world's carrying trade.

American Advantages. Americans had several advantages in building ships, most notably in their access to good timber. Shipyards tended to follow the forests, moving up the coast of Maine in the 1790s. Boston and New York shipbuilders invested in canals to help bring timber to their shipyards. Even with the forests closest to

---

AMERICA RULES THE WAVES

The resurgence of foreign trade after the end of the Revolutionary War in 1783 allowed for the American ship industry to reestablish itself. Shipping became one of the most significant parts of the American economy. From 1790 to 1807 American shippers more than doubled their carrying capacity. In 1790 American ships carried 40.5 percent of the value of goods carried in the nation's foreign trade; by 1807 they were carrying 92 percent. Shipbuilding naturally became a vibrant part of the American economy, helped by abundant timber and naval stores and a skilled workforce. Tenche Coxe described these advantages in 1794:

Ship-building is an art for which the United States are peculiarly qualified by their skill in the construction, and by the materials, with which this country abounds: and they are strongly tempted to pursue it by their commercial spirit, by the capital fisheries in their bays and on their coasts, and by the productions of a great and rapidly increasing agriculture. They build their oak vessels on lower terms than the cheapest European vessels of fir, pine, and larch. The cost of an oak ship in New England is about twenty-four Mexican dollars per ton fitted for sea: a fir vessel costs in the ports of the Baltic, thirty-five Mexican dollars: and the American ship will be much the most durable. The cost of a vessel of the American live-oak and cedar, which will last (if salted in her timbers) thirty years, is only thirty-six to thirty-eight dollars in our different ports; and an oak ship in the cheapest part of England, Holland, or France, fitted in the same manner will cost 55 to 60 dollars. In such a country, the fisheries and commerce, with due care and attention on the part of government, must be profitable.

Source: Tenche Coxe, *A View of the United States of America* (Philadelphia: William Hall, Wrigley & Berriman, 1794), pp. 99–100.

New York and Boston depleted, the country still had vast timber reserves, making the cost of construction much lower. An American ship, built of New England oak, would cost twenty-four dollars per ton; a similar ship built of fir along the Baltic coast would cost thirty-five dollars per ton. An American vessel made of more expensive live oak and cedar would cost thirty-six dollars to thirty-eight dollars per ton, while a similar vessel made of oak in England, France, or Holland would cost fifty-five dollars to sixty dollars per ton.

Live Oak. More important than the quantity of timber was its quality. The live oak found in Georgia and South Carolina will not rot quickly. Under normal use a ship with a live-oak frame would last thirty years, three times as long as a ship made of inferior wood. Live oak is also somewhat denser than regular oak or other kinds of wood, making the ship much stronger. In fact, the U.S.

An 1800 engraving depicting the construction of the frigate *Philadelphia*

frigate *Constitution*, built in Boston in 1797, has such a strong frame that British cannonballs bounced off her hull in 1812, earning the ship the nickname "Old Ironsides." Merchant ships made of live oak would not be expected to repel cannonballs but would resist rot and other enemies of wooden ships such as the teredo worm. In 1797 Congress appropriated $200,000 to preserve groves of live oak in the nation.

Wages and Exports. Another advantage to American shipbuilding was a well-trained labor force. International trade became so important to businesses that sailors' wages rose from eight dollars per month in the 1790s to thirty dollars a month by 1815, and the demand for good ships expanded so much that buyers would pay cash in advance to shipbuilders, who thus were able to pay their workers in hard currency. Shipwrights would earn about a dollar a day, more than farm laborers, and about the same wage as sailors or skilled carpenters. With the value of American exports growing from $23 million in 1790 to $52 million in 1815, good ships were in great demand. While shipbuilders did not become wealthy, they did earn good livings: in 1815 one New York shipbuilder earned $30,000. American shipbuilders earned a reputation for producing the world's best ships in this period.

Speed and Size. In addition to needing more ships, American businesses needed faster ones. Remarkable as the steamboat was, sailing technology made astonishing advances in this period. Merchants sought two different qualities in a ship: speed and size. The two could not be easily reconciled; a large ship which could carry bulky cargo could not sail as fast as a narrow ship which could quickly cut through the water. Boston shipbuilder John Peck experimented with long, narrow ships, which could both carry large cargoes and sail quickly. Elias Derby built a ship which sailed from Salem to Ireland in just eleven days; another of Derby's ships sailed to France

and back in five weeks, the time it took some sailing ships to make one crossing. Massachusetts builders favored smaller vessels. In 1795 E. H. Derby's second *Grand Turk*, built at his Salem shipyard, had to be sold in New York because it was too large for Salem's harbor and for Derby's preferred method of trade. New York merchants preferred larger ships while New England merchants favored smaller, faster ones. With this greater speed, American ships were able to make two, three, or four trading voyages each year, while English ships typically made only one trip each year.

Algiers. The high quality of materials and the skills of the labor force made American ships the envy of the world. The Dey of Algiers in 1795 asked the American consul to send him some American shipbuilders. Send them poor, he told the consul, and they would return home rich. After making a treaty with the United States, the Dey contracted to have two merchant vessels built for his commercial fleet. The United States also built a frigate, the *Crescent*, as a special gift for the Dey. When this small fleet arrived in Algiers in 1798, it impressed all with the skills of American builders. No one, the American consul reported, had ever seen such beautiful ships, and the Dey, who had been threatening to attack American merchant ships, became convinced that the United States would be a dangerous enemy.

Freedom of the Seas. The U.S. merchants did a tremendous business during the wars between England and France (1793–1815). The United States followed a policy of neutrality and argued that neutral ships should be allowed to trade freely on the world's seas. U.S. merchants grew wealthy at the expense of England and France while they supplied each side with American grain and took up much of the carrying trade merchants from those nations had formerly enjoyed. The French were first to object to this, and in 1797 they began capturing American merchant ships in the West Indies and Europe. The Adams administration responded with the use of the new navy, begun in 1793 to fight Algiers. In a series of naval battles the United States defeated the French all but once. In 1800 the two sides agreed to peace. One year later Tripoli announced that it would begin seizing American merchant vessels. The United States responded by sending its navy to blockade and bombard Tripoli. Arguing again for freedom of the seas, the United States declared war on England in 1812, and while the war at home went very badly, with the city of Washington burned and coastal New England blockaded, the navy, on the ocean and the Great Lakes, proved superior to the British. American sailors, trained in the merchant fleets, and shipbuilders, challenged to build sturdy, fast-sailing ships, defeated the British in many naval engagements. Free international commerce was vital to the survival of the American nation; the U.S. government would go to war to protect this principle. Thanks to the tremendous skill of American shipbuilders and sailors, the United States was able to maintain this principle. The frigate U.S.S. *Constitution,* completed in October 1797, remains in commission to this day, demonstrating the technological skill of American shipbuilders.

Sources:

Samuel Eliot Morison, *The Maritime History of Massachusetts, 1783–1860* (Boston: Houghton Mifflin, 1961);

Curtis P. Nettels, *The Emergence of a National Economy, 1775–1815* (New York: Holt, Rinehart & Winston, 1962).

SLAVE TRADE

Africans. The purchase and sale of African people was a major part of the early American economy. It was one of the most obvious ways Americans were linked to the global trading economy. From 1783 to 1815, around 150,000 Africans were forced to migrate to the United States, many of them carried on American ships, and sold through networks of traders after their arrival. Thousands more were carried by American slavers to other parts of the Americas, especially Cuba, until trade there was banned in 1794. The United States accounted for an increasing proportion of the slave trade, as many as 16 percent of all people taken from Africa from 1801 to 1805. The trade centered in New England, especially Rhode Island, but leading merchants in every colony were slavers. Traders would send ships to the west coast of Africa with stores of guns, manufactured goods, and rum. These items would be traded for people brought from the interior by networks of African and European traders centered in the "factories," or forts, along the coast. The ships would then return to America, stopping at the Caribbean colonies and southern states, before returning to the North, loaded with sugar (often in the form of molasses), rice, and other agricultural produce. (This was the so-called triangular trade, although few ships actually made the complete trip.) The trade was complex, with American and European slavers bartering among themselves off the African coast in order to acquire the most desirable variety of goods and selling slaves at various ports along the way home. Rhode Island

SLAVE SMUGGLING

After the end of the legal importation of slaves from Africa in 1808, some traders did continue to bring Africans in by smuggling. While never very significant economically, this trade still took its toll in human terms on the individuals involved. An 1812 venture described in an abolitionist memoir conveys something of the scope and nature of the traffic:

After resting a few days at St. Augustine, . . . I agreed to accompany Diego on a land trip through the United States, where a *kaffle* [gang] of negroes was to precede us, for whose disposal the shrewd Portuguese had already made arrangements. . . . I soon learned how readily, and at what profits, the Florida negroes were sold into the neighboring American States. The *kaffle*, under charge of negro drivers, was to strike up the Escambia River, and thence cross the boundary into Georgia, where some of our wild Africans were mixed with various squads of native blacks, and driven inland, till sold off, singly or by couples, on the road. . . . The Spanish possessions were thriving on this inland exchange of negroes and mulattoes; Florida was a sort of nursery for slave-breeders, and many American citizens grew rich by trafficking in Guinea negroes, and smuggling them continually, in small parties, through the southern United States.

Source: Philip Drake, *Revelations of a Slave Smuggler* (New York: Robert M. DeWitt, 1860), p. 51.

slavers, for instance, sold half their slaves in Cuba between 1783 and 1802, dispersing the others around the West Indies and on the mainland. The ships themselves were often owned by groups of investors of different nationalities. The trade as a whole also included traffic between Europe and America, with many kinds of commercial goods, of which slaves were only one part. The profits New Englanders enjoyed from the slave trade also helped expand their trading efforts elsewhere; Samuel Brown of Boston, a leader in opening trade to China in the late 1780s, made his initial fortune as a slaver.

Middle Passage. One of the most notorious aspects of the slave trade was the conditions Africans endured on their voyage to America. They were crowded onto small ships, most of the men chained together in pairs. Even without chains the conditions were harsh. Slaves stayed in holds as small as five feet high, and food and water were scarce. If the weather permitted they were forced to exercise or "dance" in their chains on deck once a day. In these conditions scurvy and other diseases flourished, and in many cases between 5 and 20 percent of the slaves died. Mortality was high among the white sailors as well, who shared at least some of these conditions, as well as the dangers of sea travel in this period. Slavers considered the slaves to be valuable property, and some did seek to protect their cargo. The Vernons of Rhode Island ordered the captain of their slave ship to let the Africans "have a sufficiency of good Diet . . . as you are Sensible your voyage depends upon their Health." Many slavers

Slavetrader branding one of his captives

carried doctors to help keep the slaves alive during the voyage. Those who lived faced the ordeal of auction, a frightening process where they were scrutinized publicly by men speaking a foreign language and usually separated from their families and friends, then led to their owners' farms.

Legislation. Although some early Americans profited from slavery, many others objected to it. Opposition was helped by a reduced demand for slaves in the years around the Revolution. The important factor here was declining tobacco production, hurt by stagnant European prices. The abuses of the slave trade were well known, and there were many efforts to end it. Eventually, only Georgia and South Carolina permitted slave ships to land, making Savannah and Charleston the largest American slave markets. Southern states inserted some protection for the trade into the Constitution, which included a clause barring Congress from ending the trade for twenty years. Most Americans understood that slave importation would end soon, and the trade boomed after 1790, bringing more Africans into the country in the next two decades than had entered in any previous twenty-year period. In 1807 Congress passed legislation ending the trade, which took effect in 1808. By the Civil War, almost all American slaves were native-born.

Cotton. Although the legal transatlantic slave trade ended in 1808, slave trading continued to be an important part of the American economy. In 1793 a young graduate of Yale College, Eli Whitney, traveled to Georgia. Although he went to pursue studies in law, he already had a reputation as an inventor. He had learned something of mechanics while working as a boy in his father's metalworking shop in Westborough, Massachusetts, and is said to have invented a mechanical apple parer when he was thirteen years old. In Georgia he no-

ticed how difficult it was to remove the seeds from the cotton grown on the plantations there and set about devising a way to mechanize that task. The result was the invention called the cotton gin (short for engine). The gin used a toothed roller to catch the tufts of cotton and pull them through a wire mesh, leaving the seeds behind, and the cotton ready for the textile mill. Whitney's idea was quickly copied, and the rapid spread of the gin changed the face of southern agriculture and affected the fates of millions of people. Before the gin extracting the seeds was so difficult that cotton was profitable only along the Georgia and South Carolina coasts, where a certain variety grew. With the gin other varieties became economical, and the cultivation of cotton spread across the South, meeting the demands of the booming textile industry in the North and in Britain. By 1803 American growers supplied 45 percent of the cotton imported into Britain, and more and more of the new southern territories devoted themselves to the crop. Where cotton went, slavery followed.

Plantation Economy. The early nineteenth century saw the firm establishment of the plantations that were the basic feature of the antebellum southern economy. This economy rested on slave labor. Plantations were large farms, single economic units run by the owner and his family, geared toward the production and sale of staple crops such as cotton. Most owners were closely involved in the work, sometimes personally overseeing the work of between five and ten slaves. Although most plantations were small, the economy was dominated by owners of larger plantations with more than fifty slaves and much higher productive capacity. As the value of cotton rose, the wealth of these slaveholders increased as well. Southern planters rivaled northern traders in economic power and displays of wealth. In the South the slaves themselves were a main source of that wealth. A principal feature of the plantation economy was the steady rate of natural increase within the slave population. Alone in the Americas, the United States slave population continued to grow despite the end of slave importations from Africa.

Domestic Trade. Behind the growth of the plantation economy lay a thriving internal slave trade, which drastically undermined the significance of the end of the transatlantic trade in 1808. The trade was well established as early as the 1780s. Around 100,000 slaves migrated internally between 1790 and the end of the foreign slave trade, and around another 100,000 migrated by 1815 as slave sales grew quickly. By 1860 over one million slaves would move from the old slave states of Virginia, Maryland, and the Carolinas to the West, first to Kentucky and Tennessee, and then to the Deep South. The domestic slave trade was deeply embedded in larger economic relations. In South Carolina, for instance, slave-rich low country planters dominated the legislature and passed regulations limiting the slave trade, in part to prevent agricultural overproduction in the back country, where slaves were in short supply. After 1808 there were no more slave ships, but the domestic trade was just as harsh. Some slaves moved with their masters as they settled new areas, but more were taken from one master in the East and sold to new ones in the West. Most of these were abruptly torn from homes and families, and had to start new lives under harsh conditions. The horrors of this domestic trade were also well known, but it was too profitable to end. The slave Charles Ball brought a price of $400 in the Charleston market in 1805. Speculators crisscrossed the country offering cash for slaves, a sign of the strength of the market. Over time, the chance that a slave born in Virginia where labor was plentiful would be sold to a trader and moved further south increased dramatically, and the threat of sale became a common disciplinary tool. Even Thomas Jefferson used it. In 1803 he sold a slave who had angered him into "so distant an exile . . . as to cut him off completely from ever being heard of [again]."

Sources:

David Eltis, *Economic Growth and the Ending of the Transatlantic Slave Trade* (New York & Oxford: Oxford University Press, 1987);

James A. Rawley, *The Transatlantic Slave Trade* (New York & London: Norton, 1981);

Michael Tadman, *Speculators and Slaves: Masters, Traders, and Slaves in the Old South* (Madison: University of Wisconsin Press, 1989).

HEADLINE MAKERS

JOHN JACOB ASTOR

1763-1848

FUR TRADER AND BUSINESSMAN

Emigration. John Jacob Astor was the richest man in America when he died, having amassed a fortune based on the unique economic opportunities of the United States in the early national period. He was born in the village of Waldorf in Germany on 17 July 1763, the son of a butcher. At the age of sixteen he worked his way on a timber boat to England, joining a brother there in the business of making and selling musical instruments. Astor immediately began to learn English and to save money to emigrate to America, arriving in Baltimore in March 1784 with about twenty-five dollars and seven flutes. He made his way to New York, joining another brother there, and soon set himself up in business. Astor got help through an advantageous marriage to Sarah Todd, a member of the elite Brevoort family, who brought $300 as a dowry.

Fur Trading. Astor soon established himself as a fur trader, a business he learned about from a man he had met on his trip to America who had previously been to the American backcountry and knew of the trade. In the 1790s Astor made many trips to the frontier, going as far as northern Michigan, making many useful contacts. Jay's Treaty between Britain and America in 1795 helped his business by limiting the English presence in this area and opening up greater trade between America and Canada. Astor pursued contacts with Canadian fur traders, greatly adding to his stock, although he failed in an attempt to contract with the dominant North West Company of Canada for importing their furs into the United States. By 1800 he had accumulated over a quarter of a million dollars.

Western Expansion. Astor soon began selling furs in China, a huge market just beginning to be exploited by American and European traders. He managed to acquire a license to trade freely in ports controlled by the British East India Company, which opened much of Asia to him, and his first venture made a profit of $50,000. The Louisiana Purchase of 1803 and the reports about the Columbia River basin in Oregon that followed the return of Lewis and Clark from their exploration of that area in 1806 fueled Astor's ambitions further. He faced competition in the fur trade in the Pacific Northwest from other companies based in Canada and Saint Louis. He countered by forming the American Fur Company in 1808 and planning to establish a huge trading post—to be called Astoria—at the mouth of the Columbia River to gather furs from smaller posts spread throughout the interior. Ships would leave that post for China, exchanging furs there for Asian goods, which they would take on to Europe and then to New York, where they would stock up on supplies for the traders and Indians in the West. Astoria was founded in 1811, but the project proved too ambitious even for Astor. The coming of the War of 1812 further undermined it as the British asserted a military presence in Oregon. Despite setbacks Astor still continued to dominate the fur trade until he sold all his fur companies in 1834.

Other Business. The fur trade was the basis of Astor's fortune, but not its only component. As early as the 1790s he began to use his fur profits to buy real estate in Manhattan, purchasing lots just north of the growing city and selling them as development advanced and drove prices up, leaving him able to purchase more land even further north. He also profited hugely during the War of 1812, buying bonds from the U.S. government on which he earned about sixty cents on the dollar, plus interest. He was also able to use his government contacts to good advantage in other areas, as when he persuaded Congress to close government fur trading posts in 1822. All his ventures left him with about $10 million at his death on 29 March 1848. He left $400,000 to found a library, which became the heart of the New York Public Library, today one of the largest in the world. Most of the rest of his wealth and businesses he left to his son William, establishing one of the great family fortunes of the early United States.

Source:

John Haeger, *John Jacob Astor: Business and Finance in the Early Republic* (Detroit: Wayne State University Press, 1991).

ELIAS HASKET DERBY

1739-1799

INTERNATIONAL MERCHANT

The House of Derby. Elias Hasket Derby's father, Richard Derby, had been one of the most prosperous merchants in Salem, Massachusetts. In 1761 Elias Derby married Elizabeth Crowninshield, daughter of another leading merchant family. After Derby took over managing his father's firm in the early 1780s, he made it one of the most successful businesses in America. During the American Revolution the Derbys had made their commercial vessels into privateers, raiding British commerce under the authority of the U.S. Congress. After the Revolution, having made a significant fortune during the war, Derby began sending his ships on longer voyages to South Africa, the Indian Ocean, and ultimately China and the Dutch East Indies.

Grand Turk. Derby supervised every aspect of his business, from the building of ships to the direction of the voyages. But he recognized the limits of his own authority and so sought out trustworthy and resourceful men as captains and supercargo, or supervisor of the ship's cargo. He differed from many of his fellow merchants, who insisted on strict adherence to schedules and plans: "Obey orders if you break owners" was a maxim in the merchant marine. But Derby trusted his agents, who would share in the profits of a successful voyage and thus grow wealthy along with him. For instance, in December 1785 Derby sent the *Grand Turk,* under Capt. Ebenezer West and William Vans, to the Cape of Good Hope. The *Grand Turk* carried a variety of goods: 35 hogsheads of tobacco, 20 casks of wine, 483 iron bars, 75 barrels of flour, 30 casks of rum, 42 casks of brandy, and 50 cases of oil, along with barrels of beef, rice, butter, cheese, fish, beer, candles, soap, prunes, and chocolate. Derby's plan was for the ship to trade in South Africa and at the Île de France, now the island of Mauritius, a leading market for coffee and sugar. After two stormy months at sea the *Grand Turk* reached South Africa, where she sold some cargo and took on some more to sell further in the voyage. In March the ship reached the Île de France; however, Vans and West found the prices of coffee and sugar too high. The voyage would not be profitable. But a French merchant asked to charter part of the ship's space to take a cargo to Canton, and in July the *Grand Turk* sailed for China. There the Americans traded their cargo for tea, hides, and porcelain, returning to Salem in May 1787 with a cargo valued at $23,000. Vans had bought the tea for about $53 per chest and sold it in New York for $120 per chest (in today's currency, about $1,500 each). On the whole, the voyage made a substantial profit. Derby had sent Vans and West to the Île de France but expected that when the opportunity arose, they would seize it.

Indian Cotton. Though this initial voyage to the Île de France was not successful in buying coffee and sugar, within a year Derby sent three more ships to that island, and in time his ships had practically a monopoly on American trade with the Île de France. Derby was prepared to sell even his ships. His son, E. H. Derby Jr., acting as the ship's supercargo on her second voyage to the Île de France in 1787–1788, was offered $13,000 for the *Grand Turk.* This was twice the value of the ship in Salem, and the younger Derby quickly closed the deal and bought two more ships and a cargo of Indian cotton for the return voyage to Salem. While this was the first cargo of Indian cotton to arrive in the United States, Derby could not sell it, as Americans did not want to buy it. The elder Derby knew that Indian cotton had a market in China, so he sent the cotton to Canton and dispatched another vessel to Bombay for cotton to sell in China.

International Home and Garden. Though E. H. Derby Sr. had a large fleet—six ships, four brigs, two ketches, a schooner, and a barque—in his career he only lost one vessel, though the crew was saved and insurance covered the lost cargo. He opened the American trade to the Indian Ocean and China and helped to make Salem, Massachusetts, one of the young nation's leading ports. On a farm outside of town he planted trees and other plants his ships brought from around the world, and he furnished his Salem mansion with items from Europe, India, and China. The elder Derby died in 1799, leaving his son the family business and an estate worth $1.5 million.

Sources:

Samuel Eliot Morison, *The Maritime History of Massachusetts, 1783–1860* (Boston: Houghton Mifflin, 1961);

Robert E. Peabody, *Merchant Venturers of Old Salem* (Cambridge, Mass.: Riverside Press, 1912).

ALBERT GALLATIN

1761-1849

SECRETARY OF THE TREASURY AND DIPLOMAT

Democratic Heritage. Albert Gallatin was born on 29 January 1761 into an aristocratic French family with a history of over four hundred years of leadership in the area around Geneva in what is now Switzerland. Geneva was the birthplace of Jean-Jacques Rousseau, the eighteenth-century democratic political philosopher, and as a young man Gallatin embraced Rousseau's romantic ideas about returning to nature and celebrating the common man. These ideas inspired him to go to the United States in 1780, rejecting an offer to be an officer in the Hessian army sent by King George III to fight the American Patriots. Once in America, Gallatin took little part in the conflict, instead attempting to set up a trading business.

Western Politics. After the Revolution, Gallatin moved to the frontier area of western Pennsylvania, settling along the Monongahela River. He was not successful as a pioneer or a land speculator, although he became deeply identified with the interests of western settlers as he began a career in politics. First in state politics and then at the federal level, he advocated reforms sought by his western constituents which were at the heart of the policies of the Jeffersonian party of the 1790s. In Pennsylvania he urged changes to the penal code, the establishment of a public-school system, and the abolition of slavery. Gallatin played an important mediating role during the 1794 Whiskey Rebellion, an uprising of western Pennsylvanians angered by federal liquor taxes. Because he had supported them in the past, the crowd listened to Gallatin's pleas for moderation, and he helped minimize the military conflict that followed.

Treasury Secretary. It was in public finance where he made his greatest contribution, however, ironically by promoting policies favored by the Federalists for both Pennsylvania and the nation. He supported the founding of a state bank, greater control over the currency, retirement of public debt, and greater accountability of the Treasury Department to the legislature. This last effort earned him Federalist enmity after Gallatin became a congressman in 1795, as Secretary of the Treasury Alexander Hamilton saw it as meddling in his job. Despite Federalist opposition, Gallatin succeeded in establishing a standing committee on finance (today the House Ways and Means Committee) to centralize legislative efforts to control the nation's finances. After Jefferson's election as president in 1800, Gallatin naturally became secretary of the treasury, a post he held into the administration of James Madison, resigning in 1814. Gallatin established a system of regular financial reports to Congress and worked hard to reduce the national debt in order to secure the nation's independence. He also sought to fund internal improvements to open up the western territories, including plans for $20 million worth of canals and roads connecting eastern rivers with the Mississippi. The Embargo of 1807 and the War of 1812 ruined these plans as government revenues sank with the disruption of trade and expenses rose for waging war. In 1811 Congress refused to recharter the Bank of the United States, despite Gallatin's objections, further undermining the currency. He resigned in the wake of intense Federalist opposition to the war and the financial policies needed to support it.

Statesman. Gallatin left for Europe in 1813 as part of a commission sent to negotiate with Britain to end the war. He was ultimately successful in framing the Treaty of Ghent of December 1814, which secured a number of economic advantages for the United States despite the nation's poor military record in the war. Over later years Gallatin pursued a distinguished diplomatic career, with periods as minister to France and Britain. He succeeded in settling many boundary disputes and negotiating many commercial treaties that served the nation well. He retired to New York City in 1827, spending some years as head of John Jacob Astor's National Bank and helping to end the financial crisis of the Panic of 1837. In his retirement he also pursued an interest in Native Americans, writing and sponsoring a number of ethnographic works about various tribes. Outliving many of his colleagues from the early days of the republic, he died on 12 August 1849.

Sources:

L. B. Kuppenheimer, *Albert Gallatin's Vision of Democratic Stability* (Westport, Conn.: Praeger, 1996);

Raymond Walters, *Albert Gallatin: Jeffersonian Financier and Diplomat* (New York: Macmillan, 1957).

STEPHEN GIRARD

1750-1831

FINANCIER AND BANKER

Early Career. Stephen Girard rose from being a cabin boy to become one of the richest men in America, an extreme example of a rags-to-riches story that was true for many early American businessmen. Girard was born on 20 May 1750 in Bordeaux, France, and received little education due to being blind in one eye. He went to sea at the age of fourteen, and by 1773 he had a pilot's license. In 1774 he traveled from France to the West Indies, trading for himself for the first time and ending up in Philadelphia in 1776 with some coffee and sugar and substantial debts. Hard work in an American shipping firm let him pay off his creditors and establish himself.

Shipping and Trading. Girard continued the common practice of trading for himself while also trading for his employers and gradually accumulated profits and an interest in his first ship, *La Jeune Babé.* The American Revolution disrupted shipping and prompted him to turn to merchandising in Pennsylvania. With the end of war he returned to foreign trade, where he was enormously successful. His excellent business instincts and careful attention to the details of the management of his ships were behind his profits. He also benefited from his early career as a common sailor, which left him with an extraordinary knowledge of shipping and shipbuilding. Over the years he owned eighteen ships, many named after the philosophers of his native France: the *Voltaire,* the *Diderot,* and the *Rousseau.* His shipping business continued to his death.

Banking. Girard invested his trading profits in other ventures, notably real estate and banking. As the War of 1812 approached, Girard gradually withdrew his wealth from Europe, anticipating safer investment opportunities in the United States. He supported the First Bank of the United States, purchasing stock and urging Congress to renew its charter in 1810. Congress refused, and Girard bought the bank's building and accounts, starting a private bank with a capital of $1.2 million. This was a huge amount of money for the time, and Girard's bank quickly established a national credit system with important contacts in England and Europe. The strength of the bank allowed Girard, along with other wealthy men such as John Jacob Astor, to help finance the War of 1812, to their personal benefit as well as the public good. After the war the United States decided to establish a national bank, and Girard took the leading role, subscribing for the full $3 million worth of stock in the Second Bank of the United States, when no other investors were willing to take the risk. Girard continued his private bank at the same time, and this also lasted to his death. In his later years Girard bought a farm in South Philadelphia and saw no contradiction in engaging in huge financial ventures and planting fruit trees at the same

time. He died on his farm on 26 December 1831, leaving much of his wealth to charity, including what is today Girard College in Philadelphia.

Sources:

Donald R. Adams, *Finance and Enterprise in Early America: A Study of Stephen Girard's Bank, 1812–1831* (Philadelphia: University of Pennsylvania Press, 1978);

George Wilson, *Stephen Girard: America's First Tycoon* (Conshohocken, Penn.: Combined Books, 1995).

ROBERT LIVINGSTON

1746-1813

STATESMAN AND BUSINESSMAN

Early Years. Robert Livingston became one of the most important financial figures of the early republic, thanks in part to his position in one of the richest families of colonial New York. Livingston was born on 27 November 1746 and followed brothers, cousins, and other relatives in attending King's College (now Columbia University) and becoming a lawyer. In 1770 he married Mary Stevens, whose brother John was an inventor and operator of steamships and who would later enter a profitable partnership with Livingston.

Revolutionary Career. Livingston represented New York in the Second Continental Congress and served on the committee to draft the Declaration of Independence, although his contribution was minimal. His later work was more important, and he became a pivotal figure in Congress, active in many areas of managing the war effort. His 14 December 1779 report on the financial aspects of the Revolution made a number of recommendations for funding the government which Congress continued to draw upon during the Confederation period. Livingston remained active in state politics as well, serving on the Court of Chancery as well as a number of committees. In 1777 Livingston, John Jay, and Gouverneur Morris drafted the state's constitution. Livingston joined Hamilton in securing New York's ratification of the Constitution, although he got no personal reward for that effort and gradually turned away from the Federalist Party to embrace the Jeffersonians.

Foreign Matters. In 1781 Livingston became head of the department of foreign affairs and in that post directed the negotiations for peace and commercial treaties carried on in Europe by Franklin, Adams, Jay, and others. After Jefferson's election in 1800, he became minister to France. There he negotiated the purchase of Louisiana for an advantageous price of $15 million, securing much of America's future wealth and security. While in Paris he met Robert Fulton, who was already experimenting with warships, submarines, and steam power.

Business Efforts. Like many early Americans, Livingston pursued private interests as well as a public career.

He was very interested in agricultural reform, as were Washington and Jefferson, and pioneered the importing of Merino sheep. He was interested in science, like Franklin, and was a founder in 1791 of the Society for the Promotion of Useful Arts, supporting the practical application of scientific advances. His most significant ventures were related to steamships. He gave technical and financial help to innovators such as his brother-in-law Stevens and was an important backer of Robert Fulton, whose *Clermont* (named for Livingston's New York estate) was the first steamship to travel the Hudson River, in 1807. New York gave a monopoly to Livingston for steamship service on the Hudson as early as 1798, which was renewed and modified several times over the years. Fulton got a share in its final form in 1808. Livingston used the profits from this enterprise to further develop steam technology, as well as to spread their business to the South and to the Mississippi River. Livingston died on 26 February 1813, before the heyday of steamship travel on America's western rivers that he helped make possible by both his business ventures and his diplomacy.

Source:
George Dangerfield, *Chancellor Robert R. Livingston of New York, 1746–1813* (New York: Harcourt, Brace & World, 1960).

PUBLICATIONS

John Frederick Amelung, *Remarks on Manufactures, principally on the new established glass-house, near FrederickTown, in the State of Maryland* (Frederick, Md., 1788)—a German immigrant and manufacturer calls for the U.S. government to encourage industry by granting monopolies to certain businesses;

Tenche Coxe, *A brief examination of Lord Sheffield's Observations on the Commerce of the United States of America* (Philadelphia: Mathew Carey, 1791)—Coxe responds to Lord Sheffield's arguments that Britain should continue to constrain American trade;

Coxe, *An enquiry into the principles, on which a commercial system for the United States of America should be founded* (Philadelphia: Printed and sold by Robert Aitken, 1787)—the author advocates congressional control over American trade, arguing that agriculture is the basis for American wealth; this pamphlet was written for members of the Constitutional Convention;

Coxe, *A Statement of the Arts and Manufactures of the United States of America for the year 1810* (Philadelphia, 1814)—a discussion of household manufacturing, brought on by the Embargo of 1807 shutting out imported goods;

Samuel Freeman, *A Valuable Assistant to Every Man; or, the American Clerk's Magazine*, second edition (Boston: Isaiah Thomas and E. T. Andrews, 1795)—provides information on exchange rates of various currencies and bank notes;

Albert Gallatin, *A Sketch of the Finances of the United States* (New York: William A. Davis, 1796)—Republican leader and later secretary of the treasury presents a plan for paying the national debt;

Gallatin, *Views of the Public Debt, Receipts, & Expenditures of the United States* (Philadelphia: Mathew Carey, 1801)—Treasury Secretary Gallatin's plan for paying national debt in sixteen years;

Alexander Hamilton, *The argument of the Secretary of the Treasury upon the Constitutionality of a National Bank* (Philadelphia, 1791)—Hamilton's argument that a national bank is constitutional;

John Holroyd, Earl of Sheffield, *Observations on the commerce of the American States with Europe and the West Indies* (London: J. Debrett, 1783)—Sheffield called for British restrictions against American trade, arguing that England could prevent the Americans from achieving economic independence;

Charles Jared Ingersoll, *A View of the Rights and Wrongs, power and policy, of the United States of America* (Philadelphia, 1808)—a Philadelphia lawyer endorsed Jefferson's embargo as a way of preventing the United States from developing into an industrial country like England;

Thomas Jefferson, *Notes on the establishment of a money unit and of a coinage for the United States* (Maryland, 1784)—Jefferson's proposal for minting American coins rather than relying on European currency;

Jefferson, *Observations on the Whale Fishery* (Paris: Printed by Jacques-Gabriel Clousier, 1788)—as American minister to France, Jefferson wrote a detailed study of whaling to convince the French of the value of American trade;

George Logan, *Five Letters, Addressed to the Yeomanry of the United States, containing some Observations on the Dangerous Scheme of Governor Duer and Mr. Secretary Hamilton, to Establish National Manufactories* (Philadelphia: Eleazer Oswald, 1792)—an attack on Hamilton's Society for Useful Manufactories;

Logan, *A Letter to the Citizens of Pennsylvania, on the Necessity of Promoting Agriculture, Manufactures, and the Useful Arts* (Lancaster, Penn.: W. & R. Dickson, 1800)—though Logan opposed Hamilton's industrial system, he called for domestic manufacturing that would fit in with Republican ideology;

James Richardson, *An Oration, Describing the Influence of Commerce, on the Prosperity, Character and Genius of Nations* (Boston: Russell & Cutler, 1808)—an address to the Phi Beta Kappa Society in Cambridge attacking the Embargo for destroying commerce, which was the source of industry, enterprise, and civilization;

James Sullivan, *The Path to Riches: An Inquiry into the Origin and Use of Money; and into the Principles of Stocks and Banks* (Boston: I. Thomas & E. T. Andrews, 1792)—urges Americans to choose honest commerce over corrupt or avaricious pursuits;

Thomas Thacher, *The Principles and Maxims on which the Security and Happiness of a Republic Depend* (Boston: Munroe & French, 1811)—a New England clergyman attacks the commercial policies of the Madison administration;

Pelatiah Webster, *Political Essays on the Nature and Operation of Money, Public Finances, and other Subjects: Published during the American War and Continued to the Present Year, 1791* (Philadelphia: Joseph Crukshank, 1791) — a former clergyman turned merchant argues against paper currency in favor of a stronger government to protect trade and stabilize the monetary system.

COMMUNICATIONS

by ROBERT J. ALLISON and JOHN O'KEEFE

CONTENTS

Sidebars and tables are listed in italics.

1783

- Thirty-five weekly newspapers are published in the United States.

30 May The *Pennsylvania Evening Post and Daily Advertiser* becomes the first daily newspaper in the country.

22 Aug. The *Pennsylvania Evening Post and Daily Advertiser* begins to use newsboys to sell papers on the street.

Oct. *Boston Magazine* begins publication.

27 Oct. Cornelius Bradford reopens the New York Merchants' Coffeehouse, which had operated under British authority during the Revolutionary War.

1784

21 Sept. The *Pennsylvania Packet,* a weekly newspaper, becomes a daily published by John Dunlap and D. C. Claypoole; it will be the most influential business paper for the next fourteen years.

1785

- The U.S. Post Office arranges for private coach operators to carry mail on north-south routes. This is the first use of private contractors to carry mail.

- The state of Massachusetts taxes newspapers and other reading materials.

- Postmaster General Ebenezer Hazard allows newspaper printers to exchange papers through the mail for free.

23 Feb. The *New York Morning Post* becomes a daily paper.

1 Mar. The *New York Daily Advertiser* becomes New York's second daily paper.

1786

Sept. Mathew Carey and four partners begin *Columbian Magazine* in Philadelphia.

Oct. *Boston Magazine* publishes its last issue.

1787

- The Constitution requires publication of debates.

Jan. Mathew Carey launches a new magazine, *American Museum.*

Apr. Francis Hopkinson assumes editorial duties at *Columbian Magazine.*

Nov.–Dec. The daily debates in the Pennsylvania constitutional convention are published.

1788

- Congress establishes the first east-west postal route, a 250-mile link between Philadelphia and Pittsburgh, Pennsylvania.

1789

- The first American religious magazine, *Arminian Magazine,* begins publishing.
- The first American juvenile magazine, the *Children's Magazine,* begins in Hartford, Connecticut.

Jan.   Isaiah Thomas begins publishing *Massachusetts Magazine.*

15 Apr. John Fenno begins publishing the *Gazette of the United States.*

1790

- There are seventy-five post offices in the United States, with 1,875 miles of post roads.

1 Oct.   The first issue of Benjamin Franklin Bache's *Philadelphia General Advertiser* is published.

1791

May   Thomas Paine's *Rights of Man,* a defense of the French Revolution, is published in the United States.

12 Aug. Despite Thomas Jefferson's lobbying to appoint Thomas Paine to the position, President George Washington names Timothy Pickering postmaster general.

31 Oct. Concerned that Fenno's *Gazette of the United States* distorts the news by presenting only Federalist ideas, James Madison and Thomas Jefferson help poet Philip Freneau launch a Republican paper, the *National Gazette.*

Nov.–Dec. Benjamin Franklin Bache writes a series of essays in the *Philadelphia General Advertiser* advocating reform of the postal system. Bache abandons the view that the purpose of the post office is to raise money for the government and instead advocates that it is to provide information to citizens.

1792

20 Feb. Congress establishes postal routes with the passage of the Post Office Act. In addition, newspapers are admitted freely into the mail for exchange purposes between printers; otherwise the postal rate for newspapers is one cent each.

Mar.   The *National Gazette* begins a series of attacks on Secretary of the Treasury Alexander Hamilton's campaign for national economic development.

4 Aug.   Hamilton launches an attack on Secretary of State Thomas Jefferson in the *Gazette of the United States.*

1793

- The Mechanic Library Society is founded in New Haven, Connecticut.
- Baltimore's *Free Universal Magazine* is launched, the first American magazine published south of Philadelphia.

Dec.   John Fenno changes his paper from a semiweekly publication to an evening daily under the revised title *Gazette of the United States and Evening Advertiser.*

1794

- Benjamin Franklin Bache renames his paper the *General Advertiser and Aurora.*

- The Typographical Society of New York secures wages of one dollar a day for printers.

20 Feb. The U.S. Senate, which had been meeting in secrecy, decides to allow journalists into its next session.

15 Apr. *Courrier Français,* the first foreign-language daily paper in the United States, is printed in Philadelphia.

8 May The Post Office extends free exchange privileges to magazines; it also limits fees for newspapers mailed within a state to one cent. At the time newspapers make up 70 percent of the mail's weight and generate 3 percent of postal revenue.

1795

- There are 453 post offices and 13,207 miles of post roads in the country.

- A social library is founded at Belpre, Ohio.

Jan. Rev. Samuel Williams publishes *Rural Magazine, or Vermont Repository,* in Rutland, Vermont.

Jan.–Dec. Philadelphian Samuel Harrison Smith begins publishing *American Monthly Review or Literary Chronicle.*

1796

- The *Massachusetts Magazine* stops publication; it is the longest-lasting eighteenth-century American magazine.

- The U.S. Post Office establishes a regular schedule of stagecoach service on a north-south post road.

- Postal clerk Abraham Bradley Jr. draws a detailed map of the north-south postal route, with arrival and departure times of the coach.

15 Aug. Samuel Harrison Smith publishes *New World,* which will become a daily paper two months later.

19 Sept. The *American Daily Advertiser* publishes George Washington's Farewell Address.

1797

Jan. The *South Carolina Weekly Museum* begins publication.

Jan.–Feb. The *Weekly Museum,* published in Baltimore every Sunday for two months, is the first Sunday newspaper in the nation.

4 Mar. English journalist William Cobbett publishes *Porcupine's Gazette and Daily Advertiser* in Philadelphia.

24 June The *Pittsburgh Gazette* begins using locally made paper.

July The *Medical Repository* is published in New York, the first American scientific and medical journal; it will continue until 1827.

16 Aug.	Samuel Harrison Smith ceases publication of *New World.*
16 Nov.	Samuel Harrison Smith purchases the *Gazetteer* from Joseph Gales and changes its name to the *Universal Gazette.*

1798

•	The state of Pennsylvania gives a $5,000 subsidy to Binney and Ronaldson to set up a modern type foundry.
29 June	Benjamin Franklin Bache appears in court to answer charge of seditious libel against President John Adams.
14 July	Congress passes the Sedition Act.
17 July	William Durrell, the New York publisher of the *Mount Pleasant Register,* is arrested for sedition.
Aug.	John Fenno, son of the editor of the *Gazette of the United States,* physically attacks Benjamin Franklin Bache on a street in Philadelphia, biting his knuckle.
10 Sept.	Benjamin Franklin Bache dies in a yellow fever epidemic.
14 Sept.	John Fenno dies of yellow fever.
1 Oct.	Congressman Matthew Lyon launches the magazine *Scourge of Aristocracy and Repository of Important Political Truths* to challenge Federalists and to contest the Sedition Act.
5 Oct.	Matthew Lyon is indicted for sedition; he is convicted three days later and sentenced to four months in jail.
Dec.	Matthew Lyon is overwhelmingly reelected to Congress.

1799

•	The Franklin Typographical Association is founded in New York and succeeds in raising wages of printers to seven dollars a week.
2 Mar.	Congress allows the postmaster general to require newspaper subscribers to pay part of the postage in advance.
Oct.	Luther Baldwin is fined $150 for critical remarks he made in July concerning President John Adams.

1800

Jan.	James Thomson Callender publishes *The Prospect Before Us.*
Feb.	Postmaster General Joseph Habersham tries to discourage post offices from renting boxes for mail; instead, he wants to establish "penny posts," which make home delivery in urban areas.
4 Apr.	William Durrell is convicted of sedition.
12 Apr.	Charles Holt is convicted of sedition. President John Adams grants a pardon to William Durrell, the only Republican he will pardon for sedition.

May	The House of Representatives votes to repeal the Sedition Act.
24 May	Callender indicted for sedition.
June	Callender convicted of sedition, sentenced to nine months in jail, and fined $480.
Aug.	Postmaster General Joseph Habersham institutes the hub-and-spoke system of sorting and delivering mail. Some post offices are designated as distribution centers while others become branch depots.
24 Oct.	Republicans in New York publish *Letter from Alexander Hamilton, Concerning the Public Conduct and Character of John Adams, Esq., President of the United States.*
31 Oct.	Samuel Harrison Smith publishes *National Intelligencer and Washington Advertiser,* the first newspaper in Washington, D.C.; it will become the official paper of the Jefferson administration.
Dec.	John Fenno, publisher of *Gazette of the United States and Evening Advertiser,* is fined $2,500 by a Pennsylvania court for libeling a Republican.

1801

Jan.	The first issue of *The Port Folio,* edited by Joseph Dennie, appears.
3 Mar.	The Sedition Act expires.
16 Mar.	President Thomas Jefferson pardons James Thomson Callender and other journalists punished under the Sedition Act.
16 Nov.	The *New-York Evening Post,* founded by Alexander Hamilton, prints its first issue.

1802

•	A social library is founded in Cincinnati, Ohio.
1 June	The first meeting of the American Company of Booksellers occurs in New York. The group offers a fifty-dollar gold medal for the best printer's ink.

1803

19 Sept.	The *New-York Evening Post* reports that the Philadelphia Typographical Society contributed $83.50 for relief of New York printers suffering in a yellow fever outbreak.
Nov.	Phineas Adams and Rev. William Emerson of Boston publish the first issue of *Monthly Anthology, or Magazine of Polite Literature.*

1804

•	Abraham Bradley revises the map of the national postal routes.
•	The American Company of Booksellers offers a fifty-dollar gold medal for best paper and binding.
•	Thomas Langroth of Pennsylvania patents a new machine for making paper.

•	The Ames, Ohio, social library is founded.

1805

•	A library is established in Dayton, Ohio.
3 Oct.	Rev. William Emerson and other Boston intellectuals form the Anthology Society to publish the *Monthly Anthology*.
23 Oct.	Members of the Anthology Society vote to establish a library.

1806

•	A library is founded in Vincennes, Indiana.
May	The Anthology Society opens a reading room in Boston, furnished with European and American newspapers and literary and political pamphlets. It is open to all who pay a ten-dollar yearly subscription fee.

1807

•	A social library is founded in New Haven, Connecticut.
1 Jan.	Members of Boston's Anthology Society announce a plan to organize a library, similar to Athenaeum in Liverpool, England.
7 Apr.	The Boston Athenaeum is opened.
Dec.	Congress discusses using an "optical telegraph" system of transmitting messages via light signals from a series of high towers from Washington, D.C., to New Orleans.

1809

•	The *New York Observer* publishes the second Sunday newspaper in the United States.
31 Aug.	Detroit's first newspaper, the *Michigan Essay, or Impartial Observer,* is printed in both English and French.
Oct.	The Presbyterian synod excludes Washington, Pennsylvania, postmaster Hugh Wylie from communion when he opens his post office on Sunday.

1810

Apr.	Congress revises the Postal Act, requiring local postmasters to deliver all mail on the day it is received and to open post offices on the day the mail arrives, including Sunday.

1811

7 Sept.	The first issue of *Niles' Weekly Register* is published in Baltimore by Hezekiah Niles.

1812

Nov.   Isaiah Thomas and others found the American Antiquarian Society in Worcester, Massachusetts, to preserve source materials on American history.

1813

•   Congress allows Dr. James Smith of Maryland to send his smallpox vaccine through the mail free of charge.

Feb.   Washington Irving, editor of *Select Review,* changes its name to *Analectic Magazine.*

1815

14 Feb.   The *Charleston Courier* prints the first news in the United States about the Treaty of Ghent.

May   *North American Review* prints its first issue.

OVERVIEW

Distances. When Thomas Jefferson became president in 1801, he described for the American people the particular blessings they enjoyed. They were "kindly separated by nature and a wide ocean from the exterminating havoc of one quarter of the globe," and they "possessed a chosen country, with room enough for our descendants to the thousandth and thousandth generation." In 1801 the western boundary of this enormous country was on the Mississippi River, while its southern border did not reach the Gulf of Mexico. Most of this territory, however, was still in the hands of Native Americans, and the possibility that they might easily be forced out was remote. For Jefferson the distances and scale of the New World were magnificent, the forests and prairies filled with promise and possibilities. For others, though, the size of the country presented problems. During the Constitutional Convention of 1787, when a delegate suggested that the task at hand was to make a government that would last, Nathaniel Gorham of Massachusetts asked, "Can it be supposed that this vast Country including the Western territory will 150 years hence remain one nation?" It seemed impossible that a government could be formed over this large country, or that the people of the various states could join together to form one nation.

Speed. It took time to connect these vast distances. In 1789 it took twenty days for a letter to get from Savannah, Georgia, to Portland, Maine, and another twenty to get a reply. The fastest way to travel was by boat, since roads did not exist in many areas. When President Jefferson returned home each year to his estate at Monticello, the one-hundred-mile trip took him several days, and he had to cross five rivers which did not have bridges.

Spreading News. Benjamin Franklin had been the first postmaster general appointed by the Continental Congress. In 1792 Congress, under the new Constitution, changed the nature of the U.S. Post Office, and Thomas Jefferson pushed to have Thomas Paine appointed postmaster. The postal service was vital to communication in many ways. The Post Office delivered not only mail but also newspapers, and ready access to the latest news was vital to American businessmen. Stagecoach drivers were contracted to carry the mail, and in the 1790s the federal government began regulating stagecoach routes and schedules. The government contracts were lucrative; it was said in the nineteenth century that the postmaster general could put most American stagecoach companies out of business. By requiring that the mail be carried into the West and Southwest, the Post Office helped develop those regions, subsidizing stage companies to bring mail as well as people and goods to the frontier. Abraham Bradley, a postal clerk, drew a detailed map of stage routes in 1796 showing the arrival and departure times of stagecoaches. The Post Office itself experimented only briefly with running its own stage to carry the mail, using private contractors for most of its transportation.

Geography and Optical Telegraph. The expanding distances of the new nation made two things necessary: a knowledge of geography, and ways to cross the wide-open spaces. Bradley's map was an important step. In the same period New England clergyman Jedidiah Morse wrote a geographical study, and in 1804 President Jefferson dispatched Lewis and Clark to explore the Louisiana Territory. In 1807 Congress considered constructing an "optical telegraph," a system of towers running from Washington, D.C., to New Orleans. From each tower a watchman could send a signal of light—visible from the next tower—which then could be transmitted to the next tower, and so on. Napoleon Bonaparte's armies had used a similar system in marching across Europe. Congress ultimately decided against the optical telegraph, but Morse's son, Samuel F. B. Morse, would help to bridge distances with a different kind of telegraph in 1837.

Rise of the Press. The Post Office was crucial to spreading news. Some 70 percent of the mail's weight was in newspapers, which were allowed to circulate for a very low rate. In the 1780s most newspapers had been trade sheets. They sold for about six cents a copy and were filled with advertisements, news of arriving ships, and accounts of foreign events that might influence markets. In the 1790s political papers developed, particularly in Philadelphia. The *Gazette of the United States* was launched in 1789 to present the American people with the Washington administration's views and policies. The newspaper had competition from Benjamin Franklin Bache's *Philadelphia General Advertiser* and from Philip

Freneau's *National Gazette,* which was subsidized by Jefferson and James Madison. During the "newspaper war" of 1792 these papers savagely attacked one another and the political figures they represented—not even George Washington was above criticism. These were national papers meant to circulate throughout the country, and local papers reprinted their views and stories. One Republican journalist, James Thomson Callender, suggested that all Republican papers share the same stories, which would be written in a central location. His idea did not take off at the time, but now most newspapers rely on shared "wire services" to fill their pages. These political papers did not entirely replace the business papers; by the early 1800s papers began covering both kinds of news. In most cases the news reported was national or international; these four-page papers did not usually give local news, since it was expected most people would learn about community affairs from their neighbors.

Constitutional Debate. James Madison had learned the value of public opinion in 1787. Jefferson in 1776 had written the Declaration of Independence with "a decent respect for the opinions of mankind." Madison in 1787 and 1788 had written with Alexander Hamilton and John Jay a series of essays to convince Americans to support the Constitution. Madison was a good writer, and his *Federalist* essays were convincing. The Constitutional debate, much more than the debate over independence, was a public, national debate, with people from across the country engaged in discussions on this important issue. *The Federalist* was just one of many voices ringing under a variety of pseudonyms: Americanus, An Old Whig, Philadelphiensis, Cato, Brutus, A Federal Farmer, A Columbian Patriot, Agrippa, An American. This public debate in the newspapers carried over into the state conventions. In fact, the state convention proceedings were covered by the local press, with daily debates reprinted in the papers of Philadelphia and Boston. This set the tone for coverage of proceedings in the new government when it met in New York. Accounts of debates in Congress filled the papers, and members of the government, such as John Adams and Alexander Hamilton, wrote essays for the press. Madison, too, in the 1790s contributed essays to the *National Gazette.* The U.S. government, Madison knew, rested on public opinion, and only by having an informed citizenry could the republic survive. The newspapers were not a perfect medium, but they were a useful one.

Magazines. Magazines were less successful than newspapers in reaching a broad audience. Publishers liked magazines because they were issued less frequently, included more material, and sold for a higher price. But the high price cut down on sales, and the Post Office Act of 1792, which allowed newspapers into the mail at a low price, required magazines to pay more, and this put some magazines out of business. Many magazines were begun in this period, but just as quickly as they began they disappeared. Magazines tended to contain a variety of material: some were religious, scientific, or historical, but most magazines presented a collection of seemingly unrelated themes, articles, and issues, as well as a mixture of prose and poetry, fiction and nonfiction. Their eclectic nature may have prevented their success.

Sedition Act. In 1798 the Federalist Congress, smarting under criticism from papers, passed the Sedition Act, making it a crime to criticize the president or Congress. Fourteen journalists were convicted of sedition and sent to jail for up to a year; this did not stop the criticism, however. Vice President Thomas Jefferson and James Madison secretly drafted resolutions passed by the Kentucky and Virginia legislatures calling the Sedition Act unconstitutional, both for violating the First Amendment and for assuming power in the federal government. Only the states could punish libel, Jefferson and Madison argued; a federal libel law was unconstitutional. Their view did not prevail at the time. However, the Sedition Act expired on 3 March 1801, the day before Jefferson became president. Under his administration the federal government would not punish libelers, but Jefferson did encourage the states to prosecute publishers who criticized the administration. Madison's ideas on the role of newspapers were less restrictive.

Election of 1800. Despite the Sedition Act, under which they were threatened with prosecution for criticizing the Adams administration, Republicans mobilized in 1800 to prepare for the election. James Madison was the key architect of the Republican victory, but he received crucial help from an unlikely source. Alexander Hamilton, the Federalists' intellectual leader, had become dissatisfied with President John Adams. Hamilton was angry that Adams, who did not trust him, had fired two of Hamilton's allies in the cabinet and was preparing to end the "Quasi War" with France. In the fall of 1800 Hamilton circulated a letter to influential Federalists, and possible presidential electors, arguing that Adams was not fit to be president and that instead of casting their electoral votes for Adams they should vote for Charles Cotesworth Pinckney. Adams, according to Hamilton, was too temperamental and emotional for the office. This private letter circulated among influential Federalists with minimal effect. In October Republican vice-presidential candidate Aaron Burr obtained a copy. Burr immediately saw the political value of a letter from the Federalists' chief intellect denouncing the Federalist president, and saw that the letter was published in the newspapers and as a pamphlet. It created a sensation, but whether it influenced the election is hard to tell. The episode does reveal the different attitudes of the two political parties. For the Federalists political decisions were made by influential men; by circulating a letter to several dozen individuals, Hamilton planned to alter the course of history. For the Republicans political decisions were made by the people at large, and they could best be reached through the newspapers and through public debate.

War of 1812. Communications were a crucial factor in the War of 1812. President Madison asked Congress to declare war against England because the British government insisted on impressing American sailors; five days after the United States declared war, England reversed its policy. By then it was too late; by the time news of the decision reached the United States the British and their Native American allies had captured Detroit, Fort Dearborn (present-day Chicago), and Michilimackinac Island, Michigan. Poor communication hindered the American war effort, as did a failure to set realistic goals. Many in New England opposed the war, particularly after the British blockaded the coast. In the late fall of 1814 England sent a large army to New Orleans. Meanwhile, delegates from the New England states met in Hartford, Connecticut, to discuss seceding from the union. On 5 January 1815 the delegates concluded their meeting and sent representatives to Washington, D.C., with a list of grievances and suggested changes to the Constitution. They reached the capital in February, but the New England delegates did not bring the only news to arrive that day. From Ghent, Belgium, came astonishing news that the war was over: on 24 December American negotiators and their British counterparts had agreed to a peace treaty on remarkable terms—neither side would lose any territory. Even more astonishing was the news that day from New Orleans: on 8 January the British army had been defeated by Gen. Andrew Jackson and a force of Kentucky and Tennessee militiamen, Choctaw and Cherokee warriors, New Orleans creoles, and Caribbean pirates. More than two thousand British soldiers were killed or wounded, while the Americans suffered only twenty-one casualties. It was an astounding victory, not less for coming after the war was over. The New England delegates quietly went home.

Changes. Madison recognized that the country needed a more sophisticated communication network. In his annual message at the end of 1815 he suggested that Congress consider building roads, canals, and other parts of a transportation infrastructure. Madison did not believe the Constitution gave Congress the power to do these things, but he advised Congress to propose an amendment that would allow the federal government to improve transportation and communication. On his last day in office, 4 March 1817, Madison was presented with an ambitious plan by Congress to build roads, bridges, and canals. But Congress had not amended the Constitution to allow it to do these things. Madison vetoed the bill. He believed in transportation, and knew the value of improved communication, but he feared the expansion of federal power. Nevertheless Madison left office marveling at the great changes in travel since he arrived at the scene of national government, then Philadelphia, in 1780 on a coach driven by a slave. In 1787 Madison and the other delegates to the Constitutional Convention had watched John Fitch demonstrate his prototype steamboat on the Delaware River. Fitch could not make a safe and efficient steamboat, but in the first decade of the nineteenth century other American inventors worked on the problem, and in 1817 James Madison left the presidency riding on a steamboat. This invention would cut the magnificent distances of the new republic and help keep Americans together as one nation.

TOPICS IN THE NEWS

CHAPBOOKS

For the People. While Mathew Carey and Isaiah Thomas created a publishing industry and prided themselves on the printer's craft, they also sold popular works at low cost. Throughout the country small presses turned out "chapbooks," small, relatively cheap editions of books printed on inexpensive paper. Some booksellers, such as Chapman Whitcomb, spent most of their time traveling and selling copies of their books for a few pennies a copy.

Itinerant Bookseller. Graduating from Dartmouth College in 1785, Whitcomb became a minister but did not succeed as one, either through his lack of faith or his eccentric nature. He taught school for a while and supplemented his income by collecting rags to sell to a local paper maker. Selling rags to make paper led Whitcomb into the other end of the paper industry, writing books. His several dozen books were printed in Leominster, Massachusetts, by Charles and John Prentiss. Whitcomb not only wrote poetry, but also the popular adventure stories and captivity tales. In 1800 he revised two books—the narrative of Mary Rowlandson, who was captured by Wampanoag Indians in 1676, and an English chapbook relating a robbery titled *The Farmer's*

Contemporary engraving of Maria Martin, the subject of the *History of the Captivity and Sufferings of Mrs. Maria Martin, who was Six Years a Slave in Algiers* (1807), the story of an American woman who resisted the advances of a Turkish ruler and was put in solitary confinement

Daughter, of Essex: Being a History of the Life and Sufferings of Miss Clarissa Dalton. With a stock of chapbooks in hand, Whitcomb walked through rural New England selling his wares.

Circulation. Most copies of these chapbooks have long since disappeared, though Isaiah Thomas made an effort to collect and preserve them in the American Antiquarian Society. Small presses such as that of the Prentiss brothers in Leominster turned out these cheap editions, and itinerant booksellers such as Whitcomb revised popular works and sold them in new areas. In the seventeenth century stories of colonists captured by Indians attracted readers, not only for the excitement but also for the moral lessons they conveyed. In the years 1785 to 1815 stories of Americans captured by Algerian pirates were also popular. In 1807 a Boston publisher printed *History of the Captivity and Sufferings of Mrs. Maria Martin, who was Six Years a Slave in Algiers,* which was reprinted in Vermont, Connecticut, New Jersey, and Ohio before 1816. One publisher bound this tale of captivity and suffering together with a *Short Account of Algiers,* originally published in 1793 by Mathew Carey; a rural New England printer, finding the two books bound together, printed Carey's *Short Account of Algiers* separately, but listed Maria Martin as the author. Because distances were so great between Philadelphia and the New England backcountry, Carey did not attempt to retrieve his book or to extract royalties from the small press running off copies.

Common Themes. Aside from its publishing history, the Maria Martin chapbook shares a common theme

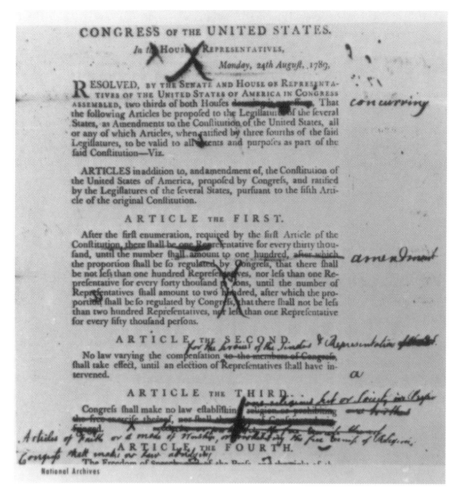

Page from the Senate's working draft of the Bill of Rights (National Archives)

with other popular stories. A young woman goes to sea with her husband and is shipwrecked. Captured by corsairs, she becomes a slave to a Turkish governor in an Algerian province. She resists his sexual advances and is put in solitary confinement. Just as her mind is about to break, she has a vision of salvation and is rescued. She returns home, where her father faints upon seeing her after seven years of absence. The story ends with Maria Martin returning to sea to find her husband. This was a powerful story of endurance and survival. It was similar to Abraham Panther's *A Very Surprising Narrative of a Young Woman, Discovered in a Rocky Cave*, which was reprinted by many small presses between 1786 and 1816. Another popular chapbook was the *Famous History of Whittington and his Cat*, which had at least nineteen editions between 1770 and 1818. It related the story of Dick Whittington, a poor English boy who arrived in London with nothing but his cat and wound up becoming the city's Lord Mayor. A rags-to-riches story, the reasons for its popularity in American society are clear.

Significance. Magazines in this period were launched and quickly sank. Newspapers devoted most of their pages to affairs of state. Chapbooks were perhaps the most significant means of spreading ideas and culture

through American society. Sold by traveling salesmen such as Whitcomb, these inexpensive books circulated throughout rural America, as well as in cities, and were meant to be read until they fell apart. The messages they conveyed—self-reliance, resistance to tyranny, family loyalty, and hard work—were the vital principles of American society.

Sources:

Robert J. Allison, *The Crescent Obscured: The United States and the Muslim World, 1776–1815* (New York: Oxford University Press, 1995);

Victor Neuberg, "Chapbooks in America: Reconstructing the Popular Reading of Early America," in *Reading in America: Literature and Social History*, edited by Cathy N. Davidson (Baltimore: Johns Hopkins University Press, 1989).

CONSTITUTIONAL DEBATE

Decision. Even if the American people had rejected the U.S. Constitution in 1787 and 1788, the ratification process would have forged a closer union. The debate over ratification, carried out in thirteen state conventions and in newspapers and pamphlets, was the first national public debate in America. The decision for independence had been made in closed session by Congress in 1776; Americans in the individual states and towns then decided to affirm it, but gradually. In contrast, the decision to ratify the Constitution was made in public conventions, and both supporters and opponents of ratification made their case with appeals to public opinion. The debates in the state conventions were reported in the daily and weekly papers, and arguments for and against ratification were reprinted in papers throughout the country. The result was that people in all the states shared their ideas; writers in Massachusetts responded to arguments made in Pennsylvania; Virginians addressed issues raised by New Yorkers; and readers in Georgia, New Hampshire, and other states could read these arguments and make their own conclusions.

Assembly of Demigods. Initially, most Americans were prepared to like the Constitution. It had been framed by an august assembly—Thomas Jefferson (who was in Paris when the debate took place) called it "an assembly of demigods"—including George Washington and Benjamin Franklin, along with less known but equally gifted men such as James Madison, Robert and Governeur Morris, James Wilson, George Wythe, Alexander Hamilton, John Dickinson, Elbridge Gerry, Roger Sherman, and Charles Cotesworth Pinckney. The Convention, meeting in Philadelphia, sent the document to Congress, which was meeting in New York.

State Conventions. Congress would have no role in approving or disapproving the document: its only task was to forward the Constitution to the states. In most states power was in the hands of legislatures, but the framers of the Constitution did not want the state legislatures to have a role in ratification (they knew the legislatures would not be happy with a system that limited their power). Instead, each state would call a convention, a body elected specifically for the purpose of considering the Constitution. A convention also represented the sovereign power of the people in the state, and thus legally would be superior to the legislature. The Constitutional Convention had met in absolute secrecy; no delegates were permitted to disclose what had been discussed each day during their proceedings. There had been great speculation outside the convention hall, and at one point the delegates did make a public statement to squelch rumors they were considering establishing a monarchy. When Washington, who presided at the convention, sent the Constitution to New York, he gave the first public account of the convention's work. Now the American people would have a chance to judge.

Support Mobilizes. Richard Henry Lee, a delegate to Congress from Virginia, wrote to George Mason on 1 October 1787 that already the proponents of the Constitution were mobilizing, joining with other interested parties to ratify the system before the American people had a chance to evaluate it. "The greatness of the powers given and the multitude of places to be created produces a coalition of monarchy men, military men, aristocrats, and drones whose noise, impudence, and zeal exceeds all belief. Whilst the commercial plunder of the south stim-ulates the rapacious trader. In this state of things, the patriot voice is raised in vain."

Federalists. The proponents realized that many Americans felt that liberty could only be preserved in a small republic and that a country as big as the United States could survive under a single national government only if that government used despotic power. Proponents of the Constitution denied that they had created a national government and pointed out the parts of the system which rested on the states, such as the Senate, with the same number of senators from each state, and the electors who chose the president. These were "federal" features. On the other hand the "national features" included a House of Representatives chosen directly by the people, a judiciary to settle disputes between the states, local judges bound to follow precedents set by the federal courts, and all the laws made by Congress. The Constitution's supporters knew that the American people would reject a "national" system. To reinforce the point that they had created a "federal" system they called themselves "Federalists"; their opponents became "Anti-Federalists."

First Responses. On 27 September 1787 a writer signing himself "Cato," at the time believed to be New York governor George Clinton, urged Americans to think for themselves and not to rush their judgment. One week later, on 5 October, Philadelphian Samuel Bryan wrote his first essay under the name "Centinel," stating that it would "not be difficult to prove" that only a despotism could "bind so great a country under one government," and that whatever system men could devise to govern ultimately would become a tyranny. The elected officers of the government would be "devoid of all responsibility or accountability to the great body of the people, and that so far from being a regular balanced government, it would be in practice a *permanent* ARISTOCRACY." Bryan went further and questioned why there was no protection for freedom of the press, religious or personal liberty, and trial by jury in civil cases. Bryan's essay was reprinted thirteen times, in Massachusetts, New York, and Virginia. Bryan's argument that the Constitution was flawed for lacking a bill of rights would stick.

James Wilson. On the evening after Bryan published his essay, James Wilson addressed a public meeting in Philadelphia. Wilson was the first member of the convention to speak out publicly on the Constitution, and his address in many ways set the tone for the rest of the debate. By the end of December 1787 Wilson's speech would be reprinted in thirty-four papers from Portland, Maine, to Augusta, Georgia. Wilson argued that the new system was unique in the world's history, maintaining that the framers had created a federal republic, that the system was partly national and partly federal, and that it all rested on representation. Wilson also addressed the lack of a bill of rights, saying that it was unnecessary to have one because the new federal government had only

Contemporary engraving of John Adams, Robert Morris, Alexander Hamilton, and
Thomas Jefferson conferring at the Continental Congress

the powers specifically given to it in the Constitution; anything not given to the federal government was reserved to the states.

Freedom of the Press. Wilson would have been well advised to stop here, but he went on to discuss the specific rights mentioned by his opponents. "For instance, the liberty of the press, which has been a copious source of declamation and opposition, what control can proceed from the federal government to shackle or destroy that sacred palladium of national freedom." By calling the free press "a copious source of declamation," Wilson undercut his later assertion that it was "a sacred palladium of national freedom." As to the charge that the new government could keep up a military force in time of peace, Wilson also dismissed this and suggested that a permanent military force would be a good thing. Wilson had a good argument about powers reserved to the states, but he went too far in suggesting that the threatened rights were not as important as Anti-Federalists were claiming. Finally, Wilson charged the Constitution's opponents with being petty, self-interested men, powerful in their own states, who feared losing their offices and prestige if a new, effective federal government was established.

Uproar. Wilson had given the Constitution's opponents something they needed—a single organizing theme. Federalists could rally around the Constitution itself, arguing that its new organization of government would cure the ills of the Confederation. The worst charge that could be leveled against them was that they were an elitist group seeking to create an aristocracy. Wilson, by sounding like an elitist, played into this fear. By dismissing concern for a bill of rights, he gave the appearance of regarding it as irrelevant. Wilson's speech came as Pennsylvania began debating the Constitution. In other states the process began with an open discussion in the legislature, with the election of delegates to a convention, and culminated in public debates in state conventions. In October and November 1787 American newspapers were filled with essays by both supporters and opponents of the Constitution. Spain's minister to America, Don Diego de Gardoqui, wrote home to his government that "the paper war in the Newspapers over the new System of Government proposed by the Convention is growing; so that each day it becomes more clear that its establishment will be delayed a long time, and that according to some respectable opinions it would not be surprising if they were to find it necessary to call another Convention next year." While opponents of ratification could not agree on what kind of government to create, their main goal was to prevent ratification so that another convention would be called. On 8 November the most influential Anti-Federalist pamphlet, *Letters from the "Federal Farmer" to "The Republican"* appeared, urging a calm, unhurried consideration of the Constitution. At the same time, Wilson and other Federalists were urging a quick acceptance.

George Mason. In early October George Mason's "Objections to the Constitution" began circulating in manuscript. Mason's arguments were sent by mail from state to state, and Anti-Federalists used Mason to argue publicly against the Constitution. Mason was reported to have said he would sooner cut off his right hand than use it to sign the Constitution. He objected to the lack of a bill of rights and believed the House of Representatives was too small to represent the people adequately; the Senate had too much power; the federal judiciary would "absorb and destroy" the state judiciaries; and the president would be the tool either of his appointed advisers or of the Senate. Mason had been horrified that the Convention allowed the slave trade to continue until 1808. Mason also objected to the fact that a simple majority, rather than two-thirds majority, could pass commercial regulations. He believed this would hurt the southern states, who exported tobacco and rice and imported manufactured goods. "This government," Mason concluded, "will commence in a moderate aristocracy; it is at present impossible to foresee whether it will, in its operation, produce a monarchy, or a corrupt oppressive aristocracy; it will most probably vibrate some years between the two, and then terminate between the one and the other." On 21 November Boston's leading Federalist paper, the *Massachusetts Centinel,* printed Mason's "Objections to the Constitution" so that all citizens, not just Anti-Federalists, could read them and so that Federalists could prepare responses. Mason's essay was reprinted thirty times and responded to by Federalists in virtually every state.

The Federalist. The Federalists were better organized and were able to make more-coherent arguments. In New York on 27 October 1787 the first of the *Federalist* essays, written by Alexander Hamilton, James Madison, and John Jay, appeared. These eighty-five essays were all signed "Publius" and published in four different New York papers. So well did the three authors understand their arguments that they turned out these essays at a rate of three or four a week, and not until the twentieth century, with the aid of computer analysis of word usage and grammatical structure, were scholars able to say definitely which author wrote which essays. Hamilton is now credited with writing fifty-one essays, Madison with twenty-six, and Jay, who became ill in the fall of 1787, five. (Hamilton and Madison also cowrote three of the essays). While they were writing, the three authors remained anonymous and did not keep track of which man authored which essay. Madison recalled that the papers "were written most of them in great haste, and without any special allotment of the different parts of the subject to the several writers. . . . It frequently happened that whilst the printer was putting into type the parts of a number, the following parts were under the pen, & to be finished in time for the press." In May 1788 the seventy-eight essays then written, along with seven new numbers, were published in book form, to be distributed in Virginia at that state's convention.

National Audience. The *Federalist* essays were addressed to the people of New York, but, like all other pamphlets and essays in this debate, their audience was truly a national one. The Anti-Federalists of Pennsylvania drew up a list of their objections, which were circulated in the other states except Massachusetts, where the Federalists controlled both the press and the post office and would not allow the document to be printed until after that state's convention had ratified the Constitution. Once Massachusetts ratified it by a vote of 187–168, Anti-Federalists in that state mobilized to prevent other states from following suit. By the spring of 1788 New York had become a central organizing point for the Anti-Federalists. Mercy Otis Warren's essay, *Observations on the Constitution by a Columbian Patriot,* published in February 1788, circulated in New York and Maryland. John Lamb, New York's customs collector, corresponded with Patrick Henry and other Virginia Anti-Federalists on goals to prevent ratification, while Madison corresponded with Hamilton on goals to secure ratification. The Anti-Federalists' goal was to prevent the necessary nine states from ratifying in order to force a second Convention.

Ratification. New Hampshire ratified in June 1788, giving the Constitution the nine necessary states to carry it into effect. Some Anti-Federalists, such as Elbridge Gerry of Massachusetts, George Mason of Virginia, and George Clinton of New York, eventually received offices under the new national government. More important, the principal Anti-Federalist objection to the Constitution, that it did not have a bill of rights, had nearly prevented ratification. When Massachusetts had ratified in February 1788, the Convention called for amendments to the Constitution. While many had come to accept the need for a new government, no one, after the bitter debate, accepted James Wilson's argument that a bill of rights was unnecessary. Instead, James Madison, in the first Congress, drafted the Bill of Rights, which was ratified by the states by the end of 1791.

Final Argument. The long debate over ratification was the first national political debate. Even if the Constitution had been rejected, this debate allowed national political communities to form, as writers in New York and Philadelphia addressed audiences in Georgia and Connecticut and arguments made in Maryland and Virginia were challenged or affirmed in Massachusetts and South Carolina. The same issues moved men and women in different parts of the country either to reject the Constitution or to support it. One of the main Anti-Federalist arguments was that the United States was simply too big to be under a single government. As James Madison wrote in *The Federalist,* number 14, printed in the *New York Packet* on 30 November 1787, "Hearken not to the unnatural voice which tells you that the people of America, knit together as they are by so many chords of affec-

BOSTON TO NEW YORK IN THREE AND ONE-HALF DAYS

An advertisement in Boston's *Columbian Centinel*, 24 April 1793, announced a new stagecoach line. It would cost eight cents a mile to ride this new stage, and each passenger could bring up to fourteen pounds of baggage free of charge.

Boston and New York Stages. The subscriber informs his friend and the public that he, in company with the other proprietors of the old line of stages, has established a new line from Boston to New York for the more rapid conveyance of the mails. The stage carriages of this new line will be small, genteel and easy, in which but four inside passengers will be admitted, with smart, good horses, and experienced and careful drivers. They will start from Boston and New York on the first Monday in May, and continue to run three times a week until the first of November, and will leave Boston every Monday, Wednesday, and Friday at four o'clock a.m. and arrive at New York in three days and a half from their departure. They will leave New York on the same days at one o'clock P.M. . . . The proprietors have been at such great expense to erect this line, they hope their exertions will give satisfaction and receive the public patronage.

Source: Seymour Dunbar, *A History of Travel in America* (New York: Tudor, 1937).

Sources:

Bernard Bailyn, ed., *The Debate on the Constitution*, 2 volumes (New York: Library of America, 1993);

Alexander Hamilton, James Madison, and John Jay, *The Federalist*, edited by Jacob E. Cooke (Middletown, Conn.: Wesleyan University Press, 1961);

John P. Kaminski and Gaspare J. Saladino, eds., *The Documentary History of the Ratification of the Constitution*, 18 volumes to date (Madison: State Historical Society of Wisconsin, 1976–).

FRENCH TRAVELER

Travel Writing. François André Michaux was a French doctor who visited America in the first decade of the nineteenth century. France's Interior Ministry had sent Michaux to inspect the plants of the Ohio River valley. Interested in more than plants, Michaux, like many other European travelers, wrote a book about his experiences, *The North American Sylva, or A Description of the Forest Trees, of the United States, Canada and Nova Scotia* (1817–1819). From his book we get a detailed picture of life in America, and because he saw more of the country than many people who would live their entire lives in it, from his account we can reconstruct the nature of travel in America. Michaux intended to explore the interior of the United States, seeing the Ohio River and the new settlements in Tennessee and Kentucky.

Charleston to Philadelphia. Michaux landed in Charleston, South Carolina, in July 1802. He discovered that to reach the Ohio River he needed to start in Philadelphia, which was fifteen days away by stage. In 1802 direct stagecoach service was begun between Boston, Massachusetts, and Savannah, Georgia; the entire trip took twenty-two and one-half days and cost seventy dollars, not counting food or lodging along the route. Meals averaged two dollars a day, lodging nearly the same. The stage from Charleston to Philadelphia would cost fifty dollars. Michaux, like most travelers, learned that on the

tion, can no longer live together as members of the same family; can no longer continue the mutual guardians of their mutual happiness, can no longer be fellow citizens of one great respectable and flourishing empire." The ratification debate brought these people into closer communication than they ever had been, and helped ensure that they would continue to be knit together as one extended family by cords of affection.

Philadelphia waterfront around 1800; watercolor by Thomas Birch (Museum of Fine Arts, Boston, Karolik Collection)

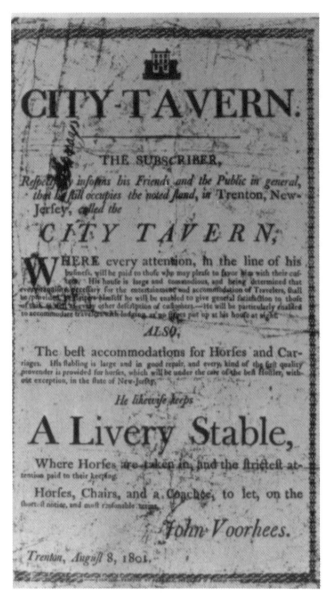

Advertisement for the City Tavern, Trenton, New Jersey, 1801 (Warshaw Collection)

to Pittsburgh. They arrived in Pittsburgh nine days after leaving Philadelphia; another traveler who walked reached Pittsburgh in twenty-seven days.

On the River. From Pittsburgh Michaux walked to Wheeling, Virginia, a town of twenty-six houses on the Ohio River. He and another traveler bought a canoe, and left Wheeling one evening, traveling twelve miles down the river before growing tired of paddling. The next morning they took to the river again, covering thirty miles that day, forty the next. For ten days they rode the river before reaching Limestone, Kentucky, a distance of 348 miles from Wheeling. Michaux was startled to see what appeared to be a fleet of six or seven enormous boxes floating down the river. "I could not conceive what such large square boxes could be, which seemed abandoned to the current, presenting alternately their ends, their sides, even their angles. As they advanced I heard a confused noise, without distinguishing anything, on account of the height of the sides. On ascending the banks of the river I perceived in these boats several families, bringing with them their horses, cows, fowls, carts, ploughs, harness, beds, instruments of husbandry; in short, all the furniture requisite for housekeeping, agriculture, and the management of a farm. These people had thus abandoned themselves to the water for several hundred miles, probably without knowing where they might stop, to exercise their industry and to enjoy in peace the fruit of their labors." This migration into the Ohio River valley had begun before the Revolution, and it would pick up in volume, though not in speed, after the United States bought the Louisiana Territory in 1803 and after the Shawnee and Creek Indians were defeated in the War of 1812. The pace of travel would not change until well after 1811, when Nicholas Roosevelt built the steamboat *New Orleans* at Pittsburgh, and brought her down the river. In 1807 another traveler on the Ohio would meet a man from Saint Louis paddling his canoe upriver. On his way to visit his brother in Pittsburgh, the man going against the current expected his trip to take ten weeks.

To Nashville. Michaux decided to go by foot to Lexington, sixty-five miles away, and he reached the town after walking for two and one-half days. He bought a horse in Lexington and rode to Nashville, Tennessee, making an average of thirty miles a day. Michaux left Nashville on 5 September, taking an old Indian road east and reaching Morgantown, North Carolina, six hundred miles away, one month later. On 18 October he returned to Charleston, South Carolina, "three months and a half after my departure from Philadelphia, having gone through a space of nearly eighteen hundred miles." Of the eighteen hundred miles, Michaux had used a stagecoach for only 140 miles. On his best days Michaux traveled between thirty and forty miles.

Sources:

Seymour Dunbar, *A History of Travel in America* (New York: Tudor, 1937);

East Coast it was much faster to go by boat. He took a packet sloop to New York, taking about ten days and costing less than fifty dollars, and then took a stage to Philadelphia, reaching that city one day and a half after leaving New York. The five-dollar stage ride did not include meals or lodging or the fifty-cent tip for the driver.

To Pittsburgh. From Philadelphia Michaux set out for Pittsburgh. After three days on the stage he learned that it only went as far as Shippensburg, 170 miles from Pittsburgh. A traveler would be "obliged to perform the rest of the journey on foot, or to purchase a horse, of which there are always many for sale; but the country people are such cheats that they always make you pay double the value for them; and on arriving at Pittsburgh you are obliged to dispose of them for half what they cost." Michaux thought of walking, but instead he and a companion bought a horse, which they took turns riding

The presentation to Liberty of a Bill of the Rights of Woman; the frontispiece of the *Lady's Magazine and Repository of Entertaining Knowledge*, 1 December 1792

François André Michaux, *The North American Sylva, or A Description of the Forest Trees, of the United States, Canada and Nova Scotia* (Philadelphia: Sold by T. Dobson / Paris: Printed by C. d'Hautel, 1817–1819).

MAGAZINES

Contents. Magazines in the early national period looked considerably different from those of today. There were no color pictures, of course. Occasionally there were woodcuts or copperplate engravings, although often crudely done. Most early magazines were simply sheets of paper stitched together. A few had thin, colored covers. There was hardly any advertising by our standards. Advertisements were usually confined to the inside covers, if there were any, or to a separate set of pages at the back of the magazine. Ads were not for nationally advertised consumer products but for local booksellers and general stores, or announcing services such as ferryboats or stagecoaches. They were more like the want ads of today's newspapers. The print in early American magazines was small, usually six-point type. The densely filled pages were made of stiff, heavy rag paper, not the glossy paper of today. Magazines ranged in size from five by six to eight by nine inches, and each issue had approximately sixty pages. Articles were opinionated and anonymous or signed with pen names. There was also little news or fiction, although both became more prominent by the end of the era. Magazines included philosophical treatises and political tracts such as Thomas Paine's *Common Sense* (1776) as well as information on the weather and the phases of the moon, like that found in the most popular early American periodical, the almanac.

Difficult Beginnings. Early American magazines faced many obstacles to success. Perhaps most significant was that before the early 1800s there were few American professional writers to count on for the contributions needed to fill the pages of the periodicals. The magazines of the period were filled with regular pleas for submissions, and reprints of English articles far outnumbered original American contributions. If writers were hard to find, so were subscribers. Most Americans had neither the time to read periodicals nor the money to buy them. The most successful American magazine of the late 1700s was Mathew Carey's *American Museum*, which listed only some 1,250 subscribers in 1792. It cost more than three dollars a year, a large amount of money at a time when a worker earned well under a dollar a day. As the era opened, printing was a difficult and expensive process. Distributing magazines was an even more daunting prospect, given the slow development of the postal system and the difficulty of traveling across a large, undeveloped country. In the late 1700s it still typically took more than a week to travel between Boston and New York, the most easily traveled route in the early United States. The few magazines that were started rarely lasted long. Before 1800 the average life span was only fourteen months and the most enduring, the *Massachusetts Magazine* and the *New-York Magazine,* lasted only eight years. After 1800 the chances for success improved. The *Port Folio* began in 1801 and continued for twenty-six years.

Post Office. The cost of sending out magazines to subscribers became an important issue to all parties involved. Both the post office and the magazine were relatively new institutions in 1783, and no one automatically assumed that mail would include magazines. Many postmasters did not like them because they were heavy and their system was strained just by delivering letters. In 1792 Congress passed the Postal Act, which allowed newspapers to be sent through the mail at discounted prices, but postmasters interpreted the law to require magazines to pay the letter rate, which was prohibitively high. A new act in 1794 changed this but still left it up to individual postmasters whether to accept magazines at all. In time most postmasters carried magazines, but as late as 1815 the postmaster general allowed only religious magazines to be sent, and these from Philadelphia and New York only.

Democratic Periodicals. Although the magazine was a new literary form in the early years of the republic (the first American magazine was Andrew Bradford's *American Magazine* of 1741), many Americans quickly sensed its potential for shaping national identity and promoting the values of the Revolutionary era. George Washington recognized this when he wrote in 1788 to Mathew

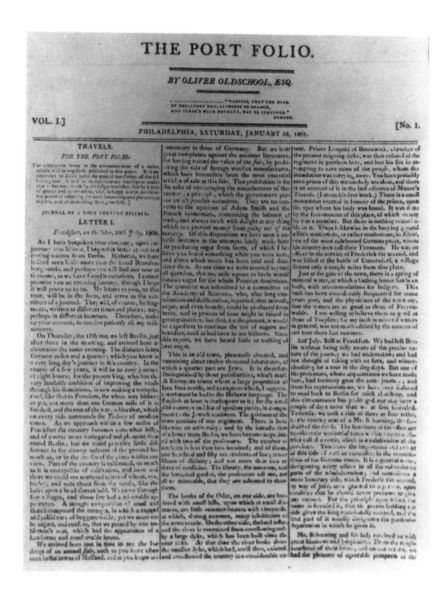

Front page of the first issue of Joseph Dennie's *The Port Folio,* which was published until 1827

Carey, the editor of the *American Museum,* that he considered "such easy vehicles of knowledge as more highly calculated than any other to preserve the liberty, stimulate the industry, and meliorate the morals of an enlightened and free people." While magazines printed all kinds of materials, political essays took up a large amount of space. Early American magazines expressed the fierce partisanship of the new republic. The controversies of the era, such as Jay's Treaty, Thomas Jefferson's election in 1800, the Embargo of 1807, and the War of 1812, were frequent essay topics. Magazines grew as they were able to give readers information about these topics, and they helped shape the opinions of their readership at the same time.

Elite Publications. The magazines of this period tried to speak to a wide readership, for obvious business reasons and also because the ideal of an informed citizenry was a basic value of the early republic. But they were not "popular" in the sense of today's press. Instead of being

supported by mass audiences and advertising, early magazines were produced by small groups of amateur writers and printers who often saw the magazine as a social event as much as a literary product. A case in point is the *Monthly Anthology,* published in Boston from 1803 to 1811. It was sustained by the members of a "Society of Gentlemen," also called the Anthology Club. This club included liberal ministers such as Joseph Stevens Buckminster and William Emerson, the father of Ralph Waldo Emerson, as well as friends associated with nearby Harvard College, such as John Kirkland, later president of that institution. These men were accomplished amateur writers, and they criticized the self-promotion required for professional success as ungentlemanly. The *Monthly Anthology* sought to improve society by raising it up to elite, genteel values. Its writers opposed what they considered the vulgar egalitarianism sweeping America, although they did not recognize that the success of their venture, and others like it, depended on marketing directed to a broad audience. Early Ameri-

Cover for an issue of Isaiah Thomas's magazine in which Judith Sargent Murray published an essay series under the pen name Constantia

can magazines promoted republicanism, but not necessarily democracy.

Women. Although the majority of contributors to early American magazines were male, women did find their way into these periodicals. Noah Webster invited "the ladies, who are the favourites of Minerva and the Muses" to contribute to his *American Magazine* in 1787. The most significant female contributor was Judith Sargent Murray, who published an essay series under the pen name Constantia in Isaiah Thomas's *Massachusetts Magazine* from 1792 to 1794. Women were especially important as contributors of poetry, which was a much more popular literary genre than it is today. They were also well represented in the subject matter of articles written by men since editors quickly recognized that women represented a significant portion of their readers. Essays on fashion were common, and there were even

some essays advocating greater equality between women and men. There was also a great deal of advice offered for women, especially about the education of girls, which was a hotly debated topic in the early republic. Some of this advice had to do with what to read, and many magazines expressed the suspicions of most Americans about the dangers to women of reading fiction, especially novels. The *Columbian Magazine* noted in 1792, for example, that "novels not only pollute the imaginations of young women, but also give them false ideas of life. . . . Good sentiments scattered in loose novels render them the more dangerous." These moralistic campaigns were not successful since the desire of many readers, especially women, for more imaginative literature made fiction writing increasingly prominent in American magazines.

Specialties. Although the most successful magazines were general magazines that included material on a wide range of topics, a growing number of periodicals targeted special groups. There were a few magazines, like the *Lady's Weekly Miscellany* (1805–1808), specifically designed for female readers, prefiguring one of the main periodical markets of the later 1800s. There were also some children's magazines, although it is hard to know what young readers might have thought of material like the mock heroic poem about apple dumplings printed in the *Juvenile Port-Folio,* begun in 1812. Children even produced magazines: thirteen-year-old John Howard Payne managed to publish the *Thespian Mirror,* a magazine of theater criticism, in 1805 and 1806. Partly on the strength of this precocious performance, Payne later became a famous actor as well as the composer of "Home, Sweet Home." There were also magazines devoted to education, medicine, science, law, and farming, although these topics all found their way into general magazines as well.

Religion. The most significant specialized magazines were religious periodicals. Their growth reflected early Americans' intense interest in religious matters during the revivals of the second Great Awakening. Methodist, Baptist, Presbyterian, and other Protestant denominations grew rapidly after 1790, and they quickly realized that magazines were an excellent way to spread God's word. The *Methodist Magazine* of 1797–1798 was an early example of the many, if short-lived, religious periodicals of the age, which were filled with sermons, hymns, news of revival meetings, and dramatic accounts of conversions to Christ. These magazines had an important role in the religious conflicts between denominations as well. The conservative Massachusetts minister Jedidiah Morse founded the *Panoplist* in 1805 to expose and combat infidelity, especially the Unitarianism then popular among New England elites. The *Panoplist* soon turned to providing news of missionary efforts both at home and abroad, and with this, religious magazines found the material that made them among the most popular nineteenth-century publications. Evangelical Americans had a seemingly inexhaustible interest in the stories of conversion and moral reform that soon were the stock-in-trade of these periodicals.

American Museum. From 1787 to 1792 Mathew Carey published what was probably the first successful magazine in the United States, the *American Museum.* Carey immigrated to Philadelphia from Ireland in 1784 after a lively publishing career in Dublin, where he defended Irish Catholicism against the oppressive English government. Carey got his American start with the help of a loan from the Revolutionary War hero the Marquis de Lafayette. He was also helped by having known Benjamin Franklin, with whom he had worked in France. The *American Museum* began soon after another journal, the *Columbian Magazine,* and had fewer than twenty subscribers. It grew quickly and after a year had about 1,250 subscribers across the country, most of whom were concentrated around Philadelphia. The magazine's success helped consolidate that city's reputation as the leading literary city in the early nation. Unfortunately, its subscribers were more eager to read it than pay for it, and the *American Museum* closed after five years, defeated in part by the high rates of the Postal Act of 1792. Nonetheless, while it lasted the *American Museum* was a good example of eighteenth-century magazine publishing. It printed mostly selections from other newspapers and journals, many of them English, as well as some original material. It covered a wide range of topics, although the new nation's constitutional politics took priority. Carey printed several of *The Federalist* essays, as well as Anti-Federalist responses, during the debate over the new constitution in 1787 and 1788. After 1790 there was an increasing emphasis on literature, with more poetry and tales that were examples of the sentimental and gothic tastes of the period. This writing was more and more popular, and in turning to it the *American Museum* and other magazines demonstrated the need for such periodicals to remain close to the developing literary tastes of the growing body of American readers.

The Port Folio. Published in Philadelphia from 1801 to 1827, *The Port Folio* illustrates the ways American magazines developed in the early nineteenth century. Like many magazines begun after 1800, *The Port Folio* was a weekly until it became a monthly in 1812. More frequent publication allowed it to keep up with the rapidly changing conditions in early America, something still of concern to magazines today. Its publisher and editor was Joseph Dennie, writing under the pen name Oliver Oldschool, which reflected the magazine's conservative political stance. Dennie had earlier edited an ambitious New Hampshire magazine, the *Farmer's Museum,* with the help of Royall Tyler, a prominent playwright. Dennie had also made a name for himself as the author of a series of humorous "Lay Preacher" essays, which he continued after moving to Philadelphia and founding *The Port Folio.* The new venture lost money but was more successful than most American magazines. Within a few months it had a circulation of two thousand. Dennie in-

THE PROSPECT BEFORE US

James Thomson Callender, Republican journalist, in January 1800 published *The Prospect Before Us,* making the case for Thomas Jefferson and against John Adams for the presidency. Callender's pamphlet earned him an indictment for sedition and nine months in the Richmond, Virginia, jail.

The reign of Mr. Adams has been one continued tempest of malignant passions. As President, he has never opened his lips, or lifted his pen without threatening and scolding; the grand object of his administration has been to exasperate the rage of contending parties to calumniate and destroy every man who differs from his opinions. . . . Adams and Washington have since been shaping a series of these paper jobbers into judges and ambassadors, as their whole courage lies in want of shame; these poltroons, without risking a manly and intelligible defense of their own measures, raise an affected yelp against the corruption of the French Directory, as if any corruption would be more venal, more notorious, more execrated than their own. The object of Mr. Adams was to recommend a French war, professedly for the sake of supporting American commerce, but in reality for yoking us into an alliance with the British tyrant. . . .

You will then make your choice between paradise and perdition; you will choose between the man who has deserted and reversed all his principles, and that man whose own example strengthens all his laws, that man whose predictions, like those of Henry, had been converted into history. You will choose between that man whose life is unspotted by crime, and that man whose hands are reeking with the blood of the poor, friendless Connecticut sailor: I see the tear of indignation starting on your cheeks! You anticipate the name of John Adams. . . . Take your choice, then, between Adams, war and beggary, and Jefferson, peace and competency.

Source: James Morton Smith, *Freedom's Fetters: The Alien and Sedition Laws and American Civil Liberties* (Ithaca, N.Y.: Cornell University Press, 1956).

tended the new magazine to include a wide range of literary pieces, and it contained a steady stream of articles on politics, the theater, books, art, travel and fashion as well as news of foreign and American affairs and translations from classical and contemporary European authors. Like most early American magazines, politics was at its heart. Its opening statement announced that "one of the primary objects of this undertaking is to combat revolutionary politics," meaning Jeffersonianism. Dennie printed many attacks on the third president and his followers in both poetry and prose. He condemned their democratic tendencies, a reminder that many early Americans were unhappy with the egalitarian society that was beginning to form in the United States. In 1805 Dennie called democracy "a fiend more terrible than any that the imagination of the classical poets ever conjured up from the vast deep of their pagan hell."

Front page of John Fenno's paper, which became the official voice of the Federalists during George Washington's administration.

Literature. After Dennie died in 1812, *The Port Folio* became less political and more literary. It printed some fiction and a great deal of criticism. It was ahead of most American periodicals in praising the new English Romantic literature of the novelist Sir Walter Scott and the poets Samuel Taylor Coleridge and William Wordsworth. *The Port Folio*, like other American magazines, also worked tirelessly to encourage the development of a distinctly American literature. Early on, it was supported by the efforts of the Tuesday Club, a group of young professional men with literary aspirations who were happy to have a forum for their writing. *The Port Folio* also praised the poems of Philip Freneau in 1807, despite Freneau's Jeffersonian politics, as well as the work of the "Connecticut Wits" (a group of nationalistic poets based in Hartford, including Timothy Dwight, Joel Barlow, and others). It also encouraged the writing of Washington Irving, who in 1807 and 1808 was publishing short sketches and satires in his occasional New York magazine, *Salmagundi*. Irving and these poets were not the only writers who got their start in the magazines of the day. Charles Brockden Brown, one of the first important American novelists, was associated with various Philadelphia magazines, including *The Port Folio*. Magazines brought these writers to the attention of a larger group of readers than they could have reached alone and, however slowly, spread their work across the entire country. They created a desire for more polished literary work, which they also tried to supply to a growing audience. Success was limited before the development of the cylinder press in 1825 made the mass production of printed material much cheaper and faster. But the work of early editors such as Carey and Dennie was the foundation for the achievements of writers such as Washington Irving and prefigured the arrival of such long-lasting and profitable periodicals as the *Saturday Evening Post*.

Sources:

Michael T. Gilmore, "Magazines, Criticism, and Essays," in *The Cambridge History of American Literature, vol. I: 1590–1820*, edited by Sacvon Bercovitch (Cambridge: Cambridge University Press, 1994);

Commercial advertising in the 21 December 1799 *New-York Gazette* with black borders marking George Washington's death

Frank Luther Mott, *A History of American Magazines, vol. I: 1741–1850* (Cambridge, Mass.: Harvard University Press, 1939);

John Tebbel and Mary Ellen Zuckerman, *The Magazine in America, 1741–1990* (New York: Oxford University Press, 1991).

NEWSPAPERS

Periodical Publications. The eighteenth century, Samuel Miller wrote in 1803, "may be emphatically called *the age of periodical publications.*" In 1780 there had been thirty-nine American newspapers; by the end of the century the United States, with a population of about three million, supported a total of 242 newspapers, twenty-four of them dailies, 180 weeklies, and the rest published two or three times a week. By 1820 there were more than four hundred papers published every week and forty-two published daily. With the first daily newspaper being printed in America in 1783, the rise of daily papers over the next twenty years was an astonishing fact.

Coffeehouses. Generally costing six cents or more a copy, newspapers were too expensive for the average person to buy. Instead, a merchant seeking information from another port would go to a coffeehouse, where he could talk with other businessmen and read copies of newspapers bought by the proprietor. Some coffeehouse keepers also printed their own papers, gathering information from the papers brought in by sea captains. In London Edward Lloyd opened his coffeehouse in 1730, eventually developing his own newspaper, as well as an insurance firm, based on the knowledge of trade and international conditions gleaned from his customers. In Philadelphia William Bradford opened the London Coffeehouse in 1754 as an adjunct to his print shop and newspaper, the *Pennsylvania Journal.* Merchants paid to join the London Coffeehouse, as Bradford would be first to receive out-of-town papers. Even the colonial governor came regularly to Bradford's coffeehouse. In New York the Ferrari family managed the Merchants' Coffeehouse until 1772; in 1776 Cornelius Bradford took it over but was driven out during the Revolution. He returned in 1783 and made the Merchants' Coffeehouse a center for news, collecting information from ships in port and publishing "Mr. Bradford's Marine List" in New York's papers. Bradford kept a book of all ships in port and invited all visitors to the city to record their names and addresses in the coffeehouse. The Merchants' Coffeehouse became an informal gathering place for men of influence and a profitable place for men who hoped to become influential.

Gilbert's Coffeehouse. These coffeehouses all functioned as news sources, and in New York and Philadelphia they were influential in establishing the first daily newspapers. In Boston, however, the successful Gilbert's Coffeehouse made a daily newspaper unnecessary. Gilbert's maintained the kind of news books other coffeehouses did, and provided out-of-town papers for its patrons. But Gilbert's also had two men with a boat ready to row out to any incoming vessel for news, and in this way the coffeehouse provided its patrons, who paid ten dollars a year, with the latest information.

Benjamin Towne. The first daily paper in America, the *Pennsylvania Evening Post, and Daily Advertiser,* began as a competitor to the traditional sources of news. Benjamin Towne was one of Philadelphia's most colorful characters. In 1775 Towne had launched Philadelphia's first successful triweekly paper, the *Pennsylvania Evening Post.* Though Towne was backed by Joseph Galloway and Thomas Wharton, both Loyalists, he attacked his rival, James Humphreys, publisher of the *Pennsylvania Ledger,* for his Tory sympathies and successfully ran him out of the city. Towne sold his paper at the unusually low rate of two pennies an issue, or ten shillings a year. When the British occupied the city, Towne stayed; when the British left, Towne's paper continued to publish, in fact giving coverage to the British evacuation.

Confession. Towne had no politics other than selling papers, although he was charged with treason by the returning Patriots. In an attempt to clear his name, Towne asked John Witherspoon, president of Princeton College, to draw up an apology for him. Witherspoon concluded the confession, "Finally I do hereby recant, draw

Tontine Coffeehouse, located on the corner of Wall and Water Streets, New York City, 1797; painting by Francis Guy (New York Historical Society)

back, eat in, and swallow down, every word that I have ever spoken, written or printed to the prejudice of the United States of America, hoping it will not only satisfy the good people in general, but also all those scatter-brained fellows, who call one another out to shoot pistols in the air, while they tremble so much they cannot hit the mark." Towne refused to sign the confession. In November 1783 he would be indicted for treason, and in 1788 would be pronounced guilty by the Pennsylvania Executive Council.

A First. Towne tried to ingratiate himself with the citizens of Philadelphia through his paper. On 17 June 1783 Towne published the first issue of the *Pennsylvania Evening Post, and Daily Advertiser*, the first daily newspaper published in America. For the first year the paper never had more than two pages, but in its second year of publication Towne was printing four-page papers, though he did not publish every day. On 22 August 1783 Towne advertised for a news hawker to sell his papers on the street. One rival printer noted contemptuously that Towne himself could be seen walking the streets selling his papers. While most papers were sold by subscription, Towne's was the first sold on the streets. Towne also priced his paper well below the prevailing price: the *Pennsylvania Evening Post, and Daily Advertiser* sold for one half or one third as much as his rivals. Towne introduced the first paper intended for mass circulation. Unfortunately, he could not win favor with the state government in Pennsylvania, could not sell advertising, and by the end of 1784 was out of business.

Dunlap and Claypoole. In 1784 John Dunlap and D.C. Claypoole, both veterans of the Continental Army, launched the second daily paper in America and the first successful one. The *Pennylvania Packet and Daily Adver-*

tiser contained shipping news, international stories, and advertising. Dunlap and Claypoole did not aim for a mass circulation; their paper looked very much like the other coffeehouse papers of the day. Its readers were men of business, eager for prices on international markets, for news of political events that might influence trade, and for confirmation of their ships reaching distant ports. Lists of ships arriving in Philadelphia were supplemented with news from other vessels the docked ships had encountered on the high seas. In this manner the *Pennsylvania Packet and Daily Advertiser* kept Philadelphia merchants informed, indirectly, of their fleets across the globe. In 1791 the two partners split, Dunlap beginning *Dunlap's American Daily Advertiser* and Claypoole starting the *Mail, or Claypoole's Daily Advertiser*. This competition lasted until 1793 when the yellow fever epidemic forced both men to suspend publication and then to join forces once again on 9 December with *Dunlap and Claypoole's American Daily Advertiser*. While Dunlap and Claypoole focused on business news, they also published stenographic reports on the proceedings in Congress, and on 19 September 1796 they were the first to publish President George Washington's Farewell Address.

Gazette of the United States. The real spark for competition between newspapers came with the creation of the federal government and the establishment of political parties. The writers of the Constitution recognized the need to provide the American people with news, and as the new government was being formed, New York Federalist leaders in April 1789 hired John Fenno, a failed Boston merchant, to launch the *Gazette of the United States*. Fenno's paper presented the views of the Washington administration. While Claypoole and Dunlap reached a small audience of businessmen, Fenno's *Ga-*

zette of the United States was meant to reach a national audience, bringing all Americans into a political community with the federal government at its center. To encourage the creation of this national community, the Washington administration proposed to allow the newspaper free postage throughout the country. Congress would not agree to this; instead, in 1792 Congress allowed all papers to circulate in the mails at a minimal charge.

National Gazette. James Madison and Thomas Jefferson at first supported the Washington administration (Jefferson was secretary of state, and Madison wrote many of Washington's speeches.) But by 1791, after Alexander Hamilton had successfully proposed a national bank, both men thought the administration was creating too strong a national government and recognized the need for opposition to the "doctrines of monarchy, aristocracy, & the exclusion of the people" advocated by Hamilton and Fenno. Three days after Washington signed the bank bill into law, Jefferson wrote to Philip Freneau, a Princeton classmate of Madison's and editor of the *New York National Advertiser.* Jefferson offered Freneau a job as translator in the State Department, paying him $250 a year for part-time work, which would leave Freneau time to edit a new newspaper, the *National Gazette.*

Newspaper War of 1792. Freneau published the *National Gazette*'s first issue in October 1791. In March 1792 Freneau began a series of newspaper essays attacking Hamilton's vision for economic development. Hamilton's financial system "has given rise to scenes of speculation calculated to aggrandize the few and the wealthy, by oppressing the great body of the people, to transfer the best resources of the country forever into the hands of the speculators, and to fix a burthen on the people of the United States and their posterity, which time . . . will serve to strengthen and increase." The whole plan, Freneau wrote, had been "copied from British statute books" and was part of a general scheme for creating a British-style government, with Hamilton as prime minister controlling the Congress through corruption and patronage. Fenno was slow to respond, waiting until June to declare that Hamilton's opponents were "persons from other countries who having lately escaped from bondage, know not how to enjoy liberty." Freneau saw an opening here, since Hamilton himself was a person from another country, and many other Americans were not native born. This made the debate on the nation's economic future into a bitter personal campaign. "Hear! Hear!," Freneau's *National Gazette* proclaimed, "ye foreigners from every country. . . . Fenno swears . . . that you foreigners are a set of rebellious turbulent dogs, a pack of *run-away slaves,* who are come here to overturn the government!" Hamilton responded in an anonymous article, charging that Jefferson was behind Freneau's attack, and that the secretary of state used his official position to support the *National Gazette.* Hamilton went on to charge Jefferson

with various counts of official misconduct while he wrote a series of essays defending his own. Jefferson prided himself on never writing a line which he did not himself sign and stayed out of the debate, though he had plenty of supporters. Madison, Freneau, James Monroe, and others eagerly took up the cause.

Aftermath. Washington was thoroughly dispirited at this falling-out in his official family. He determined to retire but was persuaded not to do so by Madison, Jefferson, and Hamilton, who agreed on nothing but Washington's importance. In 1793 Washington was reelected and Jefferson retired. The *National Gazette* folded the same year, but the *General Advertiser and Aurora* (commonly known as the *Aurora*) carried on the campaign. In Philadelphia the dispute between Hamilton and the opposition continued with increasing vehemence during the 1790s as the Washington administration made a treaty with England and the opposition created "Democratic-Republican Societies" to discuss political issues. These Democratic-Republican clubs, like the businessmen's coffeehouses, functioned as gathering places for leaders and interested citizens to exchange news, though their favored topic was politics, not commerce. Newspaper circulation increased, and though Washington and Hamilton despaired of the country's fate in this bitterly divisive time, the political press actually helped forge a stronger national identity. The *Gazette of the United States, National Gazette,* and *Aurora* circulated throughout the union, and in all parts of the United States men and women identified themselves with the policies of either Hamilton or Jefferson rather than with local personalities and issues.

Sedition Act. When John Adams became president in 1797, the United States and France were practically at war. To help foster a sense of national unity, the Adams administration and the Federalist Congress in 1798 passed a series of laws aimed at enemies of the United States. One of these laws, the Sedition Act, made it a federal offense to write, publish, or utter anything which might excite the American people's hatred of their government. This meant that any criticism of the Adams administration would be against the law. Secretary of State Timothy Pickering put one of his clerks to work studying all newspapers to find evidence of sedition. By this time the opposition papers recognized the need for concerted action, and so Pickering determined to strike at the source by moving against the most influential papers first. By 1800 seventeen individuals would be charged with sedition, including Benjamin Franklin Bache of the *Aurora;* James Thomson Callender; Charles Holt, editor of the *New London Bee;* and Congressman Matthew Lyon. The prosecutions backfired; though the papers did have a break in service, by being officially silenced their editors achieved a kind of martyrdom, and the opposition found other ways to present its case. In 1801 the Sedition Act expired, and the Adams administration died with it. "What a lesson to America & the

LETTERS AND NEWSPAPERS TRANSMITTED BY THE POSTAL SYSTEM

Year	Letters (Millions)	Letters per capita	Newspapers (millions)	Newspapers per capita
1790	0.3	0.1	0.5	0.2
1800	2.0	0.5	1.9	0.4
1810	3.9	0.7	n. a.	n. a.
1820	8.9	1.1	6.0	0.7
1830	13.8	1.3	16.0	1.5
1840	40.9	2.9	39.0	2.7

Source: Richard R. John, *Spreading the News: The American Postal System from Franklin to Morse* (Cambridge, Mass.: Harvard University Press, 1995), p. 4.

world," James Madison wrote of this demonstration of the power of public opinion "when there is no army to be turned against it."

The Washington Scene. In 1800 the federal government moved to Washington, D.C. In Philadelphia and New York there had already been newspapers when the U.S. government arrived; the political papers had become additional voices in the local media. But Washington had no paper until Samuel Harrison Smith, a Jeffersonian and editor of the *Universal Gazette,* decided to move to the newly formed city. For Smith much depended on the election of 1800; as a committed Republican, he had plenty to gain if Thomas Jefferson became president. On the other hand, if the Federalists maintained control of Congress or the executive branch, Smith could not expect success. When he approached Federalist Speaker of the House Theodore Sedgwick in December 1800 for permission to put a stenographer's desk on the House floor where he would be able to hear debates, Sedgwick refused. In Philadelphia reporters had been admitted to the House floor, Sedgwick and the Federalists said, because their meeting place had room. In the new Capitol building there was not room for reporters. When Smith argued the point, he found himself threatened with censure by the Federalists in Congress. Jefferson's election changed this, and Smith was able to secure the printing contract for both the House of Representatives and the executive branch. "Can you believe it?," Smith wrote to his sister. "I scarcely can. . . . A republican, printing the President's speech, etc.—Can it be possible? Truly these are strange times." Smith's *National Intelligencer and Washington Advertiser* acted as the official paper of the Jefferson administration, though, unlike the "official" party papers of the 1790s, it did not engage in the personal attacks and heated rhetorical passions of the day.

New-York Evening Post. With Smith and the Republican press ensconced in Washington, the Federalists also abandoned Philadelphia as their capital. The Federalists had been decisively beaten in the election of 1800. The presidential election had been close, with Jefferson narrowly edging out John Adams. But the congressional races were an overwhelming Republican victory. The Sixth Congress, elected in 1798, had sixty-four Federalists and forty-two Republicans; the Seventh Congress had sixty-nine Republicans and thirty-six Federalists. Many Federalists blamed their defeat on the maneuvering of Alexander Hamilton, who had continued to guide the party after his return to private life. Hamilton had written to influential Federalists attacking John Adams's character; when the letter fell into the hands of Aaron Burr, it was republished throughout the country. Hamilton, aware of his falling political stock and concerned that the principles of Federalism might die out, decided that the Federalists needed a new vigorous voice. In the fall of 1801 he and a group of New York's leading businessmen quickly raised thousands of dollars to launch a new paper. *The New-York Evening Post,* under the editorship of William Coleman but with significant editorial assistance from Hamilton, began publication on 16 November 1801 and continues to be published today.

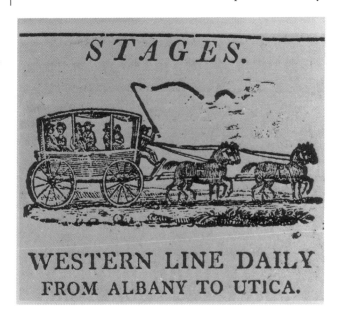

Stage line subsidized by the Post Office to carry mail; advertisement from the 17 December 1810 *Albany Gazette*

THE EXPANSION OF THE POSTAL NETWORK

Year	Post offices	Population per post office	Settled area per post office
		(thousands of square miles)	
1790	75	43,084	3492.7
1800	903	4,876	339.3
1810	2,300	2,623	180.2
1820	4,500	1,796	116.3
1830	8,450	1,289	75.5
1840	13,468	1,087	61.4

Source: Richard R. John, *Spreading the News: The American Postal System from Franklin to Morse* (Cambridge, Mass.: Harvard University Press, 1995), p. 51.

The newspaper's mission was "to diffuse among the people the correct information on all interesting subjects, to inculcate just principles in religion, morals, and politics; and to cultivate a taste for sound literature." Its real mission at its founding was to criticize the Jefferson administration, which it did with robust glee. When Jefferson proposed to cut government spending by reducing the navy to a flotilla of small gunboats which he thought better for defending rivers and harbors, the *New-York Evening Post* criticized and ridiculed him. An 1805 hurricane lifted Gunboat No. 1 from its berth in Savannah, Georgia, and tossed it into a field, where, the paper said, it was "defending the agricultural interest." The newspaper reprinted a Boston toast, "If our gunboats are of no use upon the water, may they at least be the best upon the earth," and suggested that Gunboat No. 1 was emulating Jefferson, who as governor of Virginia had fled from an advancing British force, taking refuge on a nearby mountain. Though the *New-York Evening Post* had no use for Jefferson or Madison, it also criticized the New England Federalists who proposed breaking the union in 1814. Unlike New York's other papers, which were commercial sheets, the *New-York Evening Post* would present both political and commercial news, reflecting the political ideas of its founders. In this way it formed the link connecting the commercial papers of the earlier years, the partisan political press of the 1790s, and the newspapers of today.

Sources:

William E. Ames, *A History of the* National Intelligencer (Chapel Hill: University of North Carolina Press, 1972);

Stanley Elkins and Eric McKitrick, *The Age of Federalism* (New York & Oxford: Oxford University Press, 1993);

Allan Nevins, *The* Evening Post: *A Century of Journalism* (New York: Boni & Liveright, 1922);

James Morton Smith, *Freedom's Fetters: The Alien and Sedition Laws and American Civil Liberties* (Ithaca, N.Y.: Cornell University Press, 1956).

THE POST OFFICE

Statute. The Post Office Act of 1792 was an important step in creating a national political community. While Americans had enjoyed a postal service under the British government, the U.S. Post Office, created in 1792, greatly expanded the federal government's role in communications. In 1790 there was one post office for every 43,084 Americans. Ten years later one post office served every 4,876 Americans, and by 1820 each post office served fewer than two thousand citizens. This was four times the rate of service enjoyed in England, and nearly twenty times the service of France. The Post Office would not only carry the mail: it also carried newspapers and subsidized stagecoach lines throughout the country, bringing the distant parts of the United States into closer contact.

Exchanging Newspapers. Printers traditionally shared copies of their newspapers with each other. In this way news could be transmitted from one part of the country to another, and printers could be kept informed of new developments in their trade. The practice of exchanging papers allowed news to circulate, provided printers with ample material to fill their papers, and spared printers the expense of subscribing to one another's papers. In 1785 Postmaster General Ebenezer Hazard allowed stages handling the mail to carry these newspapers in the official portmanteau. However, where the mail was carried on horseback, these exchange newspapers would have to fit in the rider's saddlebags. The rider could leave the newspapers behind if his bags were too heavy. Though Philadelphia printers pressed Hazard, he feared that requiring all post riders to carry newspapers would burden them with too much weight, and since the Post Office had been created, he said, "for the purpose of facilitating commercial correspondence," it had "no connection with the press." Hazard did not regard newspapers as suitable for mailing.

A road in western Pennsylvania used by stage lines. The Post Office Act of 1792
designated such roads as official mail routes.

Selective Circulation. After the new government took shape under the Constitution, Congress considered ways of keeping all parts of the country informed of its actions. One way was for members of Congress to send newspapers free of charge to their constituents. The practice of franking correspondence continues to this day. Another proposal was to allow one newspaper, John Fenno's *Gazette of the United States,* into the mail at a minimal cost. President George Washington saw the Post Office's goal as spreading the government's point of view to its citizenry; Fenno's goal was to "diffuse information to all parts of the Union from the seat of government, as from a common center." Fenno was a vigorous supporter of the Washington administration. The proposal to allow the *Gazette of the United States* to circulate roused opposition from some of the administration's opponents, notably Aedaneus Burke of South Carolina and Elbridge Gerry of Massachusetts. They saw the beginnings of a "court press and court gazette" in this policy. James Madison joined Burke and Gerry in seeing a different purpose behind the Post Office: not to encourage loyalty to one administration, but to mobilize citizens as guardians of their own liberty. They would have ready access to newspapers and so be informed of what their government was doing.

New Plan. In 1791 Fenno and his political adversary, Benjamin Franklin Bache, both supported a new proposal to allow all newspapers in the country to circulate for free. Bache called for free admission of newspapers into the mail to allow citizens throughout the country to know what their elected representatives were doing. He held that newspapers were essential to this knowledge and should be freely accessible to all Americans. Congress decided to charge all newspapers the same modest fee (one cent for one hundred miles, one and one-half cents for more than one hundred miles) for circulation. This was one-quarter of what Fenno had paid private carriers to deliver his paper and guaranteed a wide circulation to his paper and others. By 1800, 1.9 million newspapers, about 10 percent of all papers printed in the United States, were being mailed each year. In addition, Congress allowed printers to exchange copies of their papers for free, and by the 1820s these exchange papers made up between one-third and one-half of the mail's weight. By 1840 each publisher in the country received on average forty-three hundred different papers each year.

Disparities. Seventy percent of the mail's weight was newspapers, but because of the low rates mandated by Congress, they only contributed 3 percent of the Post Office's revenues. A single-page letter cost six cents to send thirty miles and twenty-five cents if it went farther than 450 miles. Thus, letter writers subsidized the newspapers. One critic estimated that if newspapers were charged the same rate as letters, their cost would increase 700 percent. Even more hard hit were magazines, which had begun to flourish in the 1780s. While the law required the Post Office to deliver newspapers and guarantee them a low rate, it did not require the delivery of magazines. Charged a disproportionate rate, most magazines went out of business. In 1794 Congress amended the Post Office Act to allow magazines into the mail, but it did not require individual post offices to deliver them, nor did it reduce the rate magazines would be charged. The result was that magazines remained more expensive to mail, and many smart publishers simply changed their magazines into newspapers.

Timothy Pickering, secretary of state during the Sedition Act; painting by Gilbert Stuart (from Hayward and Blanche Cirker, eds., *Dictionary of American Portraits*, 1967)

National Network. The Post Office Act encouraged circulation of newspapers. Americans at distant points were eager to learn of developments in Philadelphia, Washington, D.C., or New York. For local news they could turn to neighbors. Newspapers in this period did not cover local news, and the Post Office Act greatly expanded the circulation of national papers. The Post Office Act encouraged the trend toward national news networks. At various times postmasters and others tried to encourage the circulation of rural papers as opposed to the national papers. These attempts were unsuccessful, and not until later in the century, when newspapers began focusing more closely on local news which would not be covered in the national papers, did circulation of local papers begin to keep pace with the national press.

Sources:

Wayne E. Fuller, *The American Mail: Enlarger of the Common Life* (Chicago: University of Chicago Press, 1972);

Richard R. John, *Spreading the News: The American Postal System from Franklin to Morse* (Cambridge, Mass.: Harvard University Press, 1995);

James Tagg, *Benjamin Franklin Bache and the Philadelphia* Aurora (Philadelphia: University of Pennsylvania Press, 1991).

POST ROADS

Post Office Act. The Constitution gave Congress the power to establish not only post offices but post roads as well. With the Post Office Act of 1792 Congress created the U.S. Post Office, and it did so on three fundamental principles. First, the Post Office would be self-supporting. It would not rely on government subsidies, but would have to generate sufficient income to cover its expenses. Second, if the Post Office generated a surplus, it would invest it in improved service: in other words, it would not keep its profits. Finally, Congress, not the postmaster general, would decide where to put post roads.

English Model. In England the postmaster general decided where to put post roads. Some members of Congress saw no reason to change the customary practice, while others did not think it would be constitutional to delegate this power to an executive officer. In addition to being unconstitutional, many thought it would be unwise. It might work in England, some congressmen said, but English examples would not work in America. Giving this power to the postmaster general might lead to monarchy, as the executive branch could control the flow of information. Congress decided not to delegate its power, but to keep control of locating post roads.

Purpose. The debate over post roads had profound political importance. If the Post Office's task was to facilitate communications for the government, and to deliver federal revenue from distant places (since virtually all federal income came from tariffs, it was being collected in port cities such as Charleston, Salem, and Boston, and then had to be delivered to the capital), it made sense to have post roads linking coastal cities. But in Congress representatives from the interior areas objected to this route. John Steele, a congressman from North Carolina, insisted that the Post Office serve a majority of the people, not just the seaboard merchants. Steele, who later served as comptroller of the U.S. Treasury, recognized the importance of the post office to deliver revenue. But more important was its function in serving the general public.

Routes. By keeping control over the post roads, Congress ensured that the Post Office would respond to the American people rather than serving the government or the business community alone. By 1800 Congress had designated 20,000 miles of post roads. The Post Office was delivering mail as far west as Natchez, Mississippi, and Vincennes, Indiana. By the time of the War of 1812, the United States had 39,378 miles of post roads and more than twenty-six hundred post offices. By 1820 Congress had designated 72,492 miles of postal routes linking forty-five hundred post offices.

Sources:

Wayne E. Fuller, *The American Mail: Enlarger of the Common Life* (Chicago: University of Chicago Press, 1972);

Richard R. John, *Spreading the News: The American Postal System from Franklin to Morse* (Cambridge, Mass.: Harvard University Press, 1995).

SEDITION ACT

French Threat. When John Adams became president in 1797, the French were angry that although the United

Benjamin Franklin Bache, editor of the Republican *Philadelphia Aurora,* explained his opposition to the Sedition Act of 1798:

The people as well as the government have certain rights prescribed by the constitution, and it is as much the sworn duty of the administration to protect the one as the other. If the government is instituted for the benefit of the people, no law ought to be made to their injury. One of the first rights of a freeman is to speak or publish his sentiments; if any government founded upon the will of the people passes any ordinance to abridge this right, it is as much a crime as if the people were, in an unconstitutional way, to curtail the government of one of the powers delegated to it. Were the people to do this, would it not be called anarchy? What name shall then be given to an unconstitutional exercise of power over the people? In Turkey the voice of the government is the law, and there it is called despotism. Here the voice of the government is likewise the law and here it is called liberty.

Source: James Tagg, *Benjamin Franklin Bache and the Philadelphia* Aurora (Philadelphia: University of Pennsylvania Press, 1991), pp. 375–376.

States was officially neutral in the war between France and England, the United States had made a treaty with England in 1795. France began seizing American ships which were trading with England and also tried to arouse American public opinion to favor the French against the English. Many Americans sympathized with the French Revolution, its ideals of liberty, equality, and fraternity and its attack on monarchy and aristocracy. Many Americans also distrusted England, and so the French had significant support in the United States.

Law of the Land. The Adams administration received dispatches from France in 1798 in which a French agent boasted that France could turn the American people against their own government. This horrified the administration, which came to believe newspapers attacking the Federalists did so out of loyalty to France. Abigail Adams said that Philadelphia *Aurora* editor Benjamin Franklin Bache "has the malice & falsehood of Satan," which an "abused and insulted publick cannot tolerate . . . much longer. . . ." An ally of Secretary of State Timothy Pickering warned that "Seditions, conspiracies, seductions, and all the Arts which the French use to fraternize and overturn nations, must be guarded against by strong and specific Acts of Congress." Among the specific acts to prevent sedition, conspiracy, and seduction the Federalist Congress passed the Naturalization Act (18 June 1798), requiring a residence period of fourteen years, rather than five, before an alien could become a citizen; the Alien Friends Act (25 June), allowing the president to deport any alien he thought dangerous to the "peace and safety" of the United States; the Alien

Enemies Act (6 July), authorizing the president to deport aliens, dangerous or not, who came from countries at war with the United States; and the Sedition Act (14 July), prohibiting any "false, scandalous, and malicious" statements that were intended to defame the president, Congress, and the government or bring them into contempt or disrepute. Violators of the Sedition Act could be fined up to $2,000 and jailed for up to two years.

War Fever. These acts passed during a fever of war preparations. As Sen. Stevens T. Mason of Virginia wrote to Vice President Thomas Jefferson, "The drums Trumpets and other martial music which surrounded us, drowned the voices of those who spoke on the Question. The military parade so attracted the attention of the majority that much the greater part of them stood with their bodies out of the windows and could not be kept to order." The Federalists in Congress were eager to shut down the Republican press and to do so on the grounds of national security. Both President Adams and envoi John Marshall, recently returned from an unsuccessful mission to France, thought the sedition law unwise, but an enthusiastic Federalist Congress pushed the measure through. As Boston's *Columbian Centinel* noted, the law made it "patriotism to write in favor of our government," but "sedition to write against it."

Free Press. While the Sedition Act was being debated, Philadelphia's *Aurora* printed the text of the act, along with the text of the Constitution's First Amendment: "Congress shall make no law . . . abridging the freedom of speech, or of the press, or the right of the people peaceably to assemble and petition their government for a redress of grievances." Though it seemed to Republican editors that the Sedition Act did abridge their freedom, the Federalists argued that "the freedom of the press" was a specific legal term, coming from British law, meaning only that the press was free from any restraint on its right to publish. This freedom from prior restraint, for the Federalists, was the defining feature of a free press. Also, the Federalists argued, because the sedition law allowed truth as a defense, it actually was an improvement over English concepts of seditious libel.

Pressure to Act. President Adams did not enforce the Alien laws; many aliens left the country willingly before the laws took effect. But Republican editors were indicted even before the Sedition Act became law. Benjamin Franklin Bache, who told Americans to "hold their tongues and make tooth picks of their pens" was charged with sedition under common law and accused of being a French agent. Federalist newspapers called for vigorous enforcement of the Sedition Act, warning that the country was in grave danger from the "long knives of Kentucky, the whiskey boys of the woods of Pennsylvania, [and] the United Irishmen of Virginia" who were all "for insurrection and confusion." The chief enemy to this insurrection and confusion was Timothy Pickering, who assigned a State Department clerk the task of searching

Engraving satirizing moralists who opposed the transportation of mail
on Sundays

"the *obnoxious papers* for suitable matter to cut them up at law."

Enforcing the Law. Pickering singled out the most influential Republican papers. The smaller papers generally filled their political columns with material from the larger circulating newspapers, the *Philadelphia Aurora*, the *Boston Independent Chronicle*, the *Richmond Examiner*, and the *New York Argus*. The editors of all these papers were indicted for sedition. If the administration could silence these papers, smaller papers would not have access to their writers; or perhaps the smaller papers would be intimidated into silence. In all, seventeen individuals were charged with sedition, fourteen under the Sedition Act and three others, including Bache, under common law. Bache died of yellow fever before his trial, but the others were convicted and given sentences ranging up to eighteen months in prison and fines of more than $1,000. The *Vermont Gazette* was the only paper that continued to publish while its editor was in jail; all the others had some break in service.

Matthew Lyon. Congressman Matthew Lyon of Vermont, an immigrant from Ireland and one of the few Republicans in New England, predicted that the Federalists would use the Sedition Act against members of Congress. Lyon was already a marked man: he and Connecticut congressman Roger Griswold had gotten into a fistfight on the House floor after Griswold accused Lyon of military cowardice and Lyon responded by spitting in Griswold's face. A Boston correspondent was "grieved that the saliva of an Irishman should be left upon the face of an American & He, a New Englandman." Accusing Lyon of being both a spitting, brawling ruffian and an agent of the United Irishmen, Federalists moved unsuccessfully to expel him from Congress.

Trial. Lyon's opponent for reelection was also a newspaper publisher, Stanley Williams. When Williams's paper, the *Rutland Herald*, refused to print a letter from Lyon, Lyon and his son James, a printer, launched their

own paper, the *Scourge of Aristocracy and Repository of Important Political Truths*, with its first issue appearing on 1 October 1798. Four days later a federal grand jury in Vermont indicted Lyon for sedition. Associate Justice William Paterson of the U.S. Supreme Court presided over Lyon's trial, with the accused acting as his own attorney. In his defense Lyon offered three points: first, the Sedition Act was unconstitutional; second, Lyon had written his "seditious" essay before the law had been passed. Lyon did not focus on either of these points in his testimony, instead focusing on his final point, that his charges were not libelous because they were true. But Lyon could not prove to the court's satisfaction that the Adams administration was bent on aggrandizing power or on ridiculous pomp and parade. On 8 October the jury deliberated for an hour before finding Lyon guilty.

Two Verdicts? Judge Paterson was determined to make an example of Lyon, who, as a member of Congress, should have been "well acquainted with the mischiefs which flow from an unlicensed abuse of government." The judge fined him $1,000 and sent him to the Vergennes, Vermont, jail for four months. "May the good God grant that this may be the case of every Jacobin," an Albany newspaper said. While Lyon was in jail he was reelected to Congress, receiving 3,482 votes to Stanley Williams's 1,554. While a judge and twelve jurors had found him guilty, Lyon said, thirty-five hundred freemen ruled him innocent. However, with several other candidates in the race, Lyon came one vote short of a majority, so he faced a runoff election in December. In the runoff Lyon, still in jail, received 4,476 votes to Williams's 2,444, a clear victory and a warning to the Adams administration that the Sedition Act was unpopular.

New London Bee. Secretary of State Pickering regarded the threat of sedition as more grave than the threat of losing an election. Prosecutions continued in 1799. In Connecticut the publishers of the *Connecticut Courant* provided the district attorney with copies of their rival's *New London Bee,* which had criticized, among others, former secretary of the Treasury Alexander Hamilton. Hamilton had been made second-in-command of the provisional army raised to repel a French invasion; the letter to the *Bee* asked, "Are our young officers and soldiers to learn virtue from general Hamilton? Or like their general are they to be found in the bed of adultery?" Charles Holt, editor of the *Bee,* published the letter and was charged with sedition, both for trying to discourage enlistments in the army and for being "a wicked, malicious, seditious, and ill-disposed person." On 12 April 1800 Holt was found guilty, sentenced to four months in jail, and fined $200.

A Little Joke. The Sedition Act made it illegal to criticize the Adams administration in any way. President Adams passed through Newark, New Jersey, on 27 July 1798. The citizens of Newark turned out for the occasion; as president and Mrs. Adams entered Broad Street that morning, the citizens fired a cannon, church bells rang, and a group of young men chanted "Behold the Chief who now commands" and gave three cheers. As Adams and his entourage moved away, the young men fired a sixteen-gun salute. Luther Baldwin was walking past a tavern as the guns were firing. A tavern customer said to him, "There goes the President and they are firing at his a—." Baldwin, having had a bit to drink himself, said "he did not care if 'they fired thro' his a—.' " The tavern keeper said, "That is seditious," and a crowd gathered. Some local Federalists, upset that Adams had not stopped in Newark, agreed, and set out to punish Luther Baldwin for sedition. He and two others were indicted, and all of them wound up pleading guilty. Their joke led to a trial in October 1799 and cost Baldwin $150, his accomplices $50 and $40. The trial showed how far the Sedition Act could go. One Republican paper noted that in England a subject may safely speak of the king's head, but in America one could not speak "of the president's a—," and another Republican paper said, "Thank God, we have shown the cursed democrats that we will let none of them speak disrespectfully of any part of that dear man."

Virginia and Kentucky Resolutions. With no public way to criticize the administration or to challenge the Sedition Act, its opponents turned to the state legislatures. In Virginia James Madison drafted a series of resolutions that declared the Sedition Act to be unconstitutional, as the First Amendment said clearly that "Congress shall make no law . . . abridging the freedom of the press." Vice President Jefferson secretly drafted a similar series of resolutions adopted by the Kentucky legislature. Virginia called on other states to join the protest; Kentucky declared that a state could "nullify" an unconstitutional law. The other states unanimously rejected Virginia's and Kentucky's pleas. Madison in 1800 wrote a long report justifying the Virginia and Kentucky resolutions and arguing that a free press could not be limited by Congress.

Revolution of 1800. Though other states would not join in opposing the laws, and though the laws did effectively shut down the Republican press, the Republicans managed to mobilize for the election of 1800. A bitterly divided Federalist party, torn between Alexander Hamilton and John Adams, made the Jeffersonians seem a safe and responsible alternative. In the sedition trials the Republicans had appeared as defenders of free exchange of ideas. In October 1800 Hamilton circulated a pamphlet to other Federalists saying that John Adams was unfit to be president. Aaron Burr, the Republican vice-presidential candidate, found a copy and had it published in the New York papers. Nonetheless, Hamilton was not charged with sedition. By May 1800 Adams had fired Pickering and was no longer urging prosecutions. Adams had also decided to seek peace with France, which his administration secured in October 1800. Adams lost the election of 1800, and in March 1801 Thomas Jefferson became president. Jefferson announced a new way to deal with dissenters. "If there should be any among us who would wish to dissolve this union," he said in his inaugural address, "or change its republican form, let them stand undisturbed as monuments of the safety with which error of opinion may be tolerated where reason is left free to combat it." The Sedition Act expired the same day, and President Jefferson pardoned all who had been convicted under it. "The reign of the witches," Jefferson said, was over.

Sources:

Stanley Elkins and Eric McKitrick, *The Age of Federalism* (New York: Oxford University Press, 1993);

James Morton Smith, *Freedom's Fetters: The Alien and Sedition Laws and American Civil Liberties* (Ithaca: Cornell University Press, 1956).

SUNDAY MAIL

Unlikely Controversy. In 1808 Hugh Wylie faced an unexpected dilemma. Wylie was the postmaster of the small town of Washington, Pennsylvania. He was also an elder of his Presbyterian church, one of the leading lay people of the congregation. As an elder Wylie had to obey the biblical rules about observing the Sabbath, which forbade doing any unnecessary labor. But as postmaster, some Sunday work was required. Mail had to be sorted the day it arrived, and mail arrived in Wylie's office every day of the week, including Sunday, on the coaches that traveled from the East Coast, through Washington, to the developing western states and territories. Wylie had also taken to opening the post office on Sunday so people could pick up their mail since he was working there anyway and they were in town to attend church. One of Wylie's neighbors complained about this desecration of the Sabbath to Postmaster General Gideon Granger. The postmaster refused to change the Post Office rules, citing among other reasons the need to keep communication easy and quick all through the country, given that war with England seemed imminent. Wylie was caught between his sincerely held religious obligations and his job; he was also caught between neighbors who divided over his behavior, as the entire nation soon did as well.

Church and Congress. The controversy grew as Wylie's church censured his behavior. In October 1809 the local Presbyterian governing body, the synod of nearby Pittsburgh, barred him from receiving communion. This was a serious punishment for a man of his beliefs and position, but when he appealed to the church's national General Assembly, he was expelled. In April 1810 the affair took on a national dimension, as Congress passed a new Post Office Act. For the first time all postmasters were required by federal law to open their offices and deliver mail every day it was received, even Sunday. This national standard provoked protests from around the country.

Sabbatarian Opposition. A broad coalition opposed the delivery of mail on Sunday. It included orthodox Congregationalists such as Lyman Beecher of Connecticut and liberal Unitarians such as William Ellery Channing of Massachusetts. The Presbyterians led the way in organizing a petition drive against the Sunday mail, and by the time the controversy ended in 1817, three hundred petitions signed by a total of more than thirteen thousand people had reached Congress. People opposed the Sunday mail for many reasons. The Bible's command to honor the Lord's Day was reason enough for many opponents, called Sabbatarians for their desire to observe the Sabbath properly. Others were against the War of 1812, and opposing the Sunday mail, which was justified in part by the need to secure communication to aid the war effort, was another way to express that feeling. Still others were ambivalent about commercial development. To them Sunday mail represented an intrusion of greed and selfishness into the sanctity of the day of rest. Some saw it as an example of how the rich oppressed the poor, since it was coachmen and other workers who had to give up their day of rest while merchants and professionals benefitted most from daily mail.

Religion and the State. Probably the most important issue the Sunday mail raised was the relation of government to religion. The Presbyterians and other opponents thought the government had a duty to uphold fundamental religious values, and they stated this position forcefully in the petition they sent to Congress in 1812. Requiring people to work on the Sabbath meant forcing them to sin, and even allowing them to work meant undermining the social order, which rested on the rules of the Bible. Many Americans sincerely believed that this was inviting punishment from God in the form of social disorder and decay and urged reform to avoid this fate. A few years later this same rationale would support antislavery arguments, as abolitionists (many of whom had opposed Sunday mail) began to say that the government had a duty to end slavery in order to preserve America's blessings from God.

Supporters. Despite the strong opposition, mail continued to be delivered on Sunday. The pressures of wartime made Congress fear a change, and business needs were also important considerations. The postmaster general also defended the practice effectively on grounds of efficiency and cost. After the end of the war the issue died away, only to resurface in 1826. Then an even more vehement popular protest started as part of a widespread religious reform movement that swept the United States during the Jacksonian era. This movement did curtail Sunday mail, but only with the help of business. After 1840 railroads carried mail, and they found it unprofitable to run mail trains on Sunday, when there was little other demand for transportation. Their opposition, together with the development of the telegraph to deliver the most urgent news, helped the Sabbatarians prevail. Even without carrying the day alone, the Sabbatarian reform movement demonstrated how many Americans were convinced that the federal government had an important role in ensuring the moral order of the nation. The Post Office may seem an odd place to learn that lesson, but it was the only significant federal bureaucracy of the time and the only contact most people had with central government. It should not surprise us that it was the touchstone for much anxiety about questions of order and power in an age of rapid social change.

Sources:

Richard R. John, *Spreading the News: The American Postal System from Franklin to Morse* (Cambridge, Mass.: Harvard University Press, 1995);

John G. West Jr., *The Politics of Revelation and Reason: Religion and Civic Life in the New Nation* (Lawrence: University Press of Kansas, 1996).

HEADLINE MAKERS

JAMES THOMSON CALLENDER

1758-1803
JOURNALIST

Flight. Born in Scotland around 1758, James Thomson Callender wrote a pamphlet called *Political Progress of Britain* (1792), which led to his indictment for sedition in 1793. He fled first to Ireland and then to the United States, where he found part-time work with both Mathew Carey, writing a section for a new edition of William Guthrie's *A New System of Modern Geography* (1770) and for John Dunlap's *American Daily Advertiser.* In December Callender was hired by the *Federal Gazette* to record congressional speeches.

Congressional Reporter. Congress did not have an official stenographer; instead, newspaper reporters would try to take down what was said in shorthand, leading to many accidental and intentional inaccuracies. Callender was a fast writer with a passion for accuracy and precision. He delighted in recording the impromptu comments of some members of Congress, sharing with newspaper readers the sometimes incomprehensible ramblings of their representatives. His *Political Register* (1795), a compilation of his recordings of the debates of 1794 and 1795, stirred congressional wrath from both Federalists and Republicans. In January 1796 Congress considered replacing the newspaper reporters with an official stenographer. Though Congress did not do this at the time, Callender's employer fired him.

Hired Writer. With a wife and four children to support, Callender began writing for pay. Philadelphia's tobacco manufacturers hired him to write *A Short History of the Nature and Consequence of Excise Laws* (1795), an attack on trade taxes and on the Federalist economic program. He followed this with a pamphlet in support of a Pennsylvania congressional candidate. Callender became more involved in Republican politics, especially in opposition to Jay's Treaty with England. But Callender went far beyond other Republicans in denouncing George Washington, writing, "If ever a nation was debauched by a man, the American nation has been debauched by

WASHINGTON." In addition he warned of Washington's "foulest designs against the liberties of the people."

Hamilton and Reynolds. Callender was not afraid to castigate America's most powerful and beloved men. In 1797 he published his *History of the United States for 1796,* which unveiled former secretary of the Treasury Alexander Hamilton's scandalous relationship with James Reynolds, a speculator in military accounts. In 1790 and 1791 the government tried to pay its soldiers; Reynolds, acting as agent for a New York investor, had obtained a list of soldiers from an accomplice in the treasury and had bought their pay certificates at a reduced price; he then hoped to collect their full share. Hamilton was probably not involved in this speculation. When Congress began investigating the story in 1792, during the height of a partisan campaign with Hamilton at its center, the secretary of the treasury had put the congressional committee (which included James Monroe) off the trail of possible corruption by telling them of his adulterous relationship with Maria Reynolds, that her husband had discovered the affair and was now using his knowledge to blackmail Hamilton. The committee, interested only in public wrongdoing, dropped their investigation. But Callender in 1796 heard rumors that Hamilton might be aspiring to the presidency. He also knew that Hamilton and other Federalists were charging Monroe with incompetence on his recent mission to France. Callender responded with his *History of the United States for 1796,* charging Hamilton with using a personal scandal to bring shame upon his own wife and family in order to cover up the more significant political scandal. Callender in fact charged that Hamilton had invented his affair with Maria Reynolds to conceal his guilt in the worse offense of speculation. Monroe believed that Hamilton had engaged in the affair with Maria Reynolds while also engaged in illicit speculation with James Reynolds. The truth is lost to history. Though Alexander Hamilton continued to be an influential Federalist, his reputation was badly tarnished.

Failure. Callender's success as a polemicist did not help to feed his family. His patron, John Swanwick, died of yellow fever, and the epidemic severely threatened the city's press. He published the *American Annual Register*

(1797) and several compilations of his newspaper essays; none was a financial success. His wife died, and Callender in 1798 was left to support his four children in an increasingly hostile city. He filled in for Benjamin Franklin Bache at the *Aurora,* and his vituperative editorials in March 1798 helped lead to the Sedition Act, after which Callender left his children with a patron and fled to Virginia.

The Prospect Before Us. Callender had been supported by some small loans from Thomas Jefferson, who recognized Callender's value as a polemicist but needed to keep a discreet distance from the controversial journalist. As the election year of 1800 approached, with the Sedition Act shutting down the Republican press, Callender promised Jefferson a "Tornado as no Govt ever got before, for there is in American history a specie of ignorance, absurdity, and imbecility unknown to the annals of any other nation." In 1800 he wrote *The Prospect Before Us* in an attempt to show the corruption and incompetence of the Adams administration.

Sedition and Jail. On 24 May 1800 Callender was indicted for sedition and in June tried in Richmond before Justice Samuel Chase. Callender was represented by Virginia attorney general Philip Nicholas, by Monroe's son-in-law George Hay, and by future U.S. attorney general William Wirt. Even though Callender was convicted, his lawyers succeeded in making the Sedition Act the central issue and in presenting their client as a persecuted victim of oppression. Justice Chase, a bitter foe of democracy, gave Callender a relatively light sentence: a $480 fine and nine months in jail. Virginia's Republicans brought his three surviving children to Richmond and started a defense fund to support them as well as pay for their father's fine. A stream of dignitaries, including Gov. James Monroe and Virginia chancellor George Wythe, visited the imprisoned journalist, who continued to write from his cell. When word arrived in January that Jefferson had been elected, Callender was ecstatic. On 2 March 1801, two days before Jefferson became president, Callender's sentence expired, and he was free.

Disappointment and Revenge. Callender expected a reward for his services to the new administration. On 16 March Jefferson pardoned Callender and ordered the fine to be repaid to him. Callender desperately needed the money, but it took over a month to resolve the legal issue of repaying a fine. Callender also expected a government job and applied for the lucrative position of Richmond postmaster. But Jefferson's administration was wary of Callender and would not reward him with a position. Callender finally found work with Henry Pace, another exile, who had fled from England to Virginia after being charged with sedition. Pace's *Richmond Recorder; or Lady's and Gentleman's Miscellany* was the fourth newspaper in Richmond, and to boost circulation Callender and Pace launched vicious attacks on the Republican administration. Callender's attacks were aimed at Virginia's aristocracy, naming prominent slave-holders who had white wives and black concubines, showing their utter moral depravity. The Republican press responded, printing exposés of Callender's own troubled life. On 25 August 1802 the *Aurora* wrote that while Callender's wife had been dying of syphilis and their children were starving, he had been "having his usual pint of brandy at breakfast."

Sally Hemings. Callender was enraged by this story and responded on 1 September by publishing a story which had circulated in Virginia since the 1790s. "It is well known that the man, *whom it delighteth the people to honor,* keeps, and for many years past has kept, as his concubine, one of his own slaves. Her name is SALLY. The name of her eldest son is TOM. His features are said to bear a striking although sable resemblance to those of the president himself. The boy is ten or twelve years of age. His mother went to France in the same vessel with Mr. Jefferson and his two daughters. The delicacy of this arrangement must strike every person of common sensibilities. What a sublime pattern for an American ambassador to place before the eyes of two young ladies! . . . By this wench Sally, our president has had several children. . . . THE AFRICAN VENUS is said to officiate, as housekeeper at Monticello."

Aftermath. The story did not destroy Jefferson, though it has continued to circulate to this day. No one will be able to prove or disprove the truth of the Sally Hemings story; it achieved its immediate goal of boosting the *Richmond Recorder's* circulation to one thousand subscribers by December 1802. Callender and Pace, in another effort to embarrass their opponents, tried to replace a rival as printer to the House of Delegates, launching an exposé of corruption among Virginia Republicans. George Hay, who had defended Callender in his 1800 trial, in December 1802 beat Callender with a stick and then had him arrested for libel. Callender emerged from jail with support, even from newspaper editors who disagreed with his falsehoods but recognized the power of his writing. In early 1803 Callender and Pace quarreled; Callender wanted a fair share of the paper's profits, but Pace disagreed and then fired him. On Saturday, 16 July 1803, Callender was seen walking through Richmond extremely drunk. Early the next morning his body was found in the James River. The coroner reported that he had drowned accidentally while intoxicated.

Sources:

Michael Durey, *"With the Hammer of Truth": James Thomson Callender and America's Early National Heroes* (Charlottesville & London: University Press of Virginia, 1990);

The Papers of Alexander Hamilton, volume 21, edited by Harold C. Syrett (New York: Columbia University Press, 1961–1981), pp. 121–144;

The Papers of Thomas Jefferson, volume 18, edited by Julian P. Boyd (Princeton: Princeton University Press, 1954–   ), pp. 611–688;

James Morton Smith, *Freedom's Fetters: The Alien and Sedition Laws and American Civil Liberties* (Ithaca, N.Y.: Cornell University Press, 1956).

MATHEW CAREY

1760-1839
PUBLISHER

Irish Rebel. By the time he was twenty-four Mathew Carey had been condemned by the British House of Commons for his outspoken defense of Irish Catholics and jailed for publishing criticism of Parliament. Born in Dublin on 28 January 1760, Carey fled to France, where a priest introduced the young printer to Benjamin Franklin. The American colonial agent then introduced Carey to the Marquis de Lafayette, who was keenly interested in Ireland's revolutionary sentiment because France was considering an invasion of Ireland. Carey fled to America in September 1784, dressing as a woman to escape detection by British authorities.

Philadelphia. Carey arrived in Philadelphia with just a few dollars and no friends. Another passenger from the ship went on to Mount Vernon, Virginia, and in the course of casual conversation with George Washington and Lafayette, who was visiting, mentioned Carey. Lafayette came to Philadelphia, found Carey, introduced him to some of the city's leading men, and gave him $400. With this money Carey began a newspaper, the *Pennsylvania Evening Herald,* which offered detailed accounts of Pennsylvania's assembly sessions. The paper was successful, but Carey had antagonized Philadelphia's leading publisher, Col. Eleazer Oswald. They attacked one another viciously in the press, and when Carey published a poem ridiculing Oswald, the colonel challenged Carey to a duel. Carey was wounded in the leg, and his paper was discontinued during his long convalescence.

A Free People. While recovering, Carey launched a magazine. The *American Museum* appeared in January 1787 and included American material, unlike other magazines which were filled with English stories, essays, and news. A compilation of useful knowledge, the *American Museum* printed essays by Franklin, Thomas Paine, and Anthony Benezet; poetry by David Humphreys and Philip Freneau; and historical documents. The *American Museum* was a bold and ambitious experiment. George Washington wrote to encourage Carey, saying he wished that "copies of the *Museum* and Magazines, as well as common Gazettes, might be spread through every city, town, and village in America." These "vehicles of knowledge," Washington wrote, were best able "to preserve the liberty, stimulate the industry, and meliorate the morals of an enlightened and free people."

Wide Circulation. By 1788 Carey's *American Museum* had subscribers in every state except New Hampshire and Vermont and included some of the most influential men of the day. In addition to American readers, the magazine had subscribers in every European country (except Spain) and in the West Indies and Calcutta, India. Subscribers were generally obtained through personal contact, or by having agents circulate throughout the country to solicit subscriptions either for magazines or books. But though the circulation was wide, Carey's *American Museum* brought him into debt, and in 1792, when the Post Office Act allowed newspapers into the mail, but excluded magazines, Carey had to suspend publication. While Carey left the magazine business, he moved into the book trade, printing and selling books.

New Career. Between 1792 and 1799 Carey would do more than $300,000 worth of business in the book trade (the equivalent of about $14 million today) and more than one hundred men would work on his printing presses. In 1794 and 1795 he sold twenty-five hundred copies of William Guthrie's *A New System of Modern Geography* (1770), priced at sixteen dollars each, and earned $40,000 in profits. He wrote to his brother, who had remained in Ireland and become a Catholic priest, "My situation never promised so fair at present. I have lately entered pretty largely into the printing & book-selling business. I have printed a considerable number of books on my own account—the history of New York—Necker on religion—Beauties of Poetry—Beatties morals—Ladies' Library—Garden of the Soul—Douay Bible—McFingal, & several smaller works. . . . I have written to London, Dublin, & Glasgow for a supply of foreign books without which I cannot have a proper assortment." Carey printed American authors, but supplemented them with a wide variety of European books. In 1801 he adopted a new method of printing, similar to stereotyping, by which an entire page of type could be cast at once. The traditional method of setting individual letters in type required printers to break up the pages of type when a book was done so that they could set and print another. With the new method a printer could keep on hand the type from a book and quickly issue new editions. In 1801 Carey published an edition of the Bible using this method and paid a clergyman $1,000 for commentary.

American Company of Booksellers. By 1800 Carey and Isaiah Thomas were the two leading publishers in the United States. Most book publishers dealt with strictly local markets and corresponded with other publishers to receive copies of books. In 1802 a proposal circulated for American booksellers to hold a book fair similar to the book fairs held in Frankfurt and Leipzig. The first meeting of the American Company of Booksellers was held in New York on 1 June 1802. This group tried to raise the standards of printing, offering a fifty-dollar gold medal for the best recipe for printer's ink and a similar award for the best paper and binding of American leather. This trade association met for a few years but was undone by its own success. Booksellers attending would bring samples of their work; less scrupulous publishers would quickly produce editions on cheaper paper to sell at a lower price. Booksellers found it less advantageous to meet together and share ideas, though Carey continued to push for some kind of a national organization.

The Olive Branch. Through his publishing house Carey became one of Philadelphia's, and the nation's, leading citizens. With Stephen Girard in 1793 he worked to relieve sufferers from the yellow fever epidemic, and he launched the Hibernian Society to aid other Irish immigrants. Though he corresponded with men and women from all across the political spectrum, by the end of the 1790s he had become a confirmed Republican and engaged in a feud with the Federalist editor William Cobbett. Carey supported the national bank and in 1810 worked to have its charter renewed. In 1814, as the nation seemed on the brink of ruin, Carey wrote and published *The Olive Branch* to encourage Republicans and Federalists to work together to save the union. This may have been his most important book and was among his most popular.

Repaying Lafayette. Carey married in 1791 and with his wife had nine children. Their oldest son, Henry C. Carey, became one of the nation's leading economists. Carey throughout his life remained committed to American political and cultural independence and to the rights of the Irish people. His publishing house encouraged some of the young country's most prominent authors, from Susannah Rowson and Charles Brockden Brown in the 1790s to James Fenimore Cooper and Edgar Allan Poe in the 1830s. In 1824, when Lafayette returned to the United States, Mathew Carey was finally able to repay him the $400 loaned to him forty years earlier. Carey died on 16 September 1839.

Sources:

Earl L. Bradsher, *Mathew Carey, Editor, Author and Publisher: A Study in American Literary Development* (New York: Columbia University Press, 1912);

David Kaser, *Messrs. Carey & Lea of Philadelphia: A Study in the History of the Booktrade* (Philadelphia: University of Pennsylvania Press, 1957).

JOHN FENNO

1751-1798

FEDERALIST NEWSPAPER EDITOR

Literary Beginnings. Although he became one of the most prominent newspaper publishers in the new republic, John Fenno was not born to that business. His father was a leather tanner and tavern keeper, and while Fenno had some schooling, he did not attend college or have the classical education that other literary figures enjoyed. Fenno was born in Boston on 23 August 1751 and worked for some years as an assistant teacher at the Old South Writing School. During the Revolution he served as secretary to Gen. Artemas Ward. He entered the pub-

lishing world after the failure of an importing business prompted him to move to New York in 1789.

Newspaper. Fenno soon began to make a name for himself among people who had favored the adoption of the new Constitution, the Federalists, headed in New York by Alexander Hamilton. Fenno devised a plan for a newspaper to promote the Federalists' programs of stronger central government and commercial development. He started the semiweekly *Gazette of the United States* in April 1789, moving it the next year to Philadelphia, soon to be the nation's capital. There Fenno countered the efforts of Jeffersonian editors such as Benjamin Franklin Bache of the *Aurora* and Philip Freneau of the *National Gazette*. An intense rivalry developed between Fenno and the other editors. At one point Bache even caned Fenno during a street brawl over political differences. Despite the rough atmosphere of the newspaper world, Fenno's *Gazette of the United States* was a dignified party paper, appealing to the genteel sensibilities of the merchants and wealthy farmers who sympathized with the Federalists. The *Gazette of the United States* was helped by having essays from John Adams and Hamilton, but it lost money steadily, as most early American periodicals did. When the 1793 yellow fever epidemic emptied Philadelphia, Fenno suspended the paper for three months, reinventing it as a daily with the help of money from Hamilton and some government printing contracts. Fenno continued editing the paper, slowly building its circulation to a peak of fourteen hundred, until his death on 14 September 1798 during a second yellow fever epidemic. His son continued the *Gazette of the United States* for two years, then sold it to others who published it until 1818.

Source:

John B. Hench, ed., "Letters of John Fenno and John Ward Fenno, 1779–1800," *Proceedings, American Antiquarian Society*, 89 (1979): 299–368; 90 (1980): 163–234.

PHILIP FRENEAU

1752-1832

JEFFERSONIAN EDITOR AND POET

Patriot. Philip Freneau was well prepared for a career as one of the most prominent literary figures in the early United States. He was born on 2 January 1752 to a wealthy New York family at the center of the cultural life of that colonial city. Freneau entered the College of New Jersey (now Princeton University) at age fifteen, and there made contacts among the emerging political and cultural leaders of America, including a future president, James Madison. He also read English poetry and began to desire a career as a poet. He had his first literary success in 1771 when he coauthored with his friend Hugh Henry Brackenridge a poem titled "The Rising Glory of America," capturing the spirit of a nation on the verge of independence. During the revolutionary years Freneau lived for a time in the West Indies and served aboard a privateer in the Caribbean Sea. This was a hazardous job, and it ended with him in a British prison ship in New York harbor. He wrote constantly of his experiences, developing a distinctively romantic poetic voice.

Political Writing. After the war ended Freneau settled in Philadelphia and became a leader of the city's literary circle. He edited magazines and published many poems praising the Patriots' efforts, earning the title of the "Poet of the American Revolution." After more travel, and a further period publishing a newspaper in New York, he returned to Philadelphia to serve under Secretary of State Thomas Jefferson, who shared his democratic principles. He founded the *National Gazette* in October 1791, and it soon became a significant mouthpiece for the Jeffersonians. The *National Gazette* was much livelier than its stately rival, the Federalist *Gazette of the United States.* Freneau poked fun at Secretary of the Treasury Alexander Hamilton as a would-be king and worked hard to shape public opinion on republican principles. Both Hamilton and President George Washington were angry at the radical democratic opinions Freneau expressed in the paper. Washington pressured Jefferson to fire Freneau from his State Department job because of his outside activities, but Jefferson refused, standing up for Freneau's right of free expression. Jefferson wrote that "no government ought to be without censors; and where the press is free, no one ever will." But even Jefferson was uneasy about Freneau's whole-hearted support of the French Revolution and of the controversial French ambassador, Edmond Genet. The *National Gazette* closed in October 1793, a victim of financial pressures and the disruption caused by a yellow fever epidemic. Freneau spent the rest of his life at sea or on his New Jersey farm, occasionally involved in publishing, and still writing poetry. In 1794 he wrote an almanac which sold well. Two years later he began a literary journal called the *Time-Piece,* but like the *National Gazette,* it suffered from inadequate financial backing and quickly closed. Freneau froze to death in a blizzard near Freehold, New Jersey, on 18 December 1832.

Sources:

Mary Weatherspoon Bowden, *Philip Freneau* (Boston: Twayne, 1976);

Lewis Leary, *That Rascal Freneau: A Study in Literary Failure* (New Brunswick, N.J.: Rutgers University Press, 1941).

JOSEPH HABERSHAM

1751-1815
POSTMASTER GENERAL

Washington's Man. Appointed postmaster general by President George Washington in 1795, Joseph Habersham designed the hub-and-spoke system of sorting mail, which transformed the Post Office's functions. He also advocated home delivery but this policy did not become standard until a half century after his death. An innovative organizer, Habersham was offered the post of U.S. treasurer by President Thomas Jefferson but declined and resigned from the Post Office to return to his native Georgia.

Georgia Leader. Habersham's father, James Habersham, had arrived in Georgia with evangelist George Whitefield in 1738. Beginning as a teacher of destitute children, James Habersham soon became a merchant trader and by the 1750s was Georgia's wealthiest and most powerful merchant and a leader in the movement to import slaves into the colony. By the 1770s Habersham's rice plantation earned him an annual income of $10,000, and he had served in every important office in the colony, including two years as acting governor. He sent his sons to Princeton College, but in 1768, worried that Joseph was not receiving a proper education, he sent him to England for his schooling.

Revolutionary Politics. Joseph Habersham returned to Georgia in 1771, where his father established him in business. Though the senior Habersham remained fiercely loyal to England and detested the Patriot movement, Joseph and his brothers all became staunch Patriots. Joseph Habersham was a leader of Georgia's revolutionary movement, helping to capture the royal powder magazine at Savannah, and ultimately served as a colonel in the Continental Army. Georgia sent him as a delegate to the Continental Congress in 1785–1786, and twice he served as speaker of the state's General Assembly.

Hub-and-Spoke System. A successful businessman and a political and military leader, Habersham turned his energies to the Post Office in February 1795. One of the most vexing problems with the Post Office was the system of transporting mail. Letters were carried in large cases, or portmanteaus, which would be opened at each local post office. The postmaster would sort through the letters, pick out those for his patrons, repack the rest, and send the portmanteau on its way. Opening every portmanteau and sorting all the letters at each post office took a lot of time and also created opportunities for tampering with the mail. Habersham created two different kinds of post offices: distribution centers and depots. Packets of letters would be sent to the distribution centers and sorted there, either to be sent to the depots or sent on to the next distribution center. This system eliminated the need for repeated sorting of mail and, as Habersham explained, would prevent opportunities for tampering. The hub-and-spoke system greatly expanded the U.S. Post Office's capacity to deliver mail and would remain in place until the Civil War, when the railroad made it possible to sort mail as it traveled.

Country Press. In the Post Office Act of 1792 Congress had allowed all newspaper printers to exchange copies of their papers with other printers free of charge, and had decided to charge only a minimal amount to mail newspapers to subscribers. This was done to help spread information; it had the effect, though, of driving magazines out of business, and it threatened to replace small local papers with papers from large urban centers. Few would want to read a local paper when a paper carrying more recent world news would be just as readily available. Habersham worried about this trend and urged local postmasters to encourage subscribers to purchase the local papers. He feared that if the local printers were driven out of the newspaper business, they would also be driven from the book business, and local interests would be subsumed by national political interests. Habersham placed the Post Office behind the "country press," encouraging circulation of state and local papers, which began to respond by printing more local news.

Penny Posts v. Pigeonholes. Habersham did not favor the use of post office boxes in urban centers. Rather he hoped to encourage the "penny posts," or delivery of mail by individual carriers and paid by individual patrons. In Philadelphia nine out of every ten pieces of mail were delivered by these carriers. The alternative to these carriers was a system of post office boxes, or "pigeonholes," which a local post office could rent out. "Receiving money for pigeonholes," Habersham wrote to the postmasters of New York, Philadelphia, Boston, and Salem in February 1800, "is . . . contrary to the spirit of the act for establishing the post office. It deprives the penny posts, who are very useful . . . of a portion of that compensation which they ought to receive. You are therefore instructed not to keep any such pigeonholes for private individuals and not to receive any pay for keeping such as may be deemed useful to public bodies." Though Habersham clearly was on the side of the penny posts and against the pigeonholes, after he resigned at the end of 1801 the balance shifted, and local postmasters discouraged the penny posts from actively delivering the mail.

Return to Georgia. President Jefferson hoped to make use of Habersham's talents in the Treasury Department, but Habersham took Jefferson's suggestion as an indication that he did not wish him to continue in the Post Office, and he retired from the federal government and returned to Savannah. Appointed president of the Savannah branch of the Bank of the United States in 1802, Habersham devoted himself to his family (he and his wife had ten children) and his business interests. He is credited with exporting the first American crop of cotton. Habersham died on 17 November 1815.

Source:
Richard R. John, *Spreading the News: The American Postal System from Franklin to Morse* (Cambridge, Mass.: Harvard University Press, 1995).

ISAIAH THOMAS

1750-1831
PRINTER AND PUBLISHER

Another Franklin. Isaiah Thomas emerged from a poor Boston family to become the most important early American printer after Benjamin Franklin. His early career was much like Franklin's. He was born on 30 January 1750 and at age six was apprenticed to work in a print shop, even though he could not yet read. He began setting type for reissues of popular works by comparing the shape of the pieces of type with the letters in the book to be reprinted. Thomas learned his trade quickly and took over management of his master's shop when he was only thirteen. He was becoming quite successful when a fight with his master prompted him to leave Boston in 1766. He hoped to go to London to perfect his trade, as Franklin had done, but only made it as far as Nova Scotia. There he did his first newspaper work, on the *Halifax Gazette,* before his opposition to the Stamp Act forced him to return to Boston. He then found his way south and worked on the *South Carolina and American General Gazette* before returning to Boston in 1770. That year he founded the *Massachusetts Spy,* one of the most successful colonial newspapers. The *Massachusetts Spy* was outspoken in its support of the Patriot cause. When the British occupied Boston, Thomas relocated to the rural town of Worcester, Massachusetts, and continued his political publishing from there.

Success. Thomas became the leading book publisher in early America. He began publishing in 1771 the first of his annual almanacs. Thomas's *New-England Alamack* was enormously successful; he printed three thousand copies in 1781 and twenty-nine thousand in 1797. He marketed it through an extensive network of shops, agents, and partners, which gave him a national presence as a publisher and bookseller. His Worcester shop grew steadily, employing 150 people working on seven presses during the 1790s. The quality of his books was unmatched in the nation. He published the third English Bible printed in the United States, the first in the large folio format, with engravings by American artists. He had type for a smaller Bible, the "standing Bible," permanently set aside in order to be able to run off copies of this steady seller as they were needed. Thomas also printed the first American dictionary and many educational, religious, and literary works, including in 1789 *The Power of Sympathy* by William Hill Brown, the first novel by a native American author. Children's books also flowed from Thomas's presses, including the first American edition of *Mother Goose's Melody* in 1786. Thomas published magazines as well, notably the *Massachusetts Magazine* (1789–1793). It was financially unsuccessful but nevertheless helped set the standards for literary success in this emerging business.

Philanthropy. After 1802 Thomas began to turn over his printing enterprises to others while turning himself into a scholar and philanthropist. He drew on his large library as well as his own experience to write the *History of Printing in America* (1810), which re-mained a standard work for more than a century. In 1812 he founded the American Antiquarian Society, and his library became the center of that institution's collection of early American materials (today it is one of the most extensive in the nation.) Many other learned societies benefited from his membership, time, and efforts, and in this work Thomas contributed greatly to the cultural development of the new nation. Like Franklin's, Thomas's career demonstrated how important the printing of books and newspapers could be to founding a new nation and shaping its identity. Thomas died in Worcester, Massachusetts, on 4 April 1831.

Sources:

Clifford K. Shipton, *Isaiah Thomas: Printer, Patriot and Philanthropist* (Rochester, N.Y.: Leo Hart, 1948);

Benjamin Franklin Thomas, "Memoir of Isaiah Thomas," in *Transactions and Collections of the American Antiquarian Society*, 5 (Albany, N.Y.: Joel Munsell, 1874), pp. xvii–lxxxvii.

PUBLICATIONS

Richard Alsop, *The Political Greenhouse, for the Year 1798* (Hartford, Conn.: Hudson & Goodwin, 1799)—Alsop, Lemuel Hopkins, and Theodore Dwight published this poem attacking Republicans;

Benjamin Franklin Bache, *Truth Will Out! The Foul Charges of the Tories against the Editor of the* Aurora *Repelled by Positive Proof and Plain Truth* (Philadelphia, 1798)—Republican journalist Bache responds to charges that he is a French agent;

James Thomson Callender, *The Prospect Before Us* (Richmond: Printed for the author, 1800)—an attack on President John Adams for which the author was convicted of sedition;

Mathew Carey, *An Address to the Printers and Booksellers throughout the United States* (Philadelphia, 1801)—a broadside calling on booksellers and printers to form an association;

Carey, *The Plagi-Scurriliad: A Hudibrastic Poem Dedicated to Colonel Eleazer Oswald* (Philadelphia: Printed & sold by the author, 1786)—pamphlet by Carey accusing rival publisher Oswald of plagiarism;

Carey, *A Plumb Pudding for the Humane, Chaste, Valiant, Enlightened Peter Porcupine* (Philadelphia: Printed for the author, 1799)—an attack on the arch-Federalist William Cobbett;

Carey, *The Porcupiniad. A Hudibrastic Poem* (Philadelphia: Printed for & sold by the author, 1799)—another attack on Cobbett;

William Cobbett, *A Bone to Gnaw, for the Democrats; or, Observations on a Pamphlet Entitled, "The Political Progress of Britain"* (Philadelphia: Printed by Thomson Bradford, 1795)—Cobbett's response to James T. Callender's pamphlet;

Harry Croswell, *The Speeches at Full Length of Mr. Van-ness, Mr. Caines, . . . Ambrose Spencer, Mr. Harrison, and General Hamilton, in the Great Cause of the People against Harry Croswell, on an Indictment for a Libel on Thomas Jefferson* (New York: G. & R. Waite, 1804);

Joseph Dennie, *The Claims of Thomas Jefferson to the Presidency, Examined at the Bar of Christianity* (Philadelphia: Asbury Dickins, 1800)—Federalist attack on Jefferson's religious views;

Alexander Hamilton, *Letter from Alexander Hamilton, Concerning the Public Conduct and Character of John Adams* (New York: John Lang, 1800)—this letter from Hamilton was meant to circulate among leading Federalists; instead, Republicans published his attack on President Adams in Boston and Philadelphia, helping to split the Federalist Party in the 1800 election;

S. S. Moore and T. W. Jones, *The Traveller's Directory, or A Pocket Companion; Showing the Course of the Main Road from Philadelphia to New York, and from Philadelphia to Washington* (Philadelphia: Printed for & published by Mathew Carey, 1802)—a pocket travel guide;

Jedidiah Morse, *The American Gazetteer* (Boston: Printed by S. Hall and Thomas & Andrews, and sold by E. Larkin, 1797)—a six-hundred-page geographic survey of the United States, with seven thousand articles on geographic features and seven maps showing postal and stage routes as well as Indian tribes and natural features;

Isaiah Thomas, *The History of Printing in America*, 2 volumes (Worcester, Mass.: From the press of Isaiah Thomas, jun., 1810);

Tunis Wortman, *Treatise, Concerning Political Enquiry, and the Liberty of the Press* (New York: Printed by George Forman, 1800)—a New York Republican's attack on the Sedition Act.

EDUCATION

by ROBERT J. ALLISON

CONTENTS

Sidebars and tables are listed in italics.

1783

Apr.   The North Carolina Assembly grants a charter to Martin Academy in what is now Washington County, Tennessee. It is the first educational institution in the Mississippi River valley.

Oct.   Noah Webster publishes *The Grammatical Institute of the English Language,* part I, his "blue-backed speller" which tries to establish an American system of spelling and punctuation. Webster's speller becomes the most influential grammar book and textbook in American schools and will remain in use for the next century, with at least twenty million copies sold.

1784

•   Quakers in Portsmouth, Rhode Island, open a school, but it will close within four years for lack of funds.

•   Judge Tapping Reeve opens a law school in Litchfield, Connecticut.

•   The first theological college is founded in New Brunswick, New Jersey.

1785

•   North Carolina charters Davidson Academy in Nashville; it will ultimately become the University of Tennessee, Nashville.

27 Jan.   A charter is granted to the University of Georgia, making it the first state university to be chartered.

1786

•   The Virginia state legislature defeats Thomas Jefferson's Bill for Diffusion of Knowledge.

Apr.   A free school for poor children is opened in Alexandria, Virginia, subsidized by George Washington and others.

1787

•   Congress passes the Northwest Ordinance, setting aside land in townships north of the Ohio River in order to build schools.

13 Apr.   The New York state legislature creates a state university to be governed by a board of regents.

June   William Samuel Johnson becomes the president of Columbia (formerly King's) College, New York, creating new professorships and briefly boosting enrollment.

28 July   Benjamin Rush addresses visitors to the Young Ladies Academy in Philadelphia.

Nov.   New York teacher Cornelius Davis opens a free school for black children; twelve students attend.

1788

- Norwich Academy, Vermont, holds a lottery to raise money for a new building.

Mar.   Nicholas Pike publishes his arithmetic text.

29 Oct.   Benjamin Rush publishes a plan for a federal university in the *Federal Gazette*.

1789

- The University of North Carolina is chartered.

- Leicester Academy, Massachusetts, holds a lottery to raise money. "As the Academy . . . is established for promoting piety and virtue and for the education of youth . . . the managers have no doubt of a speedy sale of tickets."

- Bishop John Carroll founds the first Roman Catholic college at Georgetown, Maryland.

- Massachusetts law requires all towns to maintain schools for at least six months each year; larger towns are to have year-round sessions, and teachers must be certified by the state.

Jan.   The only issue of *The Children's Magazine* is published in Hartford, Connecticut.

July   The Charleston College, South Carolina, building is opened.

15 Oct.   Boston adopts a new school law, creating an elected school committee.

1790

8 Jan.   In his first annual message to Congress, President George Washington calls for a national university.

5 Apr.   Noah Webster donates some proceeds from sale of his spelling book as a prize for best essay on ethics, moral philosophy, or belles lettres by a student at Yale College.

1791

- Sarah Pierce opens a school for girls in her home in Litchfield, Connecticut.

- David Ker opens a Presbyterian academy in Fayetteville, North Carolina.

Sept.   Trustees of Hallowell Academy meet in Maine.

1792

- A Westford, Massachusetts, group opens an academy. The town buys twenty shares at six pounds a share.

- The town of Gilmanton, New Hampshire, votes to give town land for a school.

- Rev. James Wallis opens Providence Academy, a Presbyterian school near Charlotte, North Carolina.

1793

•	Westfield, Massachusetts, votes to raise £300 to start an academy.
July	The Massachusetts state legislature votes to establish Williams College in Berkshire County.
2 Oct.	Connecticut passes an act to establish a school fund from money raised by selling land in the Ohio River valley.

1794

•	The African Free School, in operation since 1787, is chartered by New York.
•	Harvard College holds a lottery to raise money for a new building.
May	The Society of Associated Teachers is formed in New York; within four months it has twenty-nine teachers.
Dec.	Former Massachusetts governor James Bowdoin's gift of $1,000 and five thousand acres of land to Hallowell Academy leads to the founding of Bowdoin College.

1795

•	Martin Academy becomes Washington College.
•	Connecticut establishes the first permanent public school fund.
•	Peacham, Vermont, chooses to be the home of the county grammar school rather than the county courthouse.
•	Union University, a nonsectarian school, is founded in Albany, New York.
9 Apr.	New York State starts to appropriate £20,000 each year for the operation of schools.
May	President John Witherspoon of Princeton College dies.
12 May	President Ezra Stiles of Yale College dies.

1796

•	The American Philosophical Society sponsors a contest on the proper system of national education.
23 Sept.	The Common Council of New York refuses to distribute state money to teachers who operate pay schools; instead, the council distributes the money to charity schools.
7 Dec.	In his final message to Congress, George Washington repeats his call for a national university and military academy.
13 Dec.	The Virginia state legislature charters the Male Charity School in Fredericksburg.

1797

- Massachusetts towns receive small land grants in Maine. The proceeds from the sale of these plots are to be used to finance academies.

- The Congregational Church in Boston opens a school.

May   The first edition of Caleb Bingham's *The Columbian Orator* is published.

Nov.   Fire destroys much of Providence College (later Brown University).

15 Dec.   Samuel Harrison Smith's system of liberal education receives a prize from the American Philosophical Society.

1800

- The Episcopal Church in Connecticut begins a movement to open church schools to the general public.

- William Samuel Johnson resigns as president of Columbia College.

Nov.   Vermont incorporates Middlebury Academy into a college, and Jeremiah Atwater is appointed the first president.

1801

- Connecticut refuses to grant Episcopalians a charter to open a school.

1802

- The Episcopal school in Cheshire, Connecticut, holds a lottery and raises $12,000.

- Pennsylvania passes the Pauper School Act to provide for education of poor children.

- The U.S. Military Academy is founded at West Point, New York.

Mar.   Fire destroys the college buildings at Princeton College, and the state legislature offers the use of the capitol building for classes.

1805

- Baptists in Maine found Hebron Academy.

- Worcester Polytechnic Institute is founded in Massachusetts.

Jan.   Samuel Holyoke opens a music school in Salem, Massachusetts.

Feb.   The Free School Society, a charitable, nonprofit organization receiving money from city and state treasuries to educate children, is formed in New York.

Nov.   Connecticut requires that the School Society examine and issue certificates to all teachers.

Dec.   Fisher Ames is elected president of Harvard College but declines to serve.

1806

* In New York City the first school opens using the Lancastrian method of monitors.

Feb.   Samuel Webber, professor of mathematics and natural philosophy, becomes president of Harvard College.

6 June   William Maclure publishes the first American article on the educational reforms of Johann Pestalozzi in the *National Intelligencer*.

12 June   John Quincy Adams is appointed professor of rhetoric and oratory at Harvard College, the first such professorship in New England.

1807

Apr.   Harvard students riot over bad food, and one hundred of them leave the college.

Princeton students riot over the expulsion of three classmates, and college administrators send home 156 pupils.

July   Rev. Joseph McKeen, the first president of Bowdoin College, dies just before the school's second commencement; Rev. Jesse Appleton of New Hampshire is elected his successor.

1808

* Green Academy in Smithfield, Rhode Island, holds a lottery to raise money.

* The Female Charity School is opened in Fredericksburg, Virginia.

Nov.   The Medical Society of New Haven proposes uniting with Yale College.

1809

* Joseph Neef opens the first American Pestalozzian school near Philadelphia.

23 May   The *Richmond Enquirer* prints a report calling for the opening of Lancastrian schools in Virginia.

11 Dec.   The opening of the Free School of New York occurs, and Gov. George Clinton speaks.

1810

Aug.   John Thornton Kirkland becomes president of Harvard College.

Nov.   Connecticut incorporates New Haven Medical Society with Yale College as the Medical Institute.

1811

Fall   Robert Ould opens a Lancastrian school in Georgetown, District of Columbia.

1812

- James Mercer Gannett opens a secular Sunday school on his farm in Essex County, Virginia.

Jan. The Academy of Natural Sciences is formed in Philadelphia.

1814

- Emma Willard opens Troy Seminary in Troy, New York.
- A school for free blacks opens in Fredericksburg, Virginia.

1815

11 Apr. Edward Everett is appointed professor of Greek literature at Harvard College.

June President John Wheelock of Dartmouth College reports to the New Hampshire state legislature that college trustees are not doing their duty; an investigation ensues.

Sept. Dartmouth trustees fire President Wheelock and appoint Rev. Francis Brown in his place.

14 Oct. A movement begins to open a public charity school in Richmond, Virginia.

OVERVIEW

New Nation. After the American Revolution, Americans began thinking of education in different ways. Traditionally education was meant to train children in various skilled trades, either through apprenticeship or through helping their parents. Many would learn to read and write, but this part of their education would also be done at home. Most children would follow the occupations of their parents, and so it was essential that they learn as their parents had done. The education they received prepared them for lives as farmers, artisans, or tradesmen of other skills.

Formal Education. Some children had been sent to school or had private tutors instruct them in reading, writing, arithmetic, and other subjects. Children selected for formal education were generally from wealthier families, and the purpose of their education was to qualify them for one of the more advanced professions, either the ministry or the law. To pass the entrance examination for college, children would have to learn Latin and Greek, and so private schools maintained by a schoolmaster, paid by the parents of his pupils, would instruct students in those languages as well as a few other subjects. Children typically would enter college at age 12 or 14. Most of the colonial colleges (Harvard, William and Mary, Yale, Princeton, Brown, Queen's, and Dartmouth) had been founded by religious groups and were devoted both to training ministers and to providing a broader education. Two other colleges, King's College, now Columbia University, and the College of Philadelphia, were not founded by religious groups, but ministers still played a large role on their faculty and in their government. Generally, faculty were ministers of a particular denomination.

Citizens and Scholars. The American Revolution brought a dramatic change in the way Americans thought about education because it brought a change in the fundamental principle of society. With independence, some American leaders began thinking of ways to change the educational system. As Benjamin Rush put it, the purpose of American education was not to turn out scholars, but to create citizens. It was essential, if the American republic was to survive, that all citizens be educated. States quickly began taking an interest in opening formal education to more people. Massachusetts in 1789 required its towns to set up common schools, and Pennsylvania's 1790 Constitution required its towns to set up schools to teach the poor for free. The states recognized the need to teach its citizens in order to ensure that they would be reliable guardians of public order.

Jefferson's Plan. Thomas Jefferson suggested that Virginia set up a system of grammar schools to provide all free children in the state with three years of free education and to teach them reading, writing, and arithmetic. After three years children who showed exceptional promise would continue for three more years of schooling, and the brightest at this level could move on to college. Jefferson envisioned a system that would teach all children to read and write and would select the brightest students to train as society's future leaders. Jefferson's ambitious plan would not be enacted until after the Civil War.

In the Classroom. Jefferson and other educational reformers had wanted to create a system of public education. For the most part they were happy with the way schools were operated, but they wanted to change the way schools were financed. One teacher, generally a young man preparing for the law or the ministry, would preside over a schoolroom holding up to fifty students who sat on benches and copied the lessons he would dictate. Students were required to memorize the lessons and were graded on their ability to recite what they had learned from memory. Books were expensive; usually only the teacher had a copy of the text, and he would read it to the pupils. This system required strict attention and concentration and built the powers of memory and concentration more than the skills of thinking and analysis.

Textbooks. With a heavy reliance on memorization, some Americans tried to produce texts that would teach reading and writing, but they would also use these lessons to instill republican values. Noah Webster, a schoolteacher in Connecticut, wrote a spelling book in 1783 which not only taught spelling but also instructed children in the tenets of republican society. Webster saw his spelling text as an intellectual declaration of independence from England: through an American system of spelling, the United States would become independent of British educational ideas and notions. Webster's "blue-backed speller," which sold over twenty million copies, and his book on grammar called for an American pronunciation of words and simplified spelling. He was not successful in having Americans spell "speak" as "speek," or in dropping the silent "gh" in "fight" and "eight," but his spelling primer and two-volume *An American Dictionary of the English Language* (1830–1832) succeeded in having the "u" dropped from "labour" and "favour," a small step away from the spelling of England. Almost as influential, Caleb Bingham, a Boston schoolmaster, produced various texts, compilations of speeches, poems, and plays for the use of schools. His *American Preceptor* (1794) sold 600,000 copies before his death in 1817.

Women. A schoolmaster might keep his school open all year or for 280 days; students, however, would attend for only 180 days. As a result Americans still looked to the family as the place for transmitting values. Girls as well as boys were expected to be educated so that they could read the Bible and transmit its values to their children. Women were raised to be "republican mothers," to keep alive in their families the ideas of civic virtue and honesty. In the colonial period "dame schools" had taught girls reading, writing, and arithmetic, and also needlework and other domestic arts. Common schools also educated both girls and boys, though females attended less often than their male counterparts. One of the most influential textbook writers of the period, Caleb Bingham, taught at a Boston school for girls. Susannah Haswell Rowson's school in Medford, Massachusetts, and Sarah Pierce's Litchfield Academy in Connecticut trained girls and young women who would marry into the elite of the next generation. Since women, as mothers, would be their children's principal educators, it was vital that they be well taught. Some women, in fact, attended schools such as Sarah Pierce's and went on to become teachers themselves. In the nineteenth century the schoolmistress began to replace the schoolmaster as the purveyor of formal education, though women would not be able to attend college until later in the century.

Sunday Schools. Begun in the 1790s, Sunday schools were mainly run by women. These schools offered secular instruction, though they were usually affiliated with churches. In any case it would be difficult to find an American school in this period that did not have some religious foundation; the New York Free School required its students to attend church on Sundays, though they could attend the denomination of their choice. The Sunday school, however, was open to all, though it would be conducted in a church. One day a week the teacher would instruct her students, who ranged from children to adults, in reading and writing, using as their basic text the Bible. These schools, like the charity schools, were designed to prevent an uneducated poor class from developing and becoming dangerous to society.

Wages. One reason women replaced men as teachers is that pay for teachers was always low. While reformers such as Jefferson and Rush argued for the value of education, it was difficult to pry funds from the hands of taxpayers. The states were slow to embrace tax-supported education for all people. It remained the responsibility of parents to pay for their children's schooling. Connecticut in 1793 passed a law to use money the state received from selling its land in the Western Reserve of Ohio for the benefit of schools. This fund became the source of great controversy, as the state would only charter Congregationalist, Presbyterian, or Episcopal schools, and as the size of the fund depended on the sale of land. Schools had to find other ways to raise money. Some would hold lotteries or would rely on wealthy benefactors. The social consequences of not teaching children to be good citizens were great, and most American leaders worried about a poorly educated generation not suited either for a successful career or for a role in protecting free government. As American cities such as New York and Philadelphia grew after the war, with children growing up in crowded cities, some began worrying about the future of the country.

New York's Free Schools. In New York in 1787 philanthropists started an African Free School for the children of former slaves and free black people to teach them to read, write, and be productive members of society. This was followed by other charity schools begun by various religious denominations. All of these schools taught reading, writing, and arithmetic, but all these lessons had a very moral basis. Religion was fundamental to these free schools. New York State in 1795 decided to support these charity schools with state funds: the counties were given money from the sale of public lands to pay the charity-school teachers, and for five years New York had a system of state-supported education. In 1800 the legislature discontinued this policy. Five years later New York philanthropists led by DeWitt Clinton created a Free School Society, which established free schools for poor children paid for by private donations.

Lancastrian System. All of these reforms focused on the way to finance schools. Two notable reforms were advanced in the ways schools should operate. The New York Free School Society adopted the educational methods of Joseph Lancaster, who ran a London school, teaching over one thousand children by himself. Lancaster's method called for the teacher to train several more-advanced students to act as "monitors" and do much of the work of drilling and listening to recitations. By this method one teacher could handle hundreds of students. This system had two advantages: reportedly, the Lancastrian schools could teach a student to read in just a few months; more importantly, this system was much less expensive than a traditional system of one teacher for every thirty or forty students.

Pestalozzian System. Another reform, this one imported from Switzerland, had been introduced by Johann

Heinrich Pestalozzi, who did not believe in the drilling and memorization practiced in most European and American schools. Pestalozzi called for educating students by awakening their curiosity, by having them explore the natural world, and once their curiosity was sufficiently awakened and engaged, to teach reading, writing, and arithmetic using concrete examples rather than abstract theories and moral lessons. A Philadelphia merchant, William Maclure, visited Pestalozzi in 1805 and saw that his system would be an ideal way to teach republican citizens in America. Maclure hired one of Pestalozzi's teachers, Joseph Neef, and brought him to America to open a Pestalozzian school. Neef, a veteran of the French army, wrote several books for Americans explaining his system and became a familiar figure in the countryside outside Philadelphia, leading his pupils on explorations of their natural environment. The Pestalozzian method also stressed physical education, and Neef was popular among his students for leading them in exercises. The small school moved to Delaware and later to Kentucky. Neef in the 1820s settled in Robert Owen's New Harmony commune in Indiana and became a teacher.

State Universities. While the period after the Revolution did not see a change in the way schools were run, there was a tremendous change in the number of schools. Throughout the new country schools were created, either by towns or by states, to educate the republic's citizens. Georgia became the first state to charter a state university in 1785, followed by New York in 1787 and North Carolina in 1789. Presidents George Washington, John Adams, Thomas Jefferson, and James Madison all tried

to persuade Congress to establish a national university, but this plan never succeeded. Jefferson failed to have Virginia establish a system of education, but after he retired from the presidency he devoted his attention to founding the University of Virginia. In 1815 New Hampshire's legislature tried to take over Dartmouth College and claim it as a state university, but the Supreme Court in 1819 stopped them.

States and Academies. In addition to universities, states chartered private academies to prepare pupils for entrance to college. The federal government, too, tried to encourage education through the sale and division of western lands. In the new territories formed in the Ohio River valley Congress in 1787 directed that the land be laid out into townships; certain lots in each township would be reserved for a schoolhouse; and other plots of land would be sold to pay for the school. This piece of legislation marks the first federal subsidy for education, though it left the control of the school in the hands of the community. Similarly, New York's 1795 school law had given money from the sale of land to communities to pay for schools, but had left it up to each community how the money would be distributed. Massachusetts in 1789 required its towns to establish schools, but left it to each town to run the schools and determine policy. It could be that state leaders simply assumed most schools would operate in the same way; the more important issue is that all shared the same vision of education as essential to creating a stable society of informed and thoughtful men and women.

TOPICS IN THE NEWS

THE LANCASTRIAN METHOD

Origins. The Lancastrian Method, named for Joseph Lancaster, actually began with Anglican missionary schools in Madras, India. Under this method one teacher could supervise hundreds of students by dividing them into groups of ten to twenty each and putting them under the direct supervision of a class monitor, a somewhat more advanced student. These monitors, selected for their deportment and attention to studies, were rewarded either by weekly tickets, which could be redeemed for money, or with room and board. The system was brought

to England in 1789 by Dr. Andrew Bell, an Anglican minister. Lancaster, a Quaker, learned the method from Bell and by 1805 was conducting his own school in London using this system, having one thousand students enrolled under his and the monitors' direction.

Success. Lancaster and his protégés were able by 1809 to open twenty schools, educating nearly ten thousand students at a cost of four shillings each every year. This system was seen by many as a miracle, one that would allow all the poor to be educated at a minimal cost. In 1805 visitors from New York were struck by Lancaster's

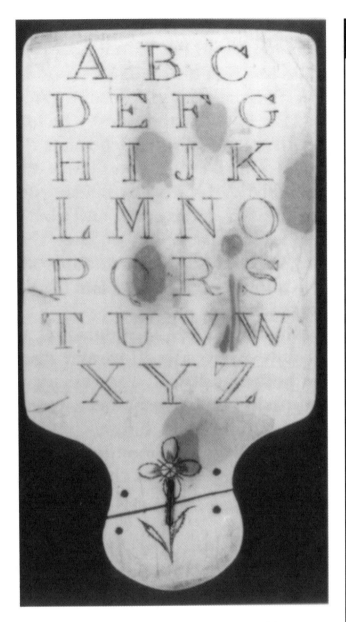

A slate alphabet board of the type invented by
Joseph Lancaster

Few Americans were as involved in reform movements as Benjamin Rush, a Philadelphia doctor. Rush saw the American Revolution as important not only for securing independence but also as the beginning of a general movement to regenerate mankind. The United States would be an example to the rest of the world, and Rush was keenly aware that everything the Americans did would have profound consequences for the world's future. He particularly interested himself in educational reform, actively supporting the establishment of schools and colleges in the new country. Here he advises on the proper role of teachers and the ways America's educational system should be different from Europe's:

In the Education of youth, let the authority of our masters be as *absolute* as possible. The government of schools, like the government of private families, should be *arbitrary,* that it may not be *severe.* By this mode of education, we prepare our youth for the subordination of laws, and thereby qualify them for becoming good citizens of the republic. I am satisfied that the most useful citizens have been formed from those youth who have never known or felt their own wills till they were one and twenty years of age, and I have often thought that society owes a great deal of its order and happiness to the deficiencies of parental government, being supplied by those habits of obedience and subordination which are contracted at schools.

I cannot help bearing a testimony, in this place, against the custom, which prevails in some parts of America, (but which is daily falling into disuse in Europe) of crowding boys together under one roof for the purpose of education. The practice is the gloomy remains of monkish ignorance, and is as unfavourable to the improvements of the mind in useful learning, as monasteries are to the spirit of religion. I grant this mode of excluding boys from the intercourse of private families, has a tendency to make them scholars, but our business is to make them men, citizens, and christians. The vices of young people are generally learned from each other. The vices of adults seldom infect them. By separating them from each other, therefore, in their hours of relaxation and study, we secure their morals from a principal source of corruption, while we improve their manners, by subjecting them to those restraints, which the difference of age and sex, naturally produce in private families.

Source: Benjamin Rush, *A Plan for the Establishment of Public Schools . . . in Pennsylvania* (1786), in *Theories of Education in Early America 1655–1819,* edited by Wilson Smith (Indianapolis: Bobbs-Merrill, 1973).

method, and the New York Free School Society, founded in that year, strictly adhered to it, hiring one of his protégés, William Smith, as its first teacher. DeWitt Clinton, mayor of New York and founder of the New York Free School Society, was a passionate advocate of Lancaster's method, which he said "created a new era in education. The system operates with the same efficacy in education as labor-saving machinery does in the useful arts."

The Sand Table. The Lancastrian schools met for five hours each day, from nine until noon and from three until five in the afternoon. Most schools of the day used dictation and memorization to teach reading and had the students learn to write by copying texts. In the Lancastrian system children learned the alphabet by practicing writing in sand: several times a day the younger children would gather around a table fifteen feet long, six inches wide, covered with a small coating of sand. Each student had a stick, about four inches long, with which to practice letters in the sand, which could then be smoothed

A Lancastrian school, from a manual published by the British and Foreign School Society, circa 1800

over and used again. Doing this work at the sand table both perfected the student's knowledge of letters and was also "a pleasing relaxation." Each classroom had an alphabet board twenty-six feet long and three feet high, placed near the ceiling, showing the upper- and lowercase letters as well as the numbers 1 through 9. To ease their learning, the Lancastrian method divided the letters into groups according to shape: perpendicular (I, H, T, L, E, F, i, and l), triangular (A, V, W, M, N, Z, K, Y, X, v, w, k, y, z, and x), and circular (O, U, C, J, G, D, P, B, R, Q, S, a, o, b, d, p, q, c, g, m, n, h, t, u, r, s, f, and j). Students would practice making these different shapes, becoming comfortable with writing each individual letter. Once students were sufficiently comfortable with writing on sand, they would be allowed to write on paper.

Comparison with Boston. Under this method thousands of children could be educated at a low cost, and Lancaster became highly regarded among educators. In 1815 a writer in the *Connecticut Courant* noted the improvements in American society of the past few years, and listed along with vaccination, the Humane Society, and the movement to abolish the slave trade, "The Lancastrian system of education, by means of which thousands of children are yearly taught the rudiments of learning, and accustomed to read the bible; who, but for that invention, must have been brought up in ignorance." While many regarded the Lancastrian system as a profound educational reform, others were skeptical. Boston's schools did not adopt the Lancastrian system; in 1818 a copy of New York's Free Schools report reached that city. Noting that the same number of pupils had been enrolled in New York's Lancastrian schools and in Boston's traditional schools, the figures for each were compared. In New York, of 1,800 students trained under the Lancastrian method, 220 had learned to write on paper; in Boston, of 1,800 students, 1,800 were writing on paper. In New York only 138 pupils were reading the Bible, while in the Boston school all of the students were

reading the Bible. The success rate for New York's pupils, according to this report, trailed off dramatically, with only five able to multiply to the rule of three, as compared to 200 Boston pupils able to do so. The Lancastrian system had its most success among students with no previous exposure to literacy. It did offer quick results in acquainting students with letters and the rudiments of learning. But with so much of its instruction resting on monitors, rather than on trained teachers, its usefulness quickly faded.

Sad End. Lancaster himself, as an educational reformer, proved disappointing. He came to the United States in 1819, appeared before the House of Representatives, was lavishly praised by Henry Clay and others, then was invited to Caracas by Simon Bolívar to establish a school. Lancaster, successful in running a large school in England, training teachers in his method, and generating publicity for his reform, proved unable either to begin a school in Caracas or to account for the $20,000 Bolívar had given him for this purpose. In 1828 he left Venezuela in disgrace, returning to New York, the American city most enthusiastic about his method, where he died in poverty in 1838.

Sources:

Vera M. Butler, *Education as Revealed by New England Newspapers Prior to 1850* (New York: Arno, 1969);

A. Emerson Palmer, *The New York Public School* (New York: Macmillan, 1905).

THE LITCHFIELD FEMALE ACADEMY

Rapid Growth. It is not known how many students Sarah Pierce had when she began teaching in her Litchfield, Connecticut, farmhouse in 1792. Six years later the Litchfield Female Academy had thirty pupils, and the town's most prominent citizens, led by law-school teacher Tapping Reeve and including congressmen, state legislators, and local judges, contributed to a campaign for "the purpose of Building a House for a Female Academy to be placed upon the land of Miss

Sally Pierce." Some 1,500 students would attend Sarah Pierce's Academy by 1814, and in 1816 alone it had enrolled 169 students. While the Academy was primarily for girls and young women, at least 125 boys are known to have attended. Students came from all parts of the country, and though a stagecoach ride from New York cost ten dollars, Litchfield was at the hub of New England's road systems, making the town accessible. Boys tended to be from the Litchfield area, but girls and young women came from as far away as Georgia, Ohio, and even Canada. It would cost as much as $350 each year for tuition, room and board, and other expenses, which made the Litchfield Academy significantly more expensive than most schools of its day, and even more expensive than Harvard or Yale, which would cost only $250 to $300 each year.

Boarding System. Students might board with the Pierce family, but most found rooms with other families in town. One widow living with her two unmarried daughters kept such a close watch on her boarders that students at Tapping Reeve's law school called her house the "convent." Rev. Lyman Beecher, who taught religion at the school in exchange for his children's education, also boarded pupils. At any given time the Beecher home would accommodate eleven of Pierce's students, a few young men studying for the ministry under Beecher, a law student or two, two servants, as well as the Reverend and Mrs. Beecher and their own eleven children. One Pierce pupil recalled that more than twenty people shared one large kitchen sink and several small wash basins, so "We could not take much of a bath—which was a great trial to me." Beecher's daughter Harriet later remembered the whole crowded scene fondly, recalling the "great household inspired by a spirit of cheerfulness and hilarity." To help the students avoid the dangers which might come from too much cheerfulness and hilarity, Sarah Pierce every Saturday would read the school rules to the students, who would have to copy them down as Miss Pierce expounded on them, noting any that had been broken during the week. Families housing the boarding students also kept a certificate on which to list student faults, and Miss Pierce conducted weekly "fault-telling" sessions, open to the public, at which students would confess their failings. The Litchfield Academy, in Sarah Pierce's eyes, acted as a bridge between the private world of childhood and the public world in which her students would live as adults. By boarding with families they were partly in the private, family world, but they were also becoming part of a community which needed to enforce its rules.

Lessons. The Litchfield Academy followed a traditional course of instruction. The teacher dictated lessons; the students copied and memorized them, and at the end of the week or the term would recite them from memory. The students studied history, geography, composition, religion, logic, chemistry, philosophy, math, and needlework. For an extra fee students could

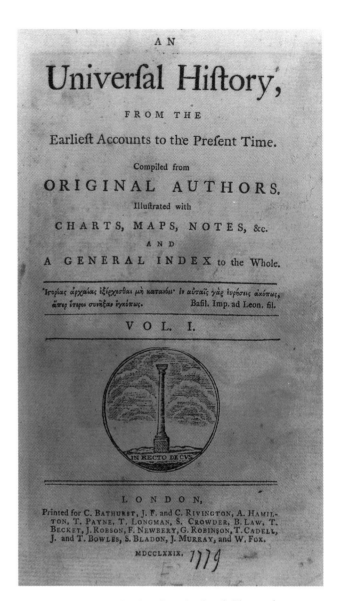

AN

Univerſal Hiſtory,

FROM THE

Earlieſt Accounts to the Preſent Time.

Compiled from

ORIGINAL AUTHORS.

Illuſtrated with

CHARTS, MAPS, NOTES, &c.

AND

A GENERAL INDEX to the Whole.

'Ιστορίας ἀρχαίας ἰξίεργιοθαι μὴ καταυθῶ· ἐν αὐταῖς γὰρ ἰυρήσεις ἀκόπως,
ἅπερ ἕτεροι συνῆξαν ἐγκόπως.   Baſil. Imp. ad Leon. fil.

VOL. I.

IN RECTO DECVS

LONDON,

Printed for C. BATHURST, J. F. and C. RIVINGTON, A. HAMILTON, T. PAYNE, T. LONGMAN, S. CROWDER, B. LAW, T. BECKET, J. ROBSON, F. NEWBERY, G. ROBINSON, T. CADELL, J. and T. BOWLES, S. BLADON, J. MURRAY, and W. FOX.

MDCCLXXIX. 1779

Title page of the textbook written by Sarah Pierce, the founder of the Litchfield Female Academy

study Latin and Greek. With four or five teachers, the Litchfield Academy had one of the largest staffs of any private school of the day: Yale College had only five professors and six tutors in 1812, and most comparable boarding schools had one headmaster and two or three assistant teachers. Sarah Pierce often hired former students to teach, and she sent her nephew, John Brace, to Williams College in 1812 to groom him as her assistant and eventual successor. The way these schools offered instruction allowed them to get by with few teachers: it required only one teacher to read the lesson and listen for proper recitation. The recitation method also allowed schools to function with few books: only the teacher needed to read the text, and the students copied from what was read aloud. The most effective way to teach using this method was through a series of questions and answers, such as in a religious catechism. Most textbooks were written in this question-and-answer format. In 1811 Sarah Pierce wrote her own *Universal History* textbook, since she had not found a satisfactory history book which used the question-and-answer method.

Wives and Mothers. Few of the students would earn a diploma. Instead, they came for a few years of study to help them become wives and mothers to the nation's leaders. Some graduates became schoolteachers, but the overwhelming majority married. Of 376 students for whom marriage information is available, 126 married lawyers, and 69 of those lawyers had attended Tapping Reeve's Litchfield law school. Thirty-seven of the lawyers became judges, and 71 held elective office, including three U.S. senators, twenty-five congressmen, three governors, and five mayors. Sixty-eight husbands were ministers, and five were college professors. Litchfield alumnae tended to marry well; at the time, only one man in one thousand attended college, but 143 of the 747 Litchfield husbands identified were college graduates. While Sarah Pierce might have presented a role model for women seeking a career without marriage, she emphasized the prevailing belief that women's proper role was in marriage as a partner. The two most famous of the school's students, though, were Catharine Beecher, who became the preceptress at the Hartford Female Seminary and wrote influential books on household economy, instructing women in how to manage their homes, and her sister, Harriet Beecher Stowe, whose *Uncle Tom's Cabin* (1852) was a savage indictment of the institution of slavery both for its brutality and, more importantly, for its violent disruption of domestic relations.

Source:
Theodore Sizer, Nancy Sizer, et al., *To Ornament Their Minds: Sarah Pierce's Litchfield Female Academy, 1792–1833* (Litchfield, Conn.: Litchfield Historical Society, 1993).

NEW YORK FREE SCHOOL SOCIETY, 1805

The Setting. New York City in 1805 had 141 teachers for a population of 75,770. Most of these teachers maintained private schools, while others taught in the charity schools run by churches, the African Free School, or the school for girls established in 1802 by the Association of Women Friends for the Relief of the Poor. About one hundred children attended the Roman Catholic school, eighty-six the Trinity Church school, and seventy a school run by the Dutch Reformed Church. Though these schools were open to all children, each religious group believed it essential to inculcate all children with religious values as well as with a knowledge of reading, writing, and arithmetic. Mayor DeWitt Clinton, nephew of New York governor and Vice President George Clinton, and other community leaders worried that even with these private charity schools many children were missing out on an education. The children most in need of instruction were those whose parents did not have religion, and so would be unlikely to send their children to a church-run school.

Foundation. In February 1805, at Clinton's urging, a group of New Yorkers met to found the New York Free School Society, committed to opening free schools for all children in New York City. Clinton himself did not attend the meeting, which decided to submit a memorial to the state legislature to incorporate their society and to lend it whatever aid the legislature "deemed proper for the promotion of the benevolent object" of education. The legislature did incorporate the society but did not give it any money. Instead, the legislature limited its income to $10,000 per year, to be raised through subscrip-

First school built by the New York Free School Society, 1809

The Society for Establishing a Free School in the City of New York, a committee of the city's leading citizens, drafted this memorial to the state legislature on 25 February 1805:

Your memorialists have viewed with painful anxiety the multiplied evils which have accrued, and are daily accruing, to this city, from the neglected education of the children of the poor. They allude more particularly to that description of children who do not belong to, or are not provided for, by any religious society; and who, therefore, do not partake of the advantages arising from the different Charity Schools established by the various religious societies of this city. The condition of this class is deplorable indeed; reared up by parents who, from a variety of concurring circumstances, are become either indifferent to the best interests of their offspring, or, through intemperate lives, are rendered unable to defray the expense of their instruction, these miserable and almost friendless objects are ushered upon the stage of life, inheriting those vices which idleness and the bad example of their parents naturally produce. The consequences of this neglect of education are ignorance and vice, and all those manifold evils resulting from every species of immorality, by which public hospitals and alms-houses are filled with objects of disease and poverty, and society burthened by taxes for their support. In addition to these melancholy facts, it is to be feared that the laboring class in the community is becoming less industrious, less moral, and less careful to lay up the fruit of their earnings. What can this alarming declension have arisen from but the existence of an error which has ever been found to produce a similar effect—a want of a virtuous education, especially at that early period of life when the impressions that are made generally stamp the future character?

The rich having ample means of educating their offspring, it must be apparent that the laboring poor—a class of citizens so evidently useful—have a superior claim to the public support.

Trusting that the necessity of providing suitable means for the prevention of the evils they have enumerated will be apparent to your honorable Body, your memorialists respectfully request the patronage and assistance of the Legislature in establishing a free school or schools, in this city, for the benevolent purpose of affording education to those unfortunate children who have no other mode of obtaining it.

On 9 April 1805 the legislature incorporated the New York Free School Society, which opened its first school on 19 May 1806.

Source: A. Emerson Palmer, *The New York Public School: Being a History of Free Education in the City of New York* (New York: Macmil-

tions. Members could join the Free School Society for eight dollars in annual dues; for twenty-five dollars a member would be entitled to send one child to the Free School; and for forty dollars a member could send two children. The Free School Society elected its trustees, with DeWitt Clinton as president, and began soliciting money both to establish a Free School and to open a Sunday school for children unable to attend school during the week. Though both the Free School and the Sunday school were to be nonsectarian, not affiliated with any particular religion, still the "primary object" of both was "without observing the particular forms of any religious Society, to inculcate the sublime truths of religion and morality contained in the Holy Scriptures."

Raising Money. Though the trustees published their appeal in all of the city's newspapers, people were slow to contribute. DeWitt Clinton gave the first pledge, for $200, but no one else gave more than $50, and most contributions were for $25. In the first year the Free School Society raised $6,501, and in May 1806, one year after it began its public campaign, it was able to open a school in New York City, with about forty pupils. In April 1806 Col. Henry Rutgers, a member of the State Board of Regents, donated a lot on Henry Street for the building of a school "to meet the wants of the indigent in that populous part of the city." Rutgers, who later served as president of the Free

School's board of trustees, was a great benefactor of education: he contributed $5,000 to help Queen's College in New Brunswick, New Jersey, remain open; the college thanked him by adopting his name.

State and City Aid. Benefactors such as Clinton and Rutgers were rare. With limited resources and the aim of educating hundreds of pupils, the trustees of the Free School Society decided to adopt the educational system of Joseph Lancaster, an English educational reformer. In January 1807 the trustees once again approached the legislature for help in educating the city's poor; this time the legislature agreed to grant the society $4,000 to build their school and another $1,000 each year. This money would come from a tax on strong liquors and licensing fees charged to inns and taverns. The City of New York agreed to give the society a building next to the almshouse, along with $500 to repair it, in return for the society's agreeing to educate fifty children from the almshouse. By early 1808, 240 pupils were attending the school, which quickly outgrew its temporary space. In 1809 the Free School Society began building a new brick schoolhouse, 120 by 40 feet, able to hold five hundred children in a single room. The lot for the school, valued at $10,000, had been donated by the city in return for the education of almshouse children. Construction cost $13,000, though much of the material was donated, and the two carpenters and master mason who supervised the labor also donated their fees. DeWitt Clinton, president of the board of trustees, spoke at the dedication ceremony for New York Free School No. 1 on 11 December 1809, reviewing the history of the Free School movement, praising the Lancastrian system, and looking ahead to the future of education in the new republic. As one contemporary historian noted, "A building, dedicated to the gratuitous instruction of five hundred children, under the care of a single individual, was a spectacle, which had never before been exhibited on the American continent."

More Schools. Building its first school and planning for others put the society into debt. With its first school in operation, fund-raising proceeded more smoothly. In 1810 the society raised $13,000, and its second school, built on land donated by Colonel Rutgers, opened in November 1811. The legislature too was willing to contribute more from the liquor tax, and Trinity Church donated land on Hudson and Christopher Streets for an additional school. By 1814 the two Free Schools in operation had an enrollment of nearly eight hundred children. In addition, the Female Association used two rooms in the schools to instruct three hundred girls in both academic subjects and needlework. The first school had been coeducational, but School No. 2 was, at first, for boys only. Gradually, the education of girls had been taken over by the Female Association.

Religious Instruction. Though one impetus for the Free School Society had been to set up a nonsectarian school for the poor, the trustees believed religious instruction necessary for the future welfare of both its students and the society in which they would live. Every Tuesday afternoon the schools would be conducted by women from various religious denominations who would instruct the students in the catechisms of the student's own church. According to school records, 271 students were Presbyterians; 186 were Episcopalians; 172 were Methodists; 119 were Baptists; 41 were Dutch Reformed; and 9 were Roman Catholic. The students were also to gather at their school on Sunday morning to be escorted to their own church by the class monitors.

Success. By 1819 the Free School Society was running four free schools in New York City, all under the Lancastrian system. In 1815 the Free Schools received $3,708.14 from the state as its part of the State Common School Fund, established by the sale of the state's public lands. This Common School Fund, the society noted with thanks, was "one of the most important laws recorded in the annals of our Legislature," as it was a practical plan "calculated to confer lasting benefits on the community." The beginning of the Free School movement in New York City, relying on private philanthropy and public support and bringing a community together to educate the poor, was one of the most important developments in the early republic.

NATIONAL UNIVERSITY

In a letter to Alexander Hamilton on 1 September 1796, President George Washington explained his thoughts on the need for a national university:

... I mean Education *generally* as one of the surest means of enlightening and giving just ways of thinking to our Citizens, but particularly the establishment of a University; where the youth from *all parts* of the United States might receive the polish of Erudition in the Arts, Sciences, and Belle Letters; and where those who were disposed to run a political course, might not only be instructed in the theory and principles, but (this Seminary being at the Seat of the General Government) where the Legislature would be in Session half the year, and the interests and politics of the Nation of course would be discussed, they would lay the surest foundation for the practical part also.

But that which would render it of the highest importance, in my opinion, is, that the Juvenile period of life, when friendships are formed, and habits established that will stick by one; the youth, or young men from different parts of the United States would be assembled together, and would by degrees discover that there was not cause for those jealousies and prejudices which one part of the Union had imbibed against another part: of course sentiments of more liberality in the general policy of the Country would result from it. What, but the mixing of people from different parts of the United States during the War rubbed off these impressions? A century in the ordinary intercourse, would not have accomplished what the Seven years association in Arms did: but that ceasing, prejudices are beginning to revive again, and never will be eradicated so effectually by any other means as the intimate intercourse of characters in early life, who, in all probability, will be at the head of the councils of this country in a more advanced stage of it.

Source: Sol Cohen, ed., *Education in the United States: A Documentary History* (New York: Random House, 1974).

Source:
A. Emerson Palmer, *The New York Public School* (New York: Macmillan, 1905).

THE NEW YORK LAW, 1795

George Clinton. New York passed a compulsory education law in 1665 which required all children and servants to be instructed in law and religion as well as reading, writing, and arithmetic. As in other colonies, most children and servants would be instructed at home; the only children sent to schools would be those destined for the ministry. In 1787 New York established a state board of regents to oversee the state's educational system, and in 1795 Gov. George Clinton had noted with pride the "general establishment and liberal endowment of academies" yet could not overlook the way this system conferred education only "on the children of the opulent" and excluded "the great proportion of the community" from the advantages of education. To overcome this persistent class barrier to education, Clinton advised "the establishment of the common school throughout the state."

Statute. The legislature on 9 April 1795 passed a sweeping act to create a system of public education in New York State. New York appropriated £100,000 (approximately $3,298,000 in today's currency) over a period of five years to support and maintain schools in the state. This amount was divided among the counties, from New York County, which received £1,888 each year (about $62,000 today), to Onondaga, which received £174 ($5,739). The people of each town would elect a school committee of two or three members to supervise the schools and would also appoint trustees for each school who were required to submit a "return" to the committee listing all students in attendance, days each student was in class, and days each teacher was conducting class. The committee would then pay the teacher from the fund established by the law. In this way, though the state would distribute money to establish schools, it left the running and organization of schools in the hands of local communities.

Charity Schools. In New York City two different systems of education had already begun operation. The city had private academies and reading schools in addition to one free school: the African Free School, established in 1787 to teach the city's free black children. This school, established by the Society for Promoting the Manumission of Slaves and for Protecting Such of Them as have been or may be Liberated, led by John Jay and Alexander Hamilton, hoped to end slavery in New York. Of New York's four thousand African Americans, about half were still slaves; the African Free School would help ease the transition to freedom and allow African Americans to be part of free society. The African Free School was followed by other "charity schools" sponsored by churches, which tried to educate poorer children and make them productive members of society. New York's private-school teachers had hoped to be reimbursed by the state under the 1795 law; instead, the city distributed the state money to the charity schools.

Reality. The only available returns for the entire state show that in 1798 New York had 1,352 schools in operation and that some 59,660 children were receiving instruction for at least part of the year (the state's total population was about 589,000). In Westchester County the school year had a maximum of 288 days, though most students attended only for one-quarter or one-half of that time. In most cases the schools enrolled both boys and girls, and in some cases white and black children attended the same school. The teacher had an interest in having students attend: he would be paid based on enrollment, attendance, and days taught. For teaching a total of 5,386 days, calculated from the attendance of

George Clinton, the New York governor who advocated the 1795 law that created a system of public education in the state

thirty-six pupils over one school year, Robert Gilmore was paid $41.07 (about $500 in today's currency).

Lottery. The law of 1795 had supported a broad system of public education. In 1800 the state decided not to extend it. The state decided not to support education through taxes but instead to have a statewide lottery, which would raise $100,000, some of which would be apportioned among private academies by the Board of Regents and the rest distributed among the common schools at the legislature's discretion. The legislature had subsidized public education for five years; in 1800 it returned the problem of paying for education to the individuals of the state.

Sources:
A. Emerson Palmer, *The New York Public School* (New York: Macmillan, 1905);

Robert F. Seybolt, *The Act of 1795 for the Encouragement of Schools and the Practice in Westchester County* (Albany: University of the State of New York, 1919).

NOAH WEBSTER AND AMERICAN CULTURAL INDEPENDENCE

Schoolmaster. Noah Webster was graduated from Yale College in 1778, and while he prepared himself for a career in law, he supported himself by teaching school.

Frontispiece and title page for the third part of *A Grammatical Institute of the English Language*,
Noah Webster's spelling book based on his educational reforms

Webster was admitted to the bar in 1781, but he would practice law only briefly, devoting his real energy to a career in education. As a schoolteacher Webster noted how difficult it was for children to learn spelling. "It is now the work of years for children to learn to spell; and after all, the business is rarely accomplished. A few men, who are bred to some business that requires constant . . . writing, finally learn to spell most words without hesitation," but most people "make mistakes, whenever they take up a pen," and would "never attempt to write a letter, without frequently consulting a dictionary."

Barriers. A student's problem with spelling also made for difficulty in pronunciation. Foreigners found it difficult to pronounce English words, as the spelling and pronunciation often varied; Americans living in different areas spoke much differently, and these regional dialects Webster saw as warning signs for a country not fully united. Unless Americans all spoke the same language and could understand one another fully, trouble was ahead.

Solution. Noah Webster had a practical solution to this problem of spelling. First, he would eliminate all silent letters. For instance, the "a" in "bread" and the "gh" in "night" and "eight" could be dropped. Second, for words such as "mean" and "near" and "speak," he would substitute an "e" for the "a," making them read "meen,"

"neer," and "speek." This would bring their spelling into line with their pronunciation. Finally, for vowels with either long or short pronunciations, Webster would add a small stroke to indicate the difference. These changes would make it easier both to write and to learn the language "and would render the pronunciation uniform, in different parts of the country, and almost prevent the possibility of changes."

Uniformity. Webster had practical as well as ideological reasons for proposing this simplicity. The most practical reason was that the reform would make it easier to learn the language, and with fewer letters books and newspapers could be shorter, thus saving paper and allowing more space for expressing ideas. (Webster estimated that his reform would eliminate one letter out of every sixteen or eighteen and thus would save one page out of every sixteen or eighteen, cutting ten pages from a 180-page book.) More importantly, Webster hoped these changes would make the pronunciation of the language as uniform as the spelling in books. This would make all Americans speak the same language and eliminate potentially dangerous regional and class differences in the spoken language, replacing prejudice and animosity with "mutual affection and respect."

Independence. This change would foster not only unity but also national independence. It would be necessary for all books to be printed in America, rather than England, and so Americans could become intellectually as well as politically independent. A national language, Webster wrote, "is a band of national union. Every engine should be employed to render the people of this country national. . . . However they may boast of Independence, . . . yet their opinions are not sufficiently independent; an astonishing respect for the arts and literature of their parent country, and a blind imitation of its manners, are still prevalent among the Americans. Thus an habitual respect for another country, deserved indeed and once laudable, turns their attention from their own interests, and prevents their respecting themselves."

A Grammatical Institute. Webster's reform proposal was enthusiastically endorsed by Benjamin Franklin, who had proposed a similar measure some years earlier. Webster was unsuccessful, though, in fully purging English of silent letters and making for uniform pronunciation. His spelling book, *A Grammatical Institute, of the English Language* (1783), had much more success in creating a national system of education. The first edition's five thousand copies were exhausted within a year, and by 1837 Webster estimated that fifteen million copies had been printed. *A Grammatical Institute,* or the "blue-backed speller," replaced Thomas Dilworth's *A New Guide to the English Tongue* (1770), written in England and full of the wrong values, Webster believed. His book was for Americans and has been called a literary declaration of independence. In it Webster advised American schoolchildren on proper pronunciation, and if he could not forge a single national dialect, he could try to purge regional variations, advising children not to drop the final "g" in "-ing," or pronounce "spirit" as "speret." He also insisted on pronunciation of "-tion" and "-cion" as one syllable ("-shun") rather than the traditional two syllables. In 1788 Webster changed the name of his speller to *An American Spelling Book.*

Part Two. Webster followed his speller with *A Grammatical Institute of the English Language* (1784), which attempted to codify and reform American grammar. Webster, with his experience as a schoolteacher, taught the language as it was spoken rather than teaching grammar through memorization of rules. Webster blasted earlier grammarians for their "stupid opinion" that the English language rested on Latin and that only by learning Latin could people understand the rules of English. Instead, English rested on a Saxon base. Webster advised reform and simplification, but his *A Grammatical Institute of the English Language* was less popular than his speller.

Other Activities. Webster's speller was published in Hartford; if Webster did not secure a copyright in every other state, printers outside of Connecticut could sell the book without paying Webster a cent. He visited all thirteen states to secure copyrights; this experience convinced him that the United States needed a uniform copyright law, and to secure this law, which would be the only way to create a national community, the country needed a stronger Consti-

tution. He was a fervent advocate for the Constitution in 1787, writing one of the first pamphlets in its defense. Webster was a staunch Federalist in the 1790s, engaging in political questions as editor of various newspapers and magazines. In the wake of the 1797 yellow fever outbreak he compiled *A Brief History of Epidemic and Pestilential Diseases* (1799), which sorted through the existing knowledge on the causes of disease. He remained fascinated by the American language, though, and in 1806 published *A Compendious Dictionary of the English Language,* a forerunner of his 1828 *An American Dictionary of the English Language.* Though Webster failed to simplify American English or to create a single national community, he led the way to America's cultural independence.

Sources:

Rena L. Vassar, ed., *Social History of American Education,* volume 1, *Colonial Times to 1860* (Chicago: Rand-McNally, 1965);

Harry R. Warfel, *Noah Webster: Schoolmaster to America* (New York: Macmillan, 1936).

SUNDAY SCHOOLS

The Idea. Fear that people without education would form a lawless mob and upset the established order motivated reformers in the late eighteenth century to establish a broad system of education and to institute schools on Sundays. The Sunday school idea had been imported from England, where the industrial system had taken women and children from their homes and put them to work in factories, making it impossible for them to enjoy the traditional home-based education. Sunday schools gave these working people a chance to learn to read and write.

Philadelphia. In 1791 Sunday schools were opened in Philadelphia to persons of all ages, both men and women, who could not afford to educate themselves. The schools were supported by charitable donations and were run by religious societies, though they were nonsectarian. The Philadelphia school required its students to attend public worship on Sundays, though it did not matter which denomination. Within two years over eight hundred students had attended this Sunday school.

Working Girls. In 1791 the Duck Manufactory, outside of Boston, opened a Sunday school for its employees, particularly the young girls working in the factory. These "young daughters of industry" were prevented from studying on any other day, so the Sunday school, run by Oliver Lane, allowed them to pay "attention to the morals and instruction" offered by their employer, whose example, the papers said, did him "infinite honor."

Churches. While some Sunday schools were opened by businesses, most were sponsored by churches. In Philadelphia virtually every religious denomination had a Sunday school, conducted by "pious young Ladies" who formed an association for this purpose. Each would instruct between ten and twenty students who met in the various churches of the city. People of all colors, ages, and social classes attended these schools, whose lessons were drawn from the Bible. Most noted by contemporaries were the older African Americans in attendance. The Sunday school in Newark, New Jersey, launched in May 1815, had over four hundred students by the end of summer.

Making Better Servants. Though originally drawing both upper and lower classes, the Sunday school's main focus quickly became the poor. It was noted in Newark that the "improvement of the blacks is said to be extraordinary and that they display as much intellect as white children could do in similar circumstances." As important to their employers, their "behavior as servants has much improved since the institution of the schools; they are tractable and sedate, and some have been reclaimed from habits of profaneness and intemperance." The Sunday school movement after 1815 continued to offer instruction to working people, though the movement itself, in the fervor of the second Great Awakening, became part of a broader evangelical movement.

Source:
Vera M. Butler, *Education as Revealed by New England Newspapers Prior to 1850* (New York: Arno, 1969).

THOMAS JEFFERSON'S PLAN

Republican Society. After independence Virginia and the other states had to revise many of their laws, which had rested on the authority of the king. In Virginia Thomas Jefferson was assigned to rewrite the state's legal code. Jefferson was not content simply to remove vestiges of British rule; his revision aimed to destroy aristocratic

privilege and any form of tyranny over the mind of man. Jefferson proposed particular laws to do this: one abolished primogeniture and entail, rules of inheritance which prevented large estates from being broken up and bequeathed to several children. This law, Jefferson said, "laid the axe to the roote of Psuedo-aristocracy." He was disappointed and frustrated that the assembly did not pass his more ambitious law on education, which would have created a statewide system of public grammar schools, elementary schools, academies, and a public college and state library. This law would have ensured that "Worth and genius" would be "sought out from every condition of life, and compleatly prepared by education for defeating the competition of wealth and birth for public trusts."

Virginia. Jefferson understood the importance of education. In Virginia only the children of wealthy men, such as Jefferson, could be sent to school. Teachers were paid by parents, and their real job was to prepare young men for college. Since entrance to college required a knowledge of Latin and Greek, these private schools and academies focused on these languages. Children were more often educated at home, but this education was meant to prepare a child for a life of farming or plying a trade rather than for college or literary pursuits. In Virginia slave children were not taught to read and write, as this might allow them to escape. Virginia's educational system encouraged elites to send their sons to college to be trained as leaders of society; children of all others, white and black, were educated to remain subservient to the educated elite.

Proposal. Jefferson's system of education was a dramatic change. He called for each county to have survey-

Lutheran schoolhouse in 1805

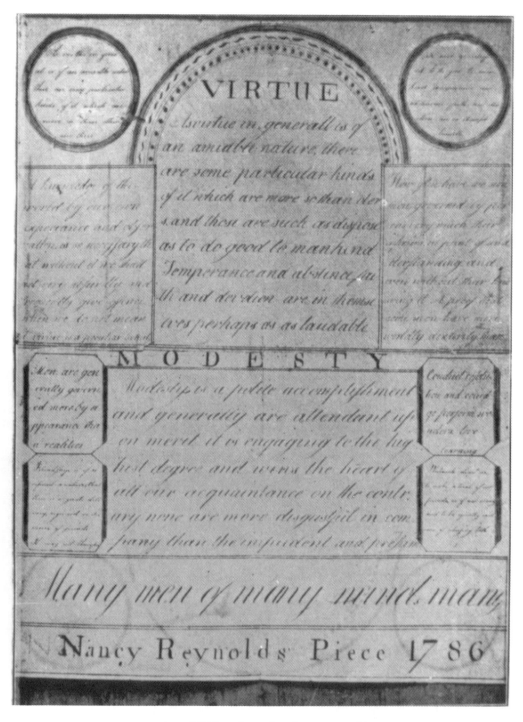

An exhibition piece of student penmanship

ors lay out the land into districts of five or six square miles and to determine the relative population of each. The free inhabitants of each district then would decide where to build a school, which would be paid for by taxes. All free children in the district, male and female, would attend the school for free. "This would throw on wealth the education of the poor," Jefferson said. The children would learn "reading, writing, and common arithmetick," and the texts used should also acquaint them with "Graecian, Roman, English, and American history."

Upward Mobility. All children would attend this school for three years; parents wanting to send their children for longer would have to pay tuition. Each year the superintendent, appointed by the alderman to supervise ten of the grammar schools, would choose one student, "of best genius in the school, of those whose parents are too poor to give them further education," and send that student on to the next level at public expense. Jefferson proposed building twenty schools throughout the state to teach Greek, Latin, geography, and higher mathematics to prepare students for college. After six years the best

I. Persons of each sex, and of any age, shall be admitted into these schools, in which they shall be taught to read and write: the hours of teaching will be, during the present season, from eight to half-past ten o'clock in the morning: and from half past four to half past six in the evening.

II. The teachers shall oblige all who are committed to their charge to attend public worship every Sunday, in the society to which they respectively belong, unless prevented by illness or any other sufficient cause.

III. The teachers shall take care that the scholars come clean to their respective schools; and if any scholar be guilty of lying, swearing, pilfering, talking in an indecent manner, or other misbehaviour, the teacher shall point out the evil of such conduct; and if, after repeated reproof, the scholar shall not be reformed, he or she shall be excluded from the school.

IV. The religious observance of the Christian Sabbath, being an essential object with the society for the institution and support of Sunday Schools, the exercise of the scholars shall be restricted to reading the Old and New Testament, and to writing copies from the same.

V. A copy of the above Rules shall be put up in the school-rooms, and read by the teacher to the scholars every Sunday.

Source: Vera M. Butler, *Education as Revealed by New England Newspapers Prior to 1850* (New York: Arno, 1969).

students would go on to college where they would learn the sciences, while the others would be qualified to go home and teach at the grammar schools. By this means, Jefferson wrote, "twenty of the best geniuses will be raked from the rubbish annually, and be instructed, at the public expense, so far as the grammar schools go." The whole plan would break the connection between wealth and power, as all children would have a chance to be educated, and the most talented would be encouraged to learn. "The ultimate result of the whole scheme of education would be the teaching all the children of the state reading, writing, and common arithmetic: turning out ten annually of superior genius, well taught in Greek, Latin, geography, and the higher branches of arithmetic: turning out ten others annually, of still superior parts, who, to those branches of learning, shall have added such of the sciences as their genius shall have led them to: the furnishing to the wealthier part of the people convenient schools, at which their children may be educated, at their own expence."

Failure of Reform. Jefferson's plan failed in the assembly. First the assembly amended his bill to allow the judges in each county to decide when the whole system of education should be created; Jefferson believed that since the judges tended to be wealthy and thus would be forced to pay taxes to educate poorer children, they would be unwilling to create this ambitious system. The assembly voted down the whole measure in 1786, but Jefferson continued to advocate creating an educational system that would reward talent rather than wealth and privilege. No state would create a system as ambitious as Jefferson's until long after his death in 1826; Virginia

The original grounds of the University of Virginia, designed by Thomas Jefferson and established in 1819

Thomas Jefferson's plan to reform Virginia's education system gave a broad outline of a progressive school structure; the details of what was taught, he thought, would be filled in by experts. Jefferson, however, had his own ideas on the proper course of instruction:

The first stage of this education being the schools of the hundreds, wherein the great mass of the people will receive their instruction, the principal foundations of future order will be laid here. Instead therefore of putting the Bible and Testament into the hands of the children, at an age when their judgments are not sufficiently matured for religious inquiries, their memories may here be stored with the most useful facts from Grecian, Roman, European, and American history. The first elements of morality too may be instilled into their minds; such as, when further developed as their judgments advance in strength, may teach them how to work out their own greatest happiness, by showing them that it does not depend on the condition of life in which chance has placed them, but is always the result of a good conscience, good health, occupation, and freedom in all just pursuits. Those whom either the wealth of their parents or the adoption of the state shall destine to higher degrees of learning, will go on to the grammar schools, which constitute the next stage, there to be instructed in the languages. The learning Greek and Latin, I am told, is going into disuse in Europe. I know not what their manners and occupations may call for: but it would be very ill-judged in us to follow their example in this instance. There is a certain period of life, say from eight to fifteen or sixteen years of age, when the mind, like the body, is not yet firm enough for laborious and close operations. If applied to such, it falls an early victim to premature exertion; exhibiting indeed at first, in these young and tender subjects, the flattering appearance of their being men while they are yet children, but ending in reducing them to be children when they should be men. The memory is then most susceptible and tenacious of impressions; and the learning of languages being chiefly a work of memory, it seems precisely fitted for the powers of this period, which is long enough too for acquiring the most useful languages ancient and modern. I do not pretend that language is science. It is only an instrument for the attainment of science. But that time is not lost which is employed in providing tools for future operation: more especially as in this case the books put into the hands of the youth for this purpose may be such as will at the same time impress their minds with useful facts and good principles. If this period be suffered to pass in idleness, the mind becomes lethargic and impotent, as would the body it inhabits if unexercised during the same time.

Source: Thomas Jefferson, *Notes on the State of Virginia* (1787), in *The Portable Thomas Jefferson*, edited by Merrill Peterson (New York: Viking, 1974).

could not create such a system until after the Civil War, when the power of the planting elite had been broken and slavery had been abolished.

College Education. Jefferson also had plans for college education. His original bill called for making his alma mater, the College of William and Mary, into a university which would teach science. The college, however, was unwilling to be taken over by the state because it was still under the control of the Anglican Church, which required all professors to subscribe to the Church's thirty-nine articles and students to learn its catechism. Moreover, Baptists opposed the measure because they feared that a university at William and Mary would help disseminate Anglicanism. As a result Jefferson turned his attention after his retirement from the presidency in 1809 to the founding of the University of Virginia, which was established in 1819.

Sources:
Merrill Peterson, ed., *The Portable Thomas Jefferson* (New York: Viking, 1974);

Wilson Smith, ed., *Theories of Education in Early America* (Indianapolis: Bobbs-Merrill, 1973);

David B. Tyack, ed., *Turning Points in American Educational History* (Waltham, Mass.: Blaisdell, 1967).

WRITING TEACHERS

Skill. In an age when all documents had to be written by hand, it was essential that these documents be written neatly and legibly. Handwriting was an important skill to learn, and there was disagreement about the best way to teach it. Most schools simply taught writing by having students learn words; the Lancastrian system and Jenkins's system both taught letters before words. Jenkins's system was specifically a way to learn penmanship, while Lancaster's system was part of a whole theory of education. Writing with a good hand was crucial to doing business, and young men trying to advance in the business world would generally enter an established firm as a clerk, responsible for copying documents. It was essential that they write clearly and quickly. One writing teacher noted that his students were graded 70 percent on legibility, 20 percent on speed, and 10 percent on elegance.

Jenkins. The first important American writing text was published in 1791 by John Jenkins of Boston. Jenkins believed that writing was "a mechanical art to be taught mechanically" and argued that all letters were based on six strokes. Jenkins ultimately published his lessons in a series of seven books titled *The Art of Writing Reduced to a Plain and Easy System, on a Plan Entirely New* (1813), and included recipes for ink, directions for making pens, and practice business forms. Writing lessons typically took one to two hours per day, as students both practiced the six basic strokes and the formation of letters. The American Academy of Arts and Sciences endorsed Jenkins's method, and it proved popular throughout the country.

School Supplies. Paper was an expensive commodity not to be wasted on teaching children to write. In the Lancastrian schools of New York City, children learned to form letters on a table covered with a layer of sand. Later, these schools began writing with chalk on boards painted black. In Vermont, where slate was plentiful, children could use it for their writing exercises. Slate was breakable, and students were often required to provide their own. Elsewhere, pupils used tree bark or other materials when writing their lessons. Students would learn to write using charcoal, rocks, or chalk. Pens were difficult to find, and pupils would have to make their own out of sticks or feathers, using a special small knife (a "penknife") to shape their point. Pupils would also learn to make lead pencils by pouring molten lead into a crack in a brick hearth. When the lead hardened, it could be removed and one end sharpened. In 1812 William Monroe of Concord, Massachusetts, found a way to manufacture pencils in quantity. He gave up the business, but John Thoreau of Concord, father of Henry David Thoreau, helped support his family by making and selling pencils to a Boston art school.

Itinerant Instructors. Many writing teachers found it difficult to support themselves in one place, so they traveled to different towns to offer writing lessons. Amos Towne, for example, had taught in Gloucester, Haverhill, Andover, and Salem, Massachusetts, before settling in Hartford, Connecticut, where he hoped to draw students both from that city and New Haven. He advertised that students could "acquire a fair regular handwriting" through his fifteen ninety-minute exercises, and after suitable practice "may acquire a habit of writing with ease and dispatch." His method was based on Jenkins's theory, as were most other systems of writing. One writing teacher in Hartford reminded readers in 1815 that "writing is the soul of commerce, the picture of the past, the regulator of the future, and the messenger of thought," and invited both young men intent on careers in business and children beginning their education to attend his school. "Let those Write now who never Wrote before," he urged, heartened at the return of peace which would bring more business to merchants and clerks and "important changes in the commercial department." The future belonged to good, clear writers, he knew, and he closed his statement with a warning: "Those parents who prefer that their children should continue their 'marking and guessing' on the common plan, to the loss of much

PEN AND INK

According to the *American Instructor* (1799), the best way to make a quill pen was as follows:

Scrape off the superfluous Scurff on the back of the Quill, so that the slit may be fine, and without the Gander's teeth. Cut Quill at end half through the back Part, and then turning up the Belly cut the other half or part quite through viz about a fourth or about half an inch at the end of the Quill which will then appear forked. Then enter the Pen knife a little back of the Notch and then putting the peg of the Pen knife Haft (or the end of another Quill) into the back Notch holding your thumb pretty hard on the back of the Quill (as high as you intend the slit to be) then with a sudden and quick Twitch force up the Slit. It must be sudden and smart that the Slit may be clearer. Then by several cuts of each Side bring the Quill into equal Shape or Form on both sides, and having brought it to a fine Point place the inside of the Nib on the Nail of your Thumb and enter the Knife at the extremity of the Nib, and cut it through a little sloping. Then with an almost downward cut of the Knife, cut the Nib, and then by other proper cuts finish the Pen, bringing it into handsome Shape and proper Form.

John Jenkins's recipe for ink was found in *The Art of Writing* (1813):

Recipe to make excellent Black Ink. For three pints.

3 oz. Aleppo Galls

3 oz. Copperas

1 oz. Gum Arabic

Boil six ounces of Logwood, strain through a cloth and mix the whole. The ink will be better if the Galls are steeped several days first and the copperas, etc., added afterwards.

time and stationary, and to the neglect of more important branches, ought not to complain, if they miss their object, disappoint their expectations, and, instead of reaching the heights of scientific eminence and profound erudition, they prove in the end but superficial scholars."

Sources:
Vera M. Butler, *Education as Revealed by New England Newspapers Prior to 1850* (New York: Arno, 1969);
Harriet Webster Marr, *The Old New England Academies Founded before 1826* (New York: Comet, 1959).

HEADLINE MAKERS

CALEB BINGHAM

1757-1817

TEXTBOOK WRITER

Background. Caleb Bingham was born in 1757 in Salisbury, Connecticut. He graduated from Dartmouth College in 1782, delivering the Latin valedictory address to his classmates. Following graduation he took charge of Moor's Indian Charity School, which prepared Indians to study at Dartmouth. By 1784 he was in Boston, where he opened a private school to teach young women "the useful branches of reading, writing, etc." Bingham would spend the rest of his life in Boston, teaching school, writing textbooks, and running his own publishing house, becoming one of the most successful and influential textbook writers in American history.

Books. Bingham's first book, *The Young Lady's Accidence: or A Short and Easy Introduction to the English Grammar* (1785), was short, concise, and clear. He followed this volume with *The American Preceptor* (1794), a collection of speeches, excerpts from plays, and poetry designed for the teaching of both reading and elocution. Specifically designed for American schools, the selections convey a sense of religious piety and patriotic honor which is even more pronounced in Bingham's most successful text, *The Columbian Orator* (1797). These books, collections of pieces from varied sources, became the most common readers in American schools. Bingham also wrote an astronomy and geography text, and a reading and spelling book designed for young children. With one of his daughters he published *Juvenile Letters; Being a Correspondence Between Children, From Eight to Fifteen Years of Age* (1803), which was a series of essays meant to introduce students to the forms of composition. Bingham opened his own bookshop and publishing house in Boston, which became a gathering place for the city's teachers.

Other Activities. Bingham advocated the changes which came with the Massachusetts school law of 1789, requiring towns to maintain schools. He was appointed master of one of Boston's new reading schools. In addi-

tion to promoting free schools, Bingham pushed for the creation of libraries and other institutions to spread knowledge. His bookshop became a center for the agitation which led Massachusetts, after his death on 6 April 1817, to create free primary schools. Bingham was a staunch Republican and an unsuccessful candidate for political office; Gov. Elbridge Gerry appointed him director of the state prison. Though he never held political office, his *Columbian Orator* influenced generations of American politicians, introducing them not only to the forms of rhetoric but also to the vibrant ideas of American democracy and republican principles.

Source:
Paul Eugen Camp, "Caleb Bingham," in *Dictionary of Literary Biography 42: American Writers for Children Before 1900* (Detroit, Mich.: Bruccoli Clark, 1985).

TIMOTHY DWIGHT

1752-1817

PRESIDENT OF YALE COLLEGE

Reformer. As president of Yale, Timothy Dwight was not only that college's most influential leader but also one of the young nation's most important educators. During Dwight's twenty-one years at Yale, he found able and inspiring teachers, launched the teaching of science and medicine, planned the creation of schools of law and theology, and gave the faculty and president a central role in running the school.

Restless Energy. Timothy Dwight was born on 14 May 1752 in Northampton, Massachusetts. Dwight's mother, the daughter of theologian Jonathan Edwards, had seen to his early education, and by the age of four he was reading the Bible; at six he taught himself Latin. Dwight had entered Yale at thirteen, and four years later graduated with the highest honors, though he made himself nearly blind in the process. He began teaching, but in 1777 he joined the Continental Army, serving at West Point, where he instructed soldiers and also wrote patriotic songs. Returning to Northampton when his father died in 1779, Dwight ran two farms, preached in the local church, and established a school which became so popular that he had to hire two assistants. His neighbors elected him to the county government in 1781 and 1782, and they would have elected him to Congress had he not decided to become a minister in 1783. At Greenfield, Connecticut, he established a school, drawing nearly a thousand students from across the country during its twelve years of operation. Dwight also wrote prolifically, publishing *The Conquest of Canaan*, an epic poem, in 1785. In 1788 he wrote *The Triumph of Infidelity*, an attack on Voltaire, and other works which made Dwight the intellectual voice of conservative Federalism, particularly after his cousin, Aaron Burr, killed Alexander Hamilton, Federalism's chief intellectual, in an 1804 duel.

Ambition. Politically and religiously conservative, Dwight, like his cousin Burr, had tremendous energy and ambition. In 1795 he declined the presidency of Union College but within a few weeks accepted the presidency of Yale, transforming that institution into a modern university, though with a firm reliance on New England Calvinism. So great was Dwight's restless ambition even he feared it, saying just before his death, "I have coveted reputation and influence to a degree which I am unable to justify." He was directly involved in all aspects of Yale: teaching rhetoric, logic, ethics, and metaphysics, serving as professor of theology and preaching in the college chapel. (He gave a series of sermons over a four-year period, so all students would hear each one.) Some students called him "Pope Dwight."

Politics. He expanded Yale's curriculum and was involved in other institutions for the betterment of mankind: the Andover Theological Seminary, the American Board of Commissioners for Foreign Missions, and the Missionary Society of Connecticut. A bitter enemy of Jeffersonian republicanism, Dwight's vision for mankind's improvement rested on a certainty of God's punishment and his belief that men could only live happily in stable and orderly societies. His sermons, *The True Means of Establishing Public Happiness* (1795), *The Nature, and Danger, of Infidel Philosophy* (1798), *The Duty of Americans, at the Present Crisis* (1798), and *Discourse . . . on the Character of George Washington* (1800) all touch on these themes. On Jefferson's election he said, "We have a country governed by blockheads and knaves; our wives and daughters are thrown into the stews; can the imagination paint anything more dreadful this side of hell." In 1799 Dwight became embroiled in a controversy with Josiah Meigs, a mathematics and natural philosophy professor. Dwight suspected him of Republican tendencies and forced him to state his political beliefs publicly and to deny that he was an "enemy to the constitution and

liberties of my country." Dwight died in New Haven on 11 January 1817.

Sources:

Charles E. Cuningham, *Timothy Dwight 1752–1817: A Biography* (New York: Macmillan, 1942);

Richard Hofstadter and Walter P. Metzger, *The Development of Academic Freedom in the United States* (New York: Columbia University Press, 1955).

SAMUEL KNOX

1756-1832
EDUCATOR

Second Prize. In 1796 the American Philosophical Society held a contest to design the best system of education for the United States. Samuel Knox entered, proposing a system of national instruction particularly designed for this "wide extent of territory, inhabited by citizens blending together almost all the various manners and customs of every country in Europe." Providing elementary education for both girls and boys, uniform training and salaries for teachers, standard textbooks produced by a national university press, with a college in every state each charging the same fees and tuition, and at "the fountain head of science" a national university, Knox's ambitious plan won second prize.

Career and Ministry. First prize had gone to Samuel Harrison Smith, who would go on to a career as a journalist and politician during the Jefferson years. Knox, on the other hand, never strayed too far from education. Born in County Armagh, Ireland, in 1756 and descended from Scotch-Irish Presbyterians, Knox first arrived in America in 1786 and stayed in Maryland for three years. He then crossed the Atlantic again to attend the University of Glasgow, winning prizes there for Greek and Latin scholarship and a master's degree in 1792. He studied for the ministry, was licensed by the Presbytery of Belfast, and returned to America in 1795 as a Presbyterian minister.

Religion, Education, Politics. Knox served as a pastor at Bladensburg (1795–1797) and Frederick, Maryland (1797–1803), and also as a schoolteacher, beginning his teaching career at Bladensburg Grammar School in 1788. From 1797 to 1803 he served as principal of the Frederick Academy, and from 1808 to 1820 he was principal of Baltimore College. In addition to his religious and educational duties, Knox engaged in the political debates of the day, writing pamphlets in 1798 on Joseph Priestley's "avowed Religious Principles" and in 1800 *A Vindication of the Religion of Mr. Jefferson and a Statement of his Services in the Cause of Religious Liberty*. Knox approved of Jefferson's Virginia Statute for Religious Freedom and also of Jefferson's proposed system of education for Virginia. Knox proposed a similar system for Maryland, with the same lack of success Jefferson had across the Potomac. Jefferson may have been influenced by Knox's essay when he designed the University of Virginia in 1816. One year later Knox was offered a professorship in languages and belles lettres at the University of Virginia, but the plans fell through. A dedicated reformer with visionary plans for America's future, Knox was also a despotic teacher and unable to bring his grandest schemes to fruition. He died on 31 August 1832 in Frederick.

Sources:

Sol Cohen, ed., *Education in the United States: A Documentary History* (New York: Random House, 1974);

Wilson Smith, ed., *Theories of Education in Early America 1655–1819* (Indianapolis: Bobbs-Merrill, 1973).

FRANCIS JOSEPH NICHOLAS NEEF

1770-1854
EDUCATIONAL REFORMER

Background. Francis Joseph Nicholas Neef was born in 1770 in Alsace, a French province on the border with Germany. Growing up he learned to speak both French and German and began to study for the priesthood, learning Latin, Greek, and Italian. The excitement of the French Revolution brought Neef out of the monastery and into the French army in 1791, and he was wounded in the Italian campaigns of 1796. Recovering from his wounds, Neef read the works of Swiss educational reformer Johann Heinrich Pestalozzi. Like many others of the age, Pestalozzi was trying to find ways to achieve personal perfection. He also sought to regenerate the poor of Europe and build a new society founded on equality and liberty. Unlike others, Pestalozzi sought liberty and perfection through developing a system of education. Neef was inspired by Pestalozzi and sought to become a schoolteacher.

Pestalozzi's System. Pestalozzi in 1800 opened a school in Burgdorf, Switzerland. His school differed from most European and American grammar schools of the day, which relied on rote learning: the teacher would read the lesson; the students would copy it down and memorize it; and at the end of the week each student would recite the lesson from memory. Pestalozzi believed education was a natural process and that children would learn best by following their natural curiosity rather than by having their minds crammed with facts. Pestalozzi's General Method, the first part of his educational program, called for the teacher to create a loving and nurturing environment for the students, who would learn best in an atmosphere of love and trust. The Specific Method, which would commence in this atmos-

phere of love and trust, called for the teacher to "begin by what is simple, plain, known, by what you find in the child; dwell on each point till the learner is perfectly master of it." The teacher would begin with an object known to the student and study it, breaking it into component parts, introducing from a concrete example more abstract principles, but going slowly and gradually so that all students would come to the same understanding.

America. Neef visited Pestalozzi's school and was hired to be an instructor in languages. After three years of training, and marriage to one of the students, Neef was sent to Paris to open a Pestalozzian school there. In 1805 William Maclure, a wealthy merchant originally from Scotland who had recently become a naturalized citizen of the United States, visited Pestalozzi. Maclure was making an informal study of educational methods and immediately saw the Pestalozzian system as an ideal reform for America. He offered to pay the salary of a Pestalozzian teacher who would open a school in the United States, and Pestalozzi recommended Neef. Arriving in Philadelphia in 1806, Neef spent two years learning English before opening his school five miles outside the city. He also published the first book on teaching method published in English in America, *Sketch of a Plan and Method of Education . . . Suitable for the Offspring of a Free People, and for All Rational Beings* (1808).

Developing Skills. Neef's book explained the Pestalozzian method. Enrollment would be limited to students between the ages of six and eight, as he wanted a fairly homogeneous group to learn together. Rather than have each student memorize passages of literature and recite individually, as was common in the schools of the day, Neef worked with all students together, helping them develop first their skills at measuring and counting by learning arithmetic by counting beans or marbles, then worked on their ability to draw, and only later began to develop writing skills. Rather than drilling the students in principles of grammar, each student would become a grammarian, learning grammatical rules from his or her own observations of language's use. Only after being thoroughly grounded by observation and conversation would students begin to read books. Like later educational reformers, Neef also rejected the teaching of Latin and Greek, focusing instead on living, practical languages rather than the classics.

Students. Neef's seventy-five students came mainly from Philadelphia, though some also came from Boston, Savannah, and small towns in Kentucky. Neef had purposely located his school outside the city so his students could enjoy fresh air and exercise: Neef thought it essential to develop the students' bodies and minds and led them on walks through the countryside, during which he would teach the principles of natural history by direct observation (Neef was elected to the Academy of Natural Sciences in 1812). He also taught gymnastic exercises and swimming. In 1813 Neef moved his school to Delaware and then to Kentucky the next year. He remained in

Kentucky until 1826 when social reformer Robert Owen, who had began a utopian community at New Harmony, Indiana, invited Neef to run the community's school. After the failure of the community Neef opened a school in Cincinnati, then returned to New Harmony in 1834. He died in 1854.

Legacy. Neef and Pestalozzi anticipated many educational reforms of the early twentieth century by stressing the learning environment, observation rather than memorization, and physical development. Many of Neef's pupils went on to become lawyers, doctors, and engineers.

Source:
Gerald Lee Gutek, *Joseph Neef: The Americanization of Pestalozzianism* (Tuscaloosa: University of Alabama Press, 1978).

PUBLICATIONS

Caleb Bingham, *The American Preceptor: Being a New Selection of lessons for reading and Speaking. Designed for the use of Schools* (Boston: Printed by I. Thomas & E. T. Andrews for the author, 1794)—some 600,000 copies of this book were sold; it went through fifty-five editions by 1818 and stayed in use until 1837;

Bingham, *An Astronomical and Geographical Catechism for the Use of Children* (Boston: Printed & sold by S. Hall, 1795)—this volume had sixteen editions by 1819;

Bingham, *The Columbian Orator: Containing a Variety of Original and Selected Pieces; Together with Rules Calculated to Improve Youth and Others in the Ornamental and Useful Art of Eloquence* (Boston: Printed by Manning & Loring, 1797)—one of the most influential textbooks of the period; Bingham's selection of speeches, plays, and poetry trained a generation of Americans in the art of rhetoric and oratory;

Bingham, *The Young Lady's Accidence: or, A Short and Easy Introduction to the English Grammar. Designed, Principally, for the Use of Young Learners, More Especially Those of the Fair Sex, Though Proper for Either* (Boston: Printed by Greenleaf & Freeman, 1785)—Bingham's first textbook, written especially for the young women in his Boston school;

Robert Coram, *Political Inquiries: to Which is Added, a Plan for the General Establishment of Schools Throughout the United States* (Wilmington, Del.: Printed by Andrews & Brynberg, 1791)—Coram, a librarian, developed a plan for educating all American children;

Jacob Abbot Cummings, *An Introduction to Ancient and Modern Geography* (Boston: Cummings & Hilliard, 1813);

Jedidiah Morse, *Geography Made Easy* (New Haven, Conn.: Meigs, Bowen & Dana, 1784)—Morse, a clergyman, and father of telegraph pioneer Samuel F. B. Morse, wrote this influential text, which became the standard work of American geography;

Joseph Neef, *The Method of Instructing Children Rationally, in the Arts of Writing and Reading* (Philadelphia: Printed for the author, 1813);

Neef, *Sketch of a Plan and Method of Education, Founded on the Analysis of the Human Faculties, and Natural Reason, Suitable for the Offspring of a Free People, and for All Rational Beings* (Philadelphia: Printed for the author, 1808)—Neef opened the first American school using the teaching methods of Johann Pestalozzi;

Sarah Pierce, *Sketches of Universal History Compiled from Several Authors for the Use of Schools*, volume 1 (New Haven, Conn., 1811)—a history textbook prepared in the form of a catechism;

Nicholas Pike, *A New and Complete System of Arithmetic, Composed for the Use of Citizens of the United States* (Newburyport, Mass.: Printed & sold by J. Mycall, 1788)—the first American arithmetic textbook;

Benjamin Rush, *Defense of the Use of the Bible as a Schoolbook, in a Letter from the Celebrated Doctor Rush to the Rev. J. Belknap* (Concord, N.H., 1806);

Rush, *A Plan for the Establishment of Public Schools and the Diffusion of Knowledge in Pennsylvania; To which are Added Thoughts Upon the Mode of Education, Proper in a Republic* (Philadelphia: Printed for Thomas Dobson, 1786);

Rush, *Thoughts upon Female Education, Accommodated to the Present State of Society, Manners and Government in the United States of America* (Philadelphia: Printed by Prichard & Hall, 1787);

Christian Gotthilf Salzmann, *Elements of Morality, for the Use of Children; With an Introductory Address to Parents. Translated by Mary Wollstonecraft* (Philadelphia: Printed by J. Hoff & H. Kammerer Jr., 1796)—a German text originally published in 1791;

Samuel Harrison Smith, *Remarks on Education: Illustrating the Close Connection between Virtue and Wisdom* (Philadelphia: Printed for John Ormrod, 1798)—Smith won first prize in an American Philosophical Society contest for this essay on education;

Noah Webster, *A Compendius Dictionary of the English Language* (New Haven: From Sidney's Press, 1806)—Webster's first attempt at a dictionary;

Webster, *A Grammatical Institute, of the English Language*, part I (Hartford, Conn.: Printed by Hudson & Goodwin for the author, 1783)—the famous "blue-backed speller," from which generations of Americans learned spelling and grammar;

Webster, *A Grammatical Institute of the English Language*, part II (Hartford, Conn.: Printed by Hudson & Goodwin for the author, 1784)—a continuation of part I, more of a grammar book than a speller.

The Wren Building at the College of William and Mary, Williamsburg, Virginia, originally built in 1695-1698 from plans by Sir Christopher Wren (Colonial Williamsburg)

CHAPTER SIX

GOVERNMENT AND POLITICS

by JAYNE TRIBER

CONTENTS

Sidebars and tables are listed in italics.

1783

15 Mar.	The Newburgh Conspiracy ends after Gen. George Washington refuses to support Continental Army officers threatening military action if Congress does not grant back pay and pensions.
8 June	Washington sends a circular letter to the states recommending that they give Congress sufficient power "to regulate and govern the general concerns of the confederated republic."
8 July	The Massachusetts Supreme Court abolishes slavery and declares it a violation of the state constitution.
3 Sept.	Great Britain and the United States sign the Treaty of Paris, ending the Revolutionary War.
7 Oct.	The Virginia legislature grants freedom to slaves who served in the Continental Army during the Revolutionary War.

1784

•	Connecticut and Rhode Island pass gradual emancipation laws.
14 Jan.	Congress ratifies the Treaty of Paris.
23 Apr.	Congress passes the Land Ordinance of 1784, establishing a national policy for settling and governing the western territories.
7 May	Congress appoints Thomas Jefferson to assist John Adams and Benjamin Franklin in negotiating commercial treaties with European nations.
26 June	Spain closes the Mississippi River to American trade.

1785

11 Jan.	Congress moves from Philadelphia to New York City.
24 Jan.	James Madison heads a congressional committee to convince the states to grant Congress more power to regulate commerce, but the effort fails.
24 Feb.	Congress appoints John Adams minister to England.
10 Mar.	Congress appoints Thomas Jefferson minister to France, replacing Benjamin Franklin.
20 May	Congress passes the Land Ordinance of 1785, revamping the system for settling western areas and setting aside land and revenue to support public education.

1786

16 Jan.	The Virginia legislature passes Thomas Jefferson's Bill for Establishing Religious Freedom, enacting the principles of religious toleration and separation of church and state.
22 Aug.	Debt-ridden farmers in western Massachusetts hold a convention in Hampshire County to discuss grievances against the state government and to demand the issuance of paper money.
29 Aug.	Armed insurgents led by Revolutionary War veteran Daniel Shays begin closing courts in western Massachusetts after the legislature ignores their list of grievances.

11–14 Sept.	Delegates from five states meet in Annapolis, Maryland, to discuss commercial problems. The Annapolis Convention votes to reconvene in Philadelphia the next year to strengthen congressional authority.

1787

25 Jan.	Gen. William Shepherd and one thousand militiamen end Shays's Rebellion by thwarting an attack on the Springfield Arsenal.
25 May	Delegates from all the states except Rhode Island begin a Constitutional Convention in Philadelphia.
29 May	Edmund Randolph submits the Virginia Plan to the Constitutional Convention, proposing a bicameral legislature based on proportional representation, a national executive and judiciary, and a congressional veto of state laws.
31 May	The Constitutional Convention votes that the people should directly elect members of the House of Representatives.
15 June	William Paterson presents the New Jersey Plan to the Convention, proposing to retain the unicameral national legislature (with each state having an equal vote) and to expand congressional control over trade and revenue.
11 July	The Constitutional Convention votes to count three-fifths of the slave population for taxation and representation purposes.
13 July	Congress passes the Northwest Ordinance, establishing the Northwest Territory (present-day Illinois, Indiana, Ohio, Michigan, Wisconsin, and parts of Minnesota). The Ordinance defines the steps for the creation and admission of new states and bars slavery in the area.
16 July	The Constitutional Convention approves the "Great Compromise," granting proportional representation in the House of Representatives and equal state representation in the Senate.
29 Aug.	The Convention gives Congress power to pass navigation acts, approves a fugitive slave clause, and forbids Congress from regulating the slave trade before 1808.
17 Sept.	The Constitutional Convention ends when all but three delegates sign the Constitution. Power is divided among three branches of the federal government and between the federal and state governments.
7 Dec.	Delaware is the first state to ratify the Constitution.
12 Dec.	Pennsylvania ratifies the Constitution.
18 Dec.	New Jersey ratifies the Constitution.

1788

2 Jan.	Georgia ratifies the Constitution.
9 Jan.	Connecticut ratifies the Constitution.
6 Feb.	Massachusetts narrowly ratifies the Constitution by a vote of 187–168.

27 Feb.– 26 Mar.	Free African Americans, led by Prince Hall, petition the Massachusetts state legislature, protesting the seizure and transportation of freed slaves to the West Indies. The legislature declares the slave trade illegal and votes to compensate the victims.
28 Apr.	Maryland ratifies the Constitution.
23 May	South Carolina ratifies the Constitution.
21 June	New Hampshire is the ninth state to ratify the Constitution. With this ratification the Constitution is declared to be in effect.
25 June	Virginia ratifies the Constitution but suggests a Bill of Rights and other amendments.
26 July	Despite strong opposition, New York ratifies the Constitution.

1789

4 Feb.	Electors unanimously choose George Washington as the first president of the United States. John Adams, who ran a distant second, becomes vice president.
4 Mar.	The first Congress to meet under the Constitution convenes in New York City.
15 Apr.	John Fenno begins publishing the Federalist newspaper *Gazette of the United States* in Philadelphia.
23 Apr.– 14 May	Congress argues over the use of presidential and vice-presidential titles.
30 Apr.	George Washington and John Adams are inaugurated as the first president and vice president of the United States.
4 July	Congress, led by James Madison, passes the Tariff Act of 1789, creating a source of revenue for the federal government.
20 July	Congress passes the Tonnage Act, imposing higher duties on foreign ships and rejecting James Madison's proposal to discriminate only against British ships.
11 Sept.	Alexander Hamilton is appointed secretary of the Treasury.
24 Sept.	Congress passes the Judiciary Act of 1789, creating a federal court system and giving the Supreme Court the right to review the constitutionality of state laws.
25 Sept.	Congress, led by James Madison, submits the first ten constitutional amendments (later known as the Bill of Rights) to the states.
26 Sept.	John Jay is appointed the first chief justice of the United States.
20 Nov.	New Jersey is the first state to ratify the Bill of Rights.
21 Nov.	North Carolina, influenced by the addition of a Bill of Rights, ratifies the Constitution.
26 Nov.	President George Washington consults department heads on foreign and military affairs, establishing the practice of regular cabinet meetings.

1790

•	According to the first United States census, the total population is 3,929,214, including 697,624 slaves and 59,557 free African Americans.

14 Jan.	Secretary of the Treasury Hamilton submits his First Report on Public Credit to Congress, recommending that Congress assume the states' debts and fund the national debt by issuing interest-bearing securities.
2 Feb.	The United State Supreme Court convenes for the first time.
11 Feb.	The Society of Friends sends Congress a petition calling for the abolition of the slave trade.
22 Mar.	Thomas Jefferson takes the office of secretary of state.
17 Apr.	Benjamin Franklin dies in Philadelphia at the age of eighty-four.
29 May	Rhode Island becomes the last state of the original thirteen to ratify the Constitution.
1 July	Congress approves a site on the Potomac River as the future capital of the United States (Washington, D.C.).
26 July	Congress passes Secretary of Treasury Hamilton's program for assuming the states' debts.
4 Aug.	Congress passes Hamilton's program for funding the national debt.
Oct.	In a series of battles Miami, Shawnee, and Delaware Indians led by Little Turtle (Mishikinakwa) defeat a U.S. military force under Gen. Josiah Harmar along the Maumee River, Northwest Territory.
6 Dec.	Congress opens its first legislative session in the temporary capital of Philadelphia.
14 Dec.	Secretary of the Treasury Alexander Hamilton submits a Second Report on Public Credit, proposing a national bank to hold government funds and issue banknotes as circulating currency.

1791

5 Jan.	Free blacks in Charleston, South Carolina, petition the state legislature against the banning of lawsuits or court testimony by African Americans; the legislature rejects the petition.
25 Feb.	President George Washington signs a bill creating the First Bank of the United States after receiving conflicting opinions of the bank's constitutionality from Secretary of the Treasury Alexander Hamilton and Secretary of State Thomas Jefferson.
3 Mar.	Congress passes an excise, or internal, tax on whiskey.
4 Mar.	Vermont becomes the fourteenth state.
31 Oct.	Philip Freneau begins publishing the Democratic-Republican newspaper *National Gazette* in Philadelphia.
4 Nov.	In the worst defeat ever inflicted by Native Americans on the U.S. military, the Miami Confederacy under Little Turtle kills over nine hundred soldiers out of a force of fourteen hundred led by Gen. Arthur St. Clair, governor of the Northwest Territory, along the Wabash River.
5 Dec.	Secretary of the Treasury Hamilton submits his Report on Manufactures, proposing protective tariffs and government support for new industries.

12 Dec.	The First Bank of the United States opens in Philadelphia with branches in other cities.
15 Dec.	The Bill of Rights becomes part of the Constitution. These ten amendments include protection of freedom of religion, speech, and the press.

1792

1 Mar.	Congress passes the Presidential Succession Act. In case of the death or disability of the president and vice president, power will pass to the president pro tempore of the Senate followed by the Speaker of the House.
1 June	Slaveholding Kentucky becomes the fifteenth state.
13 Oct.	The cornerstone of the new Executive Mansion is laid in Washington, D.C.

1793

23 Jan.– 28 Feb.	The House of Representatives examines charges of corruption against Secretary of the Treasury Alexander Hamilton, but a vote to censure him fails.
12 Feb.	Congress passes the first Fugitive Slave Law, enforcing part of Article IV, Section 2 of the Constitution.
13 Feb.	President George Washington is unanimously reelected.
18 Feb.	In *Chisholm* v. *Georgia* the Supreme Court rules that states can be sued in federal court by citizens of other states.
4 Mar.	President George Washington and Vice President John Adams are inaugurated for a second term.
8 Apr.– 16 May	Edmond Genet, the new minister from the French Republic, travels from Charleston, South Carolina, to Philadelphia, Pennsylvania, recruiting Americans to serve in privateering expeditions against Britain and Spain.
22 Apr.	Determined to keep the United States out of the war between France and Britain, President Washington issues the Proclamation of Neutrality.
8 June	Britain orders the seizure of neutral vessels, including American ships, carrying provisions to French ports.
18 Sept.	President Washington lays the cornerstone for the Capitol building in Washington, D.C.
6 Nov.	After issuing an order-in-council forbidding neutral trade with the West Indies, Britain begins seizing American ships and impressing crewmen.
31 Dec.	Secretary of State Thomas Jefferson resigns.

1794

3 Jan.	In response to the British seizure of American ships, James Madison recommends that Congress penalize countries discriminating against American commerce; the resolution fails.

10 Feb.	Sir Guy Carleton, British governor of Lower Canada, makes a speech encouraging Indian resistance in the Northwest Territory.
22 Mar.	Congress passes a bill forbidding the slave trade with foreign nations.
27 Mar.	President Washington signs a bill authorizing construction of six frigates for the United States Navy, responding to threats against American shipping from Great Britain, France, and the Barbary states.
19 Apr.	The Senate confirms the nomination of Supreme Court Chief Justice John Jay as special envoy to negotiate a treaty with Great Britain.
5 June	Congress passes the Neutrality Act, forbidding Americans from joining foreign military forces or provisioning foreign vessels in American ports.
July–Nov.	Farmers in western Pennsylvania resist officials trying to collect the whiskey tax and threaten to attack Pittsburgh. President Washington and Secretary of the Treasury Hamilton lead nearly thirteen thousand militiamen to enforce the law, but the Whiskey Rebellion is over by the time they arrive.
20 Aug.	Gen. Anthony Wayne and three thousand American soldiers rout one thousand Native Americans led by Blue Jacket at the Battle of Fallen Timbers near Detroit.
19 Nov.	Jay's Treaty is signed in London. Britain will evacuate its posts in the Northwest by 1796 and allow limited American trade in the West Indies. However, the treaty stipulations say nothing about British impressment of American seamen or compensation for slaves taken by the British army during the Revolutionary War.

1795

2 Jan.	The Georgia state legislature grants the Yazoo Tract to four land companies on very favorable terms.
31 Jan.	Secretary of the Treasury Alexander Hamilton resigns.
24 June	After secret debates, the Senate ratifies Jay's Treaty by a vote of 20–10.
3 Aug.	The United States and twelve Indian tribes in the Northwest sign the Treaty of Greenville, opening much of present-day Ohio to white settlement.
19 Aug.	Secretary of State Edmund Randolph resigns after corruption charges (later proven untrue) are leveled against him.
5 Sept.	The United States signs a treaty with Algiers, promising to pay $800,000 in tribute to the dey of Algiers and for ransom of over one hundred American sailors.
27 Oct.	The United States and Spain sign the Pinckney Treaty, recognizing the thirty-first parallel as the southern boundary of the United States and granting Americans free navigation of the Mississippi River.

1796

	The state of Georgia rescinds the Yazoo land grants because all but two members of the legislature had been bribed.
15 Feb.	The French foreign minister informs U.S. minister to France James Monroe that Jay's Treaty annuls all previous treaties between France and the United States.

3 Mar.	The Senate unanimously ratifies Pinckney's Treaty.
7 Mar.	In *Ware* v. *Hylton* the United States Supreme Court declares a state law unconstitutional for the first time.
8 Mar.	In *Hylton* v. *U.S.* the Supreme Court upholds the constitutionality of an act of Congress for the first time.
25 Mar.	By a vote of 62–37 the House of Representatives passes a motion asking President George Washington to submit all papers on Jay's Treaty to a House committee.
30 Mar.	President Washington refuses to turn over papers on Jay's Treaty to the House, establishing the precedent of executive privilege.
30 Apr.	By a vote of 51–48 the House of Representatives passes appropriations to implement Jay's Treaty.
1 June	Slaveholding Tennessee becomes the sixteenth state.
17 Sept.	In his Farewell Address, President George Washington expresses concern over party politics and reaffirms his commitment to neutrality.
4 Nov.	The United States signs a treaty with the Barbary state of Tripoli, agreeing to pay annual tributes to protect American ships and sailors.
7 Dec.	In the nation's first contested presidential election, Federalist John Adams defeats Democratic-Republican Thomas Jefferson by a narrow electoral vote of 71–68; Jefferson becomes vice president.
7 Dec.	The French foreign minister refuses to meet with Charles Cotesworth Pinckney, the new United States minister to France, until "grievances have been redressed."

1797

30 Jan.	Free blacks unsuccessfully petition Congress against a state law returning freedmen to slavery in North Carolina.
4 Mar.	President John Adams and Vice President Thomas Jefferson are inaugurated.
16 May	President Adams recommends that Congress approve a three-man diplomatic mission to France, arm merchant vessels, create a navy, fortify harbors, and enlarge the army.
28 Aug.	The United States signs a treaty with the North African state of Tunis, agreeing to pay annual tributes to protect American ships and sailors.
4 Oct.	American peace commissioners John Marshall, Charles Cotesworth Pinckney, and Elbridge Gerry arrive in Paris to negotiate an end to the seizure of U.S. vessels.
18 Oct.	Three agents of French foreign minister Charles de Talleyrand (publicly identified as "X," "Y," and "Z") demand a bribe from the American envoys before negotiations can begin. Charles Cotesworth Pinckney responds: "No, no, not a sixpence!"

1798

•	The United States and France begin the "Quasi-War," an undeclared naval conflict in the Caribbean.

8 Jan.	The Eleventh Amendment, reversing *Chisholm* v. *Georgia* (1793), is ratified. The amendment declares that states cannot be sued by citizens of another state or foreign country in federal court.
3 Apr.	President John Adams releases diplomatic dispatches to Congress on the "XYZ Affair." Within a week the "XYZ Papers" are published in newspapers throughout the country, exciting outrage against France.
May–July	Congress revokes all treaties with France and approves an enlarged army, a new Navy Department, harbor defenses, and the seizure of all French vessels interfering with American shipping.
18 June	Congress passes the Naturalization Act, the first of four Alien and Sedition Acts, limiting freedom of speech and the press and the rights of foreigners. The act also increases the residency period for citizenship to fourteen years.
25 June	Congress passes the Act Concerning Aliens, allowing the president to deport any alien, during war or peace, judged "dangerous to the peace and safety of the United States"; President Adams never uses this authority.
27 June	Benjamin Franklin Bache, grandson of Benjamin Franklin and editor of the Philadelphia Republican newspaper *Aurora,* is charged with libeling President Adams.
6 July	Congress passes the Act Respecting Alien Enemies, authorizing the president to deport or imprison enemy aliens during wartime.
9 July	Congress passes a direct tax on land, houses, and slaves to pay for the Quasi-War with France.
14 July	Congress passes the Act for the Punishment of Certain Crimes (the Sedition Act) by a vote of 44–41. The act imposes heavy fines and imprisonment on anyone convicted of writing, publishing, or speaking anything of "a false scandalous and malicious nature" against the government or its officers.
Oct.–Nov.	Peace envoy Elbridge Gerry and Dr. George Logan, a private citizen from Philadelphia, return to the United States convinced that France is ready to negotiate peace.
5 Oct.	Republican representative Matthew Lyon of Vermont is indicted under the Sedition Act for libeling President Adams. He is fined $1,000 and imprisoned for four months, during which he is reelected to Congress.
16 Nov.	The Kentucky Resolutions, drafted by Thomas Jefferson and passed by the Kentucky state legislature, declare that states can judge the constitutionality of federal laws, and that the Alien and Sedition Acts are unconstitutional and thus "void and of no force."
24 Dec.	The Virginia state legislature passes the Virginia Resolutions, a less radical version of the Kentucky Resolutions, written by James Madison.

1799

30 Jan.	Congress passes the Logan Act, forbidding private citizens from engaging in diplomatic negotiations.
Feb.	Farmers in Pennsylvania, led by John Fries, rebel against the direct tax of 1798. Federal troops put down Fries Rebellion, and the leader is convicted of treason but pardoned by President Adams.
18 Feb.	President Adams nominates William Vans Murray as minister to France.

29 Mar.	The New York state legislature passes a gradual emancipation law.
16 Oct.	President John Adams sends Oliver Ellsworth and William R. Davie to join William Vans Murray in negotiating peace with France.
22 Nov.	The Kentucky state legislature passes resolutions reaffirming nullification as a proper constitutional solution.
14 Dec.	George Washington dies at Mount Vernon at age sixty-seven.

1800

- The second U.S. Census records a population of 5,308,483, including 896,849 slaves. Free African Americans are not counted.
- The Virginia state legislature passes a resolution proposing that freed slaves be resettled in Africa.

2 Jan.	Free African Americans petition Congress in opposition to slavery and the slave trade. By a vote of 85–1, Congress refuses to accept the petition.
10 May	The Land Act of 1800 offers federal land for sale in tracts of 320 acres and under generous payment terms.
30 Aug.	Authorities in Richmond, Virginia, are prewarned and stop a planned slave revolt led by Gabriel Prosser. Thirty-eight members of Gabriel's Rebellion (including Prosser) are hanged.
30 Sept.	The United States and France sign an agreement ending the Quasi-War, during which the United States seized ninety-three French privateers and France took only one American warship. Under the Convention of 1800 the 1778 treaties of alliance and commerce are suspended, and compensation for the seizure of American merchant ships is left to future negotiations.
17 Nov.	Congress convenes in Washington, D.C., for the first time. John Adams becomes the first president to live in the new Executive Mansion.

1801

- News of Spain's cession of the Louisiana Territory to France reaches the United States in May, spurring President Thomas Jefferson to inquire about purchasing West Florida.

20 Jan.	John Marshall is appointed chief justice of the United States, serving until his death in 1835.
10–17 Feb.	John Adams receives sixty-five electoral votes and Thomas Jefferson and Aaron Burr each receive seventy-three votes, throwing the presidential election into the House of Representatives. On the thirty-sixth ballot Jefferson is elected, and Aaron Burr becomes vice president.
13 Feb.	Congress passes the Judiciary Act of 1801, reducing the number of Supreme Court justices from six to five, establishing sixteen circuit courts, and increasing the number of judicial officers.
3 Mar.	On his last day in office President John Adams appoints several Federalist judges under the Judiciary Act of 1801.
4 Mar.	Thomas Jefferson is the first president to be inaugurated in Washington, D.C.

14 May	Yusuf Karamanli, pasha of Tripoli, orders soldiers to cut down the flagpole at the U.S. Consulate.
8 Dec.	President Jefferson delivers his annual message to Congress in writing, setting a precedent that lasts until 1913.
21 Dec.	The Convention of 1800 between the United States and France goes into effect after the United States gives in to French demands that claims for compensation to American shipowners be withdrawn.

1802

6 Feb.	Congress authorizes the president to arm American ships as protection against Tripolitan corsairs.
8 Mar.	Congress repeals the Judiciary Act of 1801.
16 Mar.	Congress passes a bill establishing a military academy at West Point, New York.
6 Apr.	Congress abolishes all internal taxes, including the unpopular whiskey tax.
14 Apr.	Congress repeals the Naturalization Act of 1798, restoring the five-year residency requirement for citizenship.
29 Apr.	Congress passes a new Judiciary Act, authorizing six Supreme Court justices, one session a year for the Supreme Court, and six circuit courts, each presided over by a Supreme Court justice.
18 Oct.	Spanish officials in New Orleans forbid American traders from depositing cargo for overseas shipment.

1803

11 Jan.	President Thomas Jefferson appoints James Monroe as minister plenipotentiary to France and Spain to assist Robert Livingston in purchasing New Orleans and Spanish Florida.
19 Feb.	Ohio becomes the seventeenth state in the Union and the first to outlaw slavery from the beginning of statehood.
24 Feb.	In *Marbury* v. *Madison* the Supreme Court declares an act of Congress (the Judiciary Act of 1789) unconstitutional for the first time and expands its power of judicial review.
11 Apr.	France offers to sell the entire Louisiana Territory to the United States.
19 Apr.	Spain restores the right of deposit at New Orleans to American traders.
30 Apr.	The United States purchases the Louisiana Territory for $15 million.
23 May	Commodore Edward Preble is appointed commander of a U.S. Navy squadron to fight Tripoli.
20 Oct.	The Senate ratifies the Louisiana Purchase treaty.
20 Dec.	French officials turn over the Louisiana Territory to the United States.

1804

15 Feb.	New Jersey passes a gradual emancipation law.

25 Feb.	In the first congressional caucus Democratic-Republicans unanimously nominate President Thomas Jefferson for a second term and nominate George Clinton for vice president.
12 Mar.	After the House of Representatives impeaches New Hampshire Federal District judge John Pickering, a Federalist, for drunkenness, profanity, and unlawful decisions, the Senate removes him from office. The House then begins impeachment proceedings against Federalist Supreme Court Justice Samuel Chase.
26 Mar.	In the Louisiana Territory Act, the federal government declares for the first time its intention to move Indians living east of the Mississippi River to the West.
	The Land Act of 1804 reduces the minimum tract for the purchase of federal land from 320 to 160 acres, increasing immigration to the West.
14 May	Meriwether Lewis and William Clark begin their exploring expedition of the Louisiana Purchase territory.
11 July	Alexander Hamilton is fatally wounded in a pistol duel with Aaron Burr and dies the next day.
25 Sept.	The Twelfth Amendment to the Constitution is ratified, providing separate ballots for president and vice president.
5 Dec.	President Thomas Jefferson is reelected with 162 electoral votes over Charles Cotesworth Pinckney with 14 votes. George Clinton is elected vice president.

1805

1 Mar.	The House of Representatives impeaches Justice Samuel Chase for improper conduct in the sedition trial of James Callender and the treason trial of John Fries but fails to get the necessary two-thirds majority vote to remove him from office.
4 Mar.	President Thomas Jefferson is inaugurated for a second term.
26–29 Apr.	William Eaton, U.S. consul to Tunis, organizes a small force of Arab mercenaries, U.S. Marines, and American naval vessels to capture Derna, Tripoli.
4 June	The United States and Tripoli sign a peace treaty granting the U.S. Navy freedom to sail the Mediterranean.
23 July	American trade with the French West Indies is threatened when Great Britain invokes its Rule of 1756, banning neutral ships from trading during wartime in ports that they did not visit during peacetime.
29 Aug.	Zebulon Pike and twenty men set out to find the source of the upper Mississippi River.

1806

•	Virginia passes a law ordering freed slaves to leave the state within a year of emancipation.
29 Mar.	Congress authorizes the construction of the National Road, connecting Cumberland, Maryland, with Wheeling, Virginia.
18 Apr.	Congress passes a Non-Importation Act, prohibiting the importation of British goods in protest against the British seizure of American ships and sailors.

15 July	Zebulon Pike begins exploring the southwestern part of the Louisiana Purchase, during which time he and his men wander into Spanish territory and are held captive.
Aug.	Aaron Burr and coconspirators begin plotting to create an independent state in the Southwest.
23 Sept.	Meriwether Lewis and William Clark arrive back in Saint Louis, completing their two-and-one-half-year expedition. They explored the region west of the Mississippi River to the Pacific Ocean by way of the Missouri and Columbia Rivers. Along the way they gathered valuable information on the vegetation, animals, natural resources, geography, and Indian tribes of the area.
27 Nov.	After Gen. James Wilkinson reveals Aaron Burr's conspiracy, President Thomas Jefferson issues a proclamation warning American citizens not to join Burr's expedition to the Southwest.

1807

2 Mar.	Congress decides to prohibit the African slave trade and importation of slaves into the United States as of 1 January 1808.
22 June	The commander of the British frigate *Leopard* stops the U.S. warship *Chesapeake* off Norfolk, Virginia, and demands the surrender of four English deserters. When Commodore James Barron refuses, the British open fire (killing three and wounding eighteen Americans), board the U.S. vessel, and seize the alleged deserters.
24 June	Aaron Burr is indicted for treason.
2 July	In response to the *Chesapeake-Leopard* incident President Thomas Jefferson orders British warships out of U.S. territorial waters.
1 Sept.	Aaron Burr is acquitted of treason in Richmond, Virginia, on grounds he was not present during an overt, treasonous act.
22 Dec.	President Thomas Jefferson signs the Embargo Act, prohibiting American ships from sailing to any foreign ports.

1808

9 Jan.	Congress passes a second Embargo Act, imposing bonds and penalties on coasting vessels and fishing and whaling ships attempting to sail for foreign ports.
12 Mar.	Congress passes a third Embargo Act, prohibiting the export of any goods by land or sea.
17 Apr.	Napoleon Bonaparte issues the Bayonne Decree, ordering the seizure of all U.S. ships entering ports of the French Empire. France seizes some $10 million worth of United States ships and cargo.
25 Apr.	Congress passes an Enforcement Act that declares that no American vessel may sail for an American port adjacent to foreign territory without permission of the president, and that customs collectors and naval commanders may stop and search any ship on suspicion.
7 Dec.	Democratic-Republican candidate James Madison is elected president with 122 electoral votes. The Federalist Charles Cotesworth Pinckney receives 47 votes, and George Clinton, the candidate of eastern Democratic-Republicans, receives 6 votes. Clinton is elected vice president.

1809

9 Jan.	Congress passes a Second Enforcement Act, authorizing customs collectors to use the army and navy to aid in the seizure of any goods suspected of being shipped abroad in violation of the Embargo Act.
1 Mar.	President Thomas Jefferson signs the Non-Intercourse Act, repealing the Embargo Act and allowing Americans to resume all foreign trade except with Great Britain and France until either nation repeals its orders against neutral trade.
4 Mar.	President James Madison is inaugurated.
19 Apr.	Based on assurances from British minister David Erskine that Great Britain will revoke its orders-in-council against neutral shipping on 10 June, President Madison resumes trade with Great Britain.
2 July	The Shawnee tribal leader Tecumseh begins forming a confederacy of Native American tribes.
9 Aug.	Learning that the English government has annulled the agreement made between American officials and British minister Erskine, President Madison reinstates the Non-Intercourse Act.
30 Sept.	William Henry Harrison, governor of Indiana Territory, signs a treaty at Fort Wayne by which Indian tribes cede three tracts of land along the Wabash River.

1810

•	The third U.S. Census records a population of 7,239,881, an increase of 1,931,398 since 1800. The African American population has increased by 481,361 to 1,378,110, of whom 186,746 are free (not counted in the 1800 census).
16 Mar.	In *Fletcher* v. *Peck* the Supreme Court rules that the Georgia state legislature could not rescind the Yazoo land grants because a state is bound by contractual obligations.
23 Mar.	Napoleon issues the Rambouillet Decree, authorizing the seizure and sale of American ships entering French-controlled ports.
1 May	Congress passes Macon's Bill No. 2, legalizing American trade with France and Great Britain. If either country stops restricting neutral trade by 3 March 1811, the president is authorized to prohibit trade with the other country unless it abolishes its restrictions within three months.
5 Aug.	Napoleon advises his minister of foreign affairs to tell the U.S. minister to France that French decrees against neutral trade will be rescinded after 1 November if Great Britain rescinds its orders-in-council.
	Napoleon issues the Trianon Decree, authorizing the confiscation of American ships that entered French-controlled ports between 20 May 1809 and 1 May 1810.
27 Oct.	President James Madison annexes West Florida between the Mississippi and Pearl Rivers after Americans in the region declare independence.
2 Nov.	Believing that French decrees against neutral shipping have been rescinded, President Madison issues a proclamation stating that trade with Great Britain will cease if British orders-in-council are not rescinded within three months.

1811

20 Feb.	The Senate votes against rechartering the Bank of the United States.
4 Mar.	The charter of the Bank of the United States expires.
26 Sept.	Gov. William Henry Harrison of the Indiana Territory and one thousand troops march for Prophet's Town, the principal village of the Shawnee Indians and allied tribes along the Wabash and Tippecanoe Rivers.
5 Nov.	President James Madison asks Congress for increased defense spending in preparation for possible war against Britain.
7 Nov.	Native Americans under Tecumseh's brother the Prophet attack Harrison's army in the Battle of Tippecanoe; they are repulsed and Prophet's Town is burnt. As a result Tecumseh and his followers cross into Canada, later joining British forces in the War of 1812.
20 Nov.	Construction begins on the National Road, increasing the flow of settlers to the West after the War of 1812.
24 Dec.	Congress authorizes the completion of enlistments in the regular army, the enlistment of twenty-five thousand additional regulars for five years' service and fifty thousand volunteers for one year's service, and the call-up of one hundred thousand militia for six months' service at the president's request, and approves additional funds for the navy.

1812

14 Mar.	Congress authorizes an $11 million loan to finance the war with England.
4 Apr.	At President James Madison's request Congress approves a ninety-day embargo.
10 Apr.	Great Britain informs the United States that since France has not rescinded its decrees against neutral trade, British orders-in-council will remain in force.
14 Apr.	Congress annexes West Florida between the Pearl and Perdido Rivers to the Mississippi Territory.
30 Apr.	Slaveholding Louisiana becomes the eighteenth state in the Union.
18 May	The Republican congressional caucus nominates President James Madison for reelection and Elbridge Gerry for vice president.
1 June	President Madison sends a war message to Congress, citing impressment, violations of American trade, and the incitement of Indian warfare as the causes for hostilities with England.
4 June	By a vote of 79–49 the House of Representatives approves a declaration of war against Great Britain.
17 June	By a vote of 19–13 the Senate approves a declaration of war.
18 June	President James Madison signs the declaration of war with Great Britain.
23 June	Great Britain suspends its orders-in-council.
2 July	Acting governor John Cotton Smith of Connecticut refuses the federal government's request for militia.
17 July	The U.S. post on Michilimackinac Island in Michigan Territory surrenders to the British and their Indian allies.
5 Aug.	Gov. Caleb Strong of Massachusetts refuses the federal government's request for militia.

15 Aug.	Native Americans attack the American garrison at Fort Dearborn, Illinois (present-day Chicago), killing eighty-five soldiers and many dependents as they attempt to evacuate the post.
16 Aug.	Gen. William Hull, fearing superior enemy numbers, surrenders Detroit to British general Isaac Brock.
19 Aug.	The U.S.S. *Constitution*, commanded by Commodore Isaac Hull, sinks the British frigate *Guerriere*.
13 Oct.	An invasion of Canada fails in the Battle of Queenston when the New York militia under Gen. Stephen Van Rensselaer refuses to cross into Canada.
25 Oct.	The U.S.S. *United States*, commanded by Capt. Stephen Decatur, captures the British frigate *Macedonian*.
19 Nov.	At Plattsburgh, New York, Gen. Henry Dearborn abandons his planned assault on Montreal when militia forces refuse to cross into Canada.
2 Dec.	President James Madison is reelected with 128 electoral votes. DeWitt Clinton, candidate of anti-Madison Democratic-Republicans and Federalists, receives 89 votes. Elbridge Gerry is elected vice president.
12 Dec.	The British navy begins blockading the Delaware and Chesapeake Bays.
29 Dec.	The U.S.S. *Constitution*, commanded by Commodore William Bainbridge, destroys the British frigate *Java*.

1813

5 Feb.	John Armstrong becomes secretary of war.
4 Mar.	President James Madison is inaugurated for a second term.
11 Mar.	President Madison accepts the offer of Czar Alexander of Russia to mediate between the United States and Great Britain, but the latter refuses.
30 Mar.	The British extend their blockade of the American coast from Long Island, New York, to New Orleans, Louisiana.
27 Apr.	American forces under Generals Henry Dearborn and Zebulon Pike briefly capture York, Canada (now Toronto), and burn public buildings. The explosion of a powder magazine kills 320 troops, including Pike.
24 Jul.– 2 Aug.	Congress imposes a direct tax on land, a duty on imported salt, and a series of internal taxes to finance the war.
	Congress authorizes a $7 million loan to finance the war.
30 Aug.	Creek Indians attack Fort Mims, near Mobile, Alabama, killing more than 250 soldiers and civilians in the first battle of the Creek War.
Sept.–Nov.	Two American armies in upstate New York converge on Montreal, one led by Gen. Wade Hampton from Plattsburgh and the other by Gen. James Wilkinson from Sackett's Harbor. The campaign is abandoned after Hampton turns back at the Chateauguay River (26 October) and Wilkinson's army is repulsed at Chrysler's Farm (11 November).
10 Sept.	Capt. Oliver Hazard Perry's destruction of the British fleet at Put-in-Bay on Lake Erie forces the British out of Detroit and gives the United States control of the Michigan Territory.

5 Oct.	Gen. William Henry Harrison crosses Lake Erie and defeats British and Indian forces at the Battle of the Thames at Moraviantown (Upper Canada). Tecumseh is killed; the Indian confederacy collapses; and the Northwest is secured.
17 Dec.	Congress passes an Embargo and Non-Importation Act.

1814

•	The British defeat Napoleon, freeing up veteran forces for service in Canada and the United States.
18 Jan.	The Senate approves the appointments of Henry Clay, Jonathan Russell, John Quincy Adams, and James A. Bayard as members of a peace commission to Great Britain; Albert Gallatin is added soon afterward.
24 Mar.	Congress authorizes a $25 million loan to finance the war.
27 Mar.	In the last major battle of the Creek War, Tennessee militia led by Generals Andrew Jackson and John Coffee defeat the Indians at Horseshoe Bend in present-day Alabama.
14 Apr.	Congress repeals the Embargo and Non-Importation Act.
25 Apr.	The British extend their blockade to New England.
5 July	American generals Jacob Brown and Winfield Scott and their army cross the Niagara River into Canada and defeat the British in the Battle of Chippewa.
25 July	Gen. Jacob Brown wages a hard-fought but inconclusive battle against the British at Lundy's Lane, Canada, near Niagara Falls.
8 Aug.	Peace negotiations begin in Ghent, Belgium.
9 Aug.	The Creek Indians sign the Treaty of Fort Jackson, ceding two-thirds of their lands in southern Georgia and eastern Mississippi Territory (Alabama) to the United States.
24–25 Aug.	A British army under Gen. Robert Ross defeats a disorganized force of American regulars and militia at Bladensburg, Maryland. The British troops then burn the Executive Mansion, Capitol, and other public buildings in Washington, D.C., in retaliation for the American burning of York.
4 Sept.	Secretary of War John Armstrong resigns, and Secretary of State James Monroe takes over the War Department.
11 Sept.	Capt. Thomas Macdonough leads an American squadron to decisive victory over the British fleet on Lake Champlain, forcing British general Sir George Prevost to abandon plans for cutting off New England from the rest of the United States.
13–14 Sept.	Heavy casualties and an unsuccessful bombardment of Fort McHenry convince the British to abandon their plans to take Baltimore.
5 Nov.	Congress authorizes a $3 million loan to finance the war.
15 Dec.	Delegates from five New England states which oppose the war hold a convention in Hartford, Connecticut.
	Congress increases taxes to finance the war.
24 Dec.	The United States and Great Britain sign a peace treaty at Ghent. There are no territorial changes, and all other issues are unresolved or postponed.

1815

5 Jan.   The Hartford Convention ends. The delegates uphold a state's right to nullify federal law and propose constitutional amendments to limit the power of the federal government.

8 Jan.   Gen. Sir Edward Pakenham's British army attacks Andrew Jackson's greatly outnumbered American army in the Battle of New Orleans. The Americans inflict more than two thousand casualties while suffering only twenty-one killed and wounded.

11 Feb.   News of the Treaty of Ghent reaches the United States.

17 Feb.   The Senate ratifies the Treaty of Ghent.

3 Mar.   Congress approves a punitive expedition against Algiers, which had taken advantage of the War of 1812 to harass American shipping.

3 Mar.   Congress approves a peacetime army of ten thousand, half the number requested by President James Madison.

30 June   The dey of Algiers is forced to sign a treaty abolishing tribute payments and freeing American prisoners after Capt. Stephen Decatur captures two Algerian ships. Tunis and Tripoli sign similar treaties within the next six weeks.

3 July   Great Britain and the United States sign a treaty abolishing discriminatory duties against each other; the United States is also permitted to trade with the East Indies.

5 Dec.   President James Madison urges Congress to approve a national bank, protective tariffs, and a program of national funding for transportation and education.

OVERVIEW

"The Age of Experiments in Government." In 1783 the Treaty of Paris acknowledged the victory of the American republic over the British Empire. In 1815 the Treaty of Ghent acknowledged the American republic's successful "second revolution" against Great Britain in the War of 1812. The period in between may be called, in Thomas Jefferson's words, "the age of experiments in government." Jefferson's Declaration of Independence in 1776 established a government based on the consent of the governed that would secure "life, liberty, and the pursuit of happiness" for its citizens. How to implement those republican principles became the responsibility of the American people. The first American constitution, the Articles of Confederation, reflected the revolutionary generation's fear that a strong central government would threaten "life, liberty, and the pursuit of happiness." The Articles created "a firm league of friendship" among the states, which retained all their powers except those "expressly delegated" to the national government. By 1787 Americans recognized the limitations of weak central government and wrote a new constitution. A system of "checks and balances" and "separation of powers" established a federal republic, dividing power between the federal and state governments and among three branches of the federal government. In the 1790s the experiments continued when two political parties—Federalists and Democratic-Republicans—emerged with different visions for republican government. Despite frequently heated political debates, Americans had established by 1815 the legitimacy of the Constitution, the federal system of government, and the peaceful transfer of power from one political party to another. In that year Gen. Andrew Jackson's victory over the British in the Battle of New Orleans, as reported in the *Boston Patriot,* seemed nothing less than confirmation of the "Rising Glory of the American Republic."

State Sovereignty. In 1787 James Winthrop of Massachusetts, author of "The Agrippa Letters," warned that in a large country like the United States government "will degenerate to a despotism, unless it be made up of a confederacy of smaller states, each having full powers of internal regulation." James Madison reassured his countrymen that the federal system of government under the Constitution would not destroy state sovereignty because power was divided between the federal and the state governments. As Madison explained in *Federalist,* number 39, the jurisdiction of the federal government is limited "to certain enumerated objects only, and leaves to the several States a residuary and inviolable sovereignty over all other objects." Opponents wondered how "inviolable" state sovereignty was when the Constitution granted the federal government a lengthy list of specific powers, imposed several restrictions on state sovereignty, and gave Congress the right "to make all laws which shall be necessary and proper" for executing "all other powers" granted under the Constitution. In 1798 and 1799 Thomas Jefferson and James Madison, alarmed by the centralizing tendencies of the federal government under the Federalists, boldly asserted state sovereignty in the Kentucky and Virginia Resolutions. They argued that the states created the U.S. government and thus retained the right to judge the constitutionality of federal laws and declare invalid those they considered unconstitutional. State sovereignty was subject to conflicting interpretations, especially after the Supreme Court gradually established its right to review the constitutionality of state and federal laws beginning in 1796, and it has remained a political issue throughout American history.

Political Parties. In 1783 Americans celebrated their political independence from Great Britain, but they still found themselves influenced by British political ideas, especially the fear of political parties. On 19 November 1783 the *Pennsylvania Gazette* published a letter from "an American lady in England to her Friend in the City," in which the writer hoped that American independence would be permanent, "that little private interests may always give way to public good," and "that all former party spirit and animosity may be done away." Most Americans in the 1780s did not accept political parties as essential elements of representative democracy. Instead, they shared James Madison's belief that parties or "factions" were combinations of individuals who organized to promote their interests "adverse to the rights of other citizens, or to the permanent and aggregate interests of the community." Yet, within a few years of creating a federal system of government that they hoped would prevent parties, Americans had established two political parties. In 1801 power passed from the Federalists to the

Democratic-Republicans, but President Thomas Jefferson tried to downplay party politics by announcing, "We are all republicans—we are all federalists." The fear of political parties gradually subsided between 1783 and 1815 because Americans came to believe, as Thomas Jefferson and James Madison did, that the more even distribution of wealth in America would control the self-interest and social conflict that led to the formation of factions. Democracy, though limited to white adult males, transformed parties from selfish and competing interest groups into vital and safe political institutions that offered alternative political ideas and programs for the common good.

"An Empire of Laws." In his "Thoughts on Government," written in 1776, John Adams proclaimed: "The very definition of a republic is 'an empire of laws, and not of men.'" In 1787 delegates to the Constitutional Convention devised a federal republic whose authority depended entirely on the consent of the people. The survival of the republic rested on the people's willingness to obey laws passed by their representatives in Congress. If the framers of the Constitution could design a government which would, in John Adams's words, "secure an impartial and exact execution of the laws," surely Americans would willingly obey laws passed by majority rule. Some individuals and states, however, believed they had a right to rebel against any law they thought to be unjust. Three times between 1786 and 1799 farmers in western Massachusetts and western Pennsylvania rebelled against what they believed to be unjust laws. Their methods of protest included petitions, conventions, and the use of force to prevent officials from executing the laws. Each time, government officials, believing that the law must be obeyed or social disorder would result, used force to end the rebellions. In 1798 and 1799, in the Kentucky and Virginia Resolutions, Thomas Jefferson and James Madison supported state nullification of unconstitutional federal laws as a legitimate method of protest against unjust laws. In the final days of the War of 1812 delegates from the New England states who opposed the war and Democratic-Republican rule met in the Hartford Convention, where they upheld nullification and presented a series of Constitutional amendments to protect their rights. In later years Americans would continue to search for ways to protect individual and states' rights, including changing laws through repeal or new legislation, constitutional amendment, appeal to the Supreme Court, civil disobedience, secession, and civil war.

Foreign Policy. With a weak army and navy, British military posts in the Northwest, and Spanish control of the Southwest and access to the Mississippi River, the U.S. government during the Washington administration chose diplomacy, not war, as the basis of its foreign policy. In his Farewell Address to the nation in September 1796 President Washington stated that "our peace and prosperity" depend on "extending our commercial relations" with foreign nations while having "as little *political* connection as possible." The prosperity of the United States rested on its ability to market goods to all nations and maintain a steady flow of revenue from tariffs on foreign trade. Neutrality seemed to be the only practical principle of foreign policy, but it was difficult to defend when American commerce got caught in the wars between Britain and France which dominated world affairs from 1793 to 1815. In an effort to protect American shipping and honor from Britain and France, the administrations of Presidents Washington, Adams, Jefferson, and Madison tried diplomacy, trade restrictions, and finally war. The search for a foreign policy that would make the United States respected at home and abroad also contributed to the belligerent party politics of the era as Federalists accused Democratic-Republicans of importing dangerous principles of equality and anarchy from France, and Democratic-Republicans accused Federalists of importing principles of monarchy and aristocracy from Britain.

The Role of the Military. From their experiences under the British monarchy Americans had learned to fear professional, or "regular," armies as tools of oppressive rulers. But as witnesses to the deficient performance of militia units in the Revolutionary War, they conceded the necessity of a small regular army under strict civilian control. In March 1783 Continental Army officers in Newburgh, New York, threatened to overthrow Congress if they did not receive their promised back pay and pensions. The Confederation Congress rapidly demobilized the Continental Army and, on 3 June 1784, established a small peacetime army of seven hundred men, each enlisted for twelve months. The army's primary function was to defend the frontier, but the army's military weakness compelled the federal government to use purchase and treaty, not warfare, to open Indian lands to white settlement. Military weakness, rooted in republican fears of military power, also guided the Washington administration's foreign policy of diplomacy and neutrality. Congress expanded the army in 1798 during an undeclared war with France, but once France and the United States signed a peace treaty in 1800 the presence of this enlarged army, with Federalist leader Alexander Hamilton as a senior officer and no external foe in sight, became a political liability for President John Adams. Thomas Jefferson and James Madison, the Democratic-Republican presidents who succeeded Adams, tried trade restrictions as a substitute for military power, but both men eventually increased the size of the regular army. When the United States declared war against Great Britain in June 1812, the regular army was still weak and poorly staffed. The lack of military preparedness was a decisive factor in the War of 1812.

Settling the Frontier. In 1780 the population of the United States was under 3 million; by 1815 it was over 8 million. The availability of open land for a growing population would expand "the Empire of Liberty" by creating opportunity for American farmers, preventing a future of overpopulated cities, increasing inequalities in wealth, and political disorder. The signing of the Treaty of Paris in 1783 set off a wave of migration into Kentucky, Tennessee, and territory northwest of the Ohio River, and the Louisiana Purchase in 1803 expanded the western migration into vast new territory beyond the Mississippi River. Americans recognized that national control over western lands was necessary for the purposes of revenue, defense, and political union, leading to the important decision to give Congress control over the settlement and administration of new territory, beginning with land ordinances passed by the Confederation Congress in the 1780s. Between 1783 and 1815 Congress passed land acts that made it easier for the common man to buy land by reducing the minimum amount of land that could be purchased, extending terms of payment, and abolishing fees. Frontier settlers often objected to property qualifications for voting, and when it was time to enter the Union, the new western states extended the vote to all adult white males. Democracy and equality of opportunity for white Americans on the frontier would not have been possible, however, without the federal government's decision to open up Indian lands to settlement through purchase, treaty, and conquest.

Native Americans. The U.S. government's Indian policy was based on several factors: a weak army, British and Spanish alliances with Native American tribes, relentless pressure from settlers to expand into Indian lands, and racial attitudes. The Confederation government in the 1780s, lacking the military power to assert its authority, tried to acquire Indian lands through treaties. However, white settlers continued to pour into Indian areas in violation of treaties, and Native Americans resisted the endless expansion into their homelands. Indian policy under the new federal government was guided by a belief in the racial superiority of white civilization and the inevitable surrender of Native American culture to that civilization. The Washington administration tried to attract Native American tribes away from their British and Spanish allies by offering to buy land and have Indians assimilate into American culture. President Jefferson continued the policy of assimilation, encouraging Handsome Lake, the Seneca religious leader, to "Persuade our red brethren to be sober and cultivate their lands, and their women to spin and weave for their families." Some Native Americans, such as the Cherokee in the South, accepted assimilation, but several tribes in the Northwest resisted by organizing confederacies and engaging in warfare in the 1790s and again between 1805 and 1815. American victory over Great Britain in the War of 1812 meant that Native Americans could no longer rely on British or Spanish support to resist American advances on their lands and culture. The war was a turning point, paving the way for the eventual removal of Native Americans to lands west of the Mississippi River.

African Americans. After the Revolutionary War, African Americans, thousands of whom fought for liberty with the Continental Army or state militias, wondered whether the United States government would make the words of the Declaration of Independence—"All men are created equal"—a reality. Unfortunately the delegates to the Constitutional Convention, knowing that states in the lower South would never support a government that abolished slavery, decided that the survival of republican government for white Americans took precedence over freeing African Americans. But the presence of slavery in the midst of a government dedicated to liberty and equality did initiate antislavery activity at the state level. The legislatures of Virginia, Maryland, and Delaware passed laws in the 1780s and 1790s making it easier to free slaves. By 1792 antislavery societies had been established from Massachusetts to Virginia. By 1804 every state from Pennsylvania north had passed gradual emancipation laws, and by 1810 nearly three-quarters of all Northern African Americans were free. Life for free African Americans in the North and the South was not easy; they were subject to legal, economic, and racial discrimination. Still, their numbers grew dramatically, from 59,466 in 1790 (7.9 percent of the total African American population) to 186,446 in 1810 (13.5 percent of the total African American population). Slavery was well on its way to becoming the South's "peculiar institution," but it was by no means a dying institution. The invention of the cotton gin in 1793 enormously increased the production and profitability of cotton, but the cultivation of that crop required fertile land and intensive labor. The expansion of the southwestern frontier after the War of 1812 provided the land, but the end of the international slave trade in 1808 meant that slave labor would have to come from the sale and transfer of slaves from the older slave states to the new plantations in the Southwest. Westward migration uprooted slaves from familiar surroundings, broke up families, and subjected slaves to harsher conditions on the frontier.

The Development of Democracy. When most American political thinkers used the word *democracy* in the 1780s, they meant either the lowest order of society—the "common people"—or a type of government in which the common people exercised direct rule. From history these thinkers had learned that democracy went hand in hand with self-interest, disorder, and dictatorship. In 1787 the framers of the Constitution created a republic, or representative democracy, to protect the rights of the people while preventing the dangers of direct democracy. Ultimate power rested with the people, but they delegated that power, either directly or indirectly, to representatives in three branches of government. For Theophilus Parsons, a conservative Massachusetts lawyer who believed that educated gentlemen like himself were best suited to make political decisions, the proper role for the people was to "look on, and observe the conduct of their servants, and continue or withdraw their favor annually, according to their merit or demerit." What Parsons did not foresee was the transformation of democracy into a desirable political principle. With the relatively equal distribution of wealth in American society and with no permanent class distinctions, the common people were not content merely to "look on" as their social superiors ruled for them. The development of two political parties in the 1790s, each with distinct ideas about the future of the United States, resulted in increased voter participation and demands to reduce or abolish property and taxpaying requirements for voting. The new western states, which attracted individuals seeking the equality of opportunity promised by the American Revolution, gave the right to vote to all adult white males. After 1800 the Federalists, who called their political opponents "Democrats" as an insult, had to acknowledge that democracy, limited though it was to white males, was becoming a sacred political principle that no politician could ignore.

TOPICS IN THE NEWS

AMERICA UNDER THE ARTICLES OF CONFEDERATION

Sovereign States. On 15 November 1777 Congress ratified the Articles of Confederation, and by March 1779 all of the states except Maryland had approved them. Maryland, which lacked claims to western lands, refused to ratify until states with extensive land claims ceded their claims to the federal government "for the good of the whole," not to mention the good of Maryland land speculators. The Articles did not legally go into effect until 1 March 1781, so during most of the Revolutionary War congressional authority rested only on the states' acceptance of that authority. The Articles of Confederation contained lessons that Americans had learned from their clash with the British government in the 1760s and 1770s. Most Americans believed their liberties were best protected by elected representatives in the state legislatures. Nevertheless, they agreed on the need to set up a confederation of sovereign states which would grant specific powers to Congress "for their common defence, the security of their liberties, and their mutual and general welfare." The states gave Congress power over war, foreign policy, foreign loans, the regulation of money, and Indian trade. But in order to prevent the Confederation Congress from becoming as tyrannical as the British government, the states retained significant powers. The states, not Congress, had the power to tax citizens. Each state had one vote in Congress; major decisions required the approval of nine of the thirteen state delegations; and amendments to the Articles of Confederation required unanimous support. Finally, each state retained "its sovereignty, freedom and independence, and every power, jurisdiction and right, which is not by

Contemporary woodcut of Daniel Shays and Job Shattuck, who led the revolt of Massachusetts farmers against tax and debt policy in 1787

this confederation expressly delegated to the United States, in Congress assembled."

Achievements. The replacement of the Confederation with a stronger national government created by the Constitution suggests that national government under the Articles of Confederation was a failure. Congress was indeed hampered by its dependence on the states for war expenses, soldiers, and military supplies; its reliance on congressional committees to make decisions; a constantly changing roster of congressmen; and the needed approval of nine states to make any substantial changes. Yet, in spite of these obstacles Congress successfully organized a federal government, raised an army that waged a victorious eight-year war, and negotiated foreign alliances, foreign loans, and a peace treaty with Great Britain in September 1783. Robert Morris, appointed superintendent of finance in 1781, established a national bank that circulated a stable currency in place of the nearly worthless Continental currency, resumed interest payments on the national debt, and introduced reforms in the military supply system. The Confederation Congress also established the important precedent of national control over western lands with passage of the Northwest Ordinance of 1787. The Northwest Ordinance guaranteed the expansion of republican government by extending "the fundamental principles of civil and religious liberty" to the territories and outlining the conditions for admission to statehood, set aside revenue from land sales to support public schools, and forbade slavery in the region.

"The Critical Period." In June 1783, as he neared retirement as commander in chief of the Continental Army, George Washington sent a circular letter to the states urging them to strengthen the federal government. If they failed "to give such a tone to our federal government, as will enable it to answer the ends of its institution," the states would be responsible for "annihilating the cement of the confederation, and exposing us to become the sport of European politics." Washington and others who favored a stronger central government may have exaggerated the disastrous conditions in the 1780s to convince Americans to approve a new Constitution, but there were several factors that supported their belief that this was a "critical period." The British government refused to evacuate its military posts in the American Northwest as required by the Treaty of Paris. In 1784 Spain closed the Mississippi River to American shipping. Robert Morris's plan to create an independent source of revenue for Congress to maintain the value of currency failed when Rhode Island and New York refused to allow Congress to impose a 5 percent duty on imported goods. After the Revolutionary War, Britain flooded America with cheap manufactured goods and placed high duties on American goods, but the states refused to give Congress more power to regulate trade. In March 1783 Continental Army officers in Newburgh, New York, threatened to seize the government if Congress refused to grant their back pay and pensions. Such conditions convinced men such as James Madison that it was essential to replace the inadequate confederation of independent republics with a powerful national government that Madison hoped would provide "a republican remedy for the diseases most incident to republican government."

Annapolis Convention. U.S. merchants suffered when the British government levied discriminatory duties on American commerce. American artisans, unprotected by import duties, could not compete with British manufactured goods. American farmers found their access to the important West Indian market blocked by British trade restrictions. Individual states passed trade regulations to their own advantage and the disadvantage of other states, and the resulting sectional tensions were, as James Madison said, "destructive of the general harmony." As a member of the Virginia Assembly in 1786, Madison played a key role in the Assembly's call for a convention of the states to meet in Annapolis, Maryland, to deal with commercial problems. Nine of the thirteen states responded favorably, but only Virginia, Delaware, Pennsylvania, New Jersey, and New York sent delegates to the Annapolis Convention, which opened on 11 September 1786. Three days later the delegates endorsed Alexander Hamilton's call for another convention to meet in Philadelphia in May 1787 "to devise such further provisions as shall appear to them necessary to render the constitution of the federal government adequate to the exigencies of the Union." Hamilton also hinted at the larger agenda that delegates to the Philadelphia convention would pursue when he alluded to the "important defects in the system of the Federal Government" and the "embarrassments which characterise the present state of our national affairs, foreign and domestic."

Shays's Rebellion. During the Revolutionary War merchants and farmers who supplied the armies prospered from the abundant circulation of paper currency issued by Congress and the states and the specie, or gold

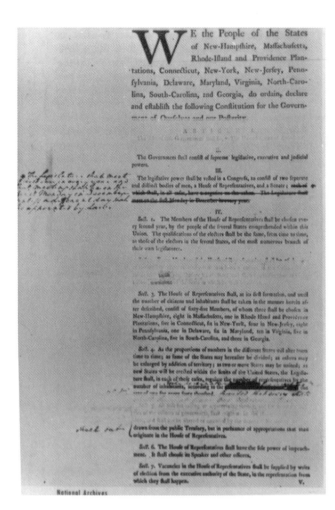

George Washinton's draft copy of the Constitution
(National Archives)

ington, and others assembled in Philadelphia in 1787, they were determined to build a strong national government to protect liberty and property and prevent another Shays's Rebellion.

Sources:

Jack P. Greene, ed., *Colonies to Nation, 1763–1789: A Documentary History of the American Revolution* (New York: Norton, 1975);

Merrill Jensen, *The New Nation: A History of the United States During the Confederation, 1781–1789,* revised edition (Boston: Northeastern University Press, 1981);

Jack N. Rakove, *The Beginnings of National Politics: An Interpretive History of the Continental Congress* (Baltimore: Johns Hopkins University Press, 1979).

THE CONSTITUTION

Constitutional Convention. Fifty-five delegates from twelve states assembled in Philadelphia on 25 May 1787. Only Rhode Island, which opposed national regulation of trade, refused to send a delegation. The delegates were the elite of the American republic: lawyers, merchants, physicians, planters, and at least nineteen slaveowners. Over half were college-educated, more than thirty were lawyers or had studied law, approximately forty had

---

and silver coin, issued by the British and French governments. By the middle of 1784, however, the amount of circulating specie dropped dramatically as American merchants and consumers used the money to buy foreign goods and states passed laws declaring that depreciating paper money should no longer be used to pay private debts or taxes. Farmers, who rarely received specie for their crops, could not pay their taxes and lost their property. Farmers from fifty western Massachusetts towns met in Hampshire County in August 1786 and petitioned the Massachusetts Legislature to issue paper money for the payment of all debts and revise the state constitution to correct inequities in taxation, representation, and the legal system. The legislature ignored their plea. The farmers, led by Revolutionary War veteran Daniel Shays, acted on the right stated in the Declaration of Independence to rebel against a government that no longer protected their interests. Beginning on 29 August 1786 Shays and his followers shut down civil courts and tried to prevent the Supreme Judicial Court from trying criminal prosecutions for debt in Springfield. Shays's Rebellion ended on 25 January 1787 when the Massachusetts militia crushed a threatened attack on the Springfield Arsenal. Shays failed, but his rebellion's impact was widely felt. When Madison, Hamilton, Wash-

THE TRADESMEN AND MECHANICKS OF BOSTON

When the Constitutional Convention convened in Massachusetts on 9 January 1788, Anti-Federalists were in the majority. Two days earlier "near four hundred of the most respectable *real* Tradesmen" of Boston, led by Paul Revere, John Lucas, and Benjamin Russell, met at the Green Dragon Tavern and approved resolutions supporting the Constitution:

the proposed frame of government is well calculated to secure the liberties, protect the property, and guard the rights of the citizens of America. . . .

trade and navigation will revive and increase, employ and subsistence will be afforded to many of our townsmen, who are now suffering from want of the necessaries of life . . . it will promote industry and morality; render us respectable as a nation; and procure us all the blessings to which we are now entitled from the natural wealth of our country, our capacity for improvement, from our industry, our freedom and independence. . . .

On 9 February 1788, three days after Massachusetts ratified the Constitution, the Committee of Tradesmen organized a procession of Boston's "tradesmen and mechanicks," "mechanicks and husbandmen from adjacent towns," and "The Ship Federal Constitution on runners drawn by thirteen horses" to "testify their approbation of the federal Constitution."

Source: *Massachusetts Centinel,* 9 January and 9 February 1788.

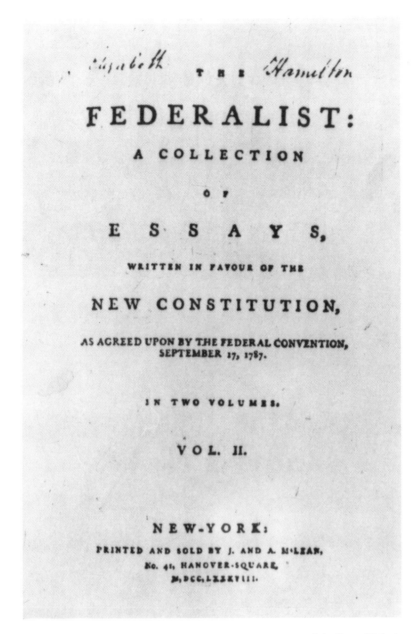

Title page for the collected edition of newspaper essays originally published
from 27 October 1787 to 28 May 1788

served in Congress, thirteen had held state offices, as many as twenty had helped write state constitutions, and one-third were Continental Army veterans. The delegates included Benjamin Franklin, Gouverneur Morris, and James Wilson of Pennsylvania; Alexander Hamilton of New York; and Edmund Randolph, George Mason, and James Madison of Virginia. (Contrary to popular belief, Thomas Jefferson did not attend the convention; he served as U.S. minister to France from 1785 to 1789.) They unanimously elected George Washington as president of the Constitutional Convention and voted to keep their deliberations secret. Men in favor of a powerful national government were in the majority, and, after little debate, the delegates voted to scrap a revision of the Articles of Confederation in favor of a new plan of government. The task at hand was a daunting one, for as James

Madison cautioned his fellow delegates: "It is more probable we are now digesting a plan which in its operation will decide forever the fate of republican government."

"Father of the Constitution." The Constitution was not the work of one person, but James Madison of Virginia earned the title of "Father of the Constitution" for his contributions as a political theorist and practical politician. In the month before the convention opened Madison consulted books on history and government and drew on his legislative experience in Congress and the Virginia legislature to analyze the "Vices of the Political System of the United States." In Madison's view the state constitutions of the period with weak governors, wider voting rights, small electoral districts, annual elections, and the voters' right to instruct their represen-

Abigail Adams (1744–1818) and Mercy Otis Warren (1728–1814) saw no conflict between their domestic responsibilities and their political activities. During the Revolutionary period, when John Adams was frequently absent due to public service, Mrs. Adams skillfully managed her home and her family's financial affairs and provided her husband with political news and analysis. Warren, sister of the patriot James Otis and wife of Massachusetts politician James Warren, expressed her support for the Revolution in poems, plays, and political satires. After the Revolution, Adams used her extensive political knowledge, acquired through voracious reading of newspapers, private conversations, and a wide circle of correspondents, to act as political adviser to both her husband and her son, John Quincy Adams. She also used private correspondence to spread her and her husband's political views. Similarly, Warren used private correspondence, often with her close friends Abigail and John Adams, to discuss politics, but she continued to play a more public role as a poet, playwright, and author of a three-volume history of the American Revolution (1805). Both women believed that domestic happiness depended on the survival of republican government, which, in turn, depended on politically enlightened and politically active citizens, including women.

Sources: Charles W. Akers, *Abigail Adams: An American Woman* (Boston: Little, Brown, 1980);

Linda K. Kerber, *Women of the Republic: Intellect and Ideology in Revolutionary America* (New York: Norton, 1980);

Warren-Adams Letters, Massachusetts Historical Society Collections, volumes 72 (1917) and 73 (1925).

tatives, all intended to protect the people from their rulers, actually contributed to a breakdown of social order. Various "interests and factions" used majority rule to pass laws to protect their private interests. Thus, Rhode Island passed paper money laws that helped farmers and hurt their creditors, and Maryland and New York passed navigation laws that favored their commercial interests over the interests of other states or the United States. To end this factionalism and self-interest, Madison advocated the establishment of a large national republic whose legislators would act in the best interests of all the people. "Extend the sphere and you take in a greater variety of parties and interests," he later wrote in *Federalist,* number 10, "and you make it less probable that a majority of the whole will have a common motive to invade the rights of other citizens."

Virginia and New Jersey Plans. Edmund Randolph submitted the Virginia Plan, representing the ideas of James Madison and the interests of the large states, to the Constitutional Convention on 29 May 1787. The plan called for a bicameral, or two-house, national legislature, with representation based on population. The people would elect the members of the lower house (House of Representatives), who would then elect the members of the upper house (Senate). The national legislature would, in turn, choose a national executive. The Virginia Plan also provided for a national judiciary and granted the national legislature the power "to negative all laws passed by the several States." William Paterson of New Jersey, representing the small states, presented his alternative plan on 15 June. The New Jersey Plan suggested giving Congress more power over commerce and revenue but keeping equal state representation in the legislature. The delegates supported the popular election of representatives in the lower house, but they argued for five weeks over representation in the Senate. Madison believed that having the lower house elect senators would filter out the "fickleness and passion" that existed in popularly elected legislatures. "A necessary fence against this danger," Madison contended, "would be to select a portion of enlightened citizens, whose limited number and firmness might seasonably interpose against impetuous counsels." Delegates from the smaller states, represented by Luther Martin of Maryland, argued that the only way to preserve a state role in the federal government was to allow the state legislatures to choose senators and to allow each state equal representation in the U.S. Senate. Under the "Great Compromise," proposed by Roger Sherman of Connecticut on 16 July, the people would elect members of the House of Representatives based on their respective states' populations (proportional representation), and the state legislatures would each choose two United States senators.

The Document. The final version of the Constitution approved on 17 September 1787 created a federal government with broad powers. Article I, Section 8 gave Congress far-reaching control over domestic, economic, and foreign affairs. In addition Congress had the power "to make all Laws which shall be necessary and proper" for executing its other powers. The Constitution also contained a long list of powers that were forbidden to the states. The president had widespread authority over the military, foreign policy, and appointments to office, and, in time, the Supreme Court would assume the power of reviewing the constitutionality of state laws that had been denied to Congress. James Madison reassured Americans that this powerful federal republic would not threaten liberty, since the powers were separated among three branches of the federal government, and a division of power between the federal and state governments would prevent any branch of government from "drawing all powers into its impetuous vortex."

Slavery. All of the delegates assembled in Philadelphia agreed with Pierce Butler of South Carolina that government "was instituted principally for the protection of property." Disagreement arose when delegates from southern states demanded protection for what George Mason of Virginia called their "peculiar species of property." The delegates' discomfort over slavery can be seen in the text of the Constitution where the word *slave* is never used; instead, slaves are called "other persons" or "such persons." Southern delegates wanted to prevent Congress from taxing or outlawing the slave trade, and they wanted to consider the slave population equal to the white population for the purpose of representation. Gouverneur Morris of Pennsylvania described his predicament of being "reduced to the dilemma of doing injustice to the Southern States or to human nature." Morris could not bring himself to protect slavery even though he knew "those States would never confederate on terms that would deprive them of that right." In the end the delegates decided that these "difficulties," as James Wilson of Pennsylvania said, "must be overruled by the necessity of compromise." On 11 July the delegates compromised by agreeing that three-fifths of the slave population would be counted for the purposes of representation and taxation. Although the delegates believed they were taking the "middle ground," they provided several protections for slavery. Article IV, Section 2 of the Constitution required the return of fugitive slaves to their masters; Article V stated that no constitutional amendments made before 1808 could affect the protection of the slave trade; and Article IV, Section 4 committed the U.S. government to protecting the states "against domestic violence," including slave revolts. Finally, the "three-fifths clause" made the southern states an important force in national politics by giving them representation for slaves who could not vote, thus making it unlikely that slavery would be abolished in the new republic.

Federalists and Anti-Federalists. Proponents of the Constitution adopted the name "Federalists," cleverly taking the name away from their opponents, who claimed that the Confederation was a true federal government. Federalist leaders included such individuals as Madison, Hamilton, and John Jay, who together wrote a series of eighty-five newspaper essays collected in a book called *The Federalist* (1788). As nationally known figures they used their prestige, education, and political skill to organize support for the Constitution. They attracted not only merchants, lawyers, planters, and other elites, but also artisans, shopkeepers, farmers, and others of the middling classes whose livelihoods would benefit from stronger national economic control. Most Anti-Federalists were not prominent national leaders; they were not an organized political party; and they opposed the Constitution for various reasons. Some were most alarmed by Congress's taxation power, others by the president's sweeping authority, and still others by the

PENNSYLVANIA CONSTITUTION

On 28 September 1776 the Pennsylvania Constitutional Convention approved the most utopian and radical of the state constitutions. Determined to erect a government that reflected America's social equality and incorporating ideas contained in Thomas Paine's pamphlet *Common Sense* (1776), the framers rejected mixed government in favor of a unicameral, or single-house, legislature and replaced the governor with an Executive Council elected by the people every three years. Other democratic features included annual elections with no property qualifications for voters and the people's right to elect a Council of Censors every seven years to determine whether the constitution required revisions. The anti-Constitutional, or Republican, Party, led by James Wilson and Robert Morris, was unsuccessful in attempts to restore mixed government and a bicameral legislature in Pennsylvania until 1790, when pressure increased to bring the state constitutions into "closer harmony" with the political principle of balanced government in the U.S. Constitution. The revised Pennsylvania Constitution approved on 2 September 1790 echoed Dr. Benjamin Rush's warning in 1777 that power was dangerous whether it was "lodged in the hands of the one or many." The solution was to establish balanced government with a bicameral legislature and a governor with veto power.

Sources: Allan Nevins, *The American States During and After the Revolution, 1775–1789*, revised edition (New York: Augustus Kelley, 1969);

Gordon S. Wood, *The Creation of the American Republic, 1776–1789* (New York: Norton, 1969).

omission of a Bill of Rights to protect individual liberties. In general, however, the Anti-Federalists, many of whom were small farmers and men of modest means, feared that the Constitution created a national government that would be dominated by aristocrats whose nearly limitless power would deprive ordinary people of their independence. Amos Singletary, a Massachusetts Anti-Federalist, warned that "lawyers, and men of learning, and moneyed men" would control the government, and with "all the power and all the money," they would "swallow up all us little folks."

Ratification. After quick ratifications by Delaware, Pennsylvania, New Jersey, Georgia, and Connecticut in the winter of 1787–1788, the first important challenge to acceptance of the document occurred in Massachusetts. When the Constitutional Convention in that state opened on 9 January 1788, Anti-Federalists were in the majority. The enthusiastic support for the Constitution expressed by Boston mechanics and tradesmen led by

A lavish reception during George Washington's administration—critics portrayed such affairs as attempts to emulate European courts; painting by Daniel Huntington (Brooklyn Museum)

Paul Revere, John Lucas, and Benjamin Russell may have played a role in convincing Samuel Adams, John Hancock, and other important leaders to vote for the Constitution. The Federalists' decision to let delegates submit proposals for future amendments to the Constitution also probably contributed to ratification by the narrow vote of 187–168 on 6 February 1788. The Constitution went into effect on 21 June 1788, when New Hampshire became the ninth state to ratify the document, but it was inconceivable to imagine the new federal republic without Virginia or New York. When the Virginia convention opened on 2 June 1788, Federalists and Anti-Federalists were present in almost equal numbers. The Federalist James Madison and the Anti-Federalist Patrick Henry, joined by the leaders of Virginia political society on both sides, debated the pros and cons of the Constitution for four weeks. Determined to play a leading role in the new republic, Virginia voted to ratify the Constitution with recommendations for a Bill of Rights and other amendments by the vote of 89–79 on 25 June 1787. In New York the well-organized Anti-Federalists were in the majority at the Constitutional Convention, but Federalist threats that New York City and the southern counties would secede convinced the delegates to approve the Constitution by a vote of 30–27 with recommendations for several amendments. North Carolina rejected the Constitution in August 1788, and

Rhode Island voters also expressed their disapproval. Both states reconsidered after the new government went into effect and a Bill of Rights was added. North Carolina ratified the Constitution on 21 November 1789, and Rhode Island ratified the Constitution by the narrow vote of 34–32 on 29 May 1790.

Jack P. Greene, ed., *Colonies to Nation, 1763–1789: A Documentary History of the American Revolution* (New York: Norton, 1975);

Alexander Hamilton, James Madison, and John Jay, *The Federalist Papers,* with an introduction by Clinton Rossiter (New York: New American Library, 1961);

Jackson Turner Main, *The Antifederalists: Critics of the Constitution, 1781–1788* (New York: Norton, 1974);

Clinton Rossiter, *1787: The Grand Convention* (New York: Macmillan, 1966);

Gordon S. Wood, *The Creation of the American Republic, 1776–1787* (New York: Norton, 1969).

ESTABLISHING THE FEDERAL GOVERNMENT

Titles, Ceremonies, and Precedents. On 4 March 1789 the first Congress under the new Constitution convened in New York City, and on 30 April George Washington and John Adams were inaugurated as the first president and vice president of the United States, respectively. One of the first issues Congress debated, from 23

206   AMERICAN ERAS: 1783-1815

April to 14 May, was the necessity of titles for the president and vice president. Members of the Senate, supported by Vice President Adams, suggested such titles for the president as "His Elective Highness" or "His Highness the President of the United States of America and Protector of Their Liberties." Members of the House were horrified by monarchical titles in a republican government. The Senate agreed to abandon fancy titles in the interest of harmony but also perhaps because they agreed with Sen. William Maclay of Pennsylvania that it was "impossible to add to the respect entertained for General Washington." Respect for Washington created respect for the office of the presidency, and his immense dignity and acute sense of history established important guidelines for the conduct of that office. In an attempt to maintain republican simplicity and presidential ceremony simultaneously, Washington decided neither to make nor accept personal social calls but only to hold formal public receptions. His decision to deliver addresses in person to Congress, as the king did to Parliament, and his transportation in an elegant carriage drawn by six fine horses and accompanied by uniformed servants set a tone of formality and legitimacy for the presidency, although critics objected that such practices were monarchical. Washington also set several other important precedents, including the presidential prerogative of appointing a special envoy to conduct diplomatic negotiations, written communications between the president and Senate to carry out the "advise and consent" clause of the Constitution regarding treaties, and the practice of holding regular cabinet meetings.

Choosing Government Officials. Washington believed that "fitness of character" and ability were essential requirements for government officials. His ideal candidates were usually well-educated men who had demonstrated their character and ability as Continental Army officers or officeholders in the Confederation or state governments. Geographical balance was a factor in choosing officers of the executive branch, and support for the Constitution was important in order to strengthen the new government. With the advice and consent of the Senate, Washington selected Alexander Hamilton of New York as secretary of the treasury, Thomas Jefferson of Virginia as secretary of state, Henry Knox of Massachusetts as secretary of war, and Edmund Randolph of Virginia as attorney general. Hamilton had served as Washington's aide-de-camp during the Revolutionary War, attended the Constitutional Convention, and penned over fifty essays in *The Federalist* (1788). Jefferson, author of the Declaration of Independence, had been a delegate to the Continental Congress, governor of Virginia, and United States minister to France under the Confederation. He had expressed some reservations about the lack of term limits for the president and a Bill of Rights in the Constitution, but he trusted that the amendment process would correct any deficiencies. Knox, a firm supporter of the Constitution, was a Conti-

nental Army artillery officer and secretary of war under the Confederation. Randolph, a member of the Continental Congress and governor of Virginia, had wavered between Federalism and Anti-Federalism as a delegate to the Constitutional Convention, but his switch to Federalism during the ratification process in Virginia made him an important political asset. As Washington explained in a letter to Supreme Court justices: "I have thought it my duty to nominate . . . such men as I conceived would give dignity and lustre to our National Character. . . ."

Tariff Act. On 8 April 1789 James Madison introduced tariff resolutions in Congress to begin the process of generating revenue for the federal government. The final version of the bill, approved on 4 July, imposed a 5 percent duty on most imported articles and higher duties on selected articles. Compromise was necessary as northern manufacturers wanted high protective tariffs, and southern planters, who imported manufactured goods, desired low tariffs. Madison also wanted Congress to impose higher duties on ships of foreign countries that had no commercial treaties with the United States. Madison's target was Great Britain, and his proposal was part of his and Thomas Jefferson's long-range goal of freeing Americans from British economic dependence. As Virginians they had long resented their subservient economic position. British merchants dictated where Virginia planters could market their produce and tied them up in long-term debt through the control of credit and American reliance on British manufactured goods. Madison hoped that discriminatory tonnage duties on British shipping would open up new avenues for American trade, particularly with America's wartime ally, France. But with Britain responsible for nearly 90 percent of American imports, the Senate refused to endorse Madison's plan. The final tonnage bill placed a duty of six cents a ton on American-owned ships and a fifty-cent duty on all foreign ships. Debate over the tariff bill revealed a developing political split between Secretary of the Treasury Alexander Hamilton's plan to tie America's economic future to Britain and James Madison and Thomas Jefferson's plan to free the United States from that dependence.

The Judiciary Act of 1789. The framers of the Constitution left it to Congress to create a judicial branch, though the Constitution stated that the Supreme Court's judicial power "shall extend to all cases, in law and equity" arising under the Constitution or laws of the United States. Sen. Oliver Ellsworth of Connecticut, who had served on the committee that produced the Great Compromise in the Constitutional Convention and who became the third chief justice of the United States in 1796, used his skill at compromise in writing the Judiciary Act of 1789. The act created a six-member Supreme Court and a system of federal district courts and courts of appeal. Both the Supreme Court and the inferior federal courts were given limited original jurisdiction, and judicial power was delegated between the federal and state governments. However, Section 25 of the Judiciary Act of 1789 did grant the Supreme Court the power to review the constitutionality of state court decisions. Sensitive to the political danger of disturbing the separation of power between the federal and state governments, the members of the Supreme Court moved cautiously to establish the power of judicial review in the first decade of the Court's existence.

The Bill of Rights. Although James Madison believed that individual liberties were protected in the state constitutions, and the delegated powers of the Constitution protected states' rights, he could not ignore the fact that the lack of a Bill of Rights in the Constitution had nearly prevented ratification in Massachusetts, Virginia, and New York and had blocked it in North Carolina and Rhode Island. Thus, Madison made the drafting of a Bill of Rights one of the first priorities of the First Congress, and, on 25 September 1789 Congress submitted twelve amendments to the states. Eight of the ten amendments that the states eventually ratified on 15 December 1791 protected individual rights rather than states' rights, satisfying Madison's goal of addressing Anti-Federalist concerns that individual rights must be protected from a "consolidated government" of unlimited powers without substantially weakening the authority of the federal government. The first eight amendments demonstrate the Revolutionary generation's belief that a powerful government must be restrained from violating essential civil liberties, including freedom of religion, speech, and the press and trial by jury. The Ninth Amendment protects all unspecified rights "retained by the people," and the Tenth Amendment reserves "powers not delegated to the United States by the Constitution, nor prohibited by it to the States" to the states or the people. The addition of the Bill of Rights probably encouraged North Carolina to ratify the Constitution on 21 November 1789 and Rhode Island to follow suit on 29 May 1790.

Sources:

Stanley Elkins and Eric McKitrick, *The Age of Federalism: The Early American Republic, 1788–1800* (New York: Oxford University Press, 1993);

John C. Miller, *The Federalist Era, 1789–1801* (New York: Harper Torchbooks, 1963);

Leonard D. White, *The Federalists: A Study in Administrative History* (New York: Macmillan, 1956).

THE FEDERALISTS' DOMESTIC PROGRAM

National Debt. On 14 January 1790 Secretary of the Treasury Alexander Hamilton submitted his First Report on Public Credit to Congress. Hamilton advised that the federal government should assume the state debts of about $25 million, add the amount to the nation's foreign debt of nearly $12 million and domestic debt of almost $42 million, and "fund," or redeem, the combined debt with new interest-bearing securities. Current holders of the depreciated Continental securities would exchange them for new securities, whose principal and interest would be guaranteed by a percentage of the national revenue. Hamilton's plan contained important principles that guided his bold agenda for the United States. Hamilton believed that a prosperous nation was a commercial nation like Great Britain, and he also believed that men were motivated by self-interest. He wanted to create a permanent national debt that would tie American merchants to their government as it did in Britain. If merchants knew that they would receive regular interest on government securities and that they could use the securities in business transactions, their self-interest would motivate them to support the new federal government and expand their businesses for the benefit of themselves and the nation. James Madison saw in Hamilton's program a calculated plan to create a government that catered to the interests of merchants, manufacturers, and speculators over the interests of honest farmers and taxpayers. Madison believed that there was "something radically immoral" about allowing current holders of Continental securities, who were often speculators, to receive new ones at face value. He thought that current holders should be paid the highest market value, with the rest going to the original holders. Madison also believed that the assumption of state debts was unfair to states such as Virginia that had paid off their obligations. Congress approved the assumption bill on 26 July and the funding bill on 4 August after a compromise in which northern congressmen agreed to a site on the Potomac River as the future United States capital in exchange for Madison and Thomas Jefferson's promise to gain southern votes for the bills.

The first Bank of the United States, which opened in Philadelphia in 1791

The National Bank. On 14 December 1790 Hamilton submitted a Second Report on Public Credit calling for the establishment of a national bank to serve as a depository for government funds and issue banknotes to private citizens. The federal government would accept the banknotes at face value for the payment of taxes, ensuring that the holders of the notes would not cash them in for scarce gold and silver but instead use them as circulating currency in business transactions. The U.S. government would own one-fourth of the bank's stock, and the rest would be held by private individuals who could purchase their shares with government securities up to three-fourths of the stock's value. The securities issued under Hamilton's funding and assumption plan and the notes issued by the Bank of the United States would provide a stable circulating currency to encourage business expansion among merchants and tie these "friends of government" closer to the federal government. Congress passed the bank bill, but James Madison's strong opposition on the grounds that the Constitution did not give Congress the explicit authority to incorporate a bank concerned President George Washington enough that he asked his cabinet members to submit written opinions on the bank's constitutionality. Secretary of State Jefferson and Attorney General Edmund Randolph endorsed Madison's argument for what became known as a strict construction of the Constitution. In opposition, Secretary of the Treasury Hamilton defended a loose, or broad, construction of the Constitution. He interpreted Article I, Section 8 granting Congress the power to "make all laws which shall be necessary and proper" to execute its ex-

plicit powers to mean that a national bank was a constitutional means to allow Congress to carry out its enumerated powers of collecting taxes and tariff revenue, regulating commerce, and providing "for the common defense and general welfare of the United States." On 25 February 1791 President Washington signed the bill creating the First Bank of the United States, but debate over a national bank contributed to the development of political parties.

Report on Manufactures. Hamilton submitted his most ambitious ideas in his Report on Manufactures on 5 December 1791. He advocated a comprehensive program of protective tariffs on imported manufactured goods, exemptions from duties on raw materials necessary for American manufacturing, and government support for the encouragement of new industries and labor-saving machinery. Hamilton's report was a criticism of Madison and Jefferson's dream that Americans could remain a nation of farmers in a world ruled by free trade. The reality was that European nations benefited by exporting their manufactured goods to the United States while restricting America's agricultural shipments abroad. Hamilton believed that a more realistic future for the United States depended on its development as a commercial and industrial society, in which domestic manufacturing would unite the North and South. Southern farmers were not happy about their projected role of supplying raw materials to northern merchants, manufacturers, and shipowners, believing that it duplicated their dependent position under the British colonial economy. Madison attacked Hamilton's program in a series of anonymous essays in the *National Gazette,* condemning the Federalists for "substituting the motive of private interest in place of public duty." By granting subsidies to privileged manufacturers, the federal government would be "accommodating its measures to the avidity of a part of the nation instead of the benefit of the whole. . . ." In the end it was not the objections of Madison, Jefferson, or southern farmers that doomed the Report on Manufactures; it was the lack of interest among members of the commercial class who were more attracted to investments in shipping, land speculation, banks, turnpikes, and canal companies. Congress incorporated some of Hamilton's tariff proposals in the Tariff of 1792 but never implemented the rest of the program.

Whiskey Rebellion. On 3 March 1791, at Alexander Hamilton's suggestion, Congress passed an excise, or internal, tax on whiskey to supplement the national revenue. Farmers in western Pennsylvania objected almost immediately. The barrier of the Appalachian Mountains and Spain's closing of the Mississippi River to American trade compelled farmers to convert their crops of rye and corn into whiskey. Liquor was also a form of currency in a region short of hard money and banknotes. Sporadic protests occurred between 1791 and 1793, but a more organized rebellion began in July 1794. By then western Pennsylvania's farmers were convinced that the federal government had consistently neglected them. The government had failed miserably at protecting frontier settlers from Indian attack in the neighboring Northwest Territory and at expelling the British from their military posts. Absentee speculators owned large tracts of western land but were not burdened with heavy property taxes. Hamilton's financial program clearly favored eastern merchants and land speculators over landless frontier farmers. Some of the disaffected farmers reacted by organizing local "Democratic Societies," which were connected to the emerging Democratic-Republican Party and its support for the French Revolution. In the summer of 1794 the "Whiskey Rebels" defended their liberty and property by stopping excise officers from collecting the whiskey tax, interfering with federal judicial proceedings, and threatening to attack Pittsburgh. In September, President Washington, accompanied by the architect of the excise tax, Secretary of the Treasury Hamilton, led nearly thirteen thousand militiamen into western Pennsylvania, but most of the rebels had already dispersed. The president pardoned two rebels who were convicted of high treason, and the outcome of the Whiskey Rebellion seemed to be a victory for "a government of laws." However, the uprising also made western Pennsylvania a Democratic-Republican stronghold.

Sources:

Lance Banning, *The Jeffersonian Persuasion* (Ithaca, N.Y.: Cornell University Press, 1978);

Stanley Elkins and Eric McKitrick, *The Age of Federalism: The Early American Republic, 1788–1800* (New York: Oxford University Press, 1993);

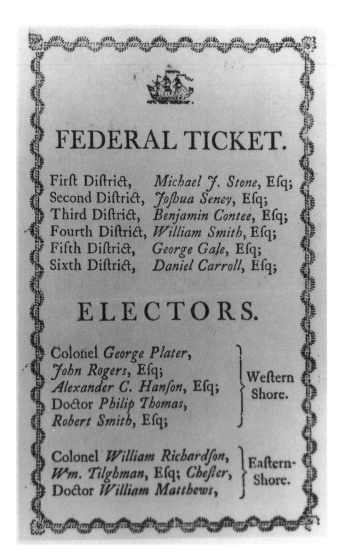

Broadside of a Maryland federal electoral ticket, 1789

Drew McCoy, *The Elusive Republic: Political Economy in Jeffersonian America* (New York: Norton, 1982);

John C. Miller, *The Federalist Era, 1789–1801* (New York: Harper Torchbooks, 1963).

THE FIRST PARTY SYSTEM

Opposition to Hamilton. As he prepared to leave office in September 1796, President George Washington published a "Farewell Address" warning his countrymen "against the baneful effects of the spirit of party. . . ." Party spirit, Washington continued, "agitates the community with ill-founded jealousies and false alarms; kindles the animosity of one part against the other . . . [and] opens the door to foreign influence and corruption. . . ." Washington hoped that party spirit would give way to national unity, and so too did James Madison and Thomas Jefferson, but Alexander Hamilton's plans for a commercial society that resembled Britain slowly led to the development of political parties. Madison and his fellow Virginian John Beckley, clerk of the House of Representatives, began organizing opposition in Con-

The political disputes of the 1790s and early 1800s divided friends, neighbors, and families. Dr. Nathaniel Ames and his younger brother, Fisher Ames, lived all their lives in Dedham, Massachusetts, and disagreed about every political issue. Nathaniel, an Anti-Federalist turned Republican, hated Federalists ("British bootlickers") and lawyers ("the Dregs of Misfortune and Misconduct"). Fisher, a Federalist congressman, lawyer, and political essayist, condemned Republicans as "Jacobins born in sin" and "trumpeters of sedition." Nathaniel supported the French Revolution and opposed the Jay Treaty, while Fisher did the opposite. Nathaniel believed Jefferson's election in 1800 would usher in a new age "with returning harmony with France—with the irresistible propagation of the Rights of Man, the eradication of hierarchy, oppression, superstition and tyranny over the world." Fisher thought, "The next thing will be, as in France, anarchy: then Jacobinism, organized with enough energy to plunder and shed blood." When Fisher Ames died on 4 July 1808, Nathaniel, although personally reconciled with his brother, refused to attend his funeral because Federalist leaders took charge of the public event. Dr. Nathaniel Ames lived until 22 July 1822, still supporting Republican policies and denouncing Federalists, lawyers, and England.

Source: Charles Warren, *Jacobin and Junto or Early American Politics As Viewed in the Diary of Dr. Nathaniel Ames* (Cambridge, Mass.: Harvard University Press, 1931).

events in 1793 changed reaction along party lines. France's declaration of war against Britain moved the United States government to declare neutrality, but Federalists sided with Britain, while Republicans sided with France. The Federalists, especially Alexander Hamilton, believed that national interests were best served by maintaining a cordial commercial relationship with Britain. Federalists were also frightened by the violent direction of the French Revolution and the possibility that similar forces of disorder could be unleashed in the United States. French radicals had taken control and launched the Reign of Terror, executing the king and queen, hundreds of aristocrats, and moderate revolutionaries before they began killing each other. The connection between Democratic Societies and the Whiskey Rebellion convinced Federalists that French ideas threatened law and order in the United States. Thomas Jefferson and James Madison had been trying since the 1780s to channel American trade away from Britain and toward France, but Republican support for the French Revolution was based more on ideological than on economic reasons. While Federalists believed Britain represented social order and stability, Republicans believed France was engaged in the cause of liberty against British tyranny and corruption. In October 1793 a public meeting in Caroline County, Virginia, warned that the breaking of "the honorable and beneficial connection" between the United States and France was "a leading step towards assimilating the American government to the form and spirit of the British monarchy."

"Jacobins and Monocrats." As political parties began to develop in the 1790s, each side claimed that it would best protect republicanism and that the other side would destroy it. Federalists attacked Republicans as "Jacobins" who, like the members of the radical Jacobin clubs in France, promised the people equality only to gain power. The Republicans' naive faith in democracy would demolish government, property, and established religion as it had in France. Only "the real friends of liberty and order," as George Cabot called the Federalists, could save the country by leading the people instead of appealing to their emotions. Republicans, in turn, attacked Federalists as lovers of monarchy and aristocracy ("monocrats") who cared only about merchants, speculators, and stockholders in the Bank of the United States and not about the common people. Each side exaggerated or misrepresented the other's ideas, but Federalists and Republicans did appeal to different segments of American society, and they did offer alternative visions of republicanism. Federalist leaders were successful lawyers, merchants, and planters. They attracted northern merchants, manufacturers, urban artisans, South Carolina planters, and some small farmers who believed that a strong national government, a sound financial system, and a realistic foreign policy that recognized Great Britain's commercial power would ensure liberty, prosperity, and social order. The Republicans' philosophy stressing limited govern-

gress early in 1790. A tour of New York, Vermont, and Connecticut in the spring and summer of 1791 gave Madison and Jefferson a chance to discuss their political concerns with local leaders and with each other. By October 1791 Madison and Jefferson had helped Philip Freneau establish the *National Gazette* in Philadelphia to provide an alternative to John Fenno's proadministration newspaper, the *Gazette of the United States.* By the end of 1792 opponents of Hamilton's policies were calling themselves "Republicans" and using the pages of the *National Gazette* and other partisan newspapers to present themselves as true republicans who would protect the people's liberties and interests from the Federalists. (Members of the opposition were also known as the Democratic-Republicans, but Jefferson and Madison did not like the term *Democratic* because it sounded too radical.)

The French Revolution. Most Americans supported the French Revolution in 1789, believing that their revolution had inspired the French struggle for liberty. But

PARTY AFFILIATIONS IN CONGRESS

Period	House	Senate	President
1st Congress (1789–1791)	38 A 26 O	17 A 9 O	Washington F
2nd Congress (1791–1793)	37 F 33 R	16 F 13 R	Washington F
3rd Congress (1793–1795)	57 R 48 F	17 F 13 R	Washington F
4th Congress (1795–1797)	54 F 52 R	19 F 13 R	Washington F
5th Congress (1797–1799)	58 F 48 R	20 F 12 R	Adams F
6th Congress (1799–1801)	64 F 42 R	19 F 13 R	Adams F
7th Congress (1801–1803)	69 R 36 F	18 R 13 F	Jefferson R
8th Congress (1803–1805)	102 R 39 F	25 R 9 F	Jefferson R
9th Congress (1805–1807)	116 R 25 F	27 R 7 F	Jefferson R
10th Congress (1807–1809)	118 R 24 F	28 R 6 F	Jefferson R
11th Congress (1809–1811)	94 R 48 F	28 R 6 F	Madison R
12th Congress (1811–1813)	108 R 36 F	30 R 6 F	Madison R
13th Congress (1813–1815)	112 R 68 F	27 R 9 F	Madison R
14th Congress (1815–1817)	117 R 65 F	25 R 11 F	Madison R

A = Administration Supporters; O = Opponents; F = Federalists; R = Republicans. The figures are for the beginning of the first session of each Congress.

Source: *Historical Statistics of the United States, Colonial Times to 1957* (Washington, D.C.: United States Bureau of the Census, 1960).

ment, the westward expansion of small farms, and the end of foreign and domestic policies that helped only the "monied aristocracy" attracted most southern planters and small farmers, especially in the new western states. Republicans also began drawing support from small merchants, artisans, and laborers in New York, Philadelphia, and other cities; non-English immigrants; and members of religious minorities—all of whom felt that the Federalists were denying them liberty, equality, and opportunity. Federalists could never let southern Republicans forget, however, that their fervent belief in democracy did not extend to the slaves that they held in chains.

Factions and Parties. The negative view of parties as "factions," or temporary gatherings of individuals interested in protecting selfish interests or receiving political patronage, affected political thought throughout the period between 1783 and 1815. Each side clung to the belief that they were forced to react to the other side's attempt to overthrow the ideals of the American Revolution. In his first administration President Washington tried to remain above party disputes, but events after 1793 made that difficult. The connection between the Democratic Societies and the Whiskey Rebellion, Republican support for the radical phase of the French Revolution, and Republican attacks on his administration's allegedly pro-British sympathies in the aftermath of the Jay Treaty moved Washington to stand with the Federalist Party as the legitimate defenders of liberty and order. Jefferson was equally opposed to parties, but after the Jay Treaty, Republicans looked to him as the leader of a political opposition forced to organize for the protection of American liberty. Jefferson regarded his presidential election in 1800 not as a victory for the Republican Party but as a victory of republican principles. In his view, the future of the republic depended not on the existence of opposing parties, but on the hope that the Federalists would abandon their party and become Republicans. As the Federalists lost national influence, however, the Republicans began to splinter into factions that argued over presidential policies and political appointments. It was the experiences of this first generation of party leaders, so uncomfortable with the idea of parties, that laid the foundation for the eventual acceptance of political parties. Their presentation of ideas and programs through newspapers, pamphlets, and political organizations in the 1790s had enlightened and stimulated voters. By the 1820s, with the spread of universal white male suffrage, voters expected to participate in politics and to choose between two parties offering coherent ideas that addressed their concerns.

Sources:

Lance Banning, *The Jeffersonian Persuasion* (Ithaca, N.Y.: Cornell University Press, 1978);

William Nisbet Chambers, *Political Parties in a New Nation: The American Experience, 1776–1809* (New York: Oxford University Press, 1963);

Richard Hofstadter, *The Idea of a Party System: The Rise of Legitimate Opposition in the United States, 1780–1840* (Berkeley: University of California Press, 1969);

Charles Warren, *Jacobin and Junto or Early American Politics as Viewed in the Diary of Dr. Nathaniel Ames* (Cambridge, Mass.: Harvard University Press, 1931).

Creamware pitcher showing the population of the United States tabulated in the first census, 1790

FOREIGN AFFAIRS IN THE WASHINGTON ADMINISTRATION

Conflicting Views. In the early 1790s the United States had a pitifully small army incapable of defending the frontier from Indian attack and no navy to defend American shipping. Economic success depended on foreign trade to provide tariff revenue and markets for American commerce. President George Washington, Secretary of State Thomas Jefferson, and Secretary of the Treasury Alexander Hamilton agreed that it was vital to maintain friendly commercial relations with European nations while remaining neutral in their political disputes. Behind this apparent agreement serious differences between Jefferson and Hamilton had surfaced during debate over Hamilton's financial program. Hamilton believed that a realistic foreign policy recognized that American economic success depended on maintaining good relations with Britain. British trade provided nearly all of the nation's tariff revenue, and, as the world's strongest naval power, Britain could enforce commercial restrictions against the United States. Jefferson, in conjunction with James Madison, developed another view of foreign policy, combining economic interest, an agrarian philosophy, and moral considerations. Jefferson believed that Hamilton's pro-British foreign policy and his support for the economic interests of merchants, manufacturers, and speculators would lead to the economic in-

equality, social disorder, and political corruption that he had witnessed in France and England during his diplomatic service. Jefferson wanted Americans to remain a nation of small farmers using their agricultural surplus as a "bargaining chip" to encourage European nations to open their markets to the United States. A commercial alliance with republican France in place of monarchical Britain would unite two republics in a moral crusade to spread liberty around the world while providing economic benefits to the United States.

France. In February 1793, when France declared war on Britain, it forced the U.S. government to reconsider its obligations to France under the Treaty of Alliance of 1778. Both Secretary of the Treasury Hamilton and Secretary of State Jefferson advised neutrality, but their respective pro-British and pro-French points of view affected their definitions of neutrality. Hamilton recommended a suspension of the Treaty of Alliance with France and an immediate declaration of neutrality. Jefferson rejected Hamilton's readiness to offer "our breech to every kick which Great Britain may choose to give" in favor of a "fair neutrality." Jefferson wanted neither to break the treaty with France nor declare an immediate neutrality, hoping to gain commercial concessions from both belligerents. On 22 April 1793 President Washington issued a Proclamation of Neutrality, committing the

United States to "a conduct friendly and impartial towards the belligerent powers." Meanwhile Edmond Genet, the new French chargé d'affaires to the United States, arrived in Charleston, South Carolina. "Citizen" Genet disregarded American prohibitions forbidding French vessels from selling their captured prizes or receiving arms in American ports, recruited American citizens to serve in privateering expeditions against British and Spanish possessions, and demanded that President Washington summon a special session of Congress to debate neutrality or he would take his case directly to the American people. Genet's actions offended American public opinion and widened the breach between Federalists and Republicans.

Great Britain. Thomas Jefferson resigned as secretary of state on 31 December 1793, but not before delivering a report to Congress recommending discriminatory duties against British shipping. James Madison's proposals for economic retaliation, presented to Congress on 3 January 1794, were in response to Britain's order to seize neutral vessels carrying supplies to the French West Indies and a renewed effort to end American dependence on British trade. Britain's seizure of more than 250 American ships between November 1793 and March 1794 was one of a series of offenses against the United States. In violation of the peace treaty ending the Revolutionary War, the British government maintained one thousand soldiers on military posts in the Northwest Territory and supplied guns, ammunition, and encouragement to the Indian tribes in the area, who successfully fought off American expansion into their lands. Southerners wanted Britain to compensate them for the loss of their slaves during the Revolutionary War. Many Americans also interpreted Britain's role in negotiating a truce between Portugal and Algiers in December 1793 as an underhanded method of attacking American shipping. Previously the Portuguese navy had controlled the Mediterranean Sea and prevented Algerian corsairs from attacking American ships, but the truce removed that protection. Madison's anti-British resolutions failed, but public hostility and continued Republican pressure for economic action against Britain led Treasury Secretary Hamilton to advise President Washington to appoint a special envoy to negotiate a treaty with Great Britain.

The Jay Treaty. The Senate approved the appointment of Supreme Court Chief Justice John Jay to negotiate a treaty with Britain in April 1794. Hamilton, not the new Secretary of State Edmund Randolph, drafted Jay's instructions. Hamilton's contention that war with Britain must be avoided at all costs guided Jay's negotiations and shaped the treaty signed on 19 November 1794. Britain's only important concession was its agreement to evacuate the northwestern posts by June 1796. Britain also agreed to allow limited American trade with the West Indies but with so many restrictions that the Senate refused to ratify that part of the treaty in June 1795. The treaty said nothing about compensation to southern slaveowners. The British government agreed to a joint arbitration commission to assess damage claims brought by Americans whose vessels had been seized, but Britain would give up neither its right to prohibit neutral trade nor its right to impress American sailors into British service. The United States also surrendered the right to impose discriminatory duties against Britain for ten years. In March 1796 Republicans in the House of Representatives tried to prevent the appropriation of funds to implement Jay's Treaty. By a vote of 62–37 the House asked the president to submit all papers relating to Jay's Treaty to the House. Washington refused to give up his constitutional right to make treaties with the advice and consent of the Senate, thus establishing the precedent of executive privilege. A shift in public opinion in favor of Jay's Treaty and threats from the Senate to delay ratification of a Spanish treaty guaranteeing American navigation of the Mississippi River induced the House of Representatives to pass appropriations for the treaty on 30 April 1796 by a vote of 51–48, with support split along party lines. The Jay Treaty prevented war with Great Britain, but it worsened relations between the United States and France and contributed to sectional and political tensions.

The Pinckney Treaty. An American victory over Indians at the Battle of Fallen Timbers in August 1794, the signing of the Treaty of Greenville with the northwestern Indians in August 1795, and British evacuation of its American military posts eliminated obstacles to western expansion, but Spain still stood in the way of expansion on the southwestern frontier. Spanish authorities in Louisiana and Florida provided arms and protection for Creeks, Choctaws, and Cherokees resisting American advancement into their lands, and for more than ten years Spain had refused to open the Mississippi River to American trade. By 1794, however, Spain's attitude toward the United States had changed. Spain's decision to ally itself with Britain against France had proved disastrous. The war damaged trade in Spain's American colonies, and news of the Jay Treaty fed Spanish fears that an Anglo-American alliance threatened her North American colonies. In the summer of 1794 the Spanish government expressed interest in negotiating with the United States. In October 1795 Thomas Pinckney, the U.S. minister to Great Britain and special envoy to Spain, negotiated a highly favorable treaty. Pinckney's Treaty established the thirty-first parallel as the southern boundary between the United States and Spain and guaranteed American navigation of the Mississippi River with the right of deposit at New Orleans. Spain also agreed not to support Indian raids in the Southwest. Pinckney's Treaty opened up new territory and economic opportunities for settlers in the South and West.

Sources:

Joseph Charles, *The Origins of the American Party System* (New York: Harper Torchbooks, 1961);

Stanley Elkins and Eric McKitrick, *The Age of Federalism: The Early American Republic, 1788–1800* (New York: Oxford University Press, 1993);

John C. Miller, *The Federalist Era, 1789–1801* (New York: Harper Torchbooks, 1963);

Paul A. Varg, *Foreign Policies of the Founding Fathers* (East Lansing: Michigan State University Press, 1963).

FOREIGN AND DOMESTIC CRISES IN THE ADAMS ADMINISTRATION

Approaching Storm. The French government, angry over Jay's Treaty, ordered the seizure of all neutral ships bound for British ports starting on 1 July 1796. On 7 December the French foreign minister refused to meet with Charles Cotesworth Pinckney, the new U.S. minister to France. Newly elected president John Adams, who had narrowly defeated the Republican candidate Thomas Jefferson, was determined to maintain an independent foreign policy that would favor neither France nor Britain. He was also determined to follow George Washington's example of trying to remain above party politics. In May 1797 Adams asked Congress to appoint a peace mission

Elbridge Gerry, a peace envoy sent to France in 1798 who was asked for a bribe by French agents in order to continue negotiations

BENJAMIN BACHE: HERO OR VILLAIN?

In June 1798 Benjamin Franklin Bache, the grandson of Benjamin Franklin and publisher of the Republican newspaper *Aurora*, published a conciliatory letter from Charles de Talleyrand, the French foreign minister, to American peace envoys before President Adams had seen the letter. Republicans defended Bache for educating the public about the French desire for peace, but William Cobbett, publisher of the Federalist *Porcupine's Gazette*, condemned Bache as a traitor:

It is here proved, that the man, who for six long years, has been incessantly employed in accusing and villifying your government, and in justifying the French in all their abominable injuries and insults, is absolutely in close correspondence with the insolent and savage despots by whom those injuries and insults have been committed, and who now demand of you an enormous TRIBUTE or threaten you, in case of disobedience, with the fate of VENICE, that is, first with subjugation, and then with being *swapped away like cattle* to that prince of state, who will give them the most in exchange for you!

Bache was charged with libel under common law two weeks before Congress passed the Sedition Act, but he died of yellow fever before he could be tried. Many Federalists believed justice had been served.

Sources: William Cobbett, "The Defection of Benjamin Bache," *Porcupine's Gazette,* 18 June 1798;

John C. Miller, *Crisis in Freedom: The Alien and Sedition Acts* (Boston: Little, Brown, 1951).

to France and authorize a series of defense measures. Congress appointed peace commissioners and appropriated money for a navy and a system of harbor fortifications, but Republicans defeated proposals for enlarging the army. Then, in April 1798, Adams released diplomatic dispatches to Congress reporting how, six months earlier, three agents of French foreign minister Charles de Talleyrand, identified only as "X," "Y," and "Z," had demanded a bribe from American peace envoys John Marshall, Charles Cotesworth Pinckney, and Elbridge Gerry before the opening of negotiations. The publication of the "XYZ Papers" created war hysteria, and between May and July, Congress passed legislation authorizing the new U.S. Navy to capture French vessels, quadrupling the regular army, and authorizing a provisional army of fifty thousand. To Republicans the undeclared "Quasi-War" with France, with its large army, taxes, and other repressive legislation, was proof that the conflict was part of a Federalist conspiracy to destroy political opposition.

The Alien and Sedition Acts. The Federalists also believed that the United States was in danger from a conspiracy between France and the Republican Party to introduce subversive ideas into the United States. Determined to suppress democracy, which Federalists believed inevitably ended in disorder and dictatorship, the Federalist-dominated Congress passed a series of four

In the aftermath of the Sedition Act, Tunis Wortman, a lawyer and New York Republican, defended the necessity of freedom of political inquiry:

> The freedom of speech and opinion, is not only necessary to the happiness of man, considered as a moral and Intellectual Being, but indispensably requisite to the perpetuation of Civil Liberty. . . .

> . . . it should therefore be established as an essential principle, that freedom of investigation is one of the most important rights of a people. It is true to a proverb, that "ignorance is the parent of vice." Knowledge is therefore a more powerful corrective than coercion. By enlightening the understanding, you lay the foundation of positive virtue and benefit. . . .

> . . . It cannot be denied, that the powers of government are not original, but strictly derivative; that the only fountain from whence its authority proceeds is public delegation. . . . It must ever remain the inherent and incontrovertible right of society, to dissolve its political constitution, whenever the voice of public opinion has declared such dissolution to be essential to the general welfare. Society must, therefore, necessarily possess the unlimited right to examine and investigate. . . . the government which attempts to coerce the progress of opinion, or to abolish the freedom of investigation into political affairs, materially violates the most essential principles of the social state.

Source: Tunis Wortman, *A Treatise Concerning Political Inquiry and the Liberty of the Press* (1800).

acts limiting freedom of speech, freedom of the press, and the rights of foreigners. Three of the acts were aimed at foreigners, targeted in the Federalist press as "the convicts, fugitives of justice, hirelings of France, and disaffected offscourings of other nations." To make it harder for foreigners to become citizens and join the Republican Party, Congress passed the Naturalization Act (18 June 1798), increasing the residency period for citizenship from five to fourteen years. The Act Concerning Aliens (25 June) allowed the president to deport any alien during war or peace judged "dangerous to the peace and safety of the United States," but President Adams did not use this authority. The Act Respecting Alien Enemies (6 July) allowed the president to deport or imprison enemy aliens during wartime, but it did not go into effect because the United States never declared war against France. The most controversial law was the Act for the Punishment of Certain Crimes, or the Sedition Act (14 July), which imposed fines and imprisonment on both citizens and aliens convicted of writing, publishing, or speaking anything of "a false, scandalous and malicious nature" against the government or its officers. Under the forceful prosecution of Federalist Secretary of State Timothy Pickering the government indicted fifteen individuals, ten of whom were convicted, including several prominent Republican newspaper editors and Congressman Matthew Lyon, "the Spitting Lyon of Vermont." (A few months earlier, Lyon had spit in the face of Roger Griswold, a Federalist congressman from Connecticut, which led to a brawl on the floor of the House of Representatives.) Federalists were thrilled when "Ragged Mat, the Democrat" was fined and imprisoned for four months for libeling President Adams, but during his imprisonment he became a national hero and was reelected to office overwhelmingly.

The Kentucky and Virginia Resolutions. According to Vice President Thomas Jefferson, the United States government after ten years of Federalist rule had become "more arbitrary, and has swallowed more of the public liberty than even that of England." In late 1798 Jefferson anonymously wrote the Kentucky Resolutions while James Madison authored the Virginia Resolutions. They presented the manifestos as respectful protests against the constitutionality of the Alien and Sedition Acts by states who professed "a warm attachment to the union of the states." Their goal was not just the immediate issue of repealing the Alien and Sedition Acts but the larger issue of protecting the states from the centralizing power of the federal government. As Jefferson and Madison interpreted the Constitution, the federal government was created by a "compact" among the states, in which the states delegated specific powers to the federal government. Since the federal government was a creation of the states, the states had the right to judge the constitutionality of federal laws. The Kentucky and Virginia Resolutions declared that the Alien and Sedition Acts were unconstitutional and thus "void and of no force." The other states did not support state nullification of unconstitutional federal laws as "the rightful remedy," but the resolutions had important effects. The goal of protecting liberty from the grasp of the Federalists gave the Republicans a party platform for the presidential election of 1800. In the long term, and with more disastrous results, nullification and the states' rights doctrine of the Kentucky and Virginia Resolutions influenced the southern states' decision to secede from the Union in 1861.

Protest, Peace, and Political Defeat. President Adams had several compelling reasons to reopen peace negotiations with France in 1799. In the fall of 1798 peace envoy Elbridge Gerry and Dr. George Logan, a private citizen from Philadelphia, returned to the United States with news that France was interested in peace. In February 1799 John Fries led a group of armed men in Pennsylvania who freed two men imprisoned for refusing to pay the direct tax on land imposed to support the enlarged army. Federal troops put down the rebellion, and Fries was convicted of treason but pardoned by the president. The Alien and Sedition Acts, the direct tax, and the use of federal soldiers to suppress the Fries Rebellion fueled Republican claims that the Federalists were deter-

Negotiations for the Treaty of Greenville, August 1795

mined to extinguish liberty. In fact, the Federalists were split between moderates under President Adams and "High Federalists" under former secretary of the Treasury Alexander Hamilton. Although he retired from office in January 1795, Hamilton continued to exert influence over High Federalists in the federal government. Robert Goodloe Harper introduced Hamilton's proposal for a provisional army of fifty thousand in Congress; Secretary of War James McHenry nominated Hamilton as major general of the enlarged army; and Hamilton drafted for several cabinet members papers opposing peace negotiations. The High Federalists also expressed expectations that the new army would have to be used against domestic enemies. In contrast, Adams had always spoken of the dangers of a large standing army. Determined to obtain peace, assert control over his cabinet, and disassociate himself from Hamilton's policies, Adams dispatched a three-man peace mission to France in November 1799. On 30 September 1800 the United States and France signed an agreement ending the Quasi-War. Adams believed that his act of sending peace envoys to France was "the most disinterested, the most determined and the most successful of my whole life." Unfortunately, his political independence split the Federalist Party and helped Republican vice president Thomas Jefferson become president in 1800.

Sources:

Richard H. Kohn, *Eagle and Sword: The Federalists and the Creation of the Military Establishment in America, 1783–1802* (New York: Macmillan, 1975);

Stephen G. Kurtz, *The Presidency of John Adams: The Collapse of Federalism, 1795–1800* (Philadelphia: University of Pennsylvania Press, 1957);

John C. Miller, *Crisis in Freedom: The Alien and Sedition Acts* (Boston: Little, Brown, 1951);

Miller, *The Federalist Era, 1789–1801* (New York: Harper Torchbooks, 1963);

Paul A. Varg, *Foreign Policies of the Founding Fathers* (East Lansing: Michigan State University Press, 1963).

THE FRONTIER AND INDIAN POLICY

Treaties, Assimilation, and Removal. The Treaty of Paris in 1783 gave the United States possession of a large unsettled territory extending west to the Mississippi River. Spain controlled Florida, Louisiana, and access to the Mississippi River, and until 1796 Britain retained possession of Forts Oswegatchie, Oswego, and Niagara in upstate New York and Forts Miami, Detroit, and Michilimackinac in the Northwest. The Confederation government lacked the military strength to stop white settlers from pouring into Indian lands or to stop Native Americans, often supported by the British and Spanish, from resisting the invasion of their lands. Yet Congress boldly claimed sovereignty over Indian lands by virtue of their victory over Britain and imposed treaties on several tribes. Both white settlers and Native Americans ignored the treaties, and the resulting conflict was passed on to the new federal government in 1789. The Washington administration, hoping to avoid costly Indian warfare or confrontation with Britain or Spain, adopted a policy of purchasing Indian lands through treaty and trying to assimilate Indians into American civilization. Jedidiah Morse, author of *The American Geography* (1789), anticipated a future "when the AMERICAN EMPIRE will comprehend millions of souls, west of the Mississippi." President Thomas Jefferson's Louisiana Purchase in 1803 made Morse's vision a reality. When Jefferson recommended that the federal government offer Native Americans land west of the Mississippi in exchange for their land in the East, he acknowledged that assimilation could only slow inevitable white settlement of the frontier. After the War of 1812 the federal government began a policy of Indian removal that reached its height in the 1830s under President Andrew Jackson, who first gained prominence by defeating the Creek nation during the War of 1812.

Northwest. The Confederation Congress asserted national control over the Northwest Territory, a large re-

THE FAILURE OF ASSIMILATION: AN INDIAN VIEW

In the years since their defeat at the Battle of Fallen Timbers in 1794 the Wyandot Indians, once members of the Miami Confederacy, had become farmers and accepted assimilation into white civilization, but they could not stop the advancing frontier. On 5 February 1812 a group of Wyandot chiefs, after having already given up "a large present of land," petitioned the United States government to protect their remaining land:

> Fathers, listen! If you really want to ameliorate our condition, let us have the land given to us; we have built valuable houses, and improvements on the same; we have learned the use of the plough; but now we are told we are to be turned off the land in fifty years.

> Fathers, listen! This has given us great uneasiness; This pretence of bettering our situation, it appears, is only for a temporary purpose: for, should we live on the land for fifty years, as farmers, and then be turned off, we will be very miserable indeed. By that time, we shall have forgot how to hunt, in which practice we are now very expert, and then you'll turn us out of doors, a poor, pitiful, helpless set of wretches. . . .

Source: *American State Papers*, Indian Affairs, volume 1 (Washington, D.C.: Gale & Seaton, 1832).

gion bounded by the Mississippi River, the Ohio River, and the Great Lakes, by passing the Northwest Ordinance of 1787 and signing treaties with several tribes in the region. Secretary of War Henry Knox believed that the new federal government could maintain peace by purchasing Indian lands. By 1789, however, the Shawnee, Miami, and Delaware Indians had organized a confederacy to resist white settlement north of the Ohio River. In 1790 Little Turtle and the Miami Confederacy defeated an American army under Gen. Josiah Harmar, and in 1791 they killed or wounded over nine hundred Americans under Gen. Arthur St. Clair, governor of the Northwest Territory. In August 1794 Gen. Anthony Wayne and an American army defeated the Miami Confederacy in the Battle of Fallen Timbers near Toledo, Ohio. Under the terms of the Treaty of Greenville, signed in August 1795, the Miami Confederacy ceded much of present-day Ohio and Indiana to the U.S. government. By 1805 a new confederacy began forming around Tenskwatawa, or "the Prophet," a Shawnee religious leader, and his brother, Tecumseh, a war chief, who urged resistance against the white invasion of Indian land and culture. By 1809 two new federal land acts and a series of Indian treaties negotiated by Gov. William Henry Harrison of Indiana Territory had taken extensive territory from Native Americans, and Tecumseh began organizing a military confederacy. In the fall of

1811, while Tecumseh was recruiting among southern tribes, Governor Harrison and one thousand men prepared to attack the headquarters of the Shawnee Confederacy on the Tippecanoe River. On 7 November the Prophet's surprise attack on the American camp failed, and the Shawnee Confederacy broke up. Tecumseh slipped away to Canada where he formed a British-Indian confederacy in the War of 1812 in a final attempt to preserve Indian culture.

Southwest. The federal government's ability to govern the southwestern frontier was impeded by aggressive expansion into Indian lands by the southern states who owned the lands and the support that Spain provided to Indians in the region. During the Confederation period Virginia rapidly settled its western lands in Kentucky, which, despite Indian warfare, became the fifteenth state in the Union in 1792. North Carolina, which did not cede its western lands in Tennessee to Congress until 1789, appropriated millions of acres of land belonging to the Creek and Cherokee Indians. Georgia, which did not cede its western lands to Congress until 1802, antagonized the Creek Indians by claiming their lands through questionable treaties in the 1780s and 1790s. The signing of the Pinckney Treaty between the United States and Spain in 1795 opened up new territory for American settlement and removed the immediate obstacle of Spanish-supported Indian warfare in the Southwest (now the southeastern United States). The federal government expanded settlement in western Tennessee by obtaining land from the Cherokees between 1798 and 1806, but they found the Creeks in Georgia and Mississippi Territory (present-day Mississippi and Alabama) resistant to offers of land and assimilation. Neither assimilation nor resistance could stop expansion, especially after President Jefferson's Louisiana Purchase encouraged further expansion into Indian lands. For many members of the Creek nation the War of 1812 was their last chance to preserve their tribal lands and culture.

The War of 1812. When the United States declared war against Britain in June 1812 after years of British harassment of American ships and sailors, Native Americans in the Northwest and the Southwest calculated that a British alliance would help them expel the American invaders from their territory forever. Britain regarded Native American tribes as useful allies to prevent the Americans from invading Canada and occupying East Florida. In the first year of war the British-Indian alliance resulted in the surrender of Fort Michilimackinac on Lake Huron and Fort Dearborn (in present-day Chicago). On 16 August 1812 Gen. William Hull abandoned plans to invade Canada and surrendered Detroit after British general Isaac Brock threatened that he could not control Tecumseh or the one thousand warriors he commanded. But Commander Oliver Hazard Perry's naval victory over the British at the Battle of Put-in-Bay in September 1813 secured American control of Lake Erie, and Gen. William Henry Har-

Harry L. Coles, *The War of 1812* (Chicago: University of Chicago Press, 1965);

Reginald Horsman, *The Frontier in the Formative Years* (Albuquerque: University of New Mexico Press, 1975);

Richard White, *The Middle Ground: Indians, Empires, and Republics in the Great Lakes Region, 1650–1815* (New York: Cambridge University Press, 1991).

THE JEFFERSONIAN REVOLUTION

"A Wise and Frugal Government." The "revolution of 1800," as Thomas Jefferson called his presidential election, was "as real a revolution in the principles of our government as that of 1776 was in its form." Federalists had attempted to insult the Republicans by calling them "Democrats," but public endorsement of their policies meant that the term *Democratic-Republican* was now an acceptable and honorable name. Symbolically, Jefferson

William Clark's sketch of a Chinook alâkân from his journal entry of 24 February 1806 (The Warder Collection)

rison's victory over a British-Indian force in the Battle of the Thames on 5 October 1813, during which Tecumseh was killed, ended Native American resistance in the Northwest. In the Southwest members of the Creek nation in Mississippi Territory decided to raid the American frontier after Tecumseh visited in 1811 and 1812 with promises of British and Spanish support and news of British victories in the Northwest. On 30 August 1813 the Creeks killed several hundred settlers and soldiers at Fort Mims near Mobile, but the American counterattack led by Gen. Andrew Jackson of the Tennessee militia was devastating. After American militia killed hundreds of Creeks in several battles in November 1813, Generals Jackson and John Coffee inflicted the final blow on 27 March 1814 in the Battle of Horseshoe Bend. Jackson's army of 2,000 militiamen, aided by 200 Cherokee allies, killed over 550 Creeks, and hundreds more died trying to escape. The destruction was completed on 9 August 1814 when the Treaty of Fort Jackson forced the Creeks to give up two-thirds of their land in eastern Georgia and most of the Mississippi Territory.

Sources:

Robert F. Berkhofer Jr., *The White Man's Indian: Images of the American Indian from Columbus to the Present* (New York: Vintage Books, 1979);

THE BURR CONSPIRACY

With his political career ruined after killing Alexander Hamilton in a duel in July 1804, Vice President Aaron Burr began plotting a conspiracy whose objects included the invasion of Mexico or the separation of the western states from the United States, depending on whom he was trying to interest in his plans. On 25 July 1806 Burr described the status of his "enterprise" in a letter to a coconspirator, Samuel Swartwout:

> Protection of England is secured. . . . navy of the United States are ready to join, and final orders are given to my friends and followers. It will be a host of choice spirits. . . . Burr guarantees the result with his life and honor—the lives, the honor, and fortune of hundreds, the best blood of our country. . . . The people of the country to which we are going [Mexico] are prepared to receive us: their agents, now with Burr, say that, if we will protect their religion, and will not subject them to a foreign Power, in three weeks all will be settled. The gods invite to glory and fortune: it remains to be seen whether we deserve the boon. . . .

After coconspirator Gen. James Wilkinson informed President Thomas Jefferson of the conspiracy, Burr was indicted for treason. He was acquitted on 1 September 1807 after Chief Justice John Marshall ruled that he was not "actually or constructively present" during an overt act of treason.

Sources: Thomas P. Abernethy, *The South in the New Nation, 1789–1819*, volume 4 of *A History of the Old South* (Baton Rouge: Louisiana State University Press, 1967);

Papers on the Burr Conspiracy in Debates in the Ninth Congress, in *Annals of Congress* (Washington, D.C.: Gale & Seaton, 1834–1856);

Marshall Smelser, *The Democratic Republic, 1801–1815* (New York: Harper Torchbooks, 1968).

marked the end of aristocracy in government by walking to the Capitol to take his oath of office instead of riding in a carriage accompanied by a military honor guard and by delivering his addresses to Congress in writing, not in person. In his first Inaugural Address in March 1801 Jefferson promised "a wise and frugal government, which shall restrain men from injuring one another, which shall leave them otherwise free to regulate their own pursuits of industry and improvement, and shall not take from the mouth of labor the bread it has earned." The Republican Congress repealed all internal taxes, including the unpopular whiskey tax; reduced the army, navy, and federal bureaucracy; and let the Sedition Act expire. Jefferson pledged to return the federal government to its legitimate and limited role of protecting life, liberty, and property. A Republican administration would also create economic opportunity for the small farmers and other productive citizens whose interests had been sacrificed to merchants and speculators by the Federalists. Jefferson's "wise and frugal government" would endure because of the support of the independent, property-owning farmers it protected. The transfer of power from Federalists to Republicans also marked a shift from pessimism about human nature, democracy, and progress to optimism about the American people and their ability to make wise decisions about the political future of the United States. As Jefferson wrote to Abigail Adams in 1804: "One [party] fears most the ignorance of the people; the other the selfishness of rulers independent of them."

Removals from Office. The overwhelming Republican victory in Congress in 1800 testified to popular support for the Republican Party. Secretary of State James Madison, a founder of the Republican Party, and Secretary of the Treasury Albert Gallatin, a Republican congressional leader from Pennsylvania, headed the cabinet. President Jefferson had the option of strengthening the people's endorsement of Republican policies by removing all Federalist officeholders. Within a month of taking office Jefferson emphasized that "good men" were in no danger of being removed from office just because they were Federalists. But in July 1801 he explained to a committee of New Haven merchants protesting his removal of a Federalist customs collector that the Federalist monopoly of government office, especially after President Adams's "midnight appointments" to the federal judiciary, could not be tolerated because it obstructed "the will of the nation." Jefferson's first priority was to remove all appointments made after 12 December 1800, when Adams's defeat was confirmed, and all officers guilty of misconduct. He also planned to appoint Republicans as U.S. attorneys and federal marshals to protect "the republican part of our fellow citizens" from the Federalist-controlled judiciary. In a letter to Secretary of the Treasury Gallatin in August 1801 Jefferson suggested that one half of government offices should be held by Republicans, and by July 1803 only 130 of 316 offices were held by Federalists. By this time, however, continuing Feder-

alist opposition had convinced Jefferson that Republicans were entitled to a much larger proportion of the offices based on their status as the majority political party. When that point was reached, Jefferson would disregard political affiliation in future appointments.

Louisiana Purchase. News that Spain had secretly ceded Louisiana to France in October 1800 threatened President Jefferson's plan for the United States to remain a nation of farmers exporting surplus crops to foreign markets. Jefferson and Secretary of State Madison instructed diplomats Robert Livingston and James Monroe to try to purchase New Orleans and as much of Spanish Florida as possible. By April 1803 France's ruler, Napoleon Bonaparte, had lost interest in a New World empire after failing to reassert control over rebellious slaves in Saint Domingue. In need of money to resume European war, Napoleon offered to sell the entire Louisiana Territory to the United States for $15 million. (The region was 885,000 square miles and stretched from the Mississippi River to the Rocky Mountains, and from the Gulf of Mexico to Canada.) Despite his concern that the Constitution did not authorize the purchase and incorporation of new territory, Jefferson approved the Louisiana Purchase as an act of national interest. The peaceful acquisition of this vast territory, doubling the size of the United States, would avoid the expense of war to secure access to the Mississippi, expand economic opportunity and independence through landownership and the growth of commercial agriculture, and supplement the national revenue through land sales. Establishing control over this large, diverse region inhabited by Native Americans, French, Spanish, American settlers, and free blacks was essential, especially after former vice president Aaron Burr organized a complicated plot in 1806–1807 involving foreign conspirators and western settlers in an attempt to establish an independent state. Jefferson and the Republican Congress passed territorial government acts that brought representative government to the region's inhabitants, including Spanish and French residents who were allowed to keep their own legal systems. Explorations of lands west of the Mississippi by Capt. Meriwether Lewis and Lt. William Clark (1804–1806) and by Lt. Zebulon Pike (1805–1806) uncovered valuable information that stimulated interest in the region. National land policies, Indian removal, and a National Road, all approved during the Jefferson administration, dramatically increased westward migration after the War of 1812, as did the decision to allow slavery in the territories of the Louisiana Purchase. Ironically, by the 1830s the "Empire of Liberty" had become a reality for millions of white Americans at the expense of Native Americans and African American slaves whose land and labor made democracy possible.

Foreign Policy. In his first Inaugural Address, President Jefferson announced a foreign policy based on "peace, commerce, and honest friendship with all nations—entangling alliances with none." Jefferson and

Secretary of State James Madison believed that commerce could be "the means of peaceable coercion" that would make war unnecessary. Unfortunately, other nations did not share their respect for freedom of the seas. When the Barbary state of Tripoli threatened to plunder American ships in demand for annual tribute, Jefferson authorized military force, blockading and bombarding Tripoli and resulting in the capture of Derna and the signing of a peace treaty in 1805. That same year Britain decided to stop allowing Americans to profit from the war with France by trading with French and Spanish colonies and reexporting goods to Europe. Britain invoked the Rule of 1756, prohibiting neutral ships from trading during wartime with ports that were closed during peacetime. Soon America's neutral trade was caught between retaliatory British and French restrictions. Britain also seized American ships and impressed, or forcibly removed, crew members whom they believed to be deserters from the Royal Navy. In April 1806 Congress passed a Non-Importation Act prohibiting the importation of British goods to protest British policies. In June 1807 the H.M.S. *Leopard* opened fire on the U.S.S. *Chesapeake* off Norfolk, Virginia, killing three Americans and wounding eighteen in the process of impressing four alleged British deserters. On 22 December 1807 President Jefferson signed the Embargo Act, forbidding the export of American commerce to any foreign ports. Jefferson and Madison overestimated the value of American trade to France and Britain and underestimated Britain's determination to maintain what it considered to be necessary policies on neutral trade and impressment. Opposition to the Embargo Act also revived the Federalist Party. Days before leaving office in March 1809, Jefferson signed the Non-Intercourse Act, allowing the resumption of foreign trade except with Britain and France until they removed their trade restrictions. For the next two years Jefferson's successor, James Madison, and Congress tried diplomacy and various nonintercourse acts, but the Republican alternative to war was now just a delaying tactic. On 23 June 1812 a new British ministry, answering the pleas of merchants and manufacturers hurt by the loss of American markets, repealed the restrictions on neutral trade, but it was too late. Days earlier the United States had decided that war against Britain was necessary to defend American honor.

Sources:

Noble E. Cunningham Jr., *The Jeffersonians in Power: Party Operations, 1801–1809* (Chapel Hill: University of North Carolina Press, 1963);

Drew R. McCoy, *The Elusive Republic: Political Economy in Jeffersonian America* (New York: Norton, 1982);

Marshall Smelser, *The Democratic Republic, 1801–1815* (New York: Harper Torchbooks, 1968);

Leonard D. White, *The Jeffersonians: A Study in Administrative History, 1801–1829* (New York: Macmillan, 1956).

Contemporary sampler celebrating George Washington's inauguration as president

NATIONAL ELECTIONS OF 1788

Electoral College. The framers of the Constitution designed a method of electing the president that grew out of their fear of democracy and political corruption and their desire to maintain the separation of powers that was the basis of the federal system of government. Under that system it was critical that the chief executive be independent of the control of any individual or body of individuals. It was also critical that the office be filled, as Alexander Hamilton wrote in *Federalist*, number 68, "by characters pre-eminent for ability and virtue." Many of the framers associated democracy with corruption. Allowing the common people to elect the president would subject them to the control of unprincipled men who could use their social position or bribes to influence the lower classes to choose the "right" candidate. The president would then become the "creature" of the individuals who had manipulated his election. Allowing Congress to elect the president, as James Madison had originally advised, could also jeopardize the president's independence because he would owe his election to the legislative branch. Instead, the framers invented the electoral college, in which the people of each state chose "electors," equal to the number of their senators and representatives in Congress. The states played an important role by deciding how the electors were chosen. In the first presidential election the legislatures in four states chose electors, while the people did in four others, and, in Massachusetts and New Hampshire electors were chosen by a combination of the people and the legislature. Each elector cast two votes for president. The candidate with the highest vote became president, and the candidate with the second highest vote became vice president. If no candidate received a majority, the House of Representatives decided the election, with each state having one vote. As Hamilton explained, this system would guarantee the high quality of candidates and prevent political intrigue. "A small number of persons, selected by their fellow-citizens from the general mass, will be most likely to possess the information and discernment requisite to so complicated an investigation."

No Party, Nomination, or Campaign. The first presidential election had none of the trappings of modern politics: nominating conventions, party platforms, or campaign speeches. No one sought the presidency. Most Americans did not accept political parties as desirable institutions, shunning them as associations of dishonest, self-interested individuals. On 4 February 1789 electors in ten states (North Carolina and Rhode Island had not yet ratified the Constitution, and a dispute in New York prevented that state from choosing electors) convened in their respective states to choose the first president of the United States. The sixty-nine electors unanimously cast their first vote for George Washington. Alexander Hamilton tried to reduce John Adams's influence in the new government by encouraging electors not to vote for him, but Hamilton's maneuvering was probably unnecessary. Adams, who received thirty-four votes, was elected vice president, with thirty-five remaining votes divided among ten other candidates. Washington had made no speeches; his countrymen declared him a candidate by their votes. His public record as a member of the Virginia House of Burgesses, delegate to the First and Second Continental Congresses, commander in chief of the Continental Army, and president of the Constitutional Convention attested to his long-standing support for republican government and the Constitution.

The First Congress. Only 5 to 8 percent of the eligible white male population voted in the first congressional elections. The absence of national political parties to attract voters through campaign rhetoric and political organization reduced voter turnout, but the anticipation of Washington's election no doubt influenced the choice of representatives who were supporters of the Constitution and a strong national government. In the First Congress, Secretary of the Treasury Alexander Hamilton took the lead in mobilizing support for his financial program by monitoring legislative debates and providing favorable arguments and statistics to congressional supporters. Congressman James Madison and Clerk of the House John Beckley of Virginia responded by organizing opposition in Congress. Members of the First Congress

objected to aspects of Hamilton's financial program, but their opposition was not yet sufficient to overcome their distrust of permanent political parties. During the second and third sessions of the First Congress, after opposition to Hamilton's policies began forming, 42 percent of the members of the House of Representatives still did not vote consistently with either of the two developing parties on at least two-thirds of all important legislation. During the Second Congress (1791–1793), as the supporters of the Washington administration more openly identified themselves as Federalists and their opponents began calling themselves Republicans, the percentage of nonparty voting in Congress dropped to an average of 20 percent. At this formative stage in party development, however, neither party could ignore nonaligned or independent members of Congress.

Sources:

William Nisbet Chambers, *Political Parties in a New Nation: The American Experience, 1776–1809* (New York: Oxford University Press, 1963);

Joseph Charles, *The Origins of the American Party System* (New York: Harper Torchbooks, 1961);

Stanley Elkins and Eric McKitrick, *The Age of Federalism: The Early American Republic, 1788–1800* (New York: Oxford University Press, 1993);

Alexander Hamilton, James Madison, and John Jay, *The Federalist Papers*, with introduction by Clinton Rossiter (New York: New American Library, 1961);

Eugene H. Roseboom and Alfred E. Eckes Jr., *A History of Presidential Elections*, fourth edition (New York: Collier, 1979).

NATIONAL ELECTIONS OF 1792

Washington Returns. At age sixty, weary of the political disputes between Secretary of the Treasury Alexander Hamilton and Secretary of State Thomas Jefferson and their respective supporters in Congress, President George Washington looked forward to retirement. The only point that Hamilton and Jefferson could agree on was that national harmony depended on Washington's reelection. Neither Federalists nor Republicans were ready for the permanent division of the United States into two opposing political parties. As in the election of 1788, there were no nominations, party labels, or campaign speeches by presidential candidates in 1792. Electors from fifteen states now in the Union unanimously cast 132 electoral votes for George Washington. This apparent unanimity and nonpartisanship is, however, somewhat misleading. The selections of a vice president and members of Congress showed unmistakable though rudimentary signs of party politics. In this sense the elections of 1792 were a transitional phase in the development of party politics. By the election of 1796, when Washington chose not to run for reelection, two competing parties had come into existence with clearly articulated ideologies, party leaders, and national political candidates.

The Vice Presidency. The Federalists quickly united behind incumbent vice president John Adams, but the Republicans engaged in a more complicated process of "nominating" their vice presidential candidate. Although the Republicans did not hold a national convention or go through a formal process of nomination, Virginia's Republican leaders James Madison, James Monroe, and John Beckley used letters and personal visits to urge New York Republicans to support New York governor George Clinton over Sen. Aaron Burr. At a meeting in Philadelphia attended by Beckley, Melancton Smith of New York, and Pierce Butler of South Carolina the Republicans decided, in Beckley's words, "to exert every endeavor for Mr. Clinton." Having informally nominated their candidate, Republican leaders used their influence within their respective states to unite support behind Clinton, with positive results. Washington was again chosen unanimously, but, unlike the elections of 1788, when thirty-five of the sixty-nine votes on the second ballot were scattered among ten candidates, in 1792 party solidarity resulted in seventy-seven votes for John Adams and fifty of the remaining fifty-five votes for George Clinton. Adams carried all of New England, New Jersey, Delaware, and Maryland, fourteen of Pennsylvania's fifteen electoral votes, and seven of South Carolina's eight votes. Clinton carried New York, Virginia, North Carolina, and Georgia and received one vote in Pennsylvania. The recently admitted state of Kentucky cast four votes for Thomas Jefferson, and South Carolina cast one vote for Aaron Burr. Victory in the electoral college went to Washington and Adams, but the growing Republican opposition in Congress meant that political harmony would not prevail during their second term.

Congressional Races. The continuing distaste for party politics was evident in the unwillingness of Federalists and Republicans to declare their affiliations openly through nominating conventions or party tickets in the elections of 1792. But the Republicans took other steps to mobilize support for their positions and their candidates. James Madison wrote a series of anonymous essays in the *National Gazette,* which, by highlighting the differences between Federalists and Republicans, served as a kind of Republican party platform. Behind the scenes, Republicans organized support for candidates. Foreign policy debates over the French Revolution and Jay's Treaty increased Republican strength in Congress, but the parties were fairly well balanced during Washington's second term. Both Federalists and Republicans began to send letters to their constituents explaining their respective party's positions and contributing to a sense of party identification among voters. Republican leaders in Congress held caucuses and appointed congressional committees to organize a unified vote on legislation. By 1796, when Congress was debating the Jay Treaty, nonparty voting had dropped to 7 percent. The existence of party caucuses and voting blocs in Congress, the use of

party newspapers and constituent letters to attract voters, and the coordinated efforts to choose candidates for national office are several features of modern party politics, but one essential element was missing. When Federalists called Republicans "Anti-Federalists" and "Jacobins," and when Republicans called Federalists "monarchists" and "British agents," they demonstrated that neither party had accepted the idea that political opposition was legitimate or desirable. Yet, even as they lamented the evils of parties, Federalists and Republicans were taking steps that would eventually establish the two-party system as one of the most important institutions of republican government.

Sources:

William Nisbet Chambers, *Political Parties in a New Nation: The American Experience, 1776–1809* (New York: Oxford University Press, 1963);

Stanley Elkins and Eric McKitrick, *The Age of Federalism: The Early American Republic, 1788–1800* (New York: Oxford University Press, 1993);

Eugene H. Roseboom and Alfred E. Eckes Jr., *A History of Presidential Elections,* fourth edition (New York: Collier, 1979);

Charles Warren, *Jacobin and Junto or Early American Politics as Viewed in the Diary of Dr. Nathaniel Ames* (Cambridge, Mass.: Harvard University Press, 1931).

NATIONAL ELECTIONS OF 1796

Federalist Successor. President George Washington's announcement that he would retire from office in September 1796 paved the way for the nation's first contested presidential election. Federalist members of Congress publicly agreed on a party ticket of Vice President John Adams of Massachusetts as their presidential candidate and Thomas Pinckney of South Carolina, negotiator of the Pinckney Treaty with Spain, as their vice-presidential candidate. Unfortunately, Article II, Section 1 of the Constitution did not provide separate ballots for electing the president and vice president, so the Federalists had no guarantee that the electors would endorse their proposed ticket. In addition former secretary of the Treasury Alexander Hamilton, who disliked Adams's moderate Federalism, not to mention his friendship with the Republican Thomas Jefferson, privately tried to arrange Pinckney's election as president. Hamilton suggested that northern electors give equal support to Adams and Pinckney, supposedly to prevent Jefferson's election. Since Hamilton expected southern electors to support Pinckney solidly, he believed that his plan would result in Pinckney's election as president. But Hamilton underestimated the support for Adams in New England, and his plan to deprive Adams of the presidency failed. Hamilton's political manipulations foreshadowed the intraparty factionalism that affected the Adams presidency and contributed to Republican electoral victory in the election of 1800.

Republican Presidential Ticket. Republican members of Congress informally nominated Thomas Jefferson of

Virginia as their presidential candidate. They could not agree on a vice-presidential candidate, but Aaron Burr of New York was the presumed candidate. John Beckley, clerk of the House of Representatives and Republican Party leader, counted on support for Burr from Pennsylvania, New York, Virginia, North Carolina, Kentucky, and Tennessee. The Republican Party's control over the presidential electors, already weakened by the lack of separate ballots for president and vice president, was further weakened by the informal, assumed, and nonbinding choice of Aaron Burr as vice president. The energetic Beckley, assuming that most of the northern electors would choose Adams and confident of solid southern support for Jefferson, turned his attention to Pennsylvania. By 1796 Pennsylvania had a highly developed two-party system, but the Federalist-controlled legislature, confident of their support from voters, passed a measure providing that presidential electors be chosen on a statewide political basis instead of by districts. Unfortunately for the Federalists, the Republicans proved to be the superior politicians. The Republican slate of presidential electors consisted of prominent men with statewide reputations while the Federalist slate consisted of less distinguished men with mostly local reputations. The Republicans also distributed fifty thousand hand-written tickets to local political leaders a week before the election. Republican electioneering paid off in Pennsylvania, where fourteen of the fifteen electors voted for Jefferson. For their second choice twelve of the fifteen electors chose Burr. Beckley also proved correct in estimating southern support for Jefferson, but electors in Virginia, North Carolina, and Georgia were decidedly cool toward Aaron Burr.

A Close Race. The national elections of 1796 had many of the characteristics of modern party politics. Candidates for the presidency and vice presidency were clearly Federalists or Republicans, and each party used newspapers and pamphlets to promote its candidates and attack the opposition. Support for or opposition to the Jay Treaty and the French Revolution were campaign issues in both the presidential and congressional elections. Many of the presidential electors were chosen on a partisan basis, either by popular vote or by the state legislatures. Both parties, however, had a long way to go in establishing a two-party system. Neither Adams nor Jefferson campaigned for the presidency. Adams expected that his long, distinguished record of public service would ensure his election, and Jefferson's lack of public commitment to his candidacy made James Madison fear that he would withdraw his name altogether. Although many presidential electors were chosen on a partisan basis, they were not bound to any candidate, and, as the final election results show, they were certainly not bound to the idea of voting for a party ticket by dividing their votes between their respective party's candidates for president and vice president. Adams received seventy-one votes, overwhelmingly from the North, while Jefferson's

An 1800 Federalist cartoon in which Thomas Jefferson is shown attempting to burn the Constitution on an "Altar to Gallic Despotism"

sixty-eight votes came primarily from the South. The failure to endorse the concept of party tickets may be seen in the vote for the vice-presidential candidates. Pinckney received fifty-nine votes, and Burr received only thirty votes, while forty-eight votes were scattered among other candidates. John Adams, a Federalist, was elected president, and Thomas Jefferson, a Republican, was vice president. The result was a damaged friendship between Adams and Jefferson and a contentious political administration. A divided administration, an increasingly partisan Congress, and divisions within his own party marred the Adams presidency and contributed to electoral defeat in 1800.

Sources:
William Nisbet Chambers, *Political Parties in a New Nation: The American Experience, 1776–1809* (New York: Oxford University Press, 1963);

Joseph Charles, *The Origins of the American Party System* (New York: Harper Torchbooks, 1961);

Stanley Elkins and Eric McKitrick, *The Age of Federalism: The Early American Republic, 1788–1800* (New York: Oxford University Press, 1993);

Eugene H. Roseboom and Alfred E. Eckes Jr., *A History of Presidential Elections,* fourth edition (New York: Collier, 1979).

NATIONAL ELECTIONS OF 1800
Federalist Divisions. Federalist victories in the 1798 congressional elections and public support for Adams's peace mission to France in November 1799 were encouraging signs for the Federalists in the presidential election of 1800. But the success of Adams's peace mission also threatened the future of Alexander Hamilton's expanded army and deprived the "High Federalists" of the position that their version of federalism was the only means to protect the nation from French invasion and Republican subversion. In May 1800 a caucus of Federalist congress-

men pledged the party's equal support to President John Adams and vice-presidential candidate Charles Cotesworth Pinckney of South Carolina, supposedly to prevent Republican victory, but Hamilton presumed that support for Pinckney in South Carolina would bring victory to Pinckney, not Adams. An outraged Adams exploded at Hamilton's political manipulations, which he believed had already cost him the election in New York, where Republican victory in the state elections resulted in control of the legislature and the choice of Republican presidential electors. In a meeting with Secretary of War James McHenry, Adams denounced Hamilton as "a man devoid of every moral principle" and McHenry as a tool of Hamilton. Adams then fired McHenry and Secretary of State Timothy Pickering, another Hamilton supporter. Hamilton responded with a pamphlet titled *Letter from Alexander Hamilton, Concerning the Public Conduct and Character of John Adams, Esq., President of the United States* (1800). Hamilton's scathing attack on Adams's "disgusting egotism," "distempered jealousy," "ungovernable indiscretion," and "vanity without bounds" became public when Aaron Burr, the Republican vice-presidential candidate, circulated Hamilton's pamphlet to the newspapers. Republicans took full advantage of the treachery, spitefulness, and political disunity among the Federalists revealed in Hamilton's pamphlet to present their party as a unified national party devoted to republican principles and the public good.

Republicans Unite. In May 1800 the Republican congressional caucus united behind Thomas Jefferson, who was no longer the reluctant candidate of 1796. Aaron Burr's successful political organizing in New York, which gave the Republicans control of the state legislature and the appointment of Republican presidential electors, earned him the vice-presidential nomination and the national support that was lacking in the 1796 elections. In pamphlets and newspapers the Republicans attacked the Federalists for high taxes and the threats to liberty posed by the enlarged army and the Alien and Sedition Acts. In their condemnations of President Adams the Republicans had plenty of quotes to choose from in Hamilton's pamphlet on Adams's multiple character defects. The Republicans also used the press to present Jefferson's "platform," promising limited government, the discharge of the national debt, and the restoration of civil liberties that the Federalists had violated. The Republicans' successful use of the press may have contributed to popular support for Jefferson, but it did not necessarily translate into electoral victory. In ten of the sixteen states the legislature chose electors, and in three states electors were chosen by district elections. In Pennsylvania popular support for the Republicans was apparent in congressional elections, where the voters elected ten Republicans and only three Federalists, but presidential electors were chosen by a more closely divided legislature. The Republican House and the Federalist Senate compromised, appointing eight Republican and seven Feder-

alist electors. District elections in Maryland and North Carolina resulted in support being divided between Federalist and Republican electors. Republican electioneering was more successful in South Carolina, where Republican Charles Pinckney, a relative of the Federalist vice-presidential candidate Charles Cotesworth Pinckney, used promises of patronage, which were honored by Jefferson, to ensure that the legislature chose eight electors committed to Jefferson and Burr.

The Revolution of 1800. In trying to influence the election of Federalist electors, Federalists denounced Jefferson as "a howling atheist," an "intellectual voluptuary," and the father of mulatto slave children. In contrast, "A Republican," writing in the Newport, Rhode Island *Guardian of Liberty*, called supporters of Jefferson "*republicans* in the true signification of the term, *patriots of '76* . . . in fine, all *true* Americans" and condemned Federalists as "Friends to monarchy . . . speculators, land jobbers, and monopolists, British agents and hirelings, degenerate Americans." Skillful party organization was evident in congressional elections, where the Republicans won 66 out of 106 seats in the House of Representatives. All Federalist electors but one divided their votes between Adams and Pinckney, while the Republican electors divided their votes equally between Jefferson and Burr. The final result showed Jefferson and Burr with seventy-three votes each, Adams with sixty-five, and Pinckney with sixty-four. The tie between Jefferson and Burr left it up to the members of the Federalist-controlled Sixth Congress, not the newly elected Republican Seventh Congress, to decide between Jefferson and Burr. For thirty-five ballots Jefferson carried eight states to Burr's six, with Vermont and Maryland divided, leaving Jefferson one short of the nine states required for election. James Bayard of Delaware, tired of waiting for Aaron Burr to solicit his support and assured by Sen. Samuel Smith of Maryland that Jefferson would not endanger Federalist economic or foreign policies or remove subordinate government officials, decided to support Jefferson. Bayard and Federalist representatives from South Carolina, Vermont, and Maryland submitted blank ballots, allowing Republican votes in Vermont and Maryland to give Jefferson the election. (Because of this election the Twelfth Amendment, providing separate ballots for president and vice president, was adopted in 1804.) The "revolution of 1800" marked a new stage in the evolution of party politics: the peaceful transition of power from one political party to another.

Sources:

William Nisbet Chambers, *Political Parties in a New Nation: The American Experience, 1776–1809* (New York: Oxford University Press, 1963);

Stanley Elkins and Eric McKitrick, *The Age of Federalism: The Early American Republic, 1788–1800* (New York: Oxford University Press, 1993);

John C. Miller, *The Federalist Era, 1789–1801* (New York: Harper Torchbooks, 1963);

Eugene H. Roseboom and Alfred E. Eckes Jr., *A History of Presidential Elections,* fourth edition (New York: Collier, 1979).

NATIONAL ELECTIONS OF 1804

The Republican Ticket. Thomas Jefferson's renomination as the Republican Party's presidential candidate in 1804 was just a formality. Jefferson had proven to be a strong executive and an effective party leader who carefully guided administration-sponsored legislation through Congress. With commanding Republican majorities in both houses of Congress, Jefferson had fulfilled his inaugural address promises of establishing "a wise and frugal government," restoring civil liberties, and creating economic opportunity by repealing internal taxes, reducing government expenses, repealing the Judiciary Act of 1801, letting the Sedition Act expire, and acquiring the Louisiana Territory. On 25 February 1804 the Republican congressional caucus, meeting openly for the first time, unanimously cast 108 votes for Jefferson. The Republican caucus, also for the first time, appointed a central committee to "promote the success of republican nominations" on a nationwide basis. The caucus was equally unanimous in their decision to drop Aaron Burr from the party's ticket, replacing him with George Clinton of New York, who received 67 out of 108 votes. The decision to remove Burr was a wise one. Burr, whose flirtation with the Federalists in the election of 1800 had stripped him of any influence in Jefferson's administration, decided to run for governor of New York in 1804. Sen. Timothy Pickering of Massachusetts and other Federalists, who were plotting secession from the republic they felt was controlled by Jefferson's democracy so they could form a northern confederacy, offered to help Burr get elected if he could bring New York into the fold. When Alexander Hamilton, who had criticized Burr's character and opposed his political ambitions for more than ten years, expressed his "despicable opinion" of Burr in print, Burr challenged him to a duel. On 11 July 1804 Burr mortally wounded Hamilton and, in the process, destroyed his own political career.

Old and Young Federalists. Public support for Jefferson and the Republican Party and its cohesive national organization were difficult obstacles for the Federalists to overcome. While Timothy Pickering and other older Federalists recoiled in disgust from Jeffersonian democracy and considered secession as a solution, a younger generation of Federalists began to adopt some of the Republicans' electioneering techniques. This second generation of Federalist political leaders, born between 1760 and 1789, whose members included Harrison Gray Otis and Josiah Quincy of Massachusetts, Robert Goodloe Harper of Maryland, and John Rutledge Jr. of South Carolina, recognized the need to organize caucuses and committees to nominate candidates and spread the Federalist message to voters through pamphlets, newspapers, mass meetings, barbecues, and other public celebrations. Most of all, the young Federalists, even though they may have been as aristocratic as the old Federalists, accepted the democratic trends in American political life. The almost universal use of secret ballots by 1800, the declining property qualifications for voters, and the phenomenal increase of voter participation after 1800 meant that no successful politician could ignore the power of this increasing body of people who could and did vote. Unfortunately, the young Federalists had only begun to organize on a statewide level by 1804. The national elections were still in the hands of the older generation of leaders who, at an informal meeting, nominated Charles Cotesworth Pinckney, the vice-presidential candidate in 1800, for president and Rufus King of New York as vice president, both of whom were Federalists of the old school.

Republican Landslide. The success of the Republican Party's philosophy and organization is evident in the final results of the presidential election of 1804. Jefferson received 162 electoral votes to Pinckney's 14. Pinckney received 9 votes from Connecticut, 3 from Delaware, and 2 of Maryland's 11 votes. To the horror of New England Federalists, Jefferson carried Massachusetts. The Republicans were just as successful in returning majorities to the House and Senate. The elections of 1804 may have lacked the excitement of 1800, but they were an important phase in American political development. Under the Twelfth Amendment the election of 1804 was the first national election with separate ballots for president and vice president, indicating the acceptance of party tickets. As evidence of the democratization of American politics, ten of the seventeen states chose presidential electors in either statewide or district popular elections, as compared to 1800, when the legislatures chose electors in ten

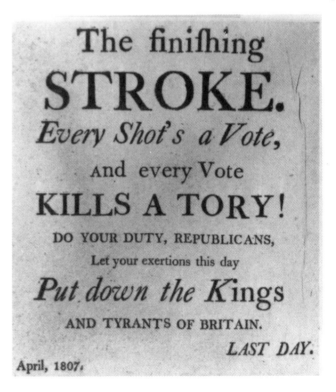

Republican broadside linking the Federalists (Tories) with the British monarchy

of sixteen states. Pinckney, the Federalist candidate, carried Connecticut and Delaware, two states where the legislature still chose electors. In addition, Connecticut had abolished the paper ballot in favor of oral voting, an undemocratic procedure that may have contributed to Federalist victory. The Federalists appeared to be headed for extinction, but reaction against Jefferson and James Madison's embargo and nonintercourse policies and the decision to declare war against England in 1812 kept the two-party system alive. The Federalists would never regain the presidency, but their organizational efforts brought some success in congressional elections during the Madison administration.

Sources:

William Nisbet Chambers, *Political Parties in a New Nation: The American Experience, 1776–1809* (New York: Oxford University Press, 1963);

Noble E. Cunningham Jr., *The Jeffersonians in Power: Party Operations, 1801–1809* (Chapel Hill: University of North Carolina Press, 1963);

David Hackett Fischer, *The Revolution of American Conservatism: The Federalist Party in the Era of Jeffersonian Democracy* (New York: Harper Torchbooks, 1965);

Marshall Smelser, *The Democratic Republic, 1801–1815* (New York: Harper Torchbooks, 1968).

NATIONAL ELECTIONS OF 1808

Contested Nomination. Thomas Jefferson's second term was marred by disputes within his party that threatened the nomination of James Madison as Jefferson's successor in 1808. Congressman John Randolph of Virginia objected to several administration measures that he believed deviated from strict republican principles, and he also resented Jefferson's successful interference in congressional affairs. When Georgia ceded its western lands to the federal government in 1802, the Jefferson administration inherited the problem of straightening out fraudulent land claims granted by the Georgia legislature in 1795. In 1804 Randolph vehemently opposed the recommendation of a committee composed of James Madison, Albert Gallatin, and Levi Lincoln that the federal government compensate the owners of the disputed Yazoo land claims, many of whom were northern speculators. In 1806 Randolph broke completely with Jefferson after the president simultaneously denounced Spain and requested that Congress appropriate funds to acquire Florida from Spain with French help. Randolph and other dissatisfied Republicans, who opposed Jefferson and Madison, their local party leaders, or various national and local policies, formed a loose opposition known as the "Tertium Quids." Their limited numbers, lack of influence in Congress, and the absence of a unified philosophy prevented the Tertium Quids from developing into a third national party or preventing Madison's presidential nomination. Randolph and some of the Tertium Quids supported James Monroe of Virginia as a presidential candidate, while other opponents of Madison favored Vice President George Clinton. Fortunately

THE GERRYMANDER

In April 1810 Massachusetts Republicans regained the governor's chair and a small majority in the legislature after a brief period of Federalist resurgence caused by opposition to the Embargo Act of 1807. In 1811 Gov. Elbridge Gerry was reelected, and the Republicans captured both branches of the legislature. Convinced that Federalist opposition to President James Madison's nonintercourse acts would lead to rebellion, Republicans proposed a series of electoral reforms to increase their numbers and throw Federalists out of office. In February 1812 the Republicans redrew the state's senatorial districts along partisan lines instead of following county boundaries, allowing their party to gain more seats. When Elkanah Tisdale, a Federalist artist, drew a map of one of the new districts, some people thought it looked like a salamander, prompting someone to suggest that it looked more like a "gerrymander." Despite having his name attached to the process of redrawing electoral districts for political purposes, Governor Gerry actually disapproved of the bill. The gerrymander helped the Republicans gain seats in the Senate, but the forty-five hundred new Federalist voters added as a result of other Republican reforms to increase the electorate allowed the Federalists to regain the governor's chair and the House of Representatives.

Sources: James M. Banner Jr., *To the Hartford Convention: The Federalists and the Origins of Party Politics in Massachusetts, 1789–1815* (New York: Knopf, 1970);

George Athan Billias, *Elbridge Gerry: Founding Father and Republican Statesman* (New York: McGraw-Hill, 1976).

for Madison, neither supporters of Monroe nor Clinton attended the Republican congressional caucus, which nominated Madison by a vote of 83-6 and renominated Clinton for vice president.

Federalist Convention. By the election of 1808 the young Federalists had established statewide organizations in New York, Massachusetts, New Hampshire, Rhode Island, Connecticut, Pennsylvania, Maryland, and Virginia, in addition to Delaware, where Federalist organization had begun in the 1790s. Opposition to the Embargo Act encouraged the Federalists to take steps toward national organization for the presidential election of 1808. Charles Willing Hare, a Philadelphia lawyer and prominent Federalist, suggested that Harrison Gray Otis of Massachusetts take the lead in organizing such an effort. Otis and other Massachusetts Federalists proposed a national meeting of Federalists in New York. Committees of correspondence in Massachusetts, New York, and Philadelphia communicated with Federalists in adjacent states to begin the process of uniting behind a

LOOK ON THIS PICTURE,   AND ON THIS.

Federalist cartoon, 1807, presenting an unfavorable comparison of
Jefferson to Washington

presidential candidate. The Federalists do not seem to have established committees of correspondence south of the Potomac. It is an exaggeration to call the meeting that convened in New York in August 1808 a "national convention." Only eight states were represented—Massachusetts, New Hampshire, Connecticut, Vermont, New York, Pennsylvania, Maryland, and South Carolina—and seven of the eight were north of the Potomac. In addition, the secrecy surrounding the convention and the number of Federalists who either criticized or ignored the convention's authority to nominate candidates demonstrates that Federalists were not yet comfortable with the legitimacy of a national nominating convention. The members of the convention considered supporting the Republican George Clinton, but they ended up renominating their party ticket from 1804: Charles Cotesworth Pinckney for president and Rufus King for vice president.

Republican Revolution Continues. Republican opponents of Madison in the key states of Virginia, Pennsylvania, and New York were unable to rally sufficient support to prevent Madison's election. Madison received 122 electoral votes (40 votes fewer than Jefferson's vote in 1804) to Pinckney's 47. New York gave 6 votes to Clinton, who was reelected vice president. The Federalists regained all of New England except Vermont, carried Delaware, and received 5 votes from Maryland and North Carolina. The results of the presidential election clearly indicate that the Federalists' secret convention in New York was unsuccess-

ful, but the Federalists did double their representation in the Eleventh Congress (1809–1811). The Federalists also made gains on the statewide level after 1808. In Massachusetts, after two years of defeat, the Federalists regained control of the state House of Representatives in the 1808–1809 session and the governorship in 1809. The Federalists controlled Maryland, Massachusetts, and Delaware and played a role in Pennsylvania politics into the 1820s. The Republicans still controlled the Eleventh Congress, with almost twice the number of seats as the Federalists, but that control, which had been an asset to Jefferson, became a liability to Madison. The Republican congressional caucus had made James Madison president, and that fact, coupled with Madison's own weaknesses as an executive, meant that Madison could never guide the Republican Congress the way Jefferson had. The result was a difficult and frustrating presidency.

Sources:

James M. Banner Jr., *To the Hartford Convention: The Federalists and the Origins of Party Politics in Massachusetts, 1789–1815* (New York: Knopf, 1970);

William Nisbet Chambers, *Political Parties in a New Nation: The American Experience, 1776–1809* (New York: Oxford University Press, 1963);

David Hackett Fischer, *The Revolution of American Conservatism: The Federalist Party in the Era of Jeffersonian Democracy* (New York: Harper Torchbooks, 1965);

Marshall Smelser, *The Democratic Republic, 1801–1815* (New York: Harper Torchbooks, 1968).

NATIONAL ELECTIONS OF 1812

"War Hawks." In the congressional elections of 1810 a younger generation of Republicans from the South and West entered Congress determined to defend the nation's honor against impressment, trade restrictions, and other policies designed to assert Britain's dominance over her former colonies. Thirty-four-year-old Henry Clay of Kentucky, chosen Speaker of the House, filled important committee posts in the Twelfth Congress (1811–1813) with fellow "War Hawks," as the Federalists called them, who pushed Congress to pass measures strengthening the army and navy in preparation for war. President James Madison's third Annual Message to Congress in November 1811, reporting the failure of diplomacy and urging Congress to pass legislation for military preparedness, indicates that Madison was moving closer to war. In April 1812 Congress, at Madison's request, approved an embargo in the hope that last-minute diplomatic developments might prevent war and to allow American ships to return home in case war was declared. The following month the Republican congressional caucus, controlled by the war hawks, unanimously renominated Madison for president. With the death of Vice President George Clinton in April, the caucus turned to Elbridge Gerry, recently defeated for reelection as governor of Massachusetts, as their vice-presidential nominee. In June, Congress declared war against Great Britain. After a series of military disasters in this first year of the War of 1812, Madison sought re-election, opposed by a member of his own party.

Federalist Challenge. As they had in 1808, the Young Federalists decided that national organization was necessary to challenge the Republicans. Federalists from eleven states met in New York in September 1812. Massachusetts Federalists, led by Harrison Gray Otis, supported DeWitt Clinton of New York, nephew of George Clinton and an antiadministration Republican who hoped to draw support from both Republicans and Federalists. New York Federalists, led by Rufus King, opposed an alliance with Clinton and recommended a separate Federalist ticket. Southern Federalists favored Supreme Court Chief Justice John Marshall of Virginia. The convention endorsed Otis's resolution against nominating a Federalist candidate but did not formally nominate Clinton. Instead, the delegates adjourned with the understanding that Clinton would get some Federalist support in each state, and that a formal nomination would be left to Federalists in the key state of Pennsylvania. The convention nominated Jared Ingersoll, a moderate Pennsylvania Federalist, for vice president. Clinton, hoping to gain votes from Federalists and Republicans, criticized the war to Federalists and criticized Madison's handling of the war to Republicans.

Madison Survives. The Young Federalists succeeded in making the presidential election of 1812 closer than the elections of 1804 and 1808, but their decision to support a Republican candidate was ultimately unsuccessful.

DeWitt Clinton, a Republican candidate for president in 1812 (New York Historical Society)

Madison won with 128 electoral votes to Clinton's 89. Clinton carried New York, New Jersey, Delaware, all of New England except Vermont, and 5 of Maryland's 11 electoral votes, but he failed to draw enough votes in Pennsylvania. The Federalists did much better in congressional elections, nearly doubling their representation in the Thirteenth Congress (1813–1815), and on the local level, where Federalist candidates won legislative and gubernatorial elections in more states than Clinton carried. Opposition to the War of 1812 and the military failures of the conflict increased Federalist unity and resulted in greater state electoral victories in 1813 and 1814. But the Federalists were still very much a minority party with little chance of challenging the policies of the Madison administration or defending their interests against the growing political influence of the new western states. By 1814 New England Federalists were reviving the idea of secession and the formation of a northern confederacy as one option to protect their interests.

Sources:
David Hackett Fischer, *The Revolution of American Conservatism: The Federalist Party in the Era of Jeffersonian Democracy* (New York: Harper Torchbooks, 1965);

Eugene H. Roseboom and Alfred E. Eckes Jr., *A History of Presidential Elections,* fourth edition (New York: Collier, 1979);

Marshall Smelser, *The Democratic Republic, 1801–1815* (New York: Harper Torchbooks, 1968).

SLAVERY AND FREEDOM

"All Men Are Created Equal." During the Revolutionary period Americans described their slavery under British rule and proclaimed their fight for liberty, equality, and natural rights. Samuel Johnson, the English author and critic, wondered: "How is it that we hear the loudest yelps for liberty among the drivers of negroes?" Americans in the Revolutionary period also questioned the hypocrisy of their devotion to liberty and their prac-

Absalom Jones in 1810, a cofounder of the African Methodist Episcopal Church

"precluded by the Constitution" and that had "a tendency to create disquiet and jealousy."

Emancipation and Discrimination. Beginning in the 1780s American discomfort over slavery resulted in a wave of antislavery activity on the state level. The Quakers, or Society of Friends, who had organized the first opposition to slavery in the mid eighteenth century, were the first to petition Congress to abolish the slave trade in February 1790. Secular antislavery societies were organized in both the North and the upper South (Virginia, Maryland, and Delaware), attacking slavery as morally degrading to both slave and master and economically inefficient. The declining demand for tobacco in the upper South beginning before the Revolutionary War and the economic depression caused by the war had resulted in a shift to less labor intensive crops and a surplus of slaves. The economic incentive to reduce the reliance on slavery, combined with the impact of evangelical Christianity, caused legislatures in the region to ease laws freeing slaves in the 1780s and 1790s. Between 1790 and 1810 the free black population as a percentage of the total African American population increased in Delaware from 30.5 percent to 75.9 percent, in Maryland from 7.2 per-

tice of slavery. No group of people was more troubled by the existence of slavery or expected more from the American Revolution and its promise of liberty and equality than African Americans, some of whom earned their freedom fighting in the Revolutionary War. The Confederation Congress did forbid slavery in the Northwest Territory in 1787, but in the Constitutional Convention economic and political self-interest defeated antislavery sentiment. Delegates from South Carolina and Georgia, whose rice planters were increasing their slave holdings in order to make up for their wartime losses, were, as James Madison said, "inflexible on the point of the slaves." In the interest of political union the delegates to the Constitutional Convention abandoned any effort to abolish slavery beyond ending the slave trade in 1808, and succeeding members of Congress were just as reluctant to deal with slavery. In January 1800 a group of "free men of color" from Philadelphia petitioned Congress to revise laws on the slave trade and adopt measures "as shall in due course emancipate the whole of their brethren." Congressman George Thacher of Massachusetts condemned slavery as "a cancer of immense magnitude, that would sometime destroy the body politic, except a proper legislation should prevent the evil." Thacher stood alone, however, and the House of Representatives voted 85–1 not to receive the petition because it asked Congress to legislate on subjects from which they were

AN AFRICAN AMERICAN PETITION

From 1789 to 1815 members of Congress were just as reluctant to abolish slavery as delegates to the Constitutional Convention had been. Still, free African Americans petitioned Congress to "hear their cause." On 30 January 1797 Jacob Nicholson, Jupiter Nicholson, John Albert, and Thomas Pritchet of North Carolina asked for relief from a North Carolina law that authorized the seizure and sale into slavery of freed slaves:

> We cannot claim the privilege of representation in your councils, yet we trust we may address you as fellow-men, who, under God . . . are entrusted with the distribution of justice, for the terror of evil-doers, the encouragement and protection of the innocent. . . . Therefore, we may hope for a share in your sympathetic attention while we represent that the unconstitutional bondage in which multitudes of our fellows in complexion are held, is to us sorrowful afflicting. . . .

Congressman James Madison of Virginia replied that the case had "no claim" on the attention of Congress:

> "If they are free by the laws of North Carolina they ought to apply to those laws. . . . If they are slaves, the Constitution gives them no hopes of being heard here."

By a vote of 50–33 the House of Representatives voted not to receive the first antislavery petition by African Americans.

Source: Debates in the Fourth Congress, in *Annals of Congress* (Washington, D.C.: Gale & Seaton, 1834–1856).

AMERICAN ERAS: 1783-1815

cent to 23.3 percent, and in Virginia from 4.2 percent to 7.2 percent. In the North, Vermont forbade slavery in its constitution (1777); Pennsylvania passed a gradual emancipation law in 1780; and in 1783 the Massachusetts Supreme Court, responding to suits brought by African Americans, ruled that slavery violated the state constitution. By 1804 the other northern states had passed gradual emancipation laws. By 1810 nearly three-quarters of all northern African Americans were free, but freedom, whether in the North or South, did not bring equality. All the northern states except Massachusetts, New Hampshire, Vermont, and New York denied the vote to freedmen. Free African Americans petitioned Congress and the state legislatures to abolish slavery and protect their rights, but their efforts were in vain. When the federal and state governments continued to ignore the twin problems of ending slavery and racial discrimination, emancipated blacks responded by establishing their own churches, schools, and social organizations to assist both the slave and free communities.

Persistence of Slavery. The brief flurry of antislavery activity subsided in the mid 1790s. The constitutional clause forbidding the slave trade after 1808, gradual emancipation laws, and statutes ending the brutal treatment of slaves allowed antislavery Americans to comfort themselves with the belief that they had laid the groundwork for the eventual extinction of slavery without confronting the issue of integrating free blacks into American society. In the South there were additional reasons to retreat from antislavery agitation. A successful slave rebellion in Saint Domingue in the 1790s culminated in the establishment of the black-ruled Republic of Haiti in 1804. Fear that the revolt in Saint Domingue would inspire a similar revolt among American slaves was at first founded on rumors of unrest and talk of rebellion among slaves. The rumors became reality in August 1800 with the discovery of a planned rebellion of slaves in Richmond, Virginia, led by Gabriel Prosser. The prospect of future slave revolts was also reinforced by the dramatic growth of the slave population, from 697,897 in 1790 to 1,191,354 in 1810, with slaves constituting one-third of the population in the South. Southern legislatures responded by making it more difficult to free slaves, requiring free slaves to leave their respective states, tightening laws enforcing slavery, and restricting the freedom of free African Americans. The invention of the cotton gin in 1793, which separated cotton seeds from the fiber, made cotton the South's most valuable crop and removed any economic incentive to abolish slavery. In fact, the westward expansion of the "Cotton Kingdom" from Georgia, South Carolina, and southeastern North Carolina into Alabama, Mississippi, Louisiana, and other southwestern territories increased both the demand for and price of slave labor. The growth of the Cotton Kingdom after 1820 also increased southern demands that the federal government protect their "peculiar institution."

Sources:

Ira Berlin, "The Revolution in Black Life," in *The American Revolution: Explorations in the History of American Radicalism,* edited by Alfred E. Young (DeKalb: Northern Illinois University Press, 1976), pp. 349–382;

Winthrop D. Jordan, *The White Man's Burden: Historical Origins of Racism in the United States* (New York: Oxford University Press, 1974);

Peter Kolchin, *American Slavery, 1619–1877* (New York: Hill & Wang, 1993).

THE WAR OF 1812

Causes. President James Madison called Congress into early session on 4 November 1811 to report on Britain's "hostile inflexibility" and continued "trampling on rights which no independent nation can relinquish." On 1 June 1812, after the latest diplomatic dispatches revealed that Britain would not revise its policies, President Madison asked Congress to declare war. Madison cited Britain's long history of abuses against the United States: impressment (over six thousand incidents between 1803 and 1812), violations of neutral trade, and incitement of Indian warfare on the western frontier. After secret debate the House of Representatives approved a declaration of war on 4 June by a vote of 79–49. The Senate approved a declaration on 17 June by a vote of 19–13. The vote for or against war was political. In the House 33 of the 49 opponents of war were Federalists. The 16 Republicans who voted against the war were generally anti-Madison Republicans such as John Randolph of Virginia. The West and the South strongly favored the war, leading some historians to conclude that fear of Indian warfare and expansionist designs on Canada and Florida were a cause of the war. While these may have been factors in swaying some western and southern congressmen to support the war, it is important to note that they also represented states that produced farm products for export and suffered from British restrictions on neutral commerce. Federalists wondered why the United States did not go to war against France for its violations of neutral trade, but Republicans believed that French abuses were in the past while Britain seemed intent on keeping her former colonies in a subordinate position forever. In the words of Republican Congressman John C. Calhoun of South Carolina, a war hawk and member of the Foreign Relations Committee: "The period has now arrived, when the United States must support their character and station among the nations of the earth, or submit to the most shameful degradation."

An Unprepared Nation. The Republicans had come to power promising to restore limited government, reduce the army and navy, and abolish internal taxes. The fulfillment of those promises impaired the ability of the United States to wage war against Britain. Beginning in December 1811, Congress quickly moved to enlarge the army that the Republicans had worked so hard to reduce. Over the next several months Congress passed legislation to bring the regular army up to its authorized strength of ten thousand, enlist an additional twenty-five thousand regulars for five years' service, and authorize the president to call up one hundred thousand state militia for six months' service. By the time war broke out in June 1812 the strength of the regular army was still under seven thousand, and its officers were either aged Revolutionary War veterans or men who owed their commissions to political connections, not military ability. The lack of central control over recruiting meant that the regular army, volunteer army, and militias often competed for the same men. The result was that the regular army probably never exceeded thirty-five thousand men during the war. Antiwar governors in Federalist New England refused to detach their militia for federal service, upholding their constitutional interpretation that the militia was an emergency army called into temporary service to repel invasion, not an offensive army. The U.S. Navy had good officers, but when the war began it numbered only sixteen vessels to face the world's strongest navy. The Republican Congress, living up to their party's antitax philosophy, did not authorize war taxes until the summer of 1813. Instead, Congress authorized the government to borrow $11 million in March 1812 and authorized additional loans throughout the war. The failure to recharter the National Bank in February 1811 forced the Treasury Department to rely on a decentralized system of state banks, which offered unattractive interest rates. Public response to the loans was poor, especially among New England's moneyed men, who stood firmly against the war. It is easy to understand why a group of congressmen who opposed the war criticized "the weakness and wildness of the project."

Military Events. The main American military objective was the conquest of Canada, but inept military leadership and reliance on the militia resulted in failure in 1812. In August plans to invade Canada from the Northwest ended when the timid and indecisive Gen. William Hull surrendered Detroit to the British. In October, American regulars lost the Battle of Queenston Heights in Canada when the New York militia refused to cross the Canadian border to support them. In November the refusal of militia forces to leave the United States ended Gen. Henry Dearborn's planned attack on Montreal. Naval victories by the U.S.S. *Constitution* and U.S.S. *United States* in 1812 boosted morale but had no strategic importance. By 1813 the Royal Navy's blockade of the American coast guaranteed Britain's dominance of the seas. Under Secretary of War John Armstrong, who took office in February 1813, younger and more capable officers such as Jacob Brown, Andrew Jackson, and Winfield Scott began to receive combat commands, but military progress in 1813 was still disappointing. In April an American army under Gen. Henry Dearborn and Gen. Zebulon Pike looted and burned York (Toronto), but in the autumn Gen. Wade Hampton's retreat at the Châteauguay River and Gen. James Wilkinson's defeat at

A peace medal, bearing the portrait of James Madison, used to gain the good will of Native Americans during the War of 1812

Chrysler's Farm ended hopes of taking Montreal. Fortunately, Capt. Oliver Hazard Perry's destruction of the British fleet at Put-in-Bay on Lake Erie in September, followed by Gen. William Henry Harrison's defeat of British-Indian forces at the Battle of the Thames in October, restored American control of the Northwest. In July 1814 Gen. Jacob Brown and Gen. Winfield Scott crossed the Niagara River into Canada, defeating the British at the Battle of Chippewa, and Brown fought the British to a standstill in the Battle of Lundy's Lane, marking the last American attempt to conquer Canada. With Napoleon Bonaparte's defeat in April 1814, Britain prepared for a final offensive. Sir George Prevost's plan to secure Canada by cutting off New England from the rest of the United States failed in September when Capt. Thomas Macdonough's American squadron defeated the British on Lake Champlain in Plattsburgh. Meanwhile, a British diversionary force occupied Washington, D.C., in August, burning the Executive Mansion and the Capitol, but successful resistance forced the British to abandon plans to capture Baltimore. The war was at a stalemate.

Hartford Convention. Several times between 1800 and 1814 New England Federalists had called for conventions to address their grievances at the hands of Republican administrations, and in 1804 they considered secession and the formation of a northern confederacy. When Federalist delegates from the New England states assembled in Hartford, Connecticut, in December 1814, Republicans might well have believed that they were plotting disunion. After all, the New England states had obstructed the war by refusing to detach their militia for federal service, not subscribing to loans financing the war, and trading with the enemy in Canada until Congress was forced to impose an embargo in December 1813. But the delegates to the Hartford Convention defended their meeting as a necessary response to their defenseless situation, caused by a Republican administration more interested in conquering Canada than in protecting its citizens from invasion. It is clear from their report, however, that the Federalists had a broader goal: how to protect their interests and restore the political power taken away by the Republicans. In seeking a solution to the problem of protecting minority rights from the majority the delegates upheld Thomas Jefferson and James Madison's doctrine of nullification, but only as a last resort. Instead, they offered seven constitutional amendments to limit the power of the federal government and the influence of the South and the West, including a one-term limit for the presidency, a two-thirds vote of both houses of Congress to admit new states, and the repeal of the three-fifths clause, which gave the South so much political power. On the same day the New England delegates reached the burned city of Washington, D.C., with their demands, news arrived that Andrew Jackson had defeated a superior British army at New Orleans, and that the United States and Britain had signed a peace treaty. The delegates, fearing that they looked like fools, or worse, traitors, quickly left the city.

The Battle of New Orleans. Andrew Jackson's performance in the Creek War earned him a major-general's commission in the regular army and command of the Seventh Military District, which included Tennessee, Louisiana, and the Mississippi Territory, in May 1814. In early December 1814 Jackson began assembling a military force made up of regular army troops; militia from Kentucky, Tennessee, and Louisiana; free African American volunteers; Choctaw Indians; and Jean Laffite's pirates. He also began building entrenchments in preparation for a British assault on New Orleans. On 1 January 1815 American artillerists and riflemen held off an assault by a British army under Sir Edward Pakenham. One week later Pakenham's reinforced army of six thousand men launched a frontal assault. Jackson directed a devastating combination of artillery and rifle fire that inflicted more than two thousand British casualties, including Pakenham and two other British generals. The Americans suffered only twenty-one casualties. Neither Jackson nor the rest of the nation knew that a peace treaty had been signed two weeks earlier, so it could be argued that the Battle of New Orleans was a wasted effort. But in a war that was short of resounding victories, Americans celebrated the Battle of New Orleans as a glorious defense of American honor.

The Treaty of Ghent. Neither nation had achieved the decisive military victory that would have allowed it to press all its demands during peace negotiations, but American commissioners John Quincy Adams, Albert Gallatin, Henry Clay, and James Bayard deserve credit for their achievements in negotiating the Treaty of Ghent. The treaty stipulations affirmed the *status quo ante bellum* (the state of affairs before the war). By December 1814, when the treaty was signed, the repeal of the British orders-in-council had solved the problem of neutral trade and the European peace had solved the problem of impressment, making it unnecessary for the American diplomats to force those issues in negotiations. However, they would not give in to British demands for the creation of an Indian buffer state in the Northwest, territorial cessions in Maine and New York, and the right of navigation on the Mississippi River. The United States had ended hostilities without losing any territory and asserted its status as an independent nation that would no longer stand for the violation of its neutral rights or the humiliation of impressment. Perhaps the best measure of the impact of the war is how Americans learned from the experiences and mistakes of the war and applied those lessons to postwar America. After the war the United States reorganized the Army, Navy, and War Department to correct the defects revealed during the War of 1812. In his message to Congress in December 1815 President Madison acknowledged the financial difficulties caused by the lack of a national bank and the supply problems caused by the poor conditions of American roads, and he recognized the value of American domestic manufacturing, stimulated by the trade disruptions of the war. Madison's recommendations that Congress approve a national bank, federal support for transportation and internal improvements, and protective tariffs were all enacted in the years immediately following the War of 1812. Americans also emerged from the war with a message to the world that their experiment in republicanism had been proven successful.

Sources:

James M. Banner Jr., *To the Hartford Convention: The Federalists and the Origins of Party Politics in Massachusetts, 1789–1815* (New York: Knopf, 1970);

Harry L. Coles, *The War of 1812* (Chicago: University of Chicago Press, 1965);

Marshall Smelser, *The Democratic Republic, 1801–1815* (New York: Harper Torchbooks, 1968);

J. C. A. Stagg, *Mr. Madison's War: Politics, Diplomacy, and Warfare in the Early American Republic, 1783–1830* (Princeton: Princeton University Press, 1983).

HEADLINE MAKERS

JOHN ADAMS

1735-1826

DIPLOMAT, VICE PRESIDENT AND PRESIDENT OF THE UNITED STATES

Independent Will. Throughout a long career culminating in a term as president, John Adams valued independence above all else. He based his political philosophy on his understanding of history and human nature, not on public opinion. As president he considered it vital to remain independent of party politics and the other branches of government. That political independence allowed Adams to remain true to his principles and prevented war with France, but it damaged his political career.

Background. John Adams was born in Braintree (now Quincy), Massachusetts, on 30 October 1735. His father, John Adams, was a farmer and cordwainer (shoemaker), church deacon, militia officer, tax collector, and selectman. His mother, Susanna Boylston Adams, was from a prominent family of merchants and physicians. After graduating from Harvard College in 1755, Adams taught school in Worcester, Massachusetts, and studied law with James Putnam. He was admitted to the bar in Boston in 1758 and opened a law practice in Braintree. In 1764 Adams married Abigail Smith, the daughter of Rev. William and Elizabeth Quincy Smith of Weymouth. Mrs. Adams was an astute political observer and her husband's "dearest friend." The Adamses had six children, including John Quincy Adams, who became the sixth president of the United States. Political events in the 1760s soon ended Adams's life as a small-town lawyer and satisfied his ambition for fame.

American Revolution. In 1765 Parliament imposed a stamp tax on the American colonists. Adams prepared Braintree's resolutions protesting the Stamp Act as an unconstitutional tax imposed without the consent of the colonists. Using his skills as a lawyer and political essay-

ist, Adams played an increasingly important role as he and his fellow patriots moved from protecting their rights as Englishmen to establishing an independent republic. As a delegate to the Continental Congress, Adams worked tirelessly in 1775 and 1776 to prepare the American colonies for independence. He pushed Congress to adopt the army assembled in Massachusetts after the Battles of Lexington and Concord and appoint George Washington commander in chief of the Continental Army and to pass resolutions authorizing the states to set up independent governments. Although Thomas Jefferson wrote the Declaration of Independence in 1776, Jefferson admitted that Adams was our "Colossus on the floor," leading the fight for its passage. From 1778 to 1788, with the exception of a brief return to the United States, during which he wrote the Massachusetts Constitution, Adams represented American diplomatic interests in Europe. In 1778 Congress appointed Adams commissioner to France to assist Benjamin Franklin and Arthur Lee in strengthening the American alliance with France. In 1782 Adams negotiated a treaty of recognition and secured the first in a series of loans from the Dutch government. Adams, Benjamin Franklin, and John Jay negotiated the peace treaty with Britain ending the Revolutionary War in 1783. Adams was minister to the Court of St. James from 1785 until he resigned in frustration in 1788. The British government, with little confidence in the future of the weak Confederation government, ignored the terms of the Peace of Paris and refused to negotiate a commercial treaty with the United States. Adams, however, returned to the United States in 1788 as a respected figure. A few months later he was elected vice president.

Political Philosophy. Adams developed his political philosophy from wide reading in English and European political thought and his observations on human nature and government. He believed that human beings were motivated by self-interest and a "passion for distinction." He also believed that society was engaged in a constant class struggle between the rich and the poor, or the aristocracy and the democracy. In his *Defence of the Constitutions of Government of the United States of America* (1787), Adams warned of the danger of a single-house legislature advocated by the French philosopher Anne-Robert-

Jacques Turgot and adopted under the Pennsylvania Constitution of 1776. Adams argued that the only way to protect liberty was to design a balanced government that would prevent either the aristocracy or the democracy from gaining too much power. The people should be represented in the lower house of the legislature, and the aristocracy should be represented in the upper house. The key to maintaining balanced government was a strong executive elected by the people with veto power over legislation. The executive must be independent from both branches of the legislature and from political parties in order to protect the interests of all the people. In *Discourses on Davila* (1805) Adams argued that the use of titles for members of the Senate would encourage the development of a natural, nonhereditary aristocracy to serve as a stabilizing force in American society. The alternative would be the establishment of hereditary aristocracy and hereditary monarchy. His political views often separated Adams from members of his own party, the opposing Republican Party, and public opinion.

Vice Presidency. Adams's critics ridiculed his support for presidential and vice-presidential titles and his practice of wearing a sword and wig to the Senate by calling him "the Duke of Braintree" and "His Rotundity." He removed the sword and the wig, but the vice presidency (1789–1797) remained a frustrating and insignificant office. He attended only two or three cabinet meetings in eight years, concentrating instead on fulfilling his constitutional responsibility of presiding over the Senate. When called upon to break tie votes, which he did more than any of his successors, he loyally supported the Washington administration and Federalist policies. Adams upheld the president's power to remove appointees without the consent of the Senate, supported the enforcement of American neutrality during the French Revolution, and defeated commercial discrimination against Britain. At the same time Adams had fundamental differences with Hamiltonian Federalists. Adams supported Hamilton on funding and the assumption of state debts because he thought those measures were necessary to establish a sound financial basis for the United States. He also approved of the National Bank as a depository of government funds. However, he did not approve of the speculative nature of federal securities or paper money designed to attract merchants, manufacturers, and speculators to support the national government out of self-interest. Adams felt that the federal government must remain independent and avoid favoring any special interests. As vice president, however, he considered it his duty to support administration policies.

Presidency. As president between 1797 and 1801 Adams held firm to the belief that he must remain free from party politics in order to rule in the best interests of the nation. Adams did not accept the developing two-party system, and his attempts at nonpartisanship led to vacillating policies and divisions within the Federalist Party. Secretary of State Timothy Pickering, Secretary of the Treasury Oliver Wolcott, and Secretary of War James McHenry took their orders not from President Adams but from former secretary of the Treasury Alexander Hamilton. Sensitive to charges that he was ambitious and spiteful toward opponents, Adams was reluctant to remove cabinet members who were plotting against him. The belief that he must remain above party politics also prevented Adams from building sufficient support for his alternative to Hamiltonian Federalism either in Congress or the nation. On the occasions when he tried to assert his independence he often lacked the political influence to back up his actions. For example, soon after taking office, Adams informed Vice President Thomas Jefferson of his intention to nominate James Madison, a Republican, as special envoy to France, but when Secretary of the Treasury Wolcott threatened to resign over the appointment, Adams withdrew the offer. In May 1797 Adams's defense preparations against France called for a navy, national system of coastal defense, and a small increase of the regular army, especially in the military specialties of artillery and cavalry. Instead, High Federalists in Congress passed Hamilton's program for a larger regular army. When Adams offered command of the army to George Washington, he was also forced to accept Washington's choice for second in command: Alexander Hamilton. Adams asserted his independence again in 1799 when he dispatched a peace mission to France. Unfortunately, he had not sufficiently established his independence from the unpopular policies of the High Federalists. A disappointed and defeated Adams left Washington, D.C., on the morning of Thomas Jefferson's inauguration.

Adamant to the End. John Adams had twenty-five years to contemplate his presidency and his place in history after he returned to Quincy, Massachusetts. Between 1809 and 1812 he published a series of letters in the *Boston Patriot* defending his record as diplomat and president. Adams also maintained his political independence, reluctantly endorsing the embargo as a temporary measure, supporting the War of 1812 but criticizing Jefferson's neglect of the navy, and opposing the Hartford Convention. He proudly observed the diplomatic and political career of his son, John Quincy Adams, whose duplication of his father's political independence cost him a Senate seat and a second presidential term. The death of Mrs. Adams in 1818 was a severe blow, but the renewal of his friendship with Thomas Jefferson in 1812 and the more flattering assessments of his career in his later years were a source of comfort. Adams freely acknowledged his character flaws of vanity and ambition and the failures of his presidency, but he was also justifiably proud of his distinguished diplomatic career and his role in restoring peace with France. His appointment of John Marshall as chief justice of the United States in 1801 also had a significant impact on U.S. constitutional history. His political independence had, on many occasions, cost him popularity and the fame he desired, but

Adams admitted that independence was "essential to my existence." John Adams died on Independence Day, 4 July 1826, just hours after the death of Thomas Jefferson.

Sources:
Manning J. Dauer, *The Adams Federalists* (Baltimore: Johns Hopkins University Press, 1953);

Peter Shaw, *The Character of John Adams* (Chapel Hill: University of North Carolina Press, 1976).

ALEXANDER HAMILTON

1755-1804
MEMBER OF CONGRESS, DELEGATE TO THE CONSTITUTIONAL CONVENTION, SECRETARY OF THE TREASURY

American Nationalism. As the first secretary of the Treasury, Alexander Hamilton formulated fiscal policies and a philosophy of American nationalism that placed him at the center of decision making in the Washington administration. Hamilton improved the financial stability of the United States, but his belief that American nationalism should be based on a union of interests between the U.S. government and wealthy merchants, manufacturers, and speculators divided the country politically.

Early Years. Alexander Hamilton was born on the island of Nevis in the British West Indies on 11 January 1755 and grew up on the neighboring Danish island of Saint Croix. He was the younger of two illegitimate sons of James Hamilton, the fourth son of an aristocratic Scottish family, and Rachel Fawcett Lavien. After James Hamilton abandoned the family in 1765, Rachel opened a small store to support her sons, but she died in 1768. For the next four years the orphaned Hamilton worked for the mercantile firm of Beekman and Cruger. His intelligence, ambition, remarkably mature business judgment, and dramatic newspaper description of a hurricane that hit Saint Croix in 1772 persuaded several prominent citizens of the island to pay for Hamilton's college education at King's College (now Columbia University) in New York. While a student, Hamilton's extensive reading and his friendship with William Livingston and other New York patriots introduced him to the ideas of the American Revolution. In 1774 and 1775, after the Reverend Samuel Seabury condemned the First Continental Congress for supporting nonimportation of British goods until Parliament repealed the Intolerable Acts, the nineteen-year-old Hamilton forcefully refuted Seabury in two pamphlets supporting colonial union as the only way to defend liberty. As a Continental Army officer Hamilton demonstrated military leadership and courage during the New Jersey campaign in 1776 and 1777 and at Yorktown in 1781. As aide-de-camp to Gen. George Washington, Hamilton impressed his superior and other important men with his intellect, organizational skills, and executive ability. He also improved his social position in 1780 by marrying Elizabeth Schuyler, daughter of Gen. Philip Schuyler, a wealthy and influential New Yorker. Hamilton was admitted to the New York bar in July 1782 after only a few months' study, but his real interest was politics and the creation of a strong national government.

Political Outlook. As a native of the West Indies, Hamilton had no attachment to any American state. His first loyalty was to the idea of national union, and his wartime experiences deepened that commitment. The states' refusal to give Congress any taxation power forced Congress and the states to finance the war with paper currency. Farmers and merchants profited from wartime inflation by raising the prices they charged to supply the American army while the army went without pay and supplies. Hamilton, influenced by Scottish philosopher David Hume's *Political Discourses* (1752), concluded that Americans could not win the war or protect their independence unless they established a national government with complete control over the economy and the states. Hamilton also accepted Hume's conclusion that men are motivated by their passions, and the strongest passion is greed. A government that could use men's greed to motivate them to support the government would become rich and powerful. Hamilton's eight months as a member of Congress in 1782 and 1783 intensified his conviction that the Confederation lacked the political and financial power to maintain national union. Shays's Rebellion in 1786 and 1787 strengthened his fear of democracy and his belief in the necessity of an effective national government to protect the property of wealthy men who would, in turn, support that government. As one of New York's delegates to the Constitutional Convention in 1787, Hamilton proposed an extraordinarily powerful national government that would have essentially abolished the states. In order to create a national government capable of providing social stability and protecting private property Hamilton recommended a senate and president elected for life and a lower house of representatives to control democracy. The final version of the Constitution provided for a weaker national government than the one Hamilton wanted, but he enthusiastically supported it as one of the authors of *The Federalist* (1788) and as a delegate to New York's Constitutional Convention.

American Prime Minister. Congress granted the secretary of the Treasury power to "digest and prepare plans for the improvement and management of the revenue, and the support of the public credit." As the first secretary of the Treasury in 1789, Alexander Hamilton took full advantage of his policy-making role in financial affairs. Hamilton's belief in the connection between national power and commerce meant that he did not limit himself to suggesting policies to stabilize the nation's credit. Instead, he injected himself into every major decision on financial, domestic, and foreign policy connected to his plan to make the United States a commercial empire. President George Washington's conception of the presidency, emphasizing independence from party politics and the legislative process, encouraged Hamilton's view of himself as an American prime minister. Hamilton acted as the chief executive of Washington's cabinet and the head of the Federalist Party, formulating policies and supervising the passage of legislation in Congress. His meetings with British diplomats to advance his agenda for America's commercial future compromised Secretary of State Thomas Jefferson's control of foreign policy and created serious divisions within the administration. By the time Hamilton retired from office in January 1795 the United States had the highest credit rating in Europe, the value of American exports had doubled, and his policies on the national debt and banking had vastly expanded American capitalistic enterprises. His policies also created vocal political opposition. Republicans attacked Federalists as pro-British monarchists and aristocrats who cared only about the rich and offered themselves as the party that would protect the interests of the common people.

Political Influence. Hamilton retired from political office in 1795, but he did not retire from politics. He remained an important party leader who advised President Washington, President John Adams's cabinet, and Federalist members of Congress on policies and presidential candidates. His influence undermined President Adams's authority and created a serious split in the Federalist Party. As the nation prepared for the possibility of war with France in 1798 Hamilton, appointed second in command of the enlarged army under George Washington, saw the conflict as an opportunity to gain military glory for himself and to expand the American "empire" by annexing Louisiana, Florida, and perhaps all of Spanish America, possibly through an alliance with Britain. Hamilton also contemplated the possibility of using the army to put down political opposition to Federalist policies such as the Alien and Sedition Acts. President Adams would not tolerate Hamilton's grandiose visions of military glory, a subservient alliance with Britain, the high taxes necessary to maintain the army, or the danger of using the army to suppress political dissent. His peace mission to France in 1799 destroyed Hamilton's plans. Hamilton had the satisfaction of seeing Adams defeated in 1800 only to have the election come down to a choice between two men he despised: Thomas Jefferson and Aaron Burr. As much as he disagreed with Jefferson's principles, Hamilton felt that the country was safer under him than under Burr, whom he denounced to his fellow Federalists as a thoroughly unprincipled man motivated only by personal and political ambition.

The Duel. Hamilton advised Federalists to respond to Jeffersonian democracy by spreading their principles to the common people he had long ignored through political organization and newspapers such as the *New-York Evening Post,* which he helped found in 1801. He was appalled when the Federalists contemplated an alliance with Aaron Burr, a long-standing political and personal rival and a man he condemned as "the most unfit and dangerous man in the community." In 1791 Burr, who had abandoned the Federalists to run as a Republican candidate for the U.S. Senate seat in New York, defeated Hamilton's father-in-law. In 1792 Burr offered to rejoin the Federalists and run against Gov. George Clinton, but Hamilton's opposition ended his candidacy. Hamilton also opposed Burr's attempt to be the Federalist vice-presidential candidate in 1792. In 1804 he denounced a Federalist plan to support Burr for governor of New York in exchange for New York's support for a northern confederacy. Burr challenged Hamilton to a duel after Hamilton refused to deny or retract derogatory statements about Burr that appeared in a New York newspaper. The death of his oldest son in a duel in 1801 had intensified Hamilton's hatred of dueling, but his honor and his principles would not allow him to step aside and allow a man like Burr to gain public office. On 11 July 1804 Hamilton and Burr met at Weehawken, New Jersey. Like his son, Hamilton had decided not to fire at his adversary, with equally fatal results. Burr shot Hamilton, and he died the next day. Hamilton's scorn for democracy made him unpopular in his day, but his support for an energetic national government that encouraged economic growth influenced later generations.

Sources:

Stanley Elkins and Eric McKitrick, *The Age of Federalism: The Early American Republic, 1788–1800* "New York: Oxford University Press, 1993);

John C. Miller, *Alexander Hamilton: Portrait in Paradox* (New York: Harper, 1959).

THOMAS JEFFERSON

1743-1826

MEMBER OF CONGRESS, SECRETARY OF STATE, VICE PRESIDENT AND PRESIDENT OF THE UNITED STATES

Unlikely Democrat. Thomas Jefferson, the Founding Father most associated with the democratic ideals that have become the basis of American society, was an unlikely champion of democracy. This slaveowning Virginia aristocrat was most definitely not one of the common people, but he put his faith in the power of reason, science, and education to enlighten the common people so that they could be trusted with the political power to establish a democratic republic that would protect "life, liberty, and the pursuit of happiness."

Early Career. Thomas Jefferson was born on 13 April 1743 at Shadwell, his family's farm in Albemarle County, Virginia. His father, Peter Jefferson, was a self-made man, a slaveowning planter, surveyor, mapmaker, justice of the peace, and member of the Virginia House of Burgesses. His mother, Jane Randolph Jefferson, was from one of Virginia's oldest and most prominent families, guaranteeing Jefferson a privileged position in colonial society. Jefferson spent most of his childhood at Tuckahoe, the plantation of his mother's late cousin William Randolph, where his father acted as guardian of Randolph's children. His education began at age five at Tuckahoe, followed by attendance at the Latin school of Rev. William Douglas beginning at age nine. At fourteen, after his father's death, Jefferson prepared for college under the direction of Rev. James Maury. At the College of William and Mary (1760–1762) Dr. William Small introduced Jefferson to the world of science, mathematics, and the Enlightenment, a European philosophical movement stressing the use of reason and observation to understand the natural world and human behavior. After college Jefferson studied law with George Wythe. He practiced law from 1767 to 1774 and managed his inheritance of nearly five thousand acres of land and twenty-two slaves. In 1772 he married Martha Wayles Skelton, a young widow and daughter of a prosperous lawyer, and brought her to live at Monticello, the home he had begun building in 1770 after fire destroyed his family home.

Revolutionary Leadership. As a member of the Virginia House of Burgesses from 1769 to 1775, Jefferson joined a group of younger men, including Patrick Henry, who led Virginia's resistance to British rule. Never an eloquent speaker, Jefferson was more persuasive in legislative committees and in his writing. In 1772 he helped draw up resolves proposing an intercolonial system of committee of correspondence. In 1774 he wrote *A Summary View of the Rights of British America,* which anticipated much of his argument in the Declaration of Independence. Jefferson asserted that Parliament "has no right to exercise authority over us," that King George III was "no more than the chief officer of the people . . . and consequently subject to their superintendance," and that the colonists possessed rights "as derived from the laws of nature, and not as the gift of their free magistrate." In 1776 Jefferson's "Reputation of a masterly Pen" won him the assignment of drafting the Declaration of Independence for Congress. Years later Jefferson wrote that the Declaration "was intended to be an expression of the American mind." The principles of equality, the right to "life, liberty, and the pursuit of happiness," and the consent of the governed that he proclaimed in the Declaration have become the most cherished beliefs in American society.

Return Home. Jefferson returned to Virginia in September 1776 and spent the next three years in the House of Delegates revising Virginia's laws. He drafted 126 bills aimed at creating a system "by which every fibre would be eradicated of ancient and future aristocracy; and a foundation laid for a government truly republican." Jefferson introduced bills abolishing inheritance laws that perpetuated an aristocracy based on birth and wealth and a bill establishing complete freedom of religion. He also proposed the Bill for the More General Diffusion of Knowledge, which recommended state funding for educating the most promising male scholars through college in order to create a natural aristocracy, but the only part of the bill that survived in 1796 was authorization for three years of public education for all children. His bills on religious freedom and education reflected Jefferson's belief in the necessity of freedom of thought and an educated citizenry to support republican government. From 1779 to 1781 Jefferson was governor of Virginia. He endured great difficulty balancing the demands of supplying arms, men, and money for the national war effort while defending the state from imminent invasion. On 4 June 1781 Jefferson barely avoided capture when the British raided Monticello. His term of office having expired two days earlier, Jefferson moved his family to safety instead of waiting for the legislature to choose a new governor on 12 June. In December the legislature absolved Jefferson of any wrongdoing, but during the presidential election of 1800 his opponents charged Jefferson with cowardice and dereliction of duty as governor.

Short Retirement. From 1781 to 1783 Jefferson wrote *Notes on the State of Virginia* in response to questions from François Marbois, secretary to the French minister in Philadelphia. In a wide-ranging analysis that included observations on climate, geography, and Native Americans; a catalogue of native minerals, trees, flowers, and animals; and criticism of inadequate political representation in Virginia, Jefferson also revealed his complex thoughts about slavery. He condemned slavery, but he also thought that blacks were intellectually inferior to whites. The "real distinctions which nature has made" between the races convinced him that the only solution was gradual emancipation and colonization. Mrs. Jefferson's death in September 1782 destroyed Jefferson's happy return to private life and scholarly study. He accepted a term in Congress in 1783 and made several important contributions, including proposals for extending republican government and prohibiting slavery in the western territories. In May 1784 Congress appointed him minister plenipotentiary to assist John Adams and Benjamin Franklin in negotiating commercial treaties in Europe, and the following year he replaced Franklin as minister to France. During his five years of diplomatic service, Jefferson gained commercial concessions from Prussia and France. He also witnessed the beginning of the French Revolution, which had a significant impact on his political ideas. He returned to America determined to create a republican government that would remove the economic, social, and political inequalities that had led to the French Revolution.

Secretary of State. When Jefferson brought his two daughters home in November 1789, he intended to return to France. Instead, he agreed to become secretary of state. Jefferson's certainty that only a nation of small, property-owning farmers would have the independence to make political decisions and preserve republican government guided his foreign policy. In Jefferson's view Treasury Secretary Alexander Hamilton's financial policies imposed an unfair burden on taxpaying farmers. Deprived of their property, farmers would fall under the political control of men upon whom they relied for their economic survival, resulting in political corruption, class conflict, and revolution. Hamilton, however, envisioned the United States as a commercial nation in close alliance with Britain, and he used every opportunity to push his foreign policy objectives. Jefferson wanted to be forceful with Britain, using commercial discrimination and American neutrality as negotiating tactics to persuade Britain to evacuate its posts in the Northwest, grant commercial concessions, and respect America's rights on the high seas. But Jefferson lost his bargaining power after Hamilton blocked tariff discrimination against Britain in Congress and held meetings with British diplomats, during which he criticized Jefferson's policies and assured them that the United States wanted a friendly relationship with Britain. In 1793 Jefferson thwarted Hamilton's attempt to break the 1778 treaty of alliance with France and gained diplomatic recognition for the first minister of the French republic to ensure that the United States would maintain a "fair neutrality" in the war between Britain and France. Bitter political divisions drove Jefferson from office in December 1793, but those same divisions guaranteed his return to public service.

Vice President. President George Washington's decision not to seek a third term ended Jefferson's retirement. Jefferson thought that James Madison, his close friend and the driving force in the Republican Party, was the logical choice to oppose John Adams in the presidential election of 1796, but Madison pushed for Jefferson's candidacy. Adams's victory, however, put Jefferson in the uncomfortable position of being a Republican vice president in a Federalist administration. With no influence over policy, Jefferson carried out his duties as presiding officer of the Senate. He also began preparing a manual of parliamentary practice, which was published in 1801 and is still used in the Senate. Madison's retirement from Congress in 1797 made Jefferson the leader of the Republican Party, and he willingly accepted the responsibility. Just a few months before he died Jefferson proudly recalled his role as vice president in heading opposition to "the federal principles and proceedings, during the administration of Mr. Adams." While the Federalists were leading the nation into war with France and depriving the people of liberty through the establishment of a large standing army, the imposition of high taxes, and especially the Alien and Sedition Acts, he and Albert Gallatin, leader of the Republicans in the House of Representatives, kept Republicans in Congress united until the state legislatures acted to protect the people from Federalist tyranny. Jefferson did not claim credit for writing the Kentucky Resolutions, but he stated that the Virginia and Kentucky Resolutions "saved the constitution at its last gasp." In 1800 Vice President Jefferson was an effective, behind-the-scenes campaigner for the presidency, circulating his party's political principles through pamphlets, newspapers, and letters.

President. Jefferson's fondness for philosophical study and his preference for communicating political ideas privately rather than through public debate led Federalists to predict that Jefferson would be a weak, indecisive, and deceitful president. President Jefferson exhibited a flexibility in adapting his principles to execute his goals that caused Federalists to denounce him as an untrustworthy demagogue. However, Jefferson, president of the American Philosophical Society from 1791 to 1815, believed that philosophical principles were useless unless they had a practical application. His persuasiveness in private meetings, conversations, letters, and written addresses allowed him to convey his ideas effectively to the public, coordinate policies with his cabinet, and supervise the passage of legislation through the Republican-controlled Congress. In Jefferson's first term (1801–1805) the repeal of internal taxes; reductions in the army, navy, and federal expenses; and the expiration of the Sedition Act conformed to his principles of restoring a republican government that protected liberty, equality of opportunity, freedom of conscience, and consent of the governed. In 1803 Federalists attacked the Louisiana Purchase as a hypocritical abandonment of Jefferson's strict constructionist interpretation of the Constitution. For Jefferson the Louisiana Purchase required him to modify his strict constructionist philosophy in order to achieve his goal of establishing an "Empire of Liberty"—an American republic of independent, property-owning farmers. The Embargo Act of 1807 was the great failure of Jefferson's second term (1805–1809) because he never clearly communicated to Congress or the public whether the embargo was a delaying tactic until the nation was prepared for war or an alternative to war. In addition Jefferson, the advocate of limited government, came under attack by Federalists for an extraordinary expansion of executive authority to enforce the embargo, including the use of the army, navy, and militia. President Jefferson, weary and disappointed by his second term, looked forward to retiring to Monticello.

The Sage of Monticello. Jefferson retired to his beloved Monticello in 1809, surrounded by his daughter and her family. His grandchildren always remembered him with a book in his hand, and when he and John Adams reconciled in 1812, many of their letters involved discussions of books on philosophy and religion. Presidents Madison and James Monroe consulted him for political advice, and a steady stream of visitors came for an audience with "The Sage of Monticello." He experimented with several agricultural techniques and other economic ventures in attempts to revive his estate. In his final years Jefferson became less hopeful about the eventual abolition of slavery and more pessimistic about the federal government's consolidation of power. Yet Jefferson put his faith in reason, science, and education to enlighten his fellow citizens and improve the rights of man. Jefferson's final achievement was the establishment of the University of Virginia in March 1825. He spent years designing buildings, planning curricula, and choosing faculty for the university, which fulfilled his belief that a democracy required educated citizens. When Thomas Jefferson died on 4 July 1826, he wanted to be remembered as the author of the Declaration of Independence and the Virginia Statute for Religious Freedom, and as the "Father of the University of Virginia."

Sources:

Noble E. Cunningham Jr., *In Pursuit of Reason: The Life of Thomas Jefferson* (Baton Rouge: Louisiana State University Press, 1987);

Adrienne Koch, ed., *Great Lives Observed: Jefferson* (Englewood Cliffs, N.J.: Prentice-Hall, 1971);

Dumas Malone, *Jefferson and His Time*, 6 volumes (Boston: Little, Brown, 1948–1981).

JAMES MADISON

1751-1836

MEMBER OF CONGRESS, DELEGATE TO THE CONSTITUTIONAL CONVENTION, SECRETARY OF STATE, PRESIDENT OF THE UNITED STATES

Founding Father. James Madison's achievements as secretary of state and president have never compared favorably with his role as "Father of the Constitution." He has also been overshadowed by his close friend and political associate, Thomas Jefferson. Madison's shyness and unimpressive oratory created a public image of ineffective leadership. But he excelled as a political thinker, essayist, and organizer who could persuade and conciliate in legislative committees and political meetings. Madison used those considerable talents to become a Founding Father of both the U.S. government and the Republican Party.

Early Life. James Madison, the oldest of twelve children of James Madison Sr. and Nellie Conway Madison, was born on 16 March 1751 at the home of his maternal grandparents in Port Conway, Virginia, and grew up at his family's plantation, Montpelier, in Orange County. His membership in a large extended family descended from several generations of Virginia planters gave Madison a strong sense of his place in Virginia society. The daily presence of slavery imparted a hatred of the institution that he nonetheless was involved in all his life. From 1769 to 1771 Madison attended the College of New Jersey (now Princeton University), where a progressive curriculum encouraged "a spirit of liberty, and free enquiry" into all fields of knowledge. Dr. John Witherspoon, president of the college and later a signer of the Declaration of Independence, was a Presbyterian minister who had fought the church hierarchy in his native Scotland. He instilled in his students an opposition to all forms of religious and political tyranny. After college Madison experienced a prolonged period of poor health and personal crisis caused by uncertainty over a career. Like other young men of his generation, Madison found a cause—liberty and republican government—and a political career in the American Revolution. In 1774 he was elected to the Committee of Safety, the revolutionary government in Virginia. Two years later he served on committees of the Virginia Convention that framed a new constitution and declaration of rights. In the Virginia Assembly from 1776 to 1777 and on the Governor's Council from 1778 to 1779, Madison worked closely with Thomas Jefferson on the bill for religious freedom, and he was deeply involved in all issues of war and government while Jefferson was governor. Their friendship would last until Jefferson's death in 1826.

The Nationalist. Madison's experiences in the Continental Congress (1780–1783) and the Virginia Assembly (1784–1786) made him a supporter of a strong national government. After only one week in Congress he wrote Thomas Jefferson about the depressing situation of an inadequately supplied army, an empty treasury, and a weak Congress, "recommending plans to the several states for execution and the states separately rejudging the expediency of such plans. . . ." The situation was no better on the state level. In a letter to Jefferson written in 1788 Madison described "the danger of oppression" caused by state legislatures acting as "the mere instrument of the major number of the constituents." As a delegate to the Annapolis Convention in 1786, Madison knew that strengthening Congress by giving it the power to regulate internal and external trade would not solve the national and state problems of factionalism, sectionalism, and the danger that majority rule posed to minority rights. In a long essay written in 1786, "Of Ancient and Modern Confederacies," Madison described what he had in mind. The solution was the creation of a government that would act as a "disinterested and dispassionate umpire" to control "disputes between different passions and interests in the State" but that "would itself be sufficiently restrained from the pursuit of interests adverse to those of the whole Society." Madison feared that the final version of the Constitution approved in September

1787 allowed the states to retain too much power through equal representation in the Senate and the lack of a national veto of state legislation, but in *The Federalist* (1788) and at the Virginia ratification convention he vigorously supported the new federal government as the best means to protect national union and liberty.

Republican Party. The Virginia Anti-Federalist Patrick Henry blocked Madison's election to the U.S. Senate, but he could not stop Madison's election to the House of Representatives in 1789. When Madison emerged as leader of House opposition to Alexander Hamilton's financial program in 1790, Federalists, including Hamilton, condemned Madison as a traitor. Madison, however, believed that Hamilton had betrayed the principles of the Constitution. Hamilton's alliance between the federal government and merchant/speculators did not conform to Madison's concept of the federal government as a "disinterested and dispassionate umpire" that would guarantee liberty and equality for all citizens. He was also alarmed at how support for Hamilton's policies in the legislative branch created a dangerous consolidation of power in the executive branch. Madison also opposed Hamilton's pro-British foreign policy, believing that it continued the subservient relationship of the colonial period. In the early 1790s Madison, with the assistance of Clerk of the House John Beckley, was far more active in organizing the Republican Party than Thomas Jefferson, especially after Jefferson retired as secretary of state in 1793. Despite his efforts in Congress and in the press, the Federalists scored one victory after another. The final blow was ratification of the Jay Treaty in 1795, which Madison regarded as obvious proof that the Federalists were "a British party." In 1797 Madison and Dolley Payne Todd, the young widow whom he had married in 1794, retired to Montpelier. The continuing "transformation of the republican system of the United States into a monarchy," most evident in the Alien and Sedition Acts, ended Madison's political retirement. As the anonymous author of the Virginia Resolutions in 1798 and as the author of a report to fellow members of the Virginia legislature in 1800, Madison maintained that the states must "interpose" their authority in order to defend civil liberties from the encroaching power of the federal government.

Secretary of State. Madison's opportunity to restore republican principles to the federal government came when Thomas Jefferson won the presidency in 1800 and chose Madison as his secretary of state. Because of their long friendship and shared beliefs, foreign policy in the Jefferson administration was very much a partnership between Jefferson and Madison. Madison's primary role in the Louisiana Purchase of 1803 may have been to implement Jefferson's instructions, but his interest in access to the Mississippi River and American settlement of western lands dated to his first term in Congress in 1780, when he argued for American claims to navigation on the Mississippi and territory in the Mississippi River Valley. Madison shared Jefferson's devotion to territorial expansion as the key to ensuring that the United States would remain a peaceful republic of independent, property-owning farmers. As secretary of state he ag-

gressively pursued the expansion of the "Empire of Liberty" through attempts to acquire Florida from Spain, finally annexing West Florida during his presidency. As the Jefferson administration's most ardent supporter of commercial coercion as an effective method of defending American commerce and American honor, Madison was instrumental in establishing and enforcing the embargo, especially after he became president-elect in December 1808. As president Madison would continue to implement the republican principles of foreign and domestic policy that he had helped formulate as secretary of state.

"Mr. Madison's War." When President Madison assumed office in March 1809, he faced the prospect of a war that would endanger the property and liberty of the American people through the introduction of high taxes, a standing army, and increased executive authority. Madison's continued reliance on commercial coercion as a substitute for war seemed naive after Britain repudiated the Erskine Agreement in 1809, which promised the removal of British restrictions on neutral trade, and France duped the United States into resuming nonintercourse with Britain in 1811 with false assurances that French trade restrictions would be removed. However, Madison's determination to maintain his republican ideals and to save the country "from the dilemma, of a mortifying peace" or war with both Britain and France compelled him to gamble on this risky policy. At the least, commercial coercion might buy time to make defense preparations and rally public support for a war against one enemy—Britain—whose long history of contempt for American economic and political independence made her the more appropriate target than France. The failure to seize Canada quickly and force Britain into peace negotiations turned the War of 1812 into a protracted struggle filled with military disasters and political opposition from Federalists, which reached its climax in the Hartford Convention of 1814–1815, as well as from antiadministration Republicans. Prosecution of the war also suffered from the mediocrity, incompetence, and political rivalry in Madison's cabinet; military and financial weaknesses due to the Republican Party's horror of standing armies, taxes, and a National Bank; and Madison's own reluctance to damage the separation-of-powers doctrine of the Constitution by consolidating power in the executive branch. Ironically, Andrew Jackson's victory at New Orleans and the signing of the Treaty of Ghent erased the many humiliations of the war, including the invasion of Washington and the burning of the Executive Mansion in August 1814, and rehabilitated President Madison's image. In 1817 Madison left office, credited with the defense of republicanism and national honor.

Elder Statesman. In retirement Madison kept a close watch on political and social issues. President James Monroe sent him diplomatic dispatches, and Madison offered foreign policy advice. He assisted Thomas Jefferson in establishing the University of Virginia, and after Jefferson's death in 1826 Madison succeeded him as rector of the university. As the number of slaves in the country increased each year with the spread of the "Cotton Kingdom," Madison believed more than ever in emancipation, but he also concluded that racial inferiority and prejudice would prevent the integration of freed slaves into American society. In 1816 he helped establish the American Colonization Society to resettle freed slaves in Africa. The Virginia constitutional convention of 1829 approved Madison's democratic proposal to extend the vote to all householders and heads of families who paid taxes. However, his proposal to use the federal three-fifths ratio to apportion representation in the lower house of the state legislature failed. Instead, the convention maintained the political dominance of slaveowners in both houses of the legislature by allowing the total slave population to be counted for representation. During the South Carolina nullification crisis of 1828–1833, Madison denied the right of states to nullify federal tariff laws that they considered unconstitutional. Madison now regretted the loose language of his Virginia Resolutions in 1798, which suggested that a state's right to "interpose" its authority included the nullification of federal laws. He explained that states should work cooperatively to repeal unjust laws. The terrible alternative was nullification, secession, and the dissolution of the Union he had worked so hard to create. James Madison died at Montpelier on 28 June 1836.

Sources:

Irving Brant, *James Madison*, 6 volumes (Indianapolis: Bobbs-Merrill, 1941–1961);

Ralph Ketcham, *James Madison: A Biography* (Charlottesville: University Press of Virginia, 1990).

GEORGE WASHINGTON

1732-1799

COMMANDER IN CHIEF OF THE CONTINENTAL ARMY, PRESIDENT OF THE CONSTITUTIONAL CONVENTION, FIRST PRESIDENT OF THE UNITED STATES

"The Father of His Country." George Washington's image as "The Father of His Country," who guided the birth and development of the American republic in war and peace, is more than a cliché. He did possess several qualities of the ideal patriarch—courage, strength, honesty, and decisive judgment tempered by patience and the ability to restrain and conciliate opposing views—which made him a skillful leader and conferred legitimacy on the offices he assumed.

Youth. George Washington, the first child of Augustine Washington and his second wife, Mary Ball Washington, was born on 22 February 1732 near Pope's Creek in Westmoreland County, Virginia. His father's death in 1743 ended Washington's chance to be educated in England like his older half brothers, but other opportunities arose in his teens when he began living mostly at Mount Vernon, the elegant home of his half brother Lawrence. Through Lawrence's marriage into the influential Fairfax family Washington met important people such as Thomas Lord Fairfax, one of the colony's largest landowners, and acquired the social skills of a Virginia gentleman. Fairfax hired the sixteen-year-old Washington to join a surveying party laying out his property in the Shenandoah Valley. By the age of eighteen Washington was a successful surveyor who was able to purchase almost fifteen hundred acres of land in the lower Shenandoah Valley.

Early Military Career. In 1752 Lawrence Washington died, and George applied for his brother's commission as a militia officer. Lt. Gov. Robert Dinwiddie's decision to oust the French from the Ohio River Valley in order to protect the interests of the Virginia-based Ohio Company and Washington's execution of the orders set off the French and Indian War, which soon widened into the Seven Years' War between Britain and France. On 27 May 1754 Washington surprised a French reconnaissance party at Laurel Mountain, killing ten and taking twenty prisoners, but on 3 July a much larger French force from Fort Duquesne surrounded Washington at his recently completed Fort Necessity. He was forced to surrender but allowed to return to Virginia. Washington resigned his commission but sought military glory in 1755 as a volunteer on Gen. Edward Braddock's expedition against Fort Duquesne. On 9 July 1755 a French and Indian force ambushed Braddock's army of regular and provincial troops. Braddock decided to maintain his troops in an orderly parade-ground formation instead of accepting Washington's offer to lead the provincial troops into the woods "and engage the enemy in their own way." The British suffered over nine hundred casualties, including Braddock. News of Washington's spurned advice to Braddock and his courageous performance under fire made him a hero in the colonies. In August 1755 the twenty-three-year-old Washington was appointed colonel and commander in chief of Virginia's militia, responsible for defending a 350-mile frontier with only a few hundred men. His experiences with inadequate supplies, undisciplined militia, and lack of cooperation from civilian officials prepared him for his position as commander in chief of the Continental Army.

The American Revolution. Between 1759 and 1774 Washington established his position as a respected leader in Virginia society. His January 1759 marriage to Martha Dandridge Custis, a wealthy widow with two children, substantially raised his economic and social status. The death of Lawrence Washington's widow and child in 1760 made him the owner of Mount Vernon. In order to free himself from an economic system that left Virginia tobacco planters heavily in debt to British merchants Washington diversified by planting wheat and corn, building a commercial mill, and hiring out his artisans to other plantations. He also increased his real estate holdings near Mount Vernon and speculated in western lands. His service as a member of the Virginia House of Burgesses for most of this period further enhanced his status in the community and gave him firsthand experience with colonial self-government. When Parliament imposed taxes and legislation to pay off the debt from the Seven Years' War and tighten colonial control, Washington participated in Virginia's resistance. In 1774 and 1775 the Virginia legislature chose him as a delegate to the Continental Congress. Washington lacked the formal education to cite scholarly works on political philosophy to support his opposition to British rule. Instead, he had extensive experience, as a provincial military officer, planter, and colonial legislator, with British arrogance and a colonial system of economic and political subjugation. Those experiences led Washington to conclude that British colonial policies were "repugnant to every principle of natural justice" and "an unexampled testimony of the most despotic system of tyranny that was ever practiced in a free government."

Continental Army. On 15 June 1775 the Continental Congress unanimously chose Washington as commander in chief of the Continental Army. John and Samuel Adams of Massachusetts, the key figures in Washington's selection, recognized that appointing a prominent southern military figure to lead what was thus far largely a New England army would unite the colonies. Washington's decision to refuse a salary reinforced his patriotic image and sent an inspirational message to his fellow citizens that private sacrifices were necessary to defend the common cause of liberty. Washington's vastly outnumbered army dictated a military strategy of surprise attacks, skillful retreats, and avoidance of direct confrontation. The states' fear of a permanent army forced Washington to rely on a small Continental Army and undisciplined, short-term state militia regiments. He was, in many ways, the chief executive of the Confederation government, endlessly pressing Congress and the states for men and supplies. In the fall of 1777 Washington's critics in the army and Congress, led by Brig. Gen. Thomas Conway, plotted to replace Washington with a new hero. Gen. Horatio Gates had won a stunning victory at Saratoga, resulting in the surrender of Gen. John Burgoyne and five thousand troops and a valuable French-American alliance, while Washington suffered the British capture of Philadelphia and defeats at Brandywine and Germantown, Pennsylvania. The "Conway Cabal" quickly collapsed after Washington publicly revealed it. After the British surrender at Yorktown in October 1781, Washington had one final contribution as commander in chief. In March 1783 a group of Continental Army officers in Newburgh, New York, threatened to use force to obtain their back pay and pensions from Congress. Washington made it clear that he would

not support the use of military force to achieve political ends, but he defended their cause to Congress and the states.

Constitutional Convention. In June 1783 Washington, approaching retirement, sent a circular letter to the states. He hoped to "demonstrate to every mind open to conviction" that "the distresses and disappointments" of the long war "resulted from a want of energy in the Continental government" and to convince the states to strengthen the federal government. Two developments in Washington's retirement contributed to his active involvement in the creation of a stronger federal government. One of Washington's chief interests was the development of a canal system linking Virginia with the West. Such a system of inland navigation required the cooperation first of Virginia and Maryland, which shared rights to the Potomac River, and eventually other states. What began in 1785 as a suggestion that Virginia and Maryland should meet annually to discuss mutual commercial concerns widened into a call for all the states to meet at the Annapolis Convention in September 1786. That, in turn, led to the Constitutional Convention. The second incident was Shays's Rebellion in 1786 and 1787, which convinced Washington that the country was "fast verging to anarchy and confusion!" As president of the Constitutional Convention in 1787, Washington took no part in debates, but he voted in favor of strengthening the federal government and executive authority. When delegates met in various social settings, Washington was there using his influence to gather support for a stronger federal government and harmonize opposing opinions. Most important, the generally accepted view that Washington would be the first chief executive was a decisive factor as the delegates framed the powers of the presidency.

The First President. Washington's beliefs in separation of powers and political independence shaped his conception of the presidency. Between 1789 and 1797 he did not participate in the passage of legislation or use the presidential veto to protect policies he favored, and he did not support partisan interests. Instead, he served as an impartial administrator of the nation's laws. He did, however, exert his constitutional authority in foreign policy. The political conflict between Secretary of the Treasury Alexander Hamilton and Secretary of State Thomas Jefferson over domestic and foreign policy spoiled Washington's hopes for a nonpartisan, harmonious administration. He supported Hamilton's policies on the national debt and the National Bank once he was convinced of its constitutionality, not as a Federalist but because he thought they would strengthen the nation's finances. Washington was not initially alarmed about Jefferson's opposition to Hamilton's policies. He liked to make decisions based on hearing a wide range of opinions, and he also prided himself on his ability to conciliate opponents. He reluctantly accepted a second term in 1793 in the interest of national unity, but as party divisions deepened over foreign policy, Washington could neither reconcile Hamilton and Jefferson nor retain his nonpartisan stance. His decisions in 1794 to march at the head of troops with the arch-Federalist Alexander Hamilton at his side to crush the Whiskey Rebellion and to link the uprising to the "self-created" Democratic Societies were based on his fear that insurrections would destroy republican government. He also believed that the Proclamation of Neutrality in 1793 and the Jay Treaty in 1795 were nonpartisan policies to preserve American neutrality and prevent war with Britain. Republicans, however, cited those policies as proof that Washington was a Federalist "monocrat" out to destroy liberty. When a weary Washington retired to Mount Vernon in 1797, the country was thriving economically, France was angry over the Jay Treaty, and party divisions seemed permanent.

Final Years. Washington became decidedly partisan in his retirement. During the French crisis of 1798 and 1799 he expected Republicans to be willing partners in a French invasion of the United States. His most overt political acts were his acceptance of the command of the Federalist-created enlarged army and his insistence that Alexander Hamilton be named second in command. However, when Federalists pleaded with Washington to protest President John Adams's peace mission to France publicly, Washington refused. He died on 14 December 1799 from a severe throat infection. Washington had served his country well in both war and peace by defending liberty and setting important precedents for the establishment of republican government. He had one final legacy: Washington never reconciled the existence of liberty and slavery as so many of his contemporaries did. In his will he provided that his slaves be freed after his wife's death, that his heirs take care of elderly or sick slaves, and that slave children be taught to read and write and learn a "useful occupation" before being freed at the age of twenty-five.

Sources:

Marcus Cunliffe, *George Washington: Man and Monument* (Boston: Little, Brown, 1958);

James Thomas Flexner, *Washington: The Indispensable Man*, revised edition (Boston: Little, Brown, 1974).

PUBLICATIONS

John Adams, *A Defence of the Constitutions of Government of the United States of America* (London: Printed for C. Dilly, 1787)—written during Adams's tenure as U.S. minister to England. He supports "balanced government," in which power is divided among the people (represented in the lower house of the legislature), the aristocracy (the senate), and an independent executive to mediate between the two groups;

Adams, *Discourses on Davila* (Boston: Russell & Cutler, 1805)—a series of papers written by Vice President Adams in 1790 in reaction to the radical phase of the French Revolution. He warns about the danger of democracy, leading critics to charge him with favoring monarchy;

John Quincy Adams, *Observations on Paine's Rights of Man, in a Series of Letters, by Publicola* (Edinburgh: J. Dickson, 1792)—the son of John Adams responds to Thomas Paine's and Thomas Jefferson's criticism of his father's principles in *Discourses on Davila*;

William Gordon, *The History of the Rise, Progress, and Establishment of the Independence of the United States of America* (London: Printed for the author, 1788; New York: Hodge, Allen & Campbell, 1789)—Reverend Gordon, an Englishman who immigrated to Massachusetts in 1770, based this study on official correspondence, conversations with military officers and members of Congress, and material copied from other publications; Americans criticized the book for being anti-American, the English for being anti-English;

Alexander Hamilton, John Jay, and James Madison, *The Federalist: A Collection of Essays, Written in Favour of the New Constitution, as agreed upon by the Federal Convention, September 17, 1787*, 2 volumes (New York: J. & A. M'Lean, 1788)—a series of anonymous essays written under the name "Publius" supporting the Constitution and a strong national government;

George Hay ("Hortensius"), *An Essay on the Liberty of the Press* (N.p., 1799)—a Virginia lawyer and Democratic-Republican attacks the Sedition Act as unconstitutional because the Constitution does not expressly give Congress the power to prosecute libel. Hay also defends "the spirit of inquiry and discussion" as being "of the utmost importance in every free country";

Richard Henry Lee, *Observations Leading to a Fair Examination of the System of Government, Proposed by the Late Convention* (New York: Thomas Greenleaf, 1787)—in a series of essays the author opposes the Constitution and a strong national government;

James Madison, *Memorial and Remonstrance, Presented to the General Assembly, of the State of Virginia, at Their Session in 1785, in consequence of a Bill Brought into that Assembly for the Establishment of Religion by Law* (Worcester: Isaiah Thomas, 1786)—a defense of the separation of church and state;

John Marshall, *The Life of George Washington* (London: Printed for R. Phillips, 1804–1807)—a lengthy biography of Washington by the chief justice of the U.S. Supreme Court;

Thomas Paine, *Rights of Man* (London: Printed for J. S. Jordan, 1791)—an attack on monarchy and the English constitution written in response to English statesman Edmund Burke's criticism of the French Revolution;

David Ramsay, *The History of the American Revolution*, 2 volumes (Philadelphia: R. Aitken & Son, 1789)—a South Carolina physician and politician analyzes both the positive and negative aspects of the Revolution, emphasizing the need for the Constitution and a strong national government to curb democratic excesses;

Mercy Otis Warren, *Observations on the New Constitution, and on the Federal and State Conventions. By a Columbian Patriot* (Boston, 1788)—written by a historian, poet, and playwright who was also the sister of the patriot leader James Otis, expressing opposition to several features of the Constitution; originally attributed to Elbridge Gerry;

Mason Locke Weems, *A History of the Life and Death, Virtues, and Exploits of General George Washington* (Georgetown, S.C.: Green & English, 1800)— "Parson Weems," a minister, writer, and bookseller, filled this popular biography with fictional anecdotes illustrating Washington's honesty and heroic nature;

Mary Wollstonecraft, *A Vindication of the Rights of Woman* (London: Printed for J. Johnson / Boston: Printed by Peter Edes for Thomas & Andrews, 1792)—a defense of the importance of women's education in a republic, written by an English feminist and philosopher;

Tunis Wortman, *A Treatise Concerning Political Enquiry and the Liberty of the Press* (N.p., 1800)—a New York lawyer and Democratic-Republican defends freedom of speech and political criticism as essential elements of civil liberty.

By the United States in Congress assembled,

SEPTEMBER 13, 1788.

WHEREAS the Convention assembled in Philadelphia, pursuant to the Resolution of Congress of the 21st February, 1787, did, on the 17th of September in the same year, report to the United States in Congress assembled, a Constitution for the People of the United States; whereupon Congress, on the 28th of the same September, did resolve unanimously, " That the said report, with the Resolutions and Letter accompanying the same, be transmitted to the several Legislatures, in order to be submitted to a Convention of Delegates chosen in each State by the people thereof, in conformity to the Resolves of the Convention made and provided in that case:" And whereas the Constitution so reported by the Convention, and by Congress transmitted to the several Legislatures, has been ratified in the manner therein declared to be sufficient for the establishment of the same, and such Ratifications duly authenticated have been received by Congress, and are filed in the Office of the Secretary---therefore,

RESOLVED, That the first Wednesday in January next, be the day for appointing Electors in the several States, which before the said day shall have ratified the said Constitution; that the first Wednesday in February next, be the day for the Electors to assemble in their respective States, and vote for a President; and that the first Wednesday in March next, be the time, and the present Seat of Congress the place for commencing Proceedings under the said Constitution.

National Archives

An announcement calling for the first presidential election (National Archives)

LAW AND JUSTICE

by JAMES ALOISI

CONTENTS

Sidebars and tables are listed in italics.

1783

- The Treaty of Paris is signed and establishes the legitimacy of Loyalist land claims.
- The Commonwealth of Massachusetts forbids slavery.

1784

- Tapping Reeve opens the first proprietary law school in Litchfield, Connecticut.

1785

- The state of New York outlaws slavery.

1786

- Pennsylvania experiments with penal reform through the "wheelbarrow law," a statute that requires convicts to labor on public works projects.
- New Jersey outlaws slavery.

1787

- Benjamin Rush writes *An Enquiry into the Effects of Public Punishments Upon Criminals, and Upon Society*, a treatise against capital punishment.

25 Jan.   Gen. William Shepherd routs insurgents under Daniel Shays at Springfield, Massachusetts.

1788

21 June   New Hampshire becomes the ninth state to ratify the Constitution. With this ratification the Constitution becomes effective.

1789

24 Sept.   Congress passes the Judiciary Act.

26 Sept.   Congress confirms President George Washington's appointments to the U.S. Supreme Court.

1790

1 Feb.   The first meeting of the U.S. Supreme Court occurs in New York City.

15 Dec.   James Wilson begins his law lectures at the College of Philadelphia.

1791

- Congress passes an excise or internal tax on whiskey.

1792

- In *Moore* v. *Cherry* the South Carolina Supreme Court affirms the power of a judge to instruct a jury on the law.

1793

- A decision is rendered in *Chisholm* v. *Georgia*, allowing a state to be sued by a citizen of another state.
- The College of William and Mary graduates America's first law-degree candidate.

1794

- The Whiskey Rebellion erupts in western Pennsylvania.

1795

1 July   John Rutledge is nominated Chief Justice of the Supreme Court after John Jay resigns from the post.

15 Dec.   The Senate rejects Rutledge's nomination as Chief Justice.

1796

- In *Ware* v. *Hylton* the Supreme Court declares that federal treaties supersede state laws.
- John Adams is elected President of the United States.

4 Mar.   Oliver Ellsworth is confirmed as Chief Justice.

1797

18 Oct.   Three agents of French Foreign Minister Charles Maurice de Talleyrand demand a bribe from American envoys Elbridge Gerry, John Marshall, and Charles Cotesworth Pinckney.

1798

- The Eleventh Amendment to the Constitution is ratified, overturning *Chisholm* v. *Georgia*.

18 June   Congress enacts the Naturalization Act.

25 June   Congress passes the Alien Act.

14 July   The Sedition Act is ratified.

21 Aug.   U.S. Supreme Court Associate Justice James Wilson dies.

20 Dec.   Bushrod Washington, nephew of George Washington, is confirmed as Associate Justice.

1799

- Fries Rebellion occurs in eastern Pennsylvania.

1800

- Thomas Jefferson is elected President of the United States.
- Following a second trial, John Fries is again found guilty of treason and sentenced to death.
- Oliver Ellsworth resigns as chief justice.
- St. George Tucker succeeds George Wythe as professor of law at the College of William and Mary.

23 May   John Fries is pardoned by President John Adams.

25 June   The Alien Act expires.

1801

- John Jay refuses reappointment as U.S. Supreme Court chief justice.

4 Feb.   John Marshall is sworn in as chief justice.

13 Feb.   Congress enacts a new Judiciary Act.

3 Mar.   The Sedition Act expires.

1802

- Congress repeals the Naturalization Act.
- Congress repeals the Judiciary Act of 1801.

1803

- The Supreme Court decision *Marbury* v. *Madison* establishes the doctrine of judicial review.
- St. George Tucker publishes his edition of Sir William Blackstone's *Commentaries on the Laws of England* (1765–1769).

Mar.   Federal District Court Judge John Pickering of New Hampshire is impeached by the House of Representatives.

1804

- Judge John Pickering is convicted by the Senate.
- Supreme Court Associate Justice Samuel Chase is impeached by the House of Representatives.

24 Mar.   Thomas Jefferson's first appointment to the Supreme Court, William Johnson, is confirmed.

1805

4 Feb.	Justice Samuel Chase's trial begins in the Senate.
1 Mar.	**Chase is acquitted of all charges.**

1806

8 June	George Wythe dies.
14 Dec.	Thomas Jefferson's second appointment to the Supreme Court, Henry Brockholst Livingston, is confirmed as associate justice.

1807

•	Congress enacts the Embargo Act.
3 Aug.	Aaron Burr goes on trial for treason.
1 Sept.	Burr is found not guilty by a circuit court in Richmond, Virginia, on the grounds that he was not present when an overt act of treason was committed.

1808

•	Supreme Court Justice William Johnson defies President Thomas Jefferson and refuses to enforce the Embargo Act.

1809

•	In the *United States* v. *Peters* the Supreme Court declares that a state legislature cannot reverse a federal court decree.

1810

•	The Supreme Court renders an opinion in *Fletcher* v. *Peck*, declaring that a state legislature cannot abrogate a contract.

1811

•	Justice Samuel Chase dies.
18 Nov.	Joseph Story and Gabriel Duvall are confirmed as associate justices.

1812

•	In the *United States* v. *Hudson & Goodwin* the Supreme Court holds that no federal court could exercise common law jurisdiction in criminal cases.

1813

•	The "American Blackstone" St. George Tucker is nominated to the circuit court in Virginia.

1814

24 Aug.   British troops capture Washington, D.C., and burn most of the public buildings. The Supreme Court chamber, located in a first-floor room in the Capitol, is gutted, and whatever furniture, books, and records remain are vandalized.

1815

Feb.   Temporary quarters for the Supreme Court are established in the Pennsylvania Avenue home of Elias Caldwell, the court clerk.

OVERVIEW

New Nation. Thomas Paine wrote on 19 April 1783, "The times that tried men's souls are over and the greatest and completest revolution the world ever knew gloriously and happily accomplished." The late eighteenth century was a time when many Americans tested the limits of their hard-won freedom, when notions of liberty were foremost in the minds of most civic-minded citizens. Thirteen British colonies had fought for their freedom and prevailed. Now loosely connected through the Articles of Confederation (adopted in 1782), the states were experiencing the benefits and challenges of independence. The Articles of Confederation established "a firm league of friendship" among the states. It soon became clear that the states needed a more unifying framework. The Constitution of 1787 marked a turning point in American legal history. The thirteen states formed a single republic, with some powers reserved to the states and other powers divided among three independent branches of a federal government. Sovereignty—the ultimate power to make decisions about the nature and form of government—was kept firmly in the hands of the people.

Need for Unity. James Madison saw the challenge of uniting "the minds of men accustomed to think and act differently." Joining the thirteen former colonies together as sovereign states within a federal framework was a daunting task; so was the task of binding the people together. Twenty-five of the fifty-six men who signed the Declaration of Independence were lawyers. The membership of the first Congress included forty-six lawyers. Men whose cultural and religious backgrounds differed and whose colonial experiences varied widely on account of geographic and economic differences naturally looked to the law to establish a unifying set of rules for the conduct of society. The noted professor of law and jurist St. George Tucker explained that because "the genius of our government differs materially from that of Great Britain, and as our laws have undergone a variety of changes since the Revolution, . . . it will not infrequently happen that we must reject or controvert the doctrines of the [old common law]."

The Study of Law. A career in the law during this time was exclusively the privilege of white men. Most young men prepared for the law by reading and serving as an apprentice to an established lawyer. Apprenticeship was the primary pathway to the law and, combined with a rigorous reading program, amounted to what John Adams referred to as a "dreary ramble." Eventually, university curricula and proprietary law schools emerged to compete with the apprenticeship program. In contrast to the craft training, which was the focal point of the apprenticeship program, these schools helped students develop practical skills as well as an understanding of legal theory, philosophy, and history. At the university level George Wythe and Tucker at the College of William and Mary and James Wilson at the College of Philadelphia led the way in the development of a uniquely American method of legal training. Wythe pioneered the use of moot courts and mock legislatures as part of his overall curriculum, while Wilson's law lectures became a foundation for the development of a new, American legal framework. Tucker wrote a "Plan for Conferring Degrees on the Students of Law in the University of William and Mary" (1800) in which he set out his views on a proper approach to the study of law. Tucker required his students to attend law lectures for two years and to study history, ethics, and political philosophy. His edition of Sir William Blackstone's *Commentaries on the Laws of England* (1803) became the most important legal tract of the early nineteenth century.

Americanization of the Common Law. When the first settlers came to colonize America, they brought with them a system of rules that had developed literally over centuries as the largely uncodified common law of England. This common law was the product of long-standing custom among a group of people, an expression of consensus designed to guarantee a measure of predictability in the administration of justice. The common law was the unquestioned cornerstone of the English legal system. Most lawyers in eighteenth-century America learned their profession in large part by reading the works of Sir Edward Coke and, later, Blackstone—the two great British exponents of common law theory. The common law was important to early American life because it helped assure a measure of order and stability. But, just as America eventually was compelled to assert its political independence, its legal community moved gradually but deliberately to develop an American system of law. In many states the first steps toward legal reform began with the adoption of state constitutions and the reform of land laws—and the explicit rejection of English laws and judicial rulings that followed the Revolution. The new constitutions were an important expression of independence and began the process of experimentation with new forms of governance. The idea of the separation of powers arose from these early state constitutions, a by-product of the revolutionary desire to limit executive power. Now it was a legislature of either one or two branches and made up of popularly elected individuals that made the laws. The executive branch was entrusted with the obligation of enforcing and carrying out legislatively mandated rule. The reform of land laws put an end to the old aristocratic rules of primogeniture (the descent of all land to the firstborn child) and entail (the legal requirement that prevented an heir and all his descendants from selling or dividing an estate). Another reform of the common law came with the relaxation of the rules of pleading, or the process of seeking relief in a court of law. Common law pleading developed into a rigid and complicated set of rules that often did not reflect the real needs of litigants. The common law pleading rules were needlessly technical and, in practice, highly unfair because the future of a legal claim was often decided not on the merits but rather on whether the claims and defenses were properly pleaded. True liberty required the fair dispensation of justice and the resolution of issues after the introduction of evidence at trial. The gradual relaxation of the strict rules of pleading to a more liberal "notice pleading" approach was an American innovation which helped democratize the justice systems by opening up access to the courts.

Judges. Not all changes in the law took place as a function of the new state and federal constitutions; much was happening at the local level. One significant development in the law that marked a departure from the common law was the gradual removal of power to decide the meaning of the law from the hands of jurors to the hands of judges. For many years the role of the judge was limited to making determinations about the merits of the pleadings. Juries were able to decide not only whose story was right, but also what the law was in each particular case. Judges rarely instructed juries on the law and almost never ventured to interpret the law. The power of juries to decide both the facts and the law worked well in the early colonial system where each colony, and, indeed, each community, often cohered to separate rules of religious belief and moral unity. The establishment and growth of a nation based upon the rule of law as established by elected state and federal legislatures ran contrary to a jury system that left the application of justice to the whim of each gathering of jurors. Judges, trained in the law, gradually took on the responsibility of integrating the statutes recently enacted by legislatures and instructing the jury as to the meaning and application of the law. As early as 1792 a South Carolina decision,

Moore v. *Cherry,* affirmed the power of the judge to instruct a jury on the law and asserted that the power of a jury must be subordinate to the legislature. This movement eventually led to the contemporary practice of judges having power not merely to instruct juries on the law, but also to overturn a jury verdict that runs contrary to the law.

Lawyers. The law enabled people to resolve disputes, enforce agreements, and establish rules for social conduct. The everyday work of the lawyer in early America was focused on the basics: drafting wills, prosecuting or defending criminal cases, and collecting debts. Many lawyers made their living as land speculators and conveyors and as agents who would assist in the elements required for the sale of property such as searching titles and writing deeds. The collection of debt and recovery of lost property were substantial areas of legal work in the years after the Revolution.

British Law Rejected. Many lawyers entered public service as a natural extension of their legal training. Some legal scholars, notably Wythe and Tucker, believed such legal training was an essential element of a young man's preparation for a career in public service. This view grew naturally out of the spirit of the Revolution, which held out the promise of unprecedented liberty for the people. The guardians of that liberty would be the citizens trained to lead and tutored in the philosophy of law and history. In the years following the ratification of the Constitution many states sought to make a clean break from the mother country by repudiating British laws. New York in 1788 enacted a law declaring that no British statutes "shall operate or be considered as laws" in that state. New Jersey in 1799 adopted a law that required that no law or legal decision made "in any court of law or equity in Great Britain" after 4 July 1776 was admissible in an American court of law. Kentucky in 1807 forbade any English rulings after 4 July 1776 from being "read or considered as authority" in court. During the Revolutionary War many states enacted laws requiring the confiscation of property abandoned by Loyalists. The collection of debts owed to British creditors was complicated by the provisions of the 1783 Treaty of Paris, which included an American promise to repay in full all debts owed to British citizens in British money. This was no small matter because Americans—mostly southern planters—owed about $28 million to British merchants. The state laws permitting confiscation and expunging debt came into conflict with the peace treaty. The seeds were sown for a clash between state sovereignty and national supremacy in foreign affairs. In a series of rulings the federal courts, and ultimately the Supreme Court, ruled that the new system of government required state laws to be subordinate to conflicting federal laws.

Federal Court System. The enactment of the Judiciary Act of 1789 established a federal court system led by a six-member Supreme Court with a circuit court system and several district courts. There were three circuit courts (Eastern, Middle, and Southern) and thirteen district courts. In its early years the Supreme Court had few significant cases before it. There was no precedent for how the justices should conduct themselves and no consensus on the proper role of the Court. As a result the judges turned to British custom for guidance. They wore powdered wigs and elaborate, colorful robes. They usually wrote separate legal opinions, so the Court rarely spoke with one voice. The Court also lacked forceful leadership. The first chief justice, John Jay, was largely occupied with foreign affairs as President George Washington's minister to Great Britain. Jay resigned from the Court in order to serve as governor of New York in 1795. His successors, John Rutledge and Oliver Ellsworth, each had brief and undistinguished service on the Court. When John Adams offered Jay the position of chief justice again in 1801, he declined. Adams, who was about to leave office, turned to his secretary of state as his second choice for the post. Thus began John Marshall's thirty-five-year career as chief justice. During those years Marshall defined a role for the Court that has guided American jurisprudence ever since. In particular Marshall established the Court as the final arbiter of the meaning of the Constitution. He also brought order to the Court, essentially ending the practice of a series of opinions on a single case and making the Court speak as often as possible with one powerful voice.

Circuit Court System. One of the provisions of the Judiciary Act of 1789 created a federal circuit court system and assigned each Supreme Court justice to one of three circuits. The Eastern Circuit comprised New York and all of New England. The Middle Circuit included Pennsylvania, Virginia, Delaware, Maryland, and New Jersey. The two Carolinas and Georgia made up the Southern Circuit. The responsibility to ride through a circuit was an enormous burden in days when transportation systems were primitive at best. The most consistent complaint recorded by these judges was the rigors of their circuit court responsibilities. The demands of office would ruin the health of several judges and, in part, cause John Jay to refuse reappointment in 1801. There was nothing glamorous about the life of a federal judge in this era. The power and role of the federal judiciary was in its formative stages and did not begin to take real shape until John Marshall began to give it shape in *Marbury* v. *Madison* (1803). The pay for federal judges varied. Chief Justice John Jay was paid $4,000 a year for his services, but district court judges made substantially less. The salaries of the district court judges were different depending on where they sat. The district court judge for Delaware made $800, in comparison to his Kentucky district counterpart who made $1,000 and his South Carolina colleague who made $1,800. In part because of these low salaries, until 1812 district court judges were legally able to continue an active law practice to supplement their income. The circuit court system initially did not require appointment of additional judges. Each circuit court was manned by two Supreme Court justices sitting with the local district court judge. For the district court judge this role was an additional uncompensated duty. For the Supreme Court judges it was a physical burden because it required much travel under difficult circumstances. The genius of the circuit court system was the way in which it helped enforce a national judicial perspective. The idea that states could be combined into regional groups was itself an important way to introduce the new federal system and acclimate citizens to the reality that certain conflicts could not be resolved exclusively on a local scale.

Threats to Judicial Independence. The use of the law to threaten or diminish liberty was an unfortunate result of the jockeying for political power in the first years of nationhood. The manipulation of the law for political gain was perpetrated by leaders of both political parties. In an effort to reduce public criticism of their policies and leaders the Federalists enacted the Sedition Act of 1798, making it illegal to write or speak against elected public officials. When Thomas Jefferson assumed power in 1801, he and his Republican allies used the weapon of impeachment and removal from office to punish their political enemies. Several efforts were made to remove Federalist judges, culminating in the failed attempt to replace Associate Justice Samuel Chase. The country emerged from these misuses of power stronger. The real revolutions in the law were the peaceable passing of power from John Adams to Thomas Jefferson and Jefferson's failure to defeat his political foes with charges of treason or the use of impeachment.

Revolts Against Federal Authority. The nation faced enormous challenges in its formative years. The concept of nationalism (a federal system that would unite all the states in a common effort) was not embraced with the same eagerness by all men. In particular, when the federal government sought to impose internal taxes or excises on the population in order to advance important national objectives, the rugged individualism of many self-appointed guardians of liberty clashed with the new federal power. In Pennsylvania western farmers revolted against an excise on whiskey. President George Washington was forced to call out armed forces to quell mob rule, which threatened federal authority. Later, President John Adams faced an antitax rebellion in eastern Pennsylvania when an auctioneer, John Fries, set out to free imprisoned tax evaders. In both cases the power of the new federal government was forcefully demonstrated, but at the price of harsh feelings that would linger for many years.

Publishing Court Decisions. The development of an American legal system was given an enormous boost by the publication of the first reports of judicial decisions. In 1789 a volume of reports of Connecticut decisions was published by Ephraim Kirby, who expressed the desire to contribute to a "permanent system of common law."

Similar reports appeared in Vermont in 1799 and in New York, New Jersey, and Massachusetts by 1810. In Pennsylvania Alexander Dallas published the state's reports in 1790. His initial volume was a success, and Dallas published another one in 1793. The second volume included a more ambitious project: a complete report of the decisions of the U.S. Supreme Court. Dallas's reports were published as an experiment; in 1804 William Cranch, the chief justice of the District of Columbia Circuit Court, took up where Dallas left off and published successive volumes of Supreme Court reports. Cranch understood the importance of a record of judicial decisions to the maintenance of "a government of laws."

TOPICS IN THE NEWS

AARON BURR AND THE DEFINITION OF TREASON

Beginnings. Aaron Burr, in Henry Adams's words, "impressed with favor all who first met him." Burr, grandson of the great theologian Jonathan Edwards, served as a colonel in the Continental Army and later studied law under Tapping Reeve in Connecticut. An intensely political and highly ambitious man, Burr centered his political career in New York. He served in the New York Assembly (1784) and as state attorney general (1789) before being elected to the U.S. Senate in 1791. In 1800, as the designated Republican candidate for vice president, Burr received the same number of electoral votes as Thomas Jefferson. Under the Constitution the House of Representatives had to decide between the two candidates. It took thirty-six ballots cast over nearly a week for Jefferson to receive the required majority of states. Burr took office as vice president but was estranged from Jefferson and had no role in the administration. Rather than seek reelection in 1804, he ran unsuccessfully for governor of New York. His service as presiding officer during the trial of Associate Justice Chase in February 1805 (his last month in office) was perhaps the high point of his service as vice president.

Conspiracy. Once out of office Burr sought to chart a course back to power. Distrusted by Jefferson and hated by Federalists for killing Alexander Hamilton in a duel in 1804, Burr traveled west. With his easy charm and famous name he befriended many, including Henry Clay and Andrew Jackson. In what is now West Virginia he made the acquaintance of Harman Blennerhassett, an Irish immigrant who owned an island in the Ohio River. Blennerhassett offered Burr friendship, accommodations, and political support. Burr had a potentially more potent ally in Gen. James Wilkinson, governor of the Louisiana Territory. Wilkinson was a man of large ambitions, and at some point he saw that an alliance with Burr would enable him to play all sides of a treacherous game. Although he would later renounce Burr and deny any complicity in Burr's goals, it seems clear that Wilkinson's offer of support gave Burr the initial boost he needed to pursue his goals. Even today there is only speculation about what Burr was really up to. The most charitable version of events has him preparing to lead an effort to liberate lands under Spanish rule. His ultimate goals:

Gen. James Wilkinson, a member of the Burr conspiracy; painting by Charles Willson Peale (Independence National Historical Park Collection, Philadelphia)

free Mexico and, eventually, Central and South America. Others believed that Burr really wanted to separate the states and territories west of the Alleghenies from the Union. Whether or not he meant to set himself up as leader of a new American Empire is, at best, ambiguous.

"Scene of Depravity." If Burr was engaged in conspiracy to disunite the nation, it was one of the most open secrets of the day. Rumors flew about across the nation and in official dispatches from British and Spanish ministers. On 22 January 1807, aware that Burr's conspiracy was the talk of Washington, D.C., President Jefferson sent a special message to Congress outlining the machinations and preparing Congress for the treason trial that would follow. Jefferson's message to Congress described the alleged conspiracy to divide the Union as "this scene of depravity" and referred to Burr's intentions as "an illegal combination . . . against the peace and safety of the Union." Jefferson declared that although it was "difficult to sift out the real facts," Burr's guilt "is placed beyond question."

Capture. When Burr heard rumors of his supposed intentions, he wrote a friend that "If there exists any design to separate the western from the eastern states, I am totally ignorant of it. I never harbored or expressed any such intention to anyone, nor did any person ever intimate such design to me." In this atmosphere of rumor and accusation government officials in Washington were prepared to try Burr for treason. First, though, he had to be found, and sixty men were sent down the Mississippi River. Burr claimed to be on his way to settle new lands in the western territories. Others believed Burr and his band of followers were bent on using force to detach American territory from the Union. Federal officials detained Burr in the Mississippi Territory and charged him with conspiracy against the United States. A grand jury exonerated him, but Burr feared for his life and went into hiding. U.S. marshals then caught him again and brought him east for trial.

Treason on Trial. In Washington two of Burr's accomplices, Dr. Justus Erich Bollman and Samuel Swartwout, were being tried for treason by virtue of their support for Burr's activities. The charges against these men were based on an alleged conspiracy hatched with Burr on Blennerhassett Island. Chief Justice John Marshall heard the case against Bollman and Swartwout and released the men for lack of evidence. Marshall noted the constitutional definition of treason—levying war against the United States or "adhering to their enemies, giving them aid and comfort"—and declared that "conspiracy is not treason." The chief justice believed that "there must be an actual assembling of men for the treasonable purpose, to constitute a levying of war." Without any such evidence, he had no choice but to release Bollman and Swartwout. Marshall was setting the standard for the upcoming treason trial of Burr. If the government failed to come forward with real evidence of an effort to levy war, it faced certain defeat in court.

Executive Privilege. Burr's trial took place in Richmond, Virginia. The former vice president assembled an impressive defense team, including Luther Martin, who had defended Samuel Chase during his 1805 impeachment trial. Burr's lawyers claimed that they required certain documents in the president's possession in order to put their case forward. The government sought to block issuance of a subpoena on the basis that the president was not subject to such a writ by a claim of executive privilege. Marshall, however, ruled that the subpoena could be issued. The president was as much subject to the law as any citizen, but the court would give due consideration to his office and prevent "vexatious and unnecessary subpoenas" from being issued. When Marshall issued the subpoena, Jefferson ignored it.

The Burr Trial. The trial finally began on 3 August 1807. Marshall reminded the government's lawyers that "Treason can be perpetrated only in open day and in the eye of the world." Burr's attorneys asked that the government be required to prove the act of treason. The government could not do so: it admitted that Burr was not present when his allies on Blennerhassett Island discussed the conspiracy to take up arms against the United States. The government's witnesses could not testify to firsthand knowledge of Burr's alleged traitorous behavior. Because they were unable to say they had seen Burr commit any overt acts against the government, they actually helped Burr's case. Marshall's charge to the jury required acquittal. The overt act of levying war "must be proved . . . by two witnesses. It is not proved by a single witness." Burr was found not guilty.

Conclusion. Aaron Burr was no saint and Thomas Jefferson no reckless political partisan. Yet, when the president sought to use the constitutional crime of treason to vanquish his adversary, he was pushing the use of the Constitution to its limits. John Marshall, no friend of the man who murdered Alexander Hamilton, nevertheless was determined to assure Burr a fair trial. His strict interpretation of the language of the Constitution defining treason prevented the use of the law as a way to harm political opponents. Marshall earned the enmity of the president, but he struck a blow for the proper and prudent use of the Constitution to achieve political ends. The American nation was young and its judicial system largely untested, but in this important instance it worked well.

Sources:

Thomas Perkins Abernethy, *The Burr Conspiracy* (New York: Oxford University Press, 1954);

Henry Adams, *History of the United States of America* (New York: Scribners, 1889–1891);

Jean Edward Smith, *John Marshall: Definer of a Nation* (New York: Holt, 1996).

ASSAULT ON THE JUDICIARY: THE USE OF IMPEACHMENT FOR PARTISAN PURPOSES

Limits of Power. The defeat of John Adams and the Federalist Congress in 1800 gave Thomas Jefferson and his Republican Party control of the mechanics of the national government. As they were leaving office, the Federalists had contrived to keep Jefferson checked by the judiciary. The Judiciary Act of 1801 decreased the size of the Supreme Court from six to five members and created several lower court positions. Adams filled these positions and famously appointed a new chief justice, John Marshall, two months before leaving office. Because federal judges had lifetime tenures, the courts would be in Federalist hands for some time.

Jefferson Responds. Gouverneur Morris, the New York Federalist, wrote that in the "heavy gale of adverse wind" represented by Jefferson the outgoing Federalists could hardly be "blamed for casting many anchors to hold their ship through the storm." Once in power Jefferson's allies in Congress enacted the Judiciary Act of 1802, repealing much of what the Federalists sought to do in 1801 and postponing the next session of the Supreme Court to 1803.

Pickering. Federal district court judge John Pickering of New Hampshire was a public embarrassment. Pickering's behavior on the bench was often marked with "ravings, cursings, and crazed incoherences" brought on by drink and growing mental instability. President Jefferson suggested to Congress that Pickering's bizarre behavior amounted to an impeachable offense. There was no other way to remove a federal judge who was no longer fit to serve but who refused to resign. In March 1803 the House of Representatives voted 45–8 to impeach Judge Pickering. The Senate convicted Pickering one year later, removing him from office. This was no small matter. The Constitution limited this power to the impeachable offenses of "treason, bribery, or other high crimes and misdemeanors." Pickering may have been wholly unfit to serve on the bench, but he had not committed an impeachable offense. Some feared that if he could be removed for raving and cursing, then Congress would impeach other judges for political offenses.

Impulse to Impeach. In 1803 the Pennsylvania legislature removed Federalist judge Alexander Addison, largely because of his intemperate judicial behavior. An attempt to impeach three of the Pennsylvania Supreme Court's four judges narrowly failed. In Congress the Pickering experience encouraged the Republicans to target a more formidable force: Supreme Court associate justice Samuel Chase of Maryland.

Federalist Firebrand. Samuel Chase was a brilliant lawyer but an intemperate judge. As Henry Adams wrote, "Chase's temper knew no laws of caution." A staunch Federalist, Chase was the scourge of Jeffersonian republicanism. He presided over some of the most controversial cases of the Adams administration, including

Samuel Chase, a diehard Federalist and member of the Supreme Court; portrait by J. W. Jarvis (Frick Art Reference Library)

the sedition trial of James Callender and the second treason trial of John Fries. Undaunted by the rejection of the Federalists at the 1800 election and furious at the Republican repeal of the 1801 Judiciary Act, Chase scolded a Baltimore grand jury in May 1803 to remember that "the late alteration of the federal judiciary, by the abolition of the office of the sixteen circuit judges . . . will in my judgment take away all security for property and personal liberty. The independence of the national judiciary is already shaken to its foundation . . . and our Republican constitution will sink into a mobocracy, the worst of all possible governments." Chase's words were harsh, but his point about the importance of judicial independence went to the core of the federal system. Chase's remarks ignited a firestorm. President Jefferson asked, after he learned of Chase's comments in Baltimore: "Ought this seditious and official attack on the principles of our Constitution . . . go unpunished?" John Randolph of Virginia, one of the most radical Republicans and one of the initiators of the move to impeach Pickering, took up the cause to remove Chase. If the Republicans in Congress succeeded in removing Chase, Chief Justice Marshall could be next in line. A constitutional crisis was in the making.

Impeachment of Chase. The eight articles of impeachment against Chase read like a litany of Republican grudges against the Adams administration. Chase was charged with prejudicial conduct during the trial of John

Fries, the Pennsylvania auctioneer turned tax rebel, and with improper conduct at the sedition trial of James Callender. Chase was also charged with inappropriate partisan conduct in his intemperate charge to the Baltimore grand jury. Chase may have been guilty of poor judgment and an ill temper, but it is debatable if his conduct rose to the level of high crimes and misdemeanors. When he read the charges against Chase, Chief Justice Marshall wrote that they were "sufficient to alarm the friends of a pure and . . . independent judiciary." The Republican majority in the House of Representatives had a different point of view, and they impeached Chase in 1804.

Trial. Chase's trial before the Senate began on 4 February 1805 with Vice President Aaron Burr presiding. The defense's legal team included Maryland attorney general Luther Martin. Often intoxicated in court, Martin was nevertheless one of the leading lawyers in the nation. Martin's opponent was Congressman John Randolph of Roanoke, the leader of radical Republicans in the House. Randolph was brilliant, but he was outmatched by Martin during the trial. Martin focused attention on the need to link Chase's conduct with a clearly expressed crime. Chase may have acted as a partisan Federalist and his rulings from the bench may have been at the far edge of correctness, but he was certainly guilty of no crime. Chase admitted that he had made "honest errors" and reminded the Senate that his outspoken behavior was not an uncommon practice—judges often expressed opinions from the bench. Luther Martin pressed the ultimate legal point: impeachment must be based on indictable offenses, not on rash or improper conduct. This decision, Martin told the assembled senators, "will establish a most important precedent as to future cases of impeachment."

Verdict. The trial lasted most of February. On 1 March Vice President Burr called for the roll of senators on each of the articles of impeachment. All nine Federalist senators voted for acquittal. Several Republicans surprised many by also voting "not guilty." A two-thirds majority was required for conviction on each count, and the Republicans could not muster anything more than a small majority vote on three of the eight articles. Chase was acquitted of all charges. Federalists, and even some Republicans, may have breathed a sigh of relief that the Senate refused to use impeachment for partisan means. The frenzy of impeachment proceedings quickly died down thereafter.

Aftermath. Samuel Chase went on to serve on the Supreme Court until his death on 19 June 1811. He continued to be outspoken and irascible and once clashed with Luther Martin when he appeared in Chase's court visibly drunk. "I am surprised that you can so prostitute your talents," Chase bellowed to Martin, who responded, "Sir, I never prostituted my talents except when I defended you and Colonel Burr." Chase threatened Martin with contempt but relented, unable to punish his old friend and defender.

Sources:

Henry Adams, *History of the United States of America* (New York: Scribners, 1889–1891);

William H. Rehnquist, *Grand Inquests* (New York: Morrow, 1992).

CHANGING VIEWS TOWARD THE PUNISHMENT OF CRIMINALS

New Way of Thinking. Public executions came to the colonies from the mother country as the ultimate demonstration of the power of the Crown in the maintenance of social order. Few people doubted the government's right to take the life of anyone who seriously violated the rules of civil society. The preservation of order was a fundamental concern of colonial governments, and public hangings were designed as much to be a warning to others as a punishment for wrongdoing.

Shays's Rebellion. The story of Shays's Rebellion of 1786 highlights this aspect of capital punishment. Unable to pay the high taxes imposed on them by the state legislature meeting in Boston, many western Massachusetts farmers were jailed or had their livestock or land confiscated to cover their unpaid debts. These disgruntled farmers, deep in debt and trying to make a living in the harsh conditions of the hills of Berkshire County, rose against the merchant leadership of Massachusetts in open and violent rebellion. The farmers joined together to stop the apparent injustice by closing down the court system. If the courts could not meet, debtors could not be jailed. Matters came to a head in January 1787 when Capt. Daniel Shays marched with a force of so-called Regulators to the Springfield Arsenal. It took several thousand militiamen to beat back the uprising, and when the dust settled, most of the regulators were pardoned. However, two participants in the revolt, John Roby and Charles Rose, were condemned to death, not for rebellion but for robbery. Roby and Rose had stolen weapons during the uprising, and in Massachusetts robbery could be a capital crime. Their execution was specifically related to antisocial behavior: robbery would not be tolerated in an orderly social system. At the hanging a sermon was offered by Rev. Stephen West, who declared that the punishment should be viewed as a "solemn warning against breaking the bond of civil society."

Personal Liberty. The view of capital punishment as a means to maintain civil order was the dominant view in the early years of the republic. As John Adams said, "public virtue is the only foundation of republics." This perception gradually gave way to emerging notions of liberty and the need to have methods of punishment that were consistent with the new nation's republican ideals. In Virginia Thomas Jefferson had been given the responsibility to write proposals for the reform of that state's penal laws. Jefferson failed to persuade his fellow lawmakers to agree with his view that the death penalty should be reserved only for the most heinous of crimes: treason and murder. Although Jefferson did not succeed

Workers moving a wooden house past the jail in Philadelphia; engraving by William Birch, circa 1800

in narrowing the use of capital punishment, he clearly had touched on an emerging national issue. The leaders of the new nation were concerned about balancing the freedoms associated with liberty with the need to maintain social order.

Social Contract. Many of the Founding Fathers were influenced by the humanitarian eighteenth-century philosophers, notably the Italian Cesare Bonesana Beccaria and the Frenchman Baron Charles-Louis de Montesquieu, who opposed capital punishment as monarchical and contrary to true liberty. These men believed that capital punishment represented an extreme form of punishment that, in practice, was not effective and did not promote the maintenance of public order. Jefferson, who was influenced by his readings of Beccaria, referred to the death penalty as "the last melancholy resource of society against its criminals." Beccaria's view was that capital punishment violated a citizen's "social contract" with his government. In other words, while all citizens in a free society give up the right to do certain things in order to establish a lawful and stable society, no one ever gives away the right to retain his or her own life. Capital punishment was a demonstration of ultimate brutality that

had no place in an enlightened and free society in which the citizens themselves were sovereign.

Benjamin Rush. The leading thinker and activist in the area of penal reform and the abolition of capital punishment was Benjamin Rush of Philadelphia. He was the preeminent American physician of his day. Like James Wilson, who taught the first structured law course at the College of Philadelphia, Rush pioneered the instruction of chemistry at the same college. Rush was not content to practice medicine but engaged in a variety of humanitarian causes, promoting the abolition of slavery and education reform. His chief contribution to public affairs was his fervent opposition to capital punishment. He wrote "we have changed our forms of government, but it remains yet to effect a Revolution in our principals, opinions, and manners so as to accommodate them to the forms of government we have adopted." Rush devoted much of his adult lifetime to reforming America's criminal justice laws.

Pennsylvania Reforms. In 1786 the Pennsylvania legislature restricted the death penalty and replaced it with public punishment by forced labor. This "wheelbarrow law" was based on the emerging view that society should reform criminals, not simply punish them. The law got its name from the notion that criminals would be required to work under hard-labor conditions and in very public settings. Convicts working on a variety of hard-labor projects soon became the subject of public ridicule. Many sought to escape; others became more hardened as a consequence of their public humiliation. The public quickly turned against the wheelbarrow law since it did not seem to work. In March 1787 Rush wrote "An Enquiry into the Effects of Public Punishments upon Criminals and upon Society," an attempt to affirm the recently enacted Pennsylvania penal reforms. His efforts could not prevent the repeal of the law, but Rush continued to speak out in favor of what he considered a more humane approach to dealing with convicted criminals.

Penitentiary System. The Pennsylvania experiment with penal reform was the precursor of a national movement to reform criminals through the penitentiary system. The idea was that criminals could be reformed through isolation from society, which forced introspection and repentance. By 1805 six states constructed penitentiaries as alternatives to the use of capital punishment, except in regard to the most heinous of crimes. In Philadelphia the penitentiary was considered a "school of reformation" and an alternative to the usual prison "scene of debauchery, idleness and profanity." The solitude of the penitentiary may seem like true reform when compared to capital punishment, but those individuals who had to endure the privations of incarceration did not view the penitentiary as a humane environment. One former inmate, Stephen Burroughs, wrote about his incarceration in the new Massachusetts prison at Castle Island that it contradicted the beliefs of "those who have tasted the bitter cup of slavery, and have known from hence the value of liberty." Burroughs asked: "How is this, that a country which has stood the foremost in asserting the cause of liberty . . . should so soon after obtaining that blessing themselves, deprive others of it?" Burroughs did not offer an alternative to the penitentiary, and indeed there were no easy answers to the problems of crime and lawlessness. All "analyzation, science and commerce have long ago failed in their attempts to improve the condition of mankind," wrote John Adams, "and even liberty itself, from which more was expected than from all other human means, has lately appeared to be insufficient for that purpose."

Sources:

Daniel J. Boorstin, *The Lost World of Thomas Jefferson* (Chicago: University of Chicago Press, 1948);

Louis P. Masur, *Rites of Execution* (New York: Oxford University Press, 1989);

Richard B. Morris, *The Forging of the Union: 1781–1789* (New York: Harper & Row, 1987).

THE DEVELOPMENT OF JUDICIAL POWER

No Clear Mandate. When the first Congress met in 1789 to determine the makeup of the new federal court

Oliver Ellsworth, successor to John Jay as chief justice of the Supreme Court; painting by John Trumbull, 1792 (Yale University Art Gallery)

system, they were writing on a blank slate. The Constitution provided no clear expression of how the federal judicial system should be organized. This may have been a natural consequence of the intense focus of the Founding Fathers on the relationship between the new chief magistrate, the president, and the elected representatives of the people in Congress. As James Madison wrote in *Federalist*, number 37, "no language is so copious as to supply words and phrases for every complex idea." Indeed, Article III does not say much about the judicial power of the United States other than it "shall be vested in one Supreme Court, and in such inferior courts as the Congress may from time to time ordain and establish."

New Law. The Judiciary Act of 1789 implemented the vague and undeveloped Article III of the Constitution. Led by Connecticut senator Oliver Ellsworth (later U.S. chief justice), Congress provided for a six-member Supreme Court consisting of five associate members and one chief justice. A district court system of thirteen courts was established, as well as three circuit courts, comprising large geographical boundaries. Each circuit court was composed of the resident district court judge plus two Supreme Court justices assigned to that particular region. In a reflection of Federalist nationalist sentiment the 1789 act brought state courts under federal appellate jurisdiction by allowing the Supreme Court to hear appeals brought from state courts in cases where the supremacy of the federal Constitution was at issue.

Loyalist Property Cases. The first cases of real significance that came to the attention of the Supreme Court concerned disputes arising from the terms of the Peace Treaty of 1783. Article IV of the treaty declared that creditors from either England or America could recover debts existing before the Revolutionary War and demand payment in British sterling money. This was a problem for many Americans because several states had passed laws expunging debts owed to British bankers and merchants. Moreover, those American debtors who had money had it in the form of state pounds, not paper currency sterling. As a result American money was not good for the repayment of these debts even if someone wanted to repay them.

Chisholm v. *Georgia.* In 1793 the Supreme Court heard the claims of a South Carolina man acting as the executor on behalf of a British merchant. The executor brought suit against the State of Georgia for the value of clothing supplied by the merchant during the war. Georgia declared that as a sovereign and independent state it was not subject to suit in a federal court. The question gave the Supreme Court its first opportunity to rule on the scope of federal authority. The Court, with only Justice James Iredell in dissent, entered a default judgment against Georgia and declared that when it joined the Union, the state left its sovereignty behind in matters such as the enforcement of national peace treaties. This decision, known as *Chisholm* v. *Georgia*, touched a nerve across the nation, where notions of federal supremacy were not universally embraced. It led to the adoption of the Eleventh Amendment, which forbids a citizen of one state to sue another state. (This remains the only time in the nation's history that a decision of the Supreme Court was reversed by constitutional amendment.) The Court again upheld the terms of the peace treaty in *Ware* v. *Hylton* (1796), when a Virginia statute attempted to negate debt repayment. The Court made its point clearly: a treaty "cannot be the supreme law of the land . . . if any act of a state legislature can stand in its way." These loyalist property cases highlighted the constitutional role of the Supreme Court as the official referee of disputes between the states and the new federal government.

Revolution of 1800. Thomas Jefferson's election to the presidency, and with him the election of a Republican Congress, created fear among Federalists that they would lose all of their national power. The last Federalist Congress took matters into its own hands with the enactment of the Judiciary Act of 1801. They created six new circuit courts and sixteen new circuit court judges, as well as several justices of the peace. The 1801 act also reduced the Supreme Court from six to five members in an effort to delay any opportunity for Jefferson to fill vacancies on the high court. John Adams, as a lame-duck president, eagerly filled these positions and was roundly criticized by Jefferson and his party for doing so. One Virginia Republican, William Branch Giles, expressed the view that "it was natural for [the Federalists] to look out for some

department of the government in which they could entrench themselves." Jefferson's Republican majority in Congress quickly repealed the 1801 act. The Republicans then enacted their own law delaying the next session of John Marshall's Supreme Court until February 1803.

No Meeting Place. When Marshall agreed to become the nation's third chief justice, he was taking on a largely undefined and unrespected role. Alexander Hamilton had tried to reassure readers of *The Federalist* (1788) that they had nothing to fear from "the natural feebleness of the judiciary." In its early years the Court's lack of significant cases and the reversal of *Chisholm* v. *Georgia* by enactment of the Eleventh Amendment proved Hamilton's prediction to be accurate. The Court was not even seen as a choice political appointment. Associate Justice John Rutledge resigned from the Court in 1791 to accept appointment as chief justice of the high court of South Carolina. When John Jay declined reappointment as chief justice in 1801, he wrote to President John Adams that the judicial branch "would not obtain the energy, weight and dignity which are essential to . . . the public confidence and respect which, as the last resort of the justice of the nation, it should possess." The Supreme Court was so poorly thought of in the pre-Marshall years that it was literally a branch of government without an official meeting place. In 1801 the outgoing Speaker of the House of Representatives proposed to Congress that the Supreme Court be housed in the Capitol Building. The Court met in a small, drafty room on the Capitol's ground floor, described by one visitor as having a "cellar-like aspect," until 1808.

Marshall Takes Command. At eleven in the morning on Wednesday, 4 February 1801, Associate Justice William Cushing of Massachusetts administered the oath of office as chief justice to John Marshall. The new Supreme Court judge was still the nation's secretary of state and would be until replaced by Republican James Madison a little over one month later. In the rush of events during the final months of John Adams's Federalist administration, Marshall left a few matters unattended. He inadvertently left behind one commission for justice of the peace for the District of Columbia. When Marshall's successor as secretary, James Madison, came across the undelivered commission, he refused to deliver it to its intended recipient, William Marbury. Without the commission Marbury could not serve, and he sued Madison, seeking to compel the delivery of the commission. This seemingly minor set of circumstances set the stage for what was arguably John Marshall's most important decision: the authority of the Supreme Court to interpret and enforce the laws.

Judicial Review. The decision of the Supreme Court in *Marbury* v. *Madison* (1803) established the doctrine of judicial review—the power of the Court to decide conclusively what the Constitution and other laws mean. Marbury brought his lawsuit directly before the Supreme Court, invoking the original jurisdiction of the Court pursuant to the Judiciary Act of 1789. Marshall took the case and asked a simple question: was Marbury entitled to his commission? The answer was "yes" because when President Adams signed it, the commission became a "vested legal right." The next question was whether Marbury had a remedy for this violation of his rights. Marbury thought he did when he presented a writ of mandamus (an order from a court commanding that a specified action be taken) pursuant to the Judiciary Act of 1789. Marshall declared, however, that Marbury had no recourse because Congress had no ability to grant the Supreme Court the power to issue a writ of mandamus. The Court's original jurisdiction came only from the Constitution. Therefore the Judiciary Act of 1789 conferring this additional authority on the Court was an unconstitutional act. Finally, Marshall declared and defended his authority to invalidate an act of Congress. The Constitution was the "fundamental and paramount" law of the land, and it was "emphatically the province and duty of the judicial department to say what the law is." "If two laws conflict with each other," Marshall reasoned, "the courts must decide on the operation of each. So if a law be in opposition to the Constitution . . . the court must determine which of these conflicting rules governs the case. This is the very essence of judicial duty." William Marbury did not receive his commission, but John Marshall found the opportunity to assert the constitutional role and purpose of the Supreme Court. From this decision all future decisions flow as a natural extension of Marshall's articulate expression of the proper function of the Court in a federal system.

The Madison Years. The authority of the Court grew significantly during the administration of James Madison (1809–1817). Weary of the lingering partisanship of the Jefferson years, the Court—which in 1809 was comprised of three Jefferson appointees—did its work unencumbered by political intrigue. In a series of decisions the Court affirmed and enlarged the principles of constitutional nationalism suggested in *Marbury* v. *Madison*. In 1809 the Court decided in *United States* v. *Peters* that the Pennsylvania legislature had no authority to enact a law designed to reverse a federal district court decree. To allow a state legislature to do so would make the Constitution "a solemn mockery," wrote Marshall. The chief justice expanded on this view in 1810 in *Fletcher* v. *Peck*, the decision that finally resolved the Yazoo Land Fraud dispute.

Corruption in Georgia. The Yazoo Land Fraud traced its beginnings back to 1794, when a corrupt Georgia legislature sold about thirty-five million acres of land (present-day Alabama and Mississippi) to four New England land companies for one and one-half cents an acre. The action was seen as a gross betrayal of the public trust, particularly since every legislator personally profited from the sale. Public outrage was so great that the entire legislature was voted out of office in 1796, replaced by new leadership which undertook as its first or-

der of business the revocation of the land sale. This put in doubt the validity of the original sale of land.

Fletcher v. *Peck*. In order to clear title on the land Robert Fletcher of New Hampshire sued John Peck of Massachusetts in 1803, claiming that Peck's attempt to sell him part of the Yazoo tract was of no effect since Peck's interest in the land had expired with the vote of the second Georgia legislature. Peck defended himself by claiming that the Georgia legislature had no right to interfere with his original grant of title. Could the state of Georgia lawfully rescind the contracts which a previous, corrupt legislature entered into? Marshall gave the Court's opinion by refusing to consider the motives of the legislature. Instead, he focused on the rights of the purchasers who acted in good faith "unaware of the injurious fraud." Georgia could not interfere with the federal Constitution which "declares that no state shall pass any . . . law impairing the obligation of contracts." Because the "power of the legislature over the lives and fortunes of individuals is expressly restrained," Georgia could not lawfully interfere with the land sale. This ruling marked the first occasion when a state law was declared invalid as contrary to the Constitution.

Impact. In the relatively short span of one decade Marshall's court had given the judiciary an important role in the governing of the nation—perhaps its most essential role, as interpreter and guardian of the Constitution. By 1810 the Supreme Court had a real constitutional role and clear judicial mandate.

Sources:

Henry Adams, *History of the United States of America* (New York: Scribners, 1889–1891);

Kermit L. Hall, *Major Problems in American Constitutional History*, volume one (Lexington, Mass.: D.C. Heath, 1992);

Alfred Kelly, Winifred Harbison, and Herman Belz, *The American Constitution, Its Origins and Development*, volume one (New York: Norton, 1991).

THE FIRST SUPREME COURT

Origins. As first president of the United States, George Washington appointed the entire membership of the Supreme Court, but he had to wait for Congress to decide, among other things, how many judges would sit on the Court. Sen. Oliver Ellsworth of Connecticut (later chief justice) drafted the Judiciary Act of 1789 providing for six judges on the Supreme Court. Washington signed the bill on 24 September 1789 and on that same day sent to the Senate the names of six men to hold the highest judicial positions in the new republic. The president wrote: "Impressed with a conviction that the due administration of justice is the firmest pillar of good government, I have considered the first arrangement of the Judicial department as essential to the happiness of our Country, and to the stability of its political system." Of the six men nominated by Washington, one (Robert Harrison of Maryland) declined appointment. The Sen-

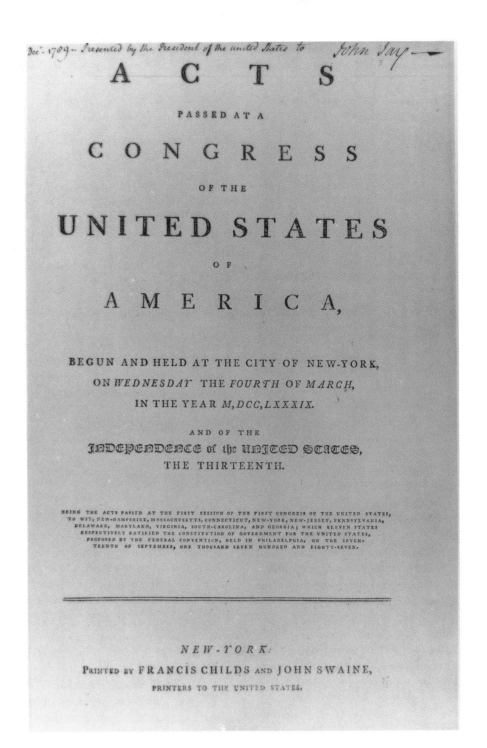

ACTS

PASSED AT A

CONGRESS

OF THE

UNITED STATES

OF

AMERICA,

BEGUN AND HELD AT THE CITY OF NEW-YORK,
ON *WEDNESDAY* THE *FOURTH* OF *MARCH*,
IN THE YEAR M,DCC,LXXXIX.

AND OF THE

INDEPENDENCE of the UNITED STATES,
THE THIRTEENTH.

BEING THE ACTS PASSED AT THE FIRST SESSION OF THE FIRST CONGRESS OF THE UNITED STATES,
TO WIT, NEW-HAMPSHIRE, MASSACHUSETTS, CONNECTICUT, NEW-JERSEY, PENNSYLVANIA,
DELAWARE, MARYLAND, VIRGINIA, SOUTH-CAROLINA, AND GEORGIA; WHICH ELEVEN STATES
RESPECTIVELY RATIFIED THE CONSTITUTION OF GOVERNMENT FOR THE UNITED STATES,
PROPOSED BY THE FEDERAL CONVENTION, HELD IN PHILADELPHIA, ON THE SEVEN-
TEENTH OF SEPTEMBER, ONE THOUSAND SEVEN HUNDRED AND EIGHTY-SEVEN.

NEW-YORK:

PRINTED BY FRANCIS CHILDS AND JOHN SWAINE,
PRINTERS TO THE UNITED STATES.

Title page of a volume presented by President George Washington to John Jay, the
first chief justice of the Supreme Court

ate confirmed the others on 26 September: Associate Justices John Rutledge of South Carolina, William Cushing of Massachusetts, James Wilson of Pennsylvania, John Blair of Virginia, and Chief Justice John Jay of New York. James Iredell of North Carolina would fill the remaining position upon his confirmation on 10 February 1790. Washington understood the need to establish an immediate sense of fairness and balance on the Supreme Court. His appointment of three northern and three southern justices reflected a wise desire to put re-

gional concerns at ease during the first days of the new government.

The Justices. The first members of the Supreme Court were very different men, chosen for their reputations as good lawyers and solid Federalists. Chief Justice Jay may have recalled his own words, in *Federalist*, number 3, that "once an efficient national government is established, the best men in the country will not only consent to serve, but also will generally be appointed to manage it." His colleagues on the bench were certainly

The Supreme Court in its first years behaved more like a British court than the Court we know today. The judges wore powdered wigs and elaborate scarlet and ermine robes, a practice taken directly from English custom. Each judge wrote a separate opinion on each case brought before the Court. This practice of separate opinions diluted the forcefulness of decisions. Deciding which opinion had more weight was difficult to assess, as was interpreting the meaning of subtle differences in concurring opinions. Too many judicial voices left a confused and weak legacy.

John Marshall, who served as chief justice from 1801 to 1835, helped the Court move toward a more American way of behavior. Marshall set an example by wearing a simple black robe in the fashion of the judges of the Virginia Court of Appeals. He also saw that the power of the Court lay in its speaking forcefully with one voice. From 1801 to 1805 Marshall wrote the sole opinion of the Court for twenty-six cases. The unanimity of the Court was broken when President Thomas Jefferson's first appointment, William Johnson of South Carolina, joined the Court in February 1805. Johnson was not awed by his colleagues (in a letter to Jefferson he referred to Justice William Cushing as "incompetent" and Justice William Paterson as "a slow man") and asserted his independence frequently.

There had always been dissents on the Court, beginning with Judge James Iredell's opinions in *Georgia* v. *Brailsford* and *Chisholm* v. *Georgia* in 1793. Johnson, however, raised dissent to new heights during his twenty-eight years on the Supreme Court, delivering thirty-three dissenting opinions and twenty-four separate concurring opinions. Yet despite his strong and steady habit of writing separate opinions, Johnson could not break Marshall's hold on the Court. Marshall enforced the power of the opinion of the Court by writing almost half of the one thousand opinions handed down by the Court during his tenure as chief justice. Marshall's power was so great that Jefferson wrote to President James Madison on 25 May 1810, "It will be difficult to find a character of firmness enough to preserve his independence on the same bench with Marshall."

Source: Kermit L. Hall, ed., *The Oxford Companion to the Supreme Court of the United States* (New York & Oxford: Oxford University Press, 1992).

among the most distinguished men of their times. John Blair of Virginia came from a family steeped in public service. Blair was one of the small number of American lawyers who could lay claim to the distinction of having been educated in the law at London's Middle Temple. Blair's early years in public service included participation in the formulation of a new Virginia state constitution and reform of the judicial system. He was a leading jurist in Virginia and participated as a delegate to the Constitutional Convention in 1787. His South Carolina colleague, John Rutledge, also studied at London's Middle Temple. Rutledge attended the Constitutional Convention and, for a brief period prior to ratification by his native state, actually held the title of President of the Republic of South Carolina. At the time of his appointment to the Supreme Court he was chief justice of South Carolina's Court of Common Pleas. Trained at Harvard University, William Cushing became a Massachusetts state court judge when he was selected to replace his father on the bench. Cushing rose to the position of chief justice of the state's highest court and may best be known for his charge to a Massachusetts jury that slavery was unconstitutional in that state. He was fifty-seven years of age when selected by Washington for national service. Two members of the first Supreme Court were foreign-born. Pennsylvania's James Wilson came to America in 1765 as an emigrant from Scotland and was a signer of the Declaration of Independence as well as a member of the Constitutional Convention. James Iredell was born in 1757 in Sussex County, England. Poverty compelled family members to send him to the colonies to work in the North Carolina port town of Edenton. Iredell studied law while serving as collector of port duties and found himself increasingly drawn to public affairs and the movement toward independence. In 1777, when the North Carolina assembly created a state judicial system, Iredell was chosen to serve as a superior court judge. He was appointed Attorney General of North Carolina in 1779 and was a highly regarded jurist when selected for service by Washington. The president explained his appointment of Iredell to the Supreme Court by noting "the reputation he sustains for abilities, legal knowledge and respectability of character."

Early Years. The first meeting of the Supreme Court on 1 February 1790 ended quickly because a quorum was not present. The next day, at New York's Federal Hall building, Chief Justice John Jay was joined by Associate Justices Wilson, Cushing, and Blair. In recognition of the importance of the occasion, many leading citizens of New York and members of Congress attended the service to observe the reading of commissions of the justices and the administration of oaths of office by Attorney General Edmund Randolph. The "first" Supreme Court ended when John Rutledge resigned on 5 March 1791 to become chief justice of the South Carolina court. George Washington appointed four more men to the Supreme Court during his presidency, including the second chief justice, the same John Rutledge, who was not confirmed by the Senate, and Oliver Ellsworth, the third chief justice, who was confirmed on 4 March 1796. For its first years the justices waited for cases to find their way to the Supreme Court for resolution. It was a slow process, since most legal disputes were brought and resolved at the state level. The full and proper role of the Supreme Court was unknown and untested, and service on the Court was viewed as a dubious honor given the limited caseload and the unusual rigors of the additional duties of each justice as a circuit court judge.

Source:
Leon Friedman and Fred Israel, *The Justices of the United States Supreme Court: Their Lives and Major Opinions* (New York: Chelsea House, 1969).

REVOLTS IN PENNSYLVANIA

Taxation with Representation. In 1789 the first secretary of the treasury, Alexander Hamilton, understood the importance of establishing a solid financial basis for the new republic. In order to achieve that goal Hamilton needed to find a way to relieve the heavy burden of debt that plagued many of the states. Hamilton's overall plan included the assumption of state debts by the federal government. This was no small matter because it implied a new, greater role for the federal government. Hamilton's plan to raise funds necessary to pay the debt included a small excise or internal tax on liquor. In 1791 Congress authorized this excise on whiskey. Despite the fact that the excise marked an important assertion of federal power, support for the excise was generally bipartisan: the senators representing North Carolina, South Carolina, and Virginia supported it. James Madison, who had opposed Hamilton's debt assumption program, nonetheless supported the whiskey excise as a fair and unavoidable way to raise necessary funds.

Document of submission signed by leaders of the Whiskey Rebellion, 1794 (Library of Congress)

Whiskey is King. For the farmers of western Pennsylvania the whiskey tax came as a bitter and unwelcome imposition of remote federal authority. Whiskey was an important local commodity, often used in place of cash as an article of barter. It was also a central element of western Pennsylvania society, where most people were involved in some fashion in the manufacture, sale, or use of the product. Taxing whiskey production touched a nerve that went to the core of the local economy. The excise itself was modest: the additional cost to a consumer of whiskey who drank an average of two gallons each month was about $1.68 a year. The real question was not the cost but the perceived challenge to liberty and the widely held view that the remote federal government was inattentive to the concerns or needs of the frontier. Moreover, the excise had a particularly harsh effect on small family distillers because it was imposed on the capacity of each still, not on the volume of whiskey actually produced. Large distillers who could operate on a more efficient basis and produced greater volumes of whiskey ended up paying less tax per gallon produced. The moment was ripe for revolt.

Reaction. Protest meetings sprang up in the western counties of Allegheny, Westmoreland, Fayette, and Washington. Federal excise officers, who were required by the law to inspect the stills, were terrorized, and as lawlessness grew, some were tarred and feathered. Tensions came to a head in 1794. The law required whiskey stills to be registered for later revenue collection purposes. John Neville, the regional excise officer responsible for collecting the tax, served papers on various men who failed to register their stills. On 16 July a group of several hundred men marched to Neville's home demanding his resignation and the return of all records associated with collection of the excise. Neville refused, defending his home with the help of a handful of soldiers from the nearby military post of Fort Pitt. Shots were fired, and after a small battle two attackers lay dead while six were wounded. The next day a second attack on the house forced Neville and his allies to flee, and the angry mob looted and burned his property.

Open Rebellion. Threats and intimidation became widespread. The insurgents had already robbed the Pittsburgh mail as an assertion of their power. On 1 August nearly seven thousand men gathered at Braddock's Field just outside Pittsburgh, menacing the town with an aggressive show of force. This call to arms was viewed as a potent and direct threat to the authority of the federal government. President George Washington, strongly encouraged by Hamilton, decided to exercise force to assert the primacy of the federal government and put an end to the violence. He called on the insurgents to disperse, but the frontiersmen paid no heed to the president's proclamation. Instead, they brazenly threatened to march to Philadelphia, then the nation's capital.

Federal Solution. Washington had no independent authority to call out the militia. The Militia Act of 1792 required the president to wait for a judge to certify that law and order could not be maintained without the use of armed forces. On 4 August 1794 Supreme Court justice James Wilson certified that the situation in western Pennsylvania could not be resolved by ordinary judicial means. Washington immediately called upon the states to form a military force of 12,900 men to quell the rebellion. A large contingent gathered in Harrisburg, Pennsylvania, in response to the call, and Washington and Hamilton rode from Philadelphia to join the militiamen. The troops moved westward, preparing to do battle with the insurgents, but no rebels could be found. Indeed, the militia met no resistance, and the march into the Alleghenies ended with no further bloodshed. Thomas Jefferson, whose sympathies did not lie with Hamilton or Washington, sniffed that "an insurrection was announced and proclaimed and armed against, but could never be found." Washington, who believed he had acted wisely, said in a message to Congress that if he had failed to act, mob rule would have "shak[en] the government to its foundations." Two leaders of the uprising were located and arrested. They were found guilty of high treason—waging war against the United States—and both were pardoned by Washington, who declared one a "simpleton" and the other "insane."

Fries Rebellion. Washington's successor, John Adams, also had to confront a Pennsylvania rebellion. The year was 1799, and the issue again was taxation, this time property taxes enacted into law in 1798. These taxes imposed levies on homes, land, and slaves. The federal government hoped to raise as much as $2 million by these levies, but many resisted the tax as an affront to their pocketbooks and their liberty. The hotbed of resistance this time was in Montgomery, Bucks, and Northampton Counties. When several tax evaders gathered to intimidate tax assessors, they were arrested by the U.S. marshal and taken to Sun Tavern in Bethlehem, Pennsylvania. John Fries, a local auctioneer, was offended by this show of federal power and assembled about 140 armed men to march on Sun Tavern. The marshal released the arrested men.

First Trial. President Adams reacted quickly and called out a federal force to suppress what he perceived as a dangerous rebellion. About sixty men were arrested as federal troops marched through the eastern Pennsylvania countryside. Fries and thirty others were indicted for treason after Justice James Iredell declared to the grand jury that if these men went unpunished "anarchy will ride triumphant and all lovers of order, decency, truth and justice will be tramped underfoot." Iredell presided over the trial along with Federal District Court Judge Richard Peters. Fries's lawyers, including Alexander Dallas, argued that his forcible release of prisoners did not amount to treason. The court disagreed and defined treason as any act of violence that could be construed as levying war against the United States. Fries was found guilty and sentenced to death by hanging.

Second Trial. Fries appealed and received a second trial. This time the judge was Samuel Chase, a staunch Federalist. Chase instructed the jury of his view that any "insurrection or rising to resist or to prevent by force or violence, the execution of any statute of the United States for levying or collecting taxes . . . is a levying war against the United States, within the Constitution." In other words Chase believed Fries's conduct amounted to treason. Fries was again found guilty and sentenced to death. Fries appealed to President Adams for clemency. Adams sought the advice of his cabinet, addressing fourteen questions of law to them. In their collective response to Adams, the cabinet unanimously supported the treason charge and the death sentence. Adams disagreed, regarding Fries's rebellion as "riot, highhanded, and dangerous indeed, but not treason." Adams saw "great danger" in applying the definition of treason to "every sudden, ignorant, inconsiderable act among a part of the people wrought up by a political dispute," and on 23 May 1800 he pardoned Fries and all those implicated in the insurrection.

Conclusion. Rebellion of any sort is a threat to public order and safety. In the early days of this nation it was also a threat to the very existence of the country. The founders understood how much effort it took to develop the fragile consensus to adopt the Constitution and a federal government. They feared that an insurrection left unchecked would undo their hard work. The primacy of that government had to be asserted in a clear, forceful, and effective manner or the very underpinnings of government would be shaken. In retrospect the Whiskey Rebellion may have been most important in the way it affirmed the general consensus of support for the office of the president and the authority of the federal government. Fries Rebellion affirmed that authority and offered the president an opportunity to demonstrate that federal power could be tempered by sensitive executive judgment.

Sources:

James MacGregor Burns, *The Vineyard of Liberty* (New York: Knopf, 1982);

Stanley Elkins and Eric McKitrick, *The Age of Federalism* (New York: Oxford University Press, 1993);

Thomas P. Slaughter, *The Whiskey Rebellion* (New York: Oxford University Press, 1986).

SEDITION ACT TRIALS

Political Parties. Despite the fears of James Madison and others that factional division would harm the nation, differences of opinion on many important issues—the federal assumption of state debts, the proper scope and use of federal power, the differences between mercantile and agrarian interests—led inevitably to separation along party lines. At the time of George Washington's retirement those parties were represented by the new president, Federalist John Adams, and the new vice president,

Cartoon of the 1798 fight on the floor of the House of Representatives between
Matthew Lyon (Vermont) and Roger Griswold (Connecticut)

Republican Thomas Jefferson. Although they would renew and maintain a close friendship in their retirement years, the 1797 inauguration of these two men from different regions and parties highlighted the deep divisions of the nation.

National Mood. The Federalists controlled both the presidency and the Congress. They had their fill of published attacks on President Adams, and they sought to control as best they could the political dialogue throughout the nation. Their efforts were aided by public fears aroused by the new French government. Flush with its own revolutionary spirit, France flexed its muscle on the high seas, seizing American ships in an effort to intimidate the new nation to support French interests in the Western Hemisphere. When Adams sent a delegation of ministers to France in 1797 to negotiate a resolution of these issues, they were met by demands for bribes. This crass attempt to extort bribes for peace was met in America with great public anger toward France. The American envoy Charles Pinckney was so appalled by the demand for money that he dismissed a corrupt French minister with the words "no, no, not a sixpence." As the rally cry "millions for defense, but not one cent for tribute" went out across the nation, the time was ripe for strong measures. Anti-France feelings reached a fever pitch, and many Americans looked inward for protection. A general sense of insecurity, understandable for a young nation

with no great navy or standing army, led to strong fears of, and feelings against, aliens.

Alien and Sedition Acts. The Federalists in Congress acted quickly. In 1798 Congress enacted four laws designed to protect the nation from foreign and domestic enemies. (The statutes also served the purpose of hurting membership in the Republican Party since many immigrants joined that group). The Naturalization Act raised the probationary period for immigrants from five years to fourteen, making immigration less appealing. The Alien Enemies Act empowered the president, in the event of war or threatened invasion, to seize, imprison, or deport all aliens who were citizens of the enemy nation. The Alien Friends Act gave the president vast powers over resident aliens, including the right to deport any alien suspected of being a threat to the United States. Finally, the Sedition Act was directed toward American citizens. It imposed penalties including fines and imprisonment on anyone who wrote, published, or spoke in a "false, scandalous, and malicious" way against "the government of the United States, or the President of the United States, with intent to defame . . . or to bring them into contempt or disrepute." In some ways the Sedition Act was ahead of its time. An individual accused of sedition could use the truth of his remarks as a defense, anticipating the twentieth-century evolution of defamation law. In this sense the Sedition Act was a moderation of English common law, which did not recognize truth as a defense. Many Federalists believed that the act encouraged responsible free speech by specifically limiting its application to those cases where malicious intent could be shown.

Free Speech. While the Sedition Act may have been more liberal than the common law, it was nevertheless contrary to the near absolute freedom of speech which was guaranteed by the First Amendment to the Constitution. Not every Federalist supported the Sedition Act. George Washington reported his misgivings, and John Marshall wrote that the act was "viewed by a great many well-meaning men as unwarranted by the Constitution." It offended the uniquely American sense of liberty. The hard-fought battles of the Revolution, and the equally hard fought political battle to pass a Constitution tempered by a Bill of Rights, set the stage for a major confrontation on the Sedition Act's limitations on speech.

The Trials. The Federalist administration brought fourteen indictments under the act, ten of which resulted in conviction and punishment. These trials of leading Republican newspaper editors, and one member of Congress, revealed a darker side of the effort to build a nation. Perhaps the most prominent case was that of the Vermont congressman Matthew Lyon, a controversial and combative figure. When Connecticut Federalist congressman Roger Griswold mocked Lyon's military record, the Vermont congressman spat in Griswold's face. Known as "the beast of Vermont" and the "spitting Lyon," congressional Federalists sought to expel him from Congress but could not muster the necessary two-thirds vote to do so. Lyon responded with personal attacks on President Adams published in the *Spooner's Vermont Journal.* He accused Adams of having "an unbounded thirst for ridiculous pomp, foolish adulation, or selfish avarice." Lyon was tried and convicted of sedition by a federal jury in Rutland, Vermont, on 8 October 1798. He spent four months in prison and was required to pay a $1,000 fine. Nevertheless, the Federalists had made a huge political error. They transformed a congressional renegade into a martyr for free speech. The conviction did not have a negative effect on Lyon's political career; he was reelected to Congress from his jail cell and continued to be a scourge toward the Federalists.

Federalists Overreact. On some occasions ordinary citizens found themselves ensnared by the Sedition Act. Daniel Brown, an eccentric pamphleteer, erected a liberty pole in Dedham, Massachusetts, and posted a spirited challenge to the Sedition Act on the pole. Charged with sedition, Brown was tried before Justice Samuel Chase in June 1799. Chase announced that "There is nothing we should more dread than . . . licentiousness." Brown pleaded guilty and received the heaviest penalty under the Sedition Act: a $450 fine and eighteen months in jail. Unable to pay his fine, Brown was kept in prison for two years before being re-

leased on the authority of President Thomas Jefferson. In Newark, New Jersey, a town drunk was charged with violating the Sedition Act for re—marks made about the president while drinking in a local tavern.

Callender. The trial that ended up having the most long-lasting repercussions was that of James Thomson Callender, a Republican pamphleteer. A hard drinker, Callender hated the Federalist government and all its allies, mocking the social order with wild charges and character assassinations. Callender's charges were hurled with reckless abandon. He called Alexander Hamilton "the Judas Iscariot of our country" and John Adams a "hoary-headed incendiary." The last straw for the Federalists was Callender's book *The Prospect Before Us* (1800), a political tract which heaped abuse on the Supreme Court and President Adams, at one point referring to him as "a repulsive pendant, a gross hypocrite, and an unprincipled oppressor." It was no surprise when Callender was indicted for violating the Sedition Act. In Samuel Chase's courtroom Callender's fate was sealed. Chase refused to allow Callender to place the Sedition Act's constitutionality before the jury and refused to hear testimony from a witness favorable to Callender. Chase allowed a juror who had already stated his belief in Callender's guilt to sit on the jury, and Callender was found guilty of sedition, fined $200, and sentenced to nine months in prison. President Jefferson pardoned him in 1801, but Callender was a broken man, consumed by hate and an addiction to alcohol. He was found dead in the James River in Richmond, Virginia, in July 1803, an apparent suicide.

Return to Normalcy. The Sedition Act did not repress the natural inclination of most Americans to think and speak freely about their government. If anything, it portrayed President Adams and his fellow Federalists as enemies of liberty and the free and open dialogue that people expected to enjoy in their new nation. Adams was concerned that Federalist partisans may have gone too far, and he eventually stopped prosecuting citizens under the act. Jefferson, understanding the strength of the national animosity toward the Federalist laws, counseled a "little patience, and we shall see the reign of witches pass over, their spells dissolved, and the people recovering their true sight, restoring their government to its true principles." His prophecy proved true. Ill feelings lingered, and Adams and his party were not returned to office by the elections of 1800. The Sedition Act expired by its own terms on 3 March 1801.

Sources:

John C. Miller, *Crisis in Freedom: The Alien and Sedition Acts* (Boston: Little, Brown, 1951);

Miller, *The Federalist Era* (New York: Harper & Row, 1960);

Merrill D. Peterson, *Thomas Jefferson and the New Nation* (New York: Oxford University Press, 1970);

William H. Rehnquist, *Grand Inquests* (New York: Morrow, 1992).

Patrick Henry, considered to be the best trial lawyer in Virginia; he defended Richard Randolph in 1793; portrait by an unidentified artist (New York Historical Society).

SOUTHERN CHIVALRY AND THE CASE OF THE CENTURY

Colonial Elite. The Randolphs were Virginia's largest and most prominent family. The founders of the Randolph family, William Randolph and Mary Isham Randolph, arrived in North America around 1673 and are known as the "Adam and Eve" of Virginia. They had nine children and thirty-seven grandchildren. Both Thomas Jefferson and John Marshall could trace their roots to this "first couple."

Two Sisters. Judith and Ann Cary were daughters of Thomas Mann Randolph. Their brother, Thomas Mann Jr., married Thomas Jefferson's daughter Martha. Ann Cary Randolph, known as Nancy, had a reputation as an independent and headstrong young woman. As one symbol of her rebelliousness, she moved out of her father's house to live with her sister and brother-in-law. Here she was courted by her brother-in-law's younger brother, Theodoric Randolph. This brought on a series of events that cast the Randolph family into a spiral of accusation and scandal.

The Tale. Nancy and Theodoric planned to marry before Theodoric's untimely death in February 1792. Nancy turned for comfort to her brother-in-law Richard, and he was solicitous of her needs. Many people considered their closeness inappropriate, and there were raised eyebrows and whispers when people observed a discernible change in Nancy's appearance, marked by an increase in weight. On 1 October 1792 Nancy joined Judith and Richard for dinner at the Glenlyvar plantation home of Richard's cousin Randolph Harrison. Nancy became ill during dinner and retired to an upstairs bedroom. That evening, screams were heard coming from her room. When the hostess sought to look in, she found Richard Randolph in Nancy's bedroom. She later found traces of blood on Nancy's bed and on the stairs leading to the room. Rumor quickly followed. Slaves on the Glenlyvar plantation opined that Nancy had delivered a child and claimed that the infant had been left for dead by Richard in a woodpile near the plantation house. Gossip followed rumor, and soon it was the talk of the county that Nancy had conceived a child by Richard Randolph, her brother-in-law, and that Richard abandoned the child in the Glenlyvar woodpile.

The Inquest. The infamous talk of adultery and infanticide was so widespread that Richard turned to John Marshall for help. Marshall noted the lack of hard evidence against Richard, most significantly the lack of an infant's body. Circumstantial evidence and rumor were all that the accusers had at their disposal. Marshall advised Richard to appear in court and demand that he be tried for murder and adultery, or that he be exonerated. At Marshall's suggestion Richard asked the semiretired Patrick Henry, still considered Virginia's premier trial lawyer, to take up his defense. Richard Randolph followed Marshall's advice and appeared in Cumberland County Court on 22 April 1793. Proceedings began one week later before a panel of county magistrates. Patrick Henry examined the witnesses against Richard. Nancy did not testify; more important, under Virginia law the Glenlyvar slaves could not give testimony about what they saw that night. Henry's examination of the witnesses proved he had lost none of his courtroom skills. Nancy's aunt, Mary Cary Page, testified that she had peered into her niece's bedroom while Nancy was undressing to see if she was carrying a child. Patrick Henry cut her to the quick, turning to the assembled magistrates and exclaiming: "Great God, deliver us from eavesdroppers." John Marshall delivered a powerful closing argument, describing Richard's relationship with Nancy as normal and affectionate for cousins-in-law. The lack of hard evidence meant that there were only rumors against Richard rather than facts, and Richard must therefore be given the benefit of the doubt. Marshall said of Nancy: "Every circumstance may be accounted for without imparting guilt to her . . . a person who may only be unfortunate." The magistrates exonerated Richard; there would be no murder trial; and all charges were dismissed.

Fallout. Virginia society did not easily accept the decision of the magistrates. Richard, Judith, and Nancy found themselves outcasts in a social order that meant everything to them. Richard died within three years, a broken and dispirited man. Nancy moved to New York, attempting to earn a living as a teacher, but she soon fell into a state of destitution. In 1808 she was befriended by Gouverneur Morris, a prominent Federalist and former senator from New York. Morris had known her father and was moved by Nancy's impoverished condition. A bachelor, Morris invited her to live with him, and the two fell in love. Morris wanted to marry Nancy but first sought out the advice of his longtime friend, John Marshall. The chief justice wrote to Morris that while the adultery charges of 1792–1793 were "very public and excited much attention," the circumstances surrounding the affair were "ambiguous, and rumor, with her usual industry, spread a thousand others which were probably invented by malignant" individuals.

The Truth Comes Out. Morris and Nancy Randolph were married on Christmas Day 1809. Nine years later, in letters she wrote to relatives, Nancy told for the first time her version of what really happened. Yes, she wrote, she did deliver a child that evening at Glenlyvar, but it was not Richard's child. She had conceived a child with her doomed lover, Richard's brother Theodoric. There would have been no scandal had Theodoric lived and married Nancy. Theodoric's untimely death left Nancy in an enormous predicament. According to Nancy, she carried the child to term, and that night after dinner at Glenlyvar, her child was stillborn. Her brother-in-law Richard knew all of this and helped her through her adversity. But he never revealed his knowledge and went to his grave the subject of suspicion and gossip because, Nancy wrote, "He was a man of honor."

Assessment. Nancy's account remains a plausible and understandable explanation of what had taken place. In 1818, when she wrote the explanation, there could be no reason for her to manufacture falsehoods. The whole truth no doubt vanished with the silence of the slaves, who knew much but could not testify, and the silence of the grave, which claimed Richard Randolph, a Virginia gentleman and man of honor.

Sources:

Dumas Malone, *Jefferson the Virginian* (Boston: Little, Brown, 1948);

Jean Edward Smith, *John Marshall: Definer of a Nation* (New York: Holt, 1996).

STRANGERS TO THE LAW

Second-Class Citizens. Women in early America did not share in the political reform that followed the Revolution. In many ways they were strangers to the law and to justice. Married women were not treated as full citizens but as extensions of their husbands. Their rights were severely limited by old common law notions that viewed the legal existence of a married woman as, in Sir William Blackstone's words, "suspended during the marriage, or at least . . . consolidated into that of her husband." This idea of consolidation was known as "coverture." Single or widowed women could sue or be sued, convey property and write wills, but a married woman generally had no such rights. Marriage meant that the husband owned his wife's labor, controlled her property

and could—as if she were property—collect damages against anyone who caused her injury. Because most women in the late eighteenth and early nineteenth centuries did marry, most suffered from a lack of independent legal identity. If her husband deserted her, she could in some states petition the legislature to grant her status as a *femme sole*, enabling her to engage in basic commercial transactions as if she were unmarried. A married woman could conduct business affairs as a "sole dealer" only with the consent of her husband, or if she petitioned the legislature for femme sole status. Legal scholar St. George Tucker declared in his 1803 "Americanized" edition of Blackstone's *Commentaries on the Laws of England* (1803): "I fear there is little reason for a compliment to our laws for their respect and favor to the female sex."

The Dower. Women had enjoyed one significant right prior to the Revolution—the dower, or the right to one-third of her husband's real estate. Ironically, the move to free land and property from restrictions, and open up commerce in land, diminished this right. In 1795 a North Carolina court, acting on a 1784 law which sought to "promote that equality of property which is the spirit and principle of a genuine republic," ruled that "the dower of the common law is abolished." In Massachusetts the courts declared the dower invalid as a "clog upon estates," and there, as in other states, this common law right of women was abolished.

Failed Marriages. The law provided little recourse for women from unfaithful or abusive husbands. Divorce in the early national period was rare; indeed more so than in colonial times. Some jurisdictions were more inclined to grant divorces than others. Connecticut had perhaps the most liberal attitude toward divorce, while in South Carolina divorce was never an option to resolve a failed marriage. Georgia's 1798 Constitution established legislative divorce. After a divorce trial a two-thirds vote of each branch of the legislature was required to obtain a divorce. This practice had roots in the English system, where divorce was only granted in rare circumstances by petition to Parliament. Many states turned away from this vestige of English custom. By 1800 Tennessee and every state from Pennsylvania northward had enacted alternatives to legislative divorce.

Grounds for Divorce. A divorce was granted only in narrow circumstances such as a proven claim of adultery or desertion. Men almost always had the upper hand. If a man was held to be the offending party, his wife would receive the equivalent of a woman's dower, or one-third of her former husband's estate. However, if a woman was found to be the offending party, her husband kept all her property. This was no small matter: a woman who left an abusive husband was often accused of desertion. She could very well be declared the offending party and left without property or means. It took much courage, fortitude, and resources for a

Caricature of St. George Tucker drawn by one of his law students (Tucker-Coleman Collection, Earl Gregg Swem Library, College of William and Mary, Virginia)

woman to prevail under such circumstances, and psychological or physical abuse were not generally accepted grounds for divorce. Men were given a great deal of leeway in the conduct of their household affairs, and that included a large measure of dominance over their wives. Physical abuse was often accepted as an appropriate response of a husband to a rebellious, independent wife. Only as the nineteenth century began and notions of reform influenced the legal world did courts begin to accept divorce petitions based on cruelty. This reform was led by Connecticut teacher and jurist Tapping Reeve, who wrote a definitive text on family law, *The Law of Baron and Femme* (1816). Reeve favored divorce in cases of cruelty, writing that "if a husband turns his wife out of doors, and so abuses her, that she cannot live with him safely, and she departs from him, this is not a willful absence on her part."

Legal Training. Preparation for a career in the law came only to men because a woman's role was seen as one properly focused on service to their families. Abigail Adams wrote to her husband John in 1798 that "you need not be told how much female education is neglected, nor how fashionable it has been to ridicule female learning. I regret the trifling, narrow contracted education of the females of my own country." In the years following the Revolution schools for girls emerged as a new way of thinking about the role of citizens in the Republic led to a growing belief that women should receive sufficient

AMERICA'S FIRST LAW DEGREE

In 1793 William Cabell of Cumberland County, Virginia, received a Bachelor of Law degree from the College of William and Mary—the first ever awarded by the college and the first in America. Cabell had been trained by legal scholar George Wythe, who was the first professor of law in the United States.

Cabell's degree was a milestone in the developing study of law in America. Young men had previously been trained for a career in the law through the apprenticeship program, where they would serve as clerks to established lawyers. Some men of financial means traveled to London to study at the Inns of Court. In the generation prior to 1783, some 115 Americans had done so. The development of a course of instruction at the College of William and Mary by Wythe and his successor, St. George Tucker, marked the beginning of the Americanization of the study of the law. Wythe's scholarly approach to the law was supplemented by his use of moot courts and mock legislatures, which he designed to prepare students for future public service. Tucker, who replaced Wythe in 1800, developed a pragmatic, less-scholarly approach to the law and relied heavily on his own edited version of Sir William Blackstone's *Commentaries on the Laws of England* (1803) as the basis for his lectures.

Cabell made immediate use of his law degree. He began practicing law in 1794 and was elected to the Virginia General Assembly in 1796. He served in the assembly until 1805, when the legislature elected him governor of Virginia. In 1808 Cabell was elected to be a judge of the General Court and in 1811 was appointed to Virginia's Supreme Court of Appeals, where he would serve until his retirement at the age of seventy-nine in 1851. Cabell died in Richmond two years later. His career demonstrates the close relationship that existed in early America between law and public service—an essential relationship if the law was to be a flexible tool for the advancement of liberty.

Source: Susan L. Trask, "In Celebration of the Bicentennial of America's First Bachelor of Law Degree Recipient," *William & Mary Law Review*, 34 (1993): 573.

education to be self-reliant. Benjamin Rush offered a model curriculum for such schools, which would include bookkeeping, geography, English grammar, composition, rhetoric, and arithmetic. In Philadelphia the Young Ladies Academy gave women the opportunity to study in a structured environment. In 1793 the school's valedictorian, Priscilla Mason, complained that men "have denied us the means of knowledge, and then reproached us for

want of it." She understood how difficult the road ahead would be when she reminded her fellow graduates that "the church, the Bar and the Senate are shut against us."

Massachusetts. The lowly status of women was highlighted by the Massachusetts case *Martin* v. *Commonwealth* (1805). William Martin Jr.'s deceased parents had been Loyalists, which caused the state to confiscate their property in 1781. Martin argued that the state could not have confiscated his mother's property because as a married woman she had no free will to challenge her husband's decision to abandon the colonies during the Revolution. Martin sued to recover his inheritance of her share of the estate. The court said that the "real question" was whether the law allowing confiscation applied to women, "persons who have, by law, no wills of their own." Martin's lawyer went so far as to argue that a married woman "has no political relation to the state any more than an alien." The state's highest court granted the son relief. None of the judges accepted the idea that his mother could have resisted her husband's political ideas. Judge Theodore Sedgwick asked: "Can we believe that a wife, for so respecting the understanding of her husband as to submit her own opinions to his, should lose her own property, and forfeit the inheritance of her children? Was she to be considered a criminal because she permitted her husband to elect his own and her place of residence? Because she did not, in violation of her marriage vows, rebel against the will of her husband?" Chief Justice Dana concluded that the statute could not apply to married women because it was unthinkable that they had freedom to "breach the duty which, by the laws of their country, and the law of God, they owed to their husbands." Ironically, the unchallenged subservience of women to their husbands led to the court's conclusion that their property rights be protected.

African Americans. The promise of liberty did not have much meaning for African Americans. The racial divide that would break the nation apart in the middle of the nineteenth century grew wide and deep in the years following the Revolution. The Constitution recognized slavery and sought to limit it, but there was no national consensus on the subject. Many leaders of the southern bar—notably the Virginians George Wythe and St. George Tucker—opposed slavery. Tucker's 1796 pamphlet *Dissertation on Slavery with a Proposal for its Gradual Abolition in Virginia* called for a gradual emancipation of slaves. This concept was followed by many northern states, which had sought to balance the individual's right to freedom with the slaveowners' right to property. As early as 1780 Pennsylvania adopted a gradual emancipation statute. Connecticut and Rhode Island created similar laws in 1784; New York in 1799; and New Jersey in 1804. Gradual emancipation was directed at the children of slaves: no slaves would be free, but after a transitional period, their children would gain freedom. Vermont did not enact such a statute because its constitution forbade slavery. In neighboring Massachusetts the constitution of 1780, written by John Adams, was interpreted as forbidding slavery.

Quock Walker. The Massachusetts Constitution provided that all "men are free and equal." When slave owner Nathaniel Jennison beat his slave Quock Walker, he was prosecuted by local authorities for assault. Jennison's defense was that Walker was his property and could be treated as he saw fit. The local authorities contended that the Constitution had freed Walker and all slaves in Massachusetts upon its adoption. In *Commonwealth* v. *Jennison* (1783) the state's highest court ruled that the Constitution had indeed abolished slavery in Massachusetts. In his charge to the jury reviewing Jennison's assault of Walker, Chief Justice William Cushing declared in judging Jennison the jurors must recognize that the Constitution had abolished slavery.

Slave Codes. Liberty for blacks in the South was another matter. Fear of slave uprisings and the enormous importance of slavery to the southern economy made its continued existence a stubborn fact of life. Most southern states presumed all blacks to be slaves and legal nonpersons, without the right to marry, enter into contracts, or testify in court. Some states, notably Virginia and North Carolina, experimented with emancipation after the Revolution, but their efforts quickly ended. In 1806 the Virginia legislature adopted the Removal Act which required that all freed slaves had to leave the state within one year or be returned to slavery. African Americans had little recourse in the federal court system. In *Scott* v. *Negro London* (1806) Chief Justice John Marshall rejected the claim of a black man that he had won his freedom as a consequence of a Virginia law which freed a slave brought into that state without his master. In *Spires* v. *Willson* (1808), *Wood* v. *Davis* (1812), and *Mimi Queen* v. *Hepburn* (1813), Marshall again upheld the laws of property even though he stated his aversion to slavery in his commentaries.

Sources:

Cornelia Hughes Dayton, *Women Before the Bar* (Chapel Hill: University of North Carolina Press, 1995);

Linda K. Kerber, *Women of the Republic* (Chapel Hill: University of North Carolina Press, 1980);

Jean Edward Smith, *John Marshall: Definer of a Nation* (New York: Holt, 1996).

THE STUDY OF LAW

Legal Tradition. The commonly expressed idea that America is "a nation of laws and not of men" traces its roots to the earliest of days of the nation, when the preservation of liberty was the foremost concern. The Founding Fathers understood that a people well educated in the law would have the tools necessary to maintain their hard-won rights. Moreover, in a time when political leaders struggled to join thirteen distinct jurisdictions into one coherent nation, the law was an important force unifying the former colonies. The system of justice

that most people were familiar with was a haphazard adaptation of ancient common law principles which were created in an English political environment whose chief organizing idea was the largely unfettered power of the monarch. The development of a truly American system of law and justice was therefore essential if this great experiment in liberty was going to succeed. The way the law was taught and studied in post-revolutionary America evolved in the late eighteenth century in order to meet those needs.

"Dreary Ramble." During most of the eighteenth century, there were two ways a young man could gain admission to the bar. The wealthy few could study in London at one of the Inns of Court, a mark of distinction shared by several prominent lawyers and jurists, including Supreme Court associate justices John Blair Jr. and John Rutledge. For most young men, though, the pathway to the bar required self-education and apprenticeship. An apprentice was basically a clerk to a practicing lawyer. A young man would pay a fee to become attached to a lawyer's office and hope to learn as much as possible by observation and reading. The work delegated to an apprentice was often routine and tedious. Thomas Jefferson complained that "placing a youth to study with an attorney was rather a prejudice than a help" because lawyers would often shift mindless tasks on their apprentice clerks. In those days before typewriters, computers, and copy machines, apprentices devoted most of their time to transcribing routine legal documents and the rest to reading. This combination of copying documents and

PROPRIETARY LAW SCHOOLS

The Litchfield school served as a model for other proprietary law schools. It cost a student approximately $350 a year to attend—$100 for tuition and the remainder for room and board. On the average a pupil studied for fourteen months before graduating.

Name	Location	Dates
Litchfield	Litchfield, Conn.	1782–1833
Van Schaack's	Kinderhook, N.Y.	1786–1830
Staples	New Haven, Conn.	1800–1849
Swift's	Windham, Conn.	1805–1823
Turner's	Fairfield, Vt.	1806–1812
Haywood's	Nashville, Tenn.	1807–1826?
Gilbert's	Hebron, Conn.	1810–1818
Taylor's	Richmond, Va.	1810–1811?
Dorsey's	Baltimore, Md.	?–1823

Sources: Lawrence A. Cremin, *American Education: The National Experience, 1783–1876* (New York: Harper & Row, 1980);

Morton J. Horwitz, *The Transformation of American Law, 1780–1860* (Cambridge, Mass.: Harvard University Press, 1977).

studying colonial statutes and ancient common law texts by such revered figures as Britain's Lord Justice Edward Coke turned into what John Adams referred to as a "dreary ramble." This highly unstructured American system was only as good as each individual tutor, and only as comprehensive as each student's reading program. A serious reader like Thomas Jefferson, blessed with a tutor of the caliber of George Wythe, was more fortunate than most. On the other hand, Patrick Henry, one of the great trial lawyers of his day, did not even have the benefit of apprenticeship. He studied the law for a grand total of six weeks prior to his admission to the Virginia bar.

Blackstone. A major development in the study of law took place in 1772 when the first American edition of Sir William Blackstone's *Commentaries on the Laws of England* (1803) was printed on a subscription basis. Approximately 840 Americans subscribed, purchasing over fifteen hundred sets priced at sixteen dollars a set. Among the first subscribers were Thomas Marshall (John Marshall's father), John Adams, John Jay, George Wythe, and James Wilson. Blackstone quickly became the centerpiece of a young man's reading program. A member of Parliament and professor of English law at Oxford University, Blackstone undertook the task of creating a guide to English law—an attempt to give order and clarity to centuries of largely uncodified common law. His *Commentaries* were considered much easier to read and understand than the four-part treatise by Sir Edward Coke, the *Institutes on the Laws of England* (1628–1644). Jefferson, who studied Coke in the years before the *Commentaries* were published, struggled with the *Institutes,* complaining that he was "tired" of the "old dull scoundrel" Coke. Jefferson eventually grew to admire Coke as a champion of the common law and the rights and liberties of the people and to despise Blackstone as the symbol of British parliamentary authority. Jefferson's views were not shared by the majority of practitioners of the law, and by the time Tucker published his Americanized version of the *Commentaries* in 1803 Blackstone's place at the center of the study of law in America was secure.

An American System. The ground was fertile for a new approach to the study of law. Yale College president Ezra Stiles wrote in 1777 that "it is scarce possible to enslave a republic of civilians, well instructed in their laws, rights and liberties." The discipline of the law was viewed as an important pillar holding up the framework of liberty. Jefferson convinced the College of William and Mary in 1779 to establish the first professorship of law in America with Wythe, then a chancellor on the High Court of Chancery, to fill the post. Wythe was a trailblazer in organizing the study of law. He combined formal lectures with a focused reading program and encouraged the development of practical skills by the use of moot courts and mock legislatures. Students spent mornings reading Blackstone, David Hume, or Baron Charles-Louis de Montesquieu and then went to lectures and moot courts. The mock legislatures brought home the importance of the political process to the making of laws and the need for lawyers to understand and participate in that process. Wythe encouraged his students to change the laws to adapt them to their needs. His reading program exposed students to the great thinkers of Europe, men who challenged and questioned the status quo. His mock legislatures were designed to give his students the tools to adapt the laws to their own needs. Wythe's combination of a lecture and reading program with the development of practical skills was not generally followed by other university professors of law, who preferred to limit their method of instruction to a more traditional series of lectures.

Wilson Law Lectures. One of the most prominent lecturers in the law was James Wilson, the Pennsylvania patriot who was also an associate Supreme Court justice. In 1790 Philadelphia lawyer Charles Smith proposed that the College of Philadelphia include a "law lecture or lectures" as a regular part of its curriculum. The trustees asked Wilson to deliver the lectures. As professor of law in the nation's largest city and temporary federal capital, Wilson assumed the heavy task of devising a truly American legal system and a comprehensive, coherent framework for the study of law. He was uniquely prepared to undertake this ambitious effort, as his entire life had been devoted to a study of the law and its origins. On the evening of 15 December 1790 in Philadelphia Wilson stood before a large audience of some of the nation's most influential citizens, including President George Washington and Vice President John Adams, and spoke of the two great American virtues: "the love of liberty, and the love of law." Wilson forcefully argued that liberty and law were connected: without liberty, law becomes oppression; without law, liberty becomes licentiousness. No one, he warned, could truly love either the law or liberty without knowledge. The law, then, should "be the study of every free citizen and of every free man." In Wilson's concept of the new American republic it was the duty of every free man to study and understand the law and "know those duties and those rights." Only by knowing the law could a man preserve his hard-won liberty.

Proprietary Schools. Wilson's law lectures ended abruptly in 1791. His exclusive focus on philosophy and legal theory at the expense of the development of practical legal skills turned many prospective students away. The trend in legal education was toward a more structured environment offering a blend of academic experiences, similar to Wythe's curriculum at William and Mary. The real proving ground for this new mode of legal education was the privately owned school of law, thirteen of which sprang up in America between 1784 and 1828. The most famous proprietary institution was Judge Tapping Reeve's law school in Litchfield, Connecticut. Reeve's curriculum in Litchfield was developed around a highly structured framework of lectures, readings, notebook writings, and moot courts. The maintenance of a comprehensive notebook was an important aspect of the training—requiring students to engage in independent thinking and enabling them to learn by repetition. This varied approach to the study of law enabled students to benefit from the best of the two prevailing pathways to a legal profession: the strictly academic aspect of lecture and reading and the practical skills-building aspect of notebook writing and moot courts. Each Saturday students were examined on the prior week's work. Students were graduated after fourteen months of training. Entrance to the bar usually followed oral examination by prominent local jurists or lawyers who, persuaded of the knowledge and ability of the applicant, would grant admission to the bar.

Sources:

L. B. Curzon, *English Legal History* (Plymouth, U.K.: Macdonald & Evans, 1979);

Lawrence M. Friedman, *A History of American Law* (New York: Simon & Schuster, 1985);

Charles Rembar, *The Law of the Land* (New York: Simon & Schuster, 1980).

HEADLINE MAKERS

JOHN JAY

1745-1829

FIRST CHIEF JUSTICE OF THE SUPREME COURT

Early Years. John Jay was born on 12 December 1745 in New York City. The son of a prosperous merchant family and nephew of a judge, Jay benefited from a solid and well-rounded education. He graduated from King's College (now Columbia University) in 1760 fluent in French, Greek, and Latin. Jay began his apprenticeship in the law in 1764, serving as clerk to Benjamin Kissam, and soon became known for quickness of mind and the strength of his reasoning. After being licensed to practice law on 26 October 1768, he began a partnership with Robert Livingston, a friend since their college days. Jay and Livingston became a preeminent New York law firm, taking on all manner of cases and building important reputations.

Public Service. Jay's public career began in 1774 as a delegate to the First Continental Congress. There followed afterward a virtual explosion of public service. In 1775 he attended the Second Continental Congress and served on the New York Provincial Congress. The following year Jay collaborated with Gouverneur Morris and William Duer to draft a new state constitution for New York. Jay served as chief justice of New York's Supreme Court from 1777 to 1779 and in 1778 served as president of the Continental Congress. He was sent to Paris in 1782, along with John Adams and Benjamin Franklin, to negotiate a peace treaty with England. Upon his return to America in 1784 he was named Secretary of Foreign Affairs for the United States under the Articles of Confederation.

Staunch Federalist. The significant question of those first years of independence was whether the former colonies, now loosely connected by the unsatisfactory Articles of Confederation, should adopt a new constitution in order to "form a more perfect union." Jay joined with James Madison and Alexander Hamilton to write *The Federalist* (1788), a series of newspaper essays that addressed the question. Overcome by illness in the fall of 1787, Jay wrote only five of the eighty-five papers—numbers 2 through 5 and 64. Nevertheless, he penned one of the most memorable lines of the series. In essay number 2 he wrote "This country and this people seem to have been made for each other."

Supreme Court. Jay's contributions to the formation and development of the new nation, and his renown as a lawyer, made him a clear candidate for selection to the Supreme Court. President George Washington, who had been lobbied by Livingston and others for the post of chief justice, turned to Jay for this high honor. In his letter of appointment to Jay, Washington wrote: "In nominating you for the important station which you now fill, I not only acted in conformity to my best judgment, but I trust I did a grateful thing to the good citizens of these United States." Jay accepted Washington's appointment and was quickly confirmed by the Senate in late 1789. He joined with Associate Justices William Cushing and

James Wilson for the first meeting of the Supreme Court in New York City on 1 February 1790.

Tenure. Jay's service as America's first chief justice is largely unremarkable. Few cases of any importance came before the Supreme Court during his tenure. Much time and energy went into the grueling requirement that the justices "ride the circuit," that is, travel throughout a designated region to hold court in places not easily accessible. Jay's circuit assignment required him to travel throughout New York and New England, a challenging task in a time when roads were either poor or nonexistent. Perhaps Jay's most important contribution as chief justice was his firm but polite refusal to advise President Washington and Treasury Secretary Alexander Hamilton on questions of public policy. Jay's refusal affirmed the separation of powers.

Test Case. The most significant decision to come before the Jay Court, and the first great case to be decided by that body, occurred in 1793. *Chisholm* v. *Georgia* raised important issues of state sovereignty. The question to be decided by the Court was whether a citizen of another state could sue the State of Georgia in federal court. Jay and the Court (except Judge James Iredell) said yes, that Georgia had abandoned its sovereignty when it joined the Union and thus could be sued. This first expression of federal primacy caused a stir throughout the states and prompted congressional reversal through the adoption of the Eleventh Amendment. In a less celebrated case Jay wrote the Court's opinion in *Glass* v. *The Sloop Betsey* (1794), where the question was whether foreign consuls or U.S. courts had authority over captured vessels brought to American ports by foreign ships. Jay struck an important blow for American sovereignty when he held that foreign consuls had no admiralty jurisdiction in the United States.

Treaty. Washington sent Jay to England in 1794 to negotiate several matters still outstanding between the new nation and the old mother country. Antagonism was particularly strong over British trade restrictions in the Caribbean and boundary lines in the Northwest. Jay's Treaty was roundly criticized by many Americans who believed he had given too much away. The most notorious item was Jay's agreement that American molasses, sugar, cotton, and coffee would not be shipped to Europe. The Senate adopted the treaty in the summer of 1795, but without the offending trade restrictions. That same year Jay resigned as chief justice to become governor of New York, a post he held until 1801.

Reappointment. On 18 December 1800 President John Adams offered Jay reappointment as chief justice to replace Oliver Ellsworth. In his letter to Jay, President Adams urged him to accept the position for a second time in order to maintain a Federalist point of view at the highest levels of government. The "firmest security we can have against the effects of visionary schemes . . . will be in a solid judiciary," wrote Adams, "and nothing will cheer the hopes of the best men so much as your acceptance of this appointment." Jay declined the honor. The rigors of riding the circuit and the relative lack of consequence of court proceedings up to that time made the post singularly unattractive, and Jay retired from public service. He died in New York on 17 May 1829.

Sources:

Leon Friedman and Fred L. Israel, *The Justices of the United States Supreme Court: Their Lives and Major Opinions* (New York: Chelsea House, 1969);

Frank Monaghan, *John Jay* (New York: AMS Press, 1935).

WILLIAM JOHNSON JR.

1771-1834
SUPREME COURT JUSTICE

Youth. William Johnson Jr. was born on 27 December 1771 in Charleston, South Carolina, the second son of William and Sara Johnson. His father was a prosperous blacksmith who took an active role in public affairs and was elected to the legislature. Young William entered the College of New Jersey (now Princeton University) in 1787 and was educated in the classics, mathematics, and history. Johnson studied law in Charleston under Charles Cotesworth Pinckney, who had studied in London under Sir William Blackstone. Johnson received his Bachelor of Arts degree in 1790 and in recognition of his outstanding scholarship was chosen to deliver the Latin Salutatory.

State Leader. Johnson was elected to the South Carolina Assembly in 1794 and later served as its speaker. He presided over the movement to reform South Carolina's judicial system and successfully advocated improved access to the courts by establishing a series of circuit courts. In 1799, at the age of twenty-seven, Johnson was appointed to the South Carolina Appellate Court, where he earned a reputation for fairness and strong reasoning skills.

High Court. On 22 March 1804 President Thomas Jefferson nominated Johnson as his first appointment to the Supreme Court. Jefferson, irritated by the Federalist leanings of the judiciary and, in particular, by the power of the formidable Chief Justice John Marshall, was delighted in 1804 to finally have a chance to appoint his own man to the Court. Johnson came recommended to Jefferson as "a zealous democrat" of "irreproachable character." Johnson was only thirty-two years old when he took the oath of office as associate justice of the Supreme Court in May 1804. Johnson has been referred to by at least one biographer as the "first dissenter," a description which is factually not true. (Judge James Iredell cast the

Court's first dissenting opinion in 1793). Johnson was, however, the High Court's most frequent dissenter in its early years, delivering a total of thirty-three dissenting opinions between 1805 and 1834. Johnson's most memorable decision came in the one matter in which he opposed the same president who appointed him.

Rebuking the President. The case arose from the application of Jefferson's controversial Embargo Act of 1807, which prohibited the export of goods from the United States to foreign ports. The embargo was an effort to keep the United States out of the war between England and France by maintaining a rigid isolationist posture. Congress had granted Jefferson sweeping enforcement powers, to which the president had added orders to local officials on maintaining the trade ban. In 1808 the collector of the port of Charleston, South Carolina, Simeon Theus, confronted a dilemma. A ship docked in his port, full of rice and cotton and, according to its owner, headed for Baltimore, appeared to be in compliance with the Embargo Act. Yet recent orders from Jefferson's Treasury Department "encouraged" the detention of all ships regardless of appearance. Faced with the possibility that he would be removed from his post for failure to follow presidential orders, Theus detained the ship even though he did not believe it was in violation of the law. The ship's owner, Adam Gilchrist, petitioned Judge Johnson, sitting as the circuit judge, to order Theus to release his ship. Johnson saw the Treasury Department rules as inappropriate executive intrusion into the decision-making of local port officials. The president was trying to take on powers not contemplated by the Embargo Act by substituting his judgment for that of local collectors. Johnson did not believe that the collector, with no evidence to detain the ship, should follow presidential orders that amounted to "an unsanctioned encroachment upon individual liberty." In a direct rebuke to President Jefferson, Johnson declared that the "officers of our government, from the highest to the lowest, are equally subjected to legal restraint." Freedom to engage in commerce was as essential a right to a person as "the air that he breathes, or the food that he consumes." On 28 May 1808 Johnson ordered the ship free.

Reaction. President Jefferson was furious at this challenge to his authority and instructed Attorney General Caesar Rodney to publish a criticism of Johnson's decision. Rodney did so, challenging Johnson's jurisdiction over the matter and accusing the justice of meddling with executive affairs. Johnson responded with a statement to the press and made the case for judicial intervention when individual liberties were at stake. The courts, he wrote, are the "constitutional expositors" of the law, and in "a country where laws govern, courts of justice necessarily are the medium of action and reaction between the government and the governed."

Republican Dissenter. For the most part Johnson was a loyal and dedicated Jeffersonian Republican, and he became a regular critic of Chief Justice John Marshall.

Johnson became a prolific dissenter and, even when he was in the majority, he often wrote a separate concurring opinion. Though he often disagreed with Marshall, Johnson supported the Court's fundamental role in constitutional decision making. Toward the end of his career, Johnson opposed John Calhoun's nullification theory, embraced by many South Carolinians, as "a silly and wicked delusion." He was also a prolific writer and active in the Charleston Horticultural Society. Johnson's health began to fail in 1832, and he died in Brooklyn, New York, on 4 August 1834.

Sources:

Percival E. Jackson, *Dissent In The Supreme Court* (Norman: University of Oklahoma Press, 1969);

Donald G. Morgan, *Justice William Johnson: The First Dissenter* (Columbia: University of South Carolina Press, 1954).

JOHN MARSHALL

1755-1835
CHIEF JUSTICE OF THE
SUPREME COURT

Second Choice. John Marshall was President John Adams's second choice for appointment to the Supreme Court when Chief Justice Oliver Ellsworth resigned in 1800. The selection of a chief justice took on heightened importance since the election of Thomas Jefferson, and a Republican Congress meant that the Federalists would no longer control the government. John Adams knew that the courts alone could impose a lasting Federalist balance to an otherwise politically lopsided government. He turned first to John Jay, former chief justice, the governor of New York, and an esteemed Federalist. Jay, however, had few fond memories of his service on the Supreme Court, with its punishing requirement of riding the circuit and the lack of a clearly defined constitutional role. He politely declined the honor, but his letter did not reach Adams until the middle of January 1801. With barely two months left in office, Adams had little time to deliberate on a substitute; he had to choose quickly. When Secretary of State John Marshall presented Jay's letter to the president, Adams looked up and asked, "Who shall I nominate now?" Answering his own question, the president told Marshall: "I believe I must nominate you."

Early Years. John Marshall was born in the frontier county of Fauquier, Virginia, on 24 September 1755, the first child of Thomas and Mary Keith Marshall. He was descended from the great Randolph family, a distinction he shared with his rival, Thomas Jefferson. Thomas Marshall made his life as a surveyor and land agent and somehow found the means to borrow or purchase a substantial library. He encouraged his young son to read history and poetry. Marshall recalled in later years great happiness in transcribing the works of Alexander Pope at the age of twelve. Marshall's youth was steeped in the revolutionary spirit, and as a captain in the Continental Army he saw action in the battles of Brandywine, Germantown, and Monmouth. Marshall returned to Virginia in late 1779 and began to study law under George Wythe at William and Mary College. Marshall was still in the Continental Army when he was studying law, and this part-time education was his only formal legal training. He was admitted to the Virginia bar on 28 August 1780. In 1783 he married Mary Ambler, known as Polly.

Lawyer. Marshall became one of Virginia's foremost lawyers, noted for his skill in thinking quickly on his feet. The 1783 Treaty of Paris had provided for repayment of prewar debts owed to British creditors, but states tried to protect their citizens from having to repay. Marshall made his fame and early fortune as a lawyer representing Virginians who sought to use state laws to stave off the claims of British creditors. In one case, *Ware* v. *Hylton* (1796), Marshall appeared before the Supreme Court to argue that a Virginia statute that allowed citizens to discharge their debts by making payments to the state treasury should be upheld. Judge James Iredell wrote that the oral argument before the Court reflected "a degree of ability equal to any occasion . . . an ingenuity, a depth of investigation, and a power of reasoning fully equal to anything I have ever witnessed." Marshall's talents were large, but he lost his case, the only one he ever argued before the Supreme Court. The Treaty of Paris had to be upheld, in Justice William Cushing's words, as "being sanctioned as the supreme law, by the Constitution of the United States, which nobody pretends to deny to be paramount and controlling to all state laws, and even state constitutions, wheresoever they interfere or disagree." Marshall would embrace these sentiments of the primacy of the federal laws and Constitution during his tenure on the Court.

"X," "Y," "Z." Marshall's commitment to the new nation led him to public service, and he was elected to the Virginia Assembly in 1782. He was an ardent nationalist and one of Virginia's foremost supporters of ratification of the Constitution. At the 1788 Virginia Constitutional Convention Marshall offered a strong defense of Article III, the judiciary article. Marshall confronted the Anti-Federalist opposition by explaining the importance of an independent judiciary to the balance of federal power. Embracing the concept of judicial review, Marshall declared that if Congress were to enact a law not warranted by the Constitution, the Court "would declare it void." In 1797 President Adams appointed Marshall, Virginia's leading Federalist after Washington, to join Charles Cotesworth Pinckney and Elbridge Gerry as a special envoy to Paris. Marshall was appalled when he and his col-

leagues were approached by French ministers soliciting bribes. In dispatches sent back to America he gave the ministers the code names "X," "Y," and "Z" and found himself something of a hero when he returned home. Marshall was elected to Congress as a Virginia Federalist, and President Adams appointed him secretary of war on 9 May 1800. Marshall requested that Adams withdraw his nomination. Adams was so determined to have Marshall in his cabinet that he dismissed Secretary of State Timothy Pickering in order to open up the post for Marshall. He did not decline this honor "for which I had vanity enough to think myself fitted." After the sweeping Federalist losses in the election of 1800 Marshall expected to retire from public service with John Adams. However, when John Jay declined a second appointment as chief justice, John Marshall found himself at the head of the third branch of government, politically isolated and lacking any practical experience. He was just forty-five years old.

On the Bench. Marshall's first act as chief justice was to administer the presidential oath to Thomas Jefferson on 4 March 1801. This was the first occasion when leadership in America passed from one party to another, a peaceful transfer of power. Resulting from a popular election, the event was a stunning demonstration of the great American experiment. As chief justice, Marshall developed the primacy of the Supreme Court in interpreting the Constitution and laws. Marshall established an overwhelming series of precedents: the doctrine of judicial review (*Marbury* v. *Madison* in 1803), a limited meaning of treason (the Aaron Burr trial of 1807), the federal government's constitutional supremacy over the states (*United States* v. *Peters* in 1809), limits on the government's power to interfere with contracts (*Fletcher* v. *Peck* in 1810), and broad powers for Congress (*McCulloch* v. *Maryland* in 1819). He also established the Supreme Court as the final voice when the states and the federal government disagreed. Marshall enhanced the Court by making it speak with one voice. He frowned on allowing each justice to write a separate opinion, and by the power of his social skills and legal reasoning he dominated the Court. Marshall's Court decided the vast majority of cases unanimously, and he wrote the opinions in about half of the decisions handed down between 1801 and 1835.

Final Years. Marshall's work on the Court was supplemented by his deep devotion to Polly, who was a sickly woman in need of regular care and attention, and to writing history. He wrote the first biography of George Washington in 1805–1807. After Polly died on Christmas Day 1831, Marshall's health began to fail; he died on 6 July 1835. At his funeral in Philadelphia, the Liberty Bell cracked while paying tribute to the great chief justice.

Source:
Jean Edward Smith, *John Marshall: Definer of a Nation* (New York: Holt, 1996).

LUTHER MARTIN

1748-1826
LAWYER AND PUBLIC OFFICIAL

Early Years. Luther Martin was one of nine children of Benjamin and Hannah Martin. The date of his birth is generally believed to be 20 February 1748. Luther worked on his father's farm in New Jersey until 1760, when he was sent away to attend the grammar school at Princeton in preparation for his attendance at the College of New Jersey (now Princeton University). Luther set out for Maryland when he graduated in 1766 and began a brief career as a schoolteacher. In April 1767 he was appointed schoolmaster of Queen Anne's County Free School, with an annual salary of twenty pounds.

Law Student. Martin began to study the law while he was teaching school, reading most evenings in the library of a benefactor and neighbor, Solomon Wright. In 1770 Martin left his position as schoolmaster to study law full-time as an apprentice to Samuel Wilson at Back Creek, Maryland. After only a few weeks of work under Wilson's tutelage Martin was approached to take on the responsibilities of superintendent of a grammar school in Accomack County, Virginia. He accepted this assignment but continued his legal studies. In September 1771, when he considered his studies complete, Martin presented himself in Williamsburg, Virginia, for oral examination for admission to the bar. His examiners were the esteemed lawyers George Wythe and John Randolph. Martin passed his examination and was admitted to the practice of law.

Attorney General. Martin began his practice on the Virginia frontier in partnership with another young lawyer, Thomas Mason. He soon returned east and in November 1772 set up his practice of law in Maryland. Martin befriended Samuel Chase, a leader of the local Sons of Liberty and an original member of the Maryland Committee on Correspondence. Martin participated in the Revolution as a member of the Baltimore Corps of Light Dragoons. With Chase's help Martin was appointed Attorney General of Maryland on 11 February 1778. As attorney general he traveled throughout the state pressing claims for property on behalf of the state, prosecuting Loyalists, and handling criminal cases. He quickly became known as a tireless worker with a reputation for diligence and honesty. On Christmas Day in 1783 Martin married Maria Cresap, daughter of the famous frontiersman Capt. Michael Cresap.

Constitution. Martin was an active participant in the Constitutional Convention of 1787. He was an especially strong proponent of proportional representation in Con-gress and fought to prohibit the further importation of slaves. The slave trade, wrote Martin, was "a solemn mockery of and insult to God." Slavery itself was "inconsistent with the genius of republicanism . . . as it lessens the sense of the equal rights of mankind and habituates us to tyranny and oppression." He would later become honorary counselor of the Maryland Society for Promoting the Abolition of Slavery. Ultimately, Martin opposed ratification of the Constitution and became a prominent Anti-Federalist in Maryland. He authored four open letters to the citizens of Maryland in which he addressed his concern that a strong federal government was bound to expand in size and scope and thereby threaten the liberties of all. His voice was a part of the larger national chorus that supported the Constitution as long as it came with a bill of rights.

Jefferson. Martin devoted himself to his legal work as attorney general of Maryland and as a prominent lawyer and was much in demand to argue cases before the Supreme Court. He skirmished with Thomas Jefferson who, in his *Notes on the State of Virginia* (1787), accused Martin's father-in-law of atrocities against Native Americans. Martin sought to have Jefferson admit that the accusations were based on rumor and demanded that the Virginian "either justify your publication, or acknowledge your error." When Jefferson did not reply, Martin complained that Jefferson had "preserved obstinate, stubborn silence." This would not be the first time that Martin found himself defending the honor of a man against accusations made by Jefferson and his allies.

Chase. When in 1805 Supreme Court Justice Samuel Chase found himself impeached by the House of Representatives and on trial in the United States Senate, he turned to his old friend Luther Martin to be part of his defense team. Chase was targeted for removal by Republicans eager to punish a prominent Federalist and regain control over the judiciary. Chase was indeed an intemperate man, given to partisan outbursts from the bench. Whether his conduct rose to the level of an impeachable offense under the Constitution (which required a demonstration of "high crimes and misdemeanors") was the question presented to the Senate. Martin gave the closing argument on Chase's behalf. He rose on Saturday, 23 February 1805, and spoke for five hours, challenging Chase's opponents to demonstrate a single impeachable offense on the justice's part and arguing that the use of impeachment proceedings against Chase was contrary to the essential American idea of liberty. When Martin completed his argument on the following Monday, he focused on the need to preserve the independence of the judiciary. Martin asked: "Would you really wish your judges, instead of acting from principle, to court only the applause of their auditors? Would you wish them to be the most contemptible of all characters, popular judges,. . .who look forward to the applause of the rabble?" Martin argued that the independence of the judiciary was an essential component of the preservation of liberty, an important check upon the executive and legislative branches. At the close of the trial the anti-Chase forces could not muster a sufficient number of votes to remove Chase, and Martin could take some satisfaction in helping an old friend and frustrating an old foe.

Burr. Luther Martin referred to the trial of Aaron Burr in 1807 as "a peculiar case." Even today there is uncertainty over the exact nature of the alleged Burr conspiracy: while some speculate that he was simply on a mission to liberate Mexico, others maintain that Burr plotted to make war upon the United States with the goal of splitting off southern and western states into a new empire under his control. President Thomas Jefferson had no doubt that Burr's conduct was treasonous, and so informed the Congress. Burr was brought to trial before Chief Justice Marshall in Richmond, Virginia, and the first encounter between the opposing lawyers raised the significant issue of executive privilege. Burr's defense team wanted certain papers in the possession of the president in order to present their case. Jefferson refused to cooperate, and the Supreme Court was asked to decide whether Jefferson could claim executive privilege and withhold the documents. Martin's observation of the situation was powerful and poignant: "Would this president of the United States, who has raised all this absurd clamor, pretend to keep back the papers which are wanted for his trial, where life itself is at stake?" Chief Justice John Marshall ruled that Jefferson must produce the requested documents. The long-standing animosity between Martin and Jefferson now broke out in full force. The president suggested that Martin also be tried for "misprision of treason at least" and referred to the Maryland lawyer as an "unprincipled and impudent federal bull dog." Martin ignored the attack and moved ahead with his defense of Burr. The trial then came to the main question of whether treason could be proved against Aaron Burr. Martin helped present the central question to Marshall: were the charges against Burr sufficient to meet the literal and specific words of the Constitution defining treason? Marshall ruled that they did not, since not one witness was presented by the government to support the claim that Burr participated in a conspiracy to overthrow the government by force of arms.

Final Years. Martin continued to enjoy a busy legal practice and presented many cases before the Supreme Court. While his professional career never lagged, his personal life suffered. His wife Maria died in 1796, and Martin had several children to look after. He was also, for most of his adult life, addicted to alcohol. Stories of Martin's prodigious drinking habits abound, and the habit took its toll on his health. In 1819 he suffered a severe stroke which left him incapacitated; he never practiced law again. Never a wealthy man, Martin was now virtually impoverished. The Maryland General Assembly enacted a law requiring each lawyer in the state to contribute five dollars annually to a fund for Martin's

use. When Aaron Burr heard of Martin's condition, he brought him to live with him in New York City. Martin lived with Burr for three years and died on 10 July 1826.

Source:
Paul S. Clarkson and R. Samuel Jett, *Luther Martin of Maryland* (Baltimore: John Hopkins University Press, 1970).

TAPPING REEVE

1744-1823
LAWYER AND EDUCATOR

Background. Tapping Reeve was born in Brookhaven on Long Island, New York, in October 1744. The son of a Presbyterian minister, Reeve graduated from the College of New Jersey (now Princeton University) in 1763. After teaching school a few years, he moved to Connecticut to study law under Judge Jesse Root. Admitted to the bar in 1772, Reeve began practicing law in Litchfield.

Public Servant. As a young lawyer in Connecticut, Tapping Reeve took a keen interest in public affairs. By December 1776 he was a committed patriot and was appointed by the Connecticut Assembly to rouse support for the Revolution through the state. Reeve accepted an officer's commission in the Continental Army but never saw battle. He served in both the legislature and the governor's council and in 1788 was nominated the state's attorney. A fervent Federalist in the 1790s, he wrote several newspaper articles supporting the Washington and Adams administrations. Reeve remained such a vocal partisan that a federal grand jury indicted him in April 1806 for libeling President Thomas Jefferson (the indictment was dismissed).

Litchfield Law School. Tapping Reeve's lasting contribution to the American legal system was the school of law he founded in Litchfield. Reeve had tutored several young apprentices in his law practice and began to reconsider apprenticeship as a way to study law. He favored a more structured approach, combining organized lectures and moot courts for practical experience. In 1784 he built a small schoolhouse next to his home. It cost a student about $350 a year to attend the law school—$100 for tuition and $250 for board and expenses. Fourteen months of training was generally required before graduation. Reeve's students were required to attend lectures on the law, undertake a carefully prescribed reading and writing program, and participate in the moot courts.

Illustrious Alumni. The Litchfield Law School's reputation grew, and its influence was extraordinary. During its existence from 1784 to 1833, two graduates would go on to serve as vice president (Aaron Burr and

John Calhoun); three would serve on the U.S. Supreme Court; and six would become cabinet members. Other illustrious alumni included 28 U.S. Senators, 101 members of the House of Representatives, 14 governors, and 16 state chief justices. For the first fourteen years, during which the school prepared two hundred students for careers in the law, Reeve taught alone. In 1798 he selected a former student, James Gould, to join him. Gould refined the school's curriculum in the nineteenth century. When the school closed its doors in 1833, some 1,016 law students had been graduated.

Community Leader. Reeve's work at his law school did not put an end to his participation in civic affairs. In 1798 he was named a judge of the Connecticut Superior Court, and in 1814 he became chief justice of the Court of Errors. He retired two years later and devoted his time to writing legal tracts related to family law. He led the state's temperance movement and helped form a society for the suppression of vice and immorality. Married twice (once to Aaron Burr's sister Sally), Reeve's only child, Aaron Burr Reeve, died in 1809. Reeve died in Litchfield on 13 December 1823.

Sources:

Stanley Elkins and Eric McKitrick, *The Age of Federalism* (New York & Oxford: Oxford University Press, 1993);

Lawrence M. Friedman, *A History of American Law* (New York: Simon & Schuster, 1985).

JAMES WILSON

1742-1798

SUPREME COURT JUSTICE

Man of Contradictions. James Wilson was unloved by the people, who thought him a wealthy, antidemocratic aristocrat, yet as a framer of the Constitution he championed the rights of the common man. A preeminent legal scholar, he was three times passed over for appointment as chief justice of the Supreme Court. One of the best educated and most energetic men of his time, he spent his last years a debtor, hunted, in his words, "like a wild beast" by anxious creditors. James Wilson's life was filled with contradictions, but it was, above all else, a life devoted to the law and to the new American republic.

Early Years. Wilson was the product of an era now known as the Scottish Enlightenment—a time when great original thinkers such as Adam Smith, David Hume, and Thomas Reid exercised enormous influence over the development of new theories and approaches to science, medicine, law, and philosophy. Born in Fifeshire, Scotland, on 14 September 1742, the eldest son of poor but deeply pious Calvinist parents, Wilson studied Latin, Greek, mathematics, and philosophy at the University of Saint Andrews. He quickly demonstrated an affinity for scholarship. Restless with ambition and confined by the limits of opportunity in Glasgow and Edinburgh, James Wilson left Scotland for America in 1765. He proceeded directly to America's largest city, Philadelphia, where he found his first job as a Latin tutor at the College of Philadelphia. Not content with the modest life of an educator, Wilson looked to the law to satisfy his need for intellectual and monetary enrichment. He studied law under John Dickinson, who himself had studied at one of the Inns of Court in London. In 1767 Wilson began his law practice in the town of Reading, Pennsylvania. He quickly established a reputation for hard work and reliable service. Four years later he married Rachel Bird, daughter of a prominent and prosperous ironworks owner. In six years James Wilson had become an established member of Pennsylvania society. He was also at the doorstep of a time of great political and social upheaval as the colonies sought their independence from England.

Patriot. In 1768 Wilson wrote *Considerations on the Nature and Extent of the Legislative Authority of the British Parliament*, a pamphlet articulating the notion of "consent of the governed." Only those who have a say in choosing their rulers, he argued, could be governed by those rulers. The theory of dominion status (the idea of a commonwealth of nations independently governed but with common allegiance to the Crown) emerged from this treatise. In 1775 and 1776 as a Pennsylvania delegate to the Continental Congress, Wilson pushed dominion status as an alternative to independence. Although his view did not prevail, he signed the Declaration of Independence and supported the cause for liberty.

Democracy. Independence enabled Wilson to explore more deeply his notions of democratic government. He believed government was like a pyramid: to reach great heights, it ought to have "as broad a basis as possible." For Wilson that foundation was the great mass of common men, the people who would choose both the form of government and its leaders. In 1774 he had written that "all men are, by nature, equal and free: no one has a right to any authority over another without his consent: all lawful government is founded on the consent of those who are subject to it." In an age where royalty ruled supreme across most of the world, and where even in America a self-appointed aristocracy of wealthy and educated men threatened to keep tight control over the reins of government, these were truly revolutionary ideas. At the Constitutional Convention of 1787 Wilson tried to make these ideas the intellectual framework for the Constitution. He believed that the simplest and surest way to secure popular support for the new government was to offer direct election of leaders. His concept of democratic nationalism led him to advocate popular elections for all members of Congress and for the chief executive.

He opposed the electoral college and the election of senators by state legislators. Wilson's contributions to the Constitutional Convention of 1787 are considered second in importance only to those of James Madison. Indeed, Wilson's insistence on a nation based on the consent of the people and not the states would become one of the essential principles of sovereignty in the union.

Lawyer. Wilson's political adventures did not stall the growth of his law practice, which became one of Philadelphia's largest and most successful. He gained the ire of patriots by defending the wealthy and Loyalist sympathizers. As his fame grew he was drawn into a life of wealth and comfort. In order to sustain his lifestyle, Wilson embarked on what would become a lifelong pursuit of land speculation and investment schemes. Wilson did not suffer from a small ego: he wrote to George Washington proposing his own appointment as the first chief justice of the Supreme Court. Put off perhaps by Wilson's reputation for aristocratic leanings and unseemly land speculations, Washington turned instead to John Jay, offering Wilson a seat as associate justice, a position he held from 1789 to 1798.

Law Lectures. In 1790 Wilson was appointed the first professor of law at the College of Philadelphia. His lectures given in 1790 and 1791 were the first serious efforts to develop an American legal system based on emerging principles of liberty and democracy. Influenced by the thinking of the Scottish Enlightenment philosopher Francis Hutcheson and others, Wilson put forward his view of popular rule based on the notion that law arises not from the state but from the consent of the governed. His perspective on popular sovereignty continues to be a foundation of American constitutional law. He held that the desire for liberty could be accommodated with the rule of law as long as that rule emanates from the free and independent exercise of sovereignty and the established custom of the common law. According to Wilson "the happiness of the society is the first law of every government." He was truly ahead of his time in his understanding of the need to establish an American legal system based on what in the eighteenth century were bold and innovative ideas. Wilson's only substantial opinion on the Supreme Court came in *Chisholm* v. *Georgia*, a 1793 case that enabled him to give full voice to his ideas of sovereignty and nationalism as they applied under the new Constitution. The case presented a fairly simple question—whether a state could be sued in a federal court by a citizen of another state—but one that raised basic questions of federalism and state sovereignty. In *Chisholm* v. *Georgia* Wilson left no doubt that as far as he was concerned, "as to the purposes of the Union, Georgia is not a sovereign state." In his opinion the people, not the states, were sovereign. It was an important decision, so much so that it precipitated the adoption of the Eleventh Amendment (1798) establishing the notion of sovereign immunity and, in effect, reversing Wilson's opin-

ion. Aside from marking the high point of his service on the Supreme Court, 1793 marked the occasion of Wilson's marriage to Hannah Gray of Boston. (His first wife, Rachel, had died in 1786).

A Sad End. Wilson's intellectual strength did not prevent him from exercising very bad judgment in his business affairs. His reckless penchant for speculation could not be abated, and his finances fell victim to the economic downturn of the late 1790s. The combination of his duties riding the circuit as an associate justice and providing for Hannah and their infant son, all the while facing continuous harassment and occasional jailings by merciless creditors, proved too much for Wilson's health. He sought refuge in a rundown inn in Edenton, North Carolina, in 1798. That July he caught malaria and several weeks later suffered a stroke. He died on 21 August 1798 a virtual pauper, with only his wife and Associate Justice James Iredell at his side.

Sources:

Leon Friedman and Fred L. Israel, *The Justices of the United States Supreme Court: Their Lives and Major Opinions* (New York: Chelsea House, 1969);

Charles Page Smith, *James Wilson* (Chapel Hill: University of North Carolina Press, 1956).

GEORGE WYTHE

1726-1806
LEGAL EDUCATOR AND INNOVATOR

Background. George Wythe (rhymes with "Smith") was born in Elizabeth City County, Virginia, in 1726, the second son of Thomas and Margaret Wythe. His father, a prosperous farmer, died when Wythe was three years old. His mother, Margaret, a devout Quaker, taught him Latin and Greek and instilled in him an enthusiasm for learning. Wythe's mother died when he was in his early adolescence, and he moved into the care of a family relation, a prominent lawyer named Stephen Dewey. He became an apprentice to Dewey and undertook a rigorous program of reading and self-education. In 1746, at the age of twenty, he passed the oral examination and was admitted to the practice of law.

Lawyer. Wythe joined John Lewis in the practice of law, riding the circuit through largely rural Virginia, enduring the punishing experience of travel on the primitive colonial roads. In December 1747 he married Lewis's sister Ann, but she died a year later. Six years later he moved to Williamsburg, Virginia's capital and educational center. Wythe brought with him a superb and wide-ranging education as well as a reputation for great legal skill and integrity. Wythe would refuse any case or client if he had the slightest doubt about the righteousness of the cause. He represented Williamsburg in the House of Burgesses in 1754 and 1755 and again from 1758 to 1761. He also served as mayor of Williamsburg in 1768. Wythe's position as a political and social leader in the capital city was firmly established by his marriage in 1755 to Elizabeth Taliaferro, daughter of a prominent family.

Jefferson. Wythe occasionally took on young men for private instruction in the law. His most famous student was Thomas Jefferson, who began his studies in 1762. Jefferson joined Wythe's lively social world—a world inhabited by local luminaries like Royal Governor Francis Fauquier and mathematics professor William Small—and later recalled Wythe as his "earliest and best friend" of whom "I am indebted for first impressions which have had the most salutary influence on the course of my life."

Political Activity. When tensions began to emerge between the colonies and England, Wythe joined with those who asserted independence. In 1764 he wrote the *Remonstrance to the House of Commons* against the stamp tax. Wythe was a careful man not given to making quick decisions. In contrast to the more bombastic Patrick Henry, Wythe urged a calm, cautious approach. He was elected to the Continental Congress in 1775 and served through 1776. He signed the Declaration of Independence but then devoted himself to the reform and codification of the laws of his native Virginia.

A Loyal Son of Virginia. Wythe collaborated on a four-year project to collate the laws of the Virginia colony and participated with Jefferson and Edmund Pendleton in the process of revising the laws of the State of Virginia. As a member of a special committee to design a seal for Virginia, Wythe is believed to have been responsible for its design and motto: *Sic semper tyrannis* (Thus Ever to Tyrants). He was strongly against slavery, and in his will he provided for the liberation of his slaves.

Teacher of Law. Wythe's most lasting contribution to the law was his tenure as the first law professor at the College of William and Mary. Then-governor of Virginia Thomas Jefferson recommended him for the position in December 1779. Wythe's actual title was Professor of Law and Policy, a title reflecting the clear link between the practice of law and the maintenance of social order. Based on the William and Mary model, other law professorships were established at the College of Philadelphia and Brown College, Rhode Island, both in 1790; Columbia College, New York, in 1794; Yale College, Connecticut, in 1801; and Middlebury College, Con-

necticut, in 1806. Wythe referred to his classes as "a training ground for republican leadership." Wythe's curriculum for the study of law included Sir William Blackstone's *Commentaries on the Laws of England* (1765–1769) and Francis Bacon's *The Elements of the Common Lawes of England* (1630). Wythe's method of instruction was notable for two reasons. First, although he used Blackstone and Bacon as the basis of readings in the law, he did not require rigid acceptance of the old common law. Rather, Wythe encouraged a process of inquiry which became one of the early efforts in adapting the common law to American needs. Wythe's second innovation was the regular conduct of moot courts and mock legislatures to provide his students with practical experience. Through the use of mock legislatures Wythe helped his students realize the importance of lawmakers in the adaptation of laws to meet contemporary needs.

Judicial Review. Wythe resigned his position at William and Mary in 1790 and moved to Richmond, where he continued to serve as chancellor on the Virginia High Court of Chancery, a position he had held since 1778. Wythe was an early proponent of the idea of judicial review. In the case of *Commonwealth v. Caton* in 1782 Wythe declared that if the legislature acted improperly he would point "to the Constitution . . . and say to them, 'here is the limit of your authority; and hither shall you go no further.' " His tenure as a judge is perhaps best remembered for his publication of his legal opinions, a spirited challenge to the reasoning of the Court of Appeals which often overturned him.

Last Years. Elizabeth Taliaferro Wythe died in 1787; her only child with Wythe had died in infancy. The legal scholar was alone in his last years except for three devoted household servants whom he intended to free upon his death. The old teacher continued to educate himself and took up the study of Hebrew—his seventh language—at the age of eighty. Wythe's death was a tragic one. His grandnephew from his first marriage, George Wythe Sweeney, had run into financial difficulties. Greed compelled Sweeney to accelerate the time of his inheritance from Wythe and to eliminate the servants who were to share in his great-uncle's will. Sweeney poisoned Wythe and the household servants with arsenic-laced coffee. The youngest servant, Michael Brown, died quickly; the two others survived. Wythe lingered long enough to disinherit his murderer. He died on 8 June 1806 and was buried in Richmond.

Sources:

Joyce Blackburn, *George Wythe of Williamsburg* (New York: Harper & Row, 1975);

Dumas Malone, *Jefferson the Virginian* (Boston: Little, Brown, 1948).

PUBLICATIONS

Mathew Bacon, *A New Abridgment of the Law*, seven volumes (Philadelphia: Farrand & Nicholas, 1811)—this first American edition, taken from the sixth London edition and with considerable additions by editor Henry Gwillim, included American decisions along with English judgments;

Cesare Bonesana, Marchese di Beccaria, *An Essay on Crimes and Punishments: Translated from the Italian with a commentary by M. de Voltaire* (New York: Stephen Gould, 1809)—the first American edition of this treatise arguing for reform of penal laws and the abolition of capital punishment;

James Callender, *The Prospect Before Us* (Richmond: Printed by the author, 1800–1801)—an incendiary tract which leveled severe criticism upon President John Adams and the Supreme Court. Callender was tried and convicted of sedition on the strength of this publication;

Alexander Hamilton and others, *The Speeches at Full Length of Mr. Van Ness, Mr. Caines, the Attorney General, Mr. Harrison, and General Hamilton, in the great cause of the People against Harry Crosswell, on an indictment for libel on Thomas Jefferson, President of the United States* (New York: G. & R. Waite, 1804)—Jefferson opposed the Sedition Act, yet he encouraged state action against newspapers which criticized his administration. Hamilton and others took up the defense of those targeted by Jefferson and his allies;

James Iredell, *Answers to Mr. Mason's Objections* (New Bern, N.C.: Hodge & Willis, 1788)—Iredell's first significant publication was a resounding expression of support for the Constitution and was influential in the ratification debates;

Iredell, *The Case of Messrs. Brailsford and Others versus James Spaulding, in the Circuit Court for the District of Georgia* (Savannah: James & Nicholas Johnston, 1792)—opinions of Judges Iredell and Nathaniel Pendleton in a complicated inheritance case;

Iredell, *Laws of the State of North Carolina* (Edenton: Hodge & Willis, 1791)—a 712-page compilation of laws covering the period 1715 to 1790;

James Madison, *Memorial and Remonstrance against the General Assessment. . .* (Worcester, Mass.: Isaiah Thomas, 1796)—a reprinting of Madison's 1785 argument in favor of religious liberty;

John Marshall, *Life of George Washington* (Philadelphia: C. P. Wayne, 1804–1807)—working with family documents provided by Associate Justice Bushrod Washington, Chief Justice Marshall wrote the first significant biography of the first president;

Benjamin Rush, *Considerations on the injustice and impolicy of punishing murder by death* (Philadelphia: Mathew Carey, 1792)—Rush was a prime advocate in favor of the abolition of the death penalty;

Rush, *Considerations upon the present Test law of Pennsylvania* (Philadelphia: Hall & Sellers, 1784)—Pennsylvania required office-holders to take an oath to support the state constitution. Quakers were forbidden by their religion to take such oaths and were thus prohibited from holding public office;

Rush, *Report of an action for Libel brought by Benjamin Rush against William Cobbett, in the Supreme Court of Pennsylvania, December Term 1799, for certain defamatory publications in a newspaper entitled* Porcupine's Gazette (Philadelphia, 1800)—Rush successfully sued William Cobbett for libel. Cobbett had attacked Rush's tendency to bleed yellow fever victims;

St. George Tucker, *Blackstone's Commentaries; with notes of reference to the Constitution and laws of the federal government of the United States and of the Commonwealth of Virginia* (Philadelphia: W. Y. Birch & A. Small, 1803);

Tucker, *Cautionary hints to Congress respecting the sale of the Western Lands belonging to the United States* (Philadelphia: William. W. Woodward, 1795)—this tract was originally attributed to James Madison and others;

Tucker, *A dissertation on Slavery, with a proposal for the gradual abolition of it in Virginia* (Philadelphia: Mathew Carey, 1796)—this essay on the abolition of slavery was part of Tucker's lectures on law and police at the College of William and Mary;

Tucker, *A letter to a member of Congress respecting the Alien and Sedition Acts* (Virginia: Published by the author, 1799)—an anonymous pamphlet written and distributed by Tucker;

Tucker, *Reflections on the cession of Louisiana to the United States* (Washington, D.C.: Samuel Harrison Smith, 1803);

Tucker, *Reflections on the policy and necessity of encouraging the commerce of the citizens of the United States and of granting them exclusive privileges of trade* (New York: Samuel & John Loudon, 1786);

James Wilson, *The Works of the Honourable James Wilson, L.L.D.*, three volumes (Philadelphia: Lorenzo Press printed for Bronson and Chauncey, 1804)—the famous law lectures of Associate Justice James Wilson were published after his death;

George Wythe, *Decisions on Cases in Virginia by the high Court of Chancery with remarks upon those decrees by the high Court of Appeals, 1788–1795* (Richmond: Thomas Nicholson, 1795)—Wythe published this in order to review and criticize the Court of Appeals which had reversed some of his own chancery opinions.

C H A P T E R   E I G H T

LIFESTYLES, SOCIAL TRENDS, AND FASHION

by ROBERT BELLINGER

CONTENTS

Sidebars and tables are listed in italics.

1783

- Noah Webster's *A Grammatical Institute, of the English Language* is published. It standardizes American orthography and helps make pronunciation more uniform.

Jan.   Street commissioners in Philadelphia recommend that farmers from outlying areas clean the city's streets in exchange for manure they will gather in the process; the experiment is a complete failure.

13 May   Continental army officers led by Henry Knox form the Society of Cincinnati to be a hereditary organization of Revolutionary War soldiers; George Washington becomes the first president.

1784

- The first bale of American cotton reaches Great Britain.

- An economic depression begins in the United States.

- Cajun cooking is established in Louisiana by Acadians who combine their recipes with those of local "injuns."

1785

- The typical American male wears "a pea-green coat, white vest, nankeen small clothes, white silk stockings, and pumps fastened with silver buckles which covered at least half the foot from instep to toe."

- The dollar becomes the basic monetary unit of the United States. The decimal system is devised by Thomas Jefferson.

1786

- The Tammany Society, or Columbian Order of New York City, is formed; this patriotic society is incorporated three years later.

- Shays's Rebellion begins in Massachusetts.

- The first American golf club is formed at Charleston's Green near Charleston, South Carolina, by local clergyman Henry Purcell.

1787

- The Free African Society is founded in Philadelphia.

1788

- Demonstrations occur in New York City protesting the activities of grave robbers.

- The first-known American advertisement for tobacco appears.

- The first bourbon whiskey is distilled by Baptist minister Elijah Craig in Kentucky. It is so refined that it becomes more popular than rum or brandy.

1789

- The Park Theater in New York City asks its male patrons to refrain from smoking cigars during performances because it is an "offensive practice to Ladies, and dangerous to the House."

26 Nov. Thanksgiving Day is celebrated for the first time as a national holiday. President George Washington, on the recommendation of Congress, declares it a day of thanksgiving for the Constitution.

25 Dec. Universalists in Boston hold special services on Christmas Day, which is not recognized as a religious holiday in Puritan New England.

1790

- The widely practiced custom of bundling, prevalent in colonial New England and Pennsylvania, begins to die out. (Bundling occurs when courting couples go to bed together, but with all their clothes on. The couple is sometimes separated by a board, or the woman's ankles are tied together.) Better heating and the construction of sturdier houses alleviate the need for this practice in the cold northern climates.

1791

- The first Bank of the United States is created.

1792

- Eli Whitney invents the cotton gin and files for a patent the next year.

- The destruction of American forests is spurred by the demand for pearl ash used in baking.

1793

- A fugitive slave act is passed by Congress.

16 Oct. A New York mob destroys the home of Mother Carey, the keeper of a local brothel.

1794

- After more than one hundred years the powdering of men's hair goes out of style. However, men's hair is still worn in a queue tied with a black ribbon.

1795

4 May A Philadelphia ordinance forbids wooden buildings south of Tenth Street.

June A bathhouse opens in Philadelphia, charging one dollar for three baths.

3 June Mayor Matthew Clarkson of Philadelphia issues a proclamation decrying the bad conduct and disorderliness of domestic servants and apprentices.

14 June A fire destroys 250 buildings in Charleston, South Carolina; three hundred families are left homeless.

1796

- Amelia Simmons publishes the first American cookbook to include Native American recipes.

- Gilbert Stuart paints George Washington.

- A Boston dispensary is founded to provide medical care for the poor in their homes and in clinics.

- The Christmas menu from Mount Vernon shows that George and Martha Washington served thirty-four dishes and wines.

6 Feb. A parade occurs in Philadelphia celebrating Gen. Anthony Wayne's victory over the Miami Indians.

1797

- Philadelphia is the first American city to develop a centralized water distribution system. Three underground tunnels pump water from the Schuylkill River and distribute it throughout the city; a reserve of water is stored in a tower in the center of town.

1798

1 Nov. Fire destroys all but twelve houses in Wilmington, North Carolina.

1799

2 Apr. The New York State legislature charters the Manhattan Company to provide water to the city of New York.

14 Dec. George Washington dies.

18 Dec. Fire in Philadelphia destroys Oeller's Hotel, one of the country's most elegant inns.

26 Dec. During his funeral oration before Congress, Henry Lee states that Washington was "First in war, first in peace, first in the hearts of his countrymen."

1800

- Four-tined forks come into use in American homes. Earlier, two- and three-tined forks had been customary.

- The Sheraton and Directoire styles of furniture, classical yet simple in design, appeal strongly to public tastes. Duncan Phyfe of New York City turns out many fine examples.

- Gabriel's Insurrection inspires Virginians to support plans for black immigration to Africa.

- Middlebury College is founded at Middlebury, Vermont.

- The Library of Congress is established with a $50,000 appropriation to purchase nine hundred books and maps that arrive from London in eleven trunks.

- *A History of the Life and Death, Virtues, and Exploits of General George Washington* by Mason Locke Weems is published.

- Washington, D.C., replaces New York City as the United States capital, and Congress convenes there for the first time. The city has 2,464 residents and 623 slaves.

- William Young of Philadelphia invents right and left shoes.

- Shoe polish is invented.

1 Jan. Two feet of snow falls in Savannah, Georgia.

Mar. Charleston citizens offer a $500 reward for the identification of arsonists who had tried to destroy the city.

1801

- The University of South Carolina is founded at Columbia, South Carolina.

- John "Johnny Appleseed" Chapman, age twenty-six, arrives in the Ohio Valley from Leominster, Massachusetts, with seeds from Philadelphia cider presses that will make the valley a rich source of apples.

1802

- In Saratoga Springs, New York, Gideon Putnam opens the Union Hotel; what distinguishes it as a hotel is its emphasis on lodging and services rather than food and drink.

- The Willard Patent Timepiece is patented by clock maker Samuel Willard, age forty-nine, of Roxbury, Massachusetts; it will become known as the "banjo clock."

- The United States Military Academy is founded at West Point, New York.

6 Mar. A fire destroys Nassau Hall at Princeton College.

1803

- The Louisiana Purchase doubles the size of the United States and extends the western border to the Rocky Mountains.

- Ohio is admitted to the Union as the seventeenth state.

- South Carolina resumes importing slaves after the cotton gin boosts the demand for field hands. Cotton passes tobacco as the leading United States export crop for the first time.

- The first ice refrigerator (icebox) is patented by Maryland farmer Thomas Moore; it will be in common use by 1838.

1804

- The Empire style in furniture and house furnishings, imported from Napoleonic France, becomes popular in the United States. Unlike the Classical style, with its straight lines and minimal carving, Empire furniture is heavier and more massive. Combinations of marble and brass and ormolu and wood are common. Carvings include animal forms such as claw feet and eagle heads, and heavy textiles are used in the upholstery.

- Alexander Hamilton is killed in a duel with Aaron Burr.

- The Lewis and Clark expedition to explore the Louisiana Purchase Territory begins.

- Ohio University is founded at Athens, Ohio.

- Capt. John Chester's schooner brings the first shipment of bananas to arrive in New York.

1805

- Tenskwatawa, called "the Open Door" or "the Prophet" by whites, becomes a leader among the Shawnee in the Ohio River Valley.

- Michigan is made a territory separate from the Indiana Territory, and Detroit becomes its capital.

- The District of Louisiana is made from the Louisiana Purchase territory, and its capital is at Saint Louis.

9 Aug.   Zebulon Pike's party leaves Saint Louis to explore the upper Mississippi River.

8 Dec.   Lewis and Clark build Fort Clatsop on the Columbia River.

1806

23 Mar.   The Lewis and Clark expedition begins its return journey up the Columbia River.

16 June   A total eclipse of the sun is visible across North America.

15 July   Zebulon Pike sets out to explore the sources of the Arkansas River.

Nov.   Pike discovers Pikes Peak in present-day Colorado.

1807

- Foreign visitors are astounded by the amount of greasy food consumed by Americans and the manner in which they eat it. A French count notes that breakfast typically includes fish, steak, ham, sausage, salt beef, and bread. He complains that "the whole day passes in heaping indigestions on one another."

- The University of Maryland is founded outside of Baltimore.

1808

- The importation of slaves into the United States is banned.

- Tecumseh and Tenskwatawa organize Native American resistance to the expansion of white settlers.

30 Oct.   The women of Marblehead, Massachusetts, tar and feather a ship captain they believe sailed away from a sinking ship because he feared losing his own vessel.

1809

- The territory of Illinois is created from the Indiana Territory.

1810

- A flight of passenger pigeons 250 miles long is sighted over Kentucky. The flock is estimated to contain two billion birds.

1811

- The New York City municipal council approves a plan for laying out streets in a grid pattern.

- A series of earthquakes centered near New Madrid, Missouri, shakes the Mississippi and Ohio River valleys.

Jan. Four hundred slaves revolt in Louisiana, kill a plantation owner's son, and march on New Orleans. Armed planters and federal soldiers put down the insurrection after killing seventy-five of the slaves.

27 Dec. A fire in a Richmond, Virginia, theater kills sixty-two people, including the governor and his wife.

1812

- Louisiana is admitted to the Union as the eighteenth state.

1813

7 Sept. "Uncle Sam" is used to designate the United States for the first time in an editorial published in the *Troy* (New York) *Post.*

1814

- "The Star Spangled Banner" by Francis Scott Key is published in the *Baltimore American* a week after the bombardment of Fort McHenry.

OVERVIEW

Distinct Culture. At the end of the Revolutionary War the United States became an independent political state, but the diverse population was hardly unified. The inhabitants were of different races and ethnicities and had no official religion or common culture. By the end of the War of 1812 the United States had begun to live up to its name. Americans were starting to develop a cultural identity that drew upon their varied heritages and assimilated them into a national character.

Statistics. The federal census of 1790 recorded the population as 3,929,214 and the land area of the country as 867,980 square miles. Men and women of British descent were the single largest group of Americans, representing 50 percent of the entire population in the original states; the rest included Africans, Germans, Dutch, French, and Native Americans. The United States at this time was predominantly rural, with only one in twenty Americans living in a city or town of more than 2,500 people. In fact, as late as 1840 only one in nine Americans lived in urban settings. Federal censuses between 1790 and 1820 reveal that an average of six people lived in each free American household. This figure, large not only by today's standards but also by those of contemporary Europe, indicated a growing country. By 1820 the American population had jumped to 9,638,453 and the country's land area to 1,753,588 square miles.

American Farmer. The English traveler Frances Trollope noted that the American people were "a busy, bustling, industrious population." Merchants and artisans played an important part in the economy, but "farming absorbed society," according to Samuel Goodrich of Connecticut. In 1800 four-fifths of all families farmed the land for themselves or others. The rhythms of farm work—plowing, planting, cultivation, and harvest—occupied the daily lives of most people. Tobacco, rice, wheat, and cotton were common crops, but the most important was corn. Across the nation families, white and black, grew corn, a staple in the diets of both people and livestock.

Ideas of Revolution. Between 1783 and 1815 Americans developed a profound sense of their virtue as a people. Not only did they successfully win their independence in 1783, but they also managed to reiterate their national integrity by defeating the British in the War of 1812. Patriotic zeal during this period helped bring the nation's first holidays and celebrations into existence, including Independence Day, Washington's Birthday, Thanksgiving Day, and Columbus Day. Democratic-Republican societies also arose to celebrate republicanism at home and abroad. Nevertheless, American notions about challenging authority were affected in the 1790s by the French and Haitian revolutions. The American spirit in the early days of the Republic was marked by consolidation, not revolution. Many Americans, particularly the New England Federalists, were horrified by the overthrow of the French monarchy in 1789 and the execution of the king and queen four years later. Southern slaveholders saw the 1791 insurrection in Haiti as an object lesson in slave revolt.

Frontiers and Freedom. Americans perceived freedom as a release from oppressive religious, political, and economic constraints. The vast frontier offered what seemed to be limitless freedom, though it was often seized at the expense of Native Americans. Westward expansion forcefully demonstrated American vision, energy, resourcefulness, and determination. It also shaped American culture as pioneers found themselves transformed by the forces of survival. Such legendary figures as Davy Crockett and Daniel Boone became national heroes because they exemplified the self-reliance that Americans came to value above all other qualities.

TOPICS IN THE NEWS

COLLECTING MAPLE SUGAR

Native Americans. Maple sugar was an important part of the Native American diet in the early spring. In late February, the "Sap Moon" in the Algonquian calender, the maple sugar season began. At this time the Indians moved to the sugar bush camps so they could be close to the maple grove. In order to keep the grove productive, the Indians maintained it by removing brush, girdling and burning old trees, and taking care of replacement saplings.

Festive Occasion. The work of maple sugaring was shared by men and women; it was one of the few times during the year that their work was integrated. The men cut wood for fires to heat the stones and kettles, and they hunted and fished for the camp. The women had the job of actually tapping the trees, which they did by cutting horizontal gashes in the tree three to four feet above the ground. They inserted cedar spiles at a downward angle, which allowed the sap to drip into elm- or birch-bark buckets. The sap was poured into wooden troughs (eventually replaced by metal pots), where it was boiled by placing hot stones into it. As it boiled it was stirred until granulation occurred. The sugar was stored in birch-bark bags, called *mococks*. Sugar making was also a festive social affair since it marked the end of winter. John James Audubon came upon a gathering in the sugar bush as he was pursuing birds through Kentucky in 1810. He wrote:

> As I approached it I observed forms of different kinds moving to and fro before [the glow of the fire], like specters; and ere long, bursts of laughter, shouts and songs apprized me of some merry-making. I thought at first that I had probably stumbled upon a camp meeting; but I soon perceived that the mirth proceeded from a band of sugar-makers. . . . At times, neighboring families join, and enjoy the labor as if it were a pastime, remaining out day and night for several weeks; for the troughs and kettles must be attended to from the moment when they are first put in requisition until the sugar is produced. The men and boys perform the most laborious part of the business, but the women and girls are not less busy.

Uses. While the sugar was being made, children loved to pour the boiling sap onto the snow to cool it into a chewy candy. Indians drank partially-rendered sap. But there were many more uses for the maple sugar than as a treat. Women used maple molasses to sweeten vegetables, fish, and meat, and they also mixed it with bear grease to store and use for basting meats. As sugar making came at the end of the winter when food stores were low, maple sugar was poured over parched corn, which was often the principal food until the spring crops became available.

Frontier. Maple sugar was also important to frontier farmers. In the early nineteenth century loaves of cane sugar were expensive for farmers who had little cash, so they used locally produced maple sugar, or wild honey, as a sweetener. They also used it to preserve sour fruits, such as crab apples and wild plums, and to cure tobacco leaves in order to produce sweet plugs. Some families wrapped the maple sugar in corn shucks and sold it at the rate of seven to thirteen cents per pound. In some sections of the frontier it was considered legal tender in trade, as was alcohol.

Source:

John Mack Faragher, *Sugar Creek, Life on the Illinois Prairie* (New Haven, Conn.: Yale University Press, 1986).

CORN SHUCKIN' ON THE PLANTATION

Ritual. Corn was a truly American crop, and the task of husking, or "shuckin'," the corn became a harvest ritual throughout the nation. In addition to consuming corn as meal or hominy, American farmers used it to feed their hogs and to make liquor. The process of taking the corn from the stalks and piling it in the yard or barn began in early November. Sometime between then and the middle of December the husk had to be removed from the corn. This was a time when most of the farm work was completed and laborers were fairly idle, so husking was a good reason for a gathering. It was called an "affair of mutual assistance" since the task was rarely done by one family. But even though corn shuckin' was performed throughout the United States, there were variations in the way it was organized and practiced. These variations were primarily regional, but other factors such as wealth also had an influence.

Regional Differences. In the western territories and the upper South, husking was male dominated and com-

A New England cornhusking, early 1800s (Museum of Fine Arts, Boston)

petitive. In these regions only men and boys husked while women prepared the food. The husking usually took place on a moonlit night. It began after two young men, nominated as captains, chose their teams and set up on opposite sides of a four-foot-high pile of corn. The side that shucked the most corn won. Liquor was provided throughout the evening but particularly after the work was completed. When the husking was done, the food was served, and "by midnight the sober were found assisting the drunken home." In the coastal regions of the South and New England corn shuckin' took on a different style. Men and women, and sometimes children, sat alternately in a circle around the pile of corn and husked together. Drink was usually a part of the ritual for men, but the emphasis in these regions was on familial relationships rather than competition.

Plantation South. In the Deep South corn shuckin' was an elaborate celebration that entwined many different activities. On a plantation the owner initiated the event by sending out word that there was going to be a corn shuckin'. As evening approached, slaves from neighboring plantations began to arrive singing. Whites, invited to watch the activities, also gathered on the portico with the planter and his family. When the slaves were gathered in the yard, which was lit by burning pine knots, the planter addressed them, in some instances even giving a formal speech to initiate the festivities.

Choosing Sides. Teams were formed and captains selected. Being chosen captain was a high honor, not only a recognition of his speed and skill as a shucker but a mark of his leadership abilities. A captain also had to be able to sing. The captains were given badges and paraded around the yard, accepting honors from slaves and whites alike. After the captains' parade each team positioned itself on one side of a pile of corn and the shuckin' began.

Singing. As the two sides competed, the captains, often seated atop the pile, sang to keep their teams moving and working together. The captain sang a verse and the team gave a response. A typical song went as follows:

Massa's [slaves] am slick and fat,
Oh! Oh! Oh!
Shine just like a new beaver hat,
Oh! Oh! Oh!
Turn out here and shuck dis corn,
Oh!Oh!Oh!
Biggest pile o' corn seen since I was born,
Oh! Oh! Oh!
Jones's [slaves] am lean and po'
Oh! Oh! Oh
Don't know whether dey got 'nough to eat or no,
Oh! Oh! Oh
Turn out here and shuck dis corn,
Oh!Oh!Oh!
Biggest pile o' corn seen since I was born,
Oh! Oh! Oh!

The captain had songs to keep the pace going or speed it up, to encourage the team, or to entertain and lighten the work.

"Chairing." When the shuckin' was over and the winning side was recognized, the host was sought out for a ride around the yard on a chair that was hoisted above the shoulders of the slaves. Since the shuckin' usually ended late at night, it was sometimes necessary to get the host up out of bed for the "chairing." After the chairing the master called for food to be served. The meal added to the festive quality of the event. It was not only the quantity of the food and drink, which alone was special for the slave, but also the variety of dishes prepared. One description listed: "Fresh meats, chicken-pie, ham, cold turkey, fried chicken, hot coffee, and several kinds of plate pies." Another recorded: "loaf, biscuits, ham, pork, chicken pie, pumpkin custard, sweet cakes, apple pie, grape pie, coffee, sweet milk, buttermilk, preserves, in short a rich feast of everything yielded by the farm." During the dinner one of the slaves, usually a captain or a particularly good speaker, acted as a master of ceremonies, commenting on the evening and toasting the host and hostess.

The Dance. When the dinner was completed, the tables were cleared away, the fiddler was called for, and the dance began. Like the corn shuckin', the dance took place in a circular pattern, or ring, on a wooden platform dance floor. The fiddler was accompanied by hand clapping; finger snapping; patting of the arms, legs, or chest; and the rhythmic sound of feet dancing on the boards. A variety of dance steps were performed to show the skill of the dancer. The dance was not reserved for any particular age group, and all of the slaves, young and old, joined in. Sometimes there were contests between dancers that continued until one gave up. The celebrations continued for hours, sometimes lasting until daybreak, at which time the slaves returned to their respective homes.

Sources:

Roger D. Abrahams, *Singing The Master, The Emergence of African American Culture in the Plantation South* (New York: Pantheon, 1992);

Jack Larkin, *The Reshaping of Every Day Life, 1790–1840* (New York: Harper & Row, 1988).

DEMOCRAT-REPUBLICAN SOCIETIES

Keeping Democracy Alive. Democrat-Republican societies were organized groups of American citizens who came together in the 1790s to reignite the "fires of '76." They wanted to keep people involved in politics to insure that the government would continue to be democratic. The societies existed during the 1790s and were concerned with both domestic and foreign affairs. Philip Freneau first wrote about the need for these societies in the *National Gazette*, which he published from October 1791 to October 1793. He challenged the idea that the government was always right, insisting that informed public opinion was needed to keep the government from becoming tyrannical. Ignoring or stifling public opinion was the result of monarchical thought and a prelude to tyranny. Freneau advocated the formation of clubs to maintain popular interest in government and to let people know when the government encroached on their rights.

Formation. The groups that began to form in the spring of 1793 supported the Constitution and the Bill of Rights but felt that Alexander Hamilton and the Federalists were trying to make the government an agency for the wealthy. This attitude was reflected by Chief Justice John Jay, who reportedly said, "those who own the country ought to govern it." In contrast the people who formed the Democrat-Republican societies believed that "it must be mechanics and farmers, or the poorer class of people that must support the freedom of America." They also disliked the way Hamilton and the Federalists seemed to accept English interference with American trade and with Americans moving into the western territories.

France and Liberty. Democratic enthusiasm was rekindled by the French Revolution. As the French monarchy fell Americans renewed their commitments to a democratic government. The French Revolution also gave energy to other antimonarchical movements in Europe. "Revolution societies" sprouted up in England, Ireland, Scotland, Germany, and France, and these societies corresponded with each other. One such immigrant society, the German Republican Society of Philadelphia, had its first meeting in March 1793. They believed that citizens were responsible for assisting in republican government by direct participation and by being alert to errors the government made. It was only through constant action that liberty would be kept alive. They believed that political societies could accomplish this through education, observation, and public expression of opinions.

Democratic Society of Pennsylvania. The largest and most influential society, the Democratic Society of Pennsylvania, was founded in the summer of 1793. It issued a circular letter calling on America to "erect the temple of LIBERTY on the ruins of *palaces and thrones*." It urged citizens to form societies and warned that if European nations succeeded in suppressing the French Revolution, Europe's monarchs would next turn their attention to the United States. Like other societies, the

Fourth of July celebration in Philadelphia, 1812

Pennsylvania group focused on the right of freedom of speech, press, and assembly. Specifically, it wanted the right to criticize the government and to demand explanations for public acts.

Growth. The Democrat-Republican societies did not have a national network, but they spread from Massachusetts to Georgia. By the end of 1793 nine more societies were founded; twenty-three were founded in 1794, three more in 1795, one in 1797, and three in 1798. Between 1793 and 1800 more than forty Democrat-Republican societies were established. Some were large, such as the Democratic Society of Pennsylvania, which had 315 members, or the Charleston society, with 114 members, but on average most attracted 20 to 25 members.

Membership. Most members were craftsmen and mechanics, but there were also merchants, investors, doctors, and editors. Most had fought in the Revolutionary War, and many had been in the Sons of Liberty. Quite a few of the members were also leaders in their communities. Publishers were heavily represented and were instrumental in making the societies popular. The southern societies had slaveholders as members, and the western groups had wealthy landowners and speculators. It is not clear if African Americans were able to become members of the societies, although there is evidence that a few attended some meetings. Members followed the custom of the French Revolution and referred to one another as "citizen" and to their officers as "citizen presidents." People joined the Democratic-Republican societies out of a common passion for political liberty and republican government, but they often disagreed about specific policies a free government should adopt. The societies tended to avoid potentially divisive issues. The wide range of interests represented in the societies affected the positions members took on all issues. Because slaveholders and abolitionists could sometimes be found in the same society, an antislavery stand could not be maintained without disrupting unity. While the societies passed many resolutions in support of the French Revolution, not one resolution passed in support of the Haitian Revolution.

Political Issues. The societies were concerned with several specific issues. They agitated against England for continuing to hold forts in the West and for acts of "piracy" against American trade and against Spain for closing the Mississippi River to American merchants. They protested the excise tax on whiskey, pushed for a uniform currency, and agitated for adequate representation for frontier areas. In South Carolina they opposed Jay's nomination as envoy to England, as well as the treaty he negotiated in 1794. Moreover, Democratic-Republican societies were against secret sessions of Congress and state legislatures.

Meetings and Holidays. The societies usually met monthly, but during elections or political crises they met

---

BECOMING AMERICANS

Sir Augustus John Foster, Baronet, a twenty-five-year-old English nobleman, visited the United States during the Jefferson administration and later just before the War of 1812. Years afterward he published his travel journals, hoping to give a balanced picture of American life. Though he did not approve of many American institutions, he understood why the United States was becoming so much different than Europe.

Even our most liberal travelers are said to have found the people too democratic. And yet they are as they were known to be and necessarily must be for ages to come. For the fact is that the well educated and well informed in the United States are few compared to the mass, and do not throw themselves into the arms of every grumbling emigrant even when he comes with his pockets full of money from England, so that the latter perhaps gets in among a set of pseudo-Americans who are greater brawlers than himself. This may easily happen, when one considers that at least four or five millions of the whole population must be new to the country they call theirs, emigrants from other states, Europeans or sons of Europeans, and that one settler being as strange as another in the back districts there is nothing to prevent an Irishman or German, a fiery red-hot zealot, from taking the lead in all discussions, browbeating, and giving a tone to the rest. To this even the state of Pennsylvania, tho' one of the oldest, was for a great while and is still from its vast extent peculiarly exposed, having long been the rendevous, on account of its rich soil. . . . Of all European emigrants, more especially Germans, who were attracted by the . . . Hessian soldiers that remained after the war and flocked there from the countries of the Rhine as well as from Hesse-Cassel. A German who has just arrived fresh and set free from serving barons or counts is like a great cart horse turned loose upon the plain, kicking and snorting in all directions. They revel in their new state and appear to be delighted with rolling about in the mire of democracy.

Source: Augustus John Foster, *Jeffersonian America: Notes on the United States of America Collected in the Years 1805–6–7 and 11–12*, edited by Richard Beale Davis (San Marino, Cal.: Huntington Library, 1954).

---

more regularly. They participated in local elections and organized public celebrations, particularly the Fourth of July, which they honored with speeches and toasts. The societies also observed Bastille Day on 14 July, commemorating the beginning of the French Revolution. The greatest efforts of the popular societies were toward creating public discussions. They composed, adopted, and issued circulars, memorials, resolutions, and addresses to the people. They also wrote complaints to the president and Congress.

Education. The Democrat-Republican societies were extremely interested in establishing a free public school system, which they felt was essential to the future of in-

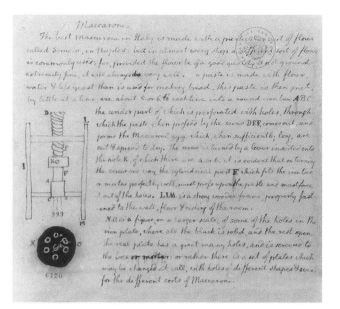

Thomas Jefferson's notes on making "maccaroni," written while he was minister to France in the 1780s

dependence and republicanism. They were vigorous supporters of the press as a key to freedom. Newspapers proliferated with the intense political discussions the societies encouraged. The number of American papers doubled to two hundred between 1790 and 1800. In 1800 there were five million copies of papers printed for a population of 5,308,483.

Foreign Impact. The French Revolution and the crisis over foreign policy in the mid 1790s most energized the Democratic-Republicans. Public support in America had begun to turn away from the French Revolution after the Paris massacres of September 1792. When the Whiskey Rebellion occurred in the summer of 1794, the Federalists blamed Democratic-Republican societies for the rebellion and then pointed to the frontier disorder as a symptom of revolutionary chaos and a beginning of an American reign of terror. President George Washington, in his annual message, publicly blamed the rebellion on "certain self-created societies." The Senate agreed with Washington that the societies had increased the severity of the rebellion and that the government was right in using force to handle it. On the other hand, the House of Representatives praised the virtuous and informed citizens. While the critical attacks took away some of their support, it was not the opposition of the president or the Senate that hurt the societies most.

Declining Influence. The failed campaign against Jay's Treaty in 1795 marked the decline of the societies. By 1796 the Democratic Society of Pennsylvania, once the largest society, no longer existed. The New York group and others remained active until 1799, and some new societies formed during the crisis years of 1798–1800. With Jefferson's election to the presidency the fears that motivated the societies abated. Nevertheless, former members stayed active in politics and continued to influence government. Jefferson appointed some former society members to state-level positions.

Source:

Philip S. Foner, *The Democratic-Republican Societies, 1790–1800* (Westport, Conn.: Greenwood Press, 1976).

FOOD IN AMERICA

Eating Habits. American eating habits, which were quite different than those of Europe, captured the attention of European visitors to the United States during the early years of the republic. Most visitors made note of the eating practices they observed in their journals, and some visitors, by publishing their observations, presented them to a wider audience. They were interested not only in the type and quantity of the food, but also in the way it was prepared, served, and eaten.

Ashe. One description of American dining habits during this period comes from Englishman Thomas Ashe, who in 1806, in a story of a fictitious journey to America, wrote about dinner in a Kentucky cabin.

> The dinner consisted of a large piece of salt bacon, a dish of hominy, and a tureen of squirrel broth. I dined entirely on the last dish, which I found incomparably good, and the meat equal to the most delicate chicken. The Kentuckian ate nothing but bacon, which indeed is the favorite diet of all the inhabitants of the State, and drank nothing but whiskey, which soon made him more than two-thirds drunk. In this last practice he is also supported by the public habit. In a country then, where bacon and spirits form the favorite summer repast, it can-

AN AMERICAN BARBECUE

Sir Augustus John Foster, a traveling English nobleman, reported on a visit to the home of President Thomas Jefferson at Monticello:

At Monticello I was present at some of the national sports and games, of which there are more in Virginia than in any other state I have visited. Horse racing is carried very far and gives rise to a great deal of gambling. Cock-fighting is on the decline, but still exists here and there. Quoits and nine-pins are much in fashion. And as to the festivities they are, especially the barbecues, most numerously attended on the Atlantic side of the Blue Ridge. A barbecue was originally a meeting in the woods to partake of a pig roasted whole. A pit was dug in the ground, firs placed in it, and a large pig supported on four stakes was put over the fire. There is always a dance afterwards, and I was told that at some places these meetings are exceedingly numerous, even the better sort of people attending them. Barbecues are now oftener held at a tavern and are very frequent in the summer. People think nothing of going ten or twelve miles to one.

Source: Augustus John Foster, *Jeffersonian America: Notes on the United States of America Collected in the Years 1805-6-7 and 11-12*, edited by Richard Beale Davis (San Marino, Cal.: Huntington Library, 1954).

A buckskin hunting shirt that reportedly belonged to Daniel Boone (Filson Club, Louisville)

not be just to attribute entirely the causes of infirmity to the climate. No people on earth live with less regard to regimen. They eat salt meat three times a day, seldom or never have any vegetables, and drink ardent spirits from morning till night. They have not only an aversion to fresh meat, but a vulgar prejudice that it is unwholesome. The truth is, their stomachs are depraved by burning liquors, and they have no appetite for anything but what is high-flavored and strongly impregnated by salt.

Vol-ney. Ashe was correct in saying that salted meat was a staple of the diet in Kentucky, but he clearly did not understand why. In the country fresh meat, other than game or poultry, was not always available. Only the wealthy could afford fresh meat regularly. However, it was possible for most people to raise hogs because they were inexpensive, and the most effective way to preserve the meat after slaughter was by salting. Also, contrary to what Ashe said, vegetables were also a part of the diet, though corn was the most commonly used vegetable. A more reliable account of American eating habits was provided by Constantin-François Chasseboeuf, Comte de Vol-ney:

I will venture to say that if a prize were proposed for the scheme of a regimen most calculated to injure the stomach, the teeth, and the health in general, no better could

be invented than that of the Americans. In the morning at breakfast they deluge their stomachs with a quart of hot water, impregnated with tea, or so slightly with coffee that it is mere colored water; and they swallow, almost without chewing, hot bread, half baked, toast soaked in butter, cheese of the fattest kind, slices of salt or hung beef, ham, etc., all which are nearly insoluble. At dinner they have boiled pastes under the name of puddings, and the fattest are esteemed the most delicious; all their sauces, even for roast beef, are melted butter; their turnips and potatoes swim in hog's lard, butter, or fat; under the name of pie or pumpkin, their pastry is nothing but a greasy paste, never sufficiently baked. To digest these viscous substances they take tea almost instantly after dinner, making it so strong that it is absolutely bitter to the taste, in which state it affects the nerves so powerfully that even the English find it brings on a more obstinate restlessness than coffee. Supper again introduces salt meats or oysters. As Chastellux says, the whole day passes in heaping indigestions on one another; and to give tone to the poor, relaxed, and wearied stomach, they drink Madeira, rum, French brandy, gin, or malt spirits, which complete the ruin of the nervous system.

Sources:
Henry Adams, *History of the United States during the First Administration of Thomas Jefferson*, volume 1 (Cambridge, Mass.: Privately printed, 1884);

Thomas Ashe, *Travels in America, 1806* (London: R. Phillips, 1808).

THE FRONTIER

Image. The expeditions of Meriwether Lewis and William Clark (1804–1806) and Zebulon Pike (1805–1807) through the vast region west of the Mississippi River illustrated the strong appeal of the frontier upon the American conscience. Some of the national legends and heroes created at this time, such as š []Appleseed, JohnnyJohnny Appleseed and Daniel Boone, came out of the frontier. They took part in bringing "civilization" to the region and represented the common man's longings, desires, and ideals. But the frontier also brought out conflicting ideas about society. On the one hand, there was an envy of the frontier and the freedom it represented; this image encouraged settlement. On the other hand, there was a feeling that the frontier needed to be civilized. As a result missionary societies went into the new territories to minister to the heathens.

Culture. Both white American and Indian hunters needed meat to feed their families and hides to clothe them. They also needed hides and furs to trade. The weapon preferred for use by both Indians and whites was the American long rifle. It was "a well-balanced, small caliber weapon" that was "accurate at distances of up to two hundred yards." Developed by German gunsmiths in southeastern Pennsylvania during the early eighteenth century, it became the preferred firearm of backwoodsmen. By the end of the eighteenth century Indians hunted with bows and arrows only when they could not get American or European weapons and ammunition. But even though American or European weapons were used, the hunting techniques were still Indian. Most European emigrants had little or no experience in stalking wild game since in Europe hunting was reserved for the nobility. They had to rely on Native American skills in knowledge in this regard.

Frontier Dress. Hunters on the frontier dressed in a combination of Indian and European styles. One contemporary observed:

> Moccasins were of deerskin but made and patched with European awls. The hunting shirt was a loose frock that reached halfway down the thighs and overlapped by as much as a foot or more in the front, sometimes fitted with a fringed cape used to cover the head. It was generally made of linsey or linen, sometimes of dressed deerskin, but this material had the disadvantage of being cold and uncomfortable in wet weather. In the front folds of the shirt hunters kept small rations of provisions. From the leather belt that pulled the shirt tight, they hung

THE INDIAN STORY OF SACAGAWEA

In the 1930s a teacher on the Wind River Reservation, Wyoming, assigned her students to record a story from an elderly person when she discovered that her students knew little about the oral traditions of their people. One of the stories recorded was the following about Sacagawea:

Sacajawea was a Shoshone girl who lived with her people in the valleys of the Rocky Mountains. Out planting one day, she and her playmates heard a war-whoop. They started to run to their teepees. Sacajawea tripped and fell, and the enemy reached her.

Sacajawea was a beautiful girl. A warrior picked her up and threw her on his horse. He rode off and carried her to his own tribe, the Minnetarees.

She lived there for many moons. Traders came there to get beaver skins in exchange for gaudy knick-knacks. Charbonneau was one of the traders. One time he saw Sacajawea.

"Who is she?" he asked the chief.

"A Shoshone captive," answered the chief. "And she eats too much."

The Frenchman wanted to buy her, but the chief said, "We will gamble for her."

Charbonneau won. He made Sacajawea his slave, but her life was no harder than it had been with the Minnetarees. Later she became his wife.

When Lewis and Clark arrived at the Mandan villages, Charbonneau and Sacajawea were there. They needed a new interpreter. So they hired Charbonneau. He took with him Sacajawea and their very young son, Baptiste.

Lewis and Clark thought that Sacajawea could help them when they reached the Shoshones. When food was scarce, she found roots and berries that were good to eat. One time she saved the records and the medicines when the boat almost overturned.

When they reached the Shoshone country, she recognized her own people. She sucked her fingers, which was a sign of joy. She and one of the Shoshone girls threw their arms around each other. This was one of her playmates when they were captured.

When Chief Cameahwait came out of his teepee, Sacajawea rushed up to him and threw her arms about him. He was her brother. He and his father had pursued the Minnetarees but had been unable to overtake them. He told her that her sister had died a short time before. So Sacajawea adopted her sisters little boy.

The Shoshones sold horses to Lewis and Clark.

Many years later, Sacajawea returned to her people and settled in the Wind River Valley. She was cared for by Bazil. She lived to be very old.

Source: Ella E. Clark and Margot Edmonds, *Sacagawea of the Lewis and Clark Expedition* (Berkeley: University of California Press, 1979).

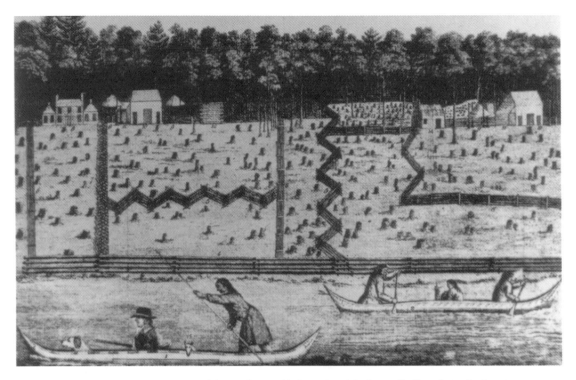

Illustration of a newly cleared farm, circa 1790 (from Patrick Campell, *Travels in the Interior Inhabited Parts of North America,* 1793)

their powder horns, bullet pouch, knife, and tomahawk. Many Americans wore breeches or drawers, but as they moved further west they took to the Indian breechclout, a length of cloth about a yard long and nine inches wide that passed between the legs, under a cloth belt, with folds hanging front and back. Long leggings stretching to above the knee were supported by garter straps. . . . Like Indian men, American hunters let their hair grow long and dressed it with bear grease, plaiting it into braids or knots. In time of war or for ritual occasions, Indian warriors might shave or pluck their scalps, leaving only a lock of hair, which they greased to stand upright or to which they attached deerskin ornaments or feathers. They painted their bodies with vermillion. American backwoodsmen heading into battle frequently adopted a similar style of ornamentation.

Values. In addition to hunting and clothing styles residents on the frontier shared general social values and certain cultural traits. They were geographically mobile and stressed personal freedom and independence. At the same time they were loyal to their families, whom they valued over the nation or tribe. They also shared a common diet (including maize, squash, wild berries, and venison) and herbal remedies.

Sources:

Stephen E. Ambrose, *Undaunted Courage: Meriwether Lewis, Thomas Jefferson, and the Opening of the West* (New York: Touchstone, 1996);

John Mack Faragher, *Daniel Boone: The Life and Legend of an American Pioneer* (New York: Holt, 1992).

HOLIDAYS

National Celebrations. An example of the growing sense of nationalism in the years after the Revolutionary War was in the holiday celebrations. Americans began to create and celebrate holidays that reflected the important events in their lives and history. Not all of the celebrations were national, and not all holidays were celebrated by the total population. During these years the government legislated some holidays to make them nationwide observances.

Washington's Birthday. The first national holiday to be recognized was George Washington's birthday. It was first celebrated near the end of the Revolutionary War in Richmond, Virginia, on 11 February 1782. The following year it was celebrated in Talbot Courthouse, Maryland; Cambridge, Massachusetts; and New York City. Since the nation was still undergoing a transition to the Gregorian Calendar, the date of Washington's Birthday—11 February—was changed to 22 February. By the time of Washington's first term as president 22 February was the accepted day; the number of celebrations had also increased. It became a tradition to celebrate Washington's Birthday by drinking thirteen toasts—one for each of the original colonies. In 1790 Congress adjourned its New York session in order to extend him congratulations. This was followed in subsequent years, and in 1792, on Washington's sixtieth birthday, there was a banquet for him in Philadelphia. However, in the following years political party affiliations began to affect the celebrations. After Washington's death in 1799 Congress passed a resolution calling for the nation to observe 22 February 1800 "with appropriate exercises." In the years to follow the celebration of the holiday became firmly established.

Independence Day. The Fourth of July became another American holiday in the postwar years. In 1783 it replaced 5 March, the day of the Boston Massacre (1770), as the day chosen to recognize American independence. It was usually celebrated with parades and speeches with the purpose of keeping the memory of the War of Independence alive. The idea of independence was also central to Bastille Day (14 July), which some Democrat-Republican societies observed during the 1790s.

Thanksgiving Day. In 1789 Thanksgiving Day was celebrated as a national holiday for the first time when, at the request of Congress, George Washington proclaimed 26 November a day of thanksgiving for the Constitution. Anti-Federalists opposed the resolution on the grounds that it violated states' rights, but the opposition did not have much influence. In New England, Thanksgiving observances were celebrations of abundant harvests and were occasions for huge feasts. This was also a time of renewing kinship ties, and family members who had moved away traveled to be with family.

Columbus Day. Americans also felt the need to commemorate the discovery of the New World by Christopher Columbus in 1492. The holiday was celebrated for the first time on 12 October 1792 under the auspices of the Society of St. Tammany Columbian Order of New York. On the same day the first memorial to Columbus was placed at Baltimore, Maryland.

African American Holidays. African Americans did not take an active part in national celebrations. They celebrated distinct holidays that were influenced by observances of the wider society but which had an African flavor. The holidays were distinctly African American in both the structure and style of the activities as noted by European American observers. It was their "Africanness" that connected and shaped the celebrations.

John Canoe Festival. In North Carolina, African Americans celebrated the John Canoe Festival held during Christmas. The celebrants paraded through town led by John Canoe, the king of the festival. As they danced through the streets singing and playing music, they would stop at the homes of prominent citizens where they would present a short play before continuing.

Election Day. In New England, African Americans celebrated Negro Election Day. This was a combination of the New England Election Day celebration and a practice by enslaved African Americans of honoring members of the community who had come from royal families in Africa. This five-day celebration included campaigning, election of a mayor and governor, an inaugural parade, and speeches.

Pinkster Festival. In New York both free and enslaved African Americans celebrated the Pinkster Festival. It was adopted from the Dutch celebration of the Pentecost and transformed into a celebration of African traditions with a parade led by elected royalty to a site where performances, music, and dancing took place. Pinkster was celebrated all along the Hudson River Valley and in Brooklyn, Long Island. New Jersey African Americans organized Pinkster festivals, but the most colorful and well-known was the one celebrated in Albany, New York. Albany's celebration included a carnival village where food was sold.

Christmas. The Americans celebrated Christmas in a variety of ways. In New England the celebration had been banned by the Puritans in the seventeenth century as they regarded Christmas as a pagan holiday. Even at the end of the American Revolution it was unusual to find Christmas observed in rural New England. In the rest of the United States, Christmas celebrations involved either visiting with family members or drunken revelry. A New York journalist in 1786 contrasted the two kinds of celebrations, as some spent the day "decently feasting with . . . friends and relatives," while others spent it "reveling in profusion, and paying . . . sincere devotion to *merry Bacchus*." In some cases the holiday revelers, such as the Boston Anticks, would invade homes, particularly those of wealthier citizens, singing bawdy songs such as a version of "Yankee Doodle":

> Christmas is a coming Boys,
> We'll go to Mother Chase's,
> And there we'll get a sugar dram [rum]
> Sweetened with Molasses.
> Heigh Ho for our Cape Cod,
> Heigh Ho for our Nantasket,
> Do not let the Boston wags
> Feel your Oyster Basket.

The revelers demanded food and drink. Taverns often served free drinks on Christmas, a custom carried over from England. In New England, Christmas was not observed as a religious holiday. The Congregational Church had services on Sunday but not on Christmas. Only in 1789, with the advent of the Universalist Church, was Christmas celebrated by a New England Protestant denomination. Catholics had celebrated the holiday, but Christmas was less important on the liturgical calendar than Easter, which marked the beginning of the year. In fact, until the 1750s the British observed the New Year on 25 March. New England Unitarians in 1800 began a push to observe Christmas, provoking fierce opposition from more traditional Congregationalists. The holiday reflected class divisions in American society. In many of the southern states the week between Christmas and New Year's Day was given to the slaves for their one yearly vacation. This release from work was seen by the slaveholders as necessary to keep the slaves from rebelling, and during the week they supplied the slaves liberally with drink and gave them their annual supply of clothing. The freedom of the week actually reinforced the bondage of the slaves during the rest of the year. The planters were the distributors of gifts, the slaves the recipients. In the rest of the country there was a distinct difference in the way the lower and upper classes celebrated Christmas. The first decades of the century saw explosive growth in the city of New York, which had a population of thirty-three thousand in 1790 and over two hundred thousand by 1825. An influx of Irish and African Americans that had begun in the middle of the eighteenth century amid an expansion of New York commerce was making the city into the commercial capital of the nation. At Christmas the Irish and African Americans tended to have wild and disruptive celebrations. In the 1810s wealthier New Yorkers sought a way to bring these rowdy elements under control. One way of doing so was by incorporating their notions of the Christmas holiday into a more orderly and genteel tradition. In the 1820s New Yorker John Pintard, who had helped create Washington's Birthday and the Fourth of July holidays, appropriated Saint Nicholas, the patron saint of Dutch New Amsterdam. Pintard in 1810 commissioned a broadside poster showing the Saint coming to either reward good children or punish bad children. It was quite a jump from this image of Saint Nicholas to the modern conception of Santa Claus, though he would be given a distinct character by Clement Clarke Moore's 1822 poem, "A Visit from St. Nicholas." Neither trees nor presents, two distinctive features of modern Christmas celebrations, were part of the tradition in early America. Christmas trees were a feature mainly in the German city of Strasbourg and were not widely used elsewhere in Europe. Apparently the Strasbourg idea was spread by German poet Johann Wolfgang von Goethe, who wrote about the city's Christmas celebration in *The Sufferings of Young Werther* (1774). By the end of the century other German cities had begun to adopt Christmas trees, though the elite in Berlin did not do so until 1810. In 1798 English poet Samuel Taylor Coleridge visited Germany, where he saw Christmas trees. His 1809 account of his journey began to spread the Christmas tree custom in Britain. German immigrants may have brought Christmas trees to America. The first recorded American Christmas tree was in 1820. Gift giving, as part of a general Christmas tradition, would not become a common custom until much later in the century.

Sources:

Jack Larkin, *The Reshaping of Everyday Life, 1790–1840* (New York: Harper, 1988);

Jacqui Malone, *Steppin' on the Blues: The Visible Rhythms of African American Dance* (Urbana: University of Illinois Press, 1996);

Stephen Nissenbaum, *The Battle for Christmas* (New York: Knopf, 1997).

THE MAMMOTH CHEESE

Jefferson. Many Americans agreed with Thomas Jefferson that his election to the presidency in 1800 marked a revolution as profound as the Revolution of 1776. Jefferson's inauguration meant not only a return to republican principles but also an affirmation of American character. Some sought to celebrate Jefferson's election by presenting the president with evidence of American greatness. From Philadelphia two butchers sent Jefferson a veal shank, the largest ever produced by a calf. Though the veal had spoiled by the time it reached Washington, D.C., in October 1801, Jefferson admired its beauty and size, which he saw as further evidence to refute the French naturalist Georges-Louis Leclerc de Buffon's theory that animals in the New World were smaller than those of Europe.

Elder Leland. In Massachusetts, Baptist leader John Leland inspired his congregation to celebrate Jefferson's election in a similar way. Leland had been born in Massachusetts but had lived in Virginia in the 1780s. There he had run against James Madison for a seat in Virginia's ratifying convention in 1788, but he had withdrawn when Madison persuaded the Baptist minister that the Constitution would not threaten religious liberty. Jefferson's and Madison's firm support for religious freedom had made Leland and other Baptists enthusiastic supporters of the Republicans. Massachusetts, overwhelmingly Federalist and Congregationalist, was not a welcoming place for those political and religious dissenters.

Special Gift. Leland's congregation sought to demonstrate their support for Jefferson by presenting him with the largest cheese ever manufactured. Nine hundred Republican cows (Leland assured the president that no Federalist cows had contributed) produced enough milk to make a block of cheese four feet across and fifteen inches thick weighing 1,235 pounds. Leland put the cheese on a sleigh in December 1801 to begin its journey to Washington.

Republican Farmer. Jefferson received the cheese as evidence of the "ebullition of the passion of republicanism in a state where it has been under heavy persecution," and he displayed it in a special room, dubbed the "mammoth room." The mammoth cheese showed not only that American farmers could produce great quantities of foods, but that even in Federalist Massachusetts ordinary farmers welcomed the accession of Jefferson. One newspaper headline called it "The greatest Cheese in America, for the Greatest Man in America." Jefferson gave Leland a $200 donation for his church and had him preach to the members of Congress during his stay in Washington. The president attended the session and heard Leland preach on the text, after which he commented, "And behold a greater than Solomon is here," which flattered Jefferson even more than had the cheese.

Federalist Reaction. Manasseh Cutler, a Congregationalist minister and Federalist representative from Massachusetts, was disgusted by this spectacle. He called Leland "a poor, illiterate, clownish creature," and of the sermon to Congress, Cutler wrote,

> Such a farrago, bawled with stunning voice, horrid tone, frightful grimaces, and extravagant gestures, I believe was never heard by any decent auditory before. Shame or laughter appeared in every countenance. Such an outrage upon

religion, the Sabbath, and common decency was extremely painful to every sober, thinking person present. But it answered to the much-wished for purpose of the Democrats, to see religion exhibited in the most ridiculous manner.

Aftermath. Cutler voiced the minority opinion on the matter. Jefferson continued to serve Leland's cheese for the next three years, finally carving out the last of it at a New Year's Day reception in 1805. By that time much of it had been discarded after mold had set in, and some Federalists went so far as to say that all of the mammoth cheese had actually been dumped into the Potomac River. The aroma of the ripe cheese filled the air at the president's mansion for most of Jefferson's first term.

Sources:

William Parker Cutler and Julia Perkins Cutler, *Life, Journal, and Correspondence of Rev. Manasseh Cutler,* 2 volumes (Cincinnati: Robert Clarke, 1888);

Dumas Malone, *Jefferson and His Time,* volume 4: *Jefferson the President, 1801–1804* (Boston: Little, Brown, 1970).

THE PATTERSON-BONAPARTE WEDDING

Belle of Baltimore. Born in 1785, Elizabeth Patterson may have been the most beautiful girl in Baltimore; she certainly was the most ambitious. "Nature never intended me for obscurity," she wrote. She dreamed of one day being a great lady, not in the small and relatively tranquil world of Baltimore, but on the grand stage of Europe. Elizabeth's father, William Patterson, had come to America from Ireland in the 1760s and through hard

Elizabeth Patterson, wife of Jerome Bonaparte, circa 1800; painting by an unknown artist (from Eugene L. Didier, *Madame Bonaparte,* 1879)

FATHER OF CHICAGO

It is believed that Jean-Baptiste Pointe Du Sable was born on the island of Saint Domingue in 1750. His mother was African, and his father was a French merchant. After his mother's death, Jean was sent to school in Paris by his father. It was common practice in Saint Domingue for white fathers to send their mulatto sons to France for an education. When he returned from Paris, Du Sable served as a seaman on his father's ships, a means of support as well as mobility.

He migrated to the French province of Louisiana in 1765 and became a fur trapper for his father's business in New Orleans. By 1779 he had traveled north and established trading posts on the modern sites of Peoria and Michigan City, Indiana. He also established a post at the mouth of a river called Checagou (Chicago) by the local Indians. During the Revolutionary War he supported the Americans, and as a result he was arrested by the British for espionage. He was released the following year and became a trader of supplies for their fort. When the British left the region in 1784, Du Sable returned to Checagou. He reestablished his trading post there and built a cabin, the first house built in present-day Chicago. He lived there for sixteen years, married a Potawatomi woman named Catherine, and had two children.

In 1800 he failed in an attempt to be elected chief of the Potawatomi. He then sold his land and businesses in the Checagou area and moved back to Peoria. He owned eight hundred acres there but lost his money and declared bankruptcy in 1814. He then moved to Saint Charles, Missouri, near Saint Louis, where he died in poverty in 1818.

Sources: Peter M. Bergman, *The Chronological History of the Negro in America* (New York: Harper & Row, 1969);

Benjamin Brawley, *A Short History of the American Negro* (New York: Macmillan, 1944).

work and fortunate opportunities had established himself as one of the country's leading merchants. He had helped finance the American Revolution, and though he shunned political life, which would have taken too much time from his family, Patterson knew the country's political leaders well. He was content to be one of Maryland's wealthiest and most successful men; his daughter was not.

French Officer. Jerome Bonaparte, one year older than Elizabeth, was the youngest brother of Napoleon Bonaparte. Napoleon, then first consul to the French Republic, had sent his younger brother to serve in the French navy. In 1803 Jerome's ship reached New York, and the young officer began a busy social schedule in the city, followed by visits to Philadelphia, Washington, and Baltimore, where he and Elizabeth Patterson caught one another's attention. She was an astonishingly beautiful and smart woman, and he was a handsome officer and, more important for Elizabeth, the brother of one of the most famous men in the world. Elizabeth, like many Americans, admired Napoleon's military genius as well as his apparent attachment to republican principles. In October 1803 Elizabeth and Jerome began courting. William Patterson, however, tried to break off the relationship and sent his daughter to Virginia. He warned her that no good would come of her marriage into the Bonaparte family, that Jerome's brother would not consider the marriage valid. Patterson had worked his way to the top and did not want to see his daughter hurt or his fortune depleted by this European adventurer. Elizabeth, though, declared she would rather be the wife of Jerome Bonaparte for one hour than the wife of any other man for a lifetime.

Marriage. William Patterson had Alexander Dallas (later U.S. secretary of the Treasury) draw up a marriage contract, providing that if any question were raised as to the validity of the union, Jerome Bonaparte would publicly affirm the marriage, and if any member of the Bonaparte family sought to annul the marriage, Elizabeth Patterson would have the right to one-third of her husband's property. To further ensure the validity, the Protestant Pattersons had the wedding performed on Christmas Eve 1803 by Rev. John Carroll, who later would become the first Roman Catholic bishop in the United States. Witnessing the wedding were the French consul and the mayor of Baltimore.

American Tour. The young couple then took an extended tour of the United States, giving Elizabeth a chance to escape what she felt to be the constraints of Baltimore and to show herself on a wider stage. In Washington she enchanted and shocked society by her dress and her sarcastic wit: "She charms by her eyes and slays by her tongue," one observer said. One Washington hostess reported that "her appearance . . . threw all the company into confusion, and no one dared to look at her but by stealth. . . . Her dress was the thinnest sarcenet and white crepe . . . there was scarcely any waist to it and no sleeves; her back, her bosom, part of her waist and her arms were uncovered and the rest of her form visible." Elizabeth was said to have the "most transcendently beautiful back and shoulders that were ever seen," and though she delighted in showing them, American society was less openly pleased to see them. Before the next Washington party, "several ladies sent her word, if she wished to meet them there she must promise to have more clothes on."

Diplomatic Difficulties. While the nuptial couple traveled, Elizabeth Patterson's brother Robert was in France, trying to ensure that his sister's marriage would be upheld by Napoleon. He met with constant disap-

pointment. Napoleon would not acknowledge the marriage, even though his mother and older brother welcomed Elizabeth into the family. Napoleon hoped to marry his brother to a European princess and in the process form a strategic alliance for the French nation. Napoleon ordered Jerome to return home and to leave the "young girl" in the United States. In October 1804 Jerome and Elizabeth sailed for France. Their ship wrecked off Delaware, but both were saved. (Elizabeth's large and extravagant gown nearly pulled her under.) In March 1805 they sailed again, this time on a safer ship owned by Elizabeth's father.

Arrival in Europe. Napoleon would not allow Jerome to bring his bride into any French port. By the time the couple arrived in Lisbon, Napoleon had been crowned emperor of France and controlled much of the European Continent. French officers were instructed to send Elizabeth back to the United States, but she was not willing to go. When a French officer in Lisbon asked what he could do for "Miss Patterson," she replied angrily, "Tell your master Madame Bonaparte is ambitious, and demands her rights as a member of the imperial family." Jerome was brought to Paris, but Elizabeth was not allowed to disembark from the ship. Jerome pledged his undying love for his bride, who was pregnant with their child, but he quickly yielded to his brother's demands. Elizabeth landed in England, where her son, Jerome Napoleon Bonaparte, was born in July.

The Pope. Napoleon denied that the marriage was valid and had a civil divorce arranged in France. He promised Elizabeth a pension of Fr 60,000 each year on the condition she not use the Bonaparte name. Elizabeth contested the divorce, though she accepted the pension (which she received as long as Napoleon was in power) and signed the receipts "Elizabeth Bonaparte." Napoleon asked Pope Pius VII to annul the marriage on the grounds that Elizabeth was a Protestant and Jerome a Catholic. To help encourage the Pope's decision, Napoleon sent him a diamond tiara. Pius VII, however, denied the annulment. The wedding had been performed according to the rules of the Church, celebrated by the leading Catholic in America. Jerome Napoleon Bonaparte, born two weeks after the Pope upheld his mother's marriage, was raised a faithful Catholic by his Protestant mother.

Jerome Remarries. In 1807 Jerome yielded to his brother's ambition and married a Westphalian princess, Fredericka Catharina of Würtemberg. Jerome, who ultimately became the king of Westphalia, offered Elizabeth a pension (Fr 200,000) if she would allow their son to be raised in his household. Elizabeth, Jerome thought, could take up residence in the principality of Smalkalden. She refused, saying Westphalia was not big enough for two queens and that she would rather be sheltered under the wing of an eagle (Jerome's brother) than to hang from the bill of a goose. Elizabeth and her son returned to Baltimore. Elizabeth may have been denied her place at Napoleon's court, but she was still determined to escape the narrow world of Baltimore. In 1815, when Napoleon fell from power, she and her son returned to Europe, but when Louis XVIII invited Elizabeth to his court, she refused. Since she had accepted a pension from Napoleon, she thought it inappropriate to accept hospitality from his deposer. In Maryland her father moved to have the legislature grant his daughter a civil divorce as he feared the Bonapartes might now try to claim some of her wealth as rightfully theirs.

"Bo." Elizabeth's two greatest concerns were for herself and her son, now ten years old. She hoped to have him educated in Europe, as "the Bonaparte talents ought to have an English education." In America "unfortunately he possesses no rank," but in Europe he was the son of a king (though only the king of Westphalia). When young Jerome Napoleon Bonaparte (called "Bo" by his family) reached a marriageable age, his mother hoped to find an appropriate European princess for him. And though his father now had a legitimate heir, young Jerome Napoleon Bonaparte was accepted into the Westphalian court family. Though it was understood in Westphalia that he would not inherit the crown, Bo and his mother seem to have expected otherwise.

Europe Again. Elizabeth Patterson Bonaparte, who would be called "Madame Bonaparte" until her death in 1879, despised the narrowness of her own country and rejoiced in living in Europe, where "the purposes of life are all fulfilled. . . . Beauty commands homage, talents secure admiration, misfortune meets with respect." Women, even at forty, fifty, or sixty years of age, "retain the glorious privilege of charming," and the word *old* was "completely banished from polite vocabulary." She became a social butterfly in Europe. Her son preferred America, telling his grandfather that "I have dined with princes and princesses and all the great people in Europe, but have not found a dish as much to my taste as the roast beef and beefsteaks I ate [at William Patterson's home] on South Street." Bo graduated from Harvard College in 1826 and married a young woman from Baltimore, much to his mother's shock.

Later Years. William Patterson died in 1835 one of the wealthiest men in Maryland. He left his children considerable estates, but Elizabeth, who he said had caused him more grief than all the others, received less property than her brothers and sisters. She still had an income of $10,000 each year and through investments managed to accumulate a large fortune by the end of her life. In the 1850s her family's royal ambitions were reawakened when Louis Napoleon Bonaparte seized power in France. Jerome Napoleon Bonaparte had established cordial relations with his cousins when they were out of power; with their restoration the American Bonapartes hoped to secure a title. Their attorney argued their case in Paris, citing among other evidence that "the great Jefferson" himself had written of the Patterson wealth. On 4 July 1856 the Bonaparte family declared that the American Bonapartes were their cousins and could continue to use the family name but that they could not inherit property or expect to share in power. Elizabeth Patterson Bonaparte was disappointed again, but not surprised. How much more surprised "the great Jefferson" would have been to hear his name invoked by an American family trying to claim a European noble title. Jerome Bonaparte died in 1860, his son in 1870. Elizabeth Pat-

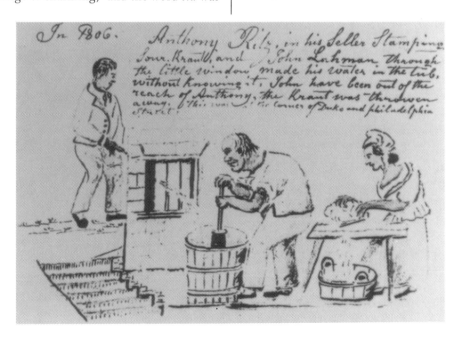

Men sometimes relieved themselves in the streets of Philadelphia. This watercolor by Lewis Miller depicts an incident in which a man urinated through a cellar window into a barrel of sauerkraut.

Medric-Louis-Elie Moreau de Saint-Mery, a French refugee in America between 1793 and 1798, wrote this account of Philadelphia:

Another veritable torture during Philadelphia's hot season is the innumerable flies which constantly light on the face and hands, stinging everywhere and turning everything black because of the filth they leave wherever they light. Rooms must be kept closed unless one wishes to be tormented in his bed at the break of day, and this need of keeping everything shut makes the heat of the night even more unbearable and sleep more difficult.

And so the heat of the day makes one long for bedtime because of weariness, and a single fly which has gained entrance to your room in spite of all precautions drives you from your bed.

I say one fly because many among them are a sort of blisterfly, and once they have attacked you, you can have no peace until they are killed. If one writes, the paper is spotted with flyspecks. If a woman is dressed in white her dress is in like manner soiled, especially her fichu [a muslin cape worn over the shoulders]. The upholstery and bellups are sticky.

At table and above all at dessert they light upon and befoul all food, all drinks. They taste everything they see. One's eyes are revolted by them; one's appetite destroyed. When a rather large room, hitherto closed, is suddenly opened in the summer, a noise is produced there which imitates the sea roaring in the distance; it is the flies who are escaping and cover you as they pass. It is because of this frightful inconvenience that the custom arose of going without [wall] hangings, and repainting apartments every autumn.

Source: *Moreau St. Mery's American Journey (1793–1798)*, translated and edited by Kenneth Roberts and Anna M. Roberts (Garden City, N.Y.: Doubleday, 1947).

terson Bonaparte lived comfortably, if not regally, to the age of ninety-four.

Sources:
Mary C. Crawford, *Romantic Days in the Early Republic* (London: Gay & Hancock, 1913);

Eugene L. Didier, *The Life and Letters of Madame Bonaparte* (New York: Scribners, 1879);

W. T. R. Saffell, *The Bonaparte-Patterson Marriage in 1803* (Philadelphia: The proprietor, 1873).

THE STREETS OF PHILADELPHIA

Problem. In the late eighteenth century city streets were filthy. With no regular trash collection or sewer system and with horses as the primary means of transportation, the streets were filled with household trash and manure. Medric-Louis-Elie Moreau de Saint-Mery, a French visitor to New York City, complained of "evil odors" and noted that "in 1791 the sewage

around the wharfs was thought to have caused the epidemic of yellow fever at the time." In smaller towns and villages the problems of public sanitation were not so severe, and in the colonial period hogs had found city streets to be promising grazing areas. But in the case of Philadelphia during the early national period, as it became a crowded city tied more to international commerce than to agriculture, its streets posed a health risk as flies and rats flourished on the garbage.

Commissioners. Philadelphia's street commissioners, charged with keeping the public ways clear, hired scavengers to cart away trash and sort through it. It was a dirty job, but scavengers and street sweepers supplemented their salaries by occasionally finding valuables or by reusing what they found in the streets. In January 1783, facing a budget deficit, Philadelphia's street commissioners decided to economize. They would find farmers in the surrounding rural areas to cart away manure and other trash. The farmers, the commissioners believed, would benefit by getting free manure, and the city would benefit by having its streets cleaned for free.

Failure. The plan did not work. Unlike the scavengers, the farmers did not clean the streets regularly. By August,

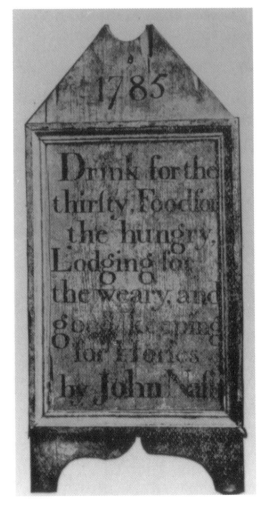

Signboard for John Nash's Tavern in Amherst, Massachusetts

Patrons drinking in a tavern in the early nineteenth century; painting by John Lewis Krimmel (Toledo Museum of Art)

Philadelphia's citizens were disgusted with the dead cats and dogs, chickens, and garbage from the marketplace. One newspaper printed a dialogue between a dead dog and cat lying in the gutter, discussing the condition of the street and the probable fate of the street commissioners. In 1784 the street commissioners abandoned the idea of allowing farmers to clean the streets in exchange for free manure and resumed the practice of paying scavengers to cart away the city's trash.

Source:
Merrill Jensen, *The New Nation: A History of the United States during the Confederation, 1781–1789* (New York: Knopf, 1950).

TEMPERANCE

Drinking Habits. In the years following the Revolution efforts were made to alter American drinking habits. This was a departure from the attitude that an alcoholic beverage was necessary to fellowship. In the South and West it was considered proper for a family to keep a full bottle of liquor for guests; not to do so was to be inhospitable. In the North hardened cider was the common table beverage, and it was customary for a man to fortify himself with a glass of it several times a day. Clergymen took drinks between services and lawyers before going to the court. Liquor was present at communal tasks, such as corn huskings and barn raisings, and also at festivities. It was also a part of slaves' festivals and celebrations. The temperance groups that appeared at the turn of the century were responding in part to the impact of technology. Improvements in the distillation process allowed for the production of stronger distilled drinks. Higher-proof liquor in itself made it dangerous to drink in the customary way. In addition the groups were trying to contest the moral evils of heavy alcohol consumption, which they believed resulted in laziness and disrupted family relations.

Early Groups. In 1789 the first temperance group was formed by two hundred farmers in Litchfield, Connecticut. They pledged not to drink alcoholic beverages during the farming season. Their goal was not to change the behavior of others or to stop consuming alcohol. Rather, these farmers changed their own behavior to improve their work. Another group was the Temperance Society for Moreau and Northumberland, formed in Saratoga County, New York, in 1808. After 1810 concerted efforts on the state level began to appear. By 1818 there were a large number of such organizations, such as the Massachusetts Society for the Suppression of Intemperance and the Connecticut Society for the Reformation of Morals, both founded in 1813.

Source:
Jack Larkin, *The Reshaping of Everyday Life, 1790–1840* (New York: Harper, 1988).

HEADLINE MAKERS

DANIEL BOONE

1734-1820
PIONEER

Birth of a Legend. Daniel Boone was born in Pennsylvania on 22 October 1734. His parents, Sarah and Squire, were Quakers, and Daniel was one of their eleven children. When Daniel was fifteen, the family immigrated to the North Carolina backcountry. Growing up on the frontier Boone learned to shoot and hunt at an early age. Although he had little formal schooling, he was able to read and write his name.

Kentucky. In 1760, at the age of twenty-six, he crossed the Blue Ridge Mountains for the first time on a winter hunt. As a "long hunter" he lived away from white settlements and civilization. Since he hunted in unsettled areas, his knowledge of the outdoors was essential to those who followed him into the western regions for permanent settlement. The pattern of Daniel Boone's life kept him on the frontier and moved him further and further west, just ahead of American settlement. Boone reached Kentucky through the Cumberland Gap for the first time in 1767. The next year he went on a long hunt in the area and was captured briefly by the Shawnee. He was able to escape from them and return home. (In total, he was captured by Indians four times and was able to escape unharmed each time.) Between 1769 and 1771 he continued to explore Kentucky and worked as a guide leading families to settlements there. In 1775 he led an advance party of the Transylvania Company and helped cut the Wilderness Road from the upper Holston River via the Cumberland Gap in southwestern Virginia to the Kentucky River. He founded the town of Boonesborough that same year and four years later founded Boone's Station. He was elected to the Virginia legislature in 1771 and again in 1791.

Hero. Boone was the embodiment of the frontier and became a living legend. In 1784, the year of Boone's fiftieth birthday, John Filson published *The Adventures of Colonel Daniel Boone;* the next year another Boone biography appeared. These books also brought Boone international fame through European editions. But this was the time that Boone began to have legal difficulties. In 1784 he entered a suit for his lands, but he did not win the claim. Along with hundreds of others Boone lost his lands because the titles issued by the Transylvania Company were not recognized by the Virginia legislature. When Kentucky became a state in 1792, Boone made another attempt to keep title to his lands, but the new state denied his request. As a result, when the Spanish government in 1797 invited him to immigrate to Missouri, Boone accepted the offer and moved there two years later. However, in 1806, after the United States had acquired the Louisiana Purchase, Boone went before a federal land commission seeking confirmation of his Spanish land grant. His petition was rejected in 1809, but in 1814 Congress agreed to recognize Boone's claims.

Death. After the death of his wife, Rebecca, in 1813, Boone moved back and forth between the homes of his children, who had settled in Missouri. In the summer of 1820, while he was at his daughter Jemima's home, he suffered recurring bouts of fever. As soon as he was well enough he traveled to his son Nathan's house, where he died on 26 September 1820, a month short of his eighty-sixth birthday. He was buried next to his wife.

Monuments. By the 1840s Boone had become a national hero for his role in exploring the West. During these years the heroes of the past were being commemorated, and Boone was no exception. In April 1845 the Kentucky legislature passed a resolution authorizing the reinternment of Boone's remains at the state capital in Kentucky. Obtaining the consent of his descendants before the Missouri legislature could react, his grave was dug up in July. On 13 September 1845 he was reinterned in the new Frankfort cemetery in Kentucky. The event was accompanied by "marching bands, state dignitaries, military companies, and fraternal organizations," and thousands of onlookers. Boone's fame helped sell many of the plots in the new cemetery, but it was not until 1860 that a monument to him was erected. In 1915 the Daughters of the American Revolution erected another monument at the original Boone grave site at Tuque Creek, Missouri.

Source:

John Mack Faragher, *Daniel Boone: The Life and Legend of an American Pioneer* (New York: Holt, 1992).

MERIWETHER LEWIS

1774-1809

ARMY OFFICER AND EXPLORER

Distinguished Family. Meriwether Lewis was born in the Virginia piedmont on 18 August 1774 into one of the state's earliest and most distinguished families. Meriwether Lewis's great-grandfather was a Welshman who served in the British army as an officer. He arrived in Virginia in 1635 with a grant from the king for 33,333 1/3 acres of land. William Lewis, Meriwether's father, inherited 1,896 acres of land, slaves, and a house when his father, Col. Robert Lewis, died. In 1769 William married his cousin Lucy Meriwether, the daughter of a land-rich Welsh family. (Between 1725 and 1774 there were eleven marriages between Lewises and Meriwethers.)

Young Boy. Meriwether Lewis was the second child of Lucy and William. In 1779, when Meriwether was five years old, his father died. He inherited £520 in cash, 147 gallons of whiskey, and a plantation of nearly two thousand acres and twenty-four slaves. It was managed by his uncle, Nicholas Meriwether, until young Meriwether became old enough to run it himself. In May 1780 Lucy married Capt. John Marks. When Meriwether was eight or nine, Marks and his new family moved to Georgia.

Frontier Life. The frontier was always a part of Meriwether Lewis's world. The Virginia piedmont was midway between the frontier and the settlements. It was a place where hunting was great and one could learn wilderness skills, but it was also a place where one could acquire the refinement of plantation society and learn about surveying, natural history, and geography. Lucy Meriwether Lewis was known far and wide for her medicinal remedies, made from herbs that she grew herself. She became a source of information for young Meriwether when he had questions about plants and animals. During the three or four years that he was in Georgia, Meriwether would often go into the forest at night with his dogs to hunt raccoons and opossums.

Education. In 1787, when he was about thirteen, Lewis returned to Virginia for an education. There were no public schools in the South at this time, and planters' sons received their educations by boarding with preachers who instructed them in Latin, mathematics, natural science, and English grammar. Lewis studied until he was eighteen and then returned to Georgia to move his family to Virginia. By that time he had not learned enough Latin to use it, and his English writing skills were poor. He loved to read journals of exploration, particularly those of Capt. James Cook. His math was good, and he had a solid base in botany and natural history.

Professional Life. In 1794 Lewis enlisted as a private in the Virginia militia. He was able to travel over much of the West, both north and south of the Ohio River. He transferred to the First U.S. Infantry Regiment in 1796 and rose to the rank of captain in 1800. In early 1801, on the basis of "a personal acquaintance with him, owing from his being of my neighborhood," Jefferson chose Lewis to be his private secretary. Jefferson also wrote to Gen. James Wilkinson, commanding general of the army, requesting that Lewis be released from active duty yet allowed to keep his commission. Jefferson wanted Lewis for this post because of his familiarity with the military, which Jefferson wanted to reduce in size, and for his familiarity and knowledge of the West, which Jefferson wanted to have explored.

Expedition. In January 1803 Jefferson requested funds for an expedition to explore the West, and Congress made the appropriation. Lewis was sent to Pennsylvania to prepare for the trip by studying with some of the nation's leading scientists, including Andrew Willcot (astronomy and mathematics), Benjamin Rush (biology), Benjamin Smith Barton (botany), and Caspar Wistar (paleontology). By the time the expedition departed in the spring of 1804, Lewis was well prepared.

Governor. The expedition reached the Pacific Ocean on 8 November 1805 and returned to Saint Louis on 23 September 1806, bringing with it great quantities of information on the flora and fauna, Native Americans, and the geography of the region. In recognition of his service Lewis was nominated by Jefferson on 28 February 1807 to be governor of the Louisiana Territory. The nomination was approved by Congress, and on 2 March, Lewis resigned his military commission. The next two years were difficult for him. He took his new position at a time when there was much interest and competition in the fur trade in the Louisiana Territory. British companies based in Montreal were actively involved in the trade on the upper Missouri River; independent hunters and trappers were flocking into the area; white settlers established homesteads; and the Lakota Indians, who controlled the area, were resisting the encroachment. At the same time Lewis was personally engaged in the fur trade and land speculation. Some of his charges to the government were being challenged, and his creditors were pressuring him for payment. Moreover, he was attempting to find a wife, but with little success.

Death. In September 1809 Lewis left for Washington to try and straighten out misunderstandings surrounding the bills he submitted. On 10 October, troubled and unsettled, he arrived at Grinder's Inn, seventy-two miles outside of Nashville. During the early hours of the next day Lewis shot himself, but the bullet only grazed his head; he then shot himself in the chest. Lewis did not die immediately and asked his servants to kill him. They did not comply with his request, but by sunrise he was dead.

Source:
Stephen E. Ambrose, *Undaunted Courage: Meriwether Lewis, Thomas Jefferson, and the Opening of the American West* (New York: Touchstone, 1996).

DOROTHY PAYNE TODD MADISON

1768-1849
FIRST LADY

Society of Friends. Dorothy Payne Todd Madison, the wife of President James Madison, was born in Guilford County, North Carolina, on 20 May 1768. Her parents, John and Mary Coles Payne, owned slaves but set them free soon after Dorothy was born. The Paynes then joined the Society of Friends and moved to Philadelphia. They raised their daughter in the Quaker faith, and in 1790 she married a young lawyer named John Todd Jr. The marriage was brief; in 1793 Todd died unexpectedly and left his wife and newborn son, John Payne, with little money. As a result Dorothy Payne Todd went to live in her mother's boardinghouse in the city.

Beauty of Philadelphia. At this time the widow relinquished her beliefs in the Quaker faith and began to dress in a more stylish manner. All who met her commented on the beauty and cheerful disposition of the young woman affectionately called "Dolley" (sometimes spelled Dolly). Among her mother's boarders were two prominent men, Congressman James Madison (Va.) and Senator Aaron Burr (N.Y.). In 1794 Madison and Dorothy Payne Todd wed.

Washington Socialite. Madison became secretary of state in 1801 and president of the United States in 1809. During her husband's long political career Dolley Madison became the center of the social scene in Washington, D.C. British diplomat Sir Augustus John Foster reported that Dolley Madison was "a very handsome woman and tho' an uncultivated mind and fond of gossiping, was so perfectly good-tempered and good-humored that she rendered her husband's house as far as depended on her agreeable to all parties." In 1803, when Thomas Jefferson opened his house for receptions on New Year's Eve and the Fourth of July, Dolley Madison served as hostess for the widower president. When James Madison assumed the presidency, the first lady had the White House refurnished to befit the dignity of her husband's high office. In May 1809 she started the first of her soon-to-be-famous Wednesday "drawing rooms," in which she invited congressmen and their wives, belles of the city, and foreign emissaries to visit the presidential pair and play the card game loo. Dolley Madison was the perfect first lady for the reserved president, and she set standards that dominated the social life of Washington until the Civil War.

Duty. During the War of 1812 a British army landed on the coast and made a quick march to the capital. After the Battle of Bladensburg, Maryland, on 24 August 1814 the president and his cabinet fled to Virginia, but the first lady felt it her duty to remain at the White House and load important documents and silver plate onto a waiting carriage. When a written message arrived from her husband imploring her to leave the city, Dolley Madison did so, but not before denying the British a trophy: she personally removed from its frame a full-length portrait of George Washington by Gilbert Stuart. When enemy troops arrived at the presidential mansion, they found the table set for forty guests, the first family having arranged a large dinner party for that day. After eating the food and drinking all the wine, British officers ordered the White House burnt.

Retirement. James Madison's term as president ended in 1817, and he and his wife retired to their Virginia home, Montpelier. After the former president died in 1836, Dolley Madison returned to Washington, where she retained much of her vivacity and grace up to her eighty-first year. She died on 12 July 1849. James and Dolley Madison had no children.

Source:
Elswyth Thane, *Dolley Madison: Her Life and Times* (New York: Crowell-Collier, 1970).

SACAGAWEA

1788?-1884?
SHOSHONE INTERPRETER

Bird Woman. Sacagawea, the Bird Woman, played an important role in opening up the western territories for settlement by Americans. She was a Shoshone born in the western Rocky Mountains around 1788. When she was about ten or eleven, she traveled east with her family to Three Forks, where the headwaters of the Missouri River begins, in present-day Montana. While there they were attacked by Minnetaree warriors, and Sacagawea and another girl were taken captive. It is not certain how long she remained the captive of the Minnetarees, but at some point she became the wife of Toussaint Charbonneau, a French-Canadian fur trapper and interpreter, and left them.

Lewis and Clark. In November 1805 she and her husband traveled to the camp of Meriwether Lewis and William Clark near the Mandan tribe in North Dakota. She was approximately sixteen years old at the time. When Lewis and Clark left Fort Mandan in the spring of 1806, Charbonneau, Sacagawea, and their infant son Baptiste, who had been born at the fort the previous February, accompanied the expedition. It was not that Lewis and Clark particularly needed Charbonneau's skills as a guide or interpreter. Lewis and Clark knew they would need to get horses from the Shoshone, and Sacagawea was the only one who spoke the language. Since they needed her, they agreed to take Charbonneau with them. Contrary to the popular belief, Sacagawea did not serve as a guide. She had not traveled in the land of the Shoshone since she was a young girl. In addition to serving the expedition as an interpreter, she knew how to find edible roots and vegetation that were important supplements to the group's diet. She also was instrumental in saving much of the group's supplies when a canoe overturned.

Reunion. When they reached the Shoshone territory, Sacagawea was reunited with her brother Chief Cameahwait and other family members. She also saw old friends, including the woman she had been kidnapped with years ago. Nonetheless, when Lewis and Clark returned to the East, she left with them. The expedition was clearly an important part of her life, and she received gifts and recognition for her role in the endeavor throughout her life. She was even given free passage on the stage lines that ran throughout the West. But her life after the expedition was equally interesting.

Mystery. When Sacagawea left the expedition in 1806, she was not even twenty years old. What happened next to her is somewhat of a mystery. Some historians believe that Sacagawea died at Fort Manuel on the Missouri River in present-day South Dakota on 20 December 1812. They base their conclusion on three recorded accounts that maintain she contracted putrid fever and died soon afterward. Other historians assert that Sacagawea lived to be nearly one hundred years old, and they base their findings on the oral tradition of the Shoshone, Comanche, Mandan, and Gros Ventre tribes. According to the oral tradition, Sacagawea traveled throughout the West living with many different Indian tribes, including the Comanche in Oklahoma. She remarried there and had children and grandchildren; after her Comanche husband died, she left. She finally settled at the Wind River Reservation, Wyoming, where she lived with her son Bazil. It is believed that Bazil was the son of Charbonneau and his other Shoshone wife. (Tribal historians argue that it was Charbonneau's second wife who died at Fort Manuel in 1812.) Sacagawea adopted him because he was treated badly by Charbonneau. The son that she had with Charbonneau, Baptiste, also lived on that reservation. Those who believe the oral tradition say that she died on 9 April 1884 and was buried, according to Bazil's request, with a Christian service and in a church cemetery because she was a friend of the whites. Bazil died the next year, followed by Baptiste in 1886.

Source:
Ella E. Clark and Margot Edmonds, *Sacagawea of the Lewis and Clark Expedition* (Berkeley: University of California Press, 1979).

TECUMSEH

1768-1813
SHAWNEE TRIBAL LEADER

Background. Tecumseh, or Panther Springing Across the Sky, was born in a small Shawnee village on the Mad River in western Ohio in 1768. His mother, Methoataske, was a Creek, and his father, Puckeshinewa, was a Shawnee. They had met in the 1750s when some Shawnees had sought refuge among the Creeks in Alabama. In 1760 the family left Alabama for Ohio. Tecumseh was the fifth child born to this couple.

Responsibility. Puckeshinewa was killed in battle with American colonials in 1774, and his fellow warriors, unable to carry him back to the village, buried him secretly in the forest. Although his oldest son, Chiksika, took over responsibility for the family, it was still difficult for them, especially since fighting and war continued for the Shawnee as more and more Americans moved into the Ohio River Valley. In 1779 their village was attacked by mounted militia under Col. John Bowen. The Shawnee repelled the attack but realized their vulnerability and migrated down the Ohio River. Some stayed in Ohio, but others, including Methoataske, continued to Missouri. Tecumseh was then raised by Chiksika and his older sister Tecumapease.

Youth. As a boy Tecumseh excelled at the games Indian boys played. He was an excellent marksman with a bow and a musket, and he often organized the other boys to go on hunts. Sometimes he divided the boys of the village into two groups to fight mock battles. He admired and looked up to the warriors, like his older brother, and tried to be like them.

The Warrior's Path. Tecumseh was known for the generosity and concern he showed for other members of his tribe, providing meat for those who had empty cooking pots. As a warrior he wanted no compromise with the Americans over territory. After the Indians suffered a major defeat at the Battle of Fallen Timbers in 1794, they were forced to sign the Treaty of Greenville, in which they agreed to remain at peace, give up all prisoners, and renounce their claims to lands in southern, central, and eastern Ohio. The Indians were able to hunt in these lands until they were actually settled. They also received $20,000 worth of trade goods and promises of annuities ranging from $500 to $10,000. Tecumseh refused to take part in the treaty negotiations, and this increased his standing among his followers, whom he led to western Ohio and Indiana.

The Prophet. By 1805 he had joined with his younger brother Lalawethika, who had a transforming vision. As a result of this vision, Lalawethika stopped drinking and changed his name to Tenskwatawa, the Open Door. He also developed a Native American theology that called for a return to traditional Indian values and practices and began efforts to help Indians return to a way of living that would save them from destruction and suffering. Tenskwatawa's teachings spread through the Ohio River Valley, and by 1807 the Shawnee settlement at Greenville was overrun by Indians who had made the pilgrimage there to become followers. The increased numbers put enormous burdens on their food supplies and increased tensions with the Americans whose settlements practically surrounded Tecumseh's camp. In the fall of 1807 Tecumseh, Tenskwatawa, and their followers accepted an invitation from the Potawatomi to settle at the mouth of the Tippecanoe River, near present-day Lafayette, Indiana. Their new village, Prophetstown, not only had more resources but also was removed from the American settlements and those of rival chiefs.

Pan-Indian Unity. While Tenskwatawa was clearly the spiritual leader of the settlement, it was Tecumseh who articulated the political ideology. As American settlements continued to expand, old treaty lines were crossed and new boundary agreements were offered. By the end of 1810 Tecumseh realized that in order for Indians to retain their culture and homelands something must be done. He left Prophetstown and traveled south, spreading a doctrine of political and military unification. In his speeches he generally outlined the injustices that Indians had suffered from Americans and their government and spoke of the way that whites had taken native homelands. He told the Indians that the only way they could resist these encroachments was to return to the ways of their fathers. He warned them that war with the Americans was inevitable and that it was necessary for Indians to unify politically and militarily. He also told

them that the British would help them defeat their enemies and that then their land would be returned and their former way of life restored. Soon Tecumseh and his brother had a following of Native American peoples stretching from the Great Lakes to Alabama.

Battle of the Thames. While Tecumseh was away among the southern tribes in the fall of 1811, American forces attacked Prophetstown, and war between the United States and Great Britain soon followed. It was in the War of 1812, at the Battle of the Thames in October 1813, that Tecumseh was killed. After the battle many of the Indians' bodies were mutilated by white frontiersmen, and Tecumseh's body could not be positively identified. Col. Richard M. Johnson of the Kentucky militia was generally believed to have been the one who killed the great Shawnee leader. In his campaigns for Congress in the 1830s Johnson used the slogan "Rumpsey dumpsey, rumpsey dumpsey, Colonel Johnson killed Tecumseh!" However, there were at least a dozen others who claimed to have killed Tecumseh at the Battle of the Thames. Meanwhile, the Shawnee maintained that some warriors returned to the battlefield the night after the engagement and recovered Tecumseh's body before it could be mutilated. They then buried their leader in a secret location.

Legend. Although an opponent of the Americans, Tecumseh has become a legendary figure, and a great deal of apocryphal material is attached to the story of his life. Much of this information attempts to link him to the Americans in some way. Some of the stories say that his father was half white or describe his skin as light. Another myth presents the story of his love for the daughter of an American frontiersman. Other stories try to make him a mystical figure by saying he could foretell future events or exaggerate the amount of territory he actually traveled while recruiting his allies. Nonetheless, Tecumseh has been elevated to the status of "noble savage" because his passing represented the last serious threat to white expansion east of the Mississippi River.

Source:
R. David Edmunds, *Tecumseh and the Quest for Indian Leadership* (Boston: Little, Brown, 1984).

PUBLICATIONS

John Quincy Adams, *An Oration, Pronounced July 4th, 1793, at the Request of the Inhabitants of the Town of Boston, in Commemoration of the Anniversary of American Independence* (Boston: Printed by Benjamin Edes & Son, 1793);

Fisher Ames, *An Oration on the Sublime Virtues of General George Washington . . .* (Boston: Printed for Young & Mims and for Manning & Loring, 1800)—one of the many books to appear on Washington following his death;

William Andrews, *Poor Will's Almanack, For the Year of Our Lord 1784* (Philadelphia: Printed and sold by Joseph Crukshank, 1783);

Jeremy Belknap, *American Biography: Or, An Historical Account of Those Persons who Have Been Distinguished in America, As Adventurers, Divines, Statesmen, Warriors, Philosophers, Authors, and Other Remarkable Characters . . . ,* 2 volumes (Boston: Printed by Isaiah Thomas & Ebenezer T. Andrews, 1794, 1798);

John Durburrow Blair, *A Sermon on the Impetuosity and Bad Effects of Passion. And the Most Likely Means of Subduing It* (Richmond: Printed by Lynch & Southgate, 1809)—a long-winded commentary on unethical behavior, including dueling;

Thomas Branagan, *The Excellency of the Female Character Vindicated; Being an Investigation Relative to the Cause and Effects of the Encroachments of Men upon the Rights of Women, and the Too Frequent Degradation and Consequent Misfortunes of the Fair Sex* (New York: Printed by Samuel Wood for the author, 1807)—the author links social injustice and sexual immorality to the male view of women "as objects of sensual convenience and domestic accommodation . . . inferior in point of intellectual faculties to the male." Branagan recommends that women receive the benefits of universal education;

Branagan, *Serious Remonstrances Addressed to the Citizens of the Northern States, and Their Representatives, Being an appeal to their natural feelings & common sense: Consisting of speculations and animadversions, on the recent revival of the Slave Trade in the American Republic . . .* (Philadelphia: Printed & published by Thomas T. Stiles, 1805)—an Irish slave trader, privateer, and plantation overseer, Branagan had a religious awakening in the early 1790s and dedicated his life thereafter to helping the nation's poor and destitute;

John Davis, *Travels of Four Years and a Half in the United States of America; During 1798, 1799, 1800, 1801, and 1802* (Bristol: Printed by R. Edwards & sold by T. Ostell in London & H. Caritat in New York, 1803);

Olaudah Equiano, *The Interesting Narrative of the Life of Olaudah Equiano, or Gustavus Vassa, the African, Written by Himself,* 2 volumes (London: Printed & sold by the author, 1789; New York: Printed & sold by W. Durell, 1791)—an autobiography by the most important African abolitionist writer in the United States before the Civil War era;

Henry Pattillo, *The Plain Planter's Family Assistant; containing an address to husbands and wives, children and servants; with some helps for instruction by catechisms: and examples of devotion for families; with a brief paraphrase on the Lord's Prayer* (Wilmington, Del.: Printed by James Adams, 1787);

Benjamin Trumbull, *An Appeal to the Public, Especially to the Learned, with respect to the Unlawfulness of Divorces, in all cases, excepting those of incontinency . . .* (New Haven: Printed by J. Meigs, 1788);

George Tucker, *Letter to a Member of the General Assembly of Virginia, on the Subject of the Late Conspiracy of the Slaves with a Proposal for Their Colonization,* as A Citizen of Virginia (Baltimore: Printed by Bonsal & Niles, 1801);

Isaac Weld Jr., *Travels Through the States of North America, and the Provinces of Upper and Lower Canada, during the Years 1795, 1796 and 1797,* 2 volumes, third edition (London: Printed for J. Stockdale, 1800).

A patriotic parade in Philadelphia, 1812; painting by John Lewis Krimmel (Springfield Art Museum)

CHAPTER NINE

RELIGION

by JOHN O'KEEFE

CONTENTS

Sidebars and tables are listed in italics.

1783

- Presbyterians found Dickinson College in Carlisle, Pennsylvania, one of some 250 colleges founded between the American Revolution and the Civil War, most of them denominational institutions.

11 Feb.   Birth of Jarena Lee, later a female African American Methodist lay preacher.

1784

9 June   John Carroll is appointed by the Pope to be "Superior of the Missions" for the Roman Catholic Church in America, the first step toward organizing an American Catholic Church.

28 Aug.   Death of Junipero Serra, Franciscan priest and leader of the Roman Catholic missionary efforts in California.

8 Sept.   Death of Mother Ann Lee, founder of the Shakers.

14 Nov.   Samuel Seabury is ordained in Scotland as first American bishop of the former Anglican Church.

24 Dec.   Methodist ministers meet at the "Christmas Conference" and organize the Methodist Episcopal Church in America, electing Francis Asbury to be their first bishop; they also take a strong stand against slavery, which they will soften over the next few years, as they grow rapidly in the southern states.

1785

- James Madison campaigns for Thomas Jefferson's Bill for Religious Freedom in Virginia; he writes his "Memorial and Remonstrance" in support of a complete separation of church and state, against Patrick Henry's position favoring state support for all Christian churches.

15 Oct.   Founding of the first American Shaker community at New Lebanon, New York.

1786

16 Jan.   Passage of the Virginia Statute for Religious Freedom.

1787

- German Reformed and German Lutheran churches jointly found Franklin College in Carlisle, Pennsylvania.

- Founding of the American Society for the Propagation of the Gospel, the first American missionary society, devoted to Indian missions in Massachusetts formerly supported by the Anglican Church.

12 Apr.   Richard Allen, Absalom Jones, and William White form the Free African Society in Philadelphia, the first step in forming an independent African American church.

Nov.   Richard Allen and Absalom Jones withdraw from Saint George's Methodist Church after being forced into the balcony by a white usher.

1788

18 Nov.   James Freeman is ordained as pastor of King's Chapel in Boston, the first Unitarian church in America.

•   Black Baptist preacher Andrew Bryan forms the First African Baptist Church in Savannah, Georgia.

1789

•   Jesse Lee, the Methodist minister, begins spreading Methodism in New England, never before considered missionary territory.

May   John Carroll is elected by his fellow American Roman Catholic priests to be their first bishop.

July–Oct.   In two General Conventions former Anglicans organize the Protestant Episcopal Church in the United States, bringing together northern and southern groups in one denomination, headed by Bishop Samuel Seabury.

14 Sept.   The Pope approves John Carroll's appointment as bishop, and places him in the newly formed diocese of Baltimore.

1790

•   Revivals begin to spread widely among New England Congregationalists, an early manifestation of the second Great Awakening.

Mar.   Jemima Wilkinson and her sect, the Universal Friends, found New Jerusalem, a millennialist utopian community, in upstate New York.

1791

•   French Sulpicians found Saint Mary's Seminary in Baltimore, the first school devoted to training American-born Roman Catholic priests.

•   Founding of Georgetown Academy, later a major Catholic university.

•   The American Sunday school movement begins with the founding of "First Day Schools" in Philadelphia.

7 Nov.   Roman Catholic bishop John Carroll convenes the First Baltimore Conference, a meeting for all American priests; about twenty attend to discuss the problems of serving Catholics throughout the United States with so few priests.

15 Dec.   Virginia's ratification of the Bill of Rights makes effective the First Amendment to the U.S. Constitution, guaranteeing religious freedom for Americans.

1792

•   The Russian Orthodox Church claims Alaska as its mission territory.

14 July   Death of Samsom Occom, a Mohegan who had become a Christian missionary to other Native Americans.

	29 Aug.	Birth of Charles Grandison Finney, the most important revivalist of the 1820s and 1830s.
1793	•	Formation of the Roman Catholic diocese of Louisiana and the two Floridas.
1794	29 June	Richard Allen and other black Methodists in Philadelphia found Bethel Church, which will become the mother church of the African Methodist Episcopal Church, the first African American denomination.
1796	•	Several African American members of the John Street Church in New York City, led by James Varick, withdraw and begin worshiping together.
	•	Presbyterian, Baptist, and Dutch Reformed Churches found the New York Missionary Society, primarily to promote missionary work among the Indians. This society is an important example of an early interdenominational missionary effort.
	25 Feb.	Death of Episcopalian bishop Samuel Seabury.
1798	•	Congregationalists organize the Missionary Society of Connecticut, the first society devoted to establishing new churches in frontier areas.
1799	June	Handsome Lake experiences his first visions and begins preaching about the renewal of traditional Iroquois religious practices.
1800	•	Philip William Otterbein forms United Brethren in Christ Church, one of the more successful American sects based in German Pietism.
	•	Presidential campaign features attacks on Thomas Jefferson for his purported atheism.
	•	South Carolina passes legislation forbidding blacks from assembling for religious meetings, even if accompanied by whites, one of the first of many southern laws restricting African American religion.
	June–July	Presbyterian minister James McGready of Logan County, Kentucky, leads revivals in Red River and Gaspar River, Kentucky, which are the first camp meetings.
	30 Aug.	Gabriel Prosser leads nearly one thousand slaves into a rebellion near Richmond, Virginia, in part inspired by reading the Bible.

1801

- Organization of the African Methodist Episcopal Zion Church in New York City, from the group that had withdrawn from the John Street Church in 1796, later to become the second African American Methodist denomination and a rival of Richard Allen's A.M.E. Church.

May   Congregational and Presbyterian Churches form a Plan of Union to unify their denominations in order to promote western missions.

Aug.   Barton W. Stone leads the largest camp meeting ever, held in Cane Ridge, Kentucky.

1802

- Timothy Dwight, president of Yale College, delivers a series of sermons attacking "freethinking," prompting a revival among the students there, many of whom (such as Lyman Beecher and Nathaniel Taylor) later become major leaders of evangelical Protestantism in America.

- Presbyterians appoint a Standing Committee on Missions.

- Philadelphia's synagogue separates when a group leaves to form a congregation following the Eastern European Ashkenazic rite, rather then the Mediterranean Sephardic rite.

14 Apr.   Birth of Horace Bushnell, later the most important theologian in the liberal wing of Congregationalism.

May   Peter Cartwright receives a "permit to exhort" from the Methodist Church, moves to Illinois, and organizes the first Methodist circuit there, beginning a career as one of the most successful circuit riders on the frontier.

1803

- Presbyterian minister Gideon Blackburn begins his missionary work among the Cherokee Indians.

21 Apr.   Thomas Jefferson writes to Benjamin Rush, Philadelphia scientist and physician, enclosing his "Syllabus . . . of the Doctrines of Jesus," which is one example of his exploration of Christianity.

1804

- Philadelphia Quakers petition the U.S. Congress against slavery.

- The Charitable Female Society of Litchfield, Connecticut, begins to contribute money for mission work to the Missionary Society of Connecticut, an early example of the importance of women's religious organizations for the funding and staffing of American missionary activity.

1805

- The German Reformed Church allows English to be used in worship services.

- The Unitarian Controversy breaks out in Boston over the question of Henry Ware's appointment as a professor at Harvard College, signaling a break between liberal and orthodox Congregationalists.

15 Feb.	George Rapp and three hundred German Pietist followers establish the utopian Harmony Society, near Pittsburgh, Pennsylvania.
14 Mar.	Elizabeth Ann Bayley Seton converts to Roman Catholicism and soon begins a career in Catholic education.
Apr.	Tenskwatawa, the "Shawnee Prophet," experiences visions and begins calling for the renewal of the Shawnee Indians through recovering their old traditions.
July	Jedidiah Morse begins publishing the *Panoplist,* the first important religious journal in America, including news of missionary activity and explanations of orthodox Calvinism.

1806

•	Shakers begin to build a community in Union Village, Ohio, a sign of their growth on the frontier, particularly in the aftermath of revivals.
20 Nov.	Death of Baptist minister Isaac Backus.

1807

•	Thomas Campbell, later a founder of the Disciples of Christ, arrives from Ireland.
•	Methodist minister Lorenzo Dow introduces the camp meeting to England.

1808

•	Andover Seminary, Massachusetts, is founded as an orthodox counterpart to Harvard College, which is run by liberal Unitarians.
8 Apr.	Pope Pius VII makes Baltimore a metropolitan see, making it the religious center for the American Catholic Church, and organizes the dioceses of Boston, New York City, Philadelphia, and Bardstown, Kentucky; at the same time, John Carroll is named archbishop of Baltimore and Jean de Cheverus becomes bishop of Boston.

1809

•	Thomas and Alexander Campbell issue their "Declaration and Address," a founding document of the Disciples of Christ movement.
•	Formation of the New York Bible Society to distribute Bibles and promote religious reading.
Mar.	Elizabeth Ann Bayley Seton and four companions take vows as Sisters of Charity, forming the first American Roman Catholic women's religious order.

1810

June	Group of Andover Seminary students band together to offer themselves for foreign missionary service, leading to the forming of the American Board of Commissioners for Foreign Missions.

1811

29 May   John H. Hobart becomes Episcopal bishop of New York and begins to promote High Church practices and liturgy.

1812

•   Presbyterians found Princeton Theological Seminary in response to their concerns about the failure of the College of New Jersey (later Princeton University) to train ministers; the seminary will later be a major center of conservative American Calvinism.

•   Founding of the New York Religious Tract Society, first American organization devoted to the publication and distribution of short, inexpensive religious works designed for mass readership.

9 June   Joseph Stevens Buckminster, pastor of the Brattle Street Church in Boston, Massachusetts, dies, after leading his church into Unitarianism.

1815

•   The American Education Society is formed.

10 Aug.   Death of Handsome Lake, Iroquois religious leader.

24 Sept.   William Dubourg is named by the Pope to be bishop of Louisiana and the Floridas and begins to assert an American Catholic missionary presence in the West, with the help of French Jesuits.

3 Dec.   Death of John Carroll, first American Roman Catholic bishop.

OVERVIEW

Old-Time Religion. The old meeting house, a barn-like building with a tall white steeple, was the center of life in the New England village of the 1790s. Every Sunday the steeple bell rang solemnly, breaking the austere stillness of the morning. Virtually the entire town gathered together for the Sunday service, just as naturally as they woke up or had breakfast. In the summer the church filled with hot sunshine; in winter months the congregation shivered as the wind rattled the loose windows. No one ever left early, however, "for everybody was there, mother, aunts, grandmother, and all the town." In the meeting house, the leading citizens, including the minister's family and the wealthier farmers, sat in front, dressed in ruffles and plush coats. Farther back were families with less money, whose clothes were not elaborate but were scrupulously clean, worn only to church. A blacksmith asserted the dignity of his work and his democratic principles by wearing a clean leather apron. On simple benches to one side sat families of Indians, descendants of the Native Americans converted by Puritan missionaries in the area a century before. In a separate gallery on the other side sat the town's blacks, some free, some slave. All listened as a minister in a flowing black robe, wearing a wig and black gloves, delivered a sermon, often an hour long. After the sermon the congregation sang a hymn or two together, although there was no organ. The minister would lead prayers for families in trouble of one kind or another, trouble the entire congregation would already know about. As they were leaving the church, people greeted each other and gossiped about the news. Sunday was a quiet time, but it was also the only break in the weekly routine of hard work. No one wanted to miss the chance to be godly and socialize at the same time.

Myth and Reality. Harriet Beecher Stowe, most famous as the author of *Uncle Tom's Cabin* (1852), offered this picture of New England religion in *Oldtown Folks* (1869), a novel that drew on her childhood experiences in Connecticut in the early 1800s. Perhaps because she was the daughter of Lyman Beecher, one of the most famous ministers of the time, she appreciated how important religion was to the lives of many Americans in the early republic. Stowe's *Oldtown Folks* is a myth about early New England, and the importance of the region for the development of American culture after the Revolution. But like all good myths, it has a large element of truth in it. Many Americans did go to their village's one church every Sunday, as Stowe described, and did meet their neighbors and their God there. This was true in New England as well as in other regions, and the independent congregation's weekly service was a basic building block of religious experience for people across the new republic. But religion was more than Sunday meetings. It was personal meditation on the Bible, as well as rowdy "camp meetings" on the frontier. It was a social force that restrained America's movement toward individualism, even as it became one of the main arenas in which newly free Americans asserted their individuality. It was an experience that changed for many Americans over the course of the early national era, as they moved from church to church seeking truth, and as the churches remade themselves for the new times. Early national religion was as varied as early national America, but some unifying themes were discernible. *Oldtown Folks* provides some understanding of what Americans meant when they talked about religion and what religion was like in the early national era.

Everyday Life. Perhaps the most important clue Stowe provides about religion in the period after the American Revolution is that it was everywhere. For many early Americans religion was not only something for Sunday or for the church. It was also something to talk and argue about at home, on the street, and in school. It was something you did by yourself, with your family, and with the whole town. It was a way of making connections to strangers, and it could also divide neighbors from each other. It was the basis for making decisions about what to do with your life, how to judge others, and what to think about the world outside your town. It shaped your whole life. One sign of the widespread presence of religion was the Bible, by far the most widely available book in early America. Between 1777 and 1799 there were sixty-eight different editions of the English Bible printed in the United States. If a family owned a book, it was sure to be the Bible. A large, illustrated family Bible was almost always on a table in a middle-class family's parlor. The Bible was physically present everywhere, but was also part of everyday conversation, a source for children's names, and a constant reference in the political speeches of the day. Its many uses indicate how religion pervaded all aspects of early American life. Few Americans distinguished sharply between religion and other parts of their culture; religion to most people meant all the things that being human meant. As Stowe suggested, being religious was as natural as having breakfast.

Changing Christianity. The presence of the Bible reminds us that the religion of *Oldtown Folks* was a specific kind of religion. Many early Americans were Calvinists. Calvinism was a branch of the Protestant movement that broke away from the Roman Catholic Church in the 1530s. Many of the Europeans settling North America held Calvinist beliefs, and those beliefs were central to several American religious groups. The most famous Calvinists were the New England Puritans, whose descendants populated Stowe's *Oldtown Folks*. Puritans or not, American Calvinists held to the idea that God is absolutely powerful, humans are fundamentally sinful, and God had sent Jesus to redeem humanity and provide a chance for some to go to heaven at the Last Judgment, all as described in the Bible. Some of these ideas were changing quickly in the early national era. Many liberal thinkers were increasingly restless with traditional ways. They wanted a wider scope for human freedom in religion as well as in politics. They found the dour Calvinist God oppressive and imagined a more benevolent and humane deity. One result of these new ideas was that Americans had a variety of religious choices in the early national period. By 1815 there were so many churches and denominations to choose from that religious diversity was rightly being seen as an essential part of American culture. So while religion for most Americans in this era meant Protestant Christianity, it also meant to many Americans a degree of freedom in their beliefs and practices.

Christianizing America. Religion was present everywhere, but that was no accident. Many Americans worked hard in the early national era to make sure Christianity was impossible to escape. In general the period was a time of unification and institution building in response to the disruption of the Revolutionary era. Part of that disruption had been a decline in church membership. The churches regrouped after 1783 and began a recruiting drive that became one of the most powerful forces in American culture. Taking seriously the biblical order to "Go and teach all nations," the Protestant churches began to Christianize America, with some spectacular results. Rates of church membership steadily rose over the period, faster than the population grew. People flocked especially to the newer denominations such as the Baptist, the Methodist, and that of the Disciples of Christ, which exploded onto the frontier west of the Appalachian Mountains. These western areas were one center of Christian evangelizing, where the churches worked hard to bring souls to Christ and civilize the wilderness at the same time. At times the religious outbursts of the period seemed quite spontaneous, but the circuit riders and revivalist preachers at the camp meetings of this era planned their work carefully, with an eye toward the needs of early Americans and the opportunities presented by conditions in the new republic. This intense evangelization produced emotional conversion experiences in many Americans, who in turn took up the job of spreading Christianity in their homes, schools, and churches.

Free Individuals. The hard work of evangelizing the United States meant that while religion was a mechanism for social unity, it was also a cause of social conflict. Stowe's picture of the entire community gathered together on Sunday morning was only partly true. There were always people who did not join a church and stood outside the social order Stowe portrayed. Even those who were in the churches often fought with each other over what they believed and what they did. Many times their differences seemed more important to them than their basic similarity as Christians. The early republic saw not only the growth of large denominations such as the Methodists, but also the emergence of hundreds of small religious groups, called sects. Several of these had very unusual views about religion; some even abandoned Christianity. This was too much religious freedom for some Americans, and they struggled to contain the new forms of religious expression. They also struggled to control more-mundane kinds of freedom that seemed to threaten religion and social order. This often meant preaching against drinking, dueling, and other disruptive social practices that were too common in the era. But it also meant wrestling with the implications of freedom itself, the republican value that had fueled the Revolution. Some people would have criticized the democratic *Oldtown Folks* blacksmith for feeling free to wear his apron to church, no matter how clean it was. One prominent Baptist minister reacted to social disorder in 1787 by reminding his listeners that "the Command of God is 'Submit yourselves to every ordinance of man for the Lord's sake.'" But for many Americans religion was a matter of individual choice, and the message of submission to authority, even divinely ordained authority, was starting to sound quite old-fashioned.

Race. Stowe described the *Oldtown Folks* blacks and Indians as sitting apart from the rest of the congregation, and this is a reminder that for many Americans the experience of religion was largely determined not by their free choice as individuals but by their race and social status. Both Native Americans and African Americans were the targets of some of the most intense evangelizing efforts in this period. To Native Americans, Protestant missionaries preached a message of Christian freedom. However, it went hand in hand with constant pressure from white Americans to give up their land and traditional cultures, so to many Indians Christianity was a sign of something lost. The situation for African Americans was even more complex because so many were enslaved. Slaveowners used Christianity to defend the system of bondage even as Christianity also offered hope for spiritual freedom to those held in slavery. A few Americans in this period, black Christians among them, used religion to attack slavery and racism. But there was no consensus on this, and American Protestants, black and white, would struggle over this issue until the Civil War, and even after. Christian unity and peace was more a hope than a reality, especially with respect to race, and religion to many Americans meant something for a future time instead of what they had now.

A Millennial America. The heady days of the American Revolution had led many to think that humanity was facing a watershed, no less than the final days of God's judgment. This feeling, called millennialism, increased with the onset of the French Revolution, and the spread of war throughout Europe, which the United States finally joined in its second conflict with England, the War of 1812. People pored over their Bibles looking for help in reading the "signs of the times." Anticipating the end times gave an intense urgency to religious tasks. It inspired evangelists in their preaching since the rapid growth of conversions to Christ was one sign that judgment was coming quickly. Millennialism made the task of social reform more urgent too since some thought the end times would begin with a thousand-year period of a perfected social order. For many, America had a special role at this particular crisis of history. As the place where the new order of freedom and equality first took hold, it was naturally the home of this perfected world. Preachers such as Ezra Stiles, the president of Yale College, spoke of America as a new Israel, meaning that Americans were the people chosen by God to lead the world into the millennial heaven. And despite the official separation of church and state, political leaders from George Washington on down regularly asked for God's blessing on America and considered the nation's work to be God's work too. So for many Americans religion was strongly mixed with national pride, and a sense of how exceptional the new country was in God's view. They strongly believed that what one poem called the "rising glory of America" was a divine sanction for optimism and activism of all kinds.

Women. When Stowe wrote that everyone in *Oldtown Folks* was at church, the ones she named specifically were all women. Females dominated the membership of churches in this era, even if few were leaders or preachers. There are many reasons for the presence of women at the heart of so much religious activity in the early republic. One was that American Protestantism was becoming for many a religion of the heart. The revivalists and other evangelicals of the era tried hard to prompt an intensely emotional response to God, one that would affect individuals so strongly that they would feel a "new birth" and convert to faith in Christ. The language they used to talk about God was filled with phrases such as "searching your heart." Emphasizing feelings of God's presence, rather than ideas about God, meant that religion was accessible to all, regardless of background or training. That a woman had not been to college was no bar to her having as much insight into religion as the most educated minister. Indeed, because women in this era were understood to be more naturally emotional than men, they supposedly had more insight into religion. This was a double-edged sword, of course, since women were probably more constrained than they were freed by the way people thought about gender. But for half of the American population, religion meant a social world especially attuned to women's feelings and needs. It reflected women's experiences even if it could not resolve the contradictions of those experiences.

Democratic Religion? Probably for all Americans in the early republic, religion was a combination of something traditional and something that was part of their time and place. They were living through the aftermath of the Revolution and trying hard to adapt older ways to new ideas and circumstances. This was as true of religion as of art, education, or politics. They had many different views about religion because they also found themselves in a wide variety of circumstances. For many the new nation meant freedom and equality, a chance for an individual to shape the world for himself or herself. Early Americans often experienced religion in the same way. In the exuberance of a frontier revival meeting, it was easy to see American Protestantism as open to all, shaped by individual participants and not by autocratic priests, a symbol of the democracy emerging in America. There is truth in this, as there is truth in Stowe's picture of the New England origins of this national phenomenon. But in freely choosing evangelical Protestantism, many early Americans also freely embraced a religion that was authoritarian and that considered humans to be sinful and saved only by God's action, not their own. America's religious culture was a mix of elements which can seem contradictory to us today. The story of early American religion is more complicated than any one telling captures, and the details of the varieties of religious experience in the new republic are just as revealing as the big story of the emergence of an evangelical culture in the newly independent United States.

TOPICS IN THE NEWS

AFRICAN AMERICANS

Slavery. During the early national period, most African Americans were slaves. Of more than 750,000 black Americans in 1790, all but 60,000 were enslaved. Their enslavement was the single most important feature of African American religious life in this period. Black Americans used religion to find some relief from slavery even as the forms of religion they practiced were shaped by this "peculiar institution." Because they were in bondage, the religious history of African Americans is a telling example of the limitations of religious freedom in early America, as well as of its growth. For despite the limitations and deprivations slavery and racism imposed on many African Americans, a richly varied religious culture evolved that was a powerful force in black life and was just as complex as the religions of white Americans.

African Religions. Africans brought their own religions with them from Africa, although we cannot know how many traditional practices and beliefs survived or how they changed once in America. The importation of these religions continued well into the early national period. Traffic in slaves was heavy from the Revolution to 1808, when the slave trade ended, with as many Africans being imported into the United States in these years as had arrived over the entire colonial period. Although the native-born black population was quickly growing, there was a steady infusion of African traditions into the slave communities. This meant that for many blacks, religion meant not Christianity, but some variant of African folk traditions. These included ideas such as reincarnation and the veneration of ancestors shared by many West African religions, as well as a wide variety of healing practices and magical beliefs, often called conjure. Conjuring was widely and informally practiced, often including such things as herbal medicines, charms, aphrodisiacs, and witchcraft lore. Sometimes conjuring became a set of more-formal practices, as was the case with the voodoo cults of French Louisiana. But usually it was extremely flexible and open to all who could find meaning in the various practices it included. African Americans were by no means alone in having such beliefs at the center of their religious lives. Many white Americans held similar beliefs, and folk traditions were a primary area of interchange between the races. Many whites took up the healing traditions of Africa, and the African American witchcraft stories that have come down to us show the important influence of the European witchcraft traditions that easily survived the Salem witch-hunts of 1692.

Christians. The presence of African traditions did not mean there was no room for Christianity in the black community. With the emergence of the revivals in the South, Christianity made important gains in the African American population during the early national period. The emotionalism and egalitarianism of the evangelical churches of the Baptists and the Methodists appealed to many black Americans. These religions resonated with their cultural legacy from Africa and spoke to their condition as slaves or, at best, second-class free people. As the numbers of black Christians grew and the racism of European Americans persisted, African Americans began to assert themselves as independent religious leaders. Black pastors emerged, and they contributed to the growth of black Christianity with their greater willingness to pursue mission work among the black community. This process was not an easy one, especially in the South, as the example of Andrew Bryan shows.

Andrew Bryan. A former slave living in Savannah, Georgia, Bryan in the late 1780s began to preach and gathered a following among other blacks. They began to meet together to worship but were harassed by whites who feared the slaves were meeting to plot their escape. Bryan and others were imprisoned and whipped, but Bryan turned persecution into opportunity and praised the chance to suffer for Christ. Finally, in 1788 Bryan was able to organize the First African Baptist Church, with the help of a white Baptist sponsor. The church had 40 members at first and grew quickly; by 1790 there were 225 communicants and 350 other baptized members. Persecution by neighboring whites let up by 1800, but it was an uneasy truce. Despite the survival of Bryan's church and the founding of two other black Baptist churches in Savannah in the early 1800s, slavery was a fact of life for most black congregants. Some were forbidden by their owners to become full members. Bryan's brother Sampson assisted in his duties while remaining a slave. And Bryan himself, despite his experiences, was a slave holder. He reported to English Baptists in 1800 that he was "well provided for . . . having a house and a

Slave preacher and his congregation

lot . . . and a fifty-six acre tract of land . . . and eight slaves; for whose education and happiness, I am enabled thro' mercy to provide."

Richard Allen. In the North the gradual abolition of slavery may have made it easier for African Americans to assert religious independence, but those assertions were still shaped by the oppression of blacks by whites. Like Andrew Bryan, Richard Allen was a former slave who had converted to Christianity and become a preacher. Despite his piety and his long membership in Saint George's Methodist Church in Philadelphia, Allen suffered the effects of discrimination against blacks. In 1787 he and two other black members of Saint George's were forced from their knees and told to go to the church's gallery by white members angry that blacks had presumed to leave their assigned area. Allen and his friends responded by separating from Saint George's and founding an independent black congregation, eventually called Bethel Methodist Church. Once again separation did not mean the end of troubles. Saint George's later tried to take control of Bethel Church's property, leading the black congregation to sue for their rights, a legal struggle that lasted until 1816, when Allen and his group were finally successful. In the meantime Allen had initiated an even more important step in securing religious independence for black Christians. Tensions continued between white church leaders and the black Methodist congregations growing up with Allen's help in Pennsylvania, New Jersey, Maryland, and Delaware. The discord led Allen to call a meeting of the black churches in 1816. When the delegates gathered, they formed the African Methodist Episcopal Church, the first African American denomination, and elected Allen as their bishop. This move gave black Christians a stronger institutional voice and was a mark of how important these new churches

were becoming to African American life and identity. Black Methodists were not alone in forming such churches. The first black Episcopal Church, established in Philadelphia in 1794, was joined in 1807 by a black Presbyterian congregation. Black Baptist churches were formed in New York City, Philadelphia, and Boston between 1804 and 1809. These institutions offered significant opportunities for leadership and public presence, and they became centers of the free black communities in these cities. They had social, economic, and political significance in addition to supporting the spiritual lives of their members. Black churches began to find their place as a key expression of African American independence and resistance to white racism, a role that continued through the civil rights movement of the twentieth century.

The "Invisible Institution." Despite these important developments in the northern states, most African Americans lived in the South. This meant that slavery was at the heart of their religious lives, in one way or another. For some whites and blacks alike, the southern evangelical emphasis on an intensely individual conversion experience gave an African American Christian a dignity that was hard to reconcile with slave status. Within the black communities slavery prompted much soul-searching. Leading black ministers such as Richard Allen were early public opponents of slavery. They articulated religious as well as political arguments against the institution and sought to ease its effects through the missionary work they sponsored. They struggled with the theological question of why God permitted the evil of slavery to exist. In the South, where black churches were not as strongly established and where the slave codes limited the public presence of black preaching, the response to slavery took a different tack. Many slaves made Christianity into a religion that spoke to their condition. They gathered together outside the view of white missionaries and their churches, creating an "invisible institution" beyond the sight of their masters. In these meetings the slaves rejected their owners' view that the Bible justified slavery and developed their own view that emphasized themes of freedom and deliverance by Christ, though for their safety they cast this in ambiguous terms. Slaves expressed these beliefs in the sermons they preached, the Bible stories they told each other, and, most dramatically, in the songs they sang. These spirituals are the deepest expressions of both their painful position and the hope they found in their form of Christianity. They expressed how their religion let African Americans accept their condition at the same time as they were resisting it. The performance of these songs, in dances called "shouts" that dramatized the stories they told, was much like the enthusiasm of many participants in the revivals of the era. In these songs African Americans were participating in one of the most important developments of American religion, while at the same time making that development distinctively their own.

Sources:

Lawrence Levine, *Black Culture and Black Consciousness* (New York & Oxford: Oxford University Press, 1977);

Donald G. Mathews, *Religion in the Old South* (Chicago: University of Chicago Press, 1977);

Albert J. Raboteau, *Slave Religion: The "Invisible Institution" in the Antebellum South* (Oxford: Oxford University Press, 1978).

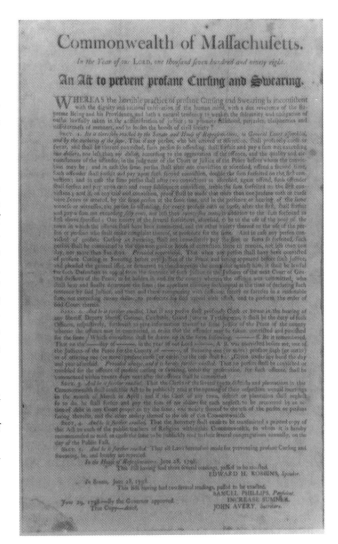

Broadside publicizing the 1798 Massachusetts law that prohibited "profane Cursing and Swearing"

CHURCH AND STATE

Separation. The separation of church and state in the United States was one of the most remarkable achievements of the new nation. The United States was unique among western nations in valuing this principle. In the late eighteenth century many people believed that without a close alliance between church and state a nation would be too unstable to survive. In Great Britain all members of Parliament and other public officials were required to be members of the established Anglican Church. In fact, in 1787 some non-Anglicans were just beginning a long effort to persuade Parliament to remove this requirement. At the same moment Americans were writing their Constitution and including in Article VI a prohibition on any such religious tests for American federal officeholders. Separating church and state was not an easy process for Americans, despite their willingness to entertain the possibility that their nation could thrive even without a state church. If the principle was important to many Americans, such as Thomas Jefferson and James Madison, turning the ideal into reality required a complex political and social struggle. Like the evolution of other features of early national society, the separation of church and state was much more than simply enshrining an ideal in a constitution.

Virginia. The factors leading to the national separation of church and state appeared first in Virginia. In January 1786 the Virginia legislature passed an Act for Establishing Religious Freedom, written some seven years earlier by Thomas Jefferson. Almost a decade passed between Jefferson's writing the bill and the state adopting it, suggesting how difficult it could be to separate church and state. Jefferson's bill started from the premise that "Almighty God hath created the mind free" and objected to the tyranny of forcing people to observe a religion they did not choose for themselves. "Our civil rights have no dependence on our religious opinions, any more than our opinions in physics or geometry," the act declared, asserting "truth is great and will prevail if left to herself," without help from the state, which would only cheapen and corrupt it. It concluded that "all men shall be free to profess, and by argument to maintain, their opinions in matters of religion, and that the same shall in no wise diminish, enlarge, or affect their civil capacities." In forbidding the state to control religious beliefs, Jefferson was clearly supporting the "inalienable rights" of humanity which he had written about in the Declaration of Independence.

Opposition. As extended to religion, however, those principles were not universally accepted at that time, even by people closely associated with the cause of American freedom. When it came time to debate Jefferson's bill in the Virginia legislature, it was opposed by Patrick Henry, whose "Give me liberty or give me death" speech in 1775 had inspired many Americans. Henry proposed a different answer to the question of the relations of church and state. Henry's bill would have made the "Christian Religion" the established religion of Virginia, and it would have provided tax support for all Christian churches. James Madison, who was promoting Jefferson's bill (Jefferson was the minister to France from 1785 to 1789), published a "Memorial and Remonstrance" in 1785, arguing against Henry's bill on grounds of natural rights and rationality. These arguments alone would probably not have carried the day against Henry, whom many considered to have a more moderate position, one that acknowledged that most Virginians were, after all, Christians, and respected religion and its social benefits.

The Baptists. Madison had some powerful, if unexpected, allies in the Baptists. The Baptists opposed Madison's and Jefferson's rationalist and deist principles, but they had their own reasons for supporting a clear separation of church and state. Before the Revolution the established Anglican Church, supported by taxes, had hindered the Baptists' every step. The Baptists reacted with intense suspicion of any government involvement with religion. They held strongly to the view that religion was a personal matter between individuals and God. State involvement, even in a positive way, would corrupt that divine relationship, thus endangering the soul of the believer. Jefferson's bill echoed these beliefs, and with support from legislators from the western part of the state, responding to the wishes of their Baptist constituents, it was passed on 16 January 1786.

Bill of Rights. When Madison came to draft the federal Bill of Rights in 1789, he remembered the lessons of the earlier struggle over religious freedom in Virginia. The First Amendment took up the question of religion, suggesting that religious freedom was a fundamental human right. Madison also considered it a political necessity, remembering how Baptist votes helped elect him to the first Congress. The First Amendment includes two clauses about religion: "Congress shall make no law respecting an establishment of religion, or prohibiting the free exercise thereof." The first clause clearly prohibits the United States from setting up a state church as in Britain. The second clause reflects the importance Americans placed on freedom of conscience. In understanding the amendment, however, it is important to keep in mind that most Americans at that time valued freedom of conscience within a Christian context. That is, many wanted religious freedom guaranteed in the

MINISTERS ON CHURCH-STATE RELATIONS

Although they were both prominent revivalists and supporters of evangelical religion, Baptist Isaac Backus and Congregationalist Lyman Beecher differed on the question of religious freedom. Backus was tireless in his efforts to limit strictly the state's role in religion, as in this excerpt from a 1779 letter proposing a bill of rights for Massachusetts:

As God is the only worthy object of all religious worship, and nothing can be true religion but a voluntary obedience unto his revealed will, of which each rational soul has an equal right to judge for itself; every person has an unalienable right to act in all religious affairs according to the full persuasion of his own mind, where others are not injured thereby. And civil rulers are so far from having any right to empower any person or persons to judge for others in such affairs, and to enforce their judgments with the sword, that their power ought to be exerted to protect all persons and societies, within their jurisdiction, from being injured or interrupted in the free enjoyment of this right.

In contrast to Backus's argument for limiting state control of religion, Beecher strenuously defended state support for the Congregational Church. He greatly feared that disestablishment would soon lead to religious and moral decline, arguing in this 1804 sermon that government and religion had to work together:

Our religion is unquestionably our greatest security, and the preservation of divine institutions, an object of the first magnitude. Let the Sabbath be annihilated and the sanctuary abandoned; let irreligion and vice be extended through the mass of our nation, and our liberties cannot be preserved. We may form free constitutions, but our vices will destroy them; we may enact laws, but they will not protect us.

Yet after his state had disestablished the Congregational Church in 1818, Beecher came to think differently, and later said it was "the best thing that ever happened to the State of Connecticut. It cut the churches loose from dependence on state support. It threw them wholly on their own resources and on God. They say ministers have lost their influence; the fact is, they have gained."

Sources: Lyman Beecher, *The Practicability of Suppressing Vice* (New London, Conn.: Printed by Samuel Green, 1804), p. 19;

Barbara M. Cross, ed., *The Autobiography of Lyman Beecher* (Cambridge, Mass.: Harvard University Press, 1961), pp. 252–253;

Isaac Backus to Noah Alden, August 1779, reprinted in William G. McLoughlin, ed., *Isaac Backus on Church, State, and Calvinism: Pamphlets, 1754–1789* (Cambridge, Mass.: Harvard University Press, 1968), pp. 487–488.

The two phrases of the First Amendment's guarantee of religious freedom took shape in the course of the congressional debates about the Bill of Rights in August 1789. In discussing the scope of American religious freedom, Rep. Daniel Carroll of Maryland (a Catholic, and the brother of John Carroll, later the first American Catholic bishop), argued in favor of a broad protection against government interference in religion, saying, "the rights of conscience are, in their nature, of peculiar delicacy, and will little bear the gentlest touch of governmental hand." He also thought these guarantees were politically important and "would tend more towards conciliating the minds of the people to the government than almost any other amendment." Others worried the protections offered were too broad; Peter Sylvester of New York "feared it might be thought to have a tendency to abolish religion altogether." Connecticut's Benjamin Huntington worried "that the words might be taken in such a latitude as to be extremely hurtful to the cause of religion," noting that his state, for one, still paid ministers with tax money. Several representatives thought the amendment unnecessary; Roger Sherman of Connecticut pointed out that "Congress had no authority whatever delegated to them by the constitution to make religious establishments." James Madison was not so certain. The constitution did give "power to Congress to make all laws necessary and proper to carry into execution the constitution, and the laws made under it [and this arguably] enabled them to make laws of such a nature as might infringe the rights of conscience, and establish a national religion." Accordingly, Madison argued for the amendment, which he said meant "that Congress should not establish a religion, and enforce the legal observation of it by law, nor compel men to worship God in any manner contrary to their conscience."

Source: Thomas Hart Benton, ed., *Abridgment of the Debates of Congress,* volume 1 (New York: Appleton, 1857), pp. 137–138.

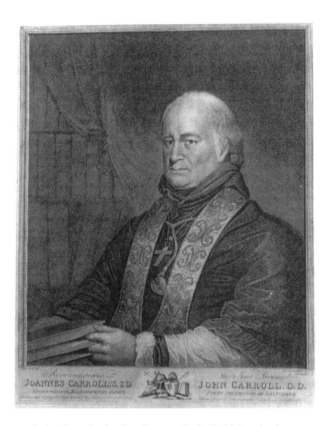

John Carroll, the first Roman Catholic bishop in the United States

principle, government involvement with religion did not cease absolutely with the First Amendment's ratification in 1791. For instance, a few days after passing the First Amendment, Congress called a day of thanksgiving for "the many signal favors of Almighty God."

State Governments. The Bill of Rights established the idea of the separation of churches from the federal government, but the same was not true of the state governments. State legislatures regulated religion far more actively than Congress. Although Virginia had passed a broad guarantee of religious freedom, and many other states had included similar statements in their constitutions or bills of rights, most state governments remained involved in religion. Many states continued to restrict public offices to Protestants, or to Christians. In Connecticut, New Hampshire, and Massachusetts the Congregational churches remained the official, established churches, supported by taxes collected from all citizens, Congregationalists and non-Congregationalists alike. There was constant agitation to change this system. Baptist minister Isaac Backus, for example, was a tireless advocate for reform. Backus spoke for many Baptists who considered any state involvement with religion as an opportunity for corruption to sneak in and undermine true godliness. More practically, Backus and the Baptists resented the need to petition for exemption from religious taxes. Officials often denied these petitions, distrusting religious scruples as attempts to avoid taxes. The Congregationalists, of course, strenuously resisted disestab-

First Amendment more because of their historical experiences with taxation to support one Protestant church at the expense of all others than because of an abstract belief that all religions are equal. One historian has called the passage of the First Amendment mainly a "symbolic act" since the exact meaning of the clauses remains debatable, despite their importance over the last two centuries. One way to think of it is as an expression of an ideal, which early Americans thought was important but which they realized only imperfectly in practice. Despite the

lishment. One of their leaders was Lyman Beecher, minister in Litchfield, Connecticut, and one of the best-known preachers of the day. Beecher considered state support for the true religion of Congregationalism as crucial, and he saw attacks on the established churches to be as bad as atheism, whether they came from deists or Baptists.

End of Established Churches. Beecher fought hard, but he lost in 1818 when Connecticut ended establishment policies (New Hampshire followed in 1819, and Massachusetts held out until 1833). Beecher was able to turn defeat to victory, however. He embraced the principle of voluntarism, that religion was strongest when people accepted God from purely spiritual reasons, with no hint of state coercion. This idea gave new fire to American Protestantism, and meant that it was still possible to see America as a godly nation, even without state support of churches. Beecher's view was justified in 1835 by the great French commentator Alexis de Tocqueville, who wrote that he found "no country in the world where the Christian religion retains a greater influence over the souls of men than in America," where there was a close union between the "spirit of religion and the spirit of freedom."

Sources:

Stephen Botein, "Religious Dimensions of the Early American State," in *Beyond Confederation*, edited by Richard Beeman and others (Chapel Hill: University of North Carolina Press, 1987);

Thomas J. Curry, *The First Freedoms* (Oxford: Oxford University Press, 1986);

Stuart C. Henry, *Unvanquished Puritan* (Grand Rapids, Mich.: Eerdmans, 1973);

William G. McLoughlin, *New England Dissent, 1630-1833: The Baptists and the Separation of Church and State* (Cambridge, Mass.: Harvard University Press, 1971);

William Lee Miller, *The First Liberty* (New York: Knopf, 1986).

EARLY AMERICAN CATHOLICS

People Set Apart. There were few Roman Catholics in the early United States, perhaps twenty-five thousand of a total population of almost four million in 1783. Like the Jews, American Catholics felt themselves to be a people set apart from Protestant Americans by their distinctive beliefs and rituals. Catholics suffered the added problem of a persistent anti-Catholic animus which had roots in the Protestant Reformation and had been reawakened in the controversy over Britain's treatment of French Catholics in Quebec in 1763. Many Protestant Americans considered the British too generous to the Catholics. American Catholics were just as engaged as Protestants in shaping the character of the new country's citizens. They eagerly embraced the republicanism of the new nation and worked hard in the 1780s to establish an American version of the Roman church. Father John Carroll wrote his *Address to the Roman Catholics of the United States of America* in 1784, which explained to Catholics the advantages to them of American religious

CHURCH MEMBERSHIP IN THE EARLY REPUBLIC

Church membership grew rapidly over the decades following American independence. Most historians consider 1780 to mark a low point in church affiliation. Probably no more than 10 percent of Americans formally claimed church membership in 1780, although many more attended church regularly. By 1820 that figure had probably at least doubled. Almost all religious groups flourished, but some grew more rapidly than others, as shown in this chart of the number of congregations in each major denomination:

Denomination	1776	1820	Percentage increase
Anglican/ Episcopalian	495	600	21
Baptist	497	2700	443
Congregational	668	1100	65
Lutheran	150	800	433
Methodist	65	2700	4050
Presbyterian	588	1700	189
Roman Catholic	56	124	121

For the Baptists and Methodists growth was spectacular. The Baptists claimed 35,000 members in 1784 and more than 170,000 in 1810. The Methodists counted fewer than 15,000 members in 1784 and almost 200,000 in 1810.

Sources: Roger Finke and Rodney Stark, *The Churching of America* (New Brunswick, N.J.: Rutgers University Press, 1992), p. 25;

Edwin S. Gaustad, *Historical Atlas of Religion in America*, revised edition (New York: Harper & Row, 1976), p. 43;

Russell E. Richey, *Early American Methodism* (Bloomington: Indiana University Press, 1991), p. 50.

freedom. Carroll attempted to assure Protestants that Catholics were firmly committed to American ways.

A Struggling Church. With few members, and those scattered across the new nation (the only significant concentration of Catholics was in Maryland), the church turned its attention to recruiting new members and supporting them with strong institutions. A crucial early step was the 1784 appointment by the Pope of John Carroll to lead American Catholics as "prefect apostolic and superior of the missions" in the United States. Carroll's dynamic leadership was crucial in establishing American Catholicism on a sound footing. The American character of the church soon emerged, as Carroll's fellow priests elected him to be their bishop in 1789, an election to which the Pope agreed. There were limits to this republican Catholicism, however, which complicated the story of the church's growth. The democratic practice of electing bishops lasted only until 1808, after which they were appointed by the Pope in Rome. Carroll's effort to promote the church was a constant struggle to accommodate the European Catholic tradition of centralized authority with the realities of American life and republican ideas. For example, Carroll was forced to rely heavily on lay help because of the shortage of priests and the conditions of the growing nation. Some lay people asserted their authority in their parishes more than Carroll would have liked, just as their Protestant neighbors were doing in their churches. This was the case in Saint Peter's Church in New York, where Carroll was caught up in a controversy with the parishioners in 1785 over which of two Irish priests should be the pastor.

Ethnic Tensions. An important part of this and other similar disputes was not only the desire of lay people to have control over their own religious lives, but also to have priests of their own national origin since the Catholic Church throughout the 1800s was largely an immigrant church. In Boston tensions ran deep between French and Irish Catholics. The French preferred to be buried with Protestants rather than the Irish, and there were arguments over what language the priests should use for services. A French and an English priest carried their personal disputes into the press, making matters worse. Carroll resolved the issue in 1792 by replacing both priests with Francis Matignon, a capable Frenchman. The community grew slowly, becoming a diocese in 1808 under the leadership of another French priest, Jean de Cheverus. Worldly figures such as Matignon and Cheverus improved the public image of American Catholics in part by mingling easily with the liberal Protestant elite of Boston, but they were also devoted to the service of poor Irish parishioners. Carroll and his successors (mostly of English Catholic origin) all faced the problem of forging a unified American church from a collection of often intensely localist parishes, many with strong ties to Europe. These difficulties were made worse in 1803 when the United States acquired the Louisiana Purchase, with its French Catholic roots. Carroll persevered, however, organizing dioceses and recruiting priests in Europe and America to meet the needs of a frontier church, just as the Methodists and Baptists were doing. His efforts were successful. There were 195,000 Catholics by 1820, even before the great waves of Irish and German immigration that would make the Catholics the largest denomination in America by 1865.

Education. If the revival tent was the characteristic structure of evangelical Protestantism, the parish school filled that role for Catholicism. Catholics became preoccupied with the task of education in this period, and it soon became a central feature of Catholic institutional

Rev. Samuel Hopkins, a Calvinist preacher who studied under Jonathan Edwards

life, as well as a form of devotional practice. Catholics shared this with Protestants, who were also experimenting with education in the early national era, but the Catholic experience was distinctive. Catholics supported education partly because of the pressing need for priests, which led to the founding of the first American seminary, Saint Mary's, in Baltimore in 1791. Before that date the few Catholic priests in America had come from Europe, like the French priests who founded Saint Mary's, or were at least trained and ordained there, as was John Carroll. Education was needed by others besides priests, however, and the same year saw the founding of Georgetown Academy, Maryland, later one of the most prestigious American Catholic colleges. These schools were restricted to men, of course, but the education of women by women soon became just as important to Catholics. An Irish laywoman, Alice Lalor, led the way by founding a Catholic women's school in Philadelphia in 1797. By 1816 Lalor had moved her school to Georgetown and founded a convent for the training of nuns to staff her schools and others like it. Even before this, in 1809, Elizabeth Ann Seton had founded the first women's religious order in America, the Sisters of Charity. These women, and those in the other religious orders that followed, devoted their lives to serving God and their church through education, health care, and other endeavors. They quickly founded schools across the

Engraving of the ordination of the first American foreign missionaries, 1812

country, and Seton, later canonized as a saint, became known as the founder of the parochial school system that is still one of the most important parts of Catholic life in many parishes. In these schools devotional practice merged with the work of education since faith was taught to children as well as reading and arithmetic. The schools performed an essential function in bringing Catholic students, increasingly the children of immigrants, into American life. Yet the firm commitment to Catholic religious instruction set these schools off from the public schools beginning to form in the early 1800s. Many Catholics succeeded socially and economically with the help of these schools, but success never fully erased the persistence of anti-Catholic and anti-immigrant bigotry. Catholics embraced American religious freedom to their institutional and devotional advantage, but their distinctive presence in early America would long remain a thorn in the side of many Protestants.

Sources:

Jay P. Dolan, *The American Catholic Experience* (Garden City, N.Y.: Doubleday, 1985);

John Tracy Ellis, *American Catholicism*, revised edition (Chicago: University of Chicago Press, 1969);

Oscar Handlin, *Boston's Immigrants, 1790–1880* (Cambridge, Mass.: Harvard University Press, 1979).

EARLY MISSIONARY WORK

The Lord's Mission. At the heart of evangelical Protestantism was the desire to spread God's word. In the early national period Americans did this in many ways, from praying with their families before meals, to attending church services and urging their neighbors to come also, to speaking out at revival meetings and inspiring others to do the same. One special form of evangelization that took shape during this period was missionary work. This was an organized outreach to non-Christians in the hope of converting them to Christianity. This work had been going on since the earliest European settlements of America. All of the first colonizing efforts had invoked the need of bringing Christ to the Indians. Later, English and Scottish missionary societies sent ministers from Europe and supported efforts to educate the Indians to assume ministerial roles themselves. Catholics as well had pursued this task; French Jesuits worked in the Mississippi and Ohio River valleys, and Spanish Franciscans, such as Father Junipero Serra, founded mission settlements in California. Some of those churches still survive today, surrounded by modern cities, but in general these colonial missionary efforts met with little success. After 1783 missionary work took on a new urgency in the United States for various reasons and also began to go in some new directions as Americans put their own stamp on this task.

New Directions. The collapse of the Anglican establishment in America after the Revolutionary War created a vacuum since much missionary work had been sponsored by the Anglican Society for the Propagation of the Gospel. Americans took over, particularly the Methodists, who were the primary heirs of the missionary tradition. Francis Asbury, the first American Methodist bishop, began his career as a missionary to America and traveled and preached across the country until his death in 1816. The Methodist evangelization of the frontier was partly a fulfillment of earlier Anglican work, but carrying God's word to the unchurched was different in

As Americans founded their republic, a French observer, Michel-Guillaume-Jean de Crèvecoeur, wrote a series of letters describing the character of the new nation and published them in Europe in the 1780s under the pen name J. Hector St. John. His main theme was the struggle to forge a single American identity from the different backgrounds and values of the American people. He saw this process in the story of early American religion:

Let us suppose you and I to be travelling; we observe that in this house, to the right, lives a catholic, who prays to God as he has been taught and believes in transubstantiation; he works and raises wheat, he has a large family of children, all hale and robust; his belief, his prayers offend nobody. About one mile farther on the same road, his next neighbour may be a good, honest, plodding German Lutheran, who addresses himself to the same God, the God of all, agreeably to the modes he has been educated in, and believes in consubstantiation; by so doing, he scandalizes nobody; he also works in his fields, embellishes the earth, clears swamps, etc. What has the world to do with his Lutheran principles? He persecutes nobody, and nobody persecutes him: he visits his neighbours, and his neighbours visit him. Next to him lives a seceder, the most enthusiastic of all sectaries. . . . He likewise raises good crops; his house is handsomely painted; his orchard is one of the fairest in the neighbourhood. How does it concern the welfare of the country, or of the province at large, what this man's religious sentiments are? He is a good farmer; he is a sober, peaceable, good citizen. . . . Thus all sects are mixed as well as all nations; thus religious indifference is imperceptibly disseminated from one end of the continent to the other; which is at present one of the strongest characteristics of the Americans.

Source: J. Hector St. John, *Letters from an American Farmer* (Philadelphia: From the Press of Mathew Carey, 1793), pp. 52–54.

early national America. After 1783 evangelical Americans shared a pervasive sense of a new beginning. Many believed that a new day was dawning for America, a day associated with the coming of the last days of God's judgment, foretold in some parts of the Bible. Some thought those days were coming quickly and that converting as many people as possible was part of the preparation needed to bring on these better times. Others thought that even if the last days of the millennium were still some time away, the job of improving the world by expanding Christianity was still an important part of bringing in a more perfect order, an earthly world where men and women might get a glimpse of heaven. A more Christian America would be the first view of that heaven. In addition to these millennial purposes, missionary work fit in well with the rebuilding of old churches and the founding of new ones, the central religious dynamic after the disruptions of the Revolutionary era.

Missions to Asia. These motivations came together for a group of young men studying for the ministry at Andover Seminary in Massachusetts in 1810. Deeply steeped in the developing orthodox position that salvation was available to all people, and caught up in the momentum of the spread of evangelical Protestantism, these men were searching for their roles in this task. Some of these men had been together in college, and had already "banded" together in a secret society, the Brethren, to spread God's word. They took a further step at Andover as they settled on the idea of a mission to foreign lands, something the English Baptists had been doing since 1792. The Andover men were inspired by reading about this work in the religious press of the age, as well as by the presence of a Hawaiian native, Henry Obookiah, at Andover. Obookiah's conversion was a living sign of the possibilities of spreading religion abroad. Adoniram Judson, Samuel Mills, and a few others brought their efforts out into the open, founding the American Board of Commissioners for Foreign Missions, with the support of the Congregationalist General Association. They began publishing materials and raising money to support this work. In 1812 Judson, with his wife and some others, left for India. They eventually reached Burma, where they would work for thirty-eight years, the first of many American foreign missions. These efforts would not only spread news of Christ, but also of America.

Missions at Home. Missionary work went forward at home as well as abroad. In some ways every revivalist and preacher was a missionary of a sort, as all ultimately sought the conversion of souls for Christ. But missionary work as a denomination's strategy for reaching out to new members took on some more-specific forms in this period. A good deal of attention was paid to Indian missions, but more-innovative forms of mission work were also pursued. The New York Tract Society, founded in 1812 to spread God's word to the unchurched, printed inexpensive pamphlets filled with Bible stories and moral messages. Philadelphia's First Day Society founded the first Sunday school, called a "First Day School," in 1791, and these schools soon became a major movement within evangelical Protestantism. Philadelphia's First Day Schools were sponsored jointly by several church groups, including the Quakers, and they taught reading and writing to poor children on Sundays, their only time free from labor. Asbury spoke out in 1796 in favor of denominational Sunday schools which would focus more directly on religious instruction, and the Methodists then took the lead in giving these efforts a more evangelical flavor. The schools continued to teach reading and writing, but they now directed those tasks toward the greater one of knowing and understanding God. The evangelical Sunday schools spread rapidly; in Philadelphia alone, where there had never been more than four First Day Schools, there were forty-one evangelical Sunday schools in 1818.

Although they focused on religious instruction, the schools had the broader goal of training moral Christian citizens. Just as the circuit riders tried to tame the frontier by introducing Christianity, so did Sunday school teachers try to tame the increasing disorder of America's quickly growing cities by introducing young people to Christian belief and godly behavior.

Disinterested Benevolence. If missionary work was securely grounded in the social and religious conditions of the new nation, it also had deep roots in America's religious past. One of the important motivations for many missionaries was actually a theological idea, the doctrine of disinterested benevolence. This idea was developed by Samuel Hopkins, the staunchly orthodox minister in Newport, Rhode Island. Hopkins preached a rigorous form of Calvinism, part of which was the idea that humans could never earn their salvation, but must receive it as a free gift from God. Yet they must nevertheless strive to do good all their lives, without any hope of reward, but simply for the glory of God. Hopkins took this disinterested benevolence to extremes, even saying people should be happy to be damned to hell since even that would be a demonstration of God's power, an idea some found hard to take. But many found a softer notion of selfless service in a world of severe hardship and few tangible rewards powerful. The criticism Hopkins received for his early antislavery preaching in Newport, where the slave trade was an important part of the economy, was itself a vivid illustration of his commitment to doing good despite the consequences. Hopkins and his followers offered a compelling rationale for the difficult life of the missionary or of any evangelical work, in America or overseas. There was in this work a strong element of self-interest, as missionaries served the purposes of national expansion, or Sunday school teachers made poor children conform to their polite standards. But Hopkins's influence should remind us that self-serving actions may also have sincerely selfless goals.

Organization. An important part of missionary work was how it was organized. Although the inspiration of people such as Judson was crucial, the work finally could not succeed without the support of the institutional church. Many denominations founded their own mission societies, beginning with the Massachusetts Congregationalists in 1787. A network of supporting groups gradually grew up around these denominational bodies. These groups raised money, planned mission trips and outposts, recruited the men and women to travel on these journeys, and published the stories of these missionaries in the growing religious press. Many of these, such as the Boston Female Society for Promoting the Diffusion of Christian Knowledge, founded in 1801, brought women into the effort. The groups were a form of mission themselves for the people, many of them women, who did this work at home. The societies were a way for mothers and children to participate in work in far-off places and to make a contribution in a way suited to their social cir-

THE CIRCUIT RIDER

Peter Cartwright was one of the most tireless Methodist circuit riders of the nineteenth century. At the end of his career he looked back on what his life was like on the early frontier around 1800:

A Methodist preacher in those days, when he felt that God had called him to preach, instead of hunting up a college or Biblical institute, hunted up a hardy pony or a horse, and some traveling apparatus, and with his library always at hand, namely, Bible, Hymn Book, and Discipline, he started, and with a text that never wore out nor grew stale, he cried, "Behold the Lamb of God, that taketh away the sin of the world!" In this way he went through storms of wind, hail, snow, and rain; climbed hills and mountains, traversed valleys, plunged through swamps, swam swollen streams, lay out all night, wet, weary, and hungry, held to his horse by the bridle all night, or tied him to a limb, slept with his saddle blanket for a bed, his saddle or saddle-bags for a pillow, and his old big coat or blanket, if he had any, for a covering. Often he slept in dirty cabins, on earthen floors, before the fire; ate roasting ears for bread, drank butter-milk for coffee, or sage tea for imperial; took, with a hearty zest, deer or bear meat, or wild turkey, for breakfast, dinner, and supper, if he could get it.

Source: *Autobiography of Peter Cartwright, the Backwoods Preacher* (New York: Hunt & Eaton, 1856), p. 164.

cumstances. Groups such as the "Cent Institution," which asked only one penny a week from its members, stressed the contribution even poor people could make to the cause. The cents added up, too: the Cent Institution raised over $2,000 from 1802 to 1808. This support was crucial for missionaries, who often were not able to farm or otherwise support themselves while doing their work, and many of whom could not have afforded the training they needed without the support of their churches. Even with this help, more was needed because of the scope of the project and its cost. Early on, Protestant churches banded together, just as the first missionaries from Andover had, to pool their resources for this important task. In 1801 Congregationalists of New England and Presbyterians of New York joined together in a "Plan of Union," a document that indicated one future direction of missionary work, as well as of American religion.

International Efforts. There was also an international aspect to the organization of missionary work in this era. As early as 1792 a group of English Baptists had formed a missionary society and sent one of their number to India. Other Protestants from England and Europe followed their lead, and the American missionaries found themselves participating in a worldwide movement of Christianization. While they considered themselves to have a special place in that task, American Protestants also were aware of the opportunity of this joint work for bringing the world together in one Christian order. The international spirit of early American missionaries, however, was tempered by the experience of the War of 1812. The end of the second war against England found Americans turning away from the world into a period of isolation which would last until after the Civil War. While some foreign missionary efforts continued, the churches put much more energy elsewhere. The home missions came to seem more important, and after 1815 American Protestantism would devote itself to spreading God's word in the expanding territory of the United States through every type of moral reform movement imaginable.

Protestant Mainstream. This development was in fact one of the principle legacies of the religious history of the early national period. The foundations were laid for the "Protestant mainstream" of American culture. The agitation for missionary endeavors brought home to many the fundamental value of preaching the gospel at every opportunity, just as the organizational efforts to start missions brought home the need for cooperation among all Protestants. Although the denominations continued to be deeply divided on matters of theology and practice, at times those divisions were less important than the basic drive to convert souls to Christ. Over time Protestants would continue to find themselves more alike religiously than not, especially as Catholics became a larger part of the American population. Protestant evangelical efforts would secure their central place in American culture since they were the most prominent shapers of that culture through their involvement in every sphere of life. The foreign mission movement was always a minority movement in this era, but its contribution to the ideological formation of American Protestantism and American culture made it important far beyond the numbers of men and women involved.

Sources:

Anne M. Boylan, *Sunday School* (New Haven: Yale University Press, 1988);

Joan Jacobs Brumberg, *Mission for Life* (New York: Free Press, 1980);

Oliver W. Elsbree, *The Rise of the Missionary Spirit in America* (N.p., 1928; reprinted, Philadelphia: Porcupine Press, 1980);

William R. Hutchison, *Errand to the World* (Chicago: University of Chicago Press, 1987).

FROM ANGLICANS TO EPISCOPALIANS

American Anglicanism. No denomination was more negatively affected by the Revolution and its outcome than the Anglicans, those who belonged to the official Church of England. The end of the war brought on a painful period of readjustment for them as they tried to create an American church that was true to their English traditions. The problem Anglicans faced in 1783 was their close identification with the English, who had lost the war for independence. Unlike all other Protestants,

John Henry Hobart, Episcopal bishop; engraving by John C. Buttre

Anglicans considered the king of England to be a spiritual leader as well as a political leader. As Americans rejected King George's right to govern them in matters of taxes and laws, Anglicans found it impossible to continue to honor him as the leader of their church. Some reshaping of the beliefs and practices of the Anglicans was clearly called for, but the group was not well prepared to bring about change. The church was greatly weakened by the war; many Anglicans, particularly ministers, had supported the British. These Loyalists were often shunned by their neighbors, and many lost their property. Others left the new country altogether, emigrating to England or Canada. Many of those remaining were part of the growing evangelical wing of Anglicanism which soon broke away as the separate Methodist church. In 1783 the Anglican churches found themselves with far fewer—and poorer—members as compared to the colonial period. They also faced divisions over how to reorganize themselves, particularly about whether they should be led by a bishop. This was a sensitive topic, partly because non-Anglicans' fears of a bishop for America had contributed to the onset of the Revolution.

Bishop Seabury. During 1783 and 1784 the churches sent delegates to a series of general meetings in the middle states to discuss the future of their denomination. Alarmed that these meetings seemed to be rejecting the idea of a bishop, a group of ten clergymen from Connecticut met and preempted the issue by electing Samuel Seabury, a former Anglican missionary, as their bishop. Seabury traveled to England for consecration as a bishop, but was rejected there because he could not swear the required oath of loyalty to the king. He had more success in Scotland and was consecrated in 1784. On returning to the United States he began to assert his authority, but he was resisted by many Episcopalians, especially those outside Connecticut, who placed more value on lay initiative in church matters. Others resented his stand against American independence during the war when he had become notorious for writing a series of Loyalist pamphlets, which had been answered by Alexander Hamilton. That Seabury was not personally well liked only made matters worse.

Episcopal Church. Eventually a compromise was reached, in two general conventions in 1785 and 1786. These meetings gave the church a national organization and paved the way for the consecration of more bishops, now approved by church authorities in London. A later meeting in 1789 finished the important work of writing an American Book of Common Prayer, the manual used for all the church's worship services. Like the compromises over organization, this book struck a balance between retaining as many traditional ways as possible in a rapidly changing world. It kept the basic Anglican rituals intact while simplifying their relatively elaborate style. The 1789 meeting also gave the church a name, the Protestant Episcopal Church, usually called the Episcopal Church, after the Greek word for bishop.

Early Growth. The Episcopalians grew slowly despite the wave of conversions bringing new members to other churches. If the Episcopalians did not have a wide appeal, they did have a select one. For all the difficulties experienced by Seabury and his followers in setting up the new Episcopal Church, they still had a significant basis for hope. Many leading citizens became Episcopalians, some drawn by its liberal theology, others by its liturgy, which was much more elaborate than the plain-style preaching of the Congregationalists and the Presbyterians. The appointment of John Hobart as bishop of New York in 1811 was important on this score since he favored such "High Church" worship services despite their association with Roman Catholicism and despite what some considered their antirepublican character. The association of Episcopalianism and the elite members of society is just one sign of the struggle this denomination had in adjusting to the Revolution.

Sources:

David L. Holmes, "The Anglican Tradition and the Episcopal Church," in *Encyclopedia of the American Religious Experience,* edited by Charles H. Lippy and Peter W. Williams (New York: Scribners, 1988), pp. 391-418.

Frederick V. Mills Sr., *Bishops by Ballot: An Eighteenth Century Ecclesiastical Revolution* (New York & Oxford: Oxford University Press, 1978);

The interior of the synagogue in Charleston, South Carolina, dedicated in 1794

Robert Bruce Mullin, *Episcopal Visions/American Reality: High Church Theology and Social Thought in Evangelical America* (New Haven: Yale University Press, 1986).

JEWS IN THE EARLY REPUBLIC

Freedom and Diversity. Although American religious culture in the early nineteenth century was dominated by Protestantism, Jews and other non-Protestants shared that culture and grew within it. The religious freedom secured by the Constitution gave these groups greater liberty than they had in the colonial period, and more than in many other nations. Like their Protestant neighbors, these people worked hard to shape practices and institutions suitable to the needs of the new nation. But they remained separated by these efforts, and so were also quickly aware of the limits of religious freedom. In the distinctive histories of Jews and other non-Protestant groups, we can see both the opportunities of religious freedom in early America and the frustrations associated with the realities of religious diversity.

Community Building. There were few Jews in the early United States, no more than fifteen hundred in 1790, growing slowly to perhaps twenty-seven hundred in 1820. They were concentrated in a few communities: Newport, New York City, Philadelphia, Lancaster, Richmond, Charleston, and Savannah. After the Revolution some of these communities were seriously unstable. Newport suffered from the long occupation of the British, and its Jewish community failed entirely by the early 1800s, although it had been well established in colonial times. In other cities Jewish communities grew and developed a richer life. There was a ritual bathhouse in Philadelphia as early as 1786, and both Philadelphia and New York had ritual slaughterers to supply kosher meat to the community. New York in 1792 reestablished the Hebrew school that had closed during the war. But maintaining a synagogue was the key to a vital Jewish community. Philadelphia built its first permanent synagogue in 1782, and Charleston had its building in 1794; New York City replaced its old building in 1818. These buildings were visible symbols of optimistic communities. They were also centers of a rich ritual life, centering on the scrolls on which the Torah, the Jewish law, is written. When the Philadelphia synagogue opened, the entire Jewish community paraded the Torah scrolls to the new building and then carried them around the reading platform and into the ark on the building's wall, where they were to be kept, all in accordance with tradition. The synagogue was the place where the community gathered together for weekly services including readings from the Torah. Like some Protestant churches, the synagogues were each led by a cantor, the hazan, for there were no trained rabbis in the United States before the 1840s.

Values. American synagogues functioned much like many American Protestant churches. They were largely independent of each other, just like the Congregational churches of New England. Like those churches, each synagogue was quite homogeneous, and most members lived within walking distance of their meeting place, which was the center of their community. The synagogues built in this period even looked like churches, Charleston's even having a spire. The hazan likewise resembled a Protestant minister, wearing simple black robes rather than more traditional garb, joining the Protestant clergy in planning citywide thanksgiving days, and preaching sermons (which even rabbis did not do before the nineteenth century). Despite important differences, American Jews experienced a religion similar to that of their Protestant neighbors, and they embraced the values behind that experience as well. Four synagogues congratulated George Washington on his 1789 inauguration in a joint "Address to the President of the United States." Both this address and a similar one issued by the Newport synagogue took up the question of religious freedom, suggesting how central this right was to their communal identity as religious Americans. Washington responded to the Jews' messages by repeating their own words, assuring them that the United States "gives bigotry no sanction, to persecution no assistance." Despite this rhetoric, Jews in the early republic also experienced the limits of religious freedom. For example, most states excluded all non-Christians from public office.

Public Roles. Many Jews entered civic life in other ways, however, often becoming leaders in business and related social activities. Solomon Simpson, for example, was a financier and a major stockholder in the Bank of New York, as well as one of the founders in 1794 of Tammany Hall, the Jeffersonian political organization that soon dominated New York politics; Simpson was even its president in 1797. Gershom Mendes Seixas, the hazan of New York's Shearith Israel synagogue, was appointed one of the regents of Columbia University. Charleston's Jewish community became the largest in America during the economic boom that city enjoyed after the Revolution. Other Jews helped open the frontier: the Monsanto family built Natchez into an important Mississippi port, and Abraham Mordecai founded Montgomery, Alabama, and introduced the cotton gin there. Their prominence did not protect Jews from bigotry, however, as many Americans were anti-Semitic and quick to conjure up illusions of Jewish financial conspiracies and other stereotypes. Federalist writer James Rivington attacked Simpson's Jeffersonian politics by writing that Simpson had "a leering underlook and malicious grin, that seem to say to the honest man—approach me not." Other forms of prejudice were not as crude, but just as damaging. Mordecai Manuel Noah of Charleston was appointed the U.S. counsel to Riga in 1811 and to Tunis in 1813, but was recalled by Secretary of State James Monroe in 1815, simply because of his religion.

Internal Divisions. Discrimination aside, early American Jews faced more-subtle threats to their viability. One was their small numbers, which made communal life hard to sustain. Migration within the United States affected Jews as well, as they moved from place to place seeking better opportunities. Communities also suffered from low rates of immigration and from differences within the Jewish community. Most immigrants before 1800 were Mediterranean, or Sephardic, Jews, whose rituals differed from those of the Eastern European, or Ashkenazic, Jews, who immigrated in greater numbers in later years. Not everyone liked the Sephardic rites that most American synagogues followed, which became clear in 1802 when a group from the Philadelphia synagogue separated and formed the first Ashkenazic synagogue. The Jewish religious communities were further weakened by the success of many Jews who intermarried with Christians and assimilated into Protestant culture. Many Protestants supported this assimilation, particularly those looking forward to the coming of the millennium, as one of the signs of Christ's return was to be the conversion of the Jews to Christianity. American Jews contended with a fundamental lack of respect for their ways from many Protestants. Hannah Adams, a cousin of the second president, indicated the extent of this problem in her two-volume *The History of the Jews* (1812), one of the first works of religious history by an American. Despite a sympathetic account, Adams was "perplexed that the race should persist in rejecting the Messiah." For all the apparent similarities between Jewish and Protestant experiences, the groups were funda-

Baptism of Native Americans by Moravian missionaries

mentally different, and the differences would only become clearer with increased Jewish immigration after 1820.

Sources:

Eli Faber, *A Time for Planting: The First Migration, 1654–1820* (Baltimore: Johns Hopkins University Press, 1992);

Ira Rosenwaike, *On the Edge of Greatness* (Cincinnati, Ohio: American Jewish Archives, 1985);

Howard M. Sachar, *A History of the Jews in America* (New York: Knopf, 1992).

NATIVE AMERICANS

Indians and Christians. Native Americans had religious beliefs and practices quite different from those of white Christians. Indians found themselves in a time of religious change as a result of contact with European Americans. In some cases Indians became Christians in European ways. Some, like the Mohegan Samsom Occom, who died in 1792, left their tribes to live and be educated among whites and then returned as missionaries to the Indians, having abandoned their original values and beliefs. Other Indians embraced Christianity in more limited ways, retaining at least some aspects of their native cultures, merging complementary elements of both together, just as many slaves combined African and European practices. Others resisted Christianity. This became increasingly evident in the early national period, as the United States developed a policy of moving Indians westward to make way for the expansion of the white population into the frontier. Efforts to convert the Indians to Christianity often went hand in hand with military actions and the signing of treaties which deprived Indians of land and independence. In the early national era, the Christian churches organized and expanded their missionary efforts to the Native Americans with the avowed purpose of destroying Indian religions; along the way, they were increasingly the agents of even greater destruction.

Handsome Lake. After the end of the Revolution, Indians, like white Americans, found themselves in a period of religious renewal. The revivalist enthusiasm that marked white Protestants at frontier camp meetings had a powerful effect on Native American cultures as well. As the nineteenth century opened, the Seneca Indians of western New York, part of the Iroquois Confederacy, had fallen far from their former political and military prowess. Many Senecas responded to their dislocation and social turmoil with destructive behaviors such as drinking, feuding, and suicide. Among these people was Ganiodaio, also known as Handsome Lake. In 1799 Handsome Lake began to experience a series of visions, which left him at times in a trancelike state similar to that experienced by converts at camp meetings. The visions made Handsome Lake into a preacher, and he began to travel among his people. He urged them to reform their lives and return to their old ways, much as Methodist circuit riders urged their listeners to repent and return to the traditional values of biblical times. A new religion developed from these teachings, called Gaiwiio, or the Longhouse Religion. It included many Senecan beliefs and rituals, including the important Thanksgiving Dance, Great Feather Dance, Personal Chants, and Bowl Game, all of which honored the traditional spirit gods and recounted ancient myths. The Bowl Game, for example, reenacted with dice made from peach pits a primal struggle between the Good Twin and the Evil Twin for control of the earth. The game lasted for several days in midwinter, with feasting and dancing at night. Handsome Lake encouraged these old practices, but his apocalyptic visions led him to all new interpretations. Influenced by the themes of the Christian gospels, he came to see the Bowl Game as not only a creation ritual but also as prefiguring a climactic war between good and evil at the end of the world, when the Senecas would be judged and sent to heaven or hell. These beliefs were new to the Senecas but were easily incorporated into their revived ritual life, which was open to such syncretism. As a practical matter Handsome Lake preached moral reform, encouraging his followers to give up drinking and abortions since they were not part of the old ways and only weakened the nation. Many Iroquois embraced this powerful message of revival, renewal, and survival. This is not surprising, given the ongoing concerns about the security of their territories. Handsome Lake failed as a political leader, and the Iroquois's political situation deteriorated steadily, although his preaching of peaceful acceptance of some white ways eventually helped relax tensions. Nevertheless, his religious success was remarkable. By the time of his death in 1815 he had sparked a major revival of Iroquois culture, both moral and spiritual. Handsome Lake's religion of Gaiwiio survives today.

Tenskwatawa. Farther west of the Appalachians a similar phenomenon occurred among the Shawnee in the Ohio River valley, but there it was even more deeply colored by the politics of Indian removal. In 1794 Gen. Anthony Wayne defeated an Indian force drawn from several tribes, including the Shawnee, at the Battle of Fallen Timbers. The resulting Treaty of Greenville was to have ended Indian resistance to white settlement of the region, which dated back to the French and Indian War (1754–1763). The British continued to rally the Indians against the white Americans, however, and fighting continued through the War of 1812. Indian resistance was based not only on Britain's support, but was also grounded in the Shawnee religion. In 1805 a Shawnee named Tenskwatawa began to experience visions. Just as Handsome Lake was doing among the Iroquois, he preached moral reform and spiritual renewal through returning to old ways. He used his visions to create a religious message grounded in resistance to white expansion. The new religion revived old rituals and added some new ones, like the ceremony of confessing sins to Tenskwatawa, that were rooted in Christianity. Tenskwatawa traveled widely among the western tribes, and people from across the trans-Appalachian region joined him. Tenskwatawa's brother was Tecumseh, the war leader of the Shawnee. As the American government continued to pressure all the western Indians for more land cessions, Tecumseh tried to forge a pan-Indian union to resist the United States, built on the pan-Indian

religious feelings preached by Tenskwatawa. Tenskwatawa's defeat at the Battle of Tippecanoe in 1811 dealt a serious setback to the revival of traditional ways, and the renewal movement gradually faded as American troops wore down the Indians. Tecumseh's alliance with the British marked the end of both the religious and military efforts, as England acknowledged American control over the Great Lakes area at the end of the conflict in 1815.

Missionaries and Acculturation. Removal was only one part of the American policy toward the Indian nations during the early national period. The other was acculturation, the effort to get Native Americans to take up European ways. Christian missions to the Indians were at the forefront of this effort. Beginning with the establishment of the American Society for the Propagation of the Gospel, American Protestants founded at least eleven organizations between 1787 and 1800 for the support of missions to the Indians. This was part of the same evangelical impulse shaping the camp meetings on the frontier, but the goals were not only religious. One missionary said his job was to instill "those habits of sobriety, cleanliness, economy, and industry, so essential to civilized life." Beginning in 1803 Congress funded Presbyterian and Moravian missionaries to pursue this "civilization program," first announced by George Washington. Partly due to the emphasis on morality in evangelical preaching, missionaries persisted in this effort long after the federal government largely abandoned the policy in the 1820s.

The Cherokee. In religious and social terms the mission to the Cherokee of Georgia and Tennessee was the most successful, but it was also a vivid sign of the limits of acculturation. The Cherokee had an elaborate culture before the Europeans' arrival, which they gradually modified over the 1700s by taking up some white ways. They sided with the British during the Revolution, however, and paid the price afterward in the loss of control over their lands. Missionaries soon arrived, led by the intensely pietistic Moravians. The effort took a distinctive form under the Presbyterian Gideon Blackburn, who arrived in 1803 to pursue the goal of acculturation with a school combining religious instruction with lessons in reading and writing. The school was better at securing political and economic change than religious conversions. Christianity spread slowly. In 1811 a revival of the traditional Cherokee religion began as several people reported visions somewhat like those of Handsome Lake and Tenskwatawa. The problem of acculturation was a recurring theme in these visions. One featured Selu, the goddess of corn and mother of the nation. She urged the Cherokee to return to growing Indian corn and give up the hybrid varieties that the Cherokee got from white farmers and were growing with only limited success. Other visions spurred the revival of traditional rituals such as the purification ceremony, which involved bathing and communal dancing by men and women, accompanied by drums and rattles. Earthquakes at the end of

Shaker furniture

1811 prompted more visions and sent many to the conjurers for an interpretation. They also asked the Christian missionaries for answers, however, and the Cherokee revival never turned against whites to the extent of the Shawnee revival. The visionaries urged the Cherokee to set limits on assimilation but not to abandon the process entirely. Many Cherokee political leaders supported this compromise; some of them were Christian and some financially benefited from closer ties to whites. These men allied the Cherokee with the United States in its war with the Creek nation, which began in 1812 and brought an end to this phase of the religious revival. The Cherokee mission revived after the end of the War of 1812 and saw the tribe pursue a remarkable combination of Christianity and republicanism, including the development of a written language. But neither their Christianity nor their cultural success kept them from being removed forcibly to Oklahoma in the 1830s.

Sources:

Robert F. Berkhofer Jr., *Salvation and the Savage* (Lexington: University Press of Kentucky, 1965);

Henry Warner Bowden, *American Indians and Christian Missions* (Chicago: University of Chicago Press, 1981);

R. David Edmunds, *The Shawnee Prophet* (Lincoln: University of Nebraska Press, 1983);

William G. McLoughlin, *Cherokees and Missionaries, 1789–1839* (Norman: University of Oklahoma Press, 1995);

Anthony F. C. Wallace, *The Death and Rebirth of the Seneca* (New York: Random House, 1969).

NEW RELIGIONS FOR A NEW REPUBLIC

Sectarian Impulses. American religion was reshaped in many ways, socially and intellectually, by the upheavals of the 1770s and 1780s. The clearest aspect of the process was the growth of new religious groups in America. As Americans established their independence from Britain, some of them sought other kinds of independence as well. Many looked for new ways of practicing their religious beliefs and new kinds of churches to join. Beginning in the 1780s, America experienced the full flowering of a sectarian impulse, the desire to break away from old churches and form new ones. Hundreds of new congregations gathered together in these decades. Some were short-lived, but others survive today. Some, like the Shakers, represented radically different alternatives to traditional Christianity.

Protestantism. In part, sectarianism represented the continuing evolution of Calvinism, the form of Protestantism most Americans at the time practiced. The teachings of John Calvin, the Protestant reformer of the 1530s, had been important to many European settlers of America, including the Puritans. One of those teachings was about the value of independent judgment in matters of religion; another was about reliance of the individual on the Bible for religious truth. In the years after the American Revolution, when republican ideas of civic equality and religious freedom were spreading rapidly, these notions seemed pertinent to many Americans. Groups taking exotic names such as the Merry Dancers, Come-Outers, and Nothingarians left the older churches and struck out on their own, seeking a better way and abandoning orthodoxy in the process. As Americans and as Protestants, they felt free to assert their right to satisfy their own consciences on religious matters.

Sects and Radicalism. Many early sects embellished traditional religion with new ideas and practices, sometimes in unsettling ways. The "Universal Friends" are an example. Jemima Wilkinson founded the group in Rhode Island in 1776 and led it until her death in 1819. Female leadership was only one mark of the radicalism of

The early national era saw the beginning of a new kind of religious singing as people turned away from chanting psalms to singing the more poetic kinds of hymns we are still familiar with today. The lyrics of these hymns offer some clues to what the singers may have believed and felt. This Shaker hymn expressed the importance of singing and dancing in worship services, a belief in the imminent second coming of Christ, and veneration for the founding "mother," Ann Lee:

"The Season of Loves"

What beautiful songs do I hear!
How sweet is the season of loves!
When Father and Mother are near,
We feel like a parcel of doves.

How pleasant the brethren do look!
How smiling the sisters appear!
And Mother delights in her flock,
I know that her spirit is here.

O this is the union I love,
Here heavenly comforts are found;
The Spirit descends like a dove,
The angels are hovering round.

With them I rejoic'd in the dance,
Their songs were so heavenly sweet;
Their love did my senses entrance, Their food such as
   angels do eat.

The Baptists sang hymns evocative of the emotions of the revival experience and the anxiety about knowing whether one was among the elect saved by Christ's death, as in this example from 1786 by Henry Alline:

"Hard Heart of Mine"

Hard heart of mine, O that the Lord
Would this hard heart subdue!
O come thou blest lifegiving word,
And form my soul anew.

I hear the heavenly pilgrims tell
Their sins are all forgiven;
And while on earth their bodies dwell,
Their souls enjoy a heaven.

The Christians sing redeeming love,
And talk of joys divine;
And soon they say in realms above,
In glory they shall shine.

But, ah! 'tis all an unknown tongue,
I never knew that love;
I cannot sing that heavenly song,
Nor tell of joys above.

I want, O God, I know not what!
I want what saints enjoy;
O let their portion be my lot,
Their work be my employ.

Sources: Henry Alline, *Hymns and Spiritual Songs* (Boston: Peter Edes, 1786), p. 14;

Benjamin Seth Youngs, comp., *Millennial Praises* (Hancock, Mass., 1813), p. 66.

this group. Wilkinson was raised as a Quaker and had experienced emotional Protestant revival meetings, as well as visions of angels announcing the imminent end of the world. She began to call herself the Public Universal Friend and to preach about the spirit within her, which was ready to save others as well. Wilkinson quickly gained a following among war-weary Americans hoping for redemption and a more perfect world. In the 1780s small congregations of Universal Friends spread across southern New England, practicing a mix of Quaker and Congregationalist worship, interrupted by charismatic episodes of healing and exorcism. In 1790 the sect founded a settlement in upstate New York called New Jerusalem. Wilkinson lived in this utopian community for thirty years with as many as 250 followers, building a base for the millennial kingdom. The Universal Friends and other sects, with their unusual beliefs such as pacifism, sexual freedom, communalism, and immortality, were clearly on the radical fringe of the day. They were often attacked for being so different. But they were also acting on the same ideas of personal freedom and the need for reform which animated many other early Americans, if not in such extreme ways.

The Shakers. The most famous early American sect was the Shakers. These people called themselves the Believers in Christ's Second Appearing, but others called them Shaking Quakers or Shakers because of their ecstatic movements during their worship services. The Shakers originated in England, coming as a group to New York in 1774, where they lived largely unnoticed until the 1780s. The leader was their "Mother," Ann Lee, a visionary like Jemima Wilkinson. Lee considered her visions to be a commission from God to complete Christ's work of redemption, eventually claiming herself to be the female incarnation of Christ's second coming. She preached the complete rejection of this world as preparation for rising to a higher plane of existence at the imminent last judgment. Considering bondage to the flesh to be the root of all evil, she also advocated celibacy and ascetic communal living. Lee led her small band on a journey across New England from 1781 to 1783, gathering followers in the hill country and eventually settling outside Albany, New York. She died in 1784, just as the movement was beginning to gather strength.

Shaker Communities. The Shakers are best known today for their villages, where they lived together by sharing their labor and resources. They founded the first of these in New Lebanon, New York, in 1785, and there were nineteen villages, with perhaps four thousand residents, by the 1820s. Today the last Shakers still live together this way in Sabbathday Lake, Maine. The villages were one reason the Shakers survived so much longer than other early American sects. In them the Shakers could work together and worship apart from neighbors put off by their ecstatic dancing and their hymns about the "simple gifts" of the spirit. They could also protect themselves better from the frequent attacks they suffered from neighbors offended and threatened by their unorthodox beliefs, including pacifism and celibacy. The villages developed into versions of the perfect world the Shakers believed was soon coming. That was to be an orderly world focused on service to God, and it was represented in the utilitarian architecture and furniture for which Shakers are admired today. Their baskets and chairs were symbolic as well as functional; they indicated the Shakers' rejection of elaborate worldly ways. Like other sectarians they seized the opportunity of American independence to build a new world for themselves. It is significant that the United States was engaged in the same experiment at this time, although on different terms.

Sources:

Stephen A. Marini, *Radical Sects of Revolutionary New England* (Cambridge, Mass.: Harvard University Press, 1982);

Stephen J. Stein, *The Shaker Experience in America* (New Haven: Yale University Press, 1992);

Herbert A. Wisbey, *Pioneer Prophetess: Jemima Wilkinson, the Public Universal Friend* (Ithaca, N.Y.: Cornell University Press, 1964).

PROTESTANT RENEWAL: THE EMERGENCE OF AMERICAN UNITARIANISM

Appointment at Harvard. In 1805 a pamphlet war erupted in Boston among some of the city's leading clergymen. The war was vicious despite its elite origins. It had its start a few years before, with the death of two professors of divinity at Harvard College. The search for re-

Jedidiah Morse, a conservative Congregationalist minister; self-portrait by Morse (collection of Mrs. Russell Colgate)

placements was complicated when Jedidiah Morse, the staunchly conservative pastor of the church in neighboring Charlestown, insisted that the new professors must be orthodox. He wanted them tested for the soundness of their theological ideas against the standard of traditional Calvinism. Morse was not alone in his struggle, but he was opposed by others with more liberal views who did not fear the new religious thinking coming into vogue in these late years of the Enlightenment. Instead of talking about human depravity and damnation, liberal Congregationalists emphasized a kindly God who had sent Jesus to redeem all people and encouraged good behavior as a means to salvation. Morse and his camp fought these unorthodox ideas strenuously but lost when Henry Ware Sr., the liberal minister from Hingham, Massachusetts, was appointed to the college. Other liberals soon followed Ware into teaching positions at Harvard, and by 1810 the college was securely in liberal hands.

The "Unitarian Controversy." The debate about liberalism at Harvard was bruising and public, but Morse took it to a further level when he published *True Reasons on Which the Election of a Hollis Professor of Divinity in Harvard College was Opposed* in 1805. He then continued his attack on the liberals in *The Panoplist*, a periodical which featured news and opinions from the orthodox perspective. The controversy raged off and on for more than ten years. Along the way, Morse helped found Andover Seminary (1808), as an orthodox counterpart to Harvard. In 1815 Morse charged his opponents with secretly being much more liberal than they publicly admitted. He went so far as to accuse them of denying the divinity of Christ. He did this by republishing the biography of an English Unitarian, Theophilus Lindsey, which included Lindsey's correspondence with several Boston liberals about these radical and unpopular views. The liberals rose to the challenge. William Ellery Channing, a leading liberal clergyman, exchanged a lively series of open letters with his orthodox opponents. This phase of the Unitarian Controversy would not conclude until 1819, when Channing preached a sermon called "Unitarian Christianity," a full defense of the liberal position. Today, it is hard to grasp the significance of this obscure struggle and to appreciate how it engaged the energy of several talented and busy men. The Unitarian Controversy was just one part of one of the most important divisions that emerged in American religion in the early national period, the division between liberalism and orthodoxy.

Unitarian Belief. Morse used the word *Unitarian* more for its shock value than as an accurate label. Unitarians denied the doctrine of the Trinity, that the one God is manifested in three divine persons—the Father, Son, and Spirit. This is such a fundamental part of Christianity, and so central to the interpretation of the Bible at that time, that orthodox Trinitarians saw Unitarianism as a radical attack on all religion. To people like Morse it was little better than deism or atheism. There had been Unitarians in Boston for some time before the Unitarian Controversy opened. King's Chapel, Boston's Anglican Church before the Revolution, became a Unitarian church in the 1780s. In 1785 James Freeman, the church's lay reader and de facto leader (the rector having left Boston with the British army in early 1776), introduced changes in the prayer book, including the removal of all references to the Trinity. In 1787 the congregation ordained Freeman and took the name of Unitarian, as had various liberal congregations in England. Morse was less concerned with these Unitarians than he was with a broader movement of liberal thinking and practice developing within New England Congregationalism. By 1805 some Congregational liberals had taken up Unitarian beliefs, but many remained committed Christians. They departed in several different ways from the orthodox Calvinist beliefs which Morse so forcefully defended. This religious liberalism, one branch of which became American Unitarianism, had deep roots in the American religious experience.

Free Will. The central themes of liberal religious thinking were a greater emphasis on free will and a confidence in the ability of individuals to affect their fate. The strictest Calvinists, like the Puritan settlers of Massachusetts, believed in the doctrine of predestination. This was the belief that God had already decided who would go to heaven and who would be damned to hell. Whether people were actually sinful or not in their lives had no effect on God's decision. If a person was saved, it was a free gift of God's mercy, not something earned by human effort.

TWO CATECHISMS

The Sunday schools springing up from the 1790s onward used catechisms as their textbooks. A catechism uses a question and answer format to describe the beliefs and rituals of a religion. Teachers would drill their students in their knowledge of their faith by asking the questions and coaching them in understanding the correct answers. By far the most common text was the *The Shorter Catechism*, first compiled in 1648 by the Westminster Assembly and reprinted thousands of times over the following centuries. This orthodox catechism began by asking "What is the chief end of man?" The answer: "Man's chief end is to glorify God and enjoy him forever." The emphasis on glorifying God through obeying him and worshiping him was sustained throughout the catechism. After describing human sinfulness, it asked "Did God leave all mankind to perish in this state of sin and misery?" Answer: "God . . . out of his mere good pleasure from all eternity elected some to everlasting life." In the orthodox view, salvation was a gift to humans, but the ultimate beneficiary was still God.

In contrast William Ellery Channing's catechism for use with Unitarian children exhibited the ways liberal religion departed from orthodox themes. The Unitarian catechism painted a more positive image of humanity, and showed a God interested in human welfare. This book started by asking "Who made you?" The answer was God, but added that God also made "all things in heaven and earth." This God offered gifts to humans that were useful in this life: "He gives me life and strength. He gives me power to see and hear, to speak and move. He gives me reason and conscience, and the means of improving in knowledge and goodness." Instead of knowing that all men are inherently sinful, the Unitarian child said "I feel that I have sinned," and it followed that Jesus was not so much a redeemer as a moral guide.

Sources: Westminster Assembly, *The Shorter Catechism* (Cambridge, Mass., 1803), pp. 3, 5;

William Ellery Channing, *Elements of Religion and Morality in the Form of a Catechism*, second edition (Boston, 1814), pp. 7, 12.

This was a difficult idea since it could easily lead to despair or to a sinful disregard for behavior. Free will was related to this doctrine because it was hard to incorporate human freedom into the Calvinist system, which could seem so fatalistic and deterministic. Yet the system demanded a free acceptance of God's foreordained action, so people had to have free will, however contradictory that seemed.

New Images of God. By the mid 1700s more and more people were thinking that human behavior must matter and that one could lose a chance at heaven by sinning. This rethinking of the Puritan tradition went on in Boston and the other coastal cities of New England, where people were most aware of new trends in English thought and in the European Enlightenment. These intellectual trends emphasized the idea of freedom of the individual and gave it a wider scope in human life than it had ever had before. The ideas had their political effect in the American Revolution, but they had a religious aspect as well. Liberal ministers such as Charles Chauncy began to preach a new message about God. They began to picture him as benevolent, not wrathful, and concerned with saving all people, not just an elect few. Chauncy gave these ideas a highly polished form in his 1784 publication *The Mystery Hid from Ages and Generations.* Chauncy focused on universal salvation rather than ideas of the Trinity. He had written this book some thirty years earlier but feared to publish it until after the egalitarianism of the Revolution made it more likely to be appreciated. In many ways the liberals' opponents were correct to see them as revolutionary in their own right.

Divisions and Evolution. Liberal ministers and lay people gradually became more influential in church matters after 1790. Many were leading citizens of New England towns, and their opinions mattered despite theological controversies. In some cases theological divisions were so intense in a church that liberal or orthodox members would break away and form new congregations. Family conflicts and lawsuits often followed such separations. More often, congregations would not especially notice the changes in their thinking and simply evolve into liberal Congregationalism or Unitarianism. In part this was because liberalism was less a break with the past than a development from the past. Even as some ideas about God and salvation developed, many other things did not change. For example, even the most radical thinkers never stopped wanting the church to be congregational, with each local church community largely independent of all others. Like other new developments in Protestantism, liberalism was the product of reform, one of the deepest impulses of Christianity. The desire to make things new, to bring them closer to God's order, is a feature of all forms of Protestantism. Liberalism and orthodoxy were both products of the process of renewal, however different they looked on the surface.

Sources:

Sidney Ahlstrom and Jonathan S. Carey, eds., *An American Reformation* (Middletown, Conn.: Wesleyan University Press, 1985);

William R. Hutchison, *The Modernist Impulse in American Protestantism* (Oxford: Oxford University Press, 1976);

Conrad Wright, *The Beginnings of Unitarianism in America* (Boston: Starr King Press, 1955);

Wright, ed., *A Stream of Light* (Boston: Skinner House, 1989).

THE RATIONAL RELIGION OF DEISM

Enlightenment Religion. A few Americans pursued more-radical roads in the early national period. The deists were perhaps the most extreme of these people, and certainly the most notorious. While there were never many American deists, they were an important group because of their elite social status, high levels of education, and prominence in the political leadership of the new nation. Deists tended to be deeply identified with the thinking of the Enlightenment, an eighteenth-century intellectual movement that stressed rationality, natural order, and an openness to scientific inquiry. Despite their distance from Europe, many Americans were part of this movement, as the well-known example of Benjamin Franklin's freethinking and scientific experiments show. Religiously, many Enlightenment thinkers came to reject biblically based Christianity in favor of a more general belief in a "divinity" or a "creator," often visualized as a being who had set up the universe to run on orderly principles, like a machine. Deism stressed religion as a moral system, and most deists rejected the idea of revelation, that is, that God had made himself known to humans through Jesus and the Bible. Deists rejected more-traditional views of God as part of a trinity, or as intervening in human history (either in the past or the present), or as being interested in punishing or rewarding people in the afterlife. These were deeply challenging views, even in Revolutionary America. Although the citizens of the new nation were exploring new kinds of freedoms, the social order was still deeply connected to a view of the universe as being created by a God for a purpose, and the Bible was still by far the most authoritative text in American culture. As a result most Americans were deeply suspicious of deism, and despite their social prominence many deists kept their views to themselves.

Priestley and Vol-ney. The close association of deists with Europeans only served to heighten these suspicions in the 1790s. The English Unitarian Joseph Priestley's materialist writings were very influential on Thomas Jefferson's thinking, and although Priestley had strongly supported the American Revolution, even moving to Philadelphia in 1794, his extreme anticlericalism set him apart from most Americans. Even more troubling was the connection to the French Enlightenment. Aside from the anticlericalism and materialism of earlier French thinkers such as Voltaire and Denis Diderot, the radical ideas of the French Revolution also found an American audience. Most significant among the French influences was Constantin-François Chasseboeuf, Comte de Vol-ney, who fled France for America. His book *Ruins: Or a Survey of the Revolutions of Empires* (1791) was one of the most widely read works of the late eighteenth century. Vol-ney explained the successive revolutions of the past (something of an obsession among American political thinkers of this time) as caused by the tyranny of priests, and thus as a function of revealed religion, which he then rejected fully. As the

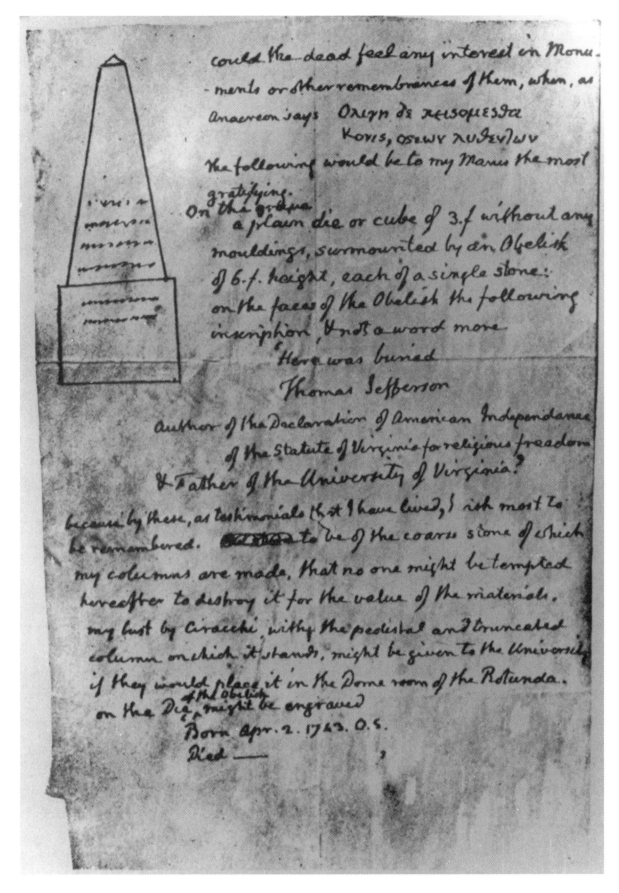

could the dead feel any interest in Monu-
-ments or other remembrances of them, when, as
Anacreon says   Ολιγη δε κεισομεϑα
          κονις, οστεων λυϑεντων
the following would be to my Manes the most
gratifying.
On the grave   a plain die or cube of 3.f without any
mouldings, surmounted by an Obelisk
of 6.f. height, each of a single stone:
on the faces of the Obelisk the following
inscription, & not a word more
          'Here was buried
          Thomas Jefferson
Author of the Declaration of American Independance
          of the Statute of Virginia for religious freedom
     & Father of the University of Virginia.'
because by these, as testimonials that I have lived, I wish most to
be remembered.   to be of the coarse stone of which
my columns are made, that no one might be tempted
hereafter to destroy it for the value of the materials.
my bust by Ciracchi, with the pedestal and truncated
column on which it stands, might be given to the University
if they would place it in the Dome room of the Rotunda.
on the Die of the Obelisk might be engraved
          Born Apr. 2. 1743. O.S.
          Died ———

Jefferson's instructions for his tombstone (Massachusetts Historical Society)

French Revolution moved through increasingly radical—and bloody—stages, Americans were alarmed at the social disorder that seemed to come from radical thinking such as deism.

Homegrown Deists. More-homegrown versions of deism fared little better as Americans continued to see them as attacks on order and so fundamentally against the direction of the postrevolutionary period. In 1784 Ethan Allen, a hero of the American Revolution, published *Reason the Only Oracle of Man,* developing a distinctly American version of deism rooted in a reaction against the revivals of the 1740s and in the revolutionary politics of the war years. Its engagement with the American scene did not make the book acceptable, however. Most copies of this infamous book were burned at the printer's shop, and after Allen's death the president of Yale College remarked that "in Hell he lifts up his eyes, being in torments," apparently sure that God would damn the infidel. A similar fate met Thomas Paine, whose *Common Sense* (1776) probably did as much as the Declaration of Independence to fuel revolutionary fervor in America. Paine had followed up with similarly spirited defenses of the French Revolution, even in the face of its increasing unpopularity in America. Again radical politics led to radical religion. Paine's deist tract, *The Age of Reason* (1794–1795), attacked revelation and the Bible. Paine endured a wave of venomous attacks and died a social outcast. American deism itself largely succumbed to these attacks and to the overwhelming growth of evangelical Protestantism after 1800. Elihu Palmer founded the Deistical Society in New York in 1794 and issued some publications over the following decade, but deism never developed a significant presence in the early 1800s. American Christianity met the threat of deism, and the limits of revolutionary thought in religion were clearly drawn.

Jefferson. Americans wrestled seriously with religious issues in the context of their revolutionary experience. One good example of this process is Thomas Jefferson. In appealing to "the laws of Nature and of Nature's God" in the Declaration of Independence, Jefferson earned for himself a reputation as the leading example of early American deism. The phrase seems to capture perfectly a deist image of a rational and impersonal god, governing the universe through the mechanical operation of the laws of nature. Jefferson did share this sense, at least in 1776, when he wrote these words. And the label of deist haunted him throughout his public career. This was most clearly the case during the presidential election of 1800 when he was repeatedly and viciously attacked as little more than an immoral atheist. But despite this, to call Jefferson a deist does a disservice to the complexity of his religious beliefs and to the importance of these beliefs in his life. Jefferson was deeply engaged with traditional religion and even produced his own version of the Bible. He tried to isolate the ethical teachings of Jesus, which he thought should be as important to good citizens as to

godly churchgoers. At the heart of Jefferson's religion was rationality. Like many Americans, Jefferson was caught up in the European Enlightenment's emphasis on reason as a path to a better world. He and other Americans thought enough of their powers of reason to want to judge truth for themselves, with open minds, using all the tools at their disposal. Many turned to nature for truth, while others continued to look in the Bible for themselves. They cared more about moral rules than about theological niceties. In a sense Jefferson practiced a unique religion of reason. But it was a highly adaptable religion, one deeply engaged with some important trends in American culture. Over time, reason would help many American Protestants realize the full potential of the Revolution in their religious beliefs and practices.

Sources:

Paul K. Conkin, "The Religious Pilgrimage of Thomas Jefferson," in *Jeffersonian Legacies,* edited by Peter S. Onuf (Charlottesville: University Press of Virginia, 1993);

Henry May, *The Enlightenment in America* (New York: Oxford University Press, 1976);

Kerry S. Walters, *The American Deists* (Lawrence: University Press of Kansas, 1992);

Walters, *Rational Infidels: The American Deists* (Durango, Colo.: Longwood Academic, 1992).

THE RISE OF EVANGELICALISM

Preaching the Word. In the early national era many Americans became intensely religious. American church membership, after declining during wartime, began to grow quickly in the 1790s. This trend continued to 1815 and well beyond. By 1850 probably 40 percent of Americans were church members, up from around 10 percent in 1790. In part this growth reflected the greater stability of the period: families returned to their pews as they resumed their previous lives. But this development was also a response to the efforts of religious leaders to recruit new members, rebuild their churches, and forge a Christian America. At the heart of this growth was the task of evangelization, that is, the preaching of the gospel. The Christian America that began to take shape during the early national era was evangelical in the sense that it was built by efforts to spread Christianity, and it devoted itself to pursuing that work even further. Evangelicalism had many different features, some of them working at cross-purposes, and had many different proponents, some of whom also worked at cross-purposes.

Revival. The most obvious and dramatic feature of America's evangelical culture was the religious revival. Beginning in the mid 1790s, a series of revivals occurred in New England as the members of Congregational churches experienced the presence of God in an especially intense, often emotional way. Sometimes sparked by an unusually moving sermon from their ministers, or sometimes by their own prayer and Bible reading, these people dedicated themselves anew to making the service of God central in their lives. These revivals were far from

Methodist camp meeting in 1808

the first New England had seen. In the 1730s and 1740s a series of these events had swept through many of the colonies, so many that the period became referred to as the "Great Awakening" for the number of people newly awakened to God's presence in their lives. Now, a new "season of grace" seemed to be getting under way as reports of revivals began arriving from many other areas besides New England. Ministers promoting this phenomenon began referring to it as a "second Great Awakening" as a way of making the revivals seem like a resurgence of older religious traditions. In some ways this was quite true. The old Puritans in New England had always appreciated emotional religious experiences similar to those their descendants were now undergoing. But there were important differences too, in the scope of the revival phenomenon, the methods ministers used during revivals, and even the character of the experiences of the people who participated in them. The revivals of the second Great Awakening are a good example of older religious practices being adapted to the new social circumstances of the new nation. One clear sign of the new directions that American religion took as a consequence of the revivals of the second Great Awakening was the phenomenal growth of the two groups most closely identified with early American evangelicalism—the Baptists and the Methodists.

Baptists and Methodists. Both the Baptists and the Methodists experienced their most rapid growth in the frontier areas of the new nation. Those areas were the lands west of the Appalachian Mountains that were rapidly settled through a westward migration of white people that started in the 1760s but quickly picked up speed after the Revolutionary War ended in 1783. Kentucky, Tennessee, upstate New York, and other frontier areas of the 1790s and early 1800s were the rough and ready West of that time, filled with boomtowns, pioneer farmers and their families clearing land and setting down roots, and drifters seeking to get rich quick, but often ending up poorer than ever. With few churches estab-

lished in these areas, revivals could not occur among settled congregations or even in church buildings, as was happening in New England. Revivals moved outside and came to be called camp meetings. Camp meetings were some of the most popular and enduring features of religion in the early national era.

Camp Meetings. Revivals taking the form of camp meetings began to appear around 1797 in rural Kentucky. The hills of Logan County were the scene of some of the first of these meetings, led by James McGready, a Presbyterian minister of Scots-Irish heritage. McGready was a powerful preacher, constantly exhorting his listeners to seek the "new birth." His work produced many converts, who began attending religious meetings around the countryside, reaching a peak in an exuberant four-day meeting at Red River in 1800. Over the next few years McGready and other ministers, joined by Methodists and Baptists, perfected the camp meeting. They became frequent events on the frontier in the summertime when the weather was good and time could best be spared from farm work. In 1801 the area of Cane Ridge, Kentucky, saw probably the largest and most raucous camp meeting of this period. As many as twenty thousand people gathered together in outdoor services over six days, camping on the fields around the open-air preaching stands. Frenzied worship continued day and night, even through heavy rainstorms, and thousands found themselves caught up in the preaching of Presbyterian Barton Stone and more than twenty other ministers. People shouted out, and one participant compared the noise to "the roar of Niagara."

Conversion Experience. Red River, Cane Ridge, and the other camp meetings were distinctly suited to frontier conditions. They brought together hundreds, sometimes thousands, of participants, often from several denominations. People came from a wide area and stayed several nights. Several preachers would lead the meeting, preaching from booths set up for the various denominations. People moved from place to place in the camp-

THE CANE RIDGE CAMP MEETING

James B. Finley was not yet converted to Christ when he attended the huge revival meeting at Cane Ridge, Kentucky, in 1801. He later became a preacher and missionary to the western Indians. He recalled how overwhelming the Cane Ridge revival had been:

The noise was like the roar of Niagara. The vast sea of human beings seemed to be agitated as if by a storm. I counted seven ministers, all preaching at one time, some on stumps, others in wagons, and one . . . was standing on a tree which had, in falling, lodged against . . . another. Some of the people were singing, others praying, some crying for mercy in the most piteous accents, while others were shouting most vociferously. While witnessing these scenes, a peculiarly-strange sensation, such as I had never felt before, came over me. My heart beat tumultuously, my knees trembled, my lip quivered, and I felt as though I must fall to the ground. A strange supernatural power seemed to pervade the entire mass of mind there collected. . . . Soon after I left and went into the woods, and there I strove to rally and man up my courage.

After some time I returned to the scene of excitement, the waves of which, if possible, had risen still higher. The same awfulness of feeling came over me. I stepped up on to a log, where I could have a better view of the surging sea of humanity. The scene that presented itself to my mind was indescribable. At one time I saw at least five hundred swept down in a moment, as if a battery of a thousand guns had been opened upon them, and then immediately followed shrieks and shouts that rent the very heavens. . . . I fled for the woods a second time, and wished I had staid at home.

Source: *Autobiography of Rev. James B. Finley; or, Life in the Pioneer West* (Cincinnati, Ohio: Cranston & Curtis, 1853), pp. 166–167.

---

ground, hearing almost continuous preaching meant to inspire an intense religious reaction, the conversion experience. Newly converted persons would think of themselves as having had a "new birth" in the Spirit. These conversion experiences often led to startling expressions from the participants, who might have spasms called "jerks" or cry out in "barks" or even fall away into trances. Congregations would often be swept up in the emotions of the moment, with mass conversions resulting. The intensity of these religious experiences was matched by the intense social life of the campground, for the experience was not solely spiritual. Families would gather together in larger groups, based on region or wider kinship ties, and would eat and live together in a temporary community, partially making up for the isolation of frontier life that was the norm the rest of the year. Many camp meetings culminated in an outdoor communion service jointly led by all the ministers present. All who had been converted during the meeting would gather together in a symbolic meal celebrating the unity they had found in their individual experiences of Christ. Those who had not been converted gathered around the group of communicants, sharing in the spirit of the service, if not in the actual sacrament, and demonstrated another level of the community formed on the campground. While many participants fell away from the intensity of the spiritual experience once they returned to their homes, even more maintained ties to the churches they joined during these meetings. For almost all, the revival, and the conversion experience embedded in it, were not once-in-a-lifetime events but rather something they would join in repeatedly, perhaps once a year.

Circuit Riders. The emphasis on conversion through preaching, as well as frontier conditions, led the Methodists in particular to embrace another religious innovation, the circuit rider. The Methodist minister on horseback, crossing the Appalachian Mountains and traveling from town to town preaching, was a familiar figure in the early national period. While there had been such itinerant preachers in the colonial period, the expansive missionary efforts of the Methodists made the circuit rider a regular feature of the religious landscape. Churches never had enough ministers to be able to provide one for each of the congregations that were springing up across America as settlement spread westward. This was not a problem for the Baptists, who had a tradition of lay leadership and local control, and this denomination boomed under these conditions. While the independence of these congregations suited the emerging democratic ethos of the new nation, church leaders in the East were concerned about sustaining the growth of these groups and providing for their spiritual needs over time. The Methodists, committed to a more centralized form of church government, including bishops, were especially worried about leaving individual congregations alone too much. Methodist congregations were organized into circuits to be served by one minister who traveled from one group to the next, taking as long as six weeks to complete his circuit. These men, intimately familiar with the rough conditions of life in these newly settling areas, could preach to the people they met in language suited to their needs, even if they were not college-trained or highly learned in biblical interpretations. They forged social cohesion among communities when travel and communication were hard and acted as a civilizing force on the frontier, encouraging family life by performing weddings and baptisms.

Spirit of Reform. In constantly preaching against drinking, gambling, and dancing, the circuit riders also gave expression to one of the most important features of the evangelicalism emerging across America, not only on the frontier: the spirit of reform. At the heart of the conversion experience was a belief that people could reject sin and be better in the future, all in response to a call from God to obey his word. The circuit riders often confronted life at its rawest and most violent, and the message they delivered was one of faith in a better world to come, not only in heaven, but here as well, if only people would act on their faith and live up to the ideals set out by Jesus in the Gospels.

Politics. The Disciples of Christ, or the Christians, as they called themselves at first, was another group to emerge in the revivals of the second Great Awakening. The Disciples are the clearest example of the impact of American republicanism on religion. Itinerant preacher Elias Smith, originally a Baptist, made this clear in sermon after sermon in New England, which he filled with a politics of religion. "Many are republicans as to government," he declared, "and yet are but half republicans, being in matters of religion still bound to a catechism, creed, covenant or a superstitious priest. Venture to be as independent in things of religion, as those which respect the government in which you live." This heady message attacking centralized religious authority in favor of a religion of the people was already being echoed across the country by others. A group of Methodists in Virginia took up this theme in rejecting the bishops of their new church. And Barton Stone, one of the leaders of the Cane Ridge revival, joined with others in issuing *The Last Will and Testament of the Springfield Presbytery* in 1803, rejecting all church authority in favor of a complete reliance on the New Testament. Also on the frontier, the Scottish immigrants Thomas Campbell and his son Alexander preached a similar message of each individual's right to pursue truth independently.

Possibilities and Limits. These men and the movements they were part of followed the ideas of civic and religious freedom out to their logical conclusions. They rejected any special status for preachers, embracing the wisdom of the common man and his access to truth. They abandoned the theological intricacies of Calvinism, yet they did not reject all authority. The Bible alone was the place to look for truth, and the Christians searched its pages for guidance. The Campbells revealed what they found there in the *Declaration and Address* (1809), a work that set out their thinking about a revolutionary new world. They found in the Bible "signs of the times" that led them to believe a new order was at hand and that God had ordained an egalitarian America to lead the way to it. The new order would actually be a restoration of the ways of the primitive church, in other words, a world stripped of all the corruption added by eighteen hundred years of Western civilization. This ethos had deep roots in colonial American religion, which was also preoccupied with apocalyptic visions, and sought to reform the world into a re-creation of the primitive church. But the movement was also a product of the special circumstances of the early republic. It capitalized on the new reality of political and social freedom and on the reality of life on the frontier to create a unique combination of republican and biblical radicalism, a truly

THE CONVERSION EXPERIENCE

An English observer at the 1801 Cane Ridge camp meeting offered this description of the behavior of the revivalists who found themselves caught up by the movements of the Spirit:

Thoughtless infidels have fallen as suddenly as if struck by lightning . . . sometimes at the very moment they are uttering blasphemies against the work. Immediately after they become totally powerless, they are seized with a general tremor, and sometimes, though not often, they utter one or two piercing shrieks in the moment of falling. Persons in this situation are affected in different degrees; . . . sometimes when unable to stand or sit, they have the use of their hands and can converse with perfect composure. In other cases, they are unable to speak, the pulse becomes weak, and they draw a difficult breath about once a minute, in some instances their extremities become cold, and pulsation, breathing, and all the signs of life, forsake them for nearly an hour. Persons who have been in this situation have uniformly avowed that they felt no bodily pain; that they had the entire use of their reason and reflection, and when recovered they could relate everything that had been said or done near them. From this it appears, that their falling is neither common fainting, nor a nervous reflection. Indeed this strange phenomenon appears to have taken every possible turn, to baffle the conjectures of those who are not willing to consider it as a supernatural work. Persons have sometimes fallen on their way from public worship, and sometimes after they had arrived at home, and in some cases, when they were pursuing their common business on the farms or when retired for secret devotion.

Source: *Methodist Magazine*, 26 (February 1803): 90–91.

popular religion. It did not last, although a huge denomination led by Stone and the Campbells emerged from this moment. But denomination survived only in building the kind of institutional church that the original participants had so strenuously rejected. The example of the Disciples of Christ suggests the radical possibilities, as well as the very real limits, of the revival movement of the early 1800s.

Theology. Although revivalists stressed the importance of a conversion experience, emphasizing the heart over the head, evangelicals did not neglect the realm of ideas completely. During the first Great Awakening the theologian Jonathan Edwards had brought traditional Puritan theology, largely based on the teachings of the French Protestant reformer John Calvin, into line with more modern thinking such as that of the English philosopher John Locke. While adhering to the Calvinist position that God had predetermined who would be saved and who would be damned (the doctrine of predestination), Edwards also stressed the role of individual responsibility in accepting God's judgment. This emphasis was a foot in the door for later revivalists. Slowly they began to emphasize the ideas of human freedom and responsibility more, in order to motivate people to accept the idea that their actions influenced God's judgment on them. This was also a way to keep religion at the forefront of peoples' lives since if what you do matters for your salvation, living a moral life is crucial. This was the position of the Methodists, who consistently stressed the importance of the free human response to God and taught that it was possible to realize holiness in this life despite the reality of sin. They preached a message for the times, and this contributed to their spectacular growth in the early national period. Congregationalists, Presbyterians, and other denominations more strongly grounded in traditional Calvinist ideas had a harder time modifying their old positions. Led by preachers such as Connecticut's Lyman Beecher, they did adjust, although the full story of the intellectual changes produced by evangelical revivalism belongs to the 1820s and 1830s.

Sources:

Nathan O. Hatch, *The Democratization of American Christianity* (New Haven: Yale University Press, 1989);

Charles A. Johnson, *The Frontier Camp Meeting* (Dallas: Southern Methodist University Press, 1955);

William G. McLoughlin, *Revivals, Awakenings, and Reform* (Chicago: University of Chicago Press, 1978);

Russell E. Richey, *Early American Methodism* (Bloomington: Indiana University Press, 1991);

Leigh Eric Schmidt, *Holy Fairs* (Princeton: Princeton University Press, 1989).

WOMEN

Going to Church. One of the most fundamental facts about American religion is that, in one historian's words, "women go to church." In almost every time period and region, and in almost every religious tradition, women participants consistently outnumber men. This was certainly true across the United States from 1783 to 1815. Women were not necessarily more religious than men, but the religious institutions of the early republic would not have existed without the help of their women members. The explosive growth of Baptist and Methodist congregations on the frontier was often due to women who attended camp meetings and were so moved by the emotional preaching there that they claimed a conversion experience and joined the church. Such women continued to attend their local churches after returning home, often bringing their husbands and children with them. Most broadly, women invested huge amounts of time and energy in religious activities, in both the public and private spheres of their lives. In these ways women's religious experiences and activities were the rocks on which American evangelical churches were built in these years.

Public Roles. While women participated actively in American churches, their public presence in these religious institutions often led to problems. Women were welcome to participate, but they were not welcome to take leadership positions in the churches. During the early national period a few women tested the limits of female participation by seeking to become preachers. The struggle over preaching by females exposed the fundamental inequality between men and women in early national America. Jarena Lee, a young African American Methodist in Philadelphia, was so affected by her minister's preaching in 1804 that she stood up and interrupted him, speaking to the congregation herself. This outburst, in itself, was not unusual, but later Lee began to feel moved to preach publicly on a regular basis. Methodist ministers at first denied her this opportunity, citing biblical passages against preaching by females, as well as women's naturally subordinate position in society. But the logic of evangelical Protestantism undercut that position. Lee and others like her responded to a religious message stressing the individual's direct relationship to God. The quality of that connection, not the individual's gender, mattered. Furthermore, God alone always initiated the relationship, so it could not be said that women were advancing themselves; rather, God had chosen them. It took Lee seven years to convince Richard Allen, the leader of the African Methodist Episcopal Church, that her feelings were genuine. He finally acknowledged that her desire to preach was a legitimate call from God. Lee embarked on a career as an itinerant preacher that became her life's work. Lee's success did not end the debates about the propriety of women preachers, which continued in all the Protestant churches until after the Civil War.

Pious Writing. Other women found other, less challenging ways to "preach" God's word to others. Notably they were able to publish religious works for a growing readership. In 1807, for example, Chloe Willey, a lay woman from rural New Hampshire, published a short account of her life. Willey linked the everyday experiences of her life to her religion, telling a story of release from worldly cares with the help of intense experiences of God's grace. Other women's lives came to public attention through funeral sermons praising them and holding them up as Christian models. The minister in Salem, Massachusetts, published such a sermon about Eleanor Emerson, a parishioner who died at age thirty-one. He included letters and other materials she had written, giving readers a full sense of her life as well as of her virtues. Readers could find models for their own lives in these accounts. The authors and subjects of these books became something like characters in novels, through whom readers could live vicariously. Many women recalled in their diaries or letters the deep impression made on them by such stories, whether true or fictional, and considered their exposure to God through these printed materials a crucial part of their own religious experiences. In doing this they were extending the logic of Bible reading, which Christians had pursued for centu-

Engraving of the Sisterhood of Loretto, founded in 1812 in Marion County, Kentucky, by the Reverend
Charles Nerinckx

ries as a way for individuals to find a path to God. As America began to develop its own literary industry in the early 1800s, women were the target audience for much pious writing of this kind.

Charity Work. It was rare to see a woman preaching publicly in this period, and most women were not published authors. Many women expressed their religion by being in the audiences of the revival preachers in the camp meetings and by joining the congregations of churches and meetinghouses around the United States. But these were rarely passive roles. Women used their churchgoing experience as the basis for a more varied religious life than we might expect. For example, bonds among women forged in the religious congregation led many to form new groups serving religious and social purposes. After 1790 women founded charitable societies in all the major towns of America in order to pursue their Christian duty of helping the poor and spreading the word of God. These groups helped some people directly and also raised money to support missionary and charitable work elsewhere. By 1817 this movement had spread so much that the Boston Female Society for Missionary Purposes was corresponding with over one hundred other such groups. Thousands of women found a sense of themselves and became part of a female-centered community in these endeavors.

At Home. While women pursued this work in the company of their female neighbors, they also labored for God in their own homes. In the early national era the family was as important as the meetinghouse as the location of religion. Sometimes, especially on the frontier where meetinghouses had not been built, the home was the only option. Family prayer services, which women could lead as easily as men, were the centers of many religious lives. Thomas Scott's *The Holy Bible* (1804–1809) was only one of thousands of prayer manuals and Bibles printed in these years to bring religion into the home. These books took their place on parlor tables and served as repositories of family history as mothers added the dates of births and deaths. At this time also, ministers were coming to see women as especially suited for religion. They talked about women as virtuous mothers rather than as heirs to the sin of Eve. This combined with the developing importance of "religion of the heart," a very emotional piety, to make it seem natural to many that women were the principal religious figures of society. So for many Protestants religion moved into the home in the early national era, where it was welcomed by a mother.

Her Sphere. Although women were central to the presence and growth of religion in the home and to the developing ideology of the Christian family, this may seem a somewhat narrow role. Religious women were limited to the domestic sphere. They worked and expressed their religion in a place given less social value than the workplaces of men, including religious men. But it is important to see that even without leaving the hearth, women had a significant influence on the American society and culture taking shape around their homes. This was because of the close association of religion and morality, and because of the emerging "civil religion" of the new nation. Christian belief and the moral behavior flowing from that belief were closely associated with the civic qualities needed for the success of the new republic. For most Americans republican virtue was largely the same as Christian virtue. Both were at the heart of a vision of a nation where all had a chance at a life of dignity and where all had a duty to help others realize their full potential. Women, especially mothers, were given the important role of teaching those values to children. Those values were increasingly in competition with other values, like individualism, but throughout the early national era they were a central part of what it meant to be American. Women had the important task of preserving and promoting them, and in this sense their private lives were very public indeed.

Sources:

Ann Braude, "Women's History *Is* American Religious History," in *Retelling U.S. Religious History*, edited by Thomas A. Tweed (Berkeley: University of California Press, 1997);

Nancy Cott, *The Bonds of Womanhood: "Woman's Sphere" in New England, 1780–1835* (New Haven: Yale University Press, 1977);

Linda Kerber, *Women of the Republic: Intellect and Ideology in Revolutionary America* (Chapel Hill: University of North Carolina Press, 1980);

Rosemary R. Reuther and Rosemary S. Keller, eds., *Women and Religion in America: A Documentary History*, volumes 1 and 2 (San Francisco: Harper & Row, 1981, 1983);

Mary Ryan, *The Cradle of the Middle Class: The Family in Oneida County, New York, 1790–1865* (Cambridge: Cambridge University Press, 1981).

HEADLINE MAKERS

RICHARD ALLEN

1760-1831

FOUNDER OF THE AFRICAN METHODIST EPISCOPAL CHURCH

Up from Slavery. Richard Allen's race and his religious experiences together shaped the course of his life and allowed him to become a leader of the free African American community in the northern states in the post-Revolutionary era. Allen was born into slavery in Philadelphia on 14 February 1760. After moving with a new owner to Delaware in 1767, Allen was converted to Methodism, drawn by its message of Christian freedom, and soon began preaching. An early success was the conversion of his owner, who allowed Allen to buy his own freedom in 1781. Moving back to Philadelphia, Allen became active as a lay preacher in the Methodist Church. By 1784 he came to the attention of Francis Asbury, the first Methodist bishop, who offered Allen the opportunity to preach in the South, although not to slaves. Allen turned this offer down, preferring instead to preach to the growing free black community in Philadelphia.

A Black Church. Allen was one of several African American members of Saint George's Methodist Church in Philadelphia. Although the church officially allowed the mixing of races, hostility toward African Americans was very much a part of the black members' experience, and an increasingly troubling one to Allen. Disturbed by the trend toward segregation, Allen and some companions founded the Free African Society on 12 April 1787, one of the first African American religious groups in the United States. Later that year the need for an independent black church became dramatically clear when Allen, Absalom Jones, and William White were pulled from their knees while praying in Saint George's and told to move to the balcony, the only place blacks were allowed. Allen and the others then withdrew and centered their religious lives on the society. When that group began to adopt Quaker principles, Allen left to form a black Episcopal church. Allen left this church in turn, forming Bethel Church in 1794, the first black Methodist church. Under Allen's leadership Bethel became the center of a network of black Methodist congregations. In 1816 sixteen of these churches joined to form the African Methodist Episcopal (AME) Church, the first African American denomination. These churches chose Allen as their first bishop, and he was installed on 11 April 1816 by the "laying on of hands" of his fellow black ministers.

Wider Visions. In keeping with the expansive goals of American evangelicalism and with the message of freedom he had found in Methodism, Allen's work was not limited to churchly duties. He had a broad vision of his mission grounded in a desire to serve God and his followers. His church sponsored a day school for the children of its members, opening in 1795. In 1804 that activity broadened as Allen founded the Society of Free People of Colour for Promoting the Instruction and School Education of Children of African Descent. Allen was also active in the early movements promoting the abolition of slavery, both in Pennsylvania and in the nation. At his death on 26 March 1831, Allen had shaped not only the basis of independent black churches, but had made a significant contribution to the development of independent African American political life in the North as well.

Sources:

Richard Allen, *The Life, Experience and Gospel Labors of the Rt. Rev. Richard Allen, Written by Himself* (N.p., 1793; reprinted, Nashville, Tenn.: Abingdon, 1983);

Carol V. R. George, *Segregated Sabbaths: Richard Allen and the Emergence of Independent Black Churches* (New York & Oxford: Oxford University Press, 1973).

FRANCIS ASBURY

1745-1816

METHODIST CIRCUIT RIDER AND BISHOP

Frontier Clergyman. Over the course of his long career as a Methodist minister and bishop, Francis Asbury traveled over 300,000 miles on horseback, crossed the Appalachian Mountains more than sixty times, preached 16,500 sermons, and ordained 4,000 other Methodist preachers. Asbury's heroic labors were only an extreme case of the incessant traveling of itinerant ministers all over the American backcountry. These men together made Methodism the fastest-growing Protestant denomination in early national America.

From England to America. Asbury was born in England in 1745 and apprenticed to be a blacksmith. After he experienced a conversion, Asbury became a Methodist lay minister instead. He immigrated to Pennsylvania in 1771 as a missionary and was the only Methodist missionary to remain in the United States during the Revolutionary War. Methodism was suspect during this period because of the views of John Wesley, its English founder, who opposed American independence. Asbury struggled to maintain contact among the scattered American Methodists during these years and was rewarded as the war ended, leaving him the leader of a movement poised for intense growth. The English Method-

ist leaders appointed Asbury a joint superintendent of American Methodism, together with Thomas Coke, whom they sent to America to ordain him. Asbury shrewdly seized the initiative, however, calling the "Christmas Conference," a gathering of leading American Methodists, in Baltimore on 24 December 1784, to discuss the matter. The conference formed the Methodist Episcopal Church as a separate American denomination. The delegates then chose Asbury as their first bishop.

Shaping American Methodism. As bishop Asbury devoted himself to the growth of the denomination, especially on the frontier. He encouraged the practice of "circuit riding," urging the Methodist clergy to travel from place to place, seeking converts everywhere rather than remain settled in one church. And he endorsed the camp-meeting style of revivals as another tool for bringing people to Christianity. During his tenure Methodism became the largest and fastest-growing denomination in the United States as thousands were drawn by its optimistic message and populist feel. Despite his leadership duties, Asbury never gave up traveling and preaching himself, and he died doing missionary work in Spotsylvania, Virginia, on 31 March 1816.

Sources:

Russell E. Richey, *Early American Methodism* (Bloomington: Indiana University Press, 1991);

L. C. Rudolph, *Francis Asbury* (Nashville, Tenn.: Abingdon, 1966).

ISAAC BACKUS

1724-1806

BAPTIST MINISTER

Religious Freedom. Isaac Backus's service as minister of the Baptist church in the small country town of Middleborough, Massachusetts, would not ordinarily ensure a place for him in the history books. Yet despite this modest position, Backus became one of the most widely known evangelical preachers in early America. He was also a key figure in the debate over the separation of church and state in the period after the American Revolution. Backus had a vision of religious freedom that complemented an intense piety, a view shared by many in these formative years of American society.

Awakening to Faith. Backus was born on a Connecticut farm on 9 January 1724. Like many other New Englanders, he experienced a dramatic conversion during the Great Awakening, a series of religious revivals that swept through American churches in the early 1740s. These revivals emphasized the importance of conversion, that is, of an intense awareness of God's grace as the centerpiece of each person's religious life. Backus held to this position for the rest of his long life despite the conflicts it created for him. The practical consequences of his religious beliefs led Backus to his ideas about religious freedom. The evangelical emphasis on conversion led some to conclude that the church should accept only those who had freely recognized this event. Backus left the Congregational Church because it refused to restrict admission in this way. He soon moved to an even more radical position and in 1756 formed a new congregation in Middleborough on Baptist principles. Baptists such as Backus abandoned the popular practice of baptizing children, arguing that it was impossible for a baby to experience conversion.

Separating Church and State. While Baptists were free to hold these beliefs, they were not free to abandon their old churches completely. The Congregational churches of Massachusetts were "established" churches, endorsed by the state government and supported with tax money. Backus became a leading spokesman for all those seeking relief from the obligation to pay taxes in support of ministers and churches they had rejected. In works such as *An Appeal to the Public for Religious Liberty Against the Oppression of the Present Day* (1773) Backus argued forcefully that state support corrupted pure Christianity, and he urged the separation of church and state. The adoption of the First Amendment to the U.S. Constitution in 1791 accomplished Backus's goal at the national level. But the states were not affected by this, and his struggle continued for the rest of his life. He continued to preach and write about this issue. Backus was not a true religious pluralist despite his views on the separation of church and state. He always believed that America should be a religious, and specifically a Baptist, nation. Religious freedom for Backus was not an abstract human right, but rather a goal to pursue in order to promote religion in a practical way. Backus died on 20 November 1806, twenty-seven years before the Congregational Church was finally disestablished in Massachusetts.

Source:

William G. McLoughlin, *Isaac Backus and the American Pietistic Tradition* (Boston: Little, Brown, 1967).

JARENA LEE

1783-?

LAY METHODIST PREACHER

A Christian Voice. Despite the limitations of being both a woman and an African American, Jarena Lee became an important religious voice in early national America. She struggled successfully to become one of the first female preachers in the United States. She later recorded her experiences in one of the first African American spiritual autobiographies to be written, a memoir still in print today.

Conversion. Jarena Lee was born in southern New Jersey in 1783. Unlike most African Americans of her day, she did not experience slavery directly, although she was removed from her parents at a young age. She considered herself "born again" af-

ter a conversion experience in 1804, and the development of her spirituality became central to her life from that point on. For many years she struggled with the implications of this experience, at times feeling deep, almost suicidal, despair, and at other times feeling that she was approaching the state of "sanctification," a sense of being always graced by God. By this time Lee had moved to Philadelphia. She became a member of Richard Allen's Bethel African Methodist Episcopal Church. One Sunday she stood up in church and interrupted a visiting male minister to witness to Jesus' saving action in her own life, a step taken by few American women, black or white, before her.

Public Preaching. In 1811 Lee went even further. She told Allen she had been called by God to preach to others. Allen discouraged Lee from pursuing this path, and for a time she took his advice. She married another minister, Joseph Lee, and moved with him to his church just outside Philadelphia. The Lees had two children, but Jarena was soon left a widow and returned to Philadelphia. In 1819 she stood up again in Bethel Church and interrupted the minister. On this occasion, rather than speak of her own experience, she gave her own interpretation of the day's Bible text, a further assertion of her spiritual authority. Richard Allen encouraged her this time and sanctioned her new vocation. Lee then became an itinerant revivalist, traveling up and down the East Coast and as far west as Ohio, seeking converts everywhere. In 1827 alone Lee traveled more than two thousand miles and preached 180 times. She spread her message even further with the 1836 publication of *The Life and Religious Experience of Jarena Lee, A Coloured Lady, Giving an Account of Her Call to Preach the Gospel.* The Methodist Church complained about the quality of the writing in this work and refused Lee's request for sponsorship for a later edition. Despite her race and lack of education, she raised the necessary money from other sources and oversaw the work herself, bringing out the new version in 1849. Unfortunately, nothing is known of Lee's life after the late 1840s.

Source:

William L. Andrews, ed., *Sisters of the Spirit: Three Black Women's Autobiographies of the Nineteenth Century* (Bloomington: Indiana University Press, 1986).

SAMUEL SEABURY

1729-1796

FIRST AMERICAN EPISCOPALIAN
BISHOP

American Anglican. Samuel Seabury was a key figure in founding the American Episcopal Church from what was left of colonial Anglicanism after the Revolution. Seabury was born into the family of the Congregational minister in Groton, Connecticut, on 30 November

1729. The next year Seabury's father converted from Congregationalism to Anglicanism, as did several other young ministers drawn by the richness of Anglican sacramental life and the association with English ways. Seabury followed his father into the priesthood in 1753 and became a missionary in New Jersey and New York, sponsored by the Anglican Society for the Propagation of the Gospel. He continued this work through the pre-Revolutionary years. During this time he became embroiled in the controversy over the ordination of an Anglican bishop for the American colonies, a possibility many Americans feared, however irrationally, as one more sign of British tyranny. Seabury, naturally, favored the proposal. He was also a notorious opponent of American independence, writing a series of Loyalist pamphlets in 1774 which Alexander Hamilton answered. The next year Seabury was captured by a Patriot mob searching for a Loyalist printer. Despite these troubles Seabury persisted in his loyalty to England and served as a chaplain to American Loyalists serving in the British army.

An American Bishop. Seabury returned to Connecticut after the war and began the effort of rebuilding the Anglican Church. The church was greatly weakened by the departure of many Loyalists for Canada and England and by anti-Anglican sentiment among the victorious American Patriots. The Connecticut clergy sent Seabury to England in 1783 to seek ordination as their bishop, feeling reconstruction of their church was impossible without the establishment of this office and the installation of a man of Seabury's abilities to fill it. Seabury faced opposition on both sides of the Atlantic. The English church refused to ordain him because it required its bishops to swear loyalty to the English king, which Seabury could not do. The Scottish Episcopal Church had no scruples on this point, however, and made Seabury the first American bishop on 14 November 1784. In exchange Seabury happily promised to promote High Church principles, namely an emphasis on the sacraments, especially holy communion, and adherence to a system of leadership by bishops and clergy. This made some American Anglicans angry, especially those from Virginia and Pennsylvania who were more skeptical about the need for a bishop and more interested in allowing for lay leadership of the church.

From Anglican to Episcopalian. Seabury returned to Connecticut and led a series of meetings of former American Anglicans which established the Protestant Episcopal Church in 1789, a church separate from the Anglican Church but in "communion" with it, that is, sharing its structure and beliefs. Seabury then began to compromise with his opponents in order to unify the denomination, a difficult process made harder by Seabury's unpleasant personality. One important task was the writing of the American Book of Common Prayer, the church's worship manual, which helped give the church a more American style, even as it adhered to its traditional En-

glish ways. As bishop Seabury led the church while also continuing his pastoral work, visiting Episcopalians and their parishes throughout New England. He died in his home parish of New London, Connecticut, on 25 February 1796.

Source:
Bruce E. Steiner, *Samuel Seabury, 1729–1796: A Study in the High Church Tradition* (Athens: Ohio University Press, 1971).

ELIZABETH ANN BAYLEY SETON

1774-1821
CATHOLIC EDUCATOR AND SAINT

A Charitable Woman. Elizabeth Ann Bayley Seton is well known today as the first Roman Catholic saint born in the United States. Her pioneering career in Catholic education and her role in founding the Sisters of Charity, as well as her own spiritual life, are the achievements behind this singular honor. Elizabeth Ann Bayley was born in New York City on 25 January 1774. Bayley's mother died soon after, and she was raised by her father, Richard Bayley, a prominent physician and later the first professor of anatomy at Columbia College. Bayley gave his daughter a broader education than most early American girls received, one that encouraged a sense of moral responsibility toward society. In 1794 she married William Seton, a businessman, and began a family that would eventually include five children. Despite her domestic duties, her earlier education prompted Seton to pursue many charitable activities. She helped to found the Society for the Relief of Poor Widows with Small Children in 1797, the first charitable society in New York.

Conversion to Rome. Seton was widowed in 1803, her husband dying from tuberculosis in Italy, where the family had traveled hoping that country's climate would cure him. While there Seton was drawn to the Roman Catholic Church and began her education in that faith. She returned to the United States and formally converted on 14 March 1805. This shocked her New York friends and family, and many abandoned her. Others, like John Hobart, later the Episcopalian bishop of New York, began a long but fruitless effort to bring her back to Protestantism. Seton started a school and struggled to support her children by teaching.

Catholic Educator. In 1808 she moved to Baltimore and started a girls' boarding school with the help of Roman Catholic archbishop John Carroll. The success of this venture encouraged a further one: the establishment of a new religious community. In March 1809 Seton and four companions took vows and formed the Sisters of

Charity, the first American order of nuns, devoting themselves to assisting the sick and poor and to education. The sisters established a center in Emmitsburg, Maryland, and there set up a new boarding school, as well as a free school for poor children. These educational ventures were among the first of many Catholic schools, and Seton in time came to be considered the founder of the American parochial school system.

American Saint. Seton led the Sisters of Charity for the rest of her life as they spread throughout the northeastern United States, founding schools, hospitals, and orphanages. She died on 4 January 1821, survived by two sons with naval careers and one daughter who later became a Sister of Mercy. Seton also left a growing group to carry on her work. These women kept her memory alive, as did others. Her half nephew, James Roosevelt Bayley, the first bishop of Newark, New Jersey, founded a college in her honor, today's Seton Hall University. Between 1935 and 1963 three people recovered from apparently fatal illnesses, and the church investigators attributed these cures to the miraculous intercession of Seton. Accordingly, in September 1975 Pope Paul VI proclaimed Mother Seton the first native-born American saint.

Sources:

Joseph I. Dirvin, *Mrs. Seton: Foundress of the American Sisters of Charity* (New York: Farrar, Straus & Cudahy, 1962);

Annabelle M. Melville, *Elizabeth Bayley Seton, 1774–1821* (New York: Scribners, 1951).

TENSKWATAWA

1775?-1836

SHAWNEE PROPHET

Assessment. Tenskwatawa is less well known today than his brother Tecumseh, who led the Shawnee people and other western tribes in a series of wars against the United States. Tecumseh may have been the greater political and military leader, but it was actually Tenskwatawa who initiated the resistance to the federal government with his unique religious vision in the early 1800s.

Renewal and Resistance. Tenskwatawa was born around 1775 to a Shawnee father, Puckeshinewa, and a Creek mother, Methoataske. Originally called Lalawethika (the Noisemaker), he was raised among his father's people but failed to distinguish himself in his youth. His life changed with a spiritual experience in 1805, and he took a new name, Tenskwatawa, "the Open Door," which signaled the role he began to carve for himself. He felt renewed by a series of revelations he received from the "Master of Life" while being taken up into the spirit world, in accordance with the shamanistic tradition of Shawnee belief. These visions were the basis of a call for renewal to the Shawnee and to other Indian tribes, a call that was the root of one of the deepest revivals of native traditions in the nineteenth century. Tenskwatawa, or, the Prophet, preached at a time of intense westward expansion by white Americans, and his visions were in part a reaction to the pressure the U.S. government was putting on the Shawnee to cede their land. To strengthen the Shawnee in their struggle he spoke out against liquor, which he saw as corrupting the Indians. He likewise tried to strengthen tribal ways by discouraging Shawnee women from marrying whites and urging the Shawnee to abandon everything introduced by whites, even guns. He also called for a return to "pure" Shawnee practices, such as holding all property in common and having the young and strong work for the benefit of the old and weak.

Defeat. Tenskwatawa reached a wide audience, well beyond the Shawnee nation. His spiritual authority seemed confirmed when he successfully predicted a solar eclipse in 1806. His call for native renewal in opposition to white America became a pan-Indian movement stretching from Florida to Saskatchewan. Tenskwatawa's message had a political effect as well. During these same years Tecumseh was forging a political and military alliance among the tribes of the Ohio River valley to resist white settlement. The Prophet joined his brother in this struggle, and his political goals gradually eclipsed his religious message. But neither Shawnee proved effective at halting the steady loss of Indian lands. Tenskwatawa suffered a serious setback at the Battle of Tippecanoe, Indiana Territory, in November 1811, losing to future president William Henry Harrison, who then burned Tenskwatawa's village, called Prophetstown. During the War of 1812 Tenskwatawa and his brother sided with the British against the Americans. Tecumseh paid for this alliance with his life, and Tenskwatawa paid with what was left of his reputation as a leader and visionary. In the peace negotiations after the war, the British once again abandoned their allies, and the long process of the displacement of the Indians by white Americans resumed. Tenskwatawa lived for a time in Canada, still preaching a message of renewal, but to a dwindling audience. He died in 1836 among the remaining Shawnee in what is now Kansas.

Source:

R. David Edmunds, *The Shawnee Prophet* (Lincoln: University of Nebraska Press, 1983).

PUBLICATIONS

Hannah Adams, *Alphabetical Compendium of the Various Sects* (Boston: Printed by B. Edes & Sons, 1784)—early U.S. example of comparative religious history;

Adams, *The History of the Jews,* 2 volumes (Boston: J. Eliot Jr., 1812)—largely sympathetic account of Judaism, including U.S. Jews, for a Protestant audience;

Ethan Allen, *Reason the Only Oracle of Man* (Bennington, Vt.: Printed by Haswell & Russell, 1784)—deist tract by a Revolutionary War hero;

American Board of Commissioners for Foreign Missions, *An Address to the Christian Public* (Boston: Printed by Samuel T. Armstrong, 1811)—manifesto justifying early foreign missionary efforts;

Isaac Backus, *A Door Opened for Equal Christian Liberty, and No Man Can Shut It* (Boston: Printed for the author and sold by Philip Freeman, 1783)—sermon supporting religious freedom;

Hosea Ballou, *A Treatise on Atonement* (Randolph, Vt.: Printed by Sereno Wright, 1805)—treatise on universalism;

Lyman Beecher, *The Remedy for Duelling* (Sag Harbor, N.Y.: Printed by Alden Spooner, 1807)—early example of the moral reform literature produced by Beecher and other evangelicals;

Thomas Belsham, *American Unitarianism* (Boston: Printed by Nathaniel Willis, 1815)—published by Jedidiah Morse, this biography included letters from Boston liberals about religion and became part of a pamphlet war about Unitarianism in the United States;

Thomas Campbell and others, *Declaration and Address of the Christian Association of Washington* (Washington, Pa.: Printed by Brown & Sample, 1809)—a formative document of the Disciples of Christ, an evangelical group that mixed Christian and democratic features on the frontier;

John Carroll, *Address to the Roman Catholics of the United States of America* (Annapolis, Md.: Printed by F. Green, 1784)—defense of Catholics against charges of being unpatriotic and less than Christian;

William Ellery Channing, *Elements of Religion and Morality in the Form of a Catechism* (Boston: Printed by John Eliot, 1813)—early Unitarian catechism for use by children;

Channing, *A Letter to the Rev. Samuel C. Thacher: on the Aspersions Contained in a Late Number of the Panoplist* (Boston: Printed and published by Wells & Lilly, 1815)—a defense of liberal religion and part of the pamphlet war over Unitarianism;

Constantin-François Chasseboeuf, Comte de Vol-ney, *The Ruins: or A Survey of the Revolutions of Empires* (New York: William A. Davis, 1796)—first American edition of the popular rationalist work, attacking the clergy as tyrants set on destroying free society;

Charles Chauncy, *The Benevolence of the Deity* (Boston: Printed by Powars & Willis, 1784)—early universalist tract by a leading Boston minister;

Chauncy, *The Mystery Hid from Ages and Generations* (London: C. Dilly, 1784)—a universalist tract;

Lorenzo Dow, *History of a Cosmopolite* (New York: Printed by John C. Totten, 1814)—systematic defense of camp meeting techniques by an early leader of U.S. Methodism;

Samuel Hopkins, *Memoirs of the Life of Mrs. Sarah Osborn* (Worcester, Mass.: Leonard Worcester, 1799)—model account of female piety;

Hopkins, *The System of Doctrines* (Boston: Isaiah Thomas & Ebenezer T. Andrews, 1793)—survey of orthodox Congregational theology by a leading orthodox minister;

Hopkins, *A Treatise on the Millennium* (Boston: Isaiah Thomas & Ebenezer T. Andrews, 1793)—a short book about the coming end of the world;

Abner Jones, *Memoirs of the Life and Experience, Travels and Preaching of Abner Jones* (Exeter, N.H.: Printed by Norris & Sawyer, 1807)—autobiography of a minister noted for mixing republicanism and revivalism;

Jesse Lee, *A Short History of the Methodists* (Baltimore: Magill & Clime, 1810)—first official history of U.S. Methodism, describing its quick growth into one of the largest U.S. denominations;

James Madison, *Memorial and Remonstrance* (Worcester, Mass.: Printed by Isaiah Thomas, 1786)—reprint of

Madison's legislative argument promoting Jefferson's Bill for Religious Freedom in Virginia;

John M. Mason, *The Voice of Warning, to Christians, on the Ensuing Election of a President of the United States* (New York: Printed and sold by G. F. Hopkins, 1800)—example of the religious attacks on Thomas Jefferson during the 1800 presidential election;

Methodist General Conference, *Form of Discipline for the Ministers, Preachers, and other Members of the Methodist Episcopal Church in America* (Philadelphia: Printed by Charles Cist, 1785)—first edition of the basic collection of rules and rituals for U.S. Methodists;

James O'Kelly, *The Author's Apology for Protesting against the Methodist Episcopal Government* (Richmond, Va.: John Dixon, 1798)—attack by a former Methodist on the hierarchical structure of that church as undemocratic and un-Christian;

Thomas Paine, *The Age of Reason* (Part I, New York: Printed by T. & J. Swords for J. Fellows, 1794; Part II, Philadelphia: Printed by Benjamin Franklin Bache for the author, 1776)—deist treatise by the author of *Common Sense;*

Joseph Priestley, *Discourses on the Evidence of Revealed Religion* (London: J. Johnson, 1794)—sermons on rationalism and religion, which influenced Thomas Jefferson's religious thinking;

Priestley, *Socrates and Jesus Compared* (Philadelphia: Printed for P. Byrne, 1803)—discussion of rational religion, emphasizing Jesus as a moral teacher;

Benjamin Rush, *Thoughts Upon Female Education* (Philadelphia: Prichard & Hall, 1787)—address about women's political and religious calling to be the moral guardians of society;

Thomas Scott, ed., *The Holy Bible . . . with Original Notes, Practical Observations, and Copious Marginal References* (Philadelphia, 1804–1809)—first U.S. version of one of the most popular family Bibles of the nineteenth century;

Elias Smith, *The Loving Kindness of God Displayed in the Triumph of Republicanism in America* (N.p., 1809)—revivalist's account of egalitarianism and religion;

Ezra Stiles, *The United States Elevated to Glory and Honor* (New Haven, Conn.: Printed by Thomas & Samuel Green, 1783)—Connecticut election sermon by the president of Yale College, describing an "American Israel" which could lead a worldwide moral reformation;

Barton W. Stone and others, *The Last Will and Testament of the Springfield Presbytery* (N.p., 1808)—early statement of principles by the Disciples of Christ;

Nathan Strong and others, comp., *The Hartford Selection of Hymns* (Hartford, Conn.: Printed by John Babcock, 1799)—anthology of more than 350 hymns for public and private devotions, prompted by an increased interest in sacred songs connected to the revivals of the 1790s;

Chloe Willey, *A Short Account of the Life of . . . Mrs. Chloe Willey* (Amherst, N.H.: Printed by Joseph Cushing, 1807)—early women's conversion narrative;

John Witherspoon, *The Works of the Rev. John Witherspoon* (Philadelphia: Printed and published by William W. Woodward, 1800–1801)—works by the president of Princeton College, including his lectures on moral philosophy and religion, which expressed a natural and rational religion within a Calvinistic framework;

Samuel Worcester, ed., *The Christian Mourning with Hope. A Sermon . . . on Occasion of the Death of Mrs. Eleanor Emerson . . . to which are Annexed Writings of Mrs. Emerson, with a Brief Sketch of her Life* (Boston: Lincoln & Edmands, 1809)—early example of a Christian biography meant as a model for other women;

Benjamin Seth Youngs, comp., *Millennial Praises* (Hancock, Mass.: Printed by Josiah Talcott Jr., 1813)—collection of 140 Shaker hymns;

Youngs, *The Testimony of Christ's Second Appearing* (Lebanon, Ohio: John M'Clean, 1808)—early Shaker theological treatise.

CHAPTER TEN

SCIENCE AND MEDICINE

by ANTHONY CONNORS

CONTENTS

Sidebars and tables are listed in italics.

1783

- Oliver Evans of Delaware invents the fully mechanized flour mill.
- Harvard Medical School is established.

1784

- Benjamin Franklin invents bifocal eyeglasses; now, he claims, at dinner he can see both his food and the person sitting across the table.

1785

10 May   Thomas Jefferson's *Notes on the State of Virginia* is first published.

1786

- The Philadelphia Dispensary, the first public clinic in America, is opened by Dr. Benjamin Rush. In its first full year 1,647 patients are treated.
- Revolutionary writer Thomas Paine builds a model of a single-span iron bridge that he hopes to erect over the five-hundred-foot-wide Schuylkill River in Philadelphia. Investors, however, are wary, and Paine eventually abandons his plans.

1787

22 Aug.   John Fitch of Connecticut demonstrates the first steamboat in America on the Delaware River; the steam engine in this boat powers oars rather than a wheel.

1788

- A New York City mob, suspecting physicians and medical students of graverobbing, attacks a group of doctors who are discovered dissecting a cadaver.

1789

- Oliver Evans designs a steam-propelled carriage.

1790

- Congress enacts the first patent law, and Secretary of State Thomas Jefferson acts as administrator of patents.
- American dentist Joseph Flagg invents the dentist's chair.
- George Washington's dentist, John Greenwood, invents the dental drill.
- Samuel Slater reproduces an Arkwright (British) mechanized textile mill on the Blackstone River in Pawtucket, Rhode Island.

31 July   The first U.S. patent is awarded to Samuel Hopkins of Vermont for his method of making pearl ash (used in glass, pigment, and soap production) from wood ashes.

1791

- John Fitch and James Rumsey are both awarded patents on their steamboats, furthering the animosity between these two rivals.

- Alexander Hamilton's Society for Establishing Useful Manufactures begins operations at the nation's first large-scale industrial village in Paterson, New Jersey, at the falls of the Passaic River.

- William Bartram, the first American-born botanist to gain international recognition, publishes *Travels through North and South Carolina, Georgia, East and West Florida, the Cherokee Country, the Extensive Territories of the Muscogulges, or Creek Confederacy, and the Country of the Chactaws,* an account of his four-year journey in quest of animal and plant specimens.

- The College of Philadelphia and the University of the State of Pennsylvania merge to form the University of Pennsylvania Medical School.

1792

- Timothy Palmer builds the first modern truss bridge (with triangular upper supports) over the Merrimack River in Massachusetts.

- John Prince builds the first microscope made in the United States.

1793

- A severe yellow fever epidemic strikes Philadelphia, killing five thousand people.

- Samuel Slater, Moses Brown, and William Almy build a new factory specifically designed for spinning cotton in Pawtucket, Rhode Island.

- The first canal for purposes of navigation in the United States is constructed in South Hadley, Massachusetts.

1794

- The Dismal Swamp Canal, connecting Virginia's Chesapeake Bay and Albemarle Sound in North Carolina, is completed.

- A sixty-six-mile-long toll road, with a top layer of crushed stone, is completed between Philadelphia and Lancaster, Pennsylvania.

14 Mar.   Eli Whitney of Connecticut receives a patent for his cotton gin; the *gin* (short for *engine*) is a wooden cylinder with protruding spikes, turned by a hand crank, that extracts the seeds from picked cotton.

1795

- The first U.S. armory is established in Springfield, Massachusetts.

- Plagued by insufficient capital, an inadequate labor force, and poor transportation, the Paterson, New Jersey, industrial village founded by Alexander Hamilton is forced to close.

1796

- James Finley of Pennsylvania builds a suspension bridge using chains.
- The first U.S. patent for a medical device is granted to Elisha Perkins of Connecticut for his metallic tractors, which supposedly cure pain by drawing off excessive "electric fluid" from the body.
- Samuel Lee Jr. of Connecticut is the first American to obtain an official patent for a medicine; he claims that his "Bilious Pills" cure yellow fever, dysentery, worms, and female complaints.

1797

- Thomas Jefferson, while vice president of the United States, is elected president of the American Philosophical Society.
- The *Medical Repository,* America's first medical journal, is published in New York.

1798

- The Sault Sainte Marie Canal is built by the Northwest Fur Company to connect Lakes Huron and Superior; its lock is the first in America.
- Robert Fulton builds a four-person submarine, called *Nautilus;* he tries to interest Napoleon Bonaparte in the idea but is unsuccessful.
- John Fitch dies, in utter despair over his failure to make his steamboat invention commercially successful.

1799

- Aaron Burr's Manhattan Company builds New York City's first public water supply; the water is pumped from wells through a system of wooden pipes.

1800

- Eli Whitney devises a method of making muskets by manufacturing interchangeable parts, rather than crafting each musket individually.
- Connecticut clock maker Eli Terry uses waterpower to speed up the process of making wooden parts for his clocks.

1801

- Robert Hare invents the hydrogen-oxygen blowpipe, the forerunner of the modern welding torch.

1802

- The city of Philadelphia builds a steam-powered municipal waterworks.

- The U.S. Patent Office is founded.

- The Massachusetts Medical Society publishes the nation's first official pharmacopoeia, a list of medicinal drugs with their preparation and use.

1803

- A steamboat built by Robert Fulton is successfully demonstrated on the Seine River in France.

1804

- John Stevens demonstrates a steamboat that uses a screw propeller, a great improvement over the paddle wheel.

- Oliver Evans builds the first steam dredge, in Philadelphia.

- Evans receives a patent for his high-pressure steam engine; it is smaller yet more powerful than low-pressure engines.

14 May   Meriwether Lewis and William Clark leave Saint Louis for their expedition to the Pacific Ocean.

1805

- Robert Fulton builds the first marine torpedo.

- The first covered bridge—covered to protect the bridge structure, not people—is built over the Schuylkill River in Philadelphia; it is a three-span wooden structure.

July   Lewis and Clark find the headwaters of the Missouri River.

8 Nov.   The Lewis and Clark expedition reaches the Pacific Ocean.

1806

- Davis Bemis lights his Waltham, Massachusetts, factory with illuminating gas.

23 Sept.   Lewis and Clark return to Saint Louis from their twenty-eight-month expedition. They bring back great quantities of information on animals, vegetation, Native Americans, and the geography of the western United States.

1807

- Robert Fulton's *North River Steam Boat* (later renamed *Clermont*) makes its maiden voyage on the East River in New York.

- Official government-sponsored mapping of the United States is begun by the Coast Survey, a federal agency that still exists today as the Coast and Geodetic Survey.

- Eli Terry creates a mechanized system to mass-produce affordable clocks.

1808

- Eli Whitney finally delivers to the War Department the four thousand mass-produced muskets that he had promised to manufacture by 1801.

- John Stevens's *Phoenix* makes the first seagoing voyage by a steamboat, from New York City to Philadelphia.

1809

- The first American suspension bridge strong enough to support vehicles is built across the Merrimack River in Massachusetts.

- Ephraim McDowell performs an ovariotomy in Danville, Kentucky, the first such operation in the world.

- William Maclure publishes *Observations on the Geology of the United States of America,* containing the first geological map of the nation.

1810

- Oliver Evans builds the first steam-powered flour mill in Pittsburgh.

1811

- Robert Fulton builds the *Chancellor Livingston,* a 160-foot, sixty-horsepower steamboat named for his partner, Robert Livingston, the former U.S. ambassador to France.

- A woolen mill in Middletown, Connecticut, is the first steam-powered industrial plant in the United States; it features a twenty-four-horsepower high-pressure engine invented by Oliver Evans.

- John Hall of Maine patents the breech-loading rifle; Hall would later supervise rifle making at the United States Armory at Harpers Ferry, where he perfected the system of manufacturing interchangeable parts.

1812

- Benjamin Rush publishes *Medical Inquiries and Observations, upon the Diseases of the Mind,* a pioneering work in mental health.

- The first issue of the *New England Medical Review and Journal* is published; today it is called the *New England Journal of Medicine.*

- John Stevens publishes *Documents Tending to Prove the Superior Advantages of Rail-ways and Steam-carriages over Canal Navigation.*

1813

- King's College and University of New York medical schools merge to form Columbia University Medical School.

- The Association for the Relief of Respectable, Aged, Indigent Females is established in New York, probably the first such agency for poor women in America.

- New Hampshire farmer Samuel Thompson receives a patent for his herbal medicine, composed mostly of lobelia, to induce vomiting. The Thompsonian system of steam baths and "purges" becomes a national phenomenon.

- Elisha Coller designs a rotating bullet chamber for a flintlock musket; Samuel Colt would later adapt this idea for his famous revolver.

1814

- Francis C. Lowell and Paul Moody perfect a power loom for use in their new textile mill in Waltham, Massachusetts.

1815

- The first steam-powered warship is built in the United States.

- John Stevens convinces the New Jersey legislature to create a company "to erect a rail road from the river Delaware near Trenton to the river Raritan at or near New Brunswick."

OVERVIEW

Assessment. The period 1783 to 1815 was a time of few great advances in medical science in America. In many ways doctors continued the crude medical practices of the colonial period, with some indications of new thinking regarding preventive medicine, mental disease, and public sanitation. The story of American technology, on the other hand, is much more dynamic, inaugurating an era of industrial revolution, mass production (interchangeable parts), and powered transportation, as well as extraordinary progress in learning about the geography, plants, animals, and native inhabitants of a nation that would double in area during this period.

Medical Science. At the time of the American Revolution, it is estimated, there were about thirty-five hundred medical practitioners in America, only four hundred of whom had formal training. After the war American medicine became more organized, with the establishment of new hospitals and medical schools. Prior to this period there were very few American medical schools (Dr. John Morgan had established the first one in 1765 at the College of Philadelphia), and many colleges were used as barracks or hospitals during the war. The few well-trained American physicians had been educated in the great medical schools of Europe, particularly Edinburgh, Scotland. The war disrupted communications with Europe, and this was especially felt by physicians. After the war there occurred a significant increase in the number of American medical schools, as well as the formation of state medical societies which established standards for licensing of physicians. Despite these changes, conditions remained primitive, and the new medical schools continued to propound dangerously outdated theories about the causes of disease.

Theory Versus Practice. Medical "theory" was in many respects caught up in old ways: folk cures, superstitions, God's wrath as the cause of disease (rather than germs, poor sanitation, or mosquitoes). There was often a fatalistic attitude toward illness. If disease was caused by sin, then only God's forgiveness—not a doctor—could help the victim. Many people simply blamed the weather or heredity: nothing could be done about it. And medical theory would be hampered by the age-old question of whether disease was to be viewed as a general problem which a single theory could explain in its en-

tirety (for example, "humors" out of balance), or whether disease was specific (for example, lesions on a particular organ indicating a localized problem or particular disease). Early American medical theory was dominated by Enlightenment thinking, which valued unified theories over experimental evidence. By the end of this period new ideas from Paris were beginning to influence American physicians. Pure theorizing was out, or at least open to new scrutiny; true scientific research based on experimentation and observation was encouraged.

General Health and Life Expectancy. Despite the shortcomings of medical science, the picture was not entirely bleak. Compared to Europeans, Americans enjoyed relatively good health, largely because of the sparsity of the population. Unlike Europeans packed in overcrowded, unsanitary cities (and thus more exposed to deadly epidemics), Americans lived primarily in rural areas. This started to change after the Revolution, as the United States began to develop cities of its own. Life expectancy was short, but that was mostly due to childhood diseases. Philadelphia records for the 1780s show that more than half of all reported deaths occurred before the age of ten. In Massachusetts and New Hampshire, according to 1789 data, the life expectancy was only 34.5 years for males and 36.4 for females. Once past the high risks of getting through childhood, though, one's life expectancy increased significantly: after reaching the age of twenty, a man could expect to live to fifty-four and a woman to fifty-six.

Hospitals and Almshouses. Only a few hospitals existed before the Revolution, most notably in Pennsylvania. During the war there had been a great many temporary hospitals in colleges or private residences, but after 1783 there was an increase—slowly, and only in the major cities—in the number of permanent hospitals. New York Hospital officially opened in 1791 and Massachusetts General Hospital in 1811. More common were the almshouses (poorhouses) that provided shelter and medical care for paupers, orphans, and the insane. By 1815 every city in the United States had an almshouse, and they were busy: the records for New York City in 1809 show that the almshouse was taking care of 538 adults and 226 children, with 168 sick in its wards. The new city hospitals, which were intended not for the destitute but for the middle class, still did not have the confidence of the general population. Most people avoided them if they possibly could, and with good reason: they were unsanitary, overcrowded, and staffed by people who knew little of human anatomy or the real causes of disease. The hospitalized patient, it was said with some truth, was just as likely to die as to recover.

Epidemics. This was a period of great outbreaks of yellow fever, smallpox, typhoid fever, and influenza. Rapid population increases in the cities led to overcrowding, inadequate water and sewage systems, and increased risks of disease. The epidemics prompted pioneering work by physicians such as Benjamin Rush and the development of better public water and sanitation systems. Philadelphia, which suffered a devastating epidemic of yellow fever in 1793, was among the first cities to build a steam-powered waterworks, in 1802. Epidemics were the most obvious killers, but not the most lethal. Diphtheria took the lives of many children each year. Respiratory diseases such as tuberculosis killed thousands annually. Because they did not strike in terrifying epidemics, these diseases were not feared as much as smallpox or yellow fever. Gout, which caused swelling and deformity of the feet and hands, was not feared. Instead, gout was believed to be a result of good living—too much fine wine, rich food, and leisure time—and therefore a sign that a man was above the working class. The victim of gout often took a strange pride in being afflicted.

Vaccination. One of the few areas of significant medical progress was vaccination against disease, in particular the new idea of infecting a healthy person with cowpox disease to ward off the more deadly smallpox. This concept struck most people, including doctors, as insane. But the English physician Edward Jenner in 1796 proved that his "vaccine" did produce an immunity to smallpox, and Harvard professor Dr. Benjamin Waterhouse, with timely support from President Thomas Jefferson, made smallpox vaccination acceptable to a larger public and saved countless lives.

Childbirth. Obstetrics began to move into general practice, at least in the cities where there were more doctors. Childbirth had always been the domain of midwives because physicians (and the population in general) had a moral opposition to male involvement in female health issues. In rural areas, though, midwives typically delivered babies—and took care of more-general medical needs as well. Although the typical midwife was poorly educated and often unable to handle serious complications, she probably did less harm than theorizing male physicians.

Mental Health. It was common practice in colonial America to ignore people suffering from mental diseases. They often roamed free or were confined in prisons, where they were at the mercy of the other prisoners. At best they were sent to public almshouses with paupers and orphans. Only Williamsburg, Virginia, had a hospital for the insane, the Mad House, founded in 1768. Dr. Benjamin Rush of Philadelphia was a pioneer in this field, among the first to insist that those suffering from psychological problems deserved special treatment. Rush wrote the first work by an American on mental illness, *Medical Inquiries and Observations, upon the Diseases of the Mind* (1812). Rush believed psychological problems were caused by "pervading vascular tension," and so could be cured by bleeding the patient. Still, in his genuine concern for those who suffered from mental illness, and his emphasis on humane treatment and the value of a trusting doctor-patient relationship, he is rightly considered the Father of American Psychiatry.

Technological Nation. Before the Revolutionary War American industry had been hampered by the colonies' great distances, sparse population, high labor costs, lack of investment capital, and British restrictions on the export of technology. With the war now over, Americans could concentrate on the major technical obstacles that faced them: how to traverse the great distances of their new nation, how to increase agricultural yields, and how to compensate for labor shortages. In the glow of post-Revolutionary enthusiasm, enterprising Americans made remarkable progress. Most technological discoveries still came from Europe, but Americans were skilled in perfecting new ideas. The steamboat, for example, was not invented by Robert Fulton, but he made steam-powered transportation practical. Although the early United States was still predominantly agricultural, the shift to an industrialized society had begun, and the basis of technology changed from craftsmanship to science.

Drawbacks to Industrialization. The Industrial Revolution had started in England, and there was occasional public outcry against its dehumanizing effects. In the United States some people also worried about the effects of industrialization, such as slums or the development of a huge underclass of laboring poor. Thomas Jefferson wrote in 1784, "While we have land to labor then, let us never wish to see our citizens occupied at a workbench." But even Jefferson had a small nail-making enterprise at Monticello, and most Americans welcomed industrialization as a means of establishing the new nation's self-sufficiency—not to mention producing great wealth. The combination of southern cotton (now more easily produced because of Eli Whitney's cotton gin) and northern industrial power temporarily united the regions of the new nation and set New England humming with the sound of waterpowered spinning and weaving. The mill machinery was operated mostly by women and children working twelve hours a day, six days a week. The first child labor law in the United States was not enacted until 1848.

American System. The period began in an age of craft production and ended on the verge of mass production. Eli Whitney, best known for his invention of the cotton gin, obtained a contract from the War Department in

1798 to manufacture four thousand muskets. At that time, all mechanical devices were made one at a time, with each part made individually and fitted to the connecting part. Challenged to devise a way to speed up the process, Whitney in 1800 invented a system of milling each part in quantity, then assembling the muskets from the interchangeable parts. Although he did not deliver on his promise until 1808, other inventors and industrial planners such as John Hall would put the theory into practice on a large scale and improve the concept. This "American system," as it became known throughout the world, may be the greatest technological innovation in American history, since it provided the basis for modern mass production.

Canals. The great age of canal building began in this period with short canals such as the Sault Sainte Marie, which allowed ships to go between Lake Huron and Lake Superior. Only a mile long, the Sault Sainte Marie canal was the first in America with a lock, to raise or lower a vessel to the elevation of the next portion of its journey. Driven by the need to bring western produce to eastern ports, engineers and hordes of laborers worked to tame longer distances and greater heights, culminating in 1825 with the 363-mile Erie Canal in upstate New York. Canal building became a national craze for engineers, politicians, and investors, enriching or impoverishing states and investors who speculated wildly on them. Unlike the Erie, most canals lost money.

Exploration. While canals, roads, and bridges were being constructed in the "civilized" states along the eastern seaboard, explorers, traders, and settlers were moving further westward, to the Mississippi River and beyond. President Jefferson had considered exploring the Missouri River watershed even before the acquisition of the vast Louisiana Territory. After the purchase in 1803, government-sponsored expeditions—most notably that of Meriwether Lewis and William Clark—explored the vast reaches west of the Mississippi River. Although some of these expeditions were scientific in nature, they all had political goals as well: there was much to learn about the native inhabitants, land, animals, and climate of regions soon to be enveloped by the expanding nation. Many other expeditions were completely independent of the government, financed by businessmen looking for wealth. Robert Gray, sailing for a fur-trading company, discovered and named the Columbia River in 1792; John Jacob Astor's American Fur Company, established in 1808, and other large corporations pushed relentlessly into America's interior. Individual farmers and hunters such as Daniel Boone also drove the expansion, drawn westward by the seemingly unlimited economic possibilities of the North American continent.

The Future. Any age of technological achievement provides an important basis for the progress of the following age. Innovations in steam power forever changed ship transportation and provided the technological foundation for the great era of steam locomotives. The interest in canal building, begun in the 1790s, became a mania by 1815 but by the 1830s canals would be put out of business by the railroads. The American system of manufacturing interchangeable parts was later applied to everything from watches to sewing machines to automobiles, and factories became a familiar (and less welcome) sight all across the American landscape. The United States was well on the way to establishing itself as a powerful, self-sustaining nation, no longer reliant on Europe for government, learning, medicine, or manufacturing.

TOPICS IN THE NEWS

CHARLATANS AND PATENT MEDICINES

Patent Medicines. Colonial Americans had imported from England a variety of patent medicines (so called because they had received official patents from the British government). When the Revolutionary War cut off the supply of Daffy's Elixir and Bateman's Pectoral Drops, enterprising Americans began creating their own packaged herbal remedies. The new confidence in the United States as strong enough to win a war against the most powerful nation on earth led to a belief that everything about America was special, including their own medications, which, because they were made from American ingredients, would have special curative powers for the people of the United States. As early as 1800 a newspaper warned that "the venders of patent medicines in almost every capital town in the United States are fattening on the weakness and folly of a deluded public." The colorful names and attractive packaging (it was often the labels rather than the ingredients that were patented) helped create an enormous market for patent medicines.

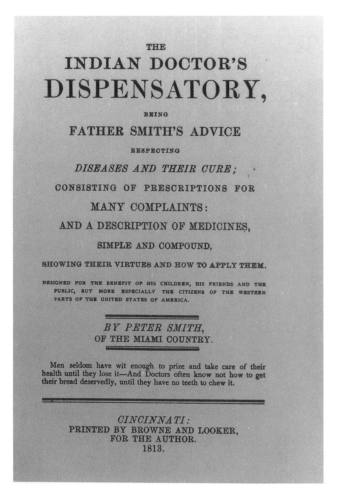

THE
INDIAN DOCTOR'S
DISPENSATORY,

BEING

FATHER SMITH'S ADVICE

RESPECTING

DISEASES AND THEIR CURE;

CONSISTING OF PRESCRIPTIONS FOR

MANY COMPLAINTS:

AND A DESCRIPTION OF MEDICINES,

SIMPLE AND COMPOUND,

SHOWING THEIR VIRTUES AND HOW TO APPLY THEM.

DESIGNED FOR THE BENEFIT OF HIS CHILDREN, HIS FRIENDS AND THE
PUBLIC, BUT MORE ESPECIALLY THE CITIZENS OF THE WESTERN
PARTS OF THE UNITED STATES OF AMERICA.

BY PETER SMITH,
OF THE MIAMI COUNTRY.

Men seldom have wit enough to prize and take care of their
health until they lose it—And Doctors often know not how to get
their bread deservedly, until they have no teeth to chew it.

CINCINNATI:
PRINTED BY BROWNE AND LOOKER,
FOR THE AUTHOR.
1813.

Title page for a book of folk remedies

And in this period of "heroic" medicine, a mild patent medicine was an appealing alternative to more-debilitating cures such as bleeding.

Mesmerism. In addition to patent medicines, new theories about universal cures were widespread. Anton Mesmer was an Austrian physician whose cures by "animal magnetism" became a popular fad in the 1780s, especially in Paris. He conducted séances in which patients were cured by contact with a universal fluid (to which of course, only Mesmer had access). What he had discovered was the power of suggestion, and the early use of what would become hypnotism; the only "magnetism" was in Mesmer's personality, and he was discredited by a group of scientists including Benjamin Franklin. The verb *mesmerize* is derived from his name.

Perkins's Metallic Tractors. Another magnetic personality who was able to exploit the power of suggestion was Connecticut physician Elisha Perkins. In 1795 Perkins introduced a theory that pain was caused by excessive "electric fluid" which could be drawn away from affected parts by metallic objects. But not just any metal object would do; only Perkins's patented "tractors," small pointed devices, supposedly made from precious metals, selling for twenty-five dollars a pair, could cure pain. Al-

though a convention of doctors in his home state declared him a fraud, Perkins sold his tractors to an eager American public as quickly as he could make them. Perkins died caring for the sick in New York's 1799 yellow fever epidemic. His son Benjamin successfully promoted the tractors in England, claiming to have cured more than 1.5 million people. However, when an English doctor declared that he obtained the same effect using tractors carved from wood and painted to look like the expensive Perkins tractors, the "electric" basis of Perkins's claim was discredited. The fad soon passed, although the popular desire for miracle cures did not.

Thompsonianism. One of the most popular health fads in American history was created by Samuel Thompson, a New Hampshire farmer who combined patent medicine with a "system" that could be administered by anyone, with no physician required. This "every-man-his-own-physician" idea was popular with independent-minded Americans. Like the theory-prone physicians of the day, Thompson was convinced that "all disease is the effect of one general cause, and may be removed by one general remedy." In the Thompsonian system the cause was cold and the cure was heat. He advocated steam baths and plants such as pepper that induced sweating, as well as enemas and purgatives (using wildflowers such as lobelia) to induce vomiting and clear out any "obstructions." Indeed, to Thompson health was very much a matter of plumbing: preserving the natural heat balance in the body was like knowing "how to clear a stove and pipe when clogged with soot, that the fire may burn free, and the whole room be warmed as before."

Medical Establishment. Thompson's simplistic theory was just as infuriating to medical doctors as it was appealing to people who feared doctors and their bloodletting practices. A rival physician had Thompson arrested for murder in 1809, charging that he had administered too much lobelia to a young patient who vomited so violently that he died. In a dramatic court scene a prosecution witness exhibited the plant that had caused the victim's death. Thompson's lawyer promptly ate the plant, which happened to be marsh rosemary rather than lobelia, with no ill effects. Thompson was cleared, and soon afterward had the added pleasure of seeing the physician who had accused him convicted of graverobbing. But the medical establishment continued its fight against quackery, to the extent that state laws forbidding the Thompsonian system were enacted. Thompson took his case to Washington and received a patent for his system in 1813. (He would later claim that President James Madison himself had endorsed it.) His system became increasingly popular in an age of intensifying democratic idealism: aristocratic, highly educated physicians were not needed when Thompson's system could make healers of everyday men and women. Yet Thompson's good fortune eventually ran out. Other charlatans stole his system, and competing systems such as homeopathy came into vogue. Thompson spent his final years unhappily trying to pro-

THE DEATH of GENERAL WASHINGTON

This most illustrious and much lamented Personage died on the 15.th of Dec.r 1799, in the 68.th year of his Age, after a short illness of 30 hours in the full Possession of all his Fame, like a Christian and an Hero, calm and collected without a groan and without a sigh.

He united and adorned many excellent Characters, at once the Patriot and Politician, the Soldier & the Citizen; the Husbandman and the Hero, the Favourite of the Genius of Liberty the Father of AMERICAN INDE-PENDENCE, the Promoter of her extensive and BROTHERLY UNION the Pillar of her CON-STITUTION, the PRESIDENT of her SENATE, and the GENERALISSIMO of her ARMIES.

He possessed and displayed extraordinary abi-lities, exalted VIRTUES, and unexampled Self command and Self denial: moderate in Prosperity, undaunted amid Danger, unbroken by adversity, firm and unmoved amid the violence or reproach of Faction, unperverted by great and general applause.

He Was GREAT in the COUNCIL, and in the FIELD.

He Was GREAT in ARTS. and in ARMS

First in War, first in Peace, first in the hearts of AMERICANS, first in the Eyes of the World, he was unrivalled as a Statesman as a Soldier, as a Senator, and he is embalmed by the tears of AMERICA, entombed in the hearts of his Countrymen, admired by the enlightened of all Lands, immortalised by his own great actions and the regrets of Mankind.

A printed cotton kerchief depicting the death of Washington (New-York Historical Society, New York City)

tect his system and died in 1843 futilely taking his own medicine. However, he was successful in one respect: his efforts helped turn the tide against the practice of bleeding.

Source:
James Harvey Young, *The Toadstool Millionaires* (Princeton: Princeton University Press, 1961).

THE DEATH OF GEORGE WASHINGTON

Cause of Alarm. On 13 December 1799, at the age of sixty-seven, former president George Washington came down with what he thought was an ordinary cold and sore throat. By the next morning he could hardly speak and was unable to swallow a soothing mixture of molasses, vinegar, and butter. Martha called for the doctor, and in the meantime Washington himself asked the plantation overseer to bleed him. This stopped only when Martha protested that he was taking too much blood.

Bleeding. Washington's insistence on being bled was typical of the time. Most doctors agreed that bleeding would lessen the excitement of the blood vessels, which in turn would reduce pain, induce sleep, and prevent relapses. Bleeding was prescribed for everything from fever to consumption to madness. The fact that Washington was bled by his overseer, in the absence of a doctor, was not unusual. Barbers or "surgeons," men with little or no formal medical training, were specialists in bleeding. They might use leeches, or would simply cut open a vein in the arm, neck, or foot and drain the blood.

The Physicians. James Craik, the first doctor to arrive at Washington's bedside, bled him again, and later a third time. Two more physicians, Elisha Dick and Gustavus Brown, arrived in the mid afternoon. Each examined the patient. Brown agreed with Craik that Washington suffered from quinsy, a severe form of tonsillitis, and recommended more bleeding. Dick, however, insisted that Washington needed a throat operation and that further bleeding would only make matters worse. "He needs his strength," Dick said, "bleeding will diminish it." Perhaps because he was the youngest of the three doctors, Dick's advice was ignored, and the former president was bled a fourth time.

Additional Treatment. Medical theory of the day recommended that bleeding be administered in conjunction with emetics to produce vomiting and purges such as calomel (mercury). The idea was to debilitate the body to the point where the disease had nothing left on which to work. All of these treatments were administered to the helpless but willing Washington. In the late afternoon, aware that the end was approaching, he examined his will and spoke with his secretary about financial matters at Mount Vernon. Then, according to his doctors, he expressed a wish "that he might be permitted to die without further interruption."

A Final Wish. As his death approached, Washington appears to have been struck with a fear of being buried alive. He gathered enough strength to ask his personal secretary, "do not let my body be put into the vault in less than three days after I am dead." When the secretary agreed, Washington replied, "Tis well." These were probably his last words. On 14 December, as midnight approached, the first president of the United States quietly passed away.

Preventable Tragedy. Had his treatment been less debilitating, it is possible that the normally healthy Washington would have lived through this sickness. Craik later admitted that he should have listened to Dick and maintained that if the physicians had "taken no more blood from him, our good friend might have been alive now," although it is by no means certain that they could have done anything about his condition. First of all, they were not sure what he suffered from: it may have been a streptococcus infection of the throat, but could have been diphtheria. Even had they diagnosed the illness correctly, they may not have had the instruments to treat him—to examine his larynx, for example. However, it is safe to say that the treatment did nothing to aid his recovery and most likely hastened his death.

Source:

James Thomas Flexner, *Washington the Indispensable Man* (Boston: Little, Brown, 1974).

EXPLORATION

Mapping the Continent. Well before Meriwether Lewis and William Clark's monumental journey from

The naturalist William Bartram, who traveled throughout the South; engraving by Thomas B. Welch

Saint Louis to the mouth of the Columbia River, explorers were mapping what would soon become the western coast of the United States. British Capt. George Vancouver explored and mapped the Pacific coast in 1790–1792, and published an atlas with the first accurate maps of that region in 1798. The federal government started mapping with the creation of the U.S. Coast Survey (today known as the Coast and Geodetic Survey) in 1807. In addition to such government-sponsored expeditions, private trade missions were often the driving force behind geographic exploration. Robert Gray of Boston, on a fur-trading mission to China, commanded the first ship to travel around the world under the American flag (1787–1789). On his next voyage (1790–1793) he was the first to explore the Columbia River, which he named after his ship. American statesmen would later use Gray's short voyage up the Columbia as the basis for the United States claim to Oregon, which was not included in the Louisiana Purchase of 1803.

The Great Von Humboldt. The most famous explorer of the age was the German Alexander von Humboldt, whom Ralph Waldo Emerson called "one of those wonders of the world . . . who appear from time to time as if to show us the possibilities of the human mind, the force and range of his faculties—a universal man." His extraordinary five-year journey throughout South America and Mexico (1799–1804) resulted in the classification of thirty-five hundred new botanical species; a better understanding of Native American cultures; the first link between volcanoes and the dynamic structure of the earth; the discovery of declining magnetic intensity from the poles to the equator; and more important, detailed maps of the Pacific coast. Humboldt was drawn to the political principles of the United States, which he described as "the only corner of the earth where man possesses liberty and where the small evils are compensated by the great goods," although he added that slavery was detestable. He also greatly admired Thomas Jefferson and visited him at Monticello in 1804. Jefferson was always pleased to meet fellow scientists, and doubly so in this case because of Humboldt's intimate knowledge and maps of the northern portion of Mexico, which bordered the newly acquired Louisiana Territory. At the time of Humboldt's visit, in fact, Lewis and Clark were on the outbound portion of their own long and extraordinary journey through the million-square-mile expanse of uncharted land.

Lewis and Clark Expedition. The greatest American scientific expedition of the time was Meriwether Lewis and William Clark's journey through the wilderness of northwestern America between 1804 and 1806. Like Humboldt's expedition, Lewis and Clark's goal was scientific discovery, but political purposes were equally important. President Thomas Jefferson planned the expedition, which resulted in an enormous increase in knowledge of American flora, fauna, geography, and native culture. It also opened up the vast Louisiana Territory, stretching from New Orleans to the headwaters of the Missouri River, to further exploration, trade, and eventual civilization. Jefferson and the American Philosophical Society had wanted to do such an expedition for years, but since the United States did not own this territory, they had been prevented. Still, the Lewis and Clark expedition had been planned before Jefferson knew he might be able to purchase this vast area. When the federal government acquired the region from France, it doubled the size of the United States, and Jefferson was prepared to find out what was there, and not just in scientific and geographical terms. The president also wanted to know the extent of the Missouri River watershed, which the United States could legally claim as part of Louisiana. If it extended far to the North, he could push the British out of the profitable western fur trade.

Journey to the Pacific. Lewis and Clark's epic journey took twenty-eight months. The company consisted of thirty-four permanent members plus fifteen soldiers and experienced rivermen for the first leg up the Missouri. The main boat, fifty-five feet long, with a sail and twenty-two oars, and two smaller open boats were crammed with supplies: firearms, gunpowder, medicine, and whiskey, plus a large supply of coats, plumed hats, glass, beads, and knives to trade with the Indians. Two horses, led along the riverbank, would be used for extended hunting trips. Leaving Saint Louis on 14 May 1804, the party traveled up the Missouri as far as the season would permit, spending the winter near the friendly Mandan Indians in what is now North Dakota. In the spring they pushed on to the headwaters of the Missouri, where they were forced to abandon their canoes and trade for horses to carry them over the Rocky Mountains in search of the "River of the West." A young Shoshone woman named Sacajawea played a vital role as interpreter for Lewis and Clark. Many legends have sprung up around her, investing her with magical powers. She was an indispensable member of the expedition and made this incredible journey carrying her infant child on her back. With help from Sacajawea and Nez Percé Indians the white explorers made it to the Snake River, then to the Columbia River, which carried them to the Pacific Ocean. After spending the rainy winter of 1805–1806 in a collection of huts they called Fort Clatsop near the mouth of the Columbia River, they retraced their steps but with notable variations, including splitting the party into two groups for several weeks, which could have left them vulnerable to hostile Indians. But they survived the return journey to arrive in Saint Louis on 23 September 1806. Along the way they had peacefully negotiated with dozens of Indian nations—many at war with each other—and recorded valuable scientific, geographical, and cultural information, including the sad state of many of the Indian villages that had been decimated by smallpox. They had traveled almost eight thousand miles amid Indians both friendly and hostile, raging rivers, bears, bitter cold, and near starvation—all with the loss of only one man.

No Northwest Passage. Lewis and Clark did not achieve one of their main goals: they did not find an all-water route from the Mississippi River to the Pacific Ocean. Between the point at which the Missouri River became too shallow for navigation and the start of the westward flowing river system were hundreds of miles of wild country, and instead of the "Stony" mountains shown on early maps were the almost impenetrable Rockies. Jefferson's hope of a Northwest Passage had been shattered, yet the West had been opened and the stage set for the expansion of the United States to the Pacific.

Exploring the East. The West was not the only scene of adventurous expeditions, for there was still much to be explored in the East. In 1791 William Bartram published his *Travels Through North and South Carolina, Georgia, East and West Florida, The Cherokee Country, The Extensive Territories of the Muscogulges, or Creek Confederacy, and the Country of the Chactaws,* an account of his journey through the forests of the Southeast from 1773 to 1777. In addition to rich descriptions of the beauty of nature in the United States, and detailed drawings of a wide variety of plants and animals, Bartram also portrayed with unusual empathy the Native Americans that he encountered along the way. Son of the British natural scientist John Bartram, William was the first American-born botanist of international stature. His writing inspired,

The Pennsylvania Hospital in Philadelphia, 1802

among others, William Wordsworth, James Fenimore Cooper, Ralph Waldo Emerson, and Henry David Thoreau.

Sources:

Stephen E. Ambrose, *Undaunted Courage: Meriwether Lewis, Thomas Jefferson and the Opening of the American West* (New York: Simon & Schuster, 1996);

Douglas Botting, *Humboldt and the Cosmos* (New York: Harper & Row, 1973);

Thomas P. Slaughter, *The Natures of John and William Bartram* (New York: Knopf, 1996);

Page Smith, *The Shaping of America* (New York: McGraw-Hill, 1980).

MEDICAL EDUCATION

Schools. Prior to the Revolution, there were very few trained physicians in the United States, and what few there were had been educated in Europe, typically in Edinburgh, Scotland. In the United States only Philadelphia and New York had medical schools, both established in the 1760s. The post–Revolutionary War period saw a significant increase in the number of medical schools affiliated with prestigious institutions. Dartmouth Medical School was established in 1781, Harvard in 1782, the University of Maryland at Baltimore in 1807, and Yale and Columbia in 1813. At the same time state licensing boards established standards for medical practice. The medical schools and state boards fought over the right to license physicians; Harvard, for example, claimed that its medical-school graduates did not have to take the state exams, and eventually the state

agreed. By about 1820 most states allowed medical schools to license physicians, and Americans began to take pride in their medical schools, reasoning that there was no need to train doctors in Europe. Unfortunately, it would be many decades before that belief would be justified.

Quality of Education. Despite the increase in the number of medical schools, nine out of ten "doctors" still had no formal training. Even the formal training was meager—medical schools would grant a license after only one year of study beyond the bachelor's degree. Doctors mainly learned "on the job." One particular problem in medical education was the difficulty in finding human cadavers, which would help prospective doctors learn human anatomy. The public had a deep revulsion to human dissection, and rarely would permission be given to dissect a body, or even to perform an autopsy. The only legal way to get human bodies was for physicians and doctors to wait for the execution of a criminal. Some medical students and doctors would rob graves to get corpses. There was even a club at Harvard called the Spunkers, who procured corpses of derelicts and criminals.

New York "Doctor's Riot." The most dramatic example of public disapproval of dissection was the "Doctor's Riot" in 1788. A group of boys climbed a ladder to look into a window at New York Hospital. They saw four men dissecting a corpse. The public was already furious over a series of grave robberies, and when news of the dissections got out, an angry mob formed to punish these suspected graverobbers. The rioters entered and ransacked

Harvard Medical School got its start in 1783 when John Warren, a surgeon in the American Revolution, began giving lectures for the Boston Medical Society. These lectures were so popular that Harvard College (from which Warren had graduated in 1771) saw the opportunity to catch up with its rivals, the College of Philadelphia and King's College (Columbia University), both of which had established medical schools.

When it was first established in 1783, the Medical Institution of Harvard College had little money, a few pieces of laboratory equipment, and a dingy classroom in the basement of Harvard Hall. Warren was appointed professor of anatomy and surgery, Benjamin Waterhouse (unpopular and pretentious, but the best-educated doctor in New England) professor of theory and practice of physic, and Aaron Dexter professor of chemistry. Students who could pay their fees were admitted; there were no entrance exams. Since some of the students could not write, the final qualifying exam was oral. To receive a bachelor of medicine degree, a student would attend college for two four-month terms and serve a six-month apprenticeship. Classroom lectures were delivered in the pompous, droning style favored by Waterhouse; students were given no opportunity to ask bothersome questions. Laboratory training was limited, and clinical experience could only be had several miles away at the "pest house" (the hospital where people with infectious diseases were quarantined) in Boston.

In 1810 the Harvard Medical School moved to Boston, and soon joined up with Massachusetts General Hospital, where students could get the clinical training they desperately needed. Yet even by 1860 there were still no entrance requirements, exams continued to be oral, and a student had to pass only five of the nine subject areas to graduate. After the Civil War, reforms instituted by Harvard president Charles William Eliot tightened entrance requirements and placed new emphasis on scientific discipline and academic rigor.

Source: John Langone, *Harvard Med* (New York: Crown, 1995).

the hospital, and would have lynched the doctors had they not escaped. The militia was called in to disperse the mob, and the riot ended, but the basic conflict between the medical profession's research needs and the individual's right to a safe burial remained unsettled.

Midwifery. Since medieval times, midwives, rather than male physicians, had helped women deliver babies. Midwives tended to be unschooled, yet many of them

had years of experience—and some medical historians claim that women were better off with a midwife than with some theorizing doctor. A few doctors believed that midwifery and professional medicine could be brought closer together. William Shippen, who had been trained in obstetrics in London, gave private lectures in midwifery in Philadelphia in 1782. He admitted midwives to these lectures—an unusual practice at the time. Like Samuel Bard in New York, he believed that midwives could handle most births, while physicians could be called in for emergencies. With the fading of the moral taboo over men's involvement in childbirth, physicians began to displace the midwives, at least in the cities, and for those who could afford it. But in the rural areas midwifery continued to flourish, as seen in the case of Martha Ballard, who from 1785 to 1815 kept a detailed diary of her life in rural Maine. She bore nine children herself, and delivered 816 others. Midwives were often the equivalent of country doctors, using their practical knowledge, herbal medicines, and empathy to meet the health-care needs of their neighbors. Ballard "knew how to manufacture salves, syrups, pills, teas, and ointments, how to prepare an oil emulsion (she called it an 'oil a mulge'), how to poultice wounds, dress burns, treat dysentery, sore throat, frostbite, measles, colic, 'hooping Cough,' 'Chin cough,' 'St. Vitas dance,' 'flying pains,' 'the salt rhume,' and 'the itch,' how to cut an infant's tongue, administer a 'cister' (enema), lance an abscessed breast, apply a 'blister' or a 'back plaster,' induce vomiting, assuage bleeding, reduce swelling, and relieve a toothache, as well as deliver babies." By any standard Ballard was a remarkable woman, as capable as any country doctor, although women as yet had never attained the status of physicians. It was not until 1849 that Elizabeth Blackwell became the first woman to obtain an M.D. degree.

Sources:

Richard Harrison Shryock, *Medicine and Society in America, 1660–1860* (New York: New York University Press, 1960);

Laurel Thatcher Ulrich, *A Midwife's Tale* (New York: Knopf, 1990).

THE PATENT OFFICE

Legal Monopoly. The U.S. Constitution (Article I, Section 8) provided for federal patents on inventions, and in 1790 Congress passed the first patent law, which granted to an inventor, for a period of fourteen years, the exclusive right to make or sell the invention covered by the patent. Some of the Founding Fathers were unsure that federal protection of inventions was a good idea. Benjamin Franklin believed that the inventor should freely give his ideas to society, and, true to his word, he never patented his famous Franklin Stove. But Franklin could afford to give his ideas for free, as could Thomas Jefferson, another inventor who never sought a patent. Jefferson was reluctant to see the government grant monopolies, but it became clear that inventors needed legal protection for their technological innovations.

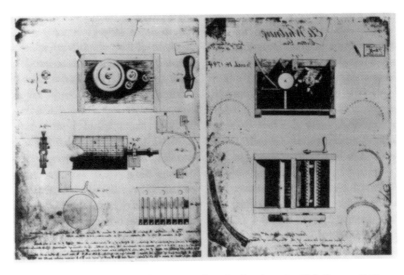

Eli Whitney's sketches of the cotton gin submitted to the U.S. Patent Office
(National Archives)

First Patents. Thomas Jefferson, as secretary of state, served as the first administrator of the patent system. A man of infinite scientific curiosity, Jefferson was well suited to the task, especially when the number of patent applications was small. There were only three patents granted the first year, the earliest on 31 July 1790 to Samuel Hopkins of Vermont for his method of producing pearl ash, or potassium carbonate (used for making glass, soap, and pigments), from wood ashes.

Expansion. As the number of applications rapidly increased, it became obvious that the secretary of state would not be able to handle them. In 1802 Secretary of State James Madison appointed architect and inventor Dr. William H. Thornton, designer of the U.S. Capitol, as superintendent of patents. Thornton is said to have single-handedly saved the Patent Office from destruction when the British burned Washington in 1814 by convincing the British that they would destroy material that was valuable to all mankind. The building housing the Patent Office was not put to the torch, as were the Capitol, the president's house, and other public buildings in Washington.

Potential for Abuse. Thornton occasionally abused his position. During his tenure he took out a surprising number of co-patents, and over time he came to believe that he, rather than John Fitch or Robert Fulton, had invented the steamboat. Thornton refused to grant a patent to John Hall, the inventor of the breech-loading rifle, unless Hall credited Thornton as coinventor. After Thornton's death in 1828, Congress reorganized the Patent Office, requiring stricter examination of patents (for example, it was no longer possible to patent a medicine with no proven benefit) and forbidding employees of the Patent Office from taking out patents.

No Guarantee. As many inventors discovered, a legal patent was not always sufficient protection, and certainly no guarantee of financial success. Fitch and James Rum-

THE AMERICAN PHILOSOPHICAL SOCIETY

Founded in Philadelphia in 1743 by Benjamin Franklin, and revived after the dislocation of the Revolutionary War, the American Philosophical Society was dedicated to the promotion of "all philosophical experiments that let light into the nature of things, tend to increase the power of man over matter, and multiply the conveniences and pleasures of life." Franklin was president from 1769 to his death in 1790. He was succeeded by astronomer and mathematician David Rittenhouse, and then by Thomas Jefferson, who presided from 1797 to 1815. Jefferson, who became president of the society at the same time he was elected vice president of the United States, claimed that the A.P.S. honor meant more to him than his political office.

The society's support of science and the practical arts was of considerable value in promoting American intellectual progress, as well as keeping the United States connected with European scientific and medical advances. In 1796 the society offered prizes for such projects as a simple method for computing longitude, improvements in fireplace and stove operation, and a design for street lamps. The emphasis was usually on the practical: how to preserve wine, raise silkworms, destroy weevils, or cure a sore throat. At the same time, radical theories were discussed and great minds engaged, as evidenced by a membership that included Benjamin Rush and James Madison.

Source: Daniel J. Boorstin, *The Lost World of Thomas Jefferson* (Chicago: University of Chicago Press, 1993).

sey both received patents on their steamboats in the same year (1791), leaving them to dispute in public each other's claim. Oliver Evans, who held several patents for factory mechanization and steam-engine improvements, was so discouraged by his long fight for royalties and the "injustice and ingratitude of the public" that he burned all the records of his inventions. Eli Whitney, the most famous of America's early inventors, made nothing on his patented but easily reproduced cotton gin. Yet the first patent system was a significant step toward encouraging American inventiveness and offering some protection to those who invested in "any useful art, manufacture, engine, machine, or device, or any improvement thereon not before known or used."

Sources:

Harry Kursh, *Inside the U.S. Patent Office* (New York: Norton, 1959);

Merritt Roe Smith, *Harpers Ferry Armory and the New Technology* (Ithaca, N.Y.: Cornell University Press, 1977).

SCIENCE, RELIGION, AND RACE

A Well-Ordered World. Enlightenment thinking encouraged Americans to make sense of their country and society, to discover the ordering principle that might explain the diversity they saw around them. One obvious, and troubling, example of diversity was skin color. The system of biological classification developed by Swedish scientist Carolus Linnaeus, used to name and categorize all living things by genus and species, was generally accepted by American scientists, but it posed difficult questions. While some believed that all human beings were of the same species, as Linnaeus suggested, others maintained that blacks and whites were of two different species (with the obvious implication that whites were superior). It was well known that the mating of animals of different species produced sterile offspring. The fact that no such reproductive problem resulted from the mixture of Caucasian and Negro parentage led some scientists to the conclusion that blacks and whites belonged to the same species. However, there were enough exceptions in the animal world to make this line of argument inconclusive.

Great Chain of Being. Another unifying principle, popularized in poetical form in Alexander Pope's *Essay on Man* (1732), was the Chain of Being, in which all matter, from minerals to God, was categorized in hierarchical order. No gaps were allowed in the chain, for that would suggest that God had not executed his creation perfectly. Why then was there a huge gap between man and the closest beast, the orangutan? Did the Negro, some wondered, fill that gap? The biblical story of Genesis raised related questions: if all humankind derived from one set of parents, why was the Negro so different? Since science and religion were not considered incompatible, scientists and philosophers tried, with varying degrees of inconsistency, to find positions that reconciled the differences among their religious, scientific, and social dispositions.

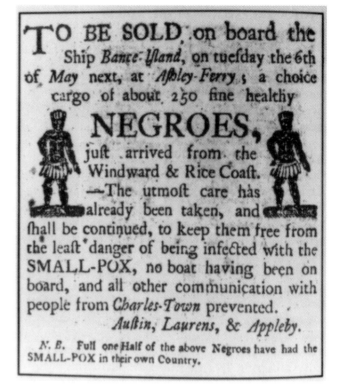

A Charleston, South Carolina, advertisement announcing the arrival of African slaves from the Windward and Rice coast

Jefferson's Unchanging Universe. As a scientist, Thomas Jefferson placed his faith in a well-ordered universe operating according to fixed laws. So firm was his belief in the Chain of Being and the unchangeable nature of the world since God's perfect creation that he denied the possibility of extinction. "Such is the economy of nature," he wrote in an attempt to prove that mammoths still existed, "that no instance can be produced of her having permitted any one race of her animals to become extinct; of her having formed any link in her great work so weak as to be broken." Yet Jefferson knew that to engage in scientific inquiry could mean encountering facts that did not fit his system. When confronted with evidence of seashells high in the Andes Mountains, he admitted that he could not explain how they got there. "Ignorance is preferable to error," he wrote in *Notes on the State of Virginia* (1785), "and he is less remote from the truth who believes nothing, than he who believes what is wrong."

Jefferson on Race. In addition to being a scientist, Jefferson was a Virginia slaveholder and refused to be pinned down on the subject of race. He was caught between his belief in a single perfect creation and his ideal of a free society, and his personal experience of Negro inferiority. "I advance it, therefore, as a suspicion only," he wrote, "that the blacks, whether originally a distinct race or made distinct by time and circumstances, are inferior to the whites in the endowments both of body and mind." Despite his vagueness on the scientific basis of his assertion, Jefferson's real opinion was clear.

On 19 August 1791 Benjamin Banneker sent a long letter to Secretary of State Thomas Jefferson, along with a copy of his almanac. It was a bold plea to the author of the Declaration of Independence to apply the same sentiments of liberty to the Negro:

Sir, I am fully sensible of the greatness of that freedom, which I take with you on the present occasion; a liberty which Seemed to me Scarcely allowable, when I reflected on that distinguished and dignified station in which you Stand, and the almost general prejudice and prepossession, which is so prevalent in the world against those of my complexion . . . . It [needs no] proof here, that we are a race of Beings, who have long labored under the abuse and censure of the world; that we have long been looked upon with an eye of contempt; and that we have long been considered rather as brutish than human, and Scarcely capable of mental endowments.

Sir, I hope . . . you will embrace every opportunity, to eradicate that train of absurd and false ideas and opinions, which so generally prevails with respect to us; and that your Sentiments are concurrent with mine, which are, that one universal Father hath given being to us all . . . and that however variable we may be in Society or religion, however diversified in Situation or colour, we are all of the Same Family. . . .

Sir, I freely and Chearfully acknowledge, that I am of the African race, and in that colour which is natural to them of the deepest dye; . . . I am not under that State of tyrannical thraldom, and inhuman captivity, to which too many of my brethren are doomed, but that I have abundantly tasted of the fruition of those blessings, which proceed from that free and unequalled liberty with which you are favored. . . .

Sir, Suffer me to recall to your mind that time, in which the Arms and tyranny of the British Crown were exerted, with every powerful effort, in order to reduce you to a State of Servitude. . . . This, Sir, was a time when you clearly saw into the injustice of a State of Slavery. . . . It was now that your abhorrence thereof was so excited, that you publicly held forth this true and invaluable doctrine, which is worthy to be recorded and remembered in all Succeeding ages: "We hold these truths to be Self-evident, that all men are created equal; that they are endowed by their Creator with certain unalienable rights, and that among these are, life, liberty, and the pursuit of happiness". . . . But, Sir, how pitiable is it to reflect, that although you were so fully convinced of the benevolence of the Father of mankind, and of his equal and impartial distribution of these rights and privileges . . . that you should at the Same time counteract his mercies, in detaining by fraud and violence so numerous a part of my brethren, under groaning captivity and cruel oppression, that you should at the Same time be found guilty of that most criminal act, which you professedly detested in others, with respect to yourselves. . . .

And now, Sir, I Shall conclude, and Subscribe my Self, with the most profound respect,

Your most Obedient humble Servant, Benjamin Banneker

Jefferson promptly replied, in a letter dated 30 August 1791, expressing his vague hope that something might be done about slavery as soon as circumstances might permit:

Sir, I Thank you sincerely for your letter of the 19th instant, and for the Almanac it contained. No body wishes more than I do, to see such proofs as you exhibit, that nature has given to our black brethren, talents equal to those of the other colors of men; and that the appearance of the want of them, is owing merely to the degraded condition of their existence, both in Africa and America. I can add with truth, that no body wishes more ardently to see a good system commenced, for raising the condition, both of their body and mind, to what it ought to be, as far as the imbecility of their present existence, and other circumstances, which cannot be neglected, will admit.

I have taken the liberty of sending your Almanac to Monsieur de Condorcet, Secretary of the Academy of Sciences at Paris, and Member of the Philanthropic Society, because I considered it as a document, to which your whole color had a right for their justification, against the doubts which have been entertained of them.

I am with great esteem, Sir, your most obedient humble servant. Thomas Jefferson.

Jefferson's letter to Banneker was reprinted and widely distributed, undoubtedly helping to publicize the *Almanac*. His letter to Condorcet was warmer and more personal regarding Banneker's accomplishments:

I am happy to be able to inform you that we have now in the United States a negro, the son of a black man born in Africa, and a black woman born in the United States, who is a very respectable mathematician. . . . He made an Almanac for the next year, which he sent me in his own hand writing, & which I enclose to you. I have seen very elegant solutions of Geometrical problems by him. Add to this that he is a very worthy & respectable member of society. He is a free man. I shall be delighted to see these instances of moral eminence so multiplied as to prove that the want of talents observed in them is merely the effect of their degraded condition, and not proceeding from any difference in the structure of the parts on which intellect depends.

Source: Silvio A. Bedini, *The Life of Benjamin Banneker* (New York: Scribners, 1972).

Environmental Argument. Jefferson's friend Dr. Benjamin Rush—an antislavery Philadelphian—working from a similar set of religious and scientific (but not social) beliefs, held to the theory that all mankind derived from the same creation and were originally white. In 1792 Rush made a presentation to the American Philosophical Society titled "Observations Intended to Favour a Supposition That the Black Color (As It Is Called) of the Negroes Is Derived from the Leprosy." Despite the total absence of scientific proof, Rush found his theory appealing, for it fit the prejudices of white European cultural superiority, while demonstrating that Negroes were on the same level of humanity with whites, but simply in need of a medical cure for their "disease." Most scientists rejected Rush's theory, yet many did believe that environmental factors accounted for differences in skin color. As Charles Crawford wrote in 1790, "the Negro is in every respect similar to us, only that his skin, or rather the skin of his ancestors, had been darkened by the sun." In the environmental argument white was the "normal" color, and all others were inferior variations, but all mankind was one and equal. There were both social and scientific problems with the environmental thesis. It could be used by defenders of slavery to justify the belief that nature had condemned the Negro to toil under conditions that whites could not tolerate. And it came under scientific attack because it could not explain why whites who lived in Africa for several generations became only somewhat darker, and still produced white children. In his satirical *Modern Chivalry* (1792) Hugh Henry Brackenridge neatly sidestepped the environmental question by proposing the idea that while Adam was a white man, Eve was black. "For what necessity to make them both of the same color, feature, and form," he wrote, "when there is beauty in variety." No one took Brackenridge seriously, yet here was a curiously logical explanation for the diversity of mankind.

Samuel Stanhope Smith. A Presbyterian minister, president of Yale, and "natural philosopher," Samuel Stanhope Smith was a major figure in this social and intellectual controversy. Elected to the American Philosophical Society in 1785, he wrote *An Essay on the Causes of the Variety of Complexion and Figure in the Human Species* (1787), in which he asserted that mankind originated in Asia as a single species. Over time, differences in climate and living conditions produced physical variations. If it were otherwise, Smith argued, no ordered scientific system would be possible: "the science of morals would be absurd; the law of nature and nations would be annihilated; and human nature . . . could not be comprehended in any system." Smith had neatly combined Linnaean order, environmental theory, and Genesis to support the antislavery cause; but even this skillful argument implied that Negroes would attain true equality only when they lost their blackness. To the majority of scientists and moral philosophers America was a country for white people. Yet despite the lack of consensus on the race question, Americans were beginning to apply disciplined scientific methods to grapple with complex intellectual problems with profound social implications.

Sources:

Daniel J. Boorstin, *The Lost World of Thomas Jefferson* (Chicago: University of Chicago Press, 1993);

Hugh Henry Brackenridge, *Modern Chivalry* (Philadelphia: Printed and sold by John M'Culloch, 1792);

Thomas Jefferson, "Notes on the State of Virginia," in *The Portable Thomas Jefferson*, edited by Merrill D. Peterson (New York: Viking, 1975);

Winthrop D. Jordan, *White Over Black: American Attitudes Toward the Negro, 1550–1812* (Chapel Hill: University of North Carolina Press, 1968).

SMALLPOX VACCINATION

The Scourge. Smallpox was a deadly fact of life in early America, just as it had been in Europe for centuries. It came to the United States among the first settlers—and every ship that visited from Europe or the West Indies had the potential for starting another epidemic. Little was known about the disease, and nothing could be done about it except to fast and pray: smallpox was God's punishment.

Early Immunization. One fact about smallpox was understood: people who contracted the disease and survived were thereafter immune to it. A crude method of inoculation had developed (possibly in India or Africa) but was rarely used in Europe: inject a healthy person with the smallpox matter taken from the sore of a person suffering a mild case, producing another mild case and lifetime immunity. But, as can be easily imagined, the idea of exposing a healthy person to smallpox was not widely accepted. Typical of the religious objection was a 1722 sermon titled "A Sermon Against the Dangerous and Sinful Practice of Inoculation." Only God, it warned, could inflict disease.

Mather and Boylston. After learning that his African slave had been immunized, Cotton Mather (himself a minister as well as a physician) tried to popularize the concept in colonial America in the early 1700s. He encouraged the experiments of Boston physician Zabdiel Boylston, who had learned of Turkish inoculations in 1721. These experiments were risky: Boylston's angry neighbors threatened to charge him with murder if any of his patients, including his own six-year-old son, died. Some Americans, including Thomas Jefferson, had been immunized by this "direct" method. However, it was still considered dangerous by many physicians, and with good reason: it was quite possible to cause the disease rather than prevent it. Benjamin Franklin believed the risk was worth taking. "In 1736 I lost one of my Sons a fine boy 4 Years old, by the Small Pox," he wrote in his autobiography. "I long regretted bitterly & still regret that I had not given it to him by Inoculation." Boylston's work had saved many lives, but a safer method would be required.

Monticello, May 14, 1806

Sir,

I have received a copy of the evidence at large respecting the discovery of the vaccine inoculation which you have been pleased to send me, and for which I return you my thanks. Having been among the early converts, in this part of the globe, to its efficiency, I avail myself of this occasion of rendering you a portion of the tribute of gratitude due to you from the whole human family. Medicine has never before produced any single improvement of such utility. Harvey's discovery of the circulation of the blood was a beautiful addition to our knowledge of the animal economy, but on a review of the practice of medicine before and since that epoch, I do not see any great amelioration which has been derived from that discovery. You have erased from the calendar of human afflictions one of its greatest. Yours is the comfortable reflection that mankind can never forget that you have lived. Future nations will know by history only that the loathsome smallpox has existed and by you has been extirpated.

Accept my fervent wishes for your health and happiness and assurances of the greatest respect and consideration

Thomas Jefferson

Source: Merrill D. Peterson, *Thomas Jefferson and the New Nation: A Biography* (New York & Oxford: Oxford University Press, 1970).

Jenner's Experiments. Beginning in the 1760s, an English country doctor named Edward Jenner had observed that English milkmaids who had contracted cowpox disease seemed to be immune to smallpox. Speculating that smallpox and the milder cowpox were related, Jenner experimented with "vaccination" using cowpox (vaccine is from *vacca*, the Latin word for cow) and proved in 1796 that it was effective against smallpox. But the medical establishment was not convinced. Britain's prestigious Royal Society rejected his findings the following year. Still, he wrote a report, *An Inquiry into the Causes and Effects of the Variolae Vaccinae, a Disease . . . Known by the Name of the Cow Pox* (1778), which was to have far-reaching consequences.

Vaccination in America. When Dr. Benjamin Waterhouse of the Harvard Medical School read Jenner's report, he began his own experiments. He injected his four children and a young servant boy with cowpox vaccine. They became mildly ill, as expected. He then exposed them to smallpox. When they did not contract the disease, Waterhouse had proved that Jenner's method was effective. Dr. Waterhouse wrote his own report on vacci-

nation, *A Prospect of Exterminating the Smallpox* (1800), which he sent along with some vaccine, to President Thomas Jefferson. The president, a great promoter of practical science, helped popularize Jenner's method by vaccinating his entire family. Recognizing the devastating effect that smallpox continued to have on Native Americans, Jefferson instructed Lewis and Clark to teach the Indians how to protect themselves against the disease.

More to Prove. But Waterhouse's work was not finished. With the popularization of Jenner's method, many people tried doing it themselves—often using impure cowpox matter. In 1802 an English sailor who had recently arrived in Boston convinced people that he had cowpox and began selling the virus from his pustules. He actually had smallpox, and a serious epidemic resulted. It took a special investigation by the Boston Board of Health to conclude that "the cow-pox is a complete security against the small-pox." As cowpox vaccine became more readily available and more doctors accepted Jenner and Waterhouse's work, there was a significant decrease in the number of deaths from smallpox.

Source:
Ola Elizabeth Winslow, *A Destroying Angel: The Conquest of Smallpox in Colonial Boston* (Boston: Houghton Mifflin, 1974).

THE STEAMBOAT

Britain. No single person was responsible for the invention of the steamboat. Rather, it was a long series of innovations and improvements, starting with the first steam engines of Thomas Savery and Thomas Newcomen in the early 1700s. Early steam engines were "atmospheric," which meant that heated water created steam that raised a piston in a cylinder; when cold water was injected into the cylinder, the steam condensed and atmospheric pressure drove the piston down, creating the power stroke. The Newcomen engine was called the "miner's friend," because it was typically used to pump water out of British coal mines. By 1725 the steam engine was also used for raising water to turn a waterwheel which then drove machinery. The next significant innovation was James Watt's invention of the separate condenser and the "double-acting" engine, both of which greatly improved the efficiency of the steam engine. With their patents and astute business sense, Watt and his partner, Matthew Boulton, dominated British steam technology throughout the last quarter of the eighteenth century.

America. John Fitch of Connecticut claimed that the idea of a steam engine came to him in a flash of insight one day in 1785. Having never heard of Watt or Newcomen, Fitch in effect reinvented the steam engine in America. His goal was to use steam power to propel a boat. With a few small investors and a great deal of ingenuity and perseverance, he was able to demonstrate to the Constitutional Convention delegates in 1787 a boat propelled by a small steam engine that drove twelve pad-

Thomas Jefferson was a devoted amateur scientist who took great pride in being president of the American Philosophical Society (1797–1815). He administered America's first patent office, although he never patented his own invention of a more efficient plow. Among his other inventions was a "polygraph" machine with a second pen that automatically copied letters as he wrote them—a handy device, since he wrote forty thousand letters in his lifetime. In 1785 Jefferson published *Notes on the State of Virginia*. Originally conceived as a refutation of a French naturalist's view that nature is "less active, less energetic" in the New World than in Europe, and that the animals of America are smaller than those of the Old World, *Notes on Virginia* covers geography, history, climate, religion, laws, and society, as well as his controversial views on slavery. As a promoter of science Jefferson helped popularize smallpox vaccination and planned the famous Lewis and Clark expedition. In addition to his skills in architecture (he designed his gracious brick home, Monticello, and the original buildings of the University of Virginia), he was also a collector of weather data, a student of American Indian languages, and a general tinker with tools and appliances.

Jefferson was an eminently practical man who had little use for the medical theories of the day, especially bleeding. As he once wrote to a friend: "The patient, treated on the fashionable theory, sometimes gets well in spite of the medicine." He was much more optimistic about science and technological invention, and understood well the process of continuous improvement, rather than isolated brilliant flashes of genius, that produced useful inventions. "One idea leads to another," he wrote, "that to a third, and so on through a course of time until someone, with whom no one of these is original, combines all together, and produces what is justly called a new creation."

Sources: Russell Bourne, *Invention in America* (Golden, Colo.: Fulcrum Press, 1996);

Noble E. Cunningham Jr., *In Pursuit of Reason: The Life of Thomas Jefferson* (New York: Ballantine, 1987).

dles. By 1790 Fitch had established commercial steamboat transportation on the Delaware River, providing service between Philadelphia and Burlington, New Jersey, traveling at a rate of four miles an hour over a distance of twenty miles. Although his boat was remarkably reliable, the venture was a financial failure, owing partly to the good roads already available in the area, and partly to Fitch's unpredictable and sour personality.

Competition. At about the same time another inventor, James Rumsey, entered the picture. Rumsey's ideas ranged from the impractical, such as a system of steam-driven poles to push boats upstream, to the futuristic: a steamboat that drew water in at the bow and squirted it out the stern. Benjamin Franklin liked Rumsey's ideas, especially the jet stream because it coincided with an idea that Franklin himself had once had. Franklin helped promote a Rumsean Society to solicit funds for the inventor. Soon the smooth-talking Rumsey had convinced influential Americans that he had invented the steamboat. The less personable Fitch could not get Franklin's endorsement. When that famous inventor, whom Fitch had asked to subscribe to his steamboat company, declined to invest but instead offered a donation, Fitch refused the money and later wrote that he wished he could have treated Franklin "with the indignity which he merited, and stomped the paltry ore under my feet." This behavior was unfortunately quite typical—Fitch had no flair for public relations.

A War over Rights. Rumsey and Fitch both patented their inventions in the same year, 1791. Federal patent laws were lax at this early stage, and inventions of dubious value (such as "patent" medicines) were accepted, and overlapping or conflicting claims sometimes left unresolved. As a result, Fitch and Rumsey were involved in a fierce pamphlet war and lawsuits against each other over their rights. Neither succeeded: Rumsey died while constructing one of his boats in England in 1792, and Fitch, unable to get along with his partners and frustrated by his lack of success, took his own life in 1798. The evidence is clearly on the side of Fitch as the earlier inventor; Rumsey was just the better businessman.

Next Wave of Inventors. Oliver Evans and John Stevens made more innovations in steam technology between 1795 and 1805. Evans put most of his energy into applying the steam engine to the mechanization of factories. His 1790 patent for an automated flour mill was only the third U.S. patent granted. In 1804 he invented a high-pressure steam engine and demonstrated a steam-powered dredger in Philadelphia's harbor. Stevens, a New Jersey inventor, patented several boiler improvements and also built practical steamboats, one of which made the first steam-powered ocean voyage in 1808. Stevens was perhaps the steamboat's primary innovator, but by luck, timing, and politics he has been overshadowed by Robert Fulton.

Success. Fulton's different sort of genius made steamboats practical. Fulton was not the lonely genius inventor of popular history. He made excellent use of partnerships and earlier advances in technology. His partner Robert Livingston, former ambassador to France, signer of the Declaration of Independence, and an influential New York politician, helped Fulton secure a monopoly on Hudson River steam transportation, and Fulton, with an engine imported from James Watt, built the boat. On 17 August 1807 Fulton's *Clermont* made its maiden voyage,

An 1810 lithograph of Robert Fulton's *Clermont* on the Hudson River

carrying passengers from New York to Albany. Because these two important cities were poorly connected by road, other modes of transportation offered little competition to his steamboat. Fulton kept improving his design (building twenty-one steamboats in all), cooperating with other mechanics and tinkering with his engines until they ran reliably.

Fulton Legend. As poor John Fitch demonstrated, technical talent alone was no guarantee of success. Fulton's achievement was so complete that he became a symbol of American business and technical genius—to the point where the other important innovators in steam engines and steam transportation are all but forgotten. Fulton may not have invented the steamboat, but he had the combination of engineering, marketing, financial, and personal skills necessary for bringing technological innovation to commercial success.

Source:
Russell Bourne, *Invention in America* (Golden, Colo.: Fulcrum, 1996).

TEXTILE MILLS

English Background. In 1769 British inventor Sir Richard Arkwright devised a mechanized system for spinning cotton into yarn, using multiple spindles. Since this machine was soon adapted to be driven by water-power, it became known as the "water frame." The frames were connected by pulleys and gears to a large wooden wheel, which was turned by water rushing through a channel. This adaptation brought about a monumental change in the efficiency of work: powerful natural forces could be harnessed to do the work of many animals or men. The water frame, unlike its predecessor, the "spinning jenny," was too large to fit in a worker's cottage, and it required a source of moving water. As a result textile production began a transition from a cottage industry to a factory system. With these innovations England completely dominated the world textile market. Having lost the American colonies, the British government intended to keep the United States at least economically dependent, and guarding this technology became an important part of British policy, with severe restrictions on the export of any technology, tools, or secrets related to textile production.

Industrial Revolution and America. A few Americans saw that the new nation would need to develop its own textile industry in order to become fully independent of England. Alexander Hamilton's industrial community at Paterson, New Jersey, had failed by 1795, but perhaps an American textile industry could succeed with imported British experts attracted by financial bonuses. Lured to America by such incentives was Samuel Slater, a twenty-one-year-old English textile mill foreman with a particular genius for the intricate mechanical workings of textile mills. After working with antiquated hand-operated machinery in New York, he heard about the wealthy Rhode Island merchant Moses Brown, who was looking for an Englishman familiar with the Arkwright machinery. Brown had set up some experiments in cotton spinning on the Blackstone River, but lacked the expertise to build a large-scale, mechanized mill. In 1790, with Brown's financial backing, Slater reproduced a waterpowered Arkwright textile mill from memory in Pawtucket, Rhode Island. This first mechanized textile mill in America was a great success, and soon waterpow-

Samuel Slater, who adapted English weaving technology to meet the needs of the American textile industry

ered mills were in use all over New England. By 1815 there were 167 cotton mills in Rhode Island alone.

Boston Money. Brown was an unusual man. Though his family had grown wealthy in the slave trade, Brown was uncomfortable with this brutal but lucrative business and wanted to invest his fortune elsewhere. Other New England shipping barons normally picked safe investments, often investing in British industries or American distilleries. But when the embargo of 1808 and the War of 1812 bottled up Boston Harbor, the city's wealthy shipping leaders became desperate and decided to put their money into the new textile factories. Their capital investment propelled the next phase of industrial development, which would use water power not only to spin the cotton yarn, but to drive power looms to do the actual weaving.

Waltham System. In 1814 a group of Boston merchants, including Francis Cabot Lowell, built a new brick mill on the Charles River at Waltham, Massachusetts. This mill was the first to house all phases of cotton textile production under one roof. The Boston investors were now becoming industrialists, in uneasy partnership with a new generation of "mechanics" who designed, built, and maintained the machinery. The aristocratic Lowell could not have succeeded without the brilliant working-class mechanic Paul Moody, who with his power loom and other innovations did as much as anyone to create the "Waltham System." This system would be further expanded with the creation of larger and more technologically advanced mills at Lowell and Lawrence, Massachusetts, and at Manchester, New Hampshire

(where the Amoskeag Mill complex would eventually stretch for a full mile along the Merrimack River).

Social Changes. Some early American manufacturing leaders, such as Moses Brown (who later endowed Brown University), believed that they could do better than their British counterparts in the treatment of workers. British industrialists seemed to care little for the social or educational needs of the workers crowding their factories. The people in the labor force at Waltham and other textile mills were as significant to the Waltham System as the power loom. The mills drew large numbers of young, educated, and industrious women from nearby farms. These female mill workers became a trademark of the New England textile industry. The factories were well lighted and surrounded by neat rows of boardinghouses where the women lived during their year or two at the mills. The women were often paid better wages than schoolteachers and went to the mills to save for a dowry or to earn money to help their families. Nevertheless, this economic success came with a social price. Instead of working in the comfort of their families and neighbors, they would now, in the words of a Vermont farmer, leave "home, friends, and paternal guardianship, to throng to the factories of Manchester, Lowell and Andover, where they are shut up for thirteen hours a day, where they are allowed but ten minutes to eat their dinners, and are forced to sleep in brick pens rather than comfortable rooms, exposed . . . to the thousand temptations of a crowded city; a promiscuous population and ill-chosen associates, and without home, friends or counselors, wearing life to decay, and weaving themselves shrouds whilst earning a gown."

Transformation. The Industrial Revolution transformed the architecture and social structure of the small town in America. Now the factory, situated on a river with clusters of millworker cottages around it, dominated the town. The factory, not the church, was at the center. While some of these "factory villages" with their redbrick mill buildings were beautifully designed and constructed, some became industrial cities, resembling in all their grim poverty the overcrowded, ugly, crime-ridden industrial centers in Britain that Thomas Jefferson had warned against. "The mobs of great cities," Jefferson wrote, "add just so much to the support of pure government, as sores do to the strength of the human body." But the goal had been achieved: cloth from Waltham factories nearly drove British imports out of the market. The revolution in textile production was just as important as the technological advances in steam transportation or precision manufacturing. All these factors contributed to America's new economic independence.

Sources:

Russell Bourne, *Invention in America* (Golden, Colo.: Fulcrum, 1996);

Noel Perrin and Kenneth Breisch, *Mills and Factories of New England* (New York: Harry N. Abrams, 1988);

Charles Singer, E. J. Holmyard, A. R. Hall, and Trevor Williams, eds., *A History of Technology* (New York & Oxford: Oxford University Press, 1958).

TRANSPORTATION

Taming Great Distances. Even in 1783, when the Mississippi River formed its western border, the United States was a huge country. The nation doubled in size with the Louisiana Purchase in 1803. Farmers traveling west in search of land, merchants looking for better means of transporting their goods, and politicians dreaming of better communications among the expanding population all needed canals, roads, and bridges. The country was still mostly wilderness, and the population small (about six million), but restless, energetic, confident Americans set to work building the infrastructure of a new nation.

Canals. Water had always presented an alternative to land travel, especially in colonies such as Virginia where an extensive network of rivers connected towns and plantations to the seaports. Throughout the settled regions of America, rivers provided the primary means for transporting produce and goods from inland farms to eastern seaports. As settlements expanded beyond the reach of navigable rivers, it was a natural step to build canals to connect rivers, or to bypass shallows or rapids. These were major undertakings, accomplished mostly by pick and shovel. Four hundred men worked nine years to construct the Middlesex Canal in Massachusetts. There was little engineering expertise available; experts were imported, or men with talent simply experimented, learning as they went along.

Building the Locks. It was especially difficult to construct the locks that compensated for differences in elevation along the route. A lock is a relatively watertight section with gates at both ends. After a boat enters the lock at one end, the gate closes behind it, and to raise or lower the boat to the water level in the next section, water is pumped into, or drained out of, the lock. Once the water level in the lock is equal to the level of the next section, the gate between them is opened, and the boat can proceed. Some ingenious alternatives to locks were tried: the two levels of the South Hadley Falls Canal in western Massachusetts were connected by an inclined plane, and boats were put in water-filled tanks and hauled up or down by cables. But no method was as effective as the lock. The first canal to employ a lock in America was the Sault Sainte Marie, constructed by the Northwest Fur Company in 1798 to connect Lakes Huron and Superior. The lock was shallow, managing a level difference of only one and a half feet, but the canal's success led to more-ambitious projects. The Middlesex Canal, connecting Boston Harbor to the Merrimack River at Chelmsford, had twenty-eight locks along its twenty-seven-mile length. Its chief engineer, Laommi Baldwin, had never actually seen a lock when he began construc-

tion and ended up hiring an expert from England to help him complete the project.

Canal Competition. By 1790 there were thirty canal companies incorporated in eight states. The Dismal Swamp Canal was constructed in 1794, the Sault Sainte Marie in 1798, and the Middlesex in 1803. George Washington personally invested in the Potomac Canal (begun in 1785 and operational in 1802) in an attempt to ensure that produce from the West would be transported to Virginia rather than to the rival state of New York, which was considering a canal of its own. New York's project was the famous Erie Canal, connecting the Great Lakes to the Hudson River and the Atlantic Ocean. All the planning and authorizations were completed prior to 1815, although the actual construction was not begun until 1817. Compared to the canals built only two decades earlier, the Erie was an amazing feat of engineering, stretching for 363 miles with eighty-three locks that would lift boats over six hundred feet.

Roads through the Wilderness. In addition to canal building, a tremendous amount of energy and money went into road construction. Roads in America were not much more than widened trails. Tree stumps and holes made the roads difficult; mud made them impassable except in dry weather. Under normal conditions it took three days to travel by coach from Boston to New York City, another day and a half to reach Philadelphia, and three days more to Baltimore. Traveling inland was even slower: going from Philadelphia to Nashville took over two weeks. Between 1792 and 1794 the Philadelphia and Lancaster Turn Pike Company built a sixty-six-mile road using a layer of small crushed stones which kept the road from deteriorating in bad weather. (This new method had been perfected by a British engineer named John McAdam, from whom we get the name of the macadam road surface used today.) The success of the Lancaster turnpike led Congress to approve the Cumberland Road in 1802, intended to stretch from the Atlantic Ocean to the Mississippi River. By 1818 it connected Cumberland, Maryland, on the Potomac River, to Wheeling, Virginia, on the Ohio River, but this "national road" ran into more political than technological roadblocks and was never fully completed. Yet it was clear that well-made roads had tremendous social and economic benefits, and state and private interests were ready to take over when the federal government abandoned its involvement in national roads.

Bridges. Sturdy wooden bridges had been built from the earliest days of the colonies. But wooden bridges could span narrow rivers only; if extended too far the bridge would weaken and crumble. By 1792 Timothy Palmer had applied the truss concept, triangular supports above the bridge's deck, to his bridge over the Merrimack River in Massachusetts. Extremely long bridges required multiple sections held up by pilings driven into the river bottom. But this trestle bridge construction did not work well in deep water, nor in the northern climate

The bridge over the Charles River—at the time of its completion in 1786 it was the 'longest bridge in America

where winter ice would destroy the supports, and bridges were constantly being rebuilt.

Charles River. In 1785 John Hancock petitioned the Massachusetts legislature for the right to build a toll bridge over the Charles River connecting Boston and Charlestown. He chose Lemuel Cox, a mechanic and wheelwright who had never built a bridge, to design and construct it. Many considered the project impossible because of the river's tidal currents, great width, and tendency to freeze. Yet on 17 June 1786 Cox completed the longest bridge in America. It was 1,503 feet long and 42 feet wide, with seventy-five sturdy timber piers and a 30-foot draw.

Iron Bridge. Bridge designers searched for materials stronger than wood to create longer spans. Thomas Paine, better known for his radical political prose, conceived a project in 1785 to build a revolutionary five-hundred-foot, single-span bridge over the Schuylkill River in Philadelphia. It would be made of wrought iron and based, he claimed, on a design of nature: the spider's web. Paine built a scale model, which he displayed at the home of his friend Benjamin Franklin. But he was unable to convince the Pennsylvania legislature or private investors that this untested concept would work in practice. Fed up with American inaction, he took his model and plans to France and England, but with no better fortune. In 1791 he abandoned his iron-bridge project and dedicated his time to writing *Rights of Man* (1791–1792). The Schuylkill River was finally crossed in 1798, but with a three-span wooden bridge. For large-scale iron-bridge construction, Paine was several decades ahead of his time.

Significance. These advances in transportation—canals, roads, and bridges—had significance far beyond their technical feats. They began to solve the problem of commercial, social, and political communication across the vast distances of America, linking what had been separate colonies into an increasingly interconnected United States. Transportation needs would also play a role in the political battle between those who favored a strong national government that would promote "internal improvements" and those who were equally convinced that this was the responsibility of the individual states.

Sources:

Henry Adams, *The History of the United States During the Administrations of Jefferson and Madison* (Chicago: University of Chicago Press, 1967);

David Freeman Hawke, *Paine* (New York: Harper & Row, 1974);

Page Smith, *The Shaping of America* (New York: McGraw-Hill, 1980);

Arthur Bernon Turtellot, *The Charles* (New York: Farrar & Rinehart, 1941).

YELLOW FEVER AND MALARIA

Dreaded Diseases. Yellow fever and malaria, two of the most feared diseases of the period, were often confused. Their symptoms—chills, aches, and high fever—are similar, and they tended to appear in hot weather. Neither is contagious—one person cannot catch it directly from another person—and both are transmitted by mosquitoes. In the late eighteenth century no one knew what caused these diseases; some thought there was a connection with swamp air or with summer heat. Yellow fever attacks the liver, producing the jaundice that makes the skin turn yellow, while with malaria, parasites build up rapidly in the liver, and the overworked spleen becomes enlarged as it tries to filter the parasites out. In severe cases blood vessels to the brain are blocked, causing delirium, coma, and death. The two diseases were apt to strike differently: yellow fever broke out in frightening epidemics, sometimes as far north as Philadelphia and New York City; malaria was a constant menace in hot, swampy areas of the Southeast, especially South Carolina and Georgia.

AN

ACCOUNT

OF THE

Bilious remitting Yellow Fever,

AS

IT APPEARED

IN THE

CITY OF PHILADELPHIA,

IN THE YEAR 1793.

By Benjamin Rush, M.D.

PROFESSOR OF THE INSTITUTES, AND OF CLINICAL MEDICINE,
IN THE UNIVERSITY OF PENNSYLVANIA.

PHILADELPHIA,
PRINTED BY THOMAS DOBSON,
AT THE STONE-HOUSE, N° 41, SOUTH SECOND-STREET.

MDCCXCIV.

Title page for a memoir of the epidemic that killed an estimated five
thousand Philadelphians

Philadelphia. The worst outbreak of yellow fever in America occurred in Philadelphia during the summer and fall of 1793. There were an estimated five thousand fatalities out of a population of forty-five thousand. A victim's first symptoms were high fever and headache, followed a day or two later by severe vomiting of blood as the internal organs degenerated. Death often occurred within four days to a week after contracting the disease. People were so afraid of catching the disease that they avoided contact even with their friends and stopped shaking hands. Relatives were afraid to bury the victims, and a familiar sight was the death cart passing by and the cry of the grave diggers: "Bring out your dead!"

Causes. Even experienced doctors who recognized the symptoms were ignorant of the cause, although there were plenty of theories. The best-known physician of the day, Benjamin Rush, believed that the contagion may have resulted from a shipment of coffee that was rotting on a Philadelphia wharf. It was also thought possible that the air itself carried the disease. Crews on ships in the harbor were advised to burn tobacco in the hope that its smoke would cleanse the air somehow. Others, convinced it was God punishing a sinful population, noted with some satisfaction that many of the victims were from the poor sections of town, and of course the poor were more wicked than the rich. And while it was true that the poor were afflicted more than the wealthy, it was because of unsanitary conditions in their neighborhoods—stagnant water and open sewage that drew mosquitoes—and not the wrath of God. But the disease attacked the rich as well, especially those brave enough to stay in the city rather than flee to the countryside. As the rich fled, there were other kinds of victims: shops and businesses had to close, leaving thousands out of work.

Prevention and Cure. Once the epidemic had struck, health officials tried to keep the contagion from getting worse by burning tobacco to clean the air and by recommending public prayer and fasting. People tried mud baths or garlic to prevent the disease from striking. Doctors would try anything to save their patients. The most common "cure" was to administer mercury pills and extract large volumes of blood. Bleeding was the fashionable theory of the day: if enough blood were removed, it was believed, the disease would have nothing to attack. One can only imagine how many lives would have been saved if the patient had simply been left alone. Although emergency hospitals were set up, it was difficult to find people brave enough to staff them, and in any case victims had no desire to go to a hospital to die.

Government Shutdown. Philadelphia's municipal government practically disintegrated during the epidemic. Only the work of an unofficial committee of public-spirited citizens, acting as a combined government and board of health, prevented total chaos. The U.S. capital was then at Philadelphia. It was common practice at the time to partially shut down the government during the hot summer months, so it was not unusual that President George Washington left for Mount Vernon. Secretary of State Thomas Jefferson, remaining calm in the midst of all the panic, tried to stay on, but found that his staff had evacuated the city, so he too went home to Virginia. Secretary of the Treasury Alexander Hamilton also went home, but not before contracting a mild case. As the time approached for the government officials to return, many feared for their lives. Washington decided to move the capital to Germantown, which became the temporary seat of government until November. By December the crisis had passed, and Congress was able to reconvene in Philadelphia.

Lessons Learned. Since there was no fundamental understanding of the cause of yellow fever, not many lessons emerged, although Benjamin Rush's critics now had more examples of the ill effects of his practice of excessive bleeding. When the disease struck Philadelphia again, mildly in 1795 and 1796 and violently in 1797, the same inadequate measures were taken. Dr. Rush did, however, correctly point out that poor sanitation appeared to be a contributing factor, and his efforts to clean up Philadelphia finally resulted in the development of a public water system. It would be years before people trusted the public health conditions in Philadelphia, and more than a century before Walter Reed would prove that the female Aedes aegypti mosquito was the carrier.

Malaria. While yellow fever also reached epidemic levels in southern cities, it was malaria that was the most prevalent killer in the South. *Malaria*—the word comes from *mala aria*, an Italian phrase for "bad air"—had been a problem in the warm, wet Southeast coastal regions of America since early colonial days. Many early settlers from Europe, with no defenses against malaria, suffered and died from what they called "fever and ague." South Carolinians were particularly susceptible to malaria because rice plants, for which large tracts of land had been cleared, grew best in shallow pools of standing water, which also formed breeding grounds for mosquitoes. Of course, at the time the mosquito was considered merely a pest, not a carrier of deadly disease.

Remedies. Although malaria's cause was unknown, it was often treated differently from yellow fever. First of all, malaria was not always life threatening, so measures such as bleeding were not considered necessary. Fevers were intermittent, and chronic fatigue was often the most debilitating effect. Second, it had been recognized from early colonial times that cinchona bark (from a South American tree) was effective in reducing the symptoms of malaria. We now know that it worked because it contains a substance similar to quinine.

Rich Versus Poor. Unlike yellow fever, which was likely to strike in the crowded cities, malaria was prevalent in the low-lying countryside (it was often called "country fever"). The wealthy landowners simply left during the hot season; in fact, some of South Carolina's richest families spent the summer in Newport, Rhode Island. That left the poor and slaves to labor in the intensely hot and mosquito-infested rice fields. It was generally believed that African slaves were not only better able than whites to endure the intense heat of southern summers, but were also resistant to malaria. Medical studies have since proved that black Africans were, in fact, partially immune, having come from areas where malaria was prevalent, and having built up antibodies, which were not genetic, but passed from mother to child during pregnancy. This immunity is curiously tied to sickle-cell anemia, a condition that causes blood circulation problems in black children, yet helps ward off malaria. The tragic social consequence was the belief in a "natural" law that blacks' immunity to malaria justified their slavery to work the plantations of the South while the white owners spent the hot months in safer regions. Like yellow fever, malaria was eventually reduced through improved public sanitation, quarantine of ships coming from infected regions, and (after 1900) control of mosquitoes.

Sources:

Dumas Malone, *Jefferson and the Ordeal of Liberty* (Boston: Little, Brown, 1962);

Page Smith, *The Shaping of America* (New York: McGraw-Hill, 1980);

Peter H. Wood, *Black Majority* (New York: Norton, 1974).

HEADLINE MAKERS

BENJAMIN BANNEKER

1731-1806
AFRICAN AMERICAN ASTRONOMER AND MATHEMATICIAN

Young Math Genius. The son of a free mulatto mother and an African father who had purchased his freedom, Benjamin Banneker gained fame as a mathematician and astronomer. He was born in 1731 and was mostly self-taught, as might be expected of an African American on an isolated Maryland tobacco farm during that time period, but it was clear that he had a genius for math. He became a local celebrity when, at the age of twenty-one, he borrowed a neighbor's pocket watch and re-created each gear out of wood, making a full-size clock—which continued to keep time for fifty years.

Astronomy. When Banneker was forty, a well-to-do Quaker family moved into the area. Despite differences in their status, age, and color, he became friendly with eighteen-year-old George Ellicott, who lent him books and a telescope and encouraged his lively interest in astronomy. Based on his own computations, Banneker created an almanac which calculated tides, phases of the moon, and the location of stars for each day of the year. His first attempt to get it published in 1791 was a failure, but it did come to the attention of George's cousin, Maj. Andrew Ellicott, himself an amateur astronomer. Major Ellicott spoke of Banneker to the president of the Pennsylvania Society for the Abolition of Slavery, who saw an opportunity to help Banneker and to further the cause of antislavery. If a free black had the genius to create an almanac, these reformers reasoned, it might finally prove that blacks were in no way inferior to whites.

Surveying. At about the same time, President George Washington appointed a commission to survey the land that was to become the District of Columbia, and he chose Major Ellicott to direct the project. Through the Ellicotts, Banneker was asked to join the team. He accepted and in February 1791, at the age of sixty, left his home area for the first time and traveled to Alexandria and Georgetown. Physically he was unable to stand the rigors of fieldwork, but he handled all the astronomical observations and calculations for the team. After three months of living in a tent and being eager to get back to his almanac, he returned home in April. He continued to work on his almanac and, through an antislavery society, came to the attention of the famous mathematician David Rittenhouse, who verified the accuracy of Banneker's astronomical calculations. "Every Instance of Genius amongst the Negroes is worthy of attention," Rittenhouse wrote, "because their oppressors seem to lay great stress on their supposed inferior mental abilities."

Correspondence with Jefferson. In 1791 Banneker sent a long and remarkable letter to Secretary of State Thomas Jefferson appealing for his help in eradicating slavery in the United States. He used Jefferson's own words from the *Declaration of Independence* to demonstrate that the same rights that Revolutionary patriots fought for were still denied to blacks in the United States. Jefferson's reply was brief and ambiguous, but he did express his hope that Banneker's example would prove that the appearance of black inferiority was merely a result of their degraded condition under slavery—a point that Jefferson's own biases never overcame. Later that year Banneker's almanac for 1792 was printed; it sold out quickly and went into various printings until 1802. Although later editions did not sell well, the almanac brought in enough money for him to quit farming and devote himself to his research and writing.

Symbolic Life. When Banneker died in 1806, his obituary in the Baltimore newspaper noted his accomplishments and the symbolism of his life's work: "Mr. Banneker is a prominent instance to prove that a descendant of Africa is susceptible of as great mental improvement and deep knowledge into the mysteries of nature as that of any nation." Thus Benjamin Banneker became a symbol of the antislavery movement.

Source:
Kevin Conley, *Benjamin Banneker* (New York: Chelsea House, 1989).

DAVID RITTENHOUSE

1732-1796
ASTRONOMER, CLOCKMAKER, AND PRESIDENT OF THE AMERICAN PHILOSOPHICAL SOCIETY

Early Years. Benjamin Franklin's successor as president of the American Philosophical Society was David Rittenhouse, America's foremost scientist in the last part of the eighteenth century. Born near Germantown, Pennsylvania, in 1732, Rittenhouse showed remarkable mechanical and mathematical abilities as a child. At seventeen he built a clock shop at the family farm. Clockmaking was his principal occupation for twenty years, although he also worked as a surveyor, establishing the official boundary line between Pennsylvania and Maryland (1763) and between New York and New Jersey (1769). His success as a clockmaker led him to other kinds of mathematical instruments. As a member of the American Philosophical Society he built an observatory at his farm. Later, at his home in Philadelphia, he built another, the first permanent astronomical observatory in America. It is also believed that Rittenhouse made the first telescope in America to observe the transit of Venus (1769).

Revolutionary Patriot. During the Revolutionary War Rittenhouse was a military engineer, supervising the manufacture of weapons and ammunition. One of his more unusual ideas in collaboration with Thomas Paine was a flaming iron arrow, which they hoped to use to destroy British fortifications at Philadelphia. Rittenhouse also became more involved in public affairs as a member of the Pennsylvania Assembly and the state constitutional convention in 1776. The next year he served as the president of the Pennsylvania Council of Safety. After the war he continued his public career, serving as Pennsylvania state treasurer until 1789, and he also returned to surveying, "running the line" between Pennsylvania and New York (1786) and New York and Massachusetts (1787). Later he was appointed professor of astronomy at the University of Pennsylvania, where he made various discoveries in the fields of astronomy, optics, and magnetism. Among his many inventions was a thermometer made of two strips of different metals, as in modern bimetallic thermostats, and a collimating telescope. In 1791 Rittenhouse began a five-year tenure as president of the American Philosophical Society. Between 1792 and 1795 he also acted as first director of the U.S. Mint, where he organized the department and supervised the minting of the first U.S. coin, a silver five-cent piece.

The Orrery. Rittenhouse was most famous in his lifetime for his elaborate mechanical planetarium, called an "orrery," that showed the movement and position of planets orbiting a sun. Originally built sometime around 1767, the mechanism was "so accurately adjusted," he wrote, "as not to differ sensibly from the tables of Astronomy in some thousands of years." His orrery also included "a most curious contrivance for exhibiting the appearance of a solar eclipse, at any particular place on the earth." (One of Rittenhouse's orreries is now at the Franklin Institute in Philadelphia, and another at Princeton University.) Jefferson was awestruck when he saw it. "He has not indeed made a world," he wrote, "but he has by imitation approached nearer its Maker than any man who has lived from the creation to this day." Rittenhouse died in 1796.

Source:
Howard C. Rice Jr., *The Rittenhouse Orrery* (Princeton, N.J.: Princeton University Library, 1954).

BENJAMIN RUSH

1745-1813
PHYSICIAN

Reformer. American patriot, signer of the Declaration of Independence, and between 1769 and 1791 professor of chemistry and medicine at the College of Philadelphia (now the University of Pennsylvania Medical School), Benjamin Rush was the best-known physician of the era. Born near Philadelphia in 1745, he was educated at Edinburgh, Scotland, considered the best medical school of the eighteenth century. He started practicing medicine in his home city in 1769. The next year he wrote *Syllabus of a Course of Lectures on Chemistry*, the first chemistry textbook in America. Rush was a deeply religious man who took a strict moral view of the issues of the day. To this active reformer, health was very much a moral issue, and he was an outspoken critic of slavery, drinking, and tobacco. Rush was the first doctor to publicly associate smoking with cancer.

Public Servant. Between 1777 and 1778 Rush served as surgeon general of the Continental Army (for which he took no pay), and in late 1785 he established the first free dispensary in the United States. As a delegate to the Pennsylvania constitutional convention in 1787, he supported ratification. Rush also served as treasurer of the U.S. Mint for seventeen years (1797–1813).

Yellow Fever Epidemic. Unlike some physicians who fled Philadelphia during the yellow fever epidemic of 1793, Rush remained in the city and worked tirelessly to care for the sick. The cause of yellow fever was unknown at the time, so most medical treatment had little benefit. Rush's remedy most likely did some harm, for he was an advocate of bleeding as a general treatment for most serious ailments. During the epidemic, he employed bleeding to such an extent that William Cobbett described his practice as "one of those great discoveries which are made from time to time for the depopulation of the earth." (Rush later sued Cobbett for libel and won.) Despite such criticism, he was one of the first physicians to link disease with poor sanitation and overcrowded living conditions.

Theory. Like many physicians influenced by Enlightenment thinking, Rush was prone to great unified theories, which were not always supported by observation. For example, he believed that fever was the result of "a spasm of the extreme arteries" (capillaries), which could be eased only by bleeding. Rush carried this idea to the extreme that all diseases resulted from capillary tension. Thus, as he told his students, there is really "only one disease in the world," and therefore one cure. Most physicians agreed with him that bleeding was an effective treatment, although few would go to his extreme. Over the course of a week's treatment he would sometimes draw as much as three quarts, half an adult's total volume of blood.

Mental Health. Rush's *Medical Inquiries and Observations, upon the Diseases of the Mind* (1812) was the first book on psychiatry written by an American. His linking of physical and mental health, his insistence that the mentally disturbed be treated in separate hospital facilities, and his personal devotion to his patients made him a pioneer in the treatment of the mentally insane. Although he believed that diseases of the mind and body arose from the same causes (and thus treated mental disorders by bleeding), Rush also emphasized the importance of dreams, encouraged patients to discuss or write about their feelings, and kept them busy at occupations that aided their rehabilitation.

Balanced Assessment. Despite Rush's fame during his lifetime, later historians were not always kind. As one nineteenth-century writer put it: "in the whole vast compass of medical literature, there cannot be found an equal number of pages containing a greater amount and variety of utter nonsense and unqualified absurdity." A more balanced view would take into account Rush's support for social reform, his devotion to his patients and students, and his pioneering work in mental health and public sanitation. Much of the progress made by the next generation of physicians would be because Rush had the courage to make his ideas public where they could be discussed and modified.

Sources:

David Freeman Hawke, *Benjamin Rush: Revolutionary Gadfly* (Indianapolis: Bobbs-Merrill, 1971);

Richard Harrison Shryock, *Medicine and Society in America, 1660–1860* (New York: New York University Press, 1960).

JOHN STEVENS

1749-1838

INVENTOR

Background. Unlike many of the inventors of this period—men who were self-educated and started out relatively poor—John Stevens was born in 1749 to a wealthy Perth Amboy, New Jersey, family. He received his education at private schools and King's College (now Columbia University). During the Revolutionary War he served as a colonel and the treasurer of New Jersey, and after the war spent several years developing his large estate and home on the Hudson River (the site of present-day Hoboken). Stevens seems to have been satisfied with this life of managing his private affairs until about 1788 when he learned of the steamboat inventions of John Fitch and James Rumsey. From that point on Stevens devoted his life (and much of his fortune) to steam-powered transportation.

Steamboat Innovator. Stevens read everything he could find on steam technology and soon was designing boilers and engines of his own. Since the federal government did not yet have a patent system, he motivated friends in Congress to pass the first U.S. patent law in 1790; the next year he was awarded patents on his boiler and engine improvements. Eager to put his ideas into practice, he formed a partnership with his brother-in-law Robert Livingston (later U.S. minister to France), and in 1798, through Livingston's political connections, they acquired the exclusive rights to steamboat transportation in New York State. In 1803 he patented a multitubular boiler. By 1804 Stevens's own steamboat, *Little Juliana*, with twin screw propellers, was operational. He made plans for a bigger boat, the one-hundred-foot *Phoenix*, which would carry passengers and freight between New York and Albany, but was beaten to it by Robert Fulton, whose *Clermont* made its historic trip in 1807. More disturbing was the fact that Fulton now had his own partnership with Livingston and had managed to get a monopoly on steamboat transportation on the Hudson River. Squeezed out of the New York market, Stevens sent his *Phoenix* to Philadelphia in 1808, the first time in history that a steamboat made a successful ocean voyage.

Railroad Pioneer. In 1810 Stevens gave the steamboat business over to his sons and turned his attention to railroads, and in 1812 published a detailed study called *Documents Tending to Prove the Superior Advantages of Rail-ways and Steam-carriages over Canal Navigation.* Three years later he received from the state of New Jersey the first railroad charter in the United States. In 1825, at the age of seventy-six, in order to prove to skeptics that steam railways were feasible, he designed and built his own steam locomotive, which he demonstrated on a track on his estate. After years of promoting his ideas, he managed to convince the New Jersey and Pennsylvania legislatures to appropriate money for railways; he is in fact considered the founder of the Pennsylvania railroad system.

Visionary. John Stevens was far ahead of his time. In addition to his steamship and railroad accomplishments, he also proposed other visionary concepts that eventually became reality, such as armored ships, a tunnel under the Hudson River, and an elevated railroad for New York City. For brilliant technical ideas as well as practical achievement he ranks with Robert Fulton. After Stevens's death in 1838, his two sons carried on his legacy by becoming engineers and inventors.

Source:
L. Sprague De Camp and Catherine C. De Camp, *The Story of Science in America* (New York: Scribners, 1967);

Bernard Jaffe, *Men of Science in America* (New York: Simon & Schuster, 1958).

BENJAMIN THOMPSON, COUNT RUMFORD

1753-1814
PHYSICIST

Early Life in America. One of the greatest American scientists of his day was in some respects not "American" at all since he did virtually all his important work in Europe. Benjamin Thompson was born in Woburn, Massachusetts, in 1753 and later taught school in Concord, New Hampshire. During the American Revolution he remained loyal to the Crown, having married a rich widow and taken to the life of the elite, and was jailed for two weeks in 1775 when American authorities suspected him of treasonous behavior. After being released he joined the British army in Boston and left for England when the British were forced out of that city by Gen. George Washington. He then served in the office of the secretary of state for several years. Thompson returned to America in 1781 and commanded a regiment of dragoons, after which he went to Europe and never again set foot on his native soil. In 1784 King George III knighted Thompson in recognition of his service.

Bavarian Noble. While in England he became acquainted with the elector of Bavaria, and with King George's permission served the elector as grand chamberlain and minister of war from 1784 to 1795. By the mid 1790s he was spending most of his time on scientific experiments. Thompson invented a revolutionary fireplace, with a tall, shallow opening to reflect more heat. He also invented the coffee percolator. Thompson was active in philanthropy, creating public-works projects for the poor and campaigning for education reform. In 1791 he was created a count of the Holy Roman Empire and chose the title of Rumford (the original name of Concord, New Hampshire).

Legacy. Thompson's scientific research on heat and friction proved productive. In 1798 he wrote a groundbreaking paper titled "An Experimental Enquiry Concerning the Source of the Heat which is Excited by Friction," in which he argued that heat is caused by the motion of particles. In 1799 he was instrumental in organizing the Royal Institution in England. During this time he also experimented with light and developed a calorimeter and photometer. Unfortunately his work was marred by his opinionated, condescending, and dictatorial style. In 1804 he moved to Auteuil, outside Paris, where he died ten years later. Thompson remembered his native land at his death, bequeathing most of his money and possessions to the government of the United States, including a fund at Harvard College for a professorship "to teach the utility of the physical and mathematical sciences for the improvement of the arts and for the extension of the industry, prosperity, happiness, and well-being of society." His grave in Auteuil is cared for today jointly by Harvard University and the American Academy of Arts and Sciences of Boston.

Source:
Sanborn C. Brown, *Benjamin Thompson, Count Rumford* (Cambridge, Mass.: MIT Press, 1979).

BENJAMIN WATERHOUSE

1754-1846
PHYSICIAN

Beginnings. Benjamin Waterhouse was born in Newport, Rhode Island, in 1754, the son of a judge. He studied medicine in his hometown for several years, but with the outbreak of the Revolutionary War in 1775 he left for England, where he was placed under the care of relatives. He continued his studies in Edinburgh, Scotland, and at Leyden in the Netherlands, where he graduated in 1780. After traveling through Europe, he returned to America.

Harvard. When the Harvard Medical School was established in 1783, Benjamin Waterhouse was appointed professor of Physic (as medicine was then called) and served in that capacity until 1812. Waterhouse was known for his emphasis on investigation, as expounded in his *The Rise, Progress, and Present State of Medicine*

(1791), which distinguished him from theoreticians such as Benjamin Rush who were often too eager to make their observations fit a unified theory. Although Waterhouse's most popular book was *Cautions to Young Persons Concerning Health . . . Shewing the Evil Tendency of the Use of Tobacco upon Young Persons; More Especially the Pernicious Effects of Smoking Cigars* (1805), he is best known now for his courageous work with smallpox vaccination.

Smallpox. In 1800, using English physician Edward Jenner's cowpox vaccine, Waterhouse vaccinated his children, then deliberately exposed them to smallpox, proving that the inoculation provided protection against the disease. That same year he wrote an explanation of his work called *A Prospect of Exterminating the Small Pox.* Waterhouse's work was supported by Thomas Jefferson, who, while president, had his entire household (including slaves) inoculated with vaccine he received from his friend at Harvard. But Waterhouse still had a battle to fight. Poor-quality vaccine and improper vaccination caused an outbreak of smallpox in Massachusetts, and a it took a special investigation by the Boston Board of Health to clear Waterhouse and prove that vaccination was effective. By 1810 Waterhouse was not on good terms with his younger colleagues at Harvard, and after failing in his attempt to set up a rival medical school, he resigned. In 1813 President James Madison appointed him medical superintendent of New England military posts, a position he held until 1820. In the last quarter century of his long life, Waterhouse turned to literary pursuits, none of which was comparable to the work he had accomplished as a pioneer American physician. He died in Cambridge, Massachusetts, in 1846.

Source:
Ola Elizabeth Winslow, *A Destroying Angel: The Conquest of Smallpox in Colonial Boston* (Boston: Houghton Mifflin, 1974).

ELI WHITNEY

1765-1825
INVENTOR

Cotton Gin. One of the most influential inventors in American history was born in Westboro, Massachusetts, in 1765. Eli Whitney was raised in poor circumstances but became so adept at making nails that he saved enough money to attend Yale College. After graduating in 1792 he traveled to Georgia to act as a tutor for a wealthy family but declined the position when he learned it did not pay what he had been promised. Fortunately, the widow of Gen. Nathanael Greene invited him to stay at her plantation at Mulberry Grove, near Savannah. While there he became intrigued with the manner in which slaves removed the seeds from picked cotton. All the work was done by hand, and Whitney began experimenting with a machine that could accomplish the same results but in an easier fashion. In 1793 he exhibited his "cotton gin" (*gin* was short for *engine*), a simple device that had profound ramifications. The machine was a hand-cranked cylinder with a series of teeth that pulled cotton from the seed. Beforehand it took one slave ten hours to clean three pounds of cotton by hand; with the cotton gin the full day's work of several laborers could be accomplished in one hour.

Impact. The significance of the invention was immediately apparent in the massive increase of cotton production: in 1790 the United States produced four thousand bales of cotton; by 1820 it was 73,222 bales; and by 1840 the figure had risen to 1,347,640. Despite patenting his machine in 1794, Whitney had difficulty protecting it from easily made reproductions, and realized little profit on his famous invention. The cotton gin was less notable for its technology than for its economic and social consequences. Whitney had hoped that by making the task of cleaning cotton so inexpensive he might help eliminate slavery. Instead the resulting boom in the cotton business in the Deep South gave new life to the institution, and southern planters became even more dependent on, and defensive about, slavery.

Mass Production. From a technical point of view Whitney's greatest contribution was his system of manufacturing guns with interchangeable parts. In late 1798, while trying to raise funds for the legal battles over his cotton gin, Whitney made the bold proposal to the War Department that he could manufacture four thousand muskets in less than two years. Rather than craft each musket by hand, as had been the custom, he designed a milling machine which would make parts exactly the same every time. Although this method would become the basis of modern mass production, Whitney at that time had no factory or tools to manufacture the muskets, and he was nine years late delivering the weapons.

Later Life. Whitney eventually built a factory with workers' residences around it, which became the town of Whitneyville, Connecticut. The inventor also devised a set of moral guidelines by which his laborers would live. Like other industrial reformers such as Samuel Slater and Francis Cabot Lowell, his goal was to have healthy, happy workers, although the employees themselves might have found the arrangements confining. In any case, at Whitneyville were the milling machines and assembly lines and efficient labor that Whitney had created, a major contribution to America's industrial transformation. Whitney died in New Haven in 1825.

Source:
Constance M. Green, *Eli Whitney and the Birth of American Technology* (Boston: Little, Brown, 1956).

PUBLICATIONS

Benjamin Banneker, *Benjamin Banneker's Pennsylvania, Delaware, Maryland and Virginia Almanack and Ephemeris* (Philadelphia: Printed and sold by Daniel Lawrence, 1791)—a collection of astronomical data and calculations, including tides, phases of the moon, and positions of stars for every day of the year, as well as predictions of solar eclipses. Banneker's almanac was a significant achievement for this self-taught African American from rural Maryland;

William Bartram, *Travels through North and South Carolina, Georgia, East and West Florida, the Cherokee Country, the Extensive Territories of the Muscogulges or Creek Confederacy, and the Country of the Chactaws* (Philadelphia: Printed by James & Johnson, 1791)—this account of Bartram's journey through the forests of the Southeast from 1773 to 1777 contained vivid descriptions and detailed drawings of a wide variety of plants and animals;

Nathaniel Bowditch, *The Improved Practical Navigator* (London: David Steel, 1802)—for many years the classic reference book of sailors;

Edward Cutbush, *Observations on the Means of Preserving the Health of Soldiers and Sailors* (Philadelphia: Printed for Thomas Dobson by Fry & Kammerer, 1808)—the first American work on naval medicine;

John Syng Dorsey, *Elements of Surgery* (Philadelphia: E. Parker, 1813)—a teaching guide, with illustrations by the author. Dorsey's book went through three editions and received considerable recognition in Great Britain;

Oliver Evans, *The Young Mill-Wright and Miller's Guide* (Philadelphia: The author, 1795)—includes a description of the inventor's automated flour mill;

Robert Fulton, *A Treatise on the Improvement of Canal Navigation* (London: I. & J. Taylor, 1796)—containing practical information on the construction and operating costs of canals as well as detailed drawings of related inventions, such as his dredging machine for cutting canal channels;

Alexander Hamilton, *Report of the Secretary of the Treasury of the United States, on the Subject of Manufactures* (New York: Printed by Childs & Swaine, 1791)—this official report stressed the need for government involvement in industrial development to ensure America's economic independence;

Thomas Jefferson, *Notes on the State of Virginia* (Paris: Privately printed, 1785)—Jefferson's only published work covers the geography, natural history, politics, economy, religion, laws, and society of his native state;

William Maclure, *Observations on the Geology of the United States of America* (1809)—contains the first geological maps of America;

Humphrey Marshall, *Arbustrum Americanum* (Philadelphia: Printed by J. Crukshank, 1785)—the first systematic study of botany in America;

Joseph Priestley, *Memoirs of Dr. Joseph Priestley* (Northumberland, Penn.: Printed by J. Binns, 1806)—the autobiography of the famous scientist and discoverer of oxygen;

Benjamin Rush, *Medical Inquiries and Observations, upon the Diseases of the Mind* (Philadelphia: Kimber & Richardson, 1812)—a pioneering work on mental health care in America;

John Stevens, *Documents Tending to Prove the Superior Advantages of Rail-ways and Steam-carriages over Canal Navigation* (New York: Printed by T. & J. Swords, 1812)—this influential work, along with Stevens's later design and construction of an experimental steam locomotive, was a significant step in the development of railroads in America;

Sir Benjamin Thompson, Count Rumford, *Philosophical Papers* (London: Printed for T. Cadell Jr. & W. Davies, 1802)—includes a 1798 article describing his discovery that heat is not a substance but a form of motion;

Benjamin Waterhouse, *A Prospect of Exterminating the Small Pox* (Cambridge, Mass.: Printed by William Hilliard, 1800)—describes the positive results he achieved in Boston with English physician Edward Jenner's cowpox vaccine;

Waterhouse, *Cautions to Young Persons Concerning Health . . . Shewing the Evil Tendency of the Use of Tobacco upon Young Persons; More Especially the Pernicious Effects of Smoking Cigars* (Cambridge, Mass.: Printed at the University Press by W. Hilliard, 1805)—in this popular antitobacco pamphlet, Dr. Waterhouse complained that Harvard students looked "pallid, languid, and unhealthy" due to excessive tobacco use;

Alexander Wilson, *American Ornithology*, 9 volumes (Philadelphia: Bradford & Inskeep, 1808–1814)—this massive study of the birds of America predated the work of John James Audubon.

CHAPTER ELEVEN

SPORTS AND RECREATION

by ROBERT BELLINGER

CONTENTS

Sidebars and tables are listed in italics.

OVERVIEW

Public Virtue. During the Revolutionary War the Continental Congress passed a resolution that "discouraged every species of extravaganza and dissipation, especially all horse racing and all kinds of gaming, cockfighting, exhibitions of shows, plays and other expensive diversions and entertainments." It was felt by the leaders of the nation that these activities were frivolous and contrary to responsible standards of morality. After the Revolution, however, the states began to lift the restrictions on games, sports, theater, and other recreations. Some people saw recreation as an expression of freedom. To them, developments in the arts and participation in leisure activity were the direct outgrowth of a free people and a successful society. Nonetheless, there were still enough people who viewed leisure as sinful, slothful, and a threat to virtue, the cornerstone of democracy. These two conflicting ideologies produced a pendulum-type response to recreation and leisure in the new nation between 1783 and 1815. The laws pertaining to theaters serve as an example. On 2 March 1789 Philadelphia re-

pealed the law prohibiting theatrical performances, and later that year George Washington attended John Street Theater in New York City. His attendance gave respectability to the practice of theatergoing, but at the same time it evoked disapproval from others. Boston closed its first theater, the New Exhibitions Room, on 5 December 1792 and arrested the manager; the law against theaters in that city was not repealed until 1807.

Relaxation and Status. The working classes engaged in recreation after work hours. Such activities as dancing, sailing, sleigh riding, chess, cards, plays, and wax museums represented a break from the monotony of their jobs. For the wealthy, leisure activities were a mark of social standing. Thomas Jefferson spoke of this when he said "[A] young [American] gentleman goes to England, he learns drinking, horse racing, and boxing . . . the peculiarities of English education." Whether educated in England or in the United States, wealthy young gentlemen were expected to learn certain social and athletic skills along with their academic studies. These in-

A spinet, an early version of the harpsichord, built by Samuel Blyth of Salem,
Massachusetts, circa 1785–1790

cluded conversation, riding, fox hunting, fencing, rowing, and dancing. The southern elite had a good amount of time to spend on sports and leisure because the work of enslaved African Americans gave them the free time to do so. Women of the wealthy class were also taught social and athletic skills, though in a much more restricted manner than the males. The world of sports at the beginning of the nineteenth century was a male domain. Women were neither allowed to participate in nor attend most sporting events; the one exception was horse racing.

Horse Racing. Of all the sporting events during this era, horse racing, considered the sport of gentlemen, was the most popular. Many racing courses—usually a round track enclosed by railings and surrounded by stands for judges and spectators—had been laid out before the Revolutionary War. However, the conflict brought a halt to most sport and leisure activities, including horse racing. After the war the sport returned, but participation in it was no longer the privilege of the wealthy. By 1800 most large towns had a race course that charged an admission fee. In 1802 the Washington, D.C., National Race Course opened, and many government officials attended the events held there. Yet even though horse racing was a sport engaged in by many segments of the population, not everyone accepted it. For some in the society, racing, and the gambling which often went with it, represented an excessive luxury that would lead to the end of virtue. The *Philadelphia Gazette* of 1802 condemned the "great mischiefs and vices" at the Germantown races, while the Philadelphia *Daily Advertiser* spoke of the "intoxication, riot, [and] lewdness." North Carolina banned horse racing in 1790, and New York followed in 1802. However, the races continued in New York, conducted by private organizations called jockey clubs. Many of these organizations had been established before the war and aimed to regulate the sport.

Jockeys. In the North horse owners relied on English jockeys, while in the South the majority of jockeys were African Americans. Slave owners valued black riders because they were usually small in stature and had grown up working with and training horses. In the South horse racing was a matter of honor, as one plantation owner pitted his best horse and rider against another planter's team. And although the owner would take the praise that came with victory, the slave and possibly the horse felt the effects of a poor showing.

Breeding. The popularity of racing was a catalyst for horse breeding in the United States. In the late eighteenth century American breeders began to import animals sired by famous racing horses in England. Top racing bloodlines were established with the purchase of Mambrina and Messenger from English aristocrats in the 1780s. Probably the most famous thoroughbred at this time was Diomed. In 1798 Sir Thomas Charles Bunbury sold the twenty-one-year-old horse to two Virginia planters for fifty guineas. Diomed quickly resold for approximately 1,500 guineas, and before his death in 1808 he sired Sir Archy, Florizel, Potomac, Hamlintonian, and seven other famous American thoroughbreds.

Pugilism. Boxing was another popular sport of the era and one in which participation differed depending on class. Wealthy young men were most often introduced to it while attending college in England, and they considered it both a leisure activity and a form of exercise. They practiced the "scientific" style developed by Daniel Mendoza, who became the English boxing champion in 1792. Mendoza introduced defense to boxing. He constantly moved in the ring to avoid being hit.

"Toe the Mark." A match conducted under the Mendoza rules differed from the brutal affair which passed as boxing among the lower classes. Far from an art or a science, it was a bare-knuckled test of strength which usually left one of the contenders bruised and broken. A typical ring, located in a tavern or back alley, had a firm dirt floor and was a circle twenty-five feet in diameter. A three-foot-long mark was drawn down the middle of the floor by the referee. The boxers had to return to this line, or "toe the mark," after a knockdown. There was no hitting below the belt or when an opponent went down and no holding below the waist. No gloves were used, and as may be expected, a match was quite bloody and could last for hours, ending only when a fighter dropped for good. Sometimes a fight resulted in the death of one of the participants. Heavy bets were placed on the outcome of these bouts.

Boxing in the South. Plantation owners in the South frequently staged boxing matches among slaves as a form of entertainment during holidays. Often these contests

---

AT THE TRACKS

In the 1790s horse racing boomed as new thoroughbred stock was imported from England. Philadelphia artisans and manufacturers became concerned because the journeymen and apprentices spent too much time at the track, drinking and gambling. In June 1802 city officials received a petition against Hart's Racecourse, located on the Hunting Park Estate; it was signed by twenty-seven hundred mechanics and businessmen:

This English dissipation of horse-racing may be agreeable to a few idle landed gentlemen, who bestow more care in training their horses than educating their children, and it may be amusing to British mercantile agents, and a few landed characters in Philadelphia; but it is in the greatest degree injurious to the mechanical and manufacturing interest, and will tend to our ruin if the nuisance is not removed by your patriotic exertions.

Source: Elliott J. Gorn and Warren Goldstein, *A Brief History of American Sports* (New York: Hill & Wang, 1993).

Self-portrait by John Durang, the first Native
American dancer

own, and many taverns had sections set aside for individuals making bets. In some drinking establishments both boxing and wrestling were staged. Other tavern activities included billiards and a card game similar to poker called brag. The dice game known as hazard came to the United States via England and France. By 1813 hazard was transformed into the game of crabs or craps by African Americans in New Orleans.

Cricket and Fox Hunting. Certain activities that came to the United States from England did not have a large following. At the time of the American Revolution cricket was a popular sport in the colonies. In the 1790s cricket clubs sprouted up in Boston, New York, and Philadelphia, but interest in the game dropped off by 1800. Fox hunting was another activity that did not attract too many participants. There was some fox hunting in New England, and the southern states, especially

matched slaves from neighboring plantations against one another. The contestants represented the honor of their masters and the reputation of the plantation, but they had other motivations as well. Sometimes enslaved African Americans who were successful as pugilists were able to use their good fortune as a way out of slavery or at least as a means to garner favors. Slave owners took a special interest in the well-being of their black boxers, and some groomed them for these contests just as they bred and trained race horses. Tom Molineaux was an example of a slave who was able to change his personal situation by success in the ring. Born a slave in either Maryland or Virginia in 1784, he fought for his owner, Algeron Molineaux, in plantation boxing matches. In 1804 he won his freedom and a cash purse by defeating a slave from the neighboring plantation of Randolph Peyton. Molineaux made his way to New York City and then to London, where he trained under William Richmond, another black boxer. In 1810 and 1811 Molineaux fought English champion Tom Crib twice and lost each time, but he demonstrated endurance and skill. Overall, Molineaux was the exception to the rule: most enslaved boxers did not receive favoritism for their endeavors in the ring.

Gambling. Betting was an important part of sports, especially boxing, horse racing, rowing, and cockfighting. In fact, gambling was in some ways a sport of its

Advertisement for stud service

Tom Molyneaux, a South Carolina slave who won his freedom by boxing, in a match with Tom Cribb at Thistleton, England, in 1811; engraving by George Cruikshank

Maryland, Virginia, and the Carolinas, had a reputation for good hunts. Only the wealthy could afford the specially imported riding outfits and the pack of dogs necessary to engage in the hunt.

Blood Events. In addition to the more accepted sports such as horse racing and boxing, Americans of the early republic had a penchant for blood sports, or contests in which the primary goal was to draw blood out of one or both of the contestants. Heavy betting accompanied these affairs, and although some, such as boxing, involved humans, animals were the usual participants. In animal baiting a dog or pack of dogs attacked a bear, bull, or badger chained in a pit. In cockfighting trained cocks, with metal spurs attached to their legs, fought to the death in specially constructed pits. Cockfighting was popular, lasting well into the nineteenth century, although it gradually lost favor among the wealthy and became associated with the lower classes.

The Frontier. In the rural areas of the West certain tasks became social occasions for whole communities. These group gatherings, or "bees" as they came to be called, brought people together to complete tasks that were too great for a single family to do on its own. Bees represent a particularly American phenomenon, and the term alludes to the social mannerisms of the insect. Husking bees brought the community together to get farmers' corn ready for milling after harvest. Quilting bees brought women together to prepare bedclothes for the winter months. There were regional variations in these activities, and a western husking bee was different

than a southern plantation corn shuckin'. Barn raisings were another communal activity in which neighbors gathered to perform a job and turned the work into a social occasion. Regardless of the reasons, once people came together, they engaged in competitive events. Contests involved such skills as hunting, fishing, target shooting, racing, log rolling, and wrestling. Gambling, card playing, and drinking were also favored.

Music. After the Revolutionary War the musical life of America resumed, and concerts, plays, and operas flourished again in the cities. A renewed interest in religious and folk music also occurred, and singing and dancing schools that had been closed during the war reopened. Professional musicians, particularly from England, came to the United States and settled in the larger cities, where they gave lessons on the pianoforte, harpsichord, and violin. One such teacher was the Reverend Andrew Law, who taught Newport Gardner, the first African American music instructor in the country.

Dancing. Americans of all classes enjoyed dancing. At the close of the eighteenth century social dancing was popular in cities and towns. Attending a ball, which was the name given to any formal occasion in which dancing occurred, became a common and important part of many community activities. For the wealthy, dancing was one of the social graces in which young men and women had to be trained. Wealthy families employed dance instructors to pass on the proper and popular dance steps to their children. In the late eighteenth century dancing teachers were usually servants, but after the French

Revolution this changed, as many French instructors sought refuge in America. In addition to providing a place to perform the steps they had been taught by their instructors, dances provided young men and women an opportunity to socialize.

Styles. Dancing instructors taught the minuet, rigadoon, cotillions, reels, jigs, and hornpipe steps. While some of the dances were done by couples, forms that allowed for group dancing were more common. In the reel and contradance, brought to North America by English and Scotch-Irish colonists, two lines, one male and one female, faced each other. The couples moved in set patterns up and down the line. Around 1800 the quadrille, or cotillion, arrived in the United States from France. Four couples danced in a square, sometimes moving in and out of the center. Dancing the cotillion in the 1790s was considered a sign of political allegiance since it was embraced by pro-French Jeffersonians and spurned by the Federalists. As political conflicts cooled, the dance spread, first through urban and then rural areas. New and old steps combined eventually to turn the cotillion into the modern square dance.

Hoedown. On the frontier dancing became a part of almost every social gathering but was not used as a mark of social status. Although a good dancer would be recognized as special, dancing was first and foremost recreational. At a hoedown people danced the same types of dances as in the cities and towns. However, since etiquette was not of the same importance and dance instructors were a rarity outside of urban areas, frontier steps were less regimented and often were performed competitively. In plank dancing two planks would be set across two barrels, and a person would dance on them as the boards bounced up and down. Other dances included Virginia reels, country jigs, and shakedowns.

African American Influence. African Americans, both free and enslaved, cultivated distinctive dance forms and styles. They danced the cakewalk, pigeon wing, jig, buck dance, buzzard lope, juba, ring dance, quadrille, cotillion, reel, and water dance. Even though some of the steps were taken from European dances, blacks improvised and added their own movements. African American dance was not completely separated from that of whites, particularly in the towns and cities. Black fiddlers were present at many balls and hoedowns. Sometimes at dances they were the set callers, singing out instructions to the dancers. It was in these roles that blacks influenced and altered European American dance styles. African American dance was also viewed as a form of entertainment by whites, particularly in the South. In the late eighteenth and early nineteenth centuries black social activity was a type of theater for whites. Enslaved blacks were often called upon to perform dance steps or to sing at social gatherings of whites. By the 1820s whites were beginning to use stereotypical imitations of black dancers and performers on the minstrel stage.

GENERAL REFERENCES

GENERAL

Joyce Appleby, *Capitalism and a New Social Order: The Republican Vision of the 1790s* (New York: New York University Press, 1984);

Daniel Boorstin, *The Americans: The National Experience* (New York: Random House, 1965);

Stanley Elkins and Eric McKitrick, *The Age of Federalism* (New York: Oxford University Press, 1993);

Marshall Smelser, *The Democratic Republic, 1801–1815* (New York: Harper & Row, 1968);

Gordon Wood, *The Creation of the American Republic, 1776–1787* (Chapel Hill: Published for the Institute of Early American History and Culture at Williamsburg, Virginia, by the University of North Carolina Press, 1969).

THE ARTS

Richard L. Bushman, *The Refinement of America: Persons, Houses, Cities* (New York: Knopf, 1992);

Cathy L. Davidson, ed., *Reading in America: Literature and Social History* (Baltimore: Johns Hopkins University Press, 1989);

Davidson, *Revolution and the Word: The Rise of the Novel in America* (New York: Oxford University Press, 1986);

Harold E. Dickson, *Arts of the Young Republic: The Age of William Dunlap* (Chapel Hill: University of North Carolina Press, 1968);

Joseph J. Ellis, *After the Revolution: Profiles of Early American Culture* (New York: Norton, 1979);

James Thomas Flexner, *America's Old Masters,* revised edition (Garden City, N.Y.: Doubleday, 1980);

Jay Fliegelman, *Prodigals and Pilgrims: The American Revolution against Patriarchal Authority, 1750–1800* (New York: Cambridge University Press, 1982);

Charles Hamm, *Music in the New World* (New York: Norton, 1983);

Kenneth Silverman, *A Cultural History of the American Revolution* (New York: Crowell, 1976).

BUSINESS AND THE ECONOMY

Bray Hammond, *Banks and Politics in America, from the Revolution to the Civil War* (Princeton: Princeton University Press, 1957);

Oscar Handlin and Mary Handlin, *Commonwealth: A Study of the Role of Government in the American Economy: Massachusetts, 1774–1861* (New York: New York University Press, 1947);

Handlin and Handlin, *The Wealth of the American People: A History of American Affluence* (New York: McGraw-Hill, 1975);

Drew R. McCoy, *The Elusive Republic: Political Economy in Jeffersonian America* (New York: Norton, 1980);

Curtis P. Nettels, *The Emergence of a National Economy, 1775–1815* (New York: Holt, Rinehart & Winston, 1962).

COMMUNICATIONS

Stanley Elkins and Eric McKitrick, *The Age of Federalism* (New York: Oxford University Press, 1993);

Wayne E. Fuller, *The American Mail: Enlarger of the Common Life* (Chicago: University of Chicago Press, 1972);

Richard R. John, *Spreading the News: The American Postal System from Franklin to Morse* (Cambridge: Harvard University Press, 1995);

James Morton Smith, *Freedom's Fetters: The Alien and Sedition Laws and American Civil Liberties* (Ithaca, N.Y.: Cornell University Press, 1956);

James Tagg, *Benjamin Franklin Bache and the Philadelphia Aurora* (Philadelphia: University of Pennsylvania Press, 1991).

EDUCATION

Bernard Bailyn, *Education in the Forming of American Society: Needs and Opportunities for Study* (Chapel Hill: Published for the Institute of Early American History and Culture at Williamsburg, Virginia, by the University of North Carolina Press, 1960);

Vera M. Butler, *Education as Revealed by New England Newspapers Prior to 1850* (New York: Arno, 1969);

A. Emerson Palmer, *The New York Public School* (New York: Macmillan, 1905);

Theodore Sizer, Nancy Sizer, and others, *To Ornament their Minds: Sarah Pierce's Litchfield Female Academy, 1792–1833* (Litchfield, Ct.: Litchfield Historical Society, 1993).

GOVERNMENT AND POLITICS

Henry Adams, *History of the United States During the Administrations of Thomas Jefferson and James Madison*, 4 volumes (New York: Scribners, 1890–1909);

Lance Banning, *The Jeffersonian Persuasion* (Ithaca, N.Y.: Cornell University Press, 1978);

William Nisbet Chambers, *Political Parties in a New Nation: The American Experience, 1776–1809* (New York: Oxford University Press, 1963);

Noble E. Cunningham Jr., *The Jeffersonians in Power: Party Operations, 1801–1809* (Chapel Hill: University of North Carolina Press, 1963);

Stanley Elkins and Eric McKitrick, *The Age of Federalism* (New York: Oxford University Press, 1993);

David Hackett Fischer, *The Revolution of American Conservatism: The Federalist Party in the Era of Jeffersonian Democracy* (New York: Harper Torchbooks, 1965);

Linda K. Kerber, *Federalists in Dissent: Imagery and Ideology in Jeffersonian America* (Ithaca, N.Y.: Cornell University Press, 1980);

Drew R. McCoy, *The Elusive Republic: Political Economy in Jeffersonian America* (New York: Norton, 1982);

John C. Miller, *The Federalist Era, 1789–1801* (New York: Harper Torchbooks, 1963);

Eugene H. Roseboom and Alfred E. Eckes Jr., *A History of Presidential Elections*, fourth edition (New York: Collier, 1979);

Gordon S. Wood, *The Creation of the American Republic, 1776–1787* (New York: Norton, 1969).

LAW AND JUSTICE

Cornelia Hughes Dayton, *Women Before the Bar* (Chapel Hill: University of North Carolina Press, 1995);

Stanley Elkins and Eric McKitrick, *The Age of Federalism* (New York: Oxford University Press, 1993);

Lawrence M. Friedman, *A History of American Law* (New York: Simon & Schuster, 1985);

Kermit Hall, *The Magic Mirror: Law in American History* (New York: Oxford University Press, 1989);

Alfred Kelly, Winifred Harbison, and Herman Belz, *The American Constitution: Its Origins and Development*, sixth edition (New York: Norton, 1983);

Louis P. Masur, *Rites of Execution: Capital Punishment and the Transformation of American Culture, 1776–1865* (New York: Oxford University Press, 1989);

Richard B. Morris, *The Forging of the Union: 1781–1789* (New York: Harper & Row, 1987);

William H. Rehnquist, *Grand Inquests* (New York: Morrow, 1992);

Thomas P. Slaughter, *The Whiskey Rebellion* (New York: Oxford University Press, 1986);

Jean Edward Smith, *John Marshall: Definer of a Nation* (New York: Holt, 1996).

LIFESTYLES, SOCIAL TRENDS, AND FASHION

Roger D. Abrahams, *Singing the Master: The Emergence of African American Culture in the Plantation South* (New York: Pantheon, 1992);

Stephen E. Ambrose, *Undaunted Courage: Meriwether Lewis, Thomas Jefferson, and the Opening of the American West* (New York: Touchstone, 1996);

R. David Edmunds, *Tecumseh and the Quest for Indian Leadership* (Boston: Little, Brown, 1984);

John Mack Faragher, *Daniel Boone: The Life and Legend of an American Pioneer* (New York: Holt, 1992);

Merrill Jensen, *The New Nation: A History of the United States during the Confederation, 1781–1789* (New York: Knopf, 1950);

Jack Larkin, *The Reshaping of Everyday Life, 1790–1840* (New York: Harper & Row, 1988);

Jacqui Malone, *Steppin' on the Blues: The Visible Rhythms of African American Dance* (Urbana, Ill.: University of Illinois Press, 1996);

Allan Nevins, *The American States During and After the Revolution, 1775–1789.* (New York: Macmillan, 1924);

Stephen Nissenbaum, *The Battle for Christmas* (New York: Knopf, 1997);

Laurel Thatcher Ulrich, *A Midwife's Tale: The Life of Martha Ballard, Based on Her Diary* (New York: Knopf, 1990).

RELIGION

Edwin S. Gaustad, *Neither King nor Prelate: Religion and the New Nation, 1776–1826* (Grand Rapids, Mich.: Erdmans, 1993);

Nathan O. Hatch, *The Democratization of American Christianity* (New Haven, Conn.: Yale University Press, 1989);

Ronald Hoffman and Peter J. Albert, *Religion in a Revolutionary Age* (Charlottesville: Published for the United States Capitol Historical Society by the University Press of Virginia, 1994);

William G. McLoughlin, *New England Dissent, 1630–1833: the Baptists and the Separation of Church and State,* 2 volumes (Cambridge: Harvard University Press, 1971);

William Lee Miller, *The First Liberty: Religion and the American Republic* (New York: Knopf, 1986);

Albert J. Raboteau, *Slave Religion: The "Invisible Institution" in the Ante-bellum South* (New York: Oxford University Press, 1978).

SCIENCE AND MEDICINE

Daniel Boorstin, *The Lost World of Thomas Jefferson* (Chicago: University of Chicago Press, 1981);

Constance M. Green, *Eli Whitney and the Birth of American Technology* (Boston: Little, Brown, 1956);

David Freeman Hawke, *Benjamin Rush: Revolutionary Gadfly* (Indianapolis: Bobbs-Merrill, 1971);

Brooke Hindle and Steven Lubar, *Engines of Change: the American Industrial Revolution, 1790–1860* (Washington, D.C.: Smithsonian Institution Press, 1986);

Winthrop S. Jordan, *White Over Black: American Attitudes toward the Negro, 1550–1812* (Chapel Hill: Published for the Institute of Early American History and Culture at Williamsburg, Virginia, by the University of North Carolina Press, 1968);

Lester S. King, *Transformations in American Medicine, from Benjamin Rush to William Osler* (Baltimore: Johns Hopkins University Press, 1991);

David Rittenhouse, *The Scientific Writings of David Rittenhouse,* edited by Brooke Hindle (New York: Arno, 1980).

SPORTS AND RECREATION

Elliot Gorn, *The Manly Art: Bare-Knuckle Prize Fighting in America* (Ithaca, N.Y.: Cornell University Press, 1986);

Gorn and Warren Goldstein, *A Brief History of American Sports* (New York: Hill & Wang, 1993);

Jack Larkin, *The Reshaping of Everyday Life, 1790–1840* (New York: Harper & Row, 1988);

Peter Levine, *American Sport: A Documentary History* (Englewood Cliffs, N.J.: Prentice Hall, 1989);

Charles E. Trevathan, *The American Thoroughbred* (New York: Macmillan, 1905).

Contributors

THE ARTS

EILEEN KA-MAY CHENG
Madison, Indiana

BUSINESS & THE ECONOMY

ROBERT J. ALLISON
Suffolk University

JOHN O'KEEFE
Cambridge, Massachussetts

COMMUNICATIONS

ROBERT J. ALLISON
Suffolk University

JOHN O'KEEFE
Cambridge, Massachussetts

EDUCATION

ROBERT J. ALLISON
Suffolk University

GOVERNMENT & POLITICS

JAYNE TRIBER
Revere, Massachussetts

LAW & JUSTICE

JAMES ALOISI
Boston, Massachussetts

LIFESTYLES, SOCIAL TRENDS,
& FASHION

ROBERT BELLINGER
Suffolk University

RELIGION

JOHN O'KEEFE
Cambridge, Massachussetts

SCIENCE & MEDICINE

ANTHONY CONNORS
Carlisle, Massachussetts

SPORTS & RECREATION

ROBERT BELLINGER
Suffolk University

INDEX

A

Abolitionism 81, 199
Academy of Natural Sciences 155, 175
Act Concerning Aliens, 1798 187, 216
Act Respecting Alien Enemies, 1798 216
Adam, Robert 43
Adams, Abigail 137, 201, 204, 220,
  234–235, 272
Adams, David Phineas 33, 54, 112
Adams, Hannah 339
Adams, Henry 256, 258
Adams, John 38, 67–68, 78, 106, 111, 116,
  128, 132–133, 136–137, 139, 144, 158,
  180, 182, 184, 186–188, 198, 201, 204,
  206, 215–216, 220, 222–225, 234–235,
  237–239, 243–244, 249–250, 253, 255,
  258–259, 261–262, 267–269, 272,
  274–279
Adams, John Sr. 234
Adams, John Quincy 154, 195, 204,
  233–235
Adams, Samuel 206, 243
Adams, Susanna Boylston 234
"Adams & Liberty" (Paine) 31, 58–59
Addison, Alexander 258
*Address to the Roman Catholics of the United
  States of America* (Carroll) 332
Adgate, Andrew 27
The Adulateur (Warrren) 68
The Adventures of Colonel Daniel Boone
  (Filson) 310
Aeneid (Virgil) 62
The Aethiop, occasional music (Taylor) 37
African American churches 328
African American holidays 303
African Free School 152, 157, 165
African Methodist Episcopal Church
  320–321, 328, 352, 354, 356
African Methodist Episcopal Zion Church,
  New York City 321
African religions 327
The Age of Reason (Paine) 348
Agricultural exports 90
"The Agrippa Letters" (Winthrop) 197
Aitken, John 27, 31
The Albany Collection (Huntington) 32
Albert, John 230
Albrecht, Charles 27

Alcuin (Brown) 31
The Algerine Captive (Tyler) 31
Alien Act of 1798 249, 250
Alien and Sedition Acts of 1798 187, 225,
  237, 239, 241, 268
Alien Enemies Act of 1798 137, 268
Alien Friends Act of 1798 137, 268
"All Hail the Power of Jesus' Name"
  (Holden) 28
Allen, Ethan 348
Allen, Richard 32, 318, 320, 321, 328, 352,
  354, 355, 356
Alline, Henry 33
Almshouses 368, 369
Almy, William 363
Alsop, Richard 31–32, 34, 59
Amelia (Wood) 33
America (Dwight) 60, 62
America (Gram) 28
"America, Commerce and Freedom"
  (Rowson and Reinagle) 29, 66
American Academy of Arts and Sciences
  171, 392
American Academy of the Fine Arts 33, 46
American Annual Register 141
American Antiquarian Society 114, 118,
  147
American Biography (Belknap) 29
American Board of Commissioners for
  Foreign Missions 174, 322, 335
American Book of Common Prayer 338, 357
American Colonization Society 242
American Company of Booksellers 112,
  143
American Daily Advertiser 110, 141
*An American Dictionary of the English
  Language* (Webster) 157, 167
American Education Society 323
American Fur Company 76, 103, 370
The American Geography (Morse) 217
American Harmony (Holden) 28
The Amercan Harmony (Shumway) 29, 32
American Instructor 172
American Magazine 125, 127
*American Monthly Review or Literary
  Chronicle* 110
American Museum 27, 108, 125–126, 128,
  143
American Philosophical Society 152–153,
  174, 239, 364, 374, 380, 390

American Poems, Select and Original
  (Hubbard, ed.) 29
The American Preceptor (Bingham) 157, 173
American Revolution 38, 52, 57, 64-68, 72,
  97, 99, 101, 103-106
—Battles:
  Brandywine 279
  Bunker Hill 67
  Germantown 279
  Lexington and Concord 67
  Monmouth 279
  Saratoga 67
American Revolution series (Trumbull) 67
The American Singing-Book (Read) 26
American Society for the Propagation of the
  Gospel 318, 341
An American Spelling Book (Webster) 167
Ames, Fisher 153, 211
Ames, Nathaniel 211
Amoskeag Mill 384
Analectic Magazine 114
The Anarchiad (Barlow, Humphreys,
  Trumbull, and Hopkins) 27, 60
Andover Theological Seminary 174 322,
  335, 344
André, John 64
André (Dunlap) 31, 64
Anglican Missionary Schools 158
Anglican Society for the Propagation of the
  Gospel 334, 357
Anglican Church 337. *See also* Episcopal
  Church.
Animal baiting 399
Anna (Hagen) 33
Annapolis Convention of 1786 72, 78, 84,
  181, 201, 243
Antes, John 28
Anthem from the 97th Psalm (Tuckey) 27
An Anthem on Peace (Wood) 26
Anthology Club 54, 113, 126
Anthracite coal 88
Anti-Federalists 120–122, 202, 205–206,
  223, 303
Antitheater laws 27, 29, 47, 49
The Apollo Harmony (Huntington) 34
An Appeal to the Public for Religious Liberty
  (Backus) 356
Appleseed, Johnny 291, 301
Appleton, Jesse 154

Burgoyne, John 67, 243
Burk, John Daly 31
Burke, Aedaneus 135
Burr, Aaron 116, 133, 139, 174, 188,
    190–191, 219–220, 223–226, 237, 251,
    256–257, 259, 279, 281, 291, 312, 364
Burr Conspiracy of 1807 191, 219, 257, 279,
    281
Burroughs, Stephen 261
Bushnell, Horace 321
Butler, Pierce 205, 223

C

Cabell, William 273
Cabot, George 211
Caldwell, Elias 252
The Caledonia Frolic (Carr) 29
Calhoun, John C. 231, 278, 282
Callender, James Thomson 111–112, 116,
    128, 132, 141–142, 190, 258–259, 269
Calvin, John 342, 351
Calvinism 59, 322, 323–325, 336, 342, 344,
    351
Cameahwait 301, 313
Camp meetings 320, 322, 324, 340,
    349–350, 355
Campbell, Alexander 322, 351
Campbell, George 91
Campbell, Thomas 322, 351
Canals 87, 370, 385
Cane Ridge revival 321, 349–351
Canoe, John 303
Capital punishment 259–260
The Capture of the Hessians at Trenton
    (Trumbull) 67
Card playing 399
Carey, Henry C. 144
Carey, Mathew 26–28, 31, 66, 108,
    117–118, 125–126, 128–129, 141, 143
Carey, Mother 289
Carleton, Sir Guy 185
Carr, Benjamin 29–33, 35–36
Carroll, Daniel 331
Carroll, Bishop 151, 306, 318–319, 322,323,
    331–333, 357
Cartwright, Peter 321, 336
Castle Island prison, Mass. 261
Catechisms 345
Catholicism 332–334
Cent Institution 336
Chambers, William 43
Chancellor Livingston (steamboat) 366
Channing, William Ellery 140, 345
Charbonneau, Baptiste 313
Charbonneau, Bazil 301, 313
Charbonneau, Toussaint 301, 312–313
Charitable Female Society 321
Charitable societies 353, 357
Charles River Bridge, Boston 87
Charleston College 151
Charleston Courier 114
Charleston slave market 102
Charlestown Collection of Sacred Songs
    (Holden) 33

Charlotte. A Tale of Truth (Rowson) 28–29,
    51, 66
Chase, Samuel 142, 190, 250–251,
    255–259, 267, 269, 280–281
Chauncy, Charles 346
Cherokee tribe 341–342
Chesapeake (ship) 89, 221
Chesapeake-Leopard incident of 1807 191
Chester, John 292
Cheverus, Jean de 322, 333
Chiksika 313
Child, Ebenezer 33
Child, Lydia Maria 33
Childbirth 369
Children's Magazine 109, 151
China trade 92–93, 104
Chisholm v. *Georgia* 184, 187, 249, 262, 265,
    277, 283
The Chorister's Companion (Jocelin) 27
The Christian Harmonist (Holyoke) 33
The Christian Harmony (Ingalls) 34
Christian Psalmody (Shaw) 37
Christmas 289, 303–304
The Churchman's Choral Companion (Smith)
    35
Cincinnatus 45
Circuit-riding ministers 321, 336, 340, 350,
    355
Clara Howard (Brown) 32, 64
Clarissa (Richardson) 51
Clark, William 115, 190, 220, 292, 301,
    313, 365, 370, 373–374, 381
Clarkson, Matthew 289
Clarkson, Thomas 81
Classical Church Musick (Huntington) 36
Clay, Henry 160, 195, 229, 233, 256
Claypoole, D. C. 108, 131
Clermont (steamship) 106, 365, 382, 391
Clinton, DeWitt 34, 157, 159, 162, 164,
    194, 229
Clinton, George 84, 120, 122, 154, 162,
    164, 190–191, 223, 226–229, 237
Clocks and clockmaking 364, 390
The Cluster (Mercer) 36
Cobb, James 29
Cobbett, William 110, 144, 215, 391
Cockfighting 399
Coffee, John 195, 219
Coffeehouses 130
Cogswell, Mason F. 34
Coinage Act of 1792 74
Coke, Sir Edward 253, 275
Coke, Thomas 355
Cole, John 32–33, 37
Cole's Collection of Psalm Tunes and Anthems
    (Cole) 33
Coleman, William 133
Coleridge, Samuel Taylor 129, 304
A Collection of Hymns for Social Worship
    (Law) 26
*A Collection of Hymns for the Use of the
    Christian Indians* (Zeisberger) 33
A Collection of Federal Songs (Reinagle) 27
Collection of Most Favorite Country Dances
    (Hewitt) 33

*A Collection of Poems, on American Affairs,
    and a Variety of Other Subjects* (Freneau)
    37
A Collection of Psalms and Hymns (Emerson)
    35
A Collection of Sacred Harmony (Brownson)
    31
A Collection of Spiritual Songs and Hymns
    (Allen) 32
College of New Jersey 144, 240, 277,
    280–281, 323. *See also* Princeton
    University.
College of Philadelphia 156, 248, 253, 260,
    275, 282–284
College of William and Mary 156, 171,
    238, 249–250, 253, 273, 275, 279, 284
Coller, Elisha 367
Colt, Samuel 367
The Columbian Orator (Bingham) 173
Columbia University 150, 153, 156, 236,
    276, 284, 339, 357. *See also* King's
    College.
—Medical School 366, 375
Columbia (ship) 73–74, 81, 93
Columbia's Glory (Prime) 28
The Columbiad (Barlow) 34, 61– 62
Columbian Centinel 43
The Columbian Harmony (Wood and Stone)
    29, 153, 173
The Columbian Harmonist (Read) 29
Columbian Magazine 108, 127–128
Columbian Melodies (Pélissier) 36
Columbian Repository of Sacred Harmony
    (Holyoke) 33
The Columbian Sacred Harmonist (Shaw) 35
Columbianum, Philadelphia 30, 65
Columbus, Christopher 61, 303
Columbus (Hagen) 32
Columbus (Hewitt) 32
Columbus (Reinagle) 31
Columbus Day 303
Commentaries on the Laws of England
    (Blackstone) 250, 253, 271, 273, 275,
    284
Committee of Safety 240
Committee of Tradesmen 202
Common law 253–255, 284
Common School Fund, New York State
    164
Common Sense (Paine) 125, 205, 348
Commonwealth v. *Caton* 284
Commonwealth v. *Jennison* 274
*A Compendious Dictionary of the English
    Language* (Webster) 34, 167
*A Compilation of the Litanies and Vespers,
    Hymns and Anthems, As They Are Sung in
    the Catholic Church* (Aitken) 27
Confederation Congress 217, 230
Congregational Church 56–57, 321, 332,
    346
Conjuring 342
Connecticut Courant 138
Connecticut Land Company 75
Connecticut Society for the Reformation of
    Morals 309
Connecticut State House 43
Connecticut Wits 27, 59, 60, 61, 129

Montrésor, John 66
Moody, Paul 367, 384
Moore, Clement Clarke 304
Moore, Thomas 291
Moore v. *Cherry* 249, 254
Moors, Hezekiah 35
Moor's Indian Charity School 173
Moral Pieces in Prose and Verse (Sigourney) 37
Moran, Peter K. 36
Moravians 341
Mordecai, Abraham 339
Morgan, George 86
Morgan, Dr. John 368
Morris, Gouverneur 72, 98, 106, 120, 203, 205, 258, 270, 276
Morris, Robert 72, 78, 80, 83, 92, 98, 120, 201, 205
Morse, Jedidiah 28, 115, 127, 217, 322, 344–345
Morse, Samuel 115
Morton, Perez 51
Morton, Sarah Wentworth 28, 31, 51
Mother Goose's Melody 147
Mount Vernon 188, 242–244
Moving pictures (Peale) 26, 65
Murray, Judith Sargent 30–31, 51, 127
Murray, William Vans 187
Music 55–58
Musica Sacra (Hastings) 57
A Musical Dictionary (Pinkington) 36
The Musical Olio (Olmstead) 34
The Musical Practitioner (Merrill) 31
Musical Preceptor (Hupfield) 35
Musical Primer (Law) 29, 37, 56
The Musical Repository (Hewitt) 32
Musical societies 57
Musical Society of New York 57
Muskets, flintlock 367
The Mysterious Marriage (Hewitt) 32
The Mysterious Monk incidental music (Pélissier) 30
The Mystery Hid from Ages and Generations (Chauncy) 346

N

Napoleonic Wars 86, 100
A Narrative of the Events Which Followed Bonaparte's Campaign in Russia (Dunlap) 37
Narratives of a Late Expedition (Brackenridge) 26
National Advertiser 132
National Bank 74, 105, 183, 196, 201, 209, 232, 233, 235, 241, 244
National debt 83–84, 183, 208
National Gazette 109, 132, 144, 145, 183, 210, 211, 223, 297
National Intelligencer and Washington Advertiser 112, 133
National Race Course, Washington, D.C. 397
National Road 190, 193
Native American religions 340–341

The Natural and Civil History of Vermont (William) 52
Natural History Museum, Philadelphia 65
Naturalization Act of 1798 137, 187, 189, 216, 249–250, 268
Nautilus (ship) 364
"Naval Song (The Pillar of Glory)" (Eckhard) 36
Neef, Joseph 154, 158, 175–176
Negro Election Day 303
Neutrality Act of 1794 185
Neville, John 266
The New American Melody (French) 27
New England Harmony (Swan) 32
New England Journal of Medicine 366
New England Medical Review and Journal 366
New Exhibitions Room, Boston 396
A New Guide to the English Tongue (Dilworth) 167
The New Harmony of Zion (Bayley) 27
New Harmony Commune 158
New Haven Gazette 27, 60
New Hymns on Various Subjects (Ballou) 26
New Jersey Plan 181, 204
New Jerusalem Settlement 319, 343
New London Bee 139
New Overture and Violin Concerto (Taylor) 30
The New-England Psalm Singer (Billings) 55
A New System of Modern Geography (Guthrie) 141, 143
New Theatre Company, Philadelphia 66
New Theatre Opera House, Philadelphia 29
New World 110–111
The New-York Evening Post 112, 237, 133
New York Daily Advertiser 108
New York Education Law of 1795 165
New York Free School Society 153, 157, 159–160, 162–164
New York Historical Society 34
New York Hospital 368, 375
New-York Magazine 125
New York Missionary Society 320
New York Morning Post 108
New York Musical Society 27
New York Observer 113
New York Public Library 103
New York Religious Tract Society 323
The New York Serenading Waltz (Weldon) 33
New York Stock Exchange 74
New York Tract Society 335
Newburgh Conspiracy 180
Newcomen, Thomas 381
The New England Harmonist (Jenks) 32
New-England Alamack (Thomas) 146
Newspaper war of 1792 116
Newspapers 108–111, 115–116, 119, 130–136, 138, 144, 299
Nez Percé 374
Nicholas, Philip 142
Nicholson, Jacob 230
Nicholson, Jupiter 230
Niles, Hezekiah 113

Niles' Weekly Register 113
Noah, Mordecai Manuel 339
Non-Importation Act 89, 190, 221
Non-Intercourse Act of 1809 76, 77, 91, 192, 221
The North American Review 37, 114
The North American Sylva, or A Description of the Forest Trees (Michaux) 123
North River Steam Boat 365
North West Company of Canada 103
Northwest Fur Company 385
Northwest Ordinance of 1787 73, 96, 150, 181, 201, 218
Northwest Passage 374
Northwest Territory 181, 185, 217, 230
Norwich Academy 151
Notes on the State of Virginia (Jefferson) 95, 238, 280, 362, 378
"Novel Reading, a Cause of Female Depravity" 51
A Number of Original Airs, Duetto's and Trio's (Hill) 33

O

Obookiah, Henry 335
Observations on the Geology of the United States of America 366
Occom, Samson 319, 340
Ode for General Hamilton's Funeral (Jackson) 33
Ode for the Fourth of July (Jackson) 35
Ode to Harmony (Jackson) 34
Ode to Peace (Jackson) 34
Ode to Spring (Wood) 27
An Ode to the New Year, An Anthem for Public or Private Worship (Taylor) 29
Of Ancient and Modern Confederacies (Madison) 240
Ohio Company of Associates 96
Ohio University 292
Old American Company, New York City 30, 64
The Old Bachelor (Wirt) 37
Oldtown Folks (Stowe) 324, 326
The Olive Branch (Carey) 144
Olmstead, Timothy 34
Orders in Council 89, 92
Oriental Harmony (Maxim) 33
The Origin of Evil. An Elegy (Tyler) 29
Original Poems (Fessenden) 33
Ormond (Brown) 31, 63
Ormond, Eleazer 143
Otis, Harrison Gray 226, 227, 229
Otis, James Jr. 67, 204
Otis, James Sr. 67
Otterbein, Philip William 320
Ouâbi, or The Virtues of Nature. An Indian Tale in Four Cantos (Morton) 28
Ould, Robert 154
Ovariotomy 366
Overture, St. Patrick's Day (Reinagle) 29
Overture in 9 Íovements Expressive of a Battle (Hewitt) 28–29
Overture to Auld Robin Gray (Moller) 30
Overture to Harlequin's Invasion (Moller) 30

Tammany, or the Indian Chief (Hewitt) 30
Target shooting, 399
Tariff Act of 1789 182, 207
Tariff Act of 1792 210
Tariff policies 73–74, 80, 93
The Tars from Tripoli (Hewitt) 35
Taylor, John 86
Taylor, Nathaniel 321
Taylor, Raynor 29–32, 36–37
Tears and Smiles (Barker and Brady) 35
Tecumapease 313
Tecumseh 192–193, 195, 218, 292, 313–314, 341, 358
Telegraph 113, 115, 140
Temperance groups 309
Templi Carmina (Mitchell) 36
Tenney, Tabitha Gilman 32, 51
Tenskwatawa 193, 218, 292, 314, 322, 341, 358
Terrible Tractoration (Fessenden) 33
Terry, Eli 364
Tertium Quids 227
Textile industry 102
Thacher, George 230
Thanksgiving Anthem (Shaw) 35
Thanksgiving Day 289, 303
Theater 47–49
Theme with Thirty Variations in D Major (Hewitt) 34
Thespian Mirror 34, 127
Theus, Simeon 278
Thirteen Easy Canons (Jackson) 35
Thirty Years Ago (Dunlap) 65
Thomas, Isaiah 26, 36, 109, 114, 117–118, 127, 143, 146
Thompson, Benjamin (Count Rumford) 392
Thompson, Samuel 366, 371
Thompsonian system 366, 371
Thoreau, John 172
Thornton, Dr. William H. 377
Thoughts on Government (Adams) 198
Three Ballads, Opus 2 (Carr) 32
Three Rondos for the Piano Forte or Harpsichord (Brown) 27
Three Sonatas for the Piano Forte, Opus 5 (Hewitt) 30
Three Songs from Shakespeare (Cook) 29
Time-Piece 145
Tisdale, Elkanah 227
"To Anacreon in Heaven" (Smith) 37, 59
"To Arms Columbia" (Paine and Hagen) 32
Tobacco 85, 91–92
Tocqueville, Alexis de 39, 332
Todd, John Jr. 312
Toll roads 87, 363
Tontine Crescent, Boston 43
Torpedoes 365
Towne, Amos 172
Towne, Benjamin 130, 131
Trade and Intercourse Act of 1790 74
Trading posts 87
Traetta, Filippo 32–33, 37
Traité d'Economie Politique (Say) 88
Transylvania Company 310

The Traveller Returned (Murray) 31
The Travellers (Reinagle) 35
Treaties:
—Alliance of 1778 213
—Fort Jackson (1814) 195, 219
—Ghent (1814) 58, 105, 195, 196–197, 233, 241
—Greenville (1795) 185, 214, 218, 313, 341
—Paris (1783) 65, 72, 82, 92, 95, 180, 197, 199, 201, 217, 248, 254, 262, 276, 279
Trenchard, John 38
Trials of the Human Heart (Rowson) 30
Triangular trade 101
Trianon Decree 192
Trinity Church, Boston 36
Trinity Church, New York City 66
Tripolitan pirates 92, 186, 190, 196, 221
The Triumph of Infidelity (Dwight) 27, 60, 174
Triumphal Arch (Peale) 65
Trollope, Frances 294
Troy Seminary 155
True Reasons on Which the Election of a Hollis Professor of Divinity in Harvard College was Opposed (Morse) 344
Trumbull, John (artist) 27, 66, 67
Trumbull, John (poet) 27, 59, 60
Tucker, St. George 26–27, 30, 250–251, 253–254, 271, 273, 275
Tucker, Thomas Tudor 207
Tuckerman, Joseph 54
Tuckey, William 27
Tudor, William 54
Tuesday Club 129
Turgot, Anne-Robert-Jacques 234
Two Years Before the Mast (Dana) 37
Tyler, Royall 27, 29, 31, 35, 49, 128
Typographical Society of New York 110

U

Uncle Tom's Cabin (Stowe) 162, 324
Union College 174
The Union Harmony (Holden) 29
Union Hotel, Saratoga Springs, N.Y. 291
Union University 152
Unitarian catechism 345
Unitarian Church 127, 345, 346
Unitarian controversy 321, 344
United States—
—Armory, Harpers Ferry, Va. 366
—Armory, Springfield, Mass. 181, 202, 259, 363
—Articles of Confederation 72, 83, 95, 98, 197, 200, 253, 276
—Capitol 29, 41, 67
—Census of 1790 95
—Circuit courts 255, 261, 277
—Coast and Geodetic Survey 365, 373
—Congress 28, 67, 78, 101, 103–105, 181, 190, 217, 222, 230, 276
—Constitution 58, 78, 86, 101, 106, 202–206, 253, 255, 263, 269, 297; *Article I, Section 8* 209; *Article II, Section 1* 223; *Article III* 261, 279; *Article IV, Section 2*

184, 205; *Article IV, Section 4* 205; *Bill of Rights* 122, 182, 206, 208, 269, 297, 330–331; *Constitutional Convention* 81, 115, 120, 181, 202, 230, 243, 265, 280; *Eleventh Amendment* 187, 249, 262, 277, 283; *First Amendment* 137, 269, 319, 330–331, 356; *Ratification* 119, 122–123, 182, 208; *Twelfth Amendment* 190, 226
—Declaration of Independence 58
—Department of Foreign Affairs 106
—District courts 255
—Electoral college 221, 283
—Geological map 366
—Marine Band 33
—Military Academy, West Point, N.Y. 153, 189, 291
—Mint 74, 98, 390
—Patent Office 365, 376
—Patent Office Superintendent 377
—Population 192, 294
—Post Office 108, 110, 112, 115, 125, 134–136, 140, 145–146
—Supreme Court 80, 182, 184, 186, 188–189, 192, 208, 248–252, 254–255, 258, 261–265, 269, 276–277, 279, 283
—Treasury Department 73, 104
United States (ship) 194
The United States and England (Paulding) 37
United States Magazine 62
United States v. Hudson & Goodwin 251
United States v. Peters 251, 263, 279
Universal Friends 319, 342
Universal Gazette 111, 133
University of Georgia 150
University of Maryland 292
University of Maryland at Baltimore Medical School 375
University of Nashville 150
University of New York Medical School 366
University of North Carolina 151
University of Pennsylvania Medical School 363
University of Saint Andrews 282
University of South Carolina 291
University of Virginia 158, 171, 175, 240, 242

V

Valentine and Orson (Pélissier) 34
Valerian: A Narrative Poem (Linn) 34
Van Hagen, Peter 31–33
Van Rensselaer, Stephen 194
Vancouver, George 373
Vanderbilt, Cornelius 77
Vans, William 103
Variations on a Swiss Waltz (Moran) 36
Varick, James 320
Vaughan, Samuel 44
Vaughan type portraits of George Washington (Stuart) 44
The Vermont Harmony (Hill) 32

GENERAL INDEX   419

PHOTO INDEX